THE

MISCELLANEOUS WRITINGS

OF

JOSEPH STORY,

ASSOCIATE JUSTICE OF THE SUPREME COURT OF THE UNITED STATES,
AND DANE PROFESSOR OF LAW AT HARVARD UNIVERSITY.

EDITED BY HIS SON,

WILLIAM W. STORY.

THE LAWBOOK EXCHANGE, LTD.
Clark, New Jersey

ISBN 978-1-58477-072-5

Lawbook Exchange edition 2001, 2017

The quality of this reprint is equivalent to the quality of the original work.

THE LAWBOOK EXCHANGE, LTD.
33 Terminal Avenue
Clark, New Jersey 07066-1321

Please see our website for a selection of our other publications and fine facsimile reprints of classic works of legal history:
www.lawbookexchange.com

Library of Congress Cataloging-in-Publication Data

Story, Joseph, 1779-1845.
The miscellaneous writings of Joseph Story, associate justice of the Supreme Court of the United States and Dane Professor of Law at Harvard University / edited by his son, William W. Story.
p. cm.
Originally published: Boston : C. C. Little and J. Brown, 1852.
ISBN 1-58477-072-4 (acid-free paper)
1. Law--United States. 2. Constitutional law--United States. I. Story, William Wetmore, 1819-1895. II. Title.

KF213 .S75 2000
349.73--dc21 99-058559

Printed in the United States of America on acid-free paper

THE

MISCELLANEOUS WRITINGS

OF

JOSEPH STORY,

ASSOCIATE JUSTICE OF THE SUPREME COURT OF THE UNITED STATES,
AND DANE PROFESSOR OF LAW AT HARVARD UNIVERSITY.

EDITED BY HIS SON,

WILLIAM W. STORY.

BOSTON:
CHARLES C. LITTLE AND JAMES BROWN.
1852.

CAMBRIDGE:
PRINTED BY HOUGHTON AND HAYWOOD.

ADVERTISEMENT.

Most of the papers contained in this volume were printed in a previous collection, which was prepared by my father in 1835, and which has been long out of print.

In the present edition a different arrangement has been adopted, and some new pieces have been added. The original Dedication by my father, to the Honorable Josiah Quincy, has been preserved.

W. W. STORY.

Boston, October, 1851.

TO

THE HONORABLE

JOSIAH QUINCY, L.L. D.,

PRESIDENT OF HARVARD UNIVERSITY.

SIR,

In dedicating this volume to you, I may, not unnaturally, be thought to indulge a wish in some sort to discharge the debt of gratitude, which I owe to the institution, over which you preside, for the many favors bestowed upon me. But, gratifying as such an expression of reverent regard for our Parent University would at all times be to me, I confess, that I seek on the present occasion rather to offer it as a testimony of my deep sense of the worth of your personal character. Few men have acquired so just a distinction for unspotted integrity, fearless justice, consistent principles, high talents, and extensive literature. Still fewer possess the merit of having justified the public confidence by the singleness of heart and purpose, with which they have devoted themselves to the best interests of society. In every station, to which you have been called by the free suffrages of the people, you have discharged its duties with the most exemplary ability, fidelity, and conscientiousness. In your present exalted station, to which you were invited by the combined voice of the guardians of the University, under the most flattering circumstances, every act of your life has conduced to establish the importance and wisdom of the choice. May you long continue to wear its honors with unsullied dignity. In the language of your own favorite Poet, I may say, *Cura Patrum . . . tuas virtutes in ævum per titulos memoresque fastos æternet.*

I have the honor to remain, most truly,

Your obliged friend,

JOSEPH STORY.

CAMBRIDGE, Massachusetts, October, 1835.

CONTENTS.

SKETCHES OF JUDGES AND LAWYERS.

AUTOBIOGRAPHY.

MISCELLANEOUS WRITINGS.

AUTOBIOGRAPHY.

Washington, 23d January, 1831.

My dear Son:

I have often resolved to write down for your use a brief memoir of my life; and having leisure at this time, I have determined not to omit it any longer. You are too young now to think much about it; but if you should live, and grow up to manhood, as I pray God you may, I am sure that it cannot fail to be of interest to you. I shall write, too, very frankly and freely, and in a manner which would not be justifiable, if this were designed for the public, or even for the eyes of a friend. But between a parent and child all forms may be dropped, and we may write as we feel; and if here and there a spice of personal vanity should appear, it would be but as the small talk of the fireside, where mutual confidence allows us to *think* aloud, and tell our honest thoughts as they arise. Perhaps, when I am in my grave you will take comfort in these little details, and say with the poet, — *Forsan et hæc olim meminisse juvabit.*

I was born at Marblehead, in the county of Essex, on the 18th of September, 1779. My father's name was Elisha Story; my mother's Mehitable Pedrick. My father was a native of Boston, and born in 1743. He was the son of William

Story of that place, who held, I believe, the office of Registrar in the Court of Admiralty at the beginning of the Revolution. My grandfather was, in fact, a Whig, but holding office under the British government, he was subjected to the common odium of the times. His house was assailed by the mob, and considerably injured. My father was a sturdy Whig, and took a very early and active part in all the revolutionary movements. He was one of the Indians who helped to destroy the tea in the famous Boston exploit. He did not receive a public education, owing, I believe, to his father's very rigid religious opinions, which would not suffer him to go to Harvard College, lest he should there imbibe those heretical tenets, which, in the form of Arminianism, were then supposed to haunt those venerable shades. He, however, was educated in the Public Latin School in Boston, then under the government of the celebrated master Lovell. After receiving the usual classical instruction there, he studied medicine with a very eminent physician, Dr. Sprague of Boston. He married, for his first wife, Miss Ruth Ruddock, daughter of John Ruddock, Esq., a man who had accumulated a considerable property in the ship-building business in Boston. She died in the year 1777, leaving seven children. In the autumn of 1778, my father married Miss Pedrick, whom you know as your grandmother still living, and by her had eleven children, of whom I am the eldest. Your grandmother's father was an opulent merchant of Marblehead, and, indeed, for that day, a very opulent merchant. He inclined, as many men of property did, to the Tory side, but never took any step except in favor of his countrymen. A considerable portion of his property being in shipping, was lost by rotting at the wharves during the war. He died in the year after I was born; and finding that like himself I was left-handed, he was extremely anxious to give me a proof of his regard by presenting me with a small messuage; but my mother, with great good sense, for the purpose of avoiding all family disagreements, declined the offer; and thus I was probably saved from the mischievous notion, that I had property in my own right, a notion with which servants are apt to fill young minds to their positive injury.

My father, soon after the commencement of the Revolution, entered the army as a surgeon, and continued in it until the close of the year 1777, when he retired, being disgusted with the management or rather mismanagement of the medical department. I am told that there is still extant a correspondence with the head of that department on the subject, somewhat excited, but I have never seen it. He was with General Washington during the campaign of 1777 in the Jerseys; and I remember to have heard him speak, in my early youth, with great enthusiasm on the subject. To the very close of his life he entertained the highest admiration of General Washington, and of John Adams, though in the political controversies between the latter and Mr. Jefferson he took side with Mr. Jefferson. He was, in a just sense, a disciple of the school of Washington, a lover of the Union, and devotedly attached to a republican government. In the party divisions of the times succeeding Washington's administration, he was a very decided Republican, and continued so to his death. But his natural moderation of character, combined as it was with great firmness and amenity, saved him from those extravagancies which but too often disgrace the history of parties.

And now that I am upon the subject of my father, I must indulge myself in a few remarks upon his character and person. He was not so tall as I am, and rather of a stronger and fuller build. He must have been an uncommonly handsome man in his youth, (and indeed so I have always heard,) for when I first recollect him with distinctness, though then quite bald, his face was still of great masculine beauty and attractiveness. His eyes were blue and of singular vivacity and sweetness, his eyebrows regularly arched, and a fine nose, and an expressive mouth, gave a perfect harmony to his features. There was, too, a slight smile which occasionally played about his face, and a general cheerfulness and ease in his conversation, which won every person who came near him. His manners were bland and approaching to elegance; modest, but at the same time with a conscious bearing of character; and there was just enough of the pride of person about him to make him solicitous to dress well, but not in showy apparel — with neatness, and yet not with too scrupulous care. My father was not a man of genius, but of plain, practical sense, and a quick insight into the deeds of men. He possessed great natural tact and sagacity, with little pretension to learning. As a physician, he was eminently successful in practice, as was established by the constant increase of his business to the very time of his decease. In one branch of it he was eminent, perhaps more so than any individual in the neighboring towns. I mean in obstetrics. In cases of this sort he was often sent for into the neighboring towns, and I remember that on several occasions, Dr. Holyoke, then very eminent in the same branch, was in the habit of requiring his presence and assistance in difficult cases.

But what I delight to dwell on with most sincere satisfaction, is my father's domestic character. He was one of the most amiable men I ever knew; kind and indulgent to his children, partaking of all their pleasures, and busy in promoting their innocent amusements. His home was full of cheerfulness. No one came there who did not receive a hearty welcome; no one departed without feeling as if leaving a home. He was liberal, charitable, and full of sympathy for the poor and afflicted. There was so much of gentleness about him, that his children felt him to be more of a companion than of a parent. His temper was very uniform, and almost an unclouded sunshine. I do not remember more than once in my whole life that he was angry with me. I have forgotten the occasion, but I know that I was quite in the wrong. I have heard him often say that his temper was naturally hasty and irascible; but that he had by perseverance and attention obtained the mastery over it. And he gave me very strong advice with parental tenderness to acquire a like mastery by the same method. I hope I have profited by that advice. I am sure that his recommendation was founded in a just observation of our power over ourselves.

I remember, that on Thanksgiving, Christmas, and New Year, my father was in the habit of joining in all the merriment and sports of his children. On some of those occasions he usually played blind-man's-buff with us, and he was really the most adroit of all the company in escaping detection. The last time he ever played with us in this manner, he could not have been far from fifty-five years of age; and upon the close of it, he said, in a manner which affected us all nearly to tears: "My children, this is the last time I shall ever play with you in this game." The remark struck us dumb; and for a few minutes we were wrapt in melancholy.

My father was a religious man, liberal and charitable in all his views. He was an Arminian in principle. My uncle, who was the minister of the church to which he belonged, was a warm, and indeed, over-zealous Calvinist. Between him and my father there were often disputes on the points of their faith, but these occasioned no alienation. One of the earliest impressions that I have, is of a conversation in which he spoke with great kindness and charity of the Roman Catholics, among whom he said there were many pious and excellent men. I was too young at the time to know who Roman Catholics were, or what was their creed. But toleration of Popery was at that time almost a deadly sin among the good old Calvinistic Puritans, and I honored his opinion the more, because it formed such a contrast to that of others who were about him. I trace back to this source my early and constant hatred of religious persecution, and my love, my inextinguishable love of freedom of opinion and inquiry in matters of religion. They have now become the guiding maxims of my life.

My father was for the last fifteen years of his life accustomed to have family prayers in the morning and evening. On Sunday, after the public afternoon service was over, all the family, including the servants, were assembled in one room, and he then read a printed sermon of some English divine, and concluded the day with reading a portion of the New Testament, and with prayer. I still remember those meetings with great pleasure. My father read with remarkable clearness and propriety, and it was a treat to sit under him, while he gave us specimens of the best eloquence of popular divines. The flexible tones of his voice, the graceful modulation, the animated zeal, and the patriarchal simplicity of his utterance on those occasions, gave me a taste for serious reading and touching eloquence, which turned my thoughts even in youth to the sober realities of life. I am sure that I was greatly a gainer by those domestic services. And when in after life I read Burns's beautiful poem of the Cotter's Saturday Night, I felt, a thousand times, that it portrayed scenes familiar to my thoughts and dear to my recollections.

I have many reasons to believe that I was somewhat of a favorite with my father from an early period. He gave me his confidence while I was yet a boy, and talked to me of his business and his situation in a manner belonging to persons of mature years and reflection. I was sensible of the value of this confidence, and retained it through his whole life. Peace to the memory of so good a man. It is still very dear to the aged inhabitants of my native town, among whom he enjoyed a singular and enviable respect and attachment. He was among them a general favorite, and often performed the truly important office of peacemaker and restorer of broken friendships and family harmony.

Marblehead is, as you know, a secluded fishing town, and having no general connection with other towns, it has not, as a thoroughfare, much of that intercourse which brings strangers to visit it, or to form an acquaintance with its inhabitants. When I was young there were many discouragements under which it was laboring. Its whole business was annihilated during the Revolutionary war. Many of its inhabitants entered the army and navy or served on board of privateers; and from the various calamities incident to such situations, the close of that war found the town with upwards of nine hundred widows whose husbands had perished in the contest. It was greatly impoverished, and indeed in my earliest recollection seemed struck with a premature and apparently irretrievable decline. The general poverty, combined with other circumstances, made the resources of education narrow; and few books were to be found, and few scholars were nurtured on its rocky shores.

The inhabitants of a town so situated, and especially of a town almost wholly engaged in the fisheries, whose voyages began and ended in the same port, and whose occupation when abroad is in sounding the depth of the ocean, and drawing their lines upon the stormy waves of the Banks of Newfoundland, have little variety in their thoughts or conversation. Their lives have few incidents but those perilous adventures which everywhere belong to a seafaring life. Their habits are necessarily plain, their morals pure, and their manners, if not rough, at least generally unpolished and unpretending. Their very equality of condition as well as uniformity of pursuit bring them all into the same circle, and there is little room for the pride of scholarship, or the triumph of superior knowledge.

The people of Marblehead are a peculiar race; and as utterly unlike their neighbors as though they belonged to another age or country. The lines of their character are perhaps a little less marked than formerly, from their wider intercourse in later years with other places, but still they are deep and permanent, strong and full of meaning. They are a generous, brave, humane, honest, straightforward people; sagacious in their own affairs, but not wise beyond them; confiding and unsuspecting; hospitable by nature, though stinted in means; with a love of home scarcely paralleled, and an indifference to the show and splendor of wealth, which cannot easily be imagined; frugal and laborious; content with their ordinary means, neither rejecting learning nor over anxious for its attainment. The very rocks of their shores, the very barrenness of the strand on which their buildings rest, the very scantiness of the mother soil on which they were born, and in which they expect to lie buried when they are dead, have to them an indescribable charm. They love it with an intensity of interest which neither time nor distance can control. They seem perpetually to exclaim, "This is my own, my native land."

It was among these people that I passed my early days; and as my father was the physician of a very large number of their families, I was familiar with them all from my youth. And if at any time in my life you have seen me sympathize with the poor, the lowly, the humble, and the unfortunate, depend upon it I learned the first lessons of charity in my father's house, and from my daily participation in the feelings and wants of those who were my daily associates.

From the circumstances to which I have above alluded, you will readily understand that, in my early days, I gathered very little from general society, or even from books, to stimulate my ambition or awaken my curiosity. I was, therefore, left very much to my own thoughts and amusements. My delight was to roam over the narrow and rude territory of my native town; to traverse its secluded beaches and its shallow inlets; to gaze upon the sleepless ocean; to lay myself down on the sunny rocks and listen to the deep tones of the rising and the falling tide; to look abroad, when the foaming waves were driven with terrific force and uproar against the barren cliffs or the rocky promontories, which everywhere opposed their immovable fronts to resist them; to seek, in the midst of the tremendous majesty of an eastern storm, some elevated spot where, in security, I could mark the mountain billow break upon the distant shore, or dash its broken waters over the lofty rocks which here and there stood along the coast naked and weather-beaten. But still more was I pleased, in a calm summer day, to lay myself down alone on one of the beautiful heights which overlook the harbor of Salem, and to listen to the broken sounds of the hammers in the distant ship yards, or to the soft dash of the oar of some swift moving boat, or to the soft ripple of the murmuring wave; or to gaze on the swelling sail, or the flying bird, or the scarcely moving smoke, in a reverie of delicious indolence.

The establishment of an academy in the town was quite an era, and gave a new turn to my thoughts and occupations. I was among the earliest scholars that belonged to it; and began there to learn the rudiments of Latin and Greek. It was for a considerable time under the superintendence of the Rev. William Harris, who was afterwards President of Columbia College, in New York. It was at this school that I first became acquainted with those admirable works, Dr. Vicesimus Knox's Elegant Extracts in Prose and Verse, an epitome of which was used daily in the exercises, and the large works were occasionally resorted to. To this source I trace back my earliest knowledge of English Literature, and my inextinguishable love of the writings of the great masters of that literature in former times. The public are almost overwhelmed by the inundation of school books in our day; but notwithstanding all our boasted improvements, there are not, in my opinion, any works so well adapted to cultivate a pure and elegant taste, and so full of excellent instruction as these. We are impatient of the old, and forever on the search for the new; and therefore Knox's compilations are now scarcely known beyond the shelves of some library formed in other days, and are deemed too antiquated for the march of modern intellect.

At school, I was diligent and ambitious, my natural temperament being cheerful, and my activity in athletic exercises great. I was generally among the foremost in our sports, and selected, if not for superior skill, at least for promptitude and strength. It is somewhat singular, however, that though

I had a good deal of the vivacity of youth, I was much given to private and contemplative reading. I had been bred up in a church, which inclined strongly to Calvinism, and my uncle (who, as I have stated, was the minister of it,) was much inclined in his preaching to dwell on the terrors of the law, upon man's depravity, and eternal torments; and he felt no scruple in mentioning hell, even to ears polite. My earliest impressions, therefore, of God were those of terror, and not of love — of awe, but not of filial affection; and in my secret devotions I approached him as a being whom I was to propitiate, rather than a parent of whom I was to ask blessings. My thoughts were on this account often gloomy; and I know not how it happened, but so the fact was, that topics respecting death, and the grave, and eternity, became more familiar with my thoughts than any other. I owned a little pocket volume of Young's Night Thoughts, which I used to carry about in my solitary rambles, and read with intense interest, I should not say with pleasure, for it was rather darkness visible.

My native town, like all other fishing towns, as I believe, was full of all sorts of superstitions; ghosts, hobgoblins, will-o'-wisps, apparitions, and premonitions were the common, I might almost say the universal subject of belief; and numberless were the stories of haunted houses, and wandering spirits, and murdered ghosts, that were told at the fire-side, and filled my imagination with all sorts of preternatural fears. It is to this circumstance that I principally owe my strong love of the marvellous in novels, and that I yet read with delight the Romances of Mrs. Radcliffe, which always appear to me to be realities with which I have been long familiar.

There is one circumstance connected with my studies at the Marblehead Academy, which has probably given a turn to my thoughts which you may easily trace. Girls as well as Boys went to the same school at the same hours, and were arranged on opposite sides of a large hall in their appropriate forms. In the simplicity of those days, it was not thought necessary to separate the sexes in their studies. Generally we studied the same books, and as we recited our lessons in the presence of each other, there was a mutual pride to do our best, and to gain an honest portion of flattery or of praise. I was early struck with the flexibility, activity, and power of the female mind. Girls of the same age were on an average of numbers quite our equals in their studies and acquirements, and had a much greater quickness of perception and delicacy of feeling than the boys. Remaining thus at school with them until I was about fifteen years old, I could not be mistaken as to their powers; and I then imbibed the opinion, which I have never since changed, that their talents are generally equal to those of men, though there are shades of difference in the character of their minds resulting from several causes. My impression is, that the principal difference in intellectual power, which is marked in after days, results not so much from their original inferiority of mind, as from the fact that education stops with females almost at the time it effectively begins with men; and that neither their habits nor pursuits in life enable them afterwards to cultivate science or literature with much diligence or success. They have no professions which constantly require, and constantly encourage them to master new sources of knowledge.

Just as I was fifteen years of age, in the autumn of 1794, an event occurred, which had some influence upon my character and destiny. I was preparing to enter Harvard College the next year, and having mastered the usual preparatory studies in Latin, and that most discouraging book, the Westminster Greek Grammar, I was beginning to study the Gospel of John, with a view to make an easy transition into Greek. Some boyish affair, I have quite forgotten what, induced me to chastise a lad belonging to the school, who boarded with my instructor, and this reaching the ears of the atter, he determined, under another pretence, to seek an occasion in school to punish me for the transaction. It is very easy to find such an occasion when we are determined on it. Some very slight peccadillo occurred on my part. I was, called up in the presence of the whole school and beaten very severely with a ferule on my hands. I bore it without shrinking, and submitted without resistance, being at that time too old to cry like a little boy, and having some pride to meet the punishment manfully. The schoolmaster was a man of violent and irascible temper when aroused, and seeing my calmness and firmness he struck me in his rage, I believe, as many as a hundred blows on my hands, until the agony was so great that I could no longer restrain myself from crying aloud. I was then ordered to my seat, and remained there suffering much pain until the school was dismissed. I never can think of this brutal and coarse treatment by this man, who was a clergyman, without a feeling of resentment and disgust. A few years after, when I had arrived at manhood, he took occasion to express his regret at the transaction, his consciousness, that he was in the wrong, and my total guiltlessness of any thing to justify the punishment. He admitted that it was a retaliation for the chastisement I had inflicted on his boarder, and that his passions had carried him beyond the bounds of moderation. I forgave him, heartily forgave him. But though in other respects a deserving man, I never desired to have any communion with him beyond the mere formalities of common respect.

With the approbation of my father, I immediately left the academy. But it was a case full of embarrassment. There was no other school in the town in which the learned languages were taught; and with so large a family the expenses attendant upon an education at a distance were not to be overlooked. Fortunately, the principal town schoolmaster (whom I shall always remember with gratitude and respect) was acquainted with Latin, and the Greek of the New Testament, and he undertook to superintend my studies in those languages in the common books. It was in the autumn, and

I formed the sudden resolution to prepare myself so as to be offered for admission at Harvard College in the ensuing January vacation as a Freshman. To do this was no small labor, and required extraordinary diligence and exertion. My master had not much time to assist me, and undertook little beyond merely hearing my recitations. My pride was roused, and my ambition stimulated. I determined to go through the labor; and though I was then but just in the beginning of Greek, and had considerable in Latin as well as in other departments to master, I was not discouraged. In the course of two short months, I had not only gone over all these studies with care, but I had several times reviewed them, and I felt confident that I could pass the necessary examinations.

Accordingly, just as the winter vacation was about to commence, (it was then a vacation of six weeks) I was taken by my uncle to Cambridge for examination, and I felt the flush of hope play on my cheeks. Great was my disappointment upon being told by the president on my arrival there, that I must be examined, not merely in the previous preparatory studies, but in all the studies which the freshman class had been pursuing for the last six months. I was completely overwhelmed. I was dumb, disconsolate, and mortified. In one moment, at a single blow, all my hopes were demolished and my labors lost. I scarcely spoke a word during my whole homeward journey. My uncle, however, had taken the precaution to ascertain to what extent the class had gone, and what were the books which I must study.

I returned home in great dejection. My father asked me what I intended to do? I replied, after some hesitation, that there were six weeks of vacation, and if he pleased, I would try to fit myself in that period for examination in the prescribed studies. I told him I could but fail, and if so, I must wait patiently until the next commencement. I went to bed, and got up the next morning with a determination to go on. All the books were obtained that day, by purchase or borrowing.

But here a new difficulty presented itself. I had no knowledge of the Greek dialects, and unluckily my master was in the same predicament; while the Iliad (which was one of the books to be studied) was full of them. All he could promise was, that he would hear me recite in Homer as well as he could. But he promised no aid in mastering these difficulties.

My task was now before me. I have a distinct recollection of the main parts. Sallust was to be read through, the Odes of Horace, two books of Livy, three books, I think, of Xenophon's Anabasis, and two books of Homer's Iliad, besides English Grammar and Rhetoric, and, I think, Logic, and some other studies. I sat down boldly to the task, reciting every morning five lessons, which I mastered during the preceding evening, and five or six more in the course of the day. It was intense labor, but I found no great difficulty except in Homer. The dialects puzzled me exceedingly, and my treacherous memory failed in preserving them accurately, so that I was often obliged to go over the same ground. For my first lesson in Homer I got five lines well; for my second, ten; for my third fifteen; and then the mystery dissolved apace. In the course of the first three weeks I had gone through all the requisite studies. I could look back upon my past labors with the silent consciousness of victory. There is nothing to a young mind, unaccustomed to the exercise of its powers, so gratifying as this. The hero who conquers in battle, the orator who triumphs in the senate or the forum, feels not a more intense delight, than the youth first perceiving, that though born of the dust he is not altogether earth, but that there is something within him of an ethereal and intellectual nature. The remaining three weeks I passed in reviewing all these studies, which I did in the most difficult, more than once, and could say without a boast, at the end of the time, that I could go through two hundred lines of Homer at a recitation. At the end of the vacation I was again offered for examination, and without difficulty obtained my matriculation.

I have forgotten to mention a circumstance which occurred at an earlier period of my life, and which had wellnigh proved fatal to me. I slept in a small chamber over the front entry of my father's house, and the bed had curtains to it. I went to bed at my usual hour, and set the candle on a chest, which was at the bottom of the bed, and so near that it touched it. From carelessness, I placed the candle close by the curtains, and being very sleepy I forgot to put it out. By some accident it afterwards fell over and the curtains and bed caught fire. I was asleep. The family were not yet retired to rest. My door was shut; but my mother, sitting in a distant room, smelt something burning. Immediate search was made in that room and in those adjoining, but nothing was found. It then occurred to her that I had gone to bed about half an hour before with a light, and she instantly exclaimed, that it must be in my chamber. My father ran up over one flight of stairs, and my mother over another. My father arrived first, opened the door, and the smoke was so intense and suffocating that he fell back breathless. My mother at this moment arrived, rushed in, and with that intrepidity and presence of mind which never desert a woman on such occasions, she caught me from the blazing clothes and carried me down stairs in her arms. I was not sensible of any thing until I was below, and then found myself in my mother's arms. She was very severely burnt. I suppose that I was nearly suffocated when I was seized. The fire was stopped, and thus my life, when in the most imminent jeopardy, was saved. This admonition was sufficient to guard me at all times from indulging in that most dangerous practice of reading by candle-light in bed.

My entrance into Harvard College gave an entirely new course to my thoughts. Every thing was new to me. I seemed to breathe a higher atmosphere, and to look abroad with a wider vision and more comprehensive powers. Instead of the narrow group of a village, I was suddenly brought into a large circle of young men engaged in literary pursuits, and warmed and cheered by the hopes of future eminence.

It was a considerable time, however, before I could acquire any familiar acquaintance with my classmates. One of the disadvantages of entering at an advanced standing is, that the associations of your class are already selected and fixed; and that you enter as a mere stranger, without rights and without sympathy. Your rank is not fixed; your scholarship is not known; your character is not ascertained; and you are viewed with a coldness and reserve peculiarly painful to the frankness of youth. I had the good fortune to chum with a young man who saw my embarrassment and gave me a kind welcome. From the first moment of my acquaintance up to this hour there has been a most unreserved friendship between us. Not a shadow has ever obscured it; not a chill has ever passed over it. I owe him much. He is one of the best and worthiest of men, and the lapse of thirty-five years enables me now to speak of him as a bosom friend, in whom I repose unlimited confidence and to whom I owe much of the truest happiness of life. May God preserve the blessing to me even to the close of my life.

Of course, on entering my class, I had no rank, and therefore silently stood at the fag-end of it. It was for me to prove that I had a title to a better place in the estimate of my judges, who were also my peers. It was some time before my classmates were inclined to form a favorable judgment, but by degrees I began to rise, and before I left college I had attained a high rank (it is not for me to say how high) for scholarship. Indeed, I was most thoroughly devoted to all the college studies, and scarcely wasted a single moment in idleness. I trace back to this cause a serious injury to my health. When I entered college I was very robust and muscular, but before I left I had become pale and feeble and was inclining to dyspepsia.

From my early years I had an inclination for poetry. I wrote verses, when I was not more than twelve years old, though I cannot say with Pope, "I lisped in numbers, for the numbers came." On the contrary, it was an exercise of skill with me, not as I imagine very successful or very attractive. One of my earliest efforts in college was a translation of an ode of Horace; of which I have now no other remembrance, than that it was thought well of by those about me. I received the usual rewards of good scholarship at the public exhibitions; delivering a poem at one exhibition, and a mathematical exercise at another in my senior year; and at the commencement at which I was graduated, I delivered the poem immediately before the closing English oration. It was received with much applause; but I burned it with some other early efforts a few years afterwards; and my memory retains no traces of it.

My college life was to me very delightful as well as instructive. I there formed several intimate friendships, which have been continued with unabated sincerity down to the present day. I believe that those friendships were highly useful to me, not merely as sources of private gratification and social intercourse; but they gave a vigor to my moral feelings, and strengthened those religious impressions of duty and those sentiments of honor, which are so important at the critical moment when a lad is passing from the feverish restlessness and unbridled passions of youth to the verge of manhood. I have some pride in saying, that I passed through this dangerous period, without a stain or reproach. I quitted college with regret; and shed many bitter tears in parting from scenes which I could never revisit with the same familiar pleasure, and classmates, whom in the future I could never expect to see again gathered in the same groups, with the buoyancy of hope, and the vivacity of unsuspecting confidence about them. I have never since read Gray's beautiful Ode on a Distant View of Eton College, without having my thoughts called back to the associations of those days with a deep and saddened feeling. I am now again an inhabitant of Cambridge; and I never pass the walls within which I spent so many happy hours, without a mixed sensation of tenderness and melancholy; for they speak to me in the voice of departed times, "departed never to return," and in the spirit of admonition of the sad inroads made by death among those who then graced its halls and guided the instructions of our Alma Mater.

Upon quitting college I returned to Marblehead, and began the study of law, under Mr. Samuel Sewall, then a distinguished counsellor at the bar, and a member of Congress, and afterwards a Judge, and finally Chief Justice of the Supreme Court of Massachusetts. With him I remained until his appointment as a Judge; and in December, 1801, I entered the office of Mr. Putnam, now Mr. Justice Putnam, in Salem, with whom I completed my preparatory studies, and was admitted to the bar at July term of the Common Pleas in Essex County, 1801.

From the causes to which I have already alluded, during my professional studies in Mr. Sewall's office, I was left very much alone, and with no literary associate in my native town. I was driven, therefore, back upon my own resources, and I not unfrequently devoted for months more than fourteen hours a day to study. Mr. Sewall's absence in Congress for about half the year also was a serious disadvantage to me, for I had no opportunity to ask for any explanation of difficulties, and no cheering encouragement to light up the dark and intricate paths of the law.

Beginning my studies in this recluse and solitary manner, I confess that I deeply felt the truth of Spelman's remarks, when he was sent to the Inns of Court for a similar purpose; my heart, like his, sunk within me, and I was tempted several times to give up the science from the firm belief that I could never master it. The case was very different then from what it is now, in respect both to the plan of studies and the facilities to acquire the elements. Then there were few elementary books; now the profession is inundated with them. Then the student, after reading that most elegant of all commentaries, Mr. Justice Blackstone's work, was hurried at once into the intricate, crabbed, and obsolete learning of Coke on Littleton. Now there are many elementary works which smooth the path towards the study of this great master of the Common Law. Then, there were scarcely any American Reports (for the whole number did not exceed five or six volumes) to enable the student to apply the learning of the Common Law to his own country, or to distinguish what was in force here, from what was not. Now, our shelves are crowded with hundreds.

Hitherto my pursuits had been wholly of a literary and classical character. I loved literature, and indulged freely in almost every variety of it to which I had access, from the profound writings of the great historians, metaphysicians, scholars, and divines, down to the lightest fiction, the enticing novel, the still more enticing romance, and the endless pageantries and imaginings of poetry. You may judge, then, how I was surprised and startled on opening works where nothing was presented but dry and technical principles, the dark and mysterious elements of the feudal system, the subtle refinements and intricacies of the middle ages of the Common Law, and the repulsive and almost unintelligible forms of processes and pleadings, for the most part wrapped up in black-letter, or in dusty folios. To me the task seemed Herculean. I should have quitted it in despair, if I had known whither to turn my footsteps, and to earn a support. My father had often told me, in the sincerity of his affection, that he should leave little property; that the most I could expect would be my education; and that I must earn my livelihood by my own labors. I felt the truth of the admonition; and it was perpetually whispered into my secret soul whenever I felt the overpowering influence of any discouragement. My destiny was to earn my bread by the sweat of my brow; and I must meet it or perish.

I shall never forget the time, when having read through Blackstone's Commentaries, Mr. Sewall, on his departure for

Washington, directed me next to read Coke on Littleton, as the appropriate succeeding study. It was a very large folio, with Hargrave and Butler's notes, which I was required to read also. Soon after his departure, I took it up, and after trying it day after day with very little success, I sat myself down and wept bitterly. My tears dropped upon the book, and stained its pages. It was but a momentary irresolution. I went on and on, and began at last to see daylight, ay, and to feel that I could comprehend and reason upon the text and the comments. When I had completed the reading of this most formidable work, I felt that I breathed a purer air, and that I had acquired a new power. The critical period was passed; I no longer hesitated. I pressed on to the severe study of special pleading, and by repeated perusals of Saunders's Reports, acquired such a decided relish for this branch of my profession, that it became for several years afterwards my favorite pursuit. Even at this day I look back upon it with a lingering fondness, although many years have elapsed since I ceased to give it an exclusive attention. It is, in my judgment, the best school for the discipline of an acute and solid lawyer. While in Mr. Sewall's office, I also read through that deep and admirable work upon one of the most intricate titles of the law, Fearne on Contingent Remainders and Executory Devises, and I made a manuscript abstract of all its principles. I am not quite sure that it may not yet be found among my manuscripts.

Upon my admission to the bar I was at a loss where to open an office, and indeed sat down in Salem, rather because I knew not where to go, than because I thought there was any real prospect of success. To young men with my political opinions the times were very discouraging. My father was a Republican, as contradistinguished from a Federalist, and I had naturally imbibed the same opinions. In Massachusetts, at that period, an immense majority of the people were Federalists. All the offices (with scarcely an exception, I believe,) were held by Federalists. The governor, the judges, the legislature, were ardent in the same cause. It cannot be disguised, too, that a great preponderance of the wealth, the rank, the talent, and the civil and literary character of the state, was in the same scale. Almost all the profession of the law were of the party. I scarcely remember more than four or five lawyers in the whole state, who *dared* avow themselves Republicans. The very name was odious, and offensive epithets (such as Jacobins) were familiarly applied to them. The great struggle was just over between Mr. Jefferson and Mr. Adams, and the former had been chosen to the Presidency. The contest had been carried on with great heat and bitterness; and the defeated party, strong at home, though not in the nation, was stimulated by resentment, and by the hope of a future triumph. Under such circumstances, there was a dreadful spirit of persecution abroad. The intercourse of families was broken up, and the most painful feuds were generated. Salem was a marked battle ground for political controversies, and for violent struggles of the parties. The Republican party was at first very small there; and its gradual growth and increasing strength, so far from mitigating, added fuel to the flame.

Such was the state of things at the time when I came to the bar. All the lawyers and all the judges in the county of Essex were Federalists, and I was the first who was obtruded upon it as a political heretic. I was not a little discouraged by this circumstance, and contemplated a removal as soon as I could find a better position or prospect elsewhere. For some time I felt the coldness and estrangement resulting from this known diversity of opinion; and taking, as I did, a firm and decided part in politics, it was not at all wonderful that I should be left somewhat solitary at the bar. Gradually, however, to my surprise, business flowed in upon me; and as I was most diligent and laborious in the discharge of my professional duties, I began in a year or two to reap the reward of my fidelity to my clients. From that time to the close of my career at the bar, my business was constantly on the increase, and at the time when I left it, my practice was probably as extensive and as lucrative as that of any gentleman in the county. Indeed, I contemplated a removal to Boston, as a wider sphere, in which I might act with more success; and I was encouraged to this by retainers from that city in very important causes.

Let me here do justice to a gentleman, whom I have always respected with the most unfeigned sincerity. I have spoken of my peculiar situation at the bar, by which I do not mean that I was treated by any one with harshness or unkindness; far from it. But I was solitary in my political opinions, and therefore in a good measure excluded from those intimacies, which warm and cheer the intercourse of the profession. I wish to speak of one then very eminent at the bar, and still, I thank God, living in the maturity of his reputation. I mean Mr. William Prescott. He was a decided Federalist, and at all times one of the ablest and most accomplished of the Federal leaders. A man of more chivalric honor, of more probity, sound sense, and discretion, I scarcely know. From the moment I came to the bar, he treated me with unhesitating kindness and respect; and when such occurrences were rare from other quarters, I constantly received from him invitations to the parties at his house, as if I belonged to the circle of his own friends. This was kindness when it was useful, and when it was felt, and when, to say the least, it would in public estimation, have been quite as much to his advantage, if he had abstained from such civilities. I have never since ceased to remember this unsought and unbought token of his respect. And I have never since had occasion, even in the bitterest periods of party spirit, to know any diminution of his regard or friendship. It is my pride to count him among those choice friends, whose regard would flatter my pride, and whose censure would infuse the most serious doubts into the estimate of my own conduct.

And this reminds me of another not unimportant circumstance in my professional life. I had not been more than three or four years at the bar, when I was engaged as junior counsel in an insurance cause then pending in the Superior Court of New Hampshire. This was an unexpected honor, and I gladly embraced the retainer. I accordingly went to New Hampshire at the term when the cause was to be tried, having prepared myself as well as I could upon a subject with which my professional experience had as yet furnished me with few practical materials. I there had the pleasure of becoming acquainted with Mr. Jeremiah Mason, then the most eminent counsellor at the bar of New Hampshire, and still maintaining, with undiminished reputation, that proud eminence. He is, as every one acquainted with him knows, a laborious, acute, learned, sagacious, and accurate lawyer, whose mind is capable of the highest reaches of reasoning, and whose comprehensiveness of view rarely leaves any thing untouched or unseen, belonging to the subject which he investigates. He and another distinguished gentleman were our adversaries, and we had the advantage of being for the plaintiff, and of course the right to open and close the cause. My leader I knew little of, but understood that he was ingenious and eloquent, and the cause had many materials for a display of this sort; for one of the vital questions was, whether there had been a fraudulent concealment of the loss before the insurance was effected; and upon the facts, it turned on the nice consideration, whether a letter coming by the mail was received on the day when the insurance was made, or on the succeeding day. Behind this, there were some difficult questions of law in respect to the liability for the loss. It was not until the day before the trial was to take place, that from causes, which it is unnecessary to mention, my leader declined the task, and left me alone in the cause under circumstances of the greatest embarrassment. A stripling, as I was, I had not the rashness to encounter such fearful odds. But it was too late to engage new counsel, and the only alternative was to consent to a verdict against my client, and take the then common remedy of a review or second trial, or to go on and lose the verdict after a struggle for victory. My client's reputation being at stake (and he was a gentleman of fair character) he thought the former course would cast an imputation upon it, and he insisted, against all my remonstrances, upon going on. I yielded, sensible of the rashness of the undertaking, and, ambitious as I was, still too sensible of my own deficiencies to hope for victory in such a struggle. By great good fortune, for I ought not to call it skill, I succeeded. This achievement gave me considerable *éclat*, and I was immediately retained in other causes, and for four or five years afterwards, I continued to practise at the Superior Court of New Hampshire, Rockingham County, with unabated reputation; and then left it, because my home business rendered such absences inconvenient.

But to conclude my story. The cause in which I was successful was tried again upon what is called a review in the local practice. Not choosing to hazard the little I had gained, I made an express stipulation with my client that other counsel should be engaged for the next trial to act as leader. But when the cause at the next term came on for trial, I was astonished to find, that instead of elder counsel, my juniors only were retained. There seemed to be a recklessness of consequences, and a confidence in results in this proceeding, which both alarmed and mortified me; and my fears were excited to a greater height, when, on entering the court, I found that Mr. Dexter, of Boston, then at the head of the Massachusetts Bar, and truly *princeps inter pares*, was to assist Mr. Mason on the other side. I utterly refused to go on; and made a motion for a continuance to the next term, alleging the facts in vindication of it. The motion was overruled; but the court thought I was entitled to the poor indulgence of two days delay to send to Massachusetts for other counsel. A messenger was accordingly despatched for Mr. Prescott, and on returning brought the information, that he was then engaged in a cause at Boston, and that it was impossible to procure his aid. This was on the evening before the day assigned for trial. I was now in utter despondency, and peremptorily declined doing any thing in the cause. My client was an aged man, and wept bitterly, and entreated me not to desert him, assuring me that if with such odds against me I lost the cause, he should be satisfied with my efforts. His tears and entreaties at last brought me over. I moved a second postponement and failed. The cause came on, and I told the real tale of my misfortunes to the jury. I was contending against talents, learning, character, experience, against my will, and conscious of my inability. I asked their indulgence, and I demanded the patient protection of the court. The cause went on, and as might be expected, my learned opponents brought a weight of eloquence and argument, which seemed destined to crush me. Fortunately, I had the reply; and being as well prepared on the law as I could be, I spoke to the matter firmly and closely, with all the vigor I could command, and all the sincerity which I felt. I was again victorious. The jury, rather against the charge of the court, found a verdict in my favor. I have ever thought that the jury felt some sympathy for me in this embarrassed situation and listened to my appeals, as one strong in faith, however wanting in professional skill. My argument, I believe, was thought well of by the bar. At all events, it was a feather in my cap. I learned, indeed, on this occasion, that the race is not always to the swift, nor the battle to the strong, nor yet favor to men of skill; but that time and chance happen unto them all.

I have dwelt longer on this circumstance than I intended: but as it had some influence on my professional career, I thought it might not be uninteresting to you. From that period I was honored with the friendship of Mr. Mason, and that friendship has continued with unabated confidence and cordiality down to the present hour.

In December, 1804, I was married to Miss Mary Lynde

Fitch Oliver, the daughter of the Rev. Thomas F. Oliver, then deceased, (who was the son of the Hon. Andrew Oliver,) and of Mrs. Sarah Oliver, his wife, who was the daughter of William Pynchon, Esq., an eminent ante-revolutionary lawyer. I will not speak to you of this marriage, from which I anticipated so much happiness. Miss Oliver, at the time of our marriage, was about twenty-two years of age, was an elegant and accomplished woman, full of fine sense, and interesting in her person and manners; most persons would have called her beautiful. We were married but a short time; she was taken suddenly ill and died, after a very short sickness on the 22d of June, 1805. This blow I felt with great severity at the time, and it quite unmanned me. It was soon followed by another which completed the prostration of my dearest hopes. My father died within two months afterwards, (in August, 1805.) I never look back upon this period of my life without feeling a sense of desolation. It left a dark and melancholy train of thoughts behind. I was new to sorrow, full of hope and ambition, with an ardent enthusiasm, and, perhaps, an almost romantic wildness of imagination. All my hopes were at once cut down and crushed. I remained for a long time like one in a painful dream, and there ever since has been at times on my mind a cloud of gloom, which sorrow, probably, always gathers, and which even the very sunshine of life does not wholly dissolve.

It was in this year, 1805, that I was first elected a member of the Legislature of Massachusetts, as a representative from Salem. I was annually rechosen until I was appointed to my present judicial office at the close of the year 1811. I was at that time Speaker of the House, having been elected to the station on the resignation of the Hon. Perez Morton, when he was appointed Attorney-General of the State.

Of my legislative career I will say a few words. Though I was a decided member of what was called the Republican party, and of course a supporter of the administration of Mr.

Jefferson and Mr. Madison, you are not to imagine that I was a mere slave to the opinions of either, or that I did not exercise an independent judgment upon public affairs. The Republican party then and at all other times embraced men of very different views on many subjects. A Virginia Republican of that day, was very different from a Massachusetts Republican, and the anti-federal doctrines of the former state then had and still have very little support or influence in the latter State, notwithstanding a concurrence in political action upon general subjects. I was at all times a firm believer in the doctrines of General Washington and an admirer of his conduct, measures, and principles during his whole administration, though they were to me mere matters of history. I read and examined his principles, and have made them in a great measure the rule and guide of my life. I was and always have been a lover, a devoted lover, of the Constitution of the United States, and a friend to the union of the States. I never wished to bring the government to a mere confederacy of States; but to preserve the power of the General Government given by all the States, in full exercise and sovereignty for the protection and preservation of all the States. I never made any concealment of these opinions, and on more than one public occasion I avowed them with a firm and unfaltering explicitness, when silence might perhaps have been deemed more prudent in point of policy. I remember that on one occasion in particular, in the debate on the celebrated resolutions of Mr. Gore, (afterwards Governor,) in 1808, it falling to my lot as a leader in opposition to them to close the debate, I avowed and vindicated my admiration of General Washington's administration in an elaborate review of it.

While a member of the legislature, though I was quite young, I was compelled, from causes to which I have already alluded, to take an important part, and generally a leading part, in every debate which brought the parties into conflict. There were few Republican lawyers in the State, and but few of them in the legislature; and in the Republican ranks, the number of good speakers, or even of tolerable speakers, was small. I thus was pushed forward to a prominence in debate, and in measures, which usually does not fall to the share of a young man in the New England States. I look back to that period of my life with some honest pride, in recollecting that I was not betrayed into any departure from a just moderation of conduct, though my party from being a minority, in the progress of events, obtained a triumphant possession of all the legislative and executive departments. The odious measures of proscription and removals I steadily opposed, and the unjustifiable districting the State into senatorial districts in 1812, which was one of the causes that precipitated the fall of the Republicans from power, I neither aided nor approved; and indeed I ceased to belong to the legislature before it passed.

There is one measure, however, which I ought to mention, because it in fact originated with me, and which without my earnest and resolute support, against the wishes of my friends, would not have passed. I refer to the Act of June, 1806, which raised the salaries of the Judges of the Supreme Court to $2400, and of the Chief Justice to $2500 per annum. Before that Act the salary was for the Chief Justice $1250 (£375) and for the other Judges 1166\frac{2}{3}$, and the Judges annually petitioned the legislature for an annual grant, which was usually given, of about $600. This kept them in a perpetual state of dependence upon the legislature, and contributed in no small degree to the retardation of any solid growth of our Jurisprudence. All the Judges of the Supreme Court were Federalists; and this constituted with many of my political friends a decided objection to the measure, as it gave independence to their enemies. I believed the measure right; and stood forth as its advocate at a time when it was unpopular even with many of our political opponents. It was carried. In June, 1809, finding that the salary was still inadequate, and having learned from Mr. Chief Justice Parsons (a most eminent and accomplished Judge) that he should be compelled to resign unless it was raised, I made another effort to procure an increase. Whether I moved the resolution for the Committee[1] or not, I do not now remember. But the measure was mine; and a favorable report having been made, in the subsequent debate I was left by all those, who were its friends, to conduct, and, indeed, to lead the debate. It encountered great opposition from several quarters, and I bore the brunt and burden of the day. It was triumphant; and the salaries fixed by the Act of June, 1809, for the Chief Justice $3500, and for the associates $3000, still remain the glory of my native State. The measure has secured to her the services of some of her ablest lawyers; and in my humble judgment has contributed more to give permanence to her institutions, dignity to her jurisprudence, and steadiness to her prosperity, than any one single measure of the State during the last forty years. This achievement, however, cost me some political friendships; and it was a long time before I recovered the popularity, which was lost by a measure so odious to some of the Republican leaders of that day.

In the autumn of 1808 I was chosen a member of Congress to fill the vacancy occasioned by the death of my honored and lamented friend, Mr. Jacob Crowninshield, a man of excellent understanding, of manly feeling, and incorruptible integrity. I remained in Congress only during one session, (that of 1808-09,) and declined being a candidate for reëlection. I have no reason to doubt that my reëlection would have been sure, for I was originally chosen without opposition; but considerations of prudence in reference to my profession induced me to withdraw. Indeed I had been long satisfied that a

1 The Committee who reported the Act of June, 1806, were, — Messrs. Story of S., Mr. Slocum, Mr. Wheaton of N., Mr. Kinsley, Mr. Parsons of Chesterfield, Mr. Perry, and Mr. Mason of B. The Committee who reported the Act of 1809, — Mr. Phelps of B., Mr. Foster of B., Mr. Story, Mr. Jackson, and Mr. Wheeler of Lanesborough. The names of the Committee will at once show who were the supporters and opponents of the measure.

continuance in public life was incompatible with complete success at the bar; and the few, though brilliant exceptions, which I have since known to the truth of the remark, and the many confirmations of it, have made me resolute at all times in my advice to ambitious young lawyers never to seek public life, if they mean to be eminent at the bar. Besides, I cannot disguise that I had lost my relish for political controversy, and I found an entire obedience to party projects required such constant sacrifices of opinion and feeling, that my solicitude was greatly increased to withdraw from the field, that I might devote myself with a singleness of heart to the study of the law, which was at all times the object of my admiration and almost exclusive devotion.

During my short career in Congress I did not take any active part in the public measures. One proposition, however, I ventured to move; and as it forms a striking proof of the mutations of party opinion, I will now refer to it. Believing that we were approaching a state of things, which would probably terminate in a war with England, and that the unprotected situation of our commerce, and our want of an effective navy, was an inducement to the continual aggressions of foreign powers, I was anxious for a gradual increase of our naval establishment. I had pondered upon the subject with a good deal of care, and had derived some aid from the experience and knowledge of those most conversant with the subject, and I was led to believe that a force of *ten* ships of the line, and of thirty frigates would, in a war of defence, be an adequate protection to our coast. I considered that Great Britain could not maintain a hostile fleet on our coast, unless at nearly triple our expense, and triple our force; that she must employ at least two squadrons, each of which, to bar accidents, ought to be superior in point of force to our whole armament; and one to relieve the other in rotation. It occurred to me, that the expense of such large fleets would be wholly disproportionate to any naval objects which Great Britain could have in view for conquest or depredations on our coast. Under these impressions, I prepared a motion, which I offered on the fourth day of January, 1809, in the following words: —

"That the committee, &c., be directed to inquire into the expediency of increasing the naval establishment of the United States, with leave to report by bill or otherwise."

I supported the motion in a speech of about an hour and a half in length, with all the ability and resources I possessed; and, without attempting any flights of eloquence, endeavored to demonstrate the propriety of an inquiry into the subject. The proposition was virtually negatived, by an almost universal vote of the Republican party in the House to lay the same on the table, with an avowed determination to defeat it. And some of the gentlemen who spoke in opposition to it, denounced the Navy, and did not hesitate to say that my support of it was pure Federalism, and utterly inconsistent with the known policy of the Republican party. This, I well knew, was true at Washington; but it was not true in respect to Republicanism in Massachusetts. On the seaboard in that State, we were friendly to a naval establishment. Mr. Jefferson was believed to be hostile to such an establishment; and the whole policy of the then administration was so notoriously against it, that I incurred no small share of odium for broaching such a heretical project. I have lived to see the time when our gallant Navy, having fought itself into favor, has become the idol of the nation, and compelled many of its most strenuous opponents to avow themselves friends. Yet its early and its true friends have been forgotten, in the general eagerness to be enrolled among its advocates, at a time when there is no longer any reproach, except in being lukewarm in its praise. Such is the mutability of public opinion!

There is one other act of my brief career, which I notice, only because it has furnished an occasion for a remark of Mr. Jefferson in the recent posthumous publication of his Correspondence, (4th vol. p. 148.) It was during the session of 1808-1809 that the embargo, unlimited in duration and extent, was passed, at the instance of Mr. Jefferson, as a retaliatory measure upon England. It prostrated the whole commerce of America, and produced a degree of distress in the New England States greater than that which followed upon the war. I always thought that it was a measure of doubtful policy, but I sustained it, however, with all my little influence for the purpose of giving it a fair experiment. A year passed away, and the evils, which it inflicted upon ourselves, were daily increasing in magnitude and extent; and in the mean time, our navigation being withdrawn from the ocean, Great Britain was enjoying a triumphant monopoly of the commerce of the world. Alive to the sufferings of my fellow-citizens, and perceiving that their necessities were driving them on to the most violent resistance of the measure, — and, indeed, to a degree which threatened the very existence of the Union, — I became convinced of the necessity of abandoning it, and as soon as I arrived at Washington I held free conversations with many distinguished members of the Republican party on the subject, which were soon followed up by consultations of a more public nature. I found that as a measure of retaliation the system had not only failed, but that Mr. Jefferson, from pride of opinion, as well as from that visionary course of speculation, which often misled his judgment, was resolutely bent upon maintaining it at all hazards. He professed a firm belief that Great Britain would abandon her orders in council, if we persisted in the embargo; and having no other scheme to offer in case of the failure of this, he maintained in private conversation the indispensable necessity of closing the session of congress without any attempt to limit the duration of the system. The consequence of this would be an aggravation for another year of all the evils which then were breaking down New England. I felt that my duty to my country called on me for a strenuous effort to prevent such calamities. And I was persuaded that if the embargo was kept on during the year, there would be an open disregard and resistance of the laws. I was unwearied, therefore, in my endeavors to impress other members of Congress with a sense of our common dangers. Mr. Jefferson has imputed mainly to me the repeal of the embargo, in a letter to which I have already alluded, and has stigmatized me on this account with the epithet of "pseudo-republican." "Pseudo-republican," of course, I must be; as every one was in Mr. Jefferson's opinion, who dared to venture upon a doubt of his infallibility. But Mr. Jefferson has forgotten to mention the reiterated attempts made by him through a committee of his particular adherents (Mr. Giles, Mr. Wilson, Mr. C. Nicholas, and Mr. G. W. Campbell,) to detach me from my object. In the course of those consultations, I learned the whole policy of Mr. Jefferson; and was surprised as well as grieved to find, that in the face of the clearest proofs of the failure of his plan, he continued to hope against facts. Mr. Jefferson has honored me by attributing to my influence the repeal of the embargo. I freely admit that I did all I could to accomplish it, though I returned home before the act passed. The very eagerness with which the repeal was supported by a majority of the Republican party ought to have taught Mr. Jefferson that it was already considered by them as a miserable and mischievous failure. It is not a little remarkable, that many years afterwards, Mr. Jefferson took great credit to himself for yielding up, *suâ sponte*, this favorite measure, to preserve, as he intimates, New England from open rebellion.[1] What in me was almost a crime, became, it seems, in him an extraordinary virtue. The truth is, that if the measure had not been abandoned when it was, it would have overturned the administration itself, and the Republican party would have been driven from power by the indignation of the people, goarded on to madness by their sufferings.

[1] See his letter to General Dearborn, dated July 16th, 1810, and his letter to William B. Giles, dated December 25th, 1825. Jefferson's *Correspondence*, vol. iv. pp. 148, 419.

I have ever considered the embargo a measure which went to the utmost limit of constructive power under the Constitution. It stands upon the extreme verge of the Constitution, being in its very form and terms an unlimited prohibition, or suspension of foreign commerce. If I were disposed to impute to Mr. Jefferson unworthy views, or unconstitutional objects, (which he so liberally attributes to others,) it would not be difficult to select from his life very strong proofs to justify them, after his manner. Who, for instance, can remember, without regret, his conduct in relation to the battue of New Orleans? Who can reconcile his treaty with France, by which Louisiana was adopted into the Union, with his acknowledged opinion, that it was beyond the reach of the Constitution? I speak not my own opinion on the latter point, but his. I never have entertained a doubt of the constitutionality of that treaty.

But I pass from these ungracious topics, to which I should not have alluded, if it had not been in self-defence. You are too young to know the real facts; and when I am dead, you may feel an interest not to have your father's character sullied by the pen of Mr. Jefferson.

In August, 1808, I was married to your mother, (then Miss Sarah Waldo Wetmore,) the daughter of Judge Wetmore. Her father was a distinguished counsellor-at-law, and her mother the granddaughter of the Brigadier General Waldo, who is so well known in our provincial annals.

Your mother was the intimate friend of my first wife, and related to her by marriage. We had the misfortune to lose all our elder children in succession. We buried three daughters and one son before either of them attained seven years of age. They were all very promising children, and our repeated losses almost broke our hearts. Your brother was a boy of very uncommon talents, and bore my name. He died in a decline, after having had the whooping cough, which entirely prostrated him. I have many agonizing recollections on this subject, and some truly pathetic touches of tenderness to tell, but I have neither the heart nor the power to go over them. You will one day learn how difficult it is to bury our sorrows, when they have struck deep into our souls.

In November, 1811, I was appointed one of the Associate Justices of the Supreme Court of the United States, by President Madison, being then thirty-two years of age, and the youngest judge that ever came on that bench. The office was conferred on me without any solicitation on my part, and came upon me quite unexpectedly. I have always supposed that my excellent friend, Mr. Ezekiel Bacon, then of Massachusetts, and now of New York, recommended the appointment.

Being at this time Speaker of the House of Representatives of Massachusetts, (a station to which I was first appointed in January, 1811,) in the following January session I took leave of the House, on resigning my place, in a short address, a copy of which is among my printed papers and pamphlets. I hope you will read it. At this day I do not feel ashamed of it.

I shall not dwell upon the circumstances attending my judicial life, because they are open to you in the decisions as well on my circuit as in the Supreme Court, in the published Reports. The time, however, when I came upon the Bench was quite unpropitious. The docket was then (owing to the protracted infirmity of my predecessor) crowded with penal actions and cases of seizure, arising under the embargo and non-intercourse systems; and in the then excited state of the people, it was no easy matter to administer the law with firmness, and at the same time without offence. The war followed close upon the heels of these measures, and New England was roused into still greater excitement by this new calamity, which seemed in her view to threaten the entire desolation of all her commercial and agricultural interests. In my circuit the principal questions of prize law were of more frequent occurrence than in any other parts of the

Union; and I need scarcely inform you that the task of performing it was ungracious and full of delicate considerations. How it was performed it is not for me to say. Let the printed decisions speak for me on this subject.

The return of peace brought with it, among the public blessings, that which was most welcome to me, the discharge of the ordinary duties of judicial life in the common course of business, free from popular prejudice and party spirit. I labored in my vocation with assiduity, never expecting again to be called into public political scenes. But in the year 1820, there being a convention called to revise the Constitution of Massachusetts, I was elected a member from Salem, and attended during the whole session. You will have an opportunity of reading, in the printed debates, the part which I took on that occasion. But my principal labors were in another body, the great committee on the subject of the representation in the House, whose debates were necessarily private. I there advocated the district system and apportionment of representatives according to population, so as to reduce the representatives to a comparatively moderate number. The plan, though supported by some of the ablest of the Committee, and particularly by Mr. Prescott, failed in Committee, and we agreed to support the next best plan, which should reduce the representation. It was that which was afterwards adopted by the Convention, but which failed with the people from causes wholly accidental, and aside from its merits. I now regret that I did not write out the substance of the speeches which I delivered in the Convention. Except in a single instance I never furnished even a note; and the best speech which I delivered (I do not mean to state what its merits were) is scarcely touched in the printed debates. I mean the speech on the question of amending the Constitution so as to allow the Legislature the power to diminish, as well as increase the salaries of the Judges. This proposition I opposed *totis viribus* in an elaborate argument; and obtained a triumphant vote in the negative, after it had been carried the other way by a very large majority. From accidental circumstances, this speech was reported less fully than any other; and indeed I may say, that not a single speech of mine is given with any thing like fulness or accuracy. Mr. Webster, with great propriety and foresight, corrected all his own. I now regret that I did not undertake a similar labor; *sed pereunt labores.*

Since that period nothing of a peculiar nature has occurred in the even tenor of my life, except my removal from Salem to Cambridge, upon being appointed Dane Professor at Law, a place to which I was carried by the voluntary and unbiased choice of that learned gentleman.

I have not said much to you in these brief memoirs about my own studies, opinions, or pursuits; perhaps at a time of more leisure I shall write some sketches to you which may lead you more thoroughly into the feelings and lucubrations of my early and my later life. In my youth I was smitten with a love of poetry, and I had the rashness to print in a first, and afterwards, in 1804, in a revised edition, a poem called the Power of Solitude, and some other poems. All except two, short and unimportant poems, were written by me.[1] Those two (I have marked them in my own copy) were written by my first wife. The work had very little success. The critics spoke unfavorably of it; and what was a little remarkable, finding from my preface that some of the minor poems were not written by me, they praised highly those which they supposed were not mine (and which in fact were mine) and censured all the others. Such is critical praise, and such critical sagacity. Henceforward I dropped poetry, except as an occasional amusement of a leisure hour; and I departed from its fairy realms with a humble belief that I was not destined to live even at the outskirts of her enchanted scenery. I took a lawyer's farewell of the Muse, and

[1] In a letter to S. P. P. Fay, dated December 26, 1798, at which time he was engaged in the composition of this poem, he speaks of it as "the sweet employment of my leisure hours."

following out the precepts of Blackstone, plunged at once into the dark labyrinths of the ancient learning of the law. Yet I cannot say, even at this distance of time, that

> "The dreams of Pindus and the Aonian maid
> Invite no more."

For though no longer a votary, I delight to visit the haunts of poetry, to listen to the lofty strains of the great masters of the lyre, to gaze on the magnificent structures reared by her worshippers, and to catch a transient inspiration, while roaming abroad through nature.

> I feel the gales that round me blow,
> A momentary bliss bestow,
> As waving wide their gladsome wing
> My weary soul they seem to soothe;
> And redolent of joy and youth
> To breathe a second spring.

But to drop metaphor. I still continue to relish poetry and fiction with a warm and vigorous love; not, indeed, in the daily outpourings of modern poets, but in the works of the great Classics of our language, of Milton, and Shakspeare, and Dryden, and Pope, and Thomson, and Gray, and Goldsmith, and others, of that true school of immortal verse. Of the more modern poets, my principal favorites are Cowper and Crabbe; the former for his singular beauty and simplicity of thought and language, and severe truth of morals; the latter for his almost supernatural illustrations of the human character in all its nicest shades and most secret workings.

But I forbear, for I have wandered from my purpose. As an appropriate close of these slight sketches, I shall subjoin a list of my literary and professional labors.[1] Some of them

[1] The accompanying list is by no means a complete one. There are other compositions (particularly legal) of which at present I shall say nothing, though the time may arrive in which it will be proper to disclose them. J. S.

[This list is so incomplete that it is here omitted. — EDITOR.]

are scarcely worth your examination, except as matters of filial curiosity; and some are in bad taste, but such as belonged to the day when they were written; others, perhaps, you may find not wholly without interest or use. Such as they are, my dear son, I commend them to your kindness.

May God in his good providence grant you many years of happiness; may your attainments far outreach those of your parent; and your genius, matured by the masculine study of the best writers, give you a just claim on the gratitude of your country, as one of its ornaments and its protectors.

I am, most affectionately,

Your father,

JOSEPH STORY.

MR. WILLIAM W. STORY.

LITERATURE AND JURISPRUDENCE.

INFRINGEMENTS OF THE NEUTRAL TRADE OF THE UNITED STATES.

A MEMORIAL ADDRESSED TO THE PRESIDENT AND CONGRESS OF THE UNITED STATES IN BEHALF OF THE INHABITANTS OF SALEM, MASSACHUSETTS.

THE Memorial of the Inhabitants, &c., humbly showeth, That on ordinary occasions they have deemed it unnecessary to apply for redress of grievances to the Government of their country, confiding in the rectitude and wisdom of its councils; and, though their confidence in this respect is undiminished, yet, as questions of national moment are now agitated, and aggressions committed on our commerce in a manner unprecedented, they deem it their duty to approach the constituted authorities, and express their sentiments with fidelity and deliberation.

It has been a source of the purest satisfaction to your Memorialists, that, while foreign nations have been engaged in wars, which in their nature and consequences have transcended the limits of human foresight, the United States have, under the benign care of Providence, been preserved in the enjoyment of peace and liberty. They have beheld with pleasure our commerce, at first feeble and confined, gradually expanding with awakened enterprise, until it has reached the farthest shores, and embraced the most inhospitable climes. This commerce, prosecuted with increasing vigor, and fostered by new aids, has continually brought to our ports the wealth of all nations, and, by opening a liberal intercourse, added fresh zeal to foreign industry and domestic labor.

Your Memorialists, considering war an evil, which cannot be confined in its consequences to belligerents, even when prosecuted with good faith and amicable intentions towards neutrals, and believing it the sound policy of the United States to avoid every entanglement in it, as injurious to internal improvement and external interests, have witnessed with unhesitating approbation the disposition to neutrality patronized by the General Government, at times when national wrongs have been pressed upon us with peculiar aggravations, and seemed to point to a summary redress. Firmness and moderation have happily secured all the advantages of successful war; and the sober appeal of reason has carried conviction to foreign nations. From considerations of a similar nature, your Memorialists have submitted to the injuries of belligerents during the late European war, and awaited with confidence the decisions of prize tribunals, instituted to adjust national rights, and afford a fair, though tardy, redress to grievances. To these tribunals, elevated in the presence of the world, as the learned and impartial courts of nations, they have hoped, that all parties might appeal for justice, and receive a righteous reward. In some instances they have been disappointed; in others they have realized their expectations. And even when they could not admit the correctness of some decisions, principles of national law have been expounded, and rules prescribed, which might serve as polestars for their future direction.

Your Memorialists, however, have witnessed, with deep regret and deep anxiety, that to some of these tribunals they can no longer appeal for safety. New interpretations of old rules, and new glosses on ancient doctrines, have been put forth to control the course of neutral commerce, and restrain, if not annihilate, its most beneficial operations. Their surprise has been greater in this respect, because the nation, which has adopted them, is one from which we had a right to expect the most conciliatory conduct; since with her ultimately centre the proceeds of our commerce, and from her we purchase the greatest portion of her staple manufactures. The interests of Great Britain and the United States seem in this respect mutual. We consume the products of her industry, and give her in return, besides large sums of money, raw materials, by which she may levy new contributions upon us. Similarity of manners and habits, of language and education, have added artificial inducements for intercourse, and gained for her among us a respect not slightly to be viewed, or inconsiderately forfeited. On all occasions, the United States have exhibited towards her an amicable disposition, and a just, and, it may be added, a generous, policy. If, therefore, we had favors to ask or receive, our claims would be peculiarly strong upon her, because we have been emphatically the sinews of her opulence. But it is believed, that the United States never asked of any nation more than justice, and are willing to be bound by the established rules of commerce. Your Memorialists, therefore, express deep regret, because the public confidence has been shaken, which may not easily be restored; and deep anxiety, because the principles alluded to, if conceded, must eventually prostrate our trade, or leave it at the arbitrary discretion of the belligerents. Whether peace or war prevail, the baneful influence of these principles will everywhere be felt; and in the latter predicament we shall, as neutrals, share the mischiefs of the war, without the chances of the benefits of it.

With these impressions, your Memorialists respectfully submit some observations on the nature and importance of the principles avowed by the British High Court of Admiralty. On the present occasion they would avoid the discussion of contested points respecting the freedom of commerce, on which civilians have entertained different opinions. They would avoid the question, how far even a direct trade, carried on by neutrals between the colony and mother country, with *bonâ fide* neutral property, is protected by the law of nations, though it may justly be a ground of national investigation. They are willing to avoid these extrinsic, though important, subjects, and meet the principle of the English courts upon the laws and usages sanctioned by the practice of nations.

The principle recently established by Great Britain is, as your Memorialists understand it, that it is not competent for a neutral to carry on in war any trade, which he is not accustomed to do in peace; and that he shall not be permitted to effect that in a circuitous, which is inhibited in a direct, trade. As corollaries from this principle, she insists, that the colonial trade, exercised by neutrals, shall not extend beyond the accustomed peace establishment; and that whenever the neutral imports into his own country colonial produce, with the intention to transship it to the mother country, if a direct intercourse be interdicted in peace, the circuity of the route shall not protect the property from confiscation. It seems admitted, that such circuitous route, with such intention, is not considered as evidence of enemy's property, confiscable within ordinary rules; but as a distinct, substantial, principle of condemnation, independent of the other both in efficacy and application. For it yields not to the most clear proof of neutral property, or innocent, though misdirected, conduct. The unaccustomed trade, or the importation with specific intentions, are the tests, by which every voyage is to be tried.

If these doctrines form a part of the law of nations, however mischievous they may be in operation, the United States must submit to them, until they are relaxed by particular conventions. Though our commerce should be oppressed, and our enterprise crushed, yet we are bound to acquiesce, if the sanction of universal justice require it.

Your Memorialists, however, beg leave, before they consider the law of nations in this particular, to advert to a few of the consequences resulting from this rule; and, if they do not greatly mistake, from thence will arise a strong argument of its inadmissibility.

In the first place, great evils must, in the nature of things, result from the indefiniteness of what is the accustomed trade. Nations are continually changing their policy, their imports and exports, their manufactures, their staples, and their commercial connections. In peace, as well as in war, peculiar circumstances induce them to open or close a traffic; and these circumstances arise as often from accidental caprice as from political wisdom. Besides these, the silent operation of time, by destroying old sources of revenue, and developing new wants, and in a more important view, by erecting the grandeur of one state on the destruction of another, with secret fatality changes the channels of commerce, and forbids it to flow in a uniform course. It seems conceded on all sides, that the rule shall not apply to every case; and that those changes, which seem not to be the result of a necessity imposed by an enemy, are exempted from its operation. But how shall these limits be defined? Every nation varies its policy in this respect in time of war; and even Great Britain relaxes her navigation acts to meet the ordinary exigencies of it. On such occasions she admits neutrals to import into her dominions articles not the growth of their own country. She admits foreigners into her mercantile, as well as her military, marine. She opens her colonies to importations strictly forbidden in peace; and allowed with jealous caution, even under the pressure of war. To changes of this nature, if they do not arise out of the predominance of the enemy's force, or out of any necessity resulting therefrom, her own civilians avow, that the rule of accustomed trade ought not to extend. According to them, it is not every convenience, or even every necessity, arising out of the state of war, but that necessity, which arises out of the impossibility of otherwise providing against the urgency of the distress, inflicted by the hand of a superior enemy, that can be admitted to produce such an effect. But in what manner shall this impossibility be determined? How shall we distinguish between the ordinary and the extraordinary necessities of war?—between those evils inflicted by a superior force, and those resulting from general embarrassment? How shall we distinguish, which is the predominant power, when one may be conqueror at one point, and conquered at another? — one all-powerful by sea, another all-powerful by land? How shall we provide for, or foresee, the changes of the day, when time with unmeasured rapidity retrieves losses in the hour of defeat, and destroys power in the hour of victory? In the opinion of your Memorialists, there is but one test of such predominancy, and that is within the old law of nations. It is, when the belligerent is able to blockade the ports of his enemy; and then his right to exclude neutrals is coëxtensive with this ability to blockade. If any other test be resorted to; if the unlimited ingenuity of the discretion of courts of admiralty be exercised in the application or denial of the rule; the rights of neutrals will change with the policy of every administration, and rise and fall with the pressure of hostilities, and the safety of depredation. Surely, no principle of the law of nations can be bottomed on so fluctuating a basis. It would reverse the nature of all law, which is fixed and determinate, and substitute a discretion little less injurious than despotism.

In another view, the rule appears to your Memorialists not less untenable and unjust. It is stated, as a part of it, that, if colonial produce be imported by any person with an intention to transship it on his own account to the mother country, it is subject to confiscation; but if imported for the purpose of general commerce, and thrown into the market for general transshipment, it is within the exception. To distinguish between general and particular intentions, and to separate things so subtile in their own natures, and almost incapable of proof, for the purposes of national decisions, seems a refinement reserved for the present age. In the nature of things it can hardly be possible to determine the intention of a merchant in importation. These may be formed and fixed at one moment, and abandoned from a change of circumstances at another. The fluctuations of foreign markets, the plenty or deficiency of the supply at home, the nature of the funds, the success of the incipient voyage, and numerous other accidents, must continually change the destination of importations, and divert them into various channels. In no case, therefore, can there arise an indisputable presumption, that a merchant imports with a determination to export. Indeed, as his intention must frequently be ambulatory, the presumption lies as strongly the other way. And even if in a few instances that intention could be ascertained, thousands of cases must arise in which it would be impossible to form a criterion for judgment. All must be doubt, caprice, or speculative construction.

These objections apply to the embarrassments attending the exercise of the rule respecting intentions of merchants. But a more serious one may be urged against it, grounded upon its inefficacy, as it respects both neutral and belligerent. As it respects the neutral, if the rule is once known, transfers of property will be immediately made. There will be an impossibility of preventing frauds in these transfers, (if they deserve the name,) by any tests applicable to them, unless restrictions are imposed, or evidence required, which no authorities could procure, and no independent nation ought to submit to. As it respects the belligerent, the same produce after sale would, according to his own principles, be admissible into the ports of his enemy; and in that way the same assistance would be supplied, and the same embarrassments be prevented. The importer will communicate a title to his vendee, which he does not himself possess, and clothe his agent with an authority, which he cannot exercise at his own hands. The rule, therefore, would require the mere formality of a sale; but it would effect none of the objects which it professes to value; and its foundation would be shaken by the extent of its exceptions. Considered in this view, your Memorialists cannot but suppose, that no such modification will ultimately prevail; but by degrees the restriction will become absolute against all neutral carriage of colonial produce to the mother country under every variety of intention. In any other way the rule might be nugatory, and with this unmeasured influence, it must be ruinous.

The foundation of this modern doctrine is laid in this principle, that the neutral has no right by an extension of this trade to afford supplies to the belligerent; because by such trade he assists the belligerent to ward off the blows of his enemy, and to oppose for a longer period the dominion of his force. But to this your Memorialists deem it a conclusive answer, that the proposition proves too much; that, if true, it is a foundation for a far more broad and sweeping principle; namely, that every commerce with a belligerent is inhibited to neutrals; for every commerce assists him in resistance, and diminishes his necessities. A doctrine thus comprehensive has never yet been avowed; and it is presumed never will be. Yet such must be the logical conclusion; and it shows irresistibly the absurdity of the assumed premises. The accustomed, as well as unaccustomed, trade, is within the terms of the principle, and must stand or fall together. Either the doctrine is unsound, and assumed as a mere pretext for predatory seizures, or neutrals have no rights as such, and must endure the calamities inflicted by belligerents in a contest, in which they have no voice, and from which they can reap only injury.

Other considerations add force to the preceding remarks. It is well known, that in time of war neutrals cannot carry on even their accustomed trade in its full extent. They are prohibited from trading in contraband goods, and to blockaded ports. Variations necessarily arise in the relations of the hostile powers, which the neutral ought to possess a right to turn to his profit, as an indemnity for the obstructions of his old trade. These obstructions are of a very serious nature. When exercised in the mildest form, they produce oppressive searches and delays, expensive litigation, and often total failure of an otherwise lucrative voyage. Reason would therefore seem to declare, that for hazards of this nature the benefits arising to neutrals from war are not more than a just equivalent. But if the obstructions be enforced, and no new channels permitted, it seems hardly too much to say, that they must lead to an extinction of all neutral commerce. If one belligerent adopt the rule, another has the same right; and regulations of colonial monopoly would then serve as false lures, only to ensnare and betray neutral navigation. It is somewhat singular, that a belligerent should invite a trade with itself, which it declares fraudulent with its enemy; and should lift the arm of power to crush the neutral, whose conduct is criminal only when it ceases to be partial.

Such are the remarks, which your Memorialists respectfully submit upon the rule considered in itself. On this examination they confess it appears to them fundamentally incorrect. It subjects commerce to fluctuating decisions, overthrows the ordinary rules of evidence, and places an immense power to be wielded at the uncontrollable discretion of magistrates appointed by a single party. It therefore wants all the discriminative features of a fundamental proposition of the law of nations,—uniformity, precision, and general applicability. It would, in their opinion, if established, create greater evils than it professes to redress, by perpetuating strife, destroying the emoluments of trade, embarrassing commercial intercourse, and letting loose the passions to prey on the miseries and plunder the property of the innocent. It would subject neutrals to hazards nearly as perilous, as those of actual hostilities; and, independently of its influence in stimulating to revenge and retaliation, it would transfer the benefits of peace to any victorious usurper of the ocean.

But your Memorialists are unwilling to rest the question on the preceding grounds, however supported by reason. They appeal to higher considerations, and deny, that the rule is, or ever has made a part of the public law, or is recognized by usage or prescription among nations. They admit, that uninterrupted and general usage, fortified by open acquiescence, forms a strong argument, perhaps a conclusive proof, of the adoption of any rule; that, if such usage had existed in the present case, and had been invariably pursued, the presumption would have been violent, that the doctrine is just, and ought not now to be shaken. But your Memorialists have in vain sought in ancient jurists, universally consulted and approved, any principle, that bears in its bosom the present. On the contrary, every page appears to give a direct contradiction to it. They adhere to the ancient interpretation of the law of nations, which pronounces, that the goods of an enemy are lawful prize, and those of a friend are free; that the neutral, except in cases of blockade and contraband, has a right to the uninterrupted pursuit of his commerce, when carried on with his own property, at all events in a direct trade from his own country. Such your Memorialists deem to have been the incontestable rights of neutrals, established for more than two centuries by universal acknowledgment, and acted upon, while a flourishing intercourse subsisted among all maritime nations. During the same period, Great Britain, France, Spain, Portugal, and Holland, have possessed extensive colonies, and engaged in commercial enterprises with an uncommon spirit of rivalry. If, therefore, any such rule, as is now claimed, had existed, innumerable cases must have occurred in the controversies of these nations to legitimate its introduction, and authorize its application. Yet no instance has been adduced in diplomatic or admiralty annals, which savors of a reference to such a rule. The approved publicists, to whom in national contests appeals are made, intimate none, and lay down the law in as broad and satisfactory terms, as your Memorialists.

Your Memorialists are aware, that even the advocates of Great Britain have not pretended to ascertain the existence of the pretended rule previous to the year 1756. To this period they refer for its first establishment, and from this origin deduce its universal reception. They pretend not to quote any foreign adjudications as in point; but rest satisfied, that their own courts were competent to establish the law, and to give it binding efficacy over all nations. To such conclusions your Memorialists confess themselves unable to bow. They conceive, that it is not within the authority of any one nation to legislate for the rest; and that the law of nations, being founded on the tacit convention of the nations that observe it, can be binding only on those nations, which have adopted it. Any other conclusion would lead to the most mischievous consequences, and oblige every nation to vindicate every other against aggressions, though its own rights might be undisputed. To give any precedent, therefore, a binding authority among nations, it must have been recognized as such by them; and no argument of its admission can be drawn from their silence, when the subject did not necessarily engage their immediate interest. An injurious pretension, when not applied to a particular state, might be easily dismissed without consideration.

But your Memorialists, after all the inquiry, which they have been able to make, confess themselves wholly ignorant of any precedent of the present rule in the year 1756. The cases of that period, which are relied on as proof, seem to them wholly inadequate for the purpose. As far as their researches extend, those cases respected the Dutch, and proceeded on a principle entirely different. They were cases, in which Dutch vessels became the carriers of colonial produce, the property of the enemies of Great Britain. This trade was vindicated on the ground of a special treaty between Great Britain and Holland, which provided, that free ships should make free goods; and it was ultimately declared illegal, because enemies' goods were protected by that treaty only in the accustomed trade. No controversy appears to have been raised as to the security of neutral property under similar circumstances. Nor should it be forgotten, that the Dutch protested, in terms of the warmest reprobation, against those condemnations, and asserted them to be contrary to the general law, as well as to the faith of treaties. Those cases seem, therefore, certainly to fail in analogy to those which they are cited to govern. In the one class, the property is neutral; in the other, hostile; in the one, the trade is for the sole benefit of the neutral; in the other, for the sole benefit of the belligerent. In a word, the one respects the rights of peaceful nations according to the public law; the other, the construction of particular treaties. The precedent seems, therefore, to want every essential similitude; and is traversable in every variety of its application.

Yet, admitting the precedent to be in point, if it stands solitary, if it has subsequently slumbered during nearly fifty years, unacknowledged abroad, and unenforced at home; it surely cannot weigh on the present occasion. It is conceded by the British civilians, that during the American Revolution the doctrine was entirely pretermitted, and the commerce of neutrals was pursued according to the ancient code. Many cases of this period might be cited from the admiralty records, which overthrow the rule, and expressly vindicate the opposite rule. If precedents are to decide, the judgments of a tribunal established in Great Britain under her sole appointment, and acting with open powers, must surely, when acquiescence creates the law, completely establish the renunciation of the contested rule. It is in vain to resort to conjectures or ingenious subtilties to fritter away authorities. The faith of the nation has been pledged by its tribunals; and it is too late now to travel out of the record. Place the whole argument of precedent in its strongest light, and it will appear, that in the year 1756 the doctrine was first assumed, and in the year 1801 was first executed.

So far, however, from being recognized, this pretended rule of the year 1756 was pointedly denied, at the moment of its introduction, by the power affected by it; and on its late resuscitation it has met the determined reprobation of the United States. Our minister at the Court of London, on the development of it in the year 1801, remonstrated against it in a spirited memorial. Indeed, Russia, France, Sweden,

Denmark, Prussia, Portugal, and Austria, in the celebrated League of the armed neutrality in the year 1780, expressly declared, and Great Britain was then compelled to admit, as the law of nations, that all neutrals may freely navigate from port to port, and on the coasts of the nations at war. Contraband articles and blockaded ports were the only admitted exceptions. This solemn protest of Europe, after an elaborate discussion, in which all neutral nations assisted, is singly opposed by the instructions of Great Britain, and is to be outweighed by an obscure and resisted precedent. Nay more, the united voice of the maritime world, and the practice of ages, must yield to the interested decisions of a single state, and change with the varying policy of its cabinet. There is, indeed, no difficulty in referring principles to former times, when it suits the public convenience; and as the argument of ancient usage is of deep concern in national pretensions, it is too often a cover for unjustifiable spoliations.

With these preliminaries, your Memorialists feel confidence in asserting, that goods not contraband, fairly purchased by the neutral, are free to the market of every country, and protected from seizure, except in cases of blockade. Guided by these principles, they perceive a plain and honorable path for commerce. Beyond them all is involved in uncertainty.

It is not the least singularity attending the conduct of the present war, that Great Britain has licensed her own subjects in a trade, which she declares fraudulent in others; that she admits them unmolested to supply her enemy with means of resistance, when she declares, that confiscation is the penalty of neutral succor. Were the rule ever so just in itself, it certainly demands relaxation, when the belligerent partakes the profits, and connives at the breach. If its foundation be the unlawfulness of affording assistance to a distressed enemy, surely it ought not to be enforced, when that assistance is an authorized object of speculation with the distressing belligerent.

Your Memorialists heartily concur with their fellow-citizens in repelling with indignation the imputation of fraud, attached by Great Britain to our colonial commerce. They conceive it to be a fair, lawful, and honorable traffic, cherished by the resources of our own country, independent of all foreign succor. Fraud may occasionally contaminate the transactions of all nations. But no one, who has estimated the extent of our resources, or the respectability of our merchants, could for a moment believe them subservient to the fraudulent purposes of any nation. It is our pride to believe, that the American merchants, with very few exceptions, are as distinguished for good faith as any on earth. The imputation thrown on them is a masked pretence to repel the odium of vexatious injuries, and to excuse violations of law, which cannot be justified.

Your Memorialists are sorry, that other instances of hostile conduct have been manifested by Great Britain, less direct in their nature, but not less derogatory to our sovereignty, than those above enumerated. The impressment of our seamen, notwithstanding clear proofs of citizenship, the violation of our jurisdiction by captures at the mouths of our harbors, and the insulting treatment of our ships on the ocean, are subjects worthy the serious consideration of our national councils, and will, we have no doubt, receive an early, prompt, and decisive attention.

Complaints also of a serious nature have arisen against other nations, on account of the conduct of piratical depredators, and the lawless plunderings by privateers on our coasts. From whatever authority these evils proceed, whether from the secret connivance of foreign powers, or the baneful machinations of individuals, we trust, that our national honor will not long be unsupported by a national naval force.

These are the considerations, which your Memorialists beg leave to submit to the wisdom of the General Government. Though they have not suffered very greatly in their individual interests, they feel deeply impressed with the opinion, that the cause is national, and the feelings should be the same. They cherish the hope, that a sense of mutual interest and good faith will successfully terminate the present embarrassments. They wish for peace, for honorable peace. They ask for no measure, but what justice approves, and reason enforces. They claim merely to pursue a fair commerce with its ordinary privileges, and to support the independence of their country by the acquisitions of lawful industry. They wish to take no part in the contests, which now convulse the world; but, acting with impartiality towards all nations, to reap the fruits of a just neutrality. If, however, conciliation cannot effect the purpose of justice, and an appeal to arms be the last and necessary protection of our honor, they feel no disposition to decline the common danger, or shrink from the common contribution.

Relying on the wisdom and firmness of the General Government in this behalf, they feel no hesitation to pledge their lives and property in support of the measures which may be adopted to vindicate the public rights, and redress the public wrongs. And, as in duty bound, will every pray.

Signed in behalf of the said Inhabitants by their authority.

John Hathorne,
Joseph Sprague,
Jonathan Mason,
Benjamin Crowninshield, Jr.
Joseph White, Jr.
Joseph Story,
} Committee.

REPORT ON THE SALARIES OF THE JUDICIARY.

IN FAVOR OF INCREASING THE SALARIES OF THE JUSTICES OF THE SUPREME COURT OF MASSACHUSETTS, MADE TO THE HOUSE OF REPRESENTATIVES OF THAT STATE, IN JUNE, 1806.[1]

THE Committee, to whom was referred the order of the House of Representatives, "to consider, whether any addition is necessary to be made to the salaries of the Judges of the Supreme Judicial Court of this Commonwealth," report: That the constitution of this Commonwealth has provided, "that permanent and honorable salaries shall be established by law for the Justices of the Supreme Judicial Court; and that if it shall be found, that any of the salaries aforesaid, so established, are insufficient, they shall, from time to time, be enlarged, as the General Court shall judge proper."

By an Act of February, 1781, soon after the constitution was adopted, the salary of the chief justice was fixed at $1066.66, and of the other justices of said court at $1000 each, per annum. These continued to be their salaries, until, by an Act of February, 1790, that of chief justice was fixed at $1233.33, and of the other justices at $1166.66. These last have ever since continued to be, and still are, the only permanent compensations of the said justices, they being debarred by law from receiving any fees or perquisites. By

1 "Permit me to recommend to your consideration the contents of a letter, addressed to me by Theophilus Parsons, Esq., Chief Justice of the Supreme Judicial Court, relating to the compensation allowed to justices of that court, and particularly to the grants made by the legislature in part of it, which are not permanent." —*Extract from Governor Strong's Message*, June, 1806.

occasional resolves, from 1794 to 1804, temporary grants have been made to the said justices, of sums, varying from $166.66 to $600; but these grants have been limited to one year. By a resolve of March, 1804, a grant was made to the said justices of $800 annually for three years, commencing in January, 1804, which, of course, expires with the present year.

The Committee further report, that, although it would be unbecoming in them to decide, that the acts of the legislature are in any manner a violation of the constitution; yet, they respectfully submit, whether the temporary grants aforesaid can be considered such a permanent compensation, as is within the purview of the article of the constitution above recited, and consistent with the clause in the Declaration of Rights, that the Justices of the Supreme Judicial Court "should have honorable salaries ascertained and established by standing laws."

Whatever may be the correct opinion on this subject, the Committee entertain great doubts of the policy of any measure, which has the immediate tendency to place the judicial department at the footstool of the legislature. They beg leave to quote for this purpose the words of the constitution, applied to the salary of the governor, and which seem, from their connection with the clause relative to the salaries of the judges, as well as from their forcible expression, to be peculiarly directed to this principle: "As the public good requires, that the governor should not be under the undue influence of any of the members of the General Court, by a dependence on them for a support; that he should in all cases act with freedom for the benefit of the public; that he should not have his attention necessarily directed from that object to his private concerns; and that he should maintain the dignity of the Commonwealth in the character of its chief magistrate; it is necessary he should have an honorable stated salary, of a fixed value, amply sufficient for those purposes, and established by standing laws."

These reasons, so applicable to a chief magistrate, certainly lose none of their force when considered in reference to courts of law. Before these tribunals, the property, the reputation, the rights and liberties, and, above all, the life, of every individual citizen of this Commonwealth, are subjects of decision. On the inflexible integrity, the profound knowledge, and strict impartiality, of the Justices of the Supreme Judicial Court, who are arbiters in the last resort, assisted by intelligent jurors, rests every thing, which is dear to us in life, and which can affect us with posterity; every thing, which is honorable in character, or valuable in enjoyment; in one word, every thing, which renders society a blessing, and secures its continuance.

The Committee would therefore inquire, whether it be not of the last importance, that judges should be elevated above the hope of reward, the influence of affection, or the fear of censure? Whether they should not be wholly exempt from any consideration of immediate support, and placed as a refuge and protection in times of political heat, beyond the necessity of bending to the changes of those times, in order to gather favor, or avert calamity? Whether they should not be placed beyond even the temptation of accommodating the law to present purposes; and, by gratifying ambition or interest, to break down the rules, that guard the security of property and the safety of rights? Whether, indeed, their compensation ought not to be such, as to command the first talents in the community, and insure to those, who are learned and honest, as well as those who are great and rich, the participation of those juridical honors, to which the lucubrations of twenty laborious years are scarcely adequate? The Committee beg leave to submit, as their opinion, that these inquiries must lead to a conclusion, that independence in compensation, as well as in tenure of office, is essential to the permanent respectability of the judicial department.

The Committee further report, that, since the year 1790, the business of the Justices of the Supreme Judicial Court has increased at least fourfold. They are obliged to travel into many counties twice a year, where formerly they travelled but once; and in some counties terms of the said Court are now held, where formerly there was none. The great extension of population and agriculture, the variety and intricacy of a new and continually increasing commerce, and the almost endless other subjects of litigation, consequent on a flourishing domestic intercourse, have swelled, and are annually swelling, the already crowded dockets of every judicial court. For six months every year the judges of the Supreme Judicial Court are travelling the circuits of the Commonwealth, and their expenses on this account are great. The other six months are absorbed in pursuits, not less fatiguing to themselves, nor less important to the people. In the vacations, they are necessarily engaged in forming and digesting opinions on special verdicts, reserved cases, cases on demurrer, and other questions of law, referred solely to the Court for decision, which are too intricate for judgment on the circuits, and require deep and minute investigation in the closet. Their whole time, therefore, both for their own reputation and for the despatch of justice, must be devoted to the public. Domestic concerns, and, much more, the active pursuit of property, are, in a great degree, inconsistent with their duties; and, as they are thus shut out from the acquisition of wealth, it would seem to be the proper office of the legislature to become the guardians of their families, and the supporters of their independence. Considering, therefore, the salaries established in 1790, either in regard to the increased duties of the judges, the greater number of circuits, and the vast addition of business in the courts, or the great depreciation of money, and consequent higher price of the necessaries of life, the Committee cannot but think, that double those salaries at the present time would hardly be a compensation equivalent to those permanently established in 1790; which, from grants almost immediately succeeding, seem to have been then deemed insufficient by the legislature.

6

With these views, the Committee respectfully report, that in their opinion it is necessary to make an addition to the salaries of the judges of the Supreme Judicial Court of this Commonwealth; and they report a bill accordingly.[1]

By order of the Committee.

JOSEPH STORY, *Chairman.*

[1] The bill passed into a law; and the salaries were again increased by another act, passed in 1809.

ADDRESS ON RESIGNING THE SPEAKER'S CHAIR,

DELIVERED IN THE HOUSE OF REPRESENTATIVES OF MASSACHUSETTS, JANUARY 17, 1812.

"COMMONWEALTH OF MASSACHUSETTS,
"*In the House of Representatives.*

"*Thursday*, 16*th January*, 1812.

"The Speaker signified that his duty elsewhere would not permit him to officiate in the House, after to-morrow.

"*Friday*, 17*th January*, 1812.

"On motion of the Hon. Mr. Bigelow, of Medford, —

"*Resolved unanimously*, That the thanks of this House be presented to the Hon. JOSEPH STORY, Esq., for his able, faithful, and impartial discharge of the duties of the chair, during the present year.

"The foregoing Resolution being passed in a very full House, and by the Clerk declared to be unanimous, the Speaker rose and addressed them as follows:"

GENTLEMEN OF THE HOUSE OF REPRESENTATIVES:

THE flattering commendations, recorded in your recent vote, claim, in return, the most sincere expressions of my gratitude. To the good opinion of my fellow-citizens I could never pretend an indifference; and I am free to confess, that the approbation of the Representatives of an enlightened people could not have been conveyed in a manner better calculated to excite my highest sensibility.

The time has now arrived, when it becomes necessary for me to ask your indulgence to retire from the chair, which your suffrages heretefore assigned me. On this occasion, which is probably the last, on which I shall ever have the privilege to address you, I feel an unusual interest mingled with inexpressible melancholy. I have to bid farewell to many distinguished friendships, which have been the pride and pleasure of my life. With many of you I have, for a series of years, shared the labors and the duties of legislation, sometimes with success, and sometimes with defeat. With all of you I have rejoiced to coöperate in support of the character and principles of our native state — a state, which was the cradle, and, I trust in God, will be the perpetual abode, of liberty.

May I be permitted to add, that, during the period, in which I have had the honor to preside over your deliberations, the manly confidence, the elevated candor, and the invariable decorum of the House, have smoothed a seat, which, though adorned with flowers and honors, is to the ingenuous mind the thorny pinnacle of anxiety and toil. Cheered, indeed, by your kindness, I have been able, in controversies marked with peculiar political zeal, to appreciate the excellence of those established rules, which invite liberal discussions, but define the boundary of right, and check the intemperance of debate. I have learned, that the rigid enforcement of these rules, while it enables the majority to mature their measures with wisdom and dignity, is the only barrier of the rights of the minority against the encroachments of power and ambition. If any thing can restrain the impetuosity of triumph, or the vehemence of opposition — if any thing can awaken the glow of oratory, and the spirit of virtue — if any thing can preserve the courtesy of generous minds, amidst the rivalries and jealousies of contending parties, — it will be found in the protection with which these rules encircle and shield every member of the legislative body. Permit me, therefore, with the sincerity of a parting friend, earnestly to recommend to your attention a steady adherence to these venerable usages.

Called, as I now am, to act in other scenes, I cannot but feel the deepest humility in weighing my own deficiencies and the new responsibility imposed upon me; at the same time I cannot but recollect, that I leave my legislative associates amidst perils which may truly be said to try men's souls. I am not unconscious of the difficulties which surround the public councils; nor of the gloom and the silence which presage approaching storms. Many of the Revolutionary worthies of our native State, to whom we might look for support, are gathered to their fathers. I might mention the names of Bowdoin, Hancock, Adams, and Sumner, and embrace no very distant period. Within my own short political life, the tomb has closed over the generous Knox, the intrepid Lincoln, the learned Dana, and the accomplished Sullivan. But the fame of their achievements has not passed away; the laurels yet freshen and repose on their sepulchres; and the memory of their deeds will animate their children boldly to dare, and gloriously to contend for their injured country. I persuade myself, that the flame kindled in the Revolution will burn with inextinguishable splendor; that, when the voice of the nation shall call to arms, this hall will witness a heroic firmness, an eloquent patriotism, and a devotion to the public weal, which have not been exceeded in the annals of our country.

COURSE OF LEGAL STUDY.

AN ARTICLE WRITTEN FOR THE NORTH AMERICAN REVIEW, IN 1817, ON "A COURSE OF LEGAL STUDY, ADDRESSED TO THE STUDENTS OF LAW IN THE UNITED STATES, BY DAVID HOFFMAN, PROFESSOR OF LAW IN THE UNIVERSITY OF MARYLAND."

THE great progress which has been made in mathematical and physical science during the last two centuries, has attracted the attention, not only of philosophers, but of men of business. So intimately, indeed, has this progress connected itself with the immediate wants and comforts of mankind, that it can scarcely escape the most careless observer. But the progress of moral, political, and juridical science during the same period, though less perceptible to the common eye, is not less wonderful; and has, quite as much, contributed to the improvement of the human race, and to the development and security of their most important rights and interests. Few persons, indeed, are sufficiently aware, how forcible, though silent, is the operation of laws upon our manners, habits, and feelings; and how much of our happiness depends upon a uniform and enlightened administration of public justice. Whatever of rational liberty and security to private rights and property is now enjoyed in England, and in the United States, may, in a great degree, be traced to the principles of the common law, as it has been moulded and fashioned, from age to age, by wise and learned judges. Not that the common law, in its origin, or early stages, was peculiarly fitted for these purposes; for the feudal system, with which it originated, or at least, became early incorporated, was a system, in many respects, the very reverse; but that it had the advantage of expanding with the improvements of the age, and of continually enlarging itself by an adoption of those maxims of civil right, which, by their intrinsic justice and propriety, commend themselves to the bosoms of all men. The narrow maxims of one age have not been permitted to present insurmountable obstacles to the improvements of another; but they have become gradually obsolete, or confined to a very insigificant range.

If it were not beside our present purpose, we might illustrate these remarks, by calling the attention of our readers to the fact, that, since the reign of Queen Elizabeth, nearly the whole system of equity has been created; and that the commercial contracts, which form so great a portion of the business of our courts, were, before that period, either wholly unknown, or, at the most, but very imperfectly understood. In respect to insurance, we may almost say, that the law has grown up within the latter half of the eighteenth century. Previously to the time of Lord Mansfield, there are but few cases in the reports, which are entitled to much respect, either for their sound interpretation of principles, or general applicability. It is to his genius, liberality, learning, and thorough understanding of the maritime jurists of the continent, of Cleirac, and Roccus, and Straccha, and Santerna, and Loccenius, and Casaregis, and Valin, and to his ardent attachment to the equitable doctrines of the civil law, that we are chiefly indebted for that beautiful and rational system, which now adorns this branch of the common law. The doctrine of bailments too, (which lies at the foundation of the law of shipments,) was almost struck out at a single heat by Lord Holt,[1] who had the good sense to incorporate into the English code that system, which the text and the commentaries of the civil law had already built up on the

[1] The case of Coggs v. Bernard, 2 Ld. Raym. R. 909.

continent of Europe. What remained, to give perfect symmetry and connection to all the parts of that system, and to refer it to its principles, has been accomplished, in our times, by the incomparable Essay of Sir William Jones, a man of whom it is difficult to say, which is most worthy of admiration, the splendor of his genius, the rareness and extent of his acquirements, or the unspotted purity of his life. Had he never written any thing but his Essay on Bailments, he would have left a name, unrivalled in the common law, for philosophical accuracy, elegant learning, and finished analysis. Even cold and cautious, as is the habit, if not the structure, of a professional mind, it is impossible to suppress enthusiasm, when we contemplate such a man.

We recall ourselves to the more immediate topics on which we have already touched. Of the law of bills of exchange and promissory notes, how little can be gleaned from works before the reign of William and Mary! And how many of its most useful principles are younger than the days (as Swift calls her) of good Queen Anne! In the reign of George III., more has been done to give a scientific cast to these doctrines than in all the preceding ages. And here, again, we may remark, how much has been gained by the accessions and alluvions of the civil law. It is impossible to read the older decisions, without reviving the memory of Marius and Casaregis; or the later, without perceiving their general coincidence with the summary, but profound treatise of Pothier. If we pass to the other branches of commercial law, we shall find the improvements not less striking, nor less important. Molloy and Malynes, feeble and inaccurate as their treatises are now confessed to be, were, until comparatively a recent period, the principal, though erring guides of the profession, in questions respecting the rights and duties of owners, masters, and mariners, of shippers and freighters, of average, salvage, and contribution. In what part of either of these writers, or of any contemporary, or more ancient reporters, shall we find the doctrines relative to the earning and loss of freight and wages, or relative to charter-parties, bills of lading, stoppage in transitu, and liens, so familiar to the modern merchant and lawyer, traced out with the important practical distinctions belonging to them? What was then despatched in a few pages would now require a large volume. Much might, even at that period, have been acquired by a diligent study of the maritime jurists of the continent; but they were either unknown, or, with one or two exceptions, passed over in silent neglect. The truth is, that maritime law had then but little attracted the attention of the courts of common law; and the only court in which the subject was much considered (we mean the Admiralty) labored under the severe hostility of these courts, and had to maintain an arduous struggle even for existence. Under such circumstances, its judgments and opinions carried little weight in Westminster Hall; for few were willing to listen to principles which had no authority beyond the narrow walks of Doctors Commons. If we except the aid borrowed from the civilians of the continent, the masterly treatise of Mr. Abbott on the law of shipping is principally founded on the adjudications since the elevation of Lord Mansfield to the Bench; and in these adjudications, the general consistency with principle is as distinguishable, as their practical importance.

We have the rather dwelt upon these improvements in maritime law, because they are most obvious to the general observer, and, therefore, most readily admitted. In the several branches of this law, instead of a few elementary principles, and a few decisions, turning upon nice distinctions, we have now a regular system; which, though not entirely perfect, exhibits such a scientific arrangement and harmony of principles, that in most of the questions arising in practice, the profession are enabled to relieve themselves from those distressing doubts, which never fail to bring discredit upon the law for its supposed uncertainty. But improvement has not been confined to commercial law. A spirit of scientific research has diffused itself over the other departments of the common law; contested questions are now, and for a long time have been, sifted with the most laborious diligence, and the limits of principles established, with a philosophical precision and accuracy, which is rarely observable in the old reports. The doctrines of uses and trusts, of last wills and testaments, of contingent remainders, of executory devises, and of legacies, although resting on ancient and immovable foundations, are reduced to a very high degree of exactness and consistency, and followed out into their regular results with a truly logical conformity to principles, for which we might search in vain in the annals of former times.

But although much has been done in modern times, to methodize the common law, and give it a systematic character, so that we may not only arrive at its principles by regular analysis, but teach its elements and distinctions by an enlarged synthesis; yet it is not to be imagined, that the profession have to encounter less labor, or to exercise less diligence, than formerly, in order to obtain a mastery of the science; or that there is little uncertainty in applying it to the solution of those questions which perpetually arise in human transactions. To a certain extent, law must forever be subject to uncertainty and doubt; not from the obscurity and fluctuation of decisions, as the vulgar erroneously suppose, but from the endless complexity and variety of human actions. However certain may be the rules of the statute or common law, they must necessarily be general in their language, and incapable of a minute and perfect application to the *boundless* circumstances of life, which may modify, limit, or affect them. It is impossible to provide by any code, however extensive, for the infinite variety of distinctions, as to civil justice, arising from the imperfection of human language and foresight, from the conflict of opposing rights, from the effect of real or apparent hardships, and from those minute equities, which are often found in different scales, adding somewhat to the weight of each, but rarely forming an exact equipoise. Until human actions are capable of being limited on every side to a definite range of circumstances, the permutations and combinations of which may be perfectly ascertained and enumerated; until there shall be an entire separation of right from wrong in all the business of life, and the elements of each shall be immiscible and repulsive; until, in short, we shall become absolutely pure and perfect in our actions, and perfectly conusant of all the operations of the past, the present, and the future; there will remain immeasurable uncertainties in the law, which will call for the exercise of professional talents, and the grave judgments of courts of justice. We must be content, since we cannot hope to realize these Utopian dreams of human excellence, to secure the upright and enlightened administration of justice, by encouraging learned advocates to fit themselves for eminence at the Bar, and by supporting with liberal salaries the dignity, the virtue, and the independence of the Bench.

We have already intimated an opinion, that the improvements in the various departments of law have in no degree lessened the necessity of laborious study to qualify gentlemen for the higher walks of the profession. The changes of two centuries have greatly facilitated the means of acquiring a thorough knowledge of the science; but they have also widened the circle to an almost incalculable extent. Sir Henry Spelman has left us a striking picture of the difficulties and discouragements of the study, of his own time. In his preface to his Glossary, he says, "Emisit me [mater] tamen sub anno altero [1579] Londinum juris nostri capessendi gratiâ; cujus cum vestibulum salutassem, reperissemque linguam peregrinam, dialectum barbaram, methodum inconcinnam, molem non ingentem solum, sed perpetuis humeris sustinendam, excidit, fateor, animus, blandioribusque subridens musis, rigidam hanc minervam, ferreis amplexibus coercendam, leni molimine delibari." To be sure, the discouragements of that day were not inconsiderable; the whole of the law was locked up in barbarous Latin, and still more barbarous Norman French. The doctrines of special pleading were obscured by the shades of a dead language, and by the embarrassing subtilties of scholastic refinement. The great body of the law was to be principally extracted from the Year Books, and the elaborate, though immethodical abridgments of Statham, Fitzherbert, and Brooke. The only guides, which could be said to illumine the way, were the brief, but profound text of Littleton on Tenures, the authoritative and methodical sketch of Glanville, the comprehensive, exact, and learned treatise of Bracton, (whom Sir William Jones has justly characterized as the best of our juridical classics,) and the perspicuous and compact work of Fleta, in which the unknown author follows with steady footsteps the path of his master. If to these we add the old Tenures, the old and the new Natura Brevium, the Register of Original Writs, the works of Britton and Staundforde, the very able dialogues of St. German between a Doctor and Student, the acute and subtile notes of Perkins, and the diffuse, but accurate and learned, commentaries of Plowden,[1] we have the bulk of juridical authors, which were to be mastered by the student at the time, to which Sir Henry Spelman refers. We do not mean to undervalue the labor, which was necessary to accomplish this arduous task; and we well know, that, what works did not then supply, could be acquired only by the dry practice of a black-letter office, and a constant and fatiguing attention upon courts of justice. But adding every thing, which the most strenuous advocate of the ancient law would ask, we may safely pronounce, that the labors of a modern student, if he means to attain eminence, must be infinitely greater. To be a sound lawyer, he must not merely taste,

[1] The other reporters of this period, Keilway, Anderson, Moore, &c., were not then published. The Mirror of Justices, though of an earlier time, did not appear until a half century afterwards. There are some few other works of this period, but they were not thought worth a distinct enumeration.

but drink deep at the ancient fountains of the law. He must acquire an accurate knowledge of the feudal tenures, and of the ancient doctrines connected therewith, because they constitute the rudiments of the law of real estates; and yet, much of this learning is remote from common use, and lies deep in the dark and uncouth text of the primitive writers. He must be initiated into the mysteries of real actions, which will at once carry him back three centuries; for, since the days of Queen Elizabeth, these actions have gradually sunk into neglect; and unless he thoroughly comprehends them, he can hardly be master of the modern actions of trespass and ejectment, not to speak of our own state, where real actions exist in their vigor, and remain the great remedies for deciding titles. If we add to this the necessary learning of personal actions, founded on torts or contracts, which in modern times have branched out into an almost endless variety, we shall have some notion of the extent of the labor, which is now requisite to the attainment of the first rank in the profession.

This view of the subject may appear appalling to young gentlemen, who are just quitting our universities, with the intention of devoting their lives to the science of jurisprudence. It ought, however, to be a great consolation to them, that the elementary writers are more faithful, more accurate, and more polished, than in former times. The paths may not always be well cleared, nor the prospects interesting; but, in almost every direction, there will be found learned guides, who cannot fail to diffuse a bright and steady cheerfulness, during the most rugged journeys.

The superior advantages, in this respect, of our own times over the past, will be apparent upon the slightest reflection. If we look back to the termination of the century, succeeding the period, to which Sir Henry Spelman alluded, we shall find, that the student had comparatively few additional elementary works to assist his progress. Lord Hale, in his preface to Rolle's Abridgment, (in 1668) gives us a list of those which were most useful, and he contents himself with adding to those already named by us, Rolle's Abridgment, Lord Coke's Institutes, and the intermediate reporters between his own time and Plowden.[1] Not but that some other elementary works had in the mean time been published; but they were not deemed by him peculiarly useful to students. We have also, yet remaining, a letter of Lord Chief Justice Reeve, addressed to his nephew about seventy years later, (9 Geo. II.) on the study of the law, by which we find, that, in his opinion, (with which we do not coincide) Finch's Law, Hale's History of the Common Law, and Wood's Institutes, were the most material elementary works, that had been added to the old stock during this whole period.[2]

The publication of Blackstone's Commentaries (in 1765) constituted a new epoch in the annals of the common law. Previously to that period, the learned author had published his Analysis of the Laws of England[3] which exhibited the outline of the method and principal divisions, which the Commentaries were intended to fill up, in pursuance, indeed, of the plan which had been previously sketched by the masterly pen of Lord Hale. Of a work, which has been so long before the public as Blackstone's Commentaries, it cannot be necessary for us to utter one word of approbation.

For luminous method, for profound research, for purity of diction, for comprehensive brevity, and pregnancy of matter, for richness in classical allusions, and for extent and variety of knowledge of foreign jurisprudence, whether introduced for illustration, or ornament, or instruction, it is not too much to say, that it stands unrivalled in ours, and, perhaps, in every other language. There have not, however, been wanting, of late years, attempts to undervalue the importance of

[1] Lord Hale's preface to Rolle is well worth the diligent perusal of students.

[2] The letter of Lord Chief Justice Reeve is published in the Collectanea Juridica, vol. i. p. 79.

[3] The Analysis was first published in 1756.

these Commentaries. It has been suggested, that in some parts the work is superficial, and in others, too general and elementary; that it cannot be safely relied on as authority; and that it teaches the science so imperfectly, that it has almost as great a tendency to mislead as to instruct. These objections seem to us founded upon a total misconception of the design of the work. The author did not undertake to exhibit a full and perfect view of the common law, but merely a summary sketch of its most important doctrines and distinctions.

That some errors may be found by a strict scrutiny cannot be denied; but, from the vast extent and variety of the materials, such errors were to be expected. The only wonder is, that so much should have been accomplished, with so little intermixture of false doctrine, and obscure and inaccurate statement. We cannot express our own sentiments better than in the language of that admirable ornament of juridical literature, Sir William Jones: "His Commentaries are the most correct and beautiful outline, that ever was exhibited of any human science; but they alone will no more form a lawyer, than a general map of the world, how accurately and elegantly soever it may be delineated, will make a geographer. If, indeed, all the titles, which he professed only to sketch in elementary discourses, were filled up with exactness and perspicuity, Englishmen might hope at length to possess a digest of their own laws, which would leave but little room for controversy, except in cases depending on their particular circumstances." — (Jones on *Bailments*, 3, 4.)

But the most incontestable proof of the excellence of the work is to be found in the striking effects which its publication produced in every department of the common law. By the elegance of its style, and the novel dress in which it clothed the elements of law, it immediately attracted universal attention in England. It was soon considered as an indispensable part of the library of every statesman and private gentleman. It invigorated the ambition of students, and relieved them at once from many of the discouragements and difficulties, which previously embarrassed every step of their progress. There are lawyers yet living, who can attest the prodigious change, which it once produced in our country. Law was no longer considered a dry and sterile study. It at once became fashionable; and this circumstance, combining with the nature of our political institutions, (which make a legal education, if not a prerequisite, at least a very important qualification, for political distinction and public office,) has contributed in a very high degree to that great increase of the bar, and that ascendency in society, which distinguish the profession, in this, more than in any other country.

It was almost impossible, that such a strong excitement should not awaken the ardor of other gentlemen of juridical learning and leisure, to follow out into its regular details a design, which had been so nobly conceived and executed by the illustrious commentator. Accordingly, there has been a larger number of treatises on the leading topics of the common law produced within the last half century, than in all preceding time. And these treatises are, in general, distinguished by a scientific distribution, exact method, propriety of style, and clear exposition of principles and authorities, which are rarely to be found in any of our older juridical essays or dissertations. In fact, the bulk of former elementary works was little more than a collection of decisions under general heads, without any successful attempt to systematize the matter, or subject it to a critical analysis. Among the most striking exceptions to this remark (for some exceptions exist) on the civil side, are the law tracts of Lord Bacon, the profound, but imperfect treatises of Lord Chief Baron Gilbert, the ingenious sketch of the Law of Tenures by Sir Martin Wright, and the brief, but very exact treatise on Equity, attributed to Mr. Ballow; and, on the criminal side, the very learned and authoritative works of Lord Hale, the copious digest of Mr. Serjeant Hawkins, and the truly admirable discourses of Sir Michael Foster. We forbear to speak at present of Comyns's Digest, intending hereafter to notice it in another place.

Among the modern works, of which we have been speaking, there are not a few on subjects of the very first importance, and of almost daily occurrence in practice, for exact information in which the student would have searched in vain in the abridgments and treatises of former ages. Where, for instance, shall we look for a work, like Mr. Fearne's Essay on Contingent Remainders and Executory Devises? This subject, which constituted one of the most obscure, and must forever remain one of the most intricate titles of the common law, had been already sketched out by the masterly hand of Lord Chief Baron Gilbert;[1] but, like all his other writings, it was left in a detached and imperfect shape. It was reserved for Mr. Fearne to honor the profession by a treatise so profound and accurate, that it became the guide of the ablest lawyers; yet so luminous in method and explanations, that it is level to the capacity of every attentive student. He has, in fact, exhausted the subject; and this *chef d'œuvre* will forever remain a monument of his skill, acuteness, and research. All that the most accomplished lawyer can reasonably hope, is to add a commentary of new cases and principles, as they arise, without venturing to touch the sacred fabric of his master. The treatise of Lord Redesdale on Pleadings in Chancery is of the same masterly and original character. It has traced out the nature and extent of the jurisdiction and practice of courts of chancery with so much brevity, perspicuity, and analytical exactness, that probably to this, more than any other work, we owe some of the most valuable improvements in the principles, as well as the proceedings, which regulate the administration of equity. Later works on the same subject (such as Mr. Cooper's) have added much valuable matter, founded on recent decisions; but the basis of these, as well as of all future works, must

[1] See Bacon's Abridgment, Guillim's Edition, title, *Remainder and Reversion.*

rest on the solid foundations, laid by the noble Chancellor. Lord Eldon pronounced its eulogy in his best manner, when he declared, that "it is a wonderful effort to collect what is deduced from authorities, speaking so little what is clear, that the surprise is not from the difficulty of understanding all he has said, but that so much can be understood."

There are many other treatises upon particular titles of the law, which might properly be taken notice of in this place, in vindication of the opinion we have expressed; but it is beside our present purpose to analyze the merits of juridical authors. We cannot, however, close these brief remarks, without calling the attention of our readers to the very excellent treatises of Mr. Park and Mr. Marshall on Insurance, which have done so much towards giving a scientific cast to doctrines so recently incorporated into the common law. Their merit is unquestionably of a very high order; and yet, probably, the most perfect theoretical work on Insurance is that of the learned Emerigon, which (strange to tell) has never been translated, although we have been almost overrun with transfusions from German and French sciolists by the enterprise or selfishness of English booksellers. We trust, that the time is not far distant, when Pothier and Emerigon and Valin will be accessible in our native tongue to every lawyer, and will be as familiarly known to them as they now are to the jurists of continental Europe.

It has been doubted by some persons, whether the present facilities in the study of law have a tendency to make as profound and accurate lawyers, as the old dry and desultory course. It is supposed, that the comparative ease with which the student may now advance into the most intricate doctrines, impairs, if it does not extinguish, that ardor of pursuit, which distinguished and disciplined the lawyers of the black-lettered times. For ourselves, we do not perceive the slightest foundation for the opinion, and we deem it radically erroneous. It might as well be contended, that turnpikes through every part of a thickly settled country have a tendency to obliterate the knowledge of its surface or its cities. It is true, that thereby the old roads are less known and less travelled; but who can doubt, that by such means the facility of intercourse and the interchange of every thing important in the commerce of life, are greatly augmented, and that public improvements circulate with tenfold rapidity and force? Nor is it very easy to perceive, how any particular science can be injuriously affected by the thorough development of its principles and practice. If the lucubrations of twenty years were necessary in former times, (as Fortescue informs us they were,) to acquire a competent knowledge of the law for ordinary practice; and if the whole of that mass can, by modern helps, be mastered in half that period, it is certainly so much time gained in the business of life; and time, in the science of law, as well as in almost every thing else, is of incalculable importance. The modern works do not teach the law in any new and superficial manner. There is no royal road to this, any more than to the science of mathematics. But the principles are now more closely investigated, the problems more fully enunciated, and the boundaries between the known and the unknown more exactly defined. Instead of sparse and scattered maxims, we have regular systems, built up with general symmetry of parts; and the necessary investigations in new and difficult cases are conducted with more safety, because they are founded on inductions from rules better established and more exactly limited. Yet, with all these advantages, to become an eminent lawyer is now a task of vast labor and difficulty. The business of the profession has extended itself, as we have already intimated, incalculably, both in quantity and variety. The most diligent study and practice of a long life are scarcely sufficient to place any gentleman beyond the necessity of continual exertions to keep pace with the current of new opinions and doctrines. It is true, that in the humbler walks of the profession, men of feeble talents and acquirements may now obtain a maintenance, and sometimes, perhaps, accumulate a fortune; but this is no more than what the experience of all ages has shown. There have always been obscure attorneys, whose industry, or cunning, or patronage, has given them the command of that portion of business, which is not without profit, if it be not attended with honor. But the sphere of professional activity is now greatly enlarged; and talents and acquirements are more easily measured, since the mysteries of the science are equally accessible to all; and little room is now left in the obscurities of a barbarous language for imaginary excellence, or for the concealment of quackery in the repetition of a technical jargon. That some titles of the common law are not as well understood, as in former times, may be safely admitted; and it is because they are either obsolete, or their relative importance is greatly diminished. But as to all the law in modern practical use, we are distinctly of opinion, that the science is better understood than in any former age. A philosophical spirit of investigation now pervades the bar and the bench, and we are freed from the blind pedantry and technical quibbles of the old schools. Many of the doctrines relative to the feudal tenures, such as reliefs, premier seisin, escuage, chivalry, villanage, grand sergeanty, homage, frank marriage, profession, attaints, and others of a similar nature, are now very little known; but, surely, it is not to be inferred, because subjects so utterly insignificant have sunk into obscurity, that the law has lost its vigor, or the profession lack learning. Probably few, if any, lawyers in our country are intimately acquainted with the law of copyholds and advowsons; yet, it would be strange to assert, that the want of such knowledge was a gross defect in professional education, when the subject-matter, upon which it can operate, has no existence in the United States.

The same remarks are in a good degree applicable to real actions, with all their accompaniments of process, essoins, aid prayers, vouchers, receit, &c. The irresistible tide of time has swept away the actions of assize, the writs of aiel, besaiel, and mort d'ancestor, cessavit, quo jure, ne injuste vexes, de rationabilibus divisis, secta ad molendinum, nuper obiit, quod permittat, and the trial by battle; and though, in our own state, writs of entry, formedon, and right still exist, yet they have been moulded into so simple a form, that most of the ancient peculiarities are utterly extinct;[1] and in England, as well as in most of the States of the Union, they are gone with the years beyond the flood, and the action of ejectment has almost universally superseded all real actions. It is, perhaps, just matter of regret, that real actions have so entirely sunk into disuse; since many doctrines applicable to modern remedies can scarcely be thoroughly understood, without reference to this department of antiquated learning. Many principles in every system of municipal law must be purely technical, and sometimes of arbitrary regulation; and the reason of them may be lost, long before the principles themselves disappear in practice. As long as such principles continue to exist, it is important to preserve the knowledge of the original reasons, on which they are founded, and the limits which regulate their application. An instance illustrative of these remarks occurred in the modern case of Taylor *v.* Horde, (1 Burr. R. 60.) It there became material to ascertain the exact nature of disseisins in the ancient law. Lord Mansfield on that occasion said, "The precise definition of what constituted a disseisin, which made the disseisor the tenant to the demandant's precipe, though the right owner's entry was not taken away, was *once* well known, but it is not *now* to be found. The more we read, unless we are careful to distinguish, the more we shall be confounded." We have

[1] We take this occasion to correct an error, into which Mr. Hoffman has inadvertently fallen, in supposing (p. 144) that real actions are in daily use in Massachusetts, with all their concomitants of voucher, counterplea of voucher, &c. &c. Real actions are here in use, and with them all those pleadings and proceedings, which are necessary for the furtherance of justice between the parties. But all the pecularities of process, essoins, and vouchers, and counterpleas, &c., are obsolete, and superseded by a great simplicity of proceeding, greater, perhaps, than attends even the *formal proceedings* in ejectments.

heard it questioned by a late learned judge, whether Lord Mansfield had gone to the bottom of this doctrine. But, however this may be, the case abundantly instructs us, how many distressing doubts may arise from the partial eclipse of lights once so familiarly known. It ought not, however, to be forgotten, that real actions have not gone into disuse by any sudden and arbitrary abolition, but from the intricacies and delays in the ancient proceedings therein, and from their unfitness for a convenient investigation of numerous questions arising from the complicated conveyances of modern times. For example, it is often a question of serious difficulty to decide, whether an estate be a fee simple, a fee tail, or an estate for life; the limitations of estates are sometimes very numerous, and the cases, in which they have lapsed, and the links of descent and heirship, are often imperfectly known. In all these cases there must be very great embarrassment thrown in the way of a demandant in a real action, and he may be turned round several times before he can obtain a decision upon his title. He may successively be driven from writs of entry of every degree to a formedon, and even to a writ of right; and, after all, he may be defeated by a mistake in the pleadings, (which he will not be allowed to amend,) having little or nothing to do with the merits of his cause. So that, if something be lost by the disuse of real actions, much (at least in England) has probably been gained in substantial justice and convenience, and even certainty of remedy.

It has been also suggested, that special pleading has suffered greatly by the modern changes in the study of law; and that it is every day less and less understood. If this were true, it might be satisfactorily accounted for upon grounds altogether distinct from the decline of professional learning. In most of the actions in modern use, special pleading is rarely necessary or advisable. When the action of assumpsit was first introduced, special pleas and issues were very common; but for more than a century they have disappeared in practice; and almost every defence, except that of the statute of limitations, is now determined under the general issue. With the exception above stated, a special plea is never heard of in actions on promissory notes, bills of exchange, policies of insurance, nor, indeed, any other simple contracts; and these form by far the largest portion of the business which at present occupies the attention of courts of justice. In actions, too, for the recovery of real estate, whether the ancient real actions, or the modern action of ejectment, almost every defence is tried under the general issue. The same remark applies to trover, and, in general, all other actions on the case; and, with the exception of actions of debt, covenant, trespass, slander, and replevin, which are, comparatively speaking, infrequent, special pleading is entirely out of use. Even in these actions, by the laxity of practice, and the provisions of statutes, the use of it has been very much abridged.

These considerations disclose a sufficient reason, why special pleading may be less regarded in practice, than in former times, and why its relative value may not always be duly appreciated in the profession. It is unquestionably a branch of learning of vast, nay, of indispensable, importance to every lawyer. Without an accurate knowledge of its principles, it is impossible to frame actions or declarations for a variety of cases arising in common practice; and, if the foundations are not well laid, the superstructure cannot stand. It is the best, and perhaps the only, method to obtain a thorough and exact knowledge of the proper boundaries of actions, upon which, frequently, the success or loss of a cause may ultimately depend. Lord Ashburton, in his celebrated letter to a student of law, observes, " It is usual to acquire some insight into real business under an eminent special pleader, previous to actual practice at the bar. This idea I beg leave strongly to second; and, indeed, I have known few great men, who have not possessed this advantage." Nor should it be forgotten, that special pleading has a most salutary effect in disciplining the mind for an accurate investigation of principles, and accustoming it, by a sort of intellectual chemistry, to the most subtile analysis and combinations. It has been truly asserted by Lord Mansfield, that "the substantial rules of special pleading are founded in strong sense and the soundest and closest logic; and so appear, when well understood and explained; though, by being misunderstood and misapplied, they are often made use of as instruments of chicane." We remember to have heard the late Chief Justice Parsons (who was an excellent special pleader) declare, that, in knotty and difficult cases, he always found more certain and satisfactory results in trying them by the rules of special pleading, than by any other method. Sir William Jones, in his preface to the speeches of Isæus, has beautifully illustrated the same thought. "Our science," says he, "of special pleading is an excellent logic; it is admirably calculated for the purpose of analyzing a cause, of extracting, like the roots of an equation, the true points in dispute, and referring them, with all imaginable simplicity, to the Court, or the jury. It is reducible to the strictest rules of pure dialectic; and, if it were scientifically taught in our public seminaries of learning, would fix the attention, give a habit of reasoning closely, quicken the apprehension, and invigorate the understanding, as effectually as the famed peripatetic system, which, how ingenious and subtile soever, is not so honorable, so laudable, or so profitable, as the science, in which Littleton exhorts his sons to employ their courage and care." Such commendation supersedes the necessity of all farther discussion of the importance of pleading.

But we doubt the fact, that special pleading is not as well understood as in former times. On the contrary, we incline to believe, that by eminent lawyers its principles are now more fully comprehended, and more philosophically examined, than in any preceding period. The age of scholastic quibbling and petty subtilty has passed away, and the quaint trifling, which disfigured and disgraced the science, is no longer in fashion. Special pleading is now applied to its original and proper purpose, the attainment of substantial justice and the introduction of certainty of remedy. The good sense and sound logic of modern times has substituted for the artificial pedantry and narrow maxims of the dark ages of the law, rules which commend themselves to all men by their intrinsic propriety and excellence for deciding contested rights. The best ancient treatise on the subject is Mr. Euer's Doctrina Placitandi, a book which Lord Chief Justice Willes pronounced, in his time, to contain more law and learning than any other book he knew (2 Wils. R. 88); yet what is this, when compared with the finished elementary and practical treatises of Mr. Lawes or Mr. Chitty? It were, indeed, desirable that modern pleaders should endeavor to imitate more generally the pointed brevity and precision of Rastall's Entries, and waste fewer words in their drafts of declarations, which,

"Like a wounded snake, drag their slow length along."

It might not be useless for them to consider, that the great aim ought to be, not how much, but how little, may be inserted with professional safety. Here, at least, the study of the ancients would amply repay all their toil, and subserve essentially the public interests. There is certainly some danger, that the current of public opinion, aided by legislative enactments, and not a little accelerated by a distaste for the prolixity of modern pleading, may bring the science itself into disrepute and neglect. If such an event should happen, it will be matter of most serious regret. We hope, that the few observations, which we have hazarded, may attract the attention of the rising generation, and call forth abler pens in the vindication and support of its principles and practice.

There are some other topics upon which it was our intention to trouble our professional readers with a few observations, in proof of the opinion that the law, as a science, never was so well understood, nor so well taught, as at the present period, and yet that a profound and comprehensive knowledge of it never was of more difficult attainment. We may, however, safely pass from general reasoning, and appeal to facts within the reach of every professional gentleman. In our own country the advancement of the knowledge of the science has been truly wonderful. The Bar and the Benches of almost every State in the Union have, within the last twenty years, very strikingly improved. There are lawyers and Judges amongst us, who would sustain the weight and dignity of Westminster Hall. And some of our Reports exhibit arguments and opinions, which, for propriety and force and logic and acuteness and erudition, have not been excelled in the proudest days of the law. This rapid improvement has, without doubt, been greatly aided by the invigorating influence of the modern treatises in almost every branch of law; but it has also owed much to the increased diligence, which a lofty ambition of excellence has stimulated among the master spirits of the profession.

But it is time for us to call the attention of our readers to the immediate subject of this article. Mr. Hoffman has published a Course of Legal Study, which he modestly addresses to students, but which is well worthy the perusal of every gentleman of the bar. Many works have been heretofore written, professedly for the direction of persons engaged in the study of the law; but, for the most part, these works have, in a didactic form, laid down elementary precepts for the moral conduct, the preparatory attainments, or the style of elocution and oratory proper for an eminent advocate. Some, indeed, are little more than a distillation from Quinctilian's Institutes and Cicero's Orator, without preserving the pungent essence or eloquence of the originals. Mr. Hoffman's work, on the contrary, is almost entirely practical; and it contains a complete course of legal study, with a catalogue of the principal books to be consulted or read under all the titles of the law. The introduction is written with a good deal of force and good taste, and in a tone of strong and sensible argumentation. In point both of matter and manner, it is highly creditable to the talents and acquirements of the author. . . .

The general course of study, proposed by Mr. Hoffman, is summed up in the following general syllabus: —

"I. Moral and Political Philosophy.

"II. The Elementary and Constitutional Principles of the Municipal Law of England; and herein,

"1st. Of the Feudal Law.

"2d. The Institutes of the Municipal Law generally.

"3d. Of the Origin and Progress of the Common Law.

"III. The Law of Real Rights and Real Remedies.

"IV. The Law of Personal Rights and Personal Remedies.

"V. The Law of Equity.

"VI. The Lex Mercatoria.

"VII. The Law of Crimes and Punishments.

"VIII. The Law of Nations.

"IX. The Maritime and Admiralty Law.

"X. The Civil or Roman Law.

"XI. The Constitution and Laws of the United States of America.

"XII. The Constitution and Laws of the several States of the Union.

"XIII. Political Economy." p. 32.

This is followed by a particular syllabus under every title of the general syllabus, in which are collected the best works on every successive subject belonging to the heads under which they are arranged. Connected with these heads is a series of notes, or perpetual commentary upon the character and relative value of the authors, whose works are cited, or the history and relative importance of the topics, which they discuss, interspersed with many judicious observations of a more general nature, which exhibit to great advantage the liberality, sound judgment, and juridical knowledge of the author. As a specimen of the style and spirit of the work, we subjoin the note on the reading of Reports, and particularly of leading cases. . . .

These observations of Mr. Hoffman are perfectly practical, and, for the most part, accurate and just. In respect to the praise bestowed on Mr. Viner's Abridgment, we are constrained to differ from the learned gentleman. We are far from thinking it the safest abridgment for reference. It is a very irregular fabric, built up on the basis of Rolle's Abridgment, with an incorporation of the principal matter of Fitzherbert, and Brooke, and other old abridgers. It abounds with inaccuracies and repetitions; and it is quite obvious, that the author more frequently consulted the works of other abridgers, than the original reports, to abbreviate and digest for himself. We agree, however, with Mr. Hargrave, (Co. Litt. 9. *a.* note 3,) that "notwithstanding all its defects and inaccuracies, it must be allowed to be a necessary part of every lawyer's library. It is, indeed, a most useful compilation, and would have been infinitely more so, if the author had been less singular and more nice in his arrangement and method, and more studious in avoiding repetitions." Bacon's (or, more properly, Gilbert's) Abridgment is more full in the development of principles and the statement of cases; and, in every respect but copiousness, is a superior production. It is incomplete; but this was the hard fate of all the writings of the most learned author, which were sent into the literary world with all their original imperfections on their head. For ourselves, we confess, that in our opinion every other abridgment suffers greatly in comparison with the Digest of Lord Chief Baron Comyns. For succinctness and brevity, for exact method and arrangement, for perspicuity and accuracy, for copiousness in principles and illustrations, and for comprehensive analysis, it stands unrivalled in the annals of the law. On one occasion, Lord Kenyon (Pasley *v.* Freeman, 3 T. R. 51, 64,) said, "I find it laid down by the Lord

C. B. Comyns, &c. He has not, indeed, cited any authority for his opinion; but his opinion alone is of great authority, since he was considered by his contemporaries, as the most able lawyer in Westminster Hall." In some other more recent cases, the Court of King's Bench have proceeded to adjudicate some very important questions, upon the sole authority of his Digest,[1] an honor, which we believe, has never been conceded to any other compiler. It has frequently occurred to us, that our professional brethren of the South did not sufficiently appreciate the merits of this work. They appear to be devoted to Bacon's Abridgment, and pass over Comyns's Digest, as a book merely of occasional reference, entitled to little either of praise or blame. How, otherwise, can we account for Mr. Hoffman's omission, under the article of pleading, to recommend the admirable title, Pleader, in the Digest, a title, which has collected and exhausted, in a most scientific order, the whole principles of the science. The title, "Pleas and Pleadings," in Bacon's Abridgment, is an excellent sketch; but it is but a sketch, and, compared with the title of Comyns, just mentioned, is but twilight to the meridian day. We would respectfully ask the attention of Mr. Hoffman, and of Southern lawyers in general, to the following observations of Mr. Hargrave: "The whole of Lord Chief Baron Comyns's work is equally remarkable for its great variety of matter, its compendious and accurate expressions, and the excellence of its methodical distribution; but the title, 'Pleader,' seems to have been the author's favorite one, and that in which he principally exerted himself." (Co. Litt. 17, *a*. note 1.)

1 We take this opportunity to enter our protest against that book-making spirit, which has disfigured all the modern editions of this incomparable work. The original edition in folio (1762) is far superior to all the later editions. These have the addition of the modern cases, it is true; but they consist of the marginal notes of the reporters, thrust into the text without order or propriety, and destroy its symmetry and connection. A supplement of modern cases and principles upon the plan of Comyns's Digest, in a distinct work, would be an invaluable present to the profession.

The remark, too, of Mr. Hoffman, that "the books of reports contain the law in the precise phraseology, in which it was administered by the judges," requires some qualification. With the exception of the Reports of Plowden, Coke, and Vaughan, and a very few great cases in other Reports, the remark can scarcely be said to be true of any Reporter, before the time of Sir James Burrow. There are some other unimportant particulars, in which we differ from Mr. Hoffman; but, with these trifling exceptions, we entirely agree in the opinions of Mr. Hoffman, as to the importance and utility of reading the original Reports. We presume, that the omission to notice the Massachusetts Reports, in company with Mr. Johnson's, Mr. Binney's, and Messrs. Henning and Munford's, was accidental; for, if we do not deceive ourselves, in point of learning and accuracy they yield to few, if any, in our country.

What particularly pleases us is the enlarged and liberal view with which Mr. Hoffman recommends the student of the common law to a full and careful study of the Admiralty, Maritime, and Civil Law. If the note on the excellence of the civil law (p. 254) were not too long, we should gladly insert it in this place. We commend it, however, as well as his observations on the law of nations and the admiralty law, most earnestly, to all those who aspire to eminence as statesmen, or scholars, or lawyers. To Mr. Hoffman's list of books, on these subjects, we beg leave to add Heineccius's Elements of the Civil Law, according to the order of the Institutes and the Pandects, whom Sir James Mackintosh has not scrupled to pronounce "the best writer of elementary books, with whom *he* is acquainted on any subject."[1] We also recommend Ferrière's Dictionnaire de Droit et de Pratique, Calvinus's Lexicon Juridicum, M.

[1] Sir James Mackintosh's Introductory Discourse on the Study of the Law of Nature and Nations, is a most finished composition, abounding in all the graces of juridical eloquence, and pregnant with most important and edifying learning.

Dessaules' Dictionnaire du Digeste, Exton and Zouch and Spelman on the Admiralty Jurisdiction, Cleirac's Us et Coutumes de la Mer, Emérigon Traité des Assurances, Pothier's Works, and particularly his Treatises on Maritime Contracts, Boucher's Translation of the Consolato del Mare, Peckius ad Rem Nauticum, D'Abreu sur les Prises, and though last, not least, Casaregis's Discursus de Commercio.

We must now hasten to a close, although there are some discussions, which the perusal of Mr. Hoffman's work has suggested, which we very reluctantly pass over. In quitting the work, we have not the slightest hesitation to declare, that it contains by far the most perfect system for the study of the law which has ever been offered to the public. The writers whom he recommends are of the very best authority; and his own notes are composed in a tone of the most enlarged philosophy, and abound in just and discriminating criticism, and in precepts calculated to elevate the moral as well as intellectual character of the profession. The course proposed by him is very ample, and would probably consume seven years of close study. But much may be omitted, where time and opportunity are wanting to exhaust it. We cordially recommend it to all lawyers, as a model for the direction of the students who may be committed to their care; and we hazard nothing in asserting, that if its precepts are steadily pursued, high as the profession now stands in our country, it will attain a higher elevation, an elevation which shall command the reverence of Europe, and reflect back light and glory upon the land and the law of our forefathers.

We have another motive, besides the intrinsic value of the work, for commending it earnestly to the perusal of our readers. It will demonstrate to the understanding of every discerning man the importance, nay, the necessity, of the law-school, which the Government of Harvard College have, so honorably to themselves, established at Cambridge. No work can sooner dissipate the common delusion, that the law may be thoroughly acquired in the immethodical, interrupted, and desultory studies of the office of a practising counsellor. Such a situation is indispensable after the student shall have laid the foundation in elementary principles, under the guidance of a learned and discreet lecturer. He will then be prepared to reap the full benefits of the practice of an attorney's office. But, without such elementary instruction, he will waste a great deal of time in useless and discouraging efforts; or become a patient drudge, versed in the forms of conveyancing and pleading, but incapable of ascending to the principles which guide and govern them; or sink into a listless indolence and inactivity, waiting for the arrival of the regular period for his admission to the bar, without one qualification to justify the honor which he receives. One year passed at the University, in attendance upon the lectures of the very respectable gentleman, who has recently been appointed to preside over the law-school there, would lay a foundation of solid learning, upon which our ingenuous and ambitious youth might confidently hope to build a fabric of professional fame, which would carry them to the first honors of the bar, and make them, on the bench, the ornaments of their country.

LITERATURE OF THE MARITIME LAW.

AN ARTICLE WRITTEN FOR THE NORTH AMERICAN REVIEW, IN 1818, ON A WORK ENTITLED, "THE LAWS OF THE SEA WITH REFERENCE TO MARITIME COMMERCE DURING PEACE AND WAR," FROM THE GERMAN OF FREDERICK J. JACOBSEN, ADVOCATE, ALTONA, 1815.

THE Ancients have left us but little on the subject of commercial law; and that little has lost much of its value in modern times. It may, perhaps, be supposed, that a great deal has perished amidst the ruins of the dark ages; or has been swallowed up in the desolations of conquest, or the overwhelming obliterations of time. Much splendid declamation has been employed in describing the maritime glory of the Phœnicians, and the Cretans, and the Rhodians, and the Egyptians, and the Greeks, and the Carthaginians, and the Romans. Without question, the coasts of the Mediterranean were, from early times, inhabited by warlike, enterprising, and industrious races of people. They had different commodities to exchange, adapted to the natural and artificial wants, the necessities and the luxuries of the different societies, into which they were divided. It was, of course, that ambition and enterprise, the love of wealth, and the desire of gratifying curiosity, should create an active interchange of these commodities, both by sea and land. The spirit of commerce, once excited, is not easily extinguished or controlled. It is a useful spirit, which imparts life and intelligence to the body politic, increases the comforts and enjoyments of every class of people, and gradually liberalizes and expands the mind, as well as fosters the best interests of humanity. Many usages must necessarily grow up in such a state of things, where many independent nations are engaged in trade with each other; which usages, at first determined by accident, or convenience, or the dictates of common sense, must gradually ripen into rights and duties, and thus regulate the concerns of commerce. It is not, therefore, to be supposed, that the nations of whom we have spoken were wholly without any principles of maritime law. But there are many reasons for believing, that nothing like an enlarged and general system of that law was ever adopted by any of them.

In the first place, the business of their commerce was extremely simple, their voyages were short, and their shipping was adapted to small cargoes and narrow reaches. They were obliged to ply the shores; and neither their interest nor their means, in the then state of navigation, allowed them to plan or execute the complicated voyages of modern times. The coasting trade of a single modern maritime power is probably far more extensive than the whole trade of many flourishing states of antiquity; at least, the operations of that trade were far less complicated; and yet the coasting trade has given rise to comparatively few of the questions of modern maritime law. In the next place, most of the ancient governments, whether despotic or free, seem to have devoted themselves more to the profession of arms, and the increase of their military and naval power, than to the encouragement of peaceful commerce. In the despotic governments, almost every thing was left to the undefined discretion of the sovereign, who would not easily be induced to circumscribe the limits of his own authority. In the free governments, the jarring of discordant interests, and the impatience of legislative control, manifested by the mass of the people, combined with the almost continual foreign warfare, in which they were engaged, to prevent any effort to systematize their civil polity. Under such circumstances, it is not very probable, that any public regulations could be framed in respect to maritime contracts, exeept in some few cases of extraordinary occurrence, or peculiar difficulty. The Romans, indeed, seem to have been the only people who attempted to methodize the principles even of their municipal law. It has been remarked by Dr. Adam Smith, (*Wealth of Nations*, b. 5, ch. 1, part 3, art. 2,) that "Though the laws of the Twelve Tables were many of them copied from those of some ancient Greek republics, yet law never seems to have grown up to be a science in any republic of ancient Greece. In Rome, it became a science very early." Nor do we recollect, that it ever has been pretended, at least in respect to maritime law, that any of the ancient nations, except the Rhodians, had formed any thing like a commercial code; and that the extent, as well as the importance, of this code has been greatly overrated, we think there are very strong reasons to believe. Whatever was most valuable in that code was, without doubt, well known to the Romans; and, so far as it suited their own more enlarged commerce, was probably transfused into their own jurisprudence. And we shall hereafter see, what have been the value and extent of the obligations of the Romans to the Rhodian Laws in this particular.

As to the manuscript, found in the library of Francis Pithou, a celebrated jurist of the sixteenth century, which was published, first at Basle, in 1561, by Simon Scardius, and afterwards at Frankfort, in 1596, by Marquardus Freer and Leunclavius, as genuine fragments of the Rhodian Laws, it may be observed, that, if their genuineness were completely established, they would not increase our veneration for the wisdom, or the commercial polity of the nation whose name they bear. But the critical sagacity of modern civilians has not hesitated to reject these fragments, as more than apocryphal, as the fictions of some jurist, as late, at least, as the middle ages. It is true, that they have been silently quoted or directly asserted as genuine, by Cujas, by Selden, Godefroi, Vinnius, and other eminent jurists. Bynkershoek first boldly denied their authenticity; the cautious and accomplished Heineccius followed in the same path; and their opinion has been generally adopted by the learned of the eighteenth century. Rejecting, therefore, as we do, the Fragments of the Rhodian Laws, as a modern fraud, there is nothing which has reached us, except the codes and the compilations of the Roman emperors, which even wears the habiliments of ancient maritime jurisprudence; and so far are we from thinking, that any thing material has been lost, that we consider the substance of all ancient maritime jurisprudence, as embraced in the titles of the Corpus Juris Civilis. The circumstances under which the Roman codes were compiled, do, as we think, fully justify these remarks.

At the period when Justinian meditated the great works, which have immortalized his memory — a monument of fame more desirable than all that conquest can bestow, and which seems destined to endure to the end of time — the Roman empire had passed through its brightest ages of military, civil, and commercial grandeur. She had been for centuries as renowned for her jurisprudence, as for her arms. A succession of learned men had adorned her courts, as judges or as lawyers, who had left behind them their arguments, opinions, and commentaries, upon most of the important branches of her law. Besides these, there were the honorary law, and edicts of her prætors, the *plebiscita* and *senatus consulta* of the days of the republic, the imperial constitutions and rescripts of her emperors, the collection of the honorary law, or perpetual edict of Julian, and the successive codes of Gregorius, Hermogenes, and Theodosius. From these materials were composed the Institutes, the Code, and the Pandects of Justinian. So that they may be truly considered, as the depository of the collected wisdom of all her sages, and as a most authentic transcript of her municipal law, in its most perfect state. Nor is this all. She had successively conquered, and incorporated into her domain, almost all the other civilized nations of the Eastern continent, including those, which had been most distinguished in commerce; and it can scarcely be doubted, that whatever was excellent in their maritime police, had been, from time to time, adopted into her own jurisprudence by the rescripts of her emperors, or by the more salutary decisions of her courts, guided by the principles of equity, and selecting, with true national comity, from the usages and the learning of foreign countries. We have direct evidence of this position in the fourteenth book of the Pandects, title second, ad Legem Rhodiam de Jactu, where, in a case of maritime law, put to the emperor Antoninus, he answered "Lege id Rhodiâ, quæ de rebus nauticis præscripta est, judicetur;" plainly importing, that the doctrines of the Rhodian Laws on this subject had been recognized and incorporated into the Roman jurisprudence. As to the manner in which they were incorporated, it is highly probable, that it was not by any imperial edict, but by the gradual operation of judicial decisions, adopting them as rules, founded in general convenience, and fitted to the commercial transactions of Rome itself. What strengthens this supposition is the fact, that the Rhodian Laws are not to be found in the text of any of the Roman codes; and the very title of the Pandects, where we should expect to find them, if they had been adopted in mass, contains nothing but the commentaries and opinions of Roman lawyers, on the principles, which regulate the application of the law of jettison, and some few other nautical questions of a kindred nature. If this be a just view of the case, and we have no doubt it is, the Roman law, as collected by Justinian, contains in itself the substance of all the maritime law of all antiquity, improved by the philosophy and the learning of Roman jurisconsults. Yet, how narrow is the compass, within which the whole maritime law of Rome is compressed! It scarcely fills a half dozen short titles in the Pandects, and about as many in the Justinian Code,[1] mixed up with matter properly appertaining to other subjects.

[1] The principal titles in the Pandects are, Lib. 4, tit. 1. Nautæ, caupones, stabularii, ut recepta restituant. Lib. 14, tit. 1. De exercitoria actione.

The most interesting and important are the titles in the Pandects; three of which treat of the responsibility of the owners and employers (exercitores) of ships for the safe keeping and delivery of goods shipped on freight, for the contracts of the master in respect to the employment, repairs, and concerns of the ship, and for the acts and defaults of the agents and mariners of the ship; one treats of bottomry and maritime loans, one of jettisons, and one of shipwrecks. Whoever expects to find, even under these heads, the minute details and practical principles of modern times, will certainly be disappointed. He will, however, find the elements of our own law on this subject, expressed with excellent sense, and often illustrated by apt examples. And brief, indeed, as are these texts of the civil law, the whole maritime world has paid them a just and voluntary homage, by adopting them as the nucleus, around which to gather their own commercial regulations. But the very circumstance, that so little is here to be found, after Rome had been for so many ages the mistress of the world in commerce and in arms, seems a decisive proof, that neither she, nor any more ancient nation, on the shores of the Mediterranean, had ever digested at any period a general system of maritime law.

The glory of having reduced the principles of maritime law to a science belongs to later times; but no one of competent judgment can doubt, that much of its intrinsic equity, as well as comprehensive liberality, is owing to a familiarity with the Roman digest, with that beautiful distribution of civil justice, which the labors of Labeo, Capito, Proculus, Gaius, Papinianus, Paulus, and Ulpianus, so much contri-

Lib. 14, tit. 2. Ad legem Rhodiam de jactu. Lib. 22, tit. 2. De nautico fœnore. Lib. 47, tit. 5. Furti adversus nautas, caupones, stabularios. Lib. 47, tit. 9. De incendio, ruina, naufragio, rate, nave expugnata. In the Code, Lib. 4, tit. 25. De institoria et exercitoria actione. Lib. 4, tit. 33. De nautico fœnore. Lib. 6, tit. 62. De hæreditatibus decurionum, navicu-lariorum, cohortalium militum et fabricensium. Lib. 11. De navicularii seu naucleris publicas species transportantibus. Variis titulis. There are a few supplementary regulations in the Novels and Authentics of Justinian, on the subjects of maritime loans and the plunder of wrecks.

buted to perfect and adorn. The whole of our own law of contracts rests upon Roman foundations; and we daily feel, how much of the enlarged equity which pervades the doctrines relative to navigation, charter-parties, liens, and shipments, is deduced by a regular descent from the times of Tribonian.

Let it not, therefore, be imagined, that the maritime law as acknowledged and practised upon by the most enlightened nations of the present day, was produced *per saltum* — by the sudden start of a single mind or nation, generalizing and analyzing the principles at a single effort. Far different is the case. It arrived at its present comparative perfection by slow and cautious steps; by the gradual accumulations of distant times, and the contributions of various nations. Industry and patience first collected the scattered rays, emitted from a thousand points through the dim vista of past ages; and philosophy reflected them back with tenfold brilliancy and symmetry. If, indeed, a professional mind might indulge in a momentary enthusiasm, it would perceive, that in this process had been realized the enchantment and wonders of the kaleidoscope, where broken and disjointed materials, however rude, are shaped into inexhaustible varieties of figures, all perfect in their order and harmonies, by the adjustment of reflected light under the guidance of philosophy.

The irruptions of the northern Barbarians over the western Empire, and the introduction of the feudal system, seem for a while to have suspended the operations of commerce. But as soon as mankind began to shake off the drowsiness of the Dark Ages, commerce revived upon the same shores of the Mediterranean, which had long been her favorite abodes. As it extended its vivifying effect, every state became sensible of the importance of collecting its own mercantile usages into some regular system, at least for its own government. One of the earliest, if not the earliest, and, considering its age, the most extraordinary collection of this kind, is the Consolato del Mare. The question, what country is entitled to the honor of its origin, has been contested with as much warmth and zeal, as the birthplace of Homer; and the exact time of its first publication has been enveloped in the like obscurity. It has been variously assigned to a date, as early as the tenth century, and as late as the fourteenth. Vinnius and Crusius appear to have thought that it was composed in the time of St. Louis, King of France. Grotius and Marquardus assign it to the age of the Crusades, and assert that it was collected by order of the ancient kings of Arragon. In this latter opinion they are followed by Targa and Casaregis. Azuni, in a very elaborate essay, endeavors to establish, that it is a revision of the maritime code, which existed in very early times in the republic of Pisa. On the other hand, Capmany, an eminent Spanish jurist, asserts that the compilation was first made at Barcelona; and in this opinion he is followed by Boucher, the learned editor of a late French translation. The earliest edition of the work, which can be traced by the diligence of its editors, is admitted on all sides to be that published by Celelles, at Barcelona, in 1494. This, as Boucher informs us, is the original of all editions and translations, that have subsequently appeared in the Castilian, the Italian, the Dutch, and French languages. The English language has not as yet been honored by any translation, except of two chapters on prize law by Dr. Robinson.[1]

The title of this curious collection, Consolato del Mare, (Consulate of the Sea,) is derived from the name consolato, (consulate or consular court,) which was, by almost all the commercial nations of the Mediterranean, given to their

[1] The principal editions, as they are collected by the best authors, are, the edition of 1494, by Celelles, printed at Barcelona in the Catalonian dialect; of 1502, at the same place; of 1539, by Francisco Romano, at Valentia, in Castilian; of 1544, by N. Pedrozano, at Venice, in Italian; of 1567, by Zeberti, in Italian; of 1576, by Zaneti & Co., in Italian; of 1577, by Mayssoni, at Marseilles, in French; of 1579, at Venice, in Italian; of 1584, in Italian; of 1592, at Barcelona, in Catalonian; of 1599, at Venice, in Italian; of 1635, at Aix, in French; of 1696 and 1720, by Casaregis, in Italian; of 1704, by Westerveen, in Italian and Dutch; of 1732, by Cayetano de Tallega, in Castilian; of 1791, by Capmany, in Castilian, at Madrid; of 1808, by Boucher, in French.

maritime courts. The value of this collection has been differently estimated in modern times by learned men. Hubner, with his usual petulance, has treated it as an ill-chosen mass of maritime usages and positive ordinances of the Middle Ages, or of times very little enlightened, which are now obsolete, and of no authority. Bynkershoek, in his usual bold and determined manner, treats it with as little ceremony. After approving of its decision in a particular case, he adds, "Vellem omnia, quæ in illa farragine legum nauticarum reperiuntur, æque proba et recta essent, sed non omnia ibi sunt tam bonæ frugis." To these opinions we might justly oppose the discreet yet liberal praise of Casaregis, Emérigon, Valin, Vinnius, and Lubeck. But in our judgment it is not necessary to resort to the *testimonia eruditorum*. The fact that the substance of its regulations was eagerly embraced, and immediately incorporated into the usages and the ordinances of all the maritime nations of the continent, pronounces a eulogy on its merits, which no formal vindication can surpass. Emérigon very justly states, that its decisions have united the suffrages of all nations; and it has furnished ample materials for the maritime ordinance of France of 1681, an ordinance, which has immortalized the ministry of Louis XIV., and which, perhaps, more than the maritime code of any other nation, deserves the praise of philosophic jurists. Nay, more, the Consolato del Mare contains the rudiments of the law of prize, as it is at present administered; and its authority has, perhaps, weighed more than any other, in settling the great controversy of our own times, relative to the question, whether free ships make free goods. England, in asserting the negative, (as we think with vast force of reasoning,) has reposed on this venerable monument, as affording the surest proof of the antiquity and the general recognition of the rule, which she has so justly sought to establish, and which has stood approved to the good sense of the three greatest civilians of modern times, Grotius, Bynkershoek, and Heineccius.

As the Consolato del Mare is a rare work in our country, it may not, perhaps, be useless to give a general outline of its method and contents. The whole work, as we now find it in the edition of Casaregis, is contained in two hundred and ninety-four chapters.[1] Of these the first forty-three chapters do not, properly speaking, belong to the original collection, but treat of the jurisdiction and forms of proceeding in the consular court of Valentia. The forty-fourth chapter is the proper commencement of the work; which contains, not as is often supposed, the positive institutions of any particular maritime nation, promulgated by its sovereign; but a collection of the general usages and customs of the sea, as approved and practised upon in the most enlightened ages. The forty-fourth chapter, which is in fact the proem of the work, states,—"These are the good institutions and good customs, which relate to the sea, which the wise men, who went abroad, began to give to our ancestors, which form the book of the knowledge of good customs in the course of which will be found the duty of the master of the ship towards the merchants, mariners, passengers, and all other persons, who go in the ship, and also the duty of the merchants, mariners, passengers, &c. towards the master of the ship; for whoever pays frieght for his person, as well as merchandise, is denominated a passenger." The work then proceeds, in an order, not very exact or methodical, to state the doctrines relative to the ownership, building, and equipment of ships; the authorities and duties of the master and owner; the rights and duties of the mariners; the responsibility of the masters, owners, and mariners, in cases of the shipment of goods, in a general ship, or under charter-parties; the earning, payment, and loss of freight and wages; and incidentally treats of ransoms, salvage, average, jettisons, and captures, and recaptures.

[1] In the edition of Boucher, which is a translation from the original edition of Celelles, the whole number of chapters is 297.

Such is the Consolato del Mare, the grand reservoir, from which, as we have already intimated, have been drawn the principal ordinances of modern maritime nations. It is remarkable, that the laws of Oleron and Wisbuy (which are of so great antiquity, that they dispute precedency with the Consolato, and by many learned men are assigned to an earlier age,) contain nothing on the subject of the law of prize; and that the Consolato stands alone, as the earliest expounder of the law of nations. In neither of them, if we except a single article (art. 66) of the laws of Wisbuy, is there the slightest allusion to the contract of insurance. There is, therefore, some reason to believe, either that the laws of Wisbuy, as we now have them, belong to a later date, than is generally assigned to it, or that the article in question is an addition to the original code.[1]

The history of commercial jurisprudence, since the publication of the Consolato, including therein also the law of bills of exchange and promissory notes, would be very interesting and instructive, at least to the professional reader. He would there have an opportunity to trace the numerous rivulets, which, in different ages and nations, have contributed to form the vast and perpetually increasing stream of commercial law. He would there learn the slow and almost imperceptible manner, in which its principles have, from minute origins, expanded to their present comprehensive and systematical equity. He would look back with admiration and surprise upon the patience, public spirit, and scientific enthusiasm of those learned men, who devoted themselves, with such unremitted labor, to the development of those principles of moral propriety and justice, which distinguished this

[1] Stypmannus, Gibalinus, Ausaldus and Casaregis suppose, that the contract of insurance was introduced in the fifteenth century. Emérigon relies on this article in the laws of Wisbuy to establish the contrary. Marshall, in his Insurance, (p. 18) doubts, whether the latter part of this article, as it stands in Cleirac, be not a mere comment upon the original text. If so, the other part of the article may well admit of an explanation, foreign from any notion of insurance. Malyne omits this clause.

branch of the law. Above all, he would, perhaps, catch a spark from the altar, which would light him on still farther in the paths of virtuous glory, and would stimulate him still more to enlarge the boundaries of the science, and vindicate to himself that immortality, which Cicero was not ashamed to court, and from which even the modesty of Sir William Jones did not retire.

But we have no space or leisure for such interesting inquiries. They belong to some philosophic spirit, who, free from the bustle and the toils of professional life, may indulge himself in juridical speculations in learned ease. Such a one may, without rashness, undertake the task, and encourage his heart with the consideration, *Numina nulla premunt.*

It may not, however, be uninstructive to review, in a rapid sketch, the merits of some of the most eminent writers, who, in different ages, from the early twilight of maritime law, contributed to give the public mind that rational direction, which has made even the technical rules of that law the dictates of philosophy itself.

About the middle of the sixteenth century, Peckius, a distinguished civilian of Belgium, published an edition of the principal texts in the Pandects and Code, on nautical affairs, and enriched them with an ample commentary, in which he has brought together all the valuable remarks of preceding jurists on this subject, and explained the reasons of the principles stated in the texts. At the distance of about a century, this work was reëdited with supplementary comments by Vinnius, who, in his best manner, has added illustrations from the maritime laws of other nations, and thereby supplied the deficiencies of his master.[1] Vinnius himself complains of these deficiencies: " Apparetque ex toto illo Peckii

[1] The works of Peckius were first collected and published together in 1646; but the edition before us was published at Antwerp in 1679. His treatise, Ad Rem Nauticam, was first published in 1556; and republished, with the commentary of Vinnius, in 12mo, at Leyden, in 1647. Vinnius died in 1657.

opere, non vidisse eum ullas alias leges de rebus maritimis quam quæ in Corpore Juris Justiniani continentur." He then very justly reproves the long digressions, in which Peckius had indulged; but concludes: "Ostendit sane in hoc opere Peckius sibi non defuisse justam eruditionem solidamque juris et multarum rerum scientiam." The work, however, such as it is, with its double commentaries, is more frequently quoted than read, in our own times.

About the same period, the work on averages of Quintin Weytsen, a counsellor of Holland, is supposed to have been first published. In the body of the work there is no reference to any decision posterior to 1551, soon after which time, it was, therefore, most probably compiled; and the editor of the edition of 1651 speaks of it, as a work which had appeared in Holland a long time before. It is certainly not without merit; and Casaregis thought so well of it, that he translated it into Latin, and put it at the beginning of the third volume of his works with the notes of Van Leeuwen and Mathieu de Vicq.

Straccha and Santerna, the first an Italian, and the last a Portugese jurist, adorned the latter part of the sixteenth century. Their works are found collected in a large work, De Mercatura, which was first published at Cologne, in 1623, and subsequently at Amsterdam in 1679.[1] The principal tracts of Straccha are De Mercatura, De Nautis, De Navibus, De Navigatione, and De Assecurationibus. In the first (De Mercatura) he treats in separate parts of the following topics: 1. who is a merchant, and what is merchandising; 2. of the condition of merchants, and things appertaining to that condition; 3. of those who are prohibited from being merchants; 4. in respect to what things (causis) merchandising may be;

[1] The title of the work is, "Benevenuti Straccha aliorumque clarissimorum jurisconsultorum de mercatura, cambiis, sponsionibus, creditoribus, fidejussoribus, debitoribus, decoctoribus, navibus, navigatione, assecurationibus, subhastionibus, aliisque mercatorum nogotiis, rebusque ad mercaturam pertinentibus, decisiones et tractatus varii."

5. of the contracts of merchants; 6. of mandates, or orders on commission; and 7. of some miscellaneous questions relative to merchandise. In the second tract (De Nautis) he treats generally of the rights, duties, and responsibility of the masters and mariners of ships, arising from their contracts or their defaults. In the third (De Navibus) he treats of the ownership, building, repairing, and freighting of ships, and other contracts relative to shipments. In the fourth (De Navigatione) he discusses some points not embraced in the preceding. In the fifth, (De Assecurationibus) after a very elaborate preface, he introduces the form of the policy of insurance used in Ancona in 1567; and taking up the several matters, in the order of the policy, he examines every sentence by itself, and in a perpetual gloss, or commentary, explains the doctrines of insurance applicable to the contract. The treatise of Santerna, which is entitled De Assecurationibus et Sponsionibus Mercatorum, is, on the other hand, a systematic treatise upon the same subject. Both of these writers draw their doctrines from the usages of merchants, from general reasoning, and above all, from the law of contracts in the Roman Code, wherever it is applicable. Considering the age in which they wrote, they are very respectable authorities; and Valin has pronounced the eulogy of Straccha, when he declares him "an author truly estimable." (Auteur vraiment estimable.)

The seventeenth century was distinguished by the labors of a great many illustrious writers on maritime law. To the beginning of that century, or, to the latter part of the preceding, is to be referred the work, entitled "Le Guidon, utile et nécessaire pour ceux qui font merchandise et qui mettent à la mer." This is an ancient French treatise on the law of insurance and bottomry, in which the various doctrines are examined in a very scientific manner, and with a practical accuracy, greatly surpassing all preceding works on the same subject. The author of the work, and the exact time of its first publication, are unknown. In 1647, Cleirac published a new edition of it, with an excellent commentary, in his "Les Us et Coutumes de la Mer." The account, he gives of it, is, that it was an old French work, drawn up for the use of the merchants of Rouen; and he adds, "Ce avec tant d'adresse et de subtilité tant déliée, que l'auteur d'icelui, en explicant les contrats ou polices d'assurance, a insinué et fait entendre avec grande facilité tout ce qu'est des autres contrats maritimes, et tout le général du commerce naval; de sorte qu'il n'a rien omis, si ce n'est seulement d'y mettre son nom pour en conserver la memoire et l'honneur qu'il mérite, d'avoir tant obligé sa patrie, et toutes les autres nations de l'Europe; lesquelles peuvent trouver en son ouvrage l'accomplissement de ce qui manque, ou la correction de ce qui est mal ordonné aux règlemens, qui chacune a fait en particulier sur semblable sujet." This is high praise; but Cleirac was a very competent judge. His own commentary on this work, and on the laws of Oleron, establishes his reputation as a maritime jurist, in the very first rank.[1] And to his collections and commentaries Lord Mansfield was unquestionably indebted for many of the best principles of commercial law, which he has infused into the English system. It is most obvious, from his decisions, that he had studied Cleirac with extraordinary attention.[2] And we may add, upon the authority of Valin, that Le Guidon formed a part of the immense compilation of law, from which was drawn the famous ordinance of 1681.

About the middle of the seventeenth century, appeared the works of Stypmannus, of Loccenius, of Kuricke, and of Roccus, on maritime law.[3] Stypmannus, in his treatise, entitled Jus Maritimum, discusses in a prolix manner most of the

[1] There have been many editions of Cleirac's work, the earliest of which is of 1647, and the latest, we believe, is the one now before us, of 1788.

[2] See, among other cases, Luke *v.* Lyde, 2 Burr. R. 882.

[3] Stypmannus was first published, as Valin says, at Stralsund in 1661. Westerveen, in his edition of Roccus, refers to an earlier edition, printed at Gryphiswaldia in 1652. Loccenius was first published at Stockholm in 1652; Kuricke, at Hamburg in 1667; and Roccus, at Naples in 1655.

questions of maritime law. Loccenius is more condensed, and more narrow in his range. The subject of insurance is treated by him in a very slight and careless manner. In other respects, the work is quite as useful as Stypmannus. There are three treatises by Kuricke. The first, Jus Maritimum Hanseaticum, contains an elaborate commentary on the several articles composing the Hanseatic ordinance of 1614. The second, Diatriba de Assecurationibus, is a very short discussion on the law of insurance. The third, Resolutio Questionum Illustrium ad Jus Maritimum pertinentium, is a collection of miscellaneous questions on maritime law, which the author is pleased to call "Illustrious Questions," but which, in our humble judgment, contain a great deal of learned trifling, and insignificant criticism. One of these "illustrious questions" is, whether a journey by sea is preferable to a journey by land; and another, whether a ship repaired is the same ship which she was before the repairs were made. From this specimen, we might, perhaps, be induced to turn with contempt from such an author. But it was the misfortune of the age, in which Stypmannus, and Loccenius, and Kuricke lived, that jurists employed a great deal of their time and talents in idle discussions upon unimportant topics, and buried matter of more worth and virtue under a cumbrous load of scholastic learning and metaphysical subtilties. Far different is the character of Roccus. He was an eminent jurist and judge at Naples, and published two tracts, (one, De Navibus et Naulo, the other, De Assecurationibus, which he modestly terms Notabilia,) which deserve, and have received the approbation of all Europe. They consist of a series of texts, remarkable for their brevity, accuracy, sound exposition of maritime law, and practical utility even in our days. His learned Dutch editor, Westerveen, has justly observed of these treatises, "Iisque casus

These works, except Roccus, were collected and published by Heineccius, with a learned preface, in a single volume, at Magdeburg in 1740, under the title of Scriptorum de Jure Nautico et Maritimo Fasciculus.

quotidianos tam breviter et absolute complexus est [Roccus] tam luculenter proposuit, tam dilucide explicavit, ut omnium Scriptorum indicem seu compendium fecisse videatur."[1] Roccus has, indeed, drawn liberally from his predecessors, and from none more frequently, or more correctly, than from Juan de Hevia Bolaños,[2] a most learned and excellent Spanish writer of his own age, whose works deserve to be better known. But Roccus was himself endowed with a clear and comprehensive mind, and, as his select responses show, with a most acute and sound judgment. His works are of more practical use to an English lawyer, than all the other maritime works, if we except Cleirac, which had been previously published. Lord Mansfield is under no inconsiderable obligations to them, and can be traced, in some of his most celebrated decisions, back to the pages of the Neapolitan.

We have now approached the times of Bynkershoek and Casaregis, two of the most eminent civilians that ever adorned the courts of any nations. In the short review already made of maritime writers since the days of the Consolato, we have purposely omitted to speak of those, who professedly wrote on the law of prize, or the more general doctrines of the law of nations. We have the more readily done this, not because there are not very ample materials for historical and critical disquisition, but because war, and conquest, and national calamity, have but too frequently brought them before the public. Who, indeed, is there, that is ignorant of the fame, or the writings, of Grotius and Puffendorf? Bynkershoek has immortalized himself by his treatise De Foro Legatorum,

1 The works of Roccus were collected and published at Naples, in a large folio volume. They consist of the tracts above mentioned, and two centuries of answers to select questions. Westerveen selected the treatises and responses on maritime law, and published them in 12mo, at Amsterdam, in 1708. An excellent translation has been recently published of the tracts De Navibus et Naulo, and De Assecuratione, by Joseph R. Ingersoll, Esq. of Philadelphia.

2 Mr. Duponceau, in his most valuable notes to his translation of Bynkershoek on the Law of War, has spoken with becoming praise of De Hevia. The tracts referred to are those published by De Hevia, on commercial contracts, in his institute of the law of Spain, called Curia Philippica.

and his Questiones Publici Juris de Rebus Bellicis.[1] It is not, perhaps, as generally known, that he has written a very neat sketch of the law of bottomry, and some very excellent dissertations on the subject of commercial law, and particularly of insurance. Every thing which came from this great man bears the marks of an original, vigorous, and independent mind. He often expresses himself with boldness and vehemence, and sometimes also with a lofty contempt for the opinions of others. But his learning, sagacity, and sound judgment, rarely if ever desert him. Alluding to Adrian Verwer, a Dutch writer on bottomry and average, he says, "Hæc etiam adhibuit, qui ante aliquot annos hunc contractum commentariolo illustrare conatus est; sed, sat scio, manes ejus non offendam, si et ipse ex penu meo aliquid proferam; ille *mercatorem* egit, ego cum maxime *jurisconsultum* agam, et sine jurisprudentia etiam hæc sacra non constant." He was conscious of his own strength, and, while acting the part of a jurisconsult in expounding doctrines, he speaks in a tone, which indicates the judge from whose sentence no appeal is permitted. Of his works it may be asserted without rashness, that the more they are studied, the more they will be admired and respected.

Casaregis was born at Genoa in 1670, and died in 1737. He was appointed a judge of the Supreme Tribunal of Tuscany; and in that office, as his biography states, he discharged the duties with great assiduity, integrity, prudence, and universal approbation, for more than twenty years. His works have been collected and published in four folio volumes, and consist of two hundred and twenty-six discourses on various topics of commercial law, of a Latin translation of Weytsen on Averages, as already mentioned, of a new edition of the

[1] Mr. Duponceau has prefixed to his translation of this last work a short but very satisfactory account of the life and writings of Bynkershoek. Why will not Mr. Duponceau increase the public gratitude by translating the works of other learned foreigners, and by a critical account of the writings of those civilians who are best entitled to the attention and study of American lawyers?

Consolato del Mare, with an excellent explanation or commentary (Spiëgazione) of his own and a treatise, entitled "Il Cambista istruito," upon bills of exchange, and other commercial securities, and of a few tracts upon municipal law.[1] His commercial discourses are by far the most valuable of all his works to a modern lawyer. They embrace the whole circle of commercial law, including the law of prize, and are written in a plain, clear style, abounding in just and practical remarks and sound learning. All that is most useful in the works of former jurists is collected and commented on with acuteness and accuracy; and for the most part the topics are examined until the whole subject-matter is exhausted. Rarely have we looked into his works upon any contested question without rising instructed and enlightened by the perusal. Higher praise cannot be bestowed upon him than the fact affords, that he is quoted by all subsequent writers on commercial law, as a leading and safe authority; and Valin does not scruple to affirm, that he is beyond all contradiction the best of all the maritime authors. In recommending him, therefore, to the diligent study of our own lawyers, we are confident that we do them a substantial service, which will be estimated the more, as familiarity with his works makes his merits more extensively known.

We had almost forgotten to speak of an author who was a countryman and contemporary of Casaregis, and is often cited by him with great respect and approbation. We allude to Targa, who, in his Reflections on Maritime Contracts, (Ponderazioni sopra la Contractazione Marittima,) has drawn from the civil and canon law, the Consolato del Mare, the usages of maritime nations, and preceding writers, the most useful learning on all the subjects of maritime law except insurance; and has adapted his work to practice by collect-

[1] The best edition of Casaregis's works is that printed at Venice in 1740, (which is now before us,) in four vols. folio. The two first volumes contain his Discursus de Commercio, in Latin; the third, Tractatus de Avariis, Cambista instruito, and Consulatus Maris; the fourth, Elucubrationes ac Resolutiones ad Statuta Januæ de Decretis ac de Successionibus ab intestato.

ing the forms of the various contracts, with hints for their proper application. He is generally esteemed as an industrious and correct author; but his fame seems lost in the superior blaze of his illustrious countryman.[1]

France was, during the seventeenth century, behind Italy, in her attention to the great interests of commerce; and her truly admirable ordinance of 1681 afforded the most ample materials for the employment of the best talents of her bar and bench. Of this masterly code, Mr. Marshall, in his Treatise on Insurance, has spoken with bare justice, when he says, "It forms a system of whatever experience and the wisdom of ages had pronounced to be most just and convenient in the marine institutions of the maritime States of Europe. And though it contains many new regulations, suggested by motives of national interest, yet it has hitherto been esteemed a code of great authority upon all questions of maritime jurisprudence." Excellent, however, as this code is, it stood in need of a philosophical commentator to explain its principles, to follow them out into all their minute consequences, and to illustrate and strengthen them by the lights borrowed from the whole body of maritime jurisprudence. The middle of the eighteenth century witnessed the perfect accomplishment of this great task after the failure of other attempts had almost extinguished every hope. Valin has the singular merit of having produced a commentary which, in celebrity, has eclipsed even the text itself, and in authority stands equally high with the positive regulations of the royal ordinance.

The illustrious author published his great work in 1760, and it immediately circulated over all Europe. He has justly observed, "Un commentaire sur l'ordonnance de la marine est un de ces projets hardis, dont le succès peut seul justifier

[1] The works of Targa are not very common in our country. A good edition was published at Genoa in 1750, and we have before us a Spanish translation, by Juan Manuel Giron, printed at Madrid in 1753, in which the author is highly praised.

l'entreprise. L'auteur des notes (imprimées in 1714) sur cette ordonnance, loin d'en avoir compris la difficulté, il ne l'a pas même soupçonnée, et j'avoué qu'elle ne m'a été bien connue, que lors qu'il n'étoit plus temps de reculer." Never, indeed, was success better earned, or more completely attained. The work is a perpetual commentary upon every article of the ordinance, and contains within itself the body of maritime jurisprudence, expounded with a philosophical precision and depth of learning, which have rarely been equalled, and can scarcely be surpassed. It is to be lamented, that the author scarcely lived long enough after the publication, to enjoy the reward of his labors.[1] His fame — it may perhaps perish — but it will cast the last stream of its light upon the last ruins of time.

England had hitherto made but slow advances in commercial law. The laws of Oleron, the articles preserved in the Black Book of the Admiralty, and the treatises of Molloy, Malynes, and Marius, formed nearly the whole stock of her written maritime jurisprudence. But the period was now arrived, when a different state of things was to be presented. The dawn of a brighter day had already diffused its pale, but increasing light, round her wide domain, and it burst upon us, with inextinguishable glory, when Lord Mansfield ascended the bench.[2] This was an epoch in English juridical history, since which the grandeur of her naval power has scarcely been more universally felt, or acknowledged, than her commercial jurisprudence has been admired and respected, for its solid principles and equity. Lord Mansfield was an accomplished scholar, whom Pope has elegantly praised in lamenting,

"How sweet an Ovid in a Murray lost!"

[1] Monsieur Valin died in 1765. His works are 1. "Nouveau Commentaire sur l'Ordonnance de la Marine," in 2 vols. 4to, first printed in 1760; the edition before us is 1766. 2. Traité des Prises, in 2 vols. 8vo, printed in 1763. 3. Commentaire sur la Coutume de la Rochelle, in 3 vols. 4to, printed in 1768.

[2] Lord Mansfield came upon the bench on the 11th of November, 1756.

He was an excellent civilian, and, from his Scotch education, he was early imbued with a reverence for the civil law. He was thoroughly versed in the maritime literature of the day, and had studied all the best works, from the Consolato del Mare to Valin. To the latter, indeed, he owes deep obligations. Mr. Marshall has observed, that "He appears to have taken much pains to possess himself of the soundest principles of marine law, and of the law of insurance; and that he seems to have drawn much of his knowledge upon these subjects from the ordinance of Louis XIV., and from the elaborate and useful commentary of Valin." With all these advantages he possessed liberal and enlarged views, a sagacious and penetrating spirit of inquiry, an unwearied diligence, a solid judgment, and a most persuasive flow of spontaneous and glowing eloquence. Whatever subject he touched was touched with a master's hand and spirit. He employed his eloquence to adorn his learning, and his learning to give solid weight to his eloquence. He was always instructive and interesting, and rarely without producing an instantaneous conviction. He broke down the narrow barrier of the common law against the prejudices of the age, and infused into it an attractive equity, which it seemed to all his predecessors incapable of sustaining. All Westminster Hall listened with admiration and delight to his judgments, and stood astonished at the extent and variety of his attainments; and, if he ever removed from the temple of English jurisprudence a single pillar of Gothic structure, it was, that he might replace it with the exquisite finish of the Corinthian order, carved in Parian marble. In short, he was one of those great men raised up by Providence, at a fortunate moment, to effect a salutary revolution in the world. If he had never existed, we should still have been in the trammels and the quibbles of technical refinements. He has lived; and the law is redeemed from feudal selfishness and barbarity. A lofty ambition of excellence, that stirring spirit, which breathes the breath of heaven and pants for immortality, sustained his genius in its perilous course. He became, what he intended, the jurist of the commercial world, the judge for every polished nation whose code is built upon virtue and principle. He lived to a good old age,[1] and could look back upon a long track illumined with glory. But even that track is but a point, compared with the splendor of his fame, as it will be seen ascending and widening by distant ages. Is it most for the honor of Valin, or of Lord Mansfield, that the commentary of the former has furnished the principal materials, or that the latter has wrought those materials with such exquisite skill, that they now form the most polished structure of commercial law that the world has ever beheld?

It is not a little remarkable, that, while Lord Mansfield was running his splendid career, two eminent scholars on the continent were devoting themselves with equal ardor to the pursuit of commercial jurisprudence. We allude to Pothier and Emérigon; the one, the author of the most finished treatise upon insurance which has yet appeared; the other, the author of distinct treatises upon almost all the branches of the law of contracts, including maritime contracts, equally remarkable for their brevity, luminous method, and apposite illustrations.[2] Whether Lord Mansfield was acquainted with the works of either of these illustrious writers is uncertain. The probability is, that he was not. Emérigon's treatise was not published until near the close of his judicial career; and we gather, from an intimation of Sir William Jones, in his Essay on Bailments, that, at the time of the publication of that work, in 1781, Pothier was unknown in England. "For my own part," says he, "I am so charmed with them [Pothier's

[1] Lord Mansfield died on the 20th of March, 1793, in the 89th year of his age.

[2] The treatise of Emérigon is entitled Traité des Assurances et des Contracts a la Grosse, and was first printed at Marseilles in 1783. The treatises of Pothier were published at different times, between 1761 and 1772, in which last year the author died. The best edition of his works is that printed at Paris in 8 vols. 4to, 1781. We have not been able to find any account of Emérigon.

treatises] that, if my undissembled fondness for the study of jurisprudence were never to produce any greater benefit to the public than barely the introduction of Pothier to the acquaintance of my countrymen, I should think, that I had in some measure discharged the debt, which every man, according to Lord Coke, owes to his profession." If, however, Emérigon and Pothier were unknown to Lord Mansfield, they have since his time instructed both the lawyers and the judges of Westminster Hall. But there is yet wanting a judge of the generalizing genius and enterprise of Lord Mansfield, or the classical enthusiasm of Sir William Jones, to naturalize them in that forum. To the honor of America, there is one man, once a chief justice, and now a chancellor, (need we name him?) whose acknowledged learning has taught us, how much judicial judgments may be enriched by the manly sense of Pothier, and the acute investigations of Emérigon.

We had intended to say something more in relation to the merits of these authors, and to have sketched a critical analysis of their works. But we are admonished, that we have already exhausted more time than we can properly devote to such speculations. We quit them with regret; but there are younger and abler pens, that can do them justice; and we trust, that it is no idle dream to anticipate, that the next age of the law will find our accomplished lawyers consulting the continental jurists with the same familiarity, with which we now cite Blackstone and Marshall.

The work which stands at the head of these remarks, and from a review of which we have been so long detained, is, as the title-page purports, a translation from the German. We have not seen the original, and, therefore, cannot speak of the exactness of the translation. But we have no reason to doubt its accuracy. Mr. Frick appears to be perfectly competent to his task, both in learning and diligence; and, so far as he has permitted himself to appear in the notes, he has acquitted himself in a manner very creditable to his talents and his acquirements. We should, indeed, have been better pleased, if the notes had been more extensive, and had embraced the various commercial decisions, and particularly the prize decisions, which have been recently made in the United States, on the various topics discussed in the text of Mr. Jacobsen. We have no right, however, to complain of this omission; and, when a gentleman offers a really valuable present to the profession, it seems hardly justice or civility to insist, that he ought to have made it still more valuable. Mr. Frick will please, therefore, to accept our thanks for the book, such as it is; and if, as we hope, it should be favorably received by the public, and a new edition be called for, we think our hint will not be unworthy of his consideration; and, from the ability of the present specimen, we are sure, that he will command the public confidence in his enlarged annotations.

We will now proceed to give some account of the work itself. We learn from the preface, that Mr. Jacobsen is himself a lawyer; and that, "Whatever practical jurists, among the Italians, French, English, Dutch, Danes, and Germans have written and suggested upon the subject, applicable to these times; whatever is contained in the sea-laws, yet in force on the subject; whatever was to be gathered from numerous legal decisions [in England]; whatever was to be gained by a correspondence for years with men who have made the subject of maritime law the study of their lives; whatever, in sixteen years' professional experience in maritime affairs, has suggested itself to the author as useful or desirable, he here proffers as a part of the debt, which every one owes to the country of his birth, and to mankind in general." And he adds, "How inconsiderable, as yet, is our proficiency in the science of maritime law, compared to our treatises of municipal law! The present, perhaps, is the first attempt to offer any thing, in a systematic form, relative to ships' papers, on which depend the fortune and the peace of so many families; for the ships' papers, with reference to the maritime laws of war, have hitherto never been treated of in any language."

Prefixed to each chapter is a catalogue of the authorities and editions of the several authors, who have discussed the subject-matter of that chapter, and from whose writings the doctrines have been drawn; and to the whole work is prefixed a catalogue of the authors, who have treated of the subject generally, or of the literature connected with it, with short comments upon their merits. This, we think, is a very useful addition; and in this catalogue we notice a number of works, which have never reached us through any English publication. It is some consolation, however, that, as far as the contents of these works are disclosed to us, they do not contain any very considerable accession to the learning already within our reach; and Mr. Jacobsen has incorporated whatever seemed most useful into his own treatise. What struck us with some degree of surprise, on the first examination, was the heavy contributions, which Mr. Jacobsen had levied from the English authorities. He appears perfectly familiar with the recent decisions in the courts of Westminster Hall, and the commercial treatises of Abbott, Lawes, Park, and Marshall; and has manifestly adopted their doctrines, from a thorough conviction of their soundness and equity. This is a flattering distinction; and is repaying to continental Europe the obligations which England, in the earliest stages of her law, owed to the enterprise and wisdom of the civilians. As to the law of prize, it is almost entirely borrowed from the Reports of the decisions of the High Court of Admiralty since the time of Sir William Scott. For this the author himself offers a very striking reason. "If," says he, "in the subsequent part of his work, he [the author] has confined himself somewhat more exclusively to the doctrines and opinions of that celebrated man, whose unrivalled decisions on maritime law, like the judgments and opinions of the Roman jurists in the civil law, will constitute an essential part of maritime law for centuries to come; *it was because the continental jurisprudence is barren of examples in those branches of the subject.* As the commercial law of Great Britain received much of its perfection through the decisions of Lord Mansfield, so the maritime laws of war of that country have attained their maturity through the decisions of Sir William Scott." This acknowledgment is extremely honorable to English jurisprudence; but it is also honorable to our author, who shows in this, as in other parts of his work, that he is far removed from the prejudices of his continental contemporaries, and that he breathes the genuine spirit of a universal jurist. It is no small praise, that he is so far above the visionary doctrines of Hubner and Schlegel, and the French and German theorists. Nor is this the least valuable portion of the work to an English lawyer. It is a remarkable fact, that no systematic treatise upon the law of prize has, as yet, appeared in England. The very superficial, hasty, and imperfect sketch of Mr. Chitty does not deserve the title which it bears, and has been egregiously overrated. Our own country has been honored with a Treatise on Captures, by Mr. Wheaton, which is, in every respect, far superior to Mr. Chitty's; and, taken in connection with his extensive notes on prize law in his Reports, it approaches very near to a complete body of this important branch of law. Are not the merits of our own authors, and especially of our own juridical authors, very slowly appreciated? In what respect is Mr. Livermore's learned Treatise, on the Law of Principal and Agent, inferior to those recently sent from the English bar?

What, however, constitutes the principal value of Mr. Jacobsen's work to an American lawyer, is the minute accuracy and fulness, with which it gives us the positive and customary law of all the maritime nations of the continent. And this, in our judgment, is a most interesting, and, in a practical view, a most important accession to our juridical literature. Of the maritime law of Russia, Prussia, Denmark, Sweden, and Germany, we have hitherto known very little. Yet with all of them we carry on an extensive trade; and the principles of their jurisprudence as to maritime affairs, both in peace and in war, are of incalculable importance to our merchants; nay more, to our government. This is not all. A great variety of curious and difficult questions are perpetually arising in our judicial tribunals, where the positive regulations or usages of other commercial nations would greatly assist us in forming decisions which should comport with general convenience, as well as with the general principles of law. Many are the cases, in which the reasoning is so nicely balanced on each side, that a settled foreign usage ought to incline the scale. We owe, indeed, a full moiety of our present commercial law to the positive ordinances or usages of France, Italy, and Spain, as they have been delivered to us by their eminent jurists. They seem now inclined to borrow from us in return; and thus, perhaps, national comity may gradually establish a nearly uniform system of commercial jurisprudence throughout the whole civilized world.

We have no hesitation, therefore, to recommend Mr. Jacobsen's treatise to the favorable attention of our lawyers and merchants. They cannot fail to be greatly instructed by the perusal. The learned author has prepared his work from very ample materials, and with the most laborious diligence, and, in general, with sound discrimination and impartiality. If Mr. Abbott's treatise were not in existence, Mr. Jacobsen's would be indispensable for every lawyer's library. As it is, it will reflect great light on points, where Mr. Abbott is deficient or unsatisfactory; and no gentleman ought to consider himself thoroughly read, who has not mastered its learning.

We notice in the translation some Germanisms, which it was not, perhaps, easy, without an awkward circumlocution or paraphrase, to avoid. There are also some words, which have not yet acquired a legitimate use in our language, such as "endorsation" and "bottomried." There may be some reason to adopt the latter word, though innovations are dangerous; but there can be no such apology for the former, since we have a genuine English word (endorsement) of the same signification. There are also some errors of the press; one, (in p. 556) which is important to the sense, and where the words should be, "the shadow of partiality," in lieu of "the shadow of impartiality." These, however, are but specks, which we have no inclination to magnify, and Mr. Frick can have no reason to wish to have concealed.

PIRACY AND THE SLAVE TRADE.

A CHARGE TO THE GRAND JURY, FIRST DELIVERED IN THE CIRCUIT COURT OF THE UNITED STATES, FOR THE JUDICIAL DISTRICT OF MAINE, AT ITS FIRST SESSION IN PORTLAND, MAY 8, 1820.

GENTLEMEN OF THE GRAND JURY:

ON this, the first occasion, that I have had the pleasure of meeting you, permit me to congratulate you on the favorable auspices, under which we are assembled. Our country enjoys a state of profound peace, under the guidance of wise and moderate councils; and though our foreign commerce is considerably abridged, both in its enterprise and prosperity, and our domestic intercourse is thus sensibly diminished; yet we have abundant reason to rejoice, as well in our exemption from the calamities, which have visited and oppressed many other nations, as in our own positive good fortune. Our agriculture yields us the most abundant products, cheapening thereby the fruits of the earth to the poor and necessitous; our really useful manufactures are increasing with a slow but solid growth; and our industry and sound morals are maturing a hardy population, which is spreading with unexampled rapidity into the wilderness, and making our forests resound with the cheering sounds of the axe and the hammer. In addition to these substantial comforts, we are indulged by a kind Providence with the blessings of civil, political, and religious liberty — blessings of inestimable value, without which life loses half its charms, property all its security, and patriotism itself sinks back from a virtue into a gross and venal prejudice.

The circumstances under which I address you at the present moment, are, perhaps, without a parallel in the annals of the other quarters of the world. This district has just been admitted into the Union, as a free, sovereign, and independent state, possessing, in common with all the others, an equality of national rights and honors, and protected by an excellent constitution, framed by its own deliberations upon principles of justice and equity.

And in what manner has this been accomplished? Not by the course, in which the division of empires has been usually sought and obtained; by civil dissension and warfare; by successful resistance, wading through the blood of friends and foes to its purpose; or by the terror of the sword, whose brightness has been stained by the sacrifice of innocence, or rusted by the tears of suffering and conquered virtue. Unhappily for mankind, a change of government has rarely taken place without involving evils of the most serious nature. It has been but the triumph of tyranny in the overthrow of the liberties of the people; or the sudden reaction of popular resentment, indignant at wrongs, and stimulated to criminal excesses.

Here a different scene, a scene of peace and good order, has been presented. The separation has been the result of cool deliberation, and cautious examination of the interests of both parties. It has been conducted in a spirit of mutual conciliation and friendship, with an anxious desire to promote the real happiness and prosperity of the people. It has been emphatically, and by no fanciful analogy, like the separation of a parent from his child, when the latter has attained maturity of years and experience. And, like that separation, I trust, it will only lay more surely the foundation of a mutual respect, sustained by the sense of independence, and chastened by grateful recollections of the past, and an earnest solicitude for the solid glory of the future.

At this new starting-point of your political existence, it cannot be disguised, that much of your future character and prosperity will depend upon the wisdom and moderation of your public councils. The great system of your government is to be put into operation, and your laws remoulded and adapted to your own peculiar circumstances. May I venture to suggest, that a liberal and comprehensive policy, in respect to your public institutions and judicial establishments, cannot fail to produce the happiest effects, by creating confidence at home and distinction abroad. Let your laws be framed for the permanent welfare of all the people, for the security of private rights and private property, and for the promotion of good education, and learning, and religion. No system, that aims *merely* at temporary, or party, or local objects, or that bends the great interests of the whole to the partial benefit of the few, ever was, or ever can be, salutary. Such a system is not only unworthy of a free and enlightened people; but brings disgrace and ruin wherever it is established. It is the harbinger of faction and discontent; and leads to animosities, from which the people can derive nothing, but bad laws, bad morals, and bad government.

May I venture, also, to add, that nothing can be of more consequence to youselves and to our common country, than that you should cherish an habitual devotion to the constitution and government of the United States. I look upon that constitution as the great security of all our most valuable political and civil rights. It is the only effectual barrier against foreign conquest and domestic feuds, against the inroads of military ambition, and the more subtile, though not less dangerous, designs of civic demagogues. It will always be the determined, though concealed, purpose of the latter, to undermine the foundations of the national government, by stirring up jealousies of its legitimate powers; and, under an affected devotion to popular rights, to take advantage of temporary prejudices, and thereby gradually withdraw the affections of the people from those principles, which the wisdom of our fathers has consecrated as the keystones of the Union. I know not, indeed, how it is possible better to express the opinion, which every sound patriot and statesman ought to entertain on this subject, than in the language of that Farewell Address, which the great and good WASHINGTON has left as his last benediction to his country.

"The unity of government, which constitutes you one people, is also now dear to you. It is justly so; for it is a main pillar in the edifice of your real independence; the support of your tranquillity at home, your peace abroad; of your safety, of your prosperity, of that very liberty, which you so highly prize. But as it is easy to foresee, that, from different causes, and from different quarters, much pains will be taken, many artifices employed, to weaken in your minds the conviction of this truth; as this is the point in your political fortress, against which the batteries of internal and external enemies will be most constantly and actively (though often covertly and insidiously) directed; it is of infinite moment, that you should properly estimate the immense value of your national union to your collective and individual happiness; that you should cherish a cordial, habitual, and immovable attachment to it; accustoming yourselves to think and speak of it, as of the palladium of your political safety and prosperity; watching for its preservation with jealous anxiety; discountenancing whatever may suggest even a suspicion, that it can in any event be abandoned. . .

"For this you have every inducement of sympathy and interest. Citizens, by birth, or choice, of a common country, that country has a right to concentrate your affections. The name of American, which belongs to you in your national capacity, must always exalt the just pride of patriotism, more than any appellation derived from local discriminations. With slight shades of difference, you have the same religion, manners, habits, and political principles. You have, in a common cause, fought and triumphed together. The independence and liberty you possess are the work of joint councils, and joint efforts, of common dangers, sufferings, and successes."

Such is the language, now speaking, as it were, from the grave of him who was "first in war, first in peace, and first in the hearts of his countrymen."

Having premised these remarks, which are drawn from me by a sense of duty, and a sincere regard to the welfare of your rising state, and which, I trust, will be received in the spirit of candor, in which they have been delivered, permit me now to call your attention to the subjects, which more immediately belong to your cognizance, as a Grand Jury of the United States.

You are impanelled to make due inquiry and presentment of all crimes, which have been committed against the United States within the judicial district of Maine. The oath of office, which has been administered to you, contains a general outline of the duty required of you. You are to inquire with diligence, and to make true and faithful presentments, unaffected by any motives, but those, which should influence conscientious and rational minds. You are to inquire without fear, favor, affection, or hope of reward, on the one side; and without the prejudices arising from hatred, envy, or malice, on the other. I am sure, that I need hardly press upon your attention the solemnity, dignity, and importance of your office. You are selected to guard the public peace, and to maintain the public laws; to accuse the guilty, and to protect the innocent. What higher objects can engage the attention of men, looking to the great interests of society? What nobler ends can be proposed, than those, which administer to the tranquillity and happiness of our friends and fellow-citizens? What can be more acceptable to God, or more conformable to the dictates of religion, than the promotion of justice, the succor of virtue, and the relief of the injured and oppressed? Nor can any one, who seriously reflects upon the invaluable blessings of a free government, hesitate to give all his aid to the due and regular administration of public justice. It is utterly impossible, that real liberty can long remain among a people sunk in vice and indifferent to crimes. The forms and shadows of its institutions may remain, to deceive the idle spectator; but that spirit, which can alone quicken into life the principles of freedom, is gone forever. The history of other nations is full of melancholy instruction on this subject. The mockery and parade of the symbols of liberty long survived the desolation of their rights. It was the amusement of their tyrants to trick out the republic in its ancient, and venerable, and tattered habiliments, when all its virtue, and its glory, and its patriotism, had passed through the last offensive stages of mortality, and dissolved into dust in its ruined sepulchres. The temples of religion, indeed, remained in their majesty; but, instead of that charity, which "believeth all things, hopeth all things, endureth all things," the sullen spirit of persecution inhabited there. The halls of legislation resounded with the voices of eloquence and learning; but they were employed to justify laws written in blood, or to wring from an afflicted and humbled people the last relics of their liberty. The courts of justice, too, entertained within their walls the grave controversies of poor and suffering suitors; but corruption deposited its deadly poison upon their ermine, and bought the patrimony of orphans and widows with bribes, and left them to perish at the very doors of the sanctuary. These are no idle pictures of the fancy. They are written on the records of many a nation, once ennobled by its freedom and enlightened policy, and now existing, only the sad monument of its own wretchedness.

Nor let us indulge the vain hope, that we shall escape a like fate, if we neglect to preserve those institutions in their purity, which sustain the great interests of society. If we grow indifferent to the progress of vice; if we silently wink at violations of the laws; if we habitually follow the current of public opinion, without pausing to consider its direction; if we cherish a sullen and irreverent disregard of the constitution of government, under which we live, or resign ourselves to factious discontent under the exercise of its legitimate powers; the time is not far distant, when we shall be separated into rival states, engaged in furious contests for paltry objects, and ultimately become the prey of some unprincipled chieftain, who will first arrive at power by flattering popular prejudices, and then secure his bad eminence by the destruction of the liberties of his country.

May this melancholy epoch never have an existence in our history! Much, indeed, may be done under the indulgence of a benign Providence, to avert such evils, if all our good citizens will unite to enforce the laws, to cherish an habitual obedience to their precepts, and to inculcate a reverence for the administration of public justice. And you, Gentlemen of the Grand Jury in particular, to whom is intrusted the high responsibility of watching over the public rights and suppressing public offences, you may do much to perpetuate our liberties by an honest, zealous, and resolute discharge of your duty.

The practice of the Court has ordinarily been to lay before you an enumeration in detail of all the crimes of which you are to take cognizance. But on the present occasion I shall feel myself better employed by dwelling somewhat at length on certain offences of a graver cast, which are unhappily but too common in our age, and require the severe animadversion of all good men from their manifest tendency to foster the foulest passions and the most unnatural cruelties. As to other crimes, as I am not aware that any of them require your very particular examination, I shall leave them to your general consideration; and if you shall have occasion for more exact information, the learned counsel for the United States, and the Court will most cheerfully aid your inquiries.

And first, gentlemen, let me call your attention to the crime of Piracy. This offence has in former times crimsoned the ocean with much innocent blood, and in its present alarming progress threatens the most serious mischiefs to our peaceful commerce. It cannot be disguised, that at the present times there are hordes of needy adventurers prowling upon the ocean, who, under the specious pretext of being in the service of the Patriot Governments of South America, commit the foulest outrages. Being united together by no common tie but the love of plunder, they assume from time to time the flag of any nation which may best favor their immediate projects, and depredate with indiscriminate ferocity upon the commerce of the neutral world, regardless of the principles of law and the dictates of justice. It often too happens, as might well be expected in such wicked associations, that, after their lawless designs are consummated, they quarrel among themselves about the division of their spoils, and their quarrels end in involving themselves in the blood of their comrades. Persons of this description are, in the most general sense of the term, pirates or freebooters, and are aptly denominated the enemies of the human race, and as such become amenable to the tribunals of all civilized nations for their crimes, and by the laws of all, as I believe, are punished with death.

While, therefore, we may properly indulge towards the South Americans a reasonable sympathy in their struggle for civil and religious liberty, and while we respect with the most guarded caution the rights of the regular commissioned ships of their governments, (as by law we are bound to do,) we should take care that our feelings are not wasted upon men who falsely assume the protection of their flag, and that our judgments are not misled by framing apologies for depredations from which virtue and patriotism turn with disgust.

Piracy, according to the common law, consists in committing those acts of depredation and robbery at sea, which, if committed upon land, would amount to felony there; and it is piracy not only when a man robs without any commission at all, but when having a commission he fraudulently, or with a thievish intent, despoils those with whom he is not warranted to fight or meddle; that is, such as are at peace with the prince or state from which he derives his commission. Piracy at sea is indeed the same crime as robbery on land at the common law. And robbery is the felonious taking away of goods or money from the person or presence of another against his will, by *force* or *violence*, or by *putting* him in *fear*. It includes, therefore, the crime of theft, and something more, namely, the taking with force or violence from a person, or in his presence, or putting him in fear. There must be either violence or putting in fear to constitute the crime; but both need not concur. Such is the definition of piracy at the common law; and it does not differ in any essential respect from that adopted in the law of nations; for in this law piracy consists in unlawful and fraudulent depredations with force upon the property of another at sea, without authority from any prince or state. The essence of the offence is the fraudulent subduction or theft of property with violence from the persons in whose custody it lawfully is. The act must be done, in the language of the law, "animo furandi," that is, with the intent to commit a theft; and it is not committed by a mere excess of lawful authority, unless combined with the intent of fraudulent gain. And, indeed, Mr. Sergeant Hawkins has given an exact description of the offence, according to the sense of the law of nations, when he declares a pirate to be "one who, to enrich himself, either by surprise or open force, sets upon merchants or others trading by sea to spoil them of their goods and treasure."

By a recent statute of the United States, in order more effectually to suppress this odious offence, it is enacted, that, if any person shall, on the high seas, commit the crime of piracy, as defined by the law of nations, and be afterwards found in the United States, he shall, on conviction, suffer death. This statute is manifestly designed to apply to all cases, whether the crime be perpetrated on board of an American ship or a foreign ship, and whether the offender be a foreigner or a citizen.

But there are other acts which the laws of the United

States have declared piracy, which are punishable as such, only when committed on board of American ships, or by persons who are justly amenable to our criminal jurisdiction. For no nation can have any right by its own legislation to bind the subjects of foreign governments as to offences, which fall within the exclusive cognizance of such governments.

The acts to which I have alluded I will now proceed to enumerate.

1. The first act is, the perpetration of murder, robbery, or any other offence on the high seas, which, if committed on land, would, by the laws of the United States, by punishable with death.

The crime of robbery here referred to is that crime, as defined by the common law, which we have already considered.

Murder consists in the unlawful killing of any reasonable creature in being, under the peace of the government, with malice aforethought. It is this malice which essentially distinguishes murder from every other kind of homicide; and it may be *express*, as when the crime is perpetrated with a sedate and deliberate mind and formed design; or it may be *implied*, as when the fact is attended with such circumstances as are the ordinary symptoms of a wicked, depraved, and malignant spirit. It matters not how sudden the transaction may have been, nor whether there was a particular malevolence or spite to the deceased or not; it is sufficient if there be either deliberate malice, or circumstances of cruelty and depravity, carrying in them "the plain indications of a heart regardless of social duty, and fatally bent on mischief."

In all charges of murder, the fact of killing being first proved, all the circumstances of accident, necessity, or infirmity, which may justify or excuse it, are to be satisfactorily proved by the prisoner at his trial unless they arise out of the evidence produced against him; for the law presumes the fact to be founded in malice, until the contrary appears.

2. A second act declared piracy by our laws, is the piratically and feloniously running away with any ship or vessel, or any goods or merchandise to the value of fifty dollars, or the voluntarily yielding up any ship or vessel to any pirate.

To constitute the offence within this clause, the crime must be committed by the captain or a mariner of the ship, and with a piratical and felonious intent; that is, with an intent fraudulently to convert the property to their own use, in violation of their trust, and against the will of the owner; and, where the piratical act is the taking of goods or merchandise, the taking must be on board a ship or vessel.

3. A third act of piracy by our laws, is the laying of violent hands by any seaman upon his commander, thereby to hinder and prevent his fighting in defence of his ship or the goods committed to his trust.

It must be understood, as a restriction upon the generality of this clause, that the fighting of the commander would be lawful; for, if it would be unlawful, as in defiance of public authority, in resistance of the right of search, or of a justifiable seizure, so far from the seamen's being guilty of a crime, they would be doing no more than their duty, and could incur no blame whatever.

4. A fourth act of piracy by our laws, is the making of a revolt by a mariner on board of the ship to which he belongs.

It is not easy to enumerate all the various circumstances which constitute "a revolt," a word, which in this clause is used in the sense of mutiny or rebellion. A mere act of disobedience to the lawful commands of the officers of the ship by the crew does not of itself constitute a revolt. But if there be a general combination of the crew to resist the lawful commands of their officers, or to usurp their authority on board of the ship; and any overt acts are done by the crew in pursuance of such design; such as the confinement of their officers, or depriving them of the control and management of the ship; these and the like acts seem properly to constitute a revolt.

5. A fifth and last act of piracy, by our laws, is, when any citizen commits any piracy or robbery aforesaid, or any act of hostility against the United States or any citizens thereof, upon the high seas, under color of any commission or authority from any foreign prince or state, or on pretence of authority from any person.

From this clause it is apparent how deeply involved in guilt are those of our citizens who enlist themselves in the armed ships of foreign states, and commit hostilities upon their countrymen, or plunder their property; since the law declares that they shall be "adjudged and taken to be pirates, felons, and robbers," and shall, on conviction, suffer death.

And I may add, that all accessories before the fact, to any of the piracies before mentioned are liable to the same capital punishment; and accessories after the fact are visited with exemplary penalties.

Another class of kindred offences to which, Gentlemen, I beg to call your particular attention, is that which respects our relations with foreign states. It has at all times been the wise determination of our government to endeavor, amidst the contests of belligerent nations, to preserve its own peace by a strict and impartial neutrality. This course, so just and reasonable in itself, and founded in the soundest, and, I may add, the noblest policy, is so intimately connected with our best interests, in a moral, commercial, and political view, that our laws have most anxiously provided for the due observance of all our neutral duties. And yet I know not how it has happened, but so the fact is, many of our citizens have been deluded by the glare of a false and hollow patriotism, deliberately to violate these laws and to engage in enterprises not only unjust, but in many instances accompanied with the most shocking barbarities. What authority have we to become the general champions of the violated rights of the human race, and to march in a general crusade for the defence of the liberties of mankind where every footstep must be traced in the mingled blood of the oppressor and the oppressed? With what justice can we complain of the wrongs of other nations if we assume the character of neutrality and yet violate all its most sacred obligations? if we present that monstrous anomaly in the history of the world, of a nation at peace and its citizens at war? Let not our honor be sullied by the just accusation, that we want the virtue to enforce our laws, or are guilty of a mean hypocrisy in suffering a collusive evasion of them. Let it be the pride of our country to preserve an honest fame without reproach; and to claim from foreign nations an observance of our own rights, only when the claim can be enforced with clean hands and pure hearts. If motives like these, so elevated and so honorable, cannot bind us to our duty, as I confidently trust they always will, let us at least take counsel of our fears and our interests, and learn the wholesome lesson, that, as good faith is the only sure foundation of national prosperity, so the breach of it will be visited sooner or later with national degradation and ruin. And, gentlemen, I entreat you, as guardians of the laws, to endeavor, by your own presentments, as well as by your counsels, to bring to punishment all persons who violate our neutrality, however specious their pretexts may be, and thus to do your part to arrest those calamities which war, even in its mildest shape, never fails to inflict upon its innocent sufferers.

Our laws have expressly prohibited our citizens from accepting and exercising, *within our jurisdiction*, a commission to serve any foreign state, colony, or people, in war, by land or by sea, against any other state, colony, or people. They have also prohibited any person whatsoever, *within our jurisdiction*, from enlisting or entering himself, or hiring or retaining another person to enlist or enter himself, or to go beyond our jurisdiction, with intent to be enlisted or entered, in the service of any foreign state, colony, or people, as a soldier, or as a mariner, or marine, in any armed ship. They have also prohibited any person whatsoever, *within our jurisdiction*, from fitting out and arming, or attempting to fit out and arm, or procuring to be fitted out and armed, or being knowingly concerned in the furnishing, fitting out, or arming, of any ship, with intent that such ship shall be employed in the service of any foreign prince or state, colony or people, to cruise or commit hostilities against the subjects or property of any foreign state, colony, or people, with whom we are at peace; and from issuing or delivering a commission for any such ship, to the intent that she shall be employed as above mentioned. They have further prohibited *our citizens, without our jurisdiction*, from fitting out and arming, or attempting to fit out and arm, or procuring to be fitted out and armed, or knowingly aiding or being concerned in the furnishing, fitting out, or arming, any private ship of war or privateer, with intent that such ship shall be employed to cruise or commit hostilities *upon our citizens or their property;* or from taking command of, or entering on board of any such, for the intent aforesaid; or from purchasing any interest in any such ship, with a view to share in the profits thereof. They have also prohibited *any person* whatsoever, *within our jurisdiction*, from increasing or augmenting, or procuring to be increased or augmented, or being knowingly concerned in increasing or augmenting the force of any ship of war or cruiser, in the service of any foreign state, colony, or people, at war with any foreign state, colony, or people, by adding to the number of her guns, or by changing those on board for guns of a larger calibre, or by the addition of any equipment solely applicable to war. And lastly, our laws have prohibited *any person* whatsoever, *within our jurisdiction*, from beginning, or setting on foot, or providing, or preparing, the means for any military expedition or enterprise, to be carried on from thence against the territory or dominions of any foreign state, colony, or people, with whom we are at peace.

Such are the prohibitions of our laws, enforced with suitable penalties, against violations of our neutrality; and so extensive are their reach, that, if our good citizens will aid the officers of the government in a vigilant discharge of their duties, and grand juries will act with the firmness befitting their office, there is little doubt, that we shall be able effectually to suppress unlawful enterprises and combinations, and to restore the brightness of our national reputation, over which the impunity of recent outrages has somewhat contributed to cast a temporary shade. Nor ought it to be forgotten, that, by a faithful performance of our duty in suppressing these offences, we shall contribute, in a very great degree, to preserve the good habits and sound morals of our seamen — a class of men of inestimable importance to our commerce, and the bulwark of our naval glory. When once they become contaminated by participating in unlawful plunder, the property of our merchants, as experience has but too fully proved, can no longer be safely confided to their care. So true is it, that the first step in vice costs us most; and we thence slip easily downward into the gulf of infamy and crime. He, who is in the pursuit of guilty plunder by violations of the laws, soon ceases to discriminate between friends and foes; and silences the voice of his conscience, by an appeal to the cravings of avarice, stimulated by a self-created necessity.

In the next place, Gentlemen, let me call your attention to that most detestable traffic, the *Slave Trade*. The existence of slavery, under any shape, is so repugnant to the natural rights of man and the dictates of justice, that it seems difficult to find for it any adequate justification. It undoubtedly had its origin in times of barbarism, and was the ordinary lot of those, who were conquered in war. It was supposed, that the conqueror had a right to take the life of his captive, and by consequence might well bind him to perpetual servitude. But the position itself, on which this supposed right is founded, is not true. No man has a right to kill his enemy, except in cases of absolute necessity; and this absolute necessity ceases to exist, even in the estimation of the conqueror himself, when he has spared the life of his prisoner. And even if in such case it were possible to contend for the right of slavery, as to the prisoner himself, it is impossible that it can justly extend to his innocent offspring through the whole line of descent. I forbear, however, to touch on this delicate topic, not because it is not worthy of the most deliberate attention of all of us; but it does not properly fall within my province on the present occasion. It is to be lamented, indeed, that slavery exists in any part of our country; but it should be considered, that it is not an evil introduced in the present age. It has been entailed upon a part of our country by their ancestors; and to provide a safe and just remedy for its gradual abolition is, undoubtedly, as much the design of many of the present owners of slaves, as of those philanthropists, who have labored with so much zeal and benevolence to effect their emancipation. It is, indeed, one of the many blessings, which we have derived from Christianity, that it prepared the way for a gradual abolition of slavery, so that, at the close of the twelfth century, it was greatly diminished in the west of Europe; and it is one of the stains on the human character, that the revival of letters and of commerce brought with it an unnatural lust of gain, and with it the plunder and slavery of the wretched Africans.

To our country belongs the honor, as a nation, of having set the first example of prohibiting the further progress of this inhuman traffic. The constitution of the United States having granted to Congress the power to regulate foreign commerce, imposed a restriction, for a limited period, upon its right of prohibiting the migration or importation of slaves. Notwithstanding this, Congress, with a promptitude, which does honor to their humanity and wisdom, proceeded, in 1794, to pass a law to prohibit the traffic of slaves by our citizens, in all cases not within the reach of the constitutional restriction; and thus cut off the whole traffic *between foreign ports.* In the year 1800 an additional law was passed to enforce the former enactments; and in the year 1807 (the epoch when the constitutional restriction was to cease, beginning with the ensuing year,) a general prohibition of the traffic, as well in our domestic as foreign trade, was proudly incorporated into our statute-book. About the same period the British Government, after the most severe opposition from slave-dealers and their West Indian friends, achieved a similar measure, and enacted a general prohibition of the trade, as well to foreign ports, as to their colonies. This act was, indeed, the triumph of virtue, of reason, and of humanity, over the hard-heartedness of avarice; and, while it was adorned by the brilliant talents of Pitt, Fox, Romilly, and Wilberforce, let us never forget that its success was principally owing to the modest, but persevering labors of the Quakers, and, above all, to the resolute patience and noble philanthropy of a man immortalized by his virtues, the intrepid Thomas Clarkson.

It is a most cheering circumstance, that the examples of the United States and Great Britain, in thus abolishing the slave trade, have, through the strenuous exertions of the latter, been generally approved throughout the continent of Europe. The Government of Great Britain has, indeed, employed the most indefatigable and persevering diligence to accomplish this desirable object; and treaties have been made by her with all the principal foreign powers, providing for a total abolition of the trade within a very short period. May America not be behind her in this glorious work; but, by a generous competition in virtuous deeds, restore the degraded African to his natural rights, and strike his manacles from the bloody hands of his oppressors.

By our laws it is made an offence for any person to import or bring, in any manner whatsoever, into the United States, or its territories, from any foreign country, any negro, mulatto, or person of color, with intent to hold, sell, or dispose of him as a slave, or to be held to service or labor. It is also made an offence for any citizen or other person, as master, owner, or factor, to build, fit, equip, load, or otherwise prepare, any vessel in any of our ports, or to cause any vessel to sail from any port whatsoever, for the purpose of procuring any negro, mulatto, or person of color, from any foreign country, to be transported to any port or place whatsoever, to be held, sold, or disposed of, as a slave, or to be held to service or labor. It is also made an offence for any citizen, or *other person resident within our jurisdiction*, to take on board, receive, or transport in any vessel from the coast of Africa, or any other foreign country, or from sea, any negro, mulatto, or person of color, not an inhabitant of, or held to service in, the United States, for the purpose of holding, selling, or disposing of, such person as a slave, or to be held to service or labor. It is also made an offence for any person within our jurisdiction to hold, purchase, sell, or otherwise dispose of any negro, mulatto or person of color, for a slave, or to be held to service or labor, who shall have been imported into the United States in violation of our laws; and, in general, the prohibitions in these cases extend to all persons who shall abet or aid in these illegal designs. These offences are visited, as well with severe pecuniary and personal penalties, as with the forfeiture of the vessels and their equipments, which have been employed in the furtherance of these illegal projects; and, in general, a moiety of the pecuniary penalties and forfeitures is given to any person who shall inform against the offenders, and prosecute them to conviction. The President of the United States is also authorized to employ our armed vessels and revenue cutters to cruise on the seas, for the purpose of arresting all vessels and persons, engaged in this traffic in violation of our laws; and bounties, as well as a moiety of the captured property, are given to the captors to stimulate them in the discharge of their duty.

Under such circumstances, it might well be supposed that the slave trade would in practice be extinguished; that virtuous men would, by their abhorrence, stay its polluted march, and wicked men would be overawed by its potent punishments. But, unfortunately, the case is far otherwise. We have but too many melancholy proofs, from unquestioned sources, that it is still carried on with all the implacable ferocity and insatiable rapacity of former times. Avarice has grown more subtile in its evasions; and watches and seizes its prey with an appetite, quickened, rather than suppressed, by its guilty vigils. American citizens are steeped up to their very mouths (I scarcely use too bold a figure) in this stream of iniquity. They throng to the coasts of Africa under the stained flags of Spain and Portugal, sometimes selling abroad "their cargoes of despair," and sometimes bringing them into some of our Southern ports, and there, under the forms of the law, defeating the purposes of the law itself, and legalizing their inhuman, but profitable, adventures. I wish I could say, that New England and New England men were free from this deep pollution. But there is reason to believe that they, who drive a loathsome traffic, "and buy the muscles and the bones of men," are to be found here also. It is to be hoped the number is small; but our cheeks may well burn with shame, while a solitary case is permitted to go unpunished.

And, Gentlemen, how can we justify ourselves or apologize for an indifference to this subject? Our constitutions of government have declared that all men are born free and equal, and have certain unalienable rights, among which are the right of enjoying their lives, liberties, and property, and of seeking and obtaining their own safety and happiness. May not the miserable African ask, "Am I not a man and a brother?" We boast of our noble struggle against the encroachments of tyranny; but do we forget, that it assumed the mildest form, in which authority ever assailed the rights of its subjects; and yet that there are men among us, who think it no wrong to condemn the shivering African to perpetual slavery?

We believe in the Christian religion. It commands us to have good-will to all men; to love our neighbors as ourselves; and to do unto all men as we would they should do unto us. It declares our accountability to the Supreme God for all our actions, and holds out to us a state of future rewards and punishments, as the sanction, by which our conduct is to be regulated. And yet there are men, calling themselves Christians, who degrade the negro by ignorance to a level with the brutes, and deprive him of all the consolations of religion. He alone, of all the rational creation, they seem to think, is to be at once accountable for his actions, and yet his actions are not to be at his own disposal; but his mind, his body, and his feelings, are to be sold to perpetual bondage. To me it appears perfectly clear, that the slave-trade is equally repugnant to the dictates of reason and religion, and is an offence equally against the laws of God and man. Yet, strange to tell, one of the pretences upon which the modern slavery of the Africans has been justified, is the "duty of converting the heathen."

I have called this an *inhuman* traffic; and, Gentlemen, with a view to enlist your sympathies, as well as your judgments, in its suppression, permit me to pass from these cold generalities, to some of those details, which are the ordinary attendants upon this trade. Here, indeed, there is no room for the play of imagination. The records of the British Parliament present us a body of evidence on this subject, taken with the most scrupulous care, while the subject of the abolition was before it; taken, too, from persons who had been engaged in, or eye-witnesses of the trade; taken, too, year after year, in the presence of those whose interests or passions were most strenuously engaged to oppose it. That it was not contradicted or disproved can be accounted for only upon the ground that it was the truth, and nothing but the truth. What, therefore, I shall briefly state to you on this subject, will be drawn principally from those records; and I am free to confess that, great as was my detestation of the trade, I had no conception, until I recently read an abstract of this evidence, of the vast extent of misery and cruelty occasioned by its ravages. And if, Gentlemen, this detail shall awaken your minds to the absolute necessity of constant vigilance in the enforcement of the laws on this subject, we may hope that public opinion, following these laws, will very soon extirpate the trade among our citizens.

The number of slaves taken from Africa in 1768 amounted to one hundred and four thousand; and though the numbers somewhat fluctuated in different years afterwards, yet it is in the highest degree probable, that the average, until the abolition, was not much below one hundred thousand a year. England alone, in the year 1786, employed one hundred and thirty ships, and carried off about forty-two thousand slaves.

The unhappy slaves have been divided into seven classes. The most considerable, and that which contains at least *half* of the whole number transported, consists of *kidnapped people.* This mode of procuring them includes every species of treachery and knavery. Husbauds are stolen from their wives, children from their parents, and bosom friends from each other. So generally prevalent are these robberies, that it is a first principle of the natives not to go unarmed, while a slave ship is on the coast, for fear of being stolen. The second class of slaves, and that *not inconsiderable,* consists of those whose villages have been depopulated for obtaining them. The parties employed in these predatory expeditions go out at night, set fire to the villages which they find, and carry off the wretched inhabitants, thus suddenly thrown into their power as slaves. The practice is, indeed, so common, that the remains of deserted and burnt villages are everywhere to be seen on the coast. The third class consists of such persons as are said to have been convicted of crimes, and are sold on this account for the benefit of their kings; and it is not uncommon to impute crimes to them falsely, and to bring on mock trials, for the purpose of bringing them within the reach of the royal traders. The fourth class includes prisoners of war, captured sometimes in ordinary wars, and sometimes in wars originated for the very purposes of slavery. The fifth class comprehends those who are slaves by birth; and some traders on the coast make a practice of breeding from their own slaves, for the purpose of selling them, like cattle, when they are arrived at a suitable age. The sixth class comprehends such as have sacrificed their liberty to the spirit of gaming. The seventh and last class consists of those who, being in debt, are seized according to the laws of the country, and sold to their creditors. But the two last classes are very inconsiderable, and scarcely deserve mention.

Having lost their liberty in one of the ways already mentioned, the slaves are conveyed to the banks of the rivers or sea-coast. Some belong to the neighborhood; others have lived in distant parts; and others are brought a thousand miles from their homes. Those who come from a distance, march in droves, or caufles, as they are called. They are secured from rising or running away by pieces of wood, which attach the necks of two and two together; or by other pieces, which are fastened by staples to their arms. They are made to carry their own water and provisions; and are watched and followed by drivers, who by force compel the weak to keep up with the strong.

They are sold, immediately upon their arrival on the rivers or coasts, either to land factors, at depots for that purpose, or directly to the ships engaged in the trade. They are then carried in boats to the various ships whose captains have purchased them. The men are immediately confined two and two together, either by the neck, leg, or arm, with fetters of solid iron. They are then put into their apartments, the men occupying the forepart, the women the after-part, and the boys the middle of the vessel. The tops of these apartments are grated, for the admission of light and air; and the slaves are stowed like any other lumber, occupying only an allotted portion of room. Many of them, while the ships are waiting for their full lading, in sight of their native shore, manifest great appearance of distress and oppression; and some instances have occurred where they have sought relief by suicide, and others, where they have been afflicted with delirium and madness. In the daytime, if the weather be fine, they are brought upon deck for air. They are placed in a long row of two and two together, on each side of the ship, a long chain is then made to pass through the shackles of each pair, and by this means each row is secured to the deck. In this state they eat their miserable meals, consisting of horse-beans, rice, and yams, with a little pepper and palm oil. After their meals, it is a custom to make them jump for exercise as high as their fetters will allow them; and if they refuse, they are whipped until they comply. This the slave merchants call dancing, and it would seem literally to be the dance of death.

When the number of slaves is completed, the ships begin what is called the middle passage, to transport them to the colonies. The height of the apartments in the ships is different, according to the size of the vessel, and is from six feet to three feet; so that it is impossible to stand erect in most of the vessels, and in some scarcely possible to sit down in the same posture. If the vessel be full, the situation of the slaves is truly deplorable. In the best-regulated ships a grown person is allowed but sixteen inches in width, thirty-two inches in height, and five feet eleven inches in length; or, to use the expressive language of a witness, not so much room as a man has in his coffin. They are, indeed, so crowded below, that it is almost impossible to walk through the groups without treading on some of them; and if they are reluctant to get into their places, they are compelled by the lash of a whip. And here their situation becomes wretched beyond description. The space between decks, where they are confined, often becomes so hot that persons who have visited them there, have found their shirts so wet with perspiration, that water might be wrung from them; and the steam from their confined bodies comes up through the gratings like smoke from a furnace. The bad effects of such confinement and want of air are soon visible in the weakness and faintness, which overcome the unhappy victims. Some go down apparently well at night, and are found dead in the morning. Some faint below, and die from suffocation before they can be brought upon deck. As the slaves, whether well or ill, always lie upon bare planks, the motion of the ship rubs the flesh from the prominent parts of their body, and leaves their bones almost bare. The pestilential breath of so many, in so confined a state, renders them also very sickly, and the vicissitudes of heat and cold generate a flux. When this is the case (which happens frequently) the whole place becomes covered with blood and mucus, like a slaughter-house; and as the slaves are fettered and wedged close together, the utmost disorder arises from endeavors to relieve themselves in the necessities of nature; and the disorder is still further increased by the healthy being not unfrequently chained to the diseased, the dying, and the dead. When the scuttles in the ship's sides are shut in bad weather, the gratings are not sufficient for airing the room; and the slaves are then seen drawing their breath with all that anxious and laborious effort for life, which we observe in animals subjected to experiments in foul air, or in an exhausted receiver of an air-pump. Many of them expire in this situation, crying out in their native tongue, "We are dying." During the time that elapses from the slaves being put on board on the African coast to their sale in the colonies, about one fourth part, or twenty-five thousand per annum, are destroyed; a mortality which may be easily credited after the preceding statement.

At length the ship arrives at her destined port, and the unhappy Africans, who have survived the voyage, are prepared for sale. Some are consigned to brokers, who sell them for the ships at private sale. With this view, they are examined by the planters who want them for their farms; and in the selection of them friends and relations are parted without any hesitation; and when they part with mutual embraces, they are severed by a lash. Others are sold at public auction, and become the property of the highest bidder. Others are sold by what is denominated a "scramble." In this case the main and quarter decks of the ship are darkened by sails hung over them at a convenient height. The slaves are then brought out of the hold and made to stand in the darkened area. The purchasers, who are furnished with long ropes, rush, at a given signal, within the awning, and endeavor to encircle as many of them as they can. Nothing can exceed the terror which the wretched Africans exhibit on these occasions. A universal shriek is immediately heard — all is consternation and dismay — the men tremble — the women cling together in each other's arms — some of them faint away, and others are known to expire.

About twenty thousand, or one fifth part of those who are annually imported, die during the "seasoning," which seasoning is said to expire when the two first years of servitude are completed; so that of the whole number about one half perish within two years from their first captivity. I forbear to trace the subsequent scenes of their miserable lives — worn out in toils, from which they can receive no profit, and oppressed with wrongs from which they can hope for no relief.

The scenes which I have described are almost literally copied from the most authentic and unquestionable narratives published under the highest authority. They present a picture of human wretchedness and human depravity, which the boldest imagination would hardly have dared to portray, and from which (one should think) the most abandoned profligate would shrink with horror. Let it be considered, that this wretchedness does not arise from the awful visitations of Providence, in the shape of plagues, famines, or earthquakes, the natural scourges of mankind; but is inflicted by man on man, from the accursed love of gold. May we not justly dread the displeasure of that Almighty Being, who is the common Father of us all, if we do not, by all means within our power, endeavor to suppress such infamous cruelties? If we cannot, like the good Samaritan, bind up the wounds and soothe the miseries of the friendless Africans, let us not, like the Levite, pass with sullen indifference on the other side. What sight can be more acceptable in the eyes of Heaven than that of good men struggling in the cause of oppressed humanity? What consolation can be more sweet, in a dying hour, than the recollection that at least one human being may have been saved from sacrifice by our vigilance in enforcing the laws?

I make no apology, Gentlemen, for having detained you so long upon this interesting subject. In vain shall we expend our wealth in missions abroad for the promotion of Christianity; in vain shall we rear at home magnificent temples to the service of the Most High. If we tolerate this traffic, our charity is but a name, and our religion little more than a faint and delusive shadow.

CHANCERY JURISDICTION.

AN ARTICLE WRITTEN FOR THE NORTH AMERICAN REVIEW, IN 1820, ON THE REPORTS OF MR. JOHNSON.

MR. CHANCELLOR KENT was appointed a puisne Judge of the Supreme Court of New York, on the 6th of February, 1798; Chief Justice of the same court, on the 2d of July, 1804; and, upon the resignation of Mr. Chancellor Lansing, succeeded to the distinguished station of Chancellor of New York, on the 25th of February, 1814. He has been long, therefore, before the public in a judicial character, which he has sustained with increasing reputation, a reputation, as pure as it is bright; and he is, at the very moment we are writing, devoting himself to the labors of jurisprudence with a diligence and enthusiasm, which excite the admiration of the veteran counsellor at the bar, even more than of the ambitious student just struggling for distinction. He has always been remarkable for an unwearied attention to business, a prompt and steady vigilance, and a sacred reverence for juridical authorities. For him the easy course of general reasoning, popular analogies, and fanciful theories, has no charms. He does not believe that judicial discretion is the *arbitrium boni judicis*, much less *boni viri;* or, that he is at liberty to promulgate rules, either of law or equity, measured by his own abstract notions of what is fit or reasonable. He contents himself with administering the common law, as he finds it, without the rashness to presume himself wiser than the law, or the vanity of distinguishing himself by innovations. His life has been devoted, sedulously and earnestly, to professional studies. He has fathomed the depths and searched the recesses of the ancient law, the black-lettered relics of former times, so much disparaged, and yet of such inestimable value. He has traced back the magnificent streams of jurisprudence to their fountains, lying dark and obscure amidst the rubbish of monkish retreats, or stealing silently from the chivalric heights of feudal grandeur. His researches have been, amidst the dust and the cobwebs of antiquated lore, pursued in the unfashionable pages of the Year Books, and Glanville, and Fleta, and Britton, and the almost classical Bracton. He has dared to examine the Abridgments of Brooke, and Fitzherbert, and Statham; books, from which the modern student starts back with doubt and apprehension, as the great reservoirs, whence have been drawn the best principles of modern times, and whence must be drawn the body and the soul of that learning, which distinguishes the professor from the sciolist. He has not stopped short at a survey of the mere Gothic structures of the law; but has examined, with eager and enlightened curiosity, the beautiful systems with which the commercial law has been adorned in our day. He has mastered all their refinements, and has, in no small degree, contributed to their beauty and perfection. He has drawn deeply from the commercial law of foreign nations; the works of Straccha, and Roccus, and Valin, and Pothier, and Emérigon are familiar to his thoughts and his writings. He has there found the principles, by which our own jurisprudence is to be illustrated; and one is at a loss which most to admire, the incomparable discernment of the judge, or the attractive excellence of the materials. If his attainments had found their boundary here, they would have entitled him to great praise; but he has nobly extended his inquiries beyond the common and commercial law, and explored the Roman jurisprudence through its texts and commentaries with uncommon acuteness and accuracy. This has been done with no idle view, to gratify a merely speculative curiosity, or to gather up the fragments of antiquarian fame. Like all his other studies, this has been made subservient to the great purposes of his life, the promotion of justice, and the establishment of a solid jurisprudence, founded in the most enlightened policy. In his decisions, we can every where trace the happy use of that marvellous system of doctrines, which Justinian collected with so much care, and which stands unrivalled in the world for its general equity, and nice adaptation to the necessities of mankind; a system, which was gradually matured by the labors of jurists and prætors, during centuries, in which Rome was the mistress of the world; and which had the singular advantage of being the combined results of experience, and general reasoning, and judicial interpretation, aided very little by imperial rescripts, and rarely marred by imperial interference. Let those who now doubt the importance of the study of the civil law by common lawyers, read diligently the opinions of Mr. Chancellor Kent, and they will find all the objections raised by indolence, and ignorance, and prejudice, practically refuted, and the civil law triumphantly sustained. They will perceive the vivid lights, which it casts on the paths of juridical science; and they will be instructed and cheered in the pursuit, though they may not hope to move in the brilliant career of such a judge with equal footsteps.

It required such a man, with such a mind, at once liberal, comprehensive, exact, and methodical; always reverencing authorities, and bound by decisions; true to the spirit, yet more true to the letter of the law; pursuing principles with a severe and scrupulous logic, yet blending with them the most persuasive equity;—it required such a man, with such a mind, to unfold the doctrines of chancery in our country, and to settle them upon immovable foundations. Without doubt, his learned predecessors had done much to systematize and amend the practice of the court. But it cannot be disguised, that the general state of the profession was not favorable to a very exact and well-regulated practice. There were, comparatively speaking, few lawyers in the country, who had devoted themselves to courts of equity. In general, the ablest men found the courts of common law the most lucrative, as well as the most attractive, for the display of their talents. They contented themselves with occasional attendance at the chancery bar; and placed their solid fame in the popular forum, where the public felt a constant interest, and where the great business of the country was done. In many of the states no court of chancery existed. In others it was a mixed jurisdiction, exercised by courts of common law. And in those where it was administered by a distinct judicature, there is great reason to fear, that the practice was very poor, and the principles of decision built upon a rational equity, resting very much in discretion, and hardly limited by any fixed rules. In short, the doctrines of the courts depended much less upon the settled analogies of the system, than upon the character of the particular judge. If he possessed a large and liberal mind, he stretched them to a most unwarrantable extent; if a cautious and cold one, the system fainted and expired under his curatorship. This description was applicable, perhaps, without any material exceptions, to the equity jurisprudence of our country; and New York comes in, probably, for a full share of it. At least, there are in the volumes now before us abundant proofs, that neither the practice nor principles of the chancery of that state had, previously to the time of Mr. Chancellor Kent, assumed a steady and well-defined shape. We see, for instance, that points of practice are often most elaborately reasoned out by this learned chancellor, in various opinions, as if the case stood *de novo* before him, and he was called upon for the first time to apply the English practice to our own. This could hardly have occurred, if there had been a constant, settled channel, in which it had previously flowed.

Nor is it difficult to account for this state of things, consistently with the highest deference for the learned judges, who had administered equity. In England, the court of chancery is, and for a long time has been, the most active, and most extensive judicature in the kingdom. From the existence of a law of descents, which gives to the eldest son the exclusive heirship of real estate, there arises a necessity for complicated marriage settlements, apportioning the property among all the children, and looking to very remote contingencies for their completion. The same circumstance makes last wills and testaments extremely intricate and perplexed, and fills them with provisions for younger sons and daughters, and remote relations, which may not be exhausted in a century. Hence we find complex entails, springing uses, contingent remainders, and express or resulting trusts, spreading over almost every estate in the kingdom, and weaving a network, which at last becomes so close, and so embarrassing, that a private act of Parliament is the only effectual remedy to disentangle the title. It is scarcely possible to form the most simple marriage-settlement, without incorporating some trusts into it. And as to last wills, even if they furnish no direct case for the application of chancery jurisdiction, which rarely happens, yet they almost invariably fall within the cognizance of that court, in virtue of its general jurisdiction as to legacies, or to compel a settlement of the accounts, and a distribution of the estate. So that it has been remarked, and probably with great correctness, that, in the course of half a century, almost every estate in the kingdom passes under the judicial review of the chancellor.

Nor is this to be wondered at, when we consider, that no trustees can safely act, without the direction of a court of equity; and that, in complicated settlements and wills, there must be a great variety of clauses, whose exact meaning and extent can never be ascertained, until they receive a judicial interpretation. This is an inexhaustible source of hostile or amicable litigation; and of itself would create more business than the diligence and talents of a half dozen chancellors could despatch, within any reasonable time. And it often happens, with all the exertions of the chancellor, the master of the rolls, the vice-chancellor, the chancery court of the exchequer, and many local courts of equity, that suits of this nature are still pending, after the lapse of twenty years, and sometimes survive all the original parties, and their immediate descendants and representatives.

It is fortunate for our country, that the genius of our institutions, and the happy structure of our laws of descents, by dividing and subdividing property among immediate and remote relatives by equitable rules, silently provides for ninety-nine cases out of a hundred of all the objects of an anxious parent or friend. We hear, therefore, of few cases of settlements, and comparatively few of wills, which are not extremely simple, and are not exhausted with the breath of the first limitations. Entails have practically ceased among us, from the facility, with which they may be turned into a fee; and, indeed, under the present circumstances of our country, they would be likely to generate family feuds and difficulties, rather than to accomplish any valuable purposes. We may, therefore, easily see in the past circumstances of our country, very strong reasons, why the chancery jurisdiction has hitherto had but a limited scope for its powers; and why its principles and practice have not hitherto assumed a very scientific cast in our own tribunals. It is but a few years ago, that our common law courts were governed by a very lax jurisprudence. There are few reports older than twenty years; and those few leave us little regret for the total oblivion cast on all preceding times in our legal annals. There were, without doubt, acute and able lawyers, and learned judges; but they were few in number; and the defects of the juridical system and practice, and the narrow walks of business, precluded any great improvements. We had scarcely any commercial law; and very few contracts, on which it could operate; and the generalizing spirit of the present day had scarcely shed a doubtful twilight over us. Our suits principally respected titles or trespasses to land, or personal wrongs, or penalties, or local topics, or debt, or bonds, or assumpsits on contracts for labor, or services, or goods sold in small parcels. Policies of insurance, bills of exchange, and promissory notes, and shipping contracts, and charter-parties, are the growth of a thriftier trade, and more extensive mercantile enterprise. They have grown up among us almost in our own day. Indeed, in England, they are not, in a practical sense, much older than the days of Lord Holt; and as to insurance law, it was almost contemporaneous with the reign of George III. If, then, our courts of common law were so limited and lax in their practice, it is not to be supposed, that our chancery courts could have been very exact or methodical. Their business was of a nature not to attract the highest talents; and, before the revolution, in some of the states, the office of chancellor was but a political appointment. We find it stated by Mr. Johnson, in the preface to the present Reports, that in New York, "The erecting of a court of chancery, by an ordinance of the 2d of September, 1701, to consist of the *Governor and Council*, rendered it extremely unpopular; and frequent but fruitless attempts were made by the Assembly to destroy the court. It continued to be held under that ordinance, though little business appears to have been transacted in it, until its organization in March, 1778, under the constitution of our state." What is true with respect to the chancery of New York, is probably true with respect to most of the other equity courts in the Union. They had little business before the Revolution. The revolution itself was not a season for building up a judicial establishment; and the times that succeeded, until after the adoption of the constitution of the United States, were times of so much difficulty, and distress, and want of capital, and want of confidence, that there was little inclination to become either an equity lawyer, or an equity judge. In better times, many years must have elapsed before there was a regular current of business; and that was, from obvious causes, slow and uncertain, and not always the clearest. Without going more into detail, it may at once be seen why, even in the busy state of New York, we are driven almost to the times of Mr. Chancellor Kent, in our search for a systematic administration of equity. The fault was not in the learned chancellors, but in the materials, and in the organization of the system, and the difficulties of the times, and the lax state of the profession.

It may, perhaps, be asked, as it has been heretofore asked, whether courts of equity be, on the whole, of any serious importance in our country, considering that many of the most fertile sources of litigation are here completely dried up, or spring up in courts of common law? We have already alluded to some of these sources. But, before we proceed to answer this inquiry, it may not be improper to advert to a few more of the subjects of chancery jurisdiction in England, which are not likely to have an extensive operation here, or, at least, to be drawn here within the same jurisdiction. We may at once dismiss all consideration of the common law jurisdiction of the chancellor, such as his authority of granting writs of scire facias to repeal patents, petitions and monstrans de droit, traverses of office, writs of scire facias upon recognizances, &c. These properly fall within the cognizance of our courts of common law, and are no appendages of chancery. In respect, also, to the statutable jurisdiction of the chancellor, such as that under the bankrupt laws, little need be said; because it must depend upon the will of the legislature, to whom shall be intrusted the summary powers exercised in such cases. Another important branch of the chancellor's jurisdiction is exercised partly under statutes, and partly under his general chancery authority, and partly under his special authority, as the immediate delegate of the crown, acting as *parens patriæ*. We allude to his jurisdiction in cases of charitable uses, a subject of great extent and difficulty, and of the deepest interest to the whole community. The English system, on this subject, has been built up with wonderful ingenuity; and the statute regulations are entitled to our most serious consideration. Mr. Wheaton, in his valuable reports, adorned, as they are, with much of his own exact learning, has given us a sketch of the English law of charities in the appendix to his fourth volume. We merely mention the fact, with the recommendation to all our legal readers, and particularly to those who are, or expect to be, legislators, to peruse it with the utmost diligence, as worthy of their most serious reflection. Having alluded to the great statute of charitable uses of 9 Geo. II., ch. 36, he emphatically concludes with the following remarks:—"And it deserves the consideration of every wise and enlightened American legislator, whether provisions similar to those of this celebrated statute are not proper to be enacted in this country, with a view to prevent undue influence and imposition upon pious and feeble minds, in their last moments, and to check that unhappy propensity, which sometimes is found to exist under a bigoted enthusiasm, the desire to gain fame, as a religious devotee and benefactor, at the expense of all the natural claims of blood and parental duty to children." Already charitable donations, to an immense extent, have been bestowed in our country, without any check being interposed by the legislature. We are in some danger, and from the same natural causes, which are forever at work in all ages, and in all countries, of having our most valuable estates locked up in mortmain, and our surplus wealth pass away in specious or mistaken charities, founded upon visionary or useless schemes, to the impoverishment of friends, and the injury of the poor and deserving of our own countrymen. Let us but look for a moment at England, where, notwithstanding all the legislative and judicial guards, interposed from time to time, abuses of the most disgraceful and dangerous nature have grown up, under the administration of their charities by trustees and by corporations, and which parliament are now seeking to redress; and let us ask ourselves whether we can hope for a better state of things, when we have not a single guard, legislative, executive, or judicial, either to check improper donations, procured by fanatical or other delusions, or to secure the just administration of them from the most gross abuses. We are not aware, that any adequate authority at present exists in any of the United States for such purposes; and, certainly, in our own state there is not a pretence to say, that we have any real substantial security. A chancery jurisdiction on this subject, to the fullest extent, seems indispensable to insure justice, as well to the intentions of the benevolent donors, as to the objects of the donations. Remedies, in courts of common law, are, and must forever be, utterly inefficient and illusory.

We have been unexpectedly led to these remarks by a deep sense of their immediate and pressing importance, and we quit the subject with great reluctance, believing, that a full development of it could not fail to be interesting to all well-wishes to our country, to statesmen, to lawyers, to pious and benevolent men, and to those who love, and those who cultivate literature, the arts, or the sciences. But this is not the time or occasion for such a discussion. At present we must go dryly on with our examination of the chancery jurisdiction. We may, however, say, that as long as charitable uses shall exist, (and in a pious, refined, and elegant society, they must always be cherished,) there is a necessity to follow up their administration with the cogent process of chancery visiting them, to quicken their diligence and their virtue.

There is another authority, which has been, from time immemorial, or at least for several hundred years, exercised by the chancellor, which is said to belong to him, not in his official capacity, but as personal delegate of the crown. We allude to his jurisdiction in the cases of idiots and lunatics, as to the guardianship of their persons, and the management of their estates, and the protection of their rights. Of an analogous character is the authority of the chancellor, as to the care of infants. The king, as *parens patriæ*, is entitled to the care of infants; and this care is delegated by him to the court of chancery, and, as it seems, to this court alone. The court of chancery, therefore, exercises a most extensive jurisdiction, as to the custody of the person and estates of infants, their maintenance, and marriages. In our country, as well from public convenience, as from considerations drawn from a respect for private interests, this jurisdiction generally belongs to probate and orphans' courts, which are instituted in every small district or county, for the purpose of granting administrations, guardianships, &c. These tribunals are so domestic, and popular, and convenient, that it is highly probable they will always retain, if not an exclusive possession of this jurisdiction, at all events, such a concurrent jurisdiction, as will absorb the great mass of cases, and, for general purposes, be as efficacious and salutary as a court of chancery. In New York, however, it appears that the chancery exercises a general superintending authority in these cases, in many respects analogous to that in England. In New England we believe the probate courts exercise an exclusive authority as to the appointment and removal of guardians, and a concurrent, and sometimes an exclusive, authority in the settlement of their accounts.

There is another class of cases, of every day's occurrence in England, which belongs exclusively to the court of chancery, and must probably have an existence in every court of chancery acting *ex æquo et bono.* We allude to bills for specific performance of contracts, in contradistinction to mere actions for damages for the breach of such contracts. The doctrines of courts of equity on this head have spread into numerous branches; and the system itself has become not a little complex and unsatisfactory. The notion, that a court of equity is at liberty to dispense with a strict compliance with the terms of the contract, when no accident, mistake, or fraud, in a strict sense, has intervened to prevent an exact compliance by the parties; and that the court may interfere with these terms, and, as to *time*, dispense with them altogether, upon the footing of mere discretion; is so repugnant to a just conception of the obligation of contracts, and of the right of the parties to stand upon their own stipulations, as well as to general convenience and justice, that one wonders, that such an extraordinary authority should have ever been assumed or tolerated. Yet it has become an inveterate rule in equity, that time is not, or at least may not be, of the essence of a contract; and, consequently, that a party may be entitled to relief and a specific performance, if a contract for the sale of lands be decreed, although he has utterly failed to comply with the conditions of sale, within the period stipulated by the express letter of his contract; and this, too, to make the case stronger, rests not on a notion that there has been fraud, or circumvention, or inevitable accident, (casus fortuitus,) or mutual and innocent mistake, but upon the mere will, we had almost said caprice, of chancery, acting upon a thousand fancies of imaginary hardship. The old doctrine on this subject was most extravagant; and it seems the inclination of the present times to narrow the ground, and reduce it more to principles of common reason and convenience. But still, there is enough of difficulty and doubt in the cases that arise, to make us wish for a thorough reformation of the whole doctrine; and to put it upon this intelligible ground, that, where the party seeks a specific performance, he must show a strict compliance with the terms of the contract, or stand for relief upon some other real principle of equity. We ourselves have known specific performance decreed of purchases of real estate after twenty years from the time of the contract, when the property had changed its value exceedingly, three or four times in opposite ways, during the intervening period. We have also known specific performance sought, and reluctantly denied, after the lapse of more than thirty years, when all the original parties were dead, and the land, which was a wilderness, was become a settled and cultivated country. If there ever was a case for a statute prohibition of suits, except they are brought within a very short period, as a lawyer might say, by *journeys' accounts*, bills of this nature would furnish the most striking occasion for salutary legislation.

Still, it is not on the whole probable that this head of equity will, in our country, ever embrace a very extensive jurisdiction. The reasons which in England have conduced to raise up so many suits of this nature do not, and perhaps never will, exist in a corresponding degree in our country. In England, from causes already attended to, conveyancing has become extremely complicated; titles are buried under loads of parchment; and the intricacies of the trusts and uses, present and future, springing and resulting, of powers, gross or appurtenant, of entails, and contingent provisions, (especially if the estate has passed through two or three great landholders' hands, or has been linked to a marriage-settlement,) become so perplexing that it requires a vast deal of time and money to evolve its material muniments, and arrive at any thing like certainty, even as to the transmission of the title. Now and then to be sure, a *fine* or a *common recovery* cures all latent defects, and gives a new start to the title. But in many cases these remedies are impracticable, and sometimes they fail, (as unfortunately happens in respect to remedies administered for physical diseases,) even in the most skilful hands, and a latent taint first infects, and in the hands of a cunning solicitor soon eats up or destroys the title, though cased as it were in its triple mail of parchment, and surrounded by its concords and its vouchers. Hence, it rarely happens upon the purchase of an estate in England, if it be of any considerable value, that conveyances are immediately executed. The title-deeds are first to be thoroughly examined through perhaps a century; and diligent search made, not as we might hastily imagine, into a few short deeds of a folio page in length, but into volumes of dark and mouldy parchment, rolled up like ancient manuscripts, and requiring as much time to unravel and study them. Abstracts of these titles are to be made out and laid before counsel for their consideration and opinion. If a doubt of fact or law occurs the search is to be renewed; outstanding terms of years are to be ascertained to be either satisfied and attendant on the inheritance, or to be subsisting for trusts, which are exhausted or still to be fulfilled; mortgages are to be traced, either as dead or living *fungi* on the trunk of the title, through one or two generations; the records of courts are to be searched for liens of judgments and conveyances; and it is to be ascertained what limitations have taken effect or failed, and at what time and under what circumstances. It is to be considered, too, that in general deeds of lands are not recorded as in our country; so that it is not easy to trace even the deeds through the various depositories. And finally, a suit in chancery for a discovery often becomes necessary to compel a reluctant or obstinate party to discover the title by which he claims an interest in the land, or which he unjustly withholds from the legitimate owner. These are not exaggerations of the actual state of things, though perhaps to a careless observer, or a young lawyer accustomed merely to our local practice, it might seem otherwise. A treatise has already appeared, or is just about appearing, (and a most important one in a practical sense it must be,) on the mere subject of *abstracts of titles*, showing what a purchaser has a right to require, and what a vendor is bound to give, as to the history of his title to the land, before he can call on the former for payment or specific performance. From these remarks it must abundantly appear how it happens, that in England few important purchases are made except by an *executory* contract, or, in other words, a contract of sale, in which there are covenants to give a good title on one side, and on the other, to accept and pay the purchase-money at a stipulated period. From unforeseen difficulties, from unexpected occurrences, and from indolence or a lax reliance upon the redeeming power of chancery, it frequently happens that the conditions of the sale are not complied with; and thus the parties are prepared for a suit in chancery. In due time it comes, when the parties are a little quickened in their course, and after reference to a master in chancery to report upon the title, and other interlocutory proceedings, a decree in the course of four or five years is obtained requiring that to be done, which some or all of the above causes had contributed to leave utterly undone.

Many of our readers, we dare say, remember the following remarks of Tristram Shandy: "Upon looking into my mother's marriage-settlement, in order to satisfy myself and reader in a point necessary to be cleared up before we could proceed any farther in this history — *I had the good fortune to pop upon the very thing I wanted before I had read a day and a half straight forwards — it might have taken me up a month.*" If we have at all impressed our readers with our own views they will begin to perceive that what they took for the coloring of romance, a bright and beaming fiction, was, or at least might have been, like many of Sterne's most beautiful and touching sketches, a mere matter of fact. There are without doubt many titles in England that could not be thoroughly investigated even upon parchment without months of close and vigorous study.

Now the state of things is, as we all know, very different in our own country. Titles are generally very simple, and from obvious causes will probably always remain so, among the bulk of our landholders. A few hours or days of diligent study will generally give us all that is worth knowing as to the titles of estates offered for sale. In cases of sales, the deeds of conveyance are usually contemporaneous with the contract of sale. In cases where it is otherwise, the contract contains few provisions, and the period for its fulfilment is rarely distant; and at the stipulated period it is usually either fulfilled or abandoned altogether, or a new contract is substituted. This is so generally true, or at least a specific performance is so little insisted on, that bills for this purpose are of not very frequent occurrence in States accustomed to the exercise of chancery jurisdiction. And we believe and hope that this happy state of things will long continue. A strict equity on this subject is the best equity. It discourages sloth, and chicanery, and management; compelling parties to forego the unjust advantage of speculating on the future chances of a profitable rise in the value of estates, contracted to be purchased; if they rise, then at the fortunate moment, long after the time fixed for the performance of the contract is gone by, to insist upon a specific performance; if they fall, then to leave the property to the owner with a claim for damages, or a suit in chancery on his hands. There is so much good sense in the remarks of Mr. Justice Livingston on this subject, in Hepburn *v.* Auld, (5 Cranch, R. 262,) that we cannot forbear to quote them. The learned Judge on that occasion said,—"The remedy by a decree for the specific performance is a departure from the common law, and ought to be granted only in cases where the party who seeks it has strictly entitled himself to it. It is said, that by the English authorities, the lapse of time may be disregarded in equity, in decreeing a specific execution of a contract for land. But there is a vast difference between contracts for land in that country and in this. There the lands have a known, fixed, and stable value. Here the price is continually fluctuating and uncertain. A single day often makes a great difference; and, in almost every case, time is a material circumstance."

Having glanced, in a cursory manner, at some of the subjects of equity jurisdiction, which will be found of but limited application in the United States, we may now turn to other subjects in which it will forever operate with a constant and salutary influence. These are cases where relief becomes necessary from accident or mistake of the parties; cases of complicated accounts, whether between partners, or factors, or merchants, or assignees, or executors and administrators, or bailees, or trustees; cases of fraud, assuming myriads of vivid or of darkened hues, and as prolific in their brood, as the motes floating in sunbeams; cases of trust and confidence, spreading through all the concerns of society, and sinking their roots deep and firm through all the foundations of refined life and domestic relations; cases where bills of discovery are indispensable to promote public justice; and lastly, cases where bills of injunction are the only solid security against irreparable mischiefs and losses. Some other cases might be mentioned; but those above named must constitute the body of every equity jurisprudence adapted to our country. And in the times to come they will probably give ample employment for all the learning, and acuteness, and diligence of the ablest chancellors in States where courts of equity are established.

The inquiry, then, whether courts of equity are, on the whole, of any serious importance to our country, is, in some measure, answered by a mere reference to the subjects of its jurisdiction. Are these of any serious concern to societies organized as ours are? Is it important to administer substantial justice, to suppress frauds, to relieve against inevitable casualties, to succor the injured, to interpose preventive checks against malice and oppression, or mistaken claims of rights?

But it may be asked why all these objects are not, and may not be, as fully accomplished by courts of law? To a certain extent, they undoubtedly are accomplished by these courts; for it would be strange if courts, created for the administration of justice, should wholly fail to answer the purposes of their institution. The true inquiry, therefore, is not whether they are not of very great utility, which will be admitted by all persons of reasonable intelligence and honesty, but whether they accomplish all that, in a refined and elevated system of jurisprudence, it is desirable to attain. Now we venture to say that no person of competent skill in the science of law, or of comprehensive knowledge as a statesman, can fairly answer in the affirmative. There are many cases in which the parties are without remedy at law, or in which the remedy is wholly inadequate to the attainment of justice. Courts of law proceed by certain established forms, and administer certain kinds of remedies; their judgments are almost invariably general, for the plaintiff or for the defendant. If a case arise in which the remedy already existing at law is inapplicable, or the established forms cannot be pursued, there is an end of relief. Now it is very easy to see that such cases must frequently arise; for human actions, and contracts, and torts, assume an infinite variety of shapes, and become fashioned by an infinite variety of circumstances. The relief must, in many of these cases, be necessarily upon principles of equity of a mixed nature, and, to a certain degree, in favor of both of the parties. It may be wholly unjust to grant the plaintiff all that he asks, and as unjust to dismiss his suit without any relief. The parties in the defence, too, may have different rights, and different equities; and a judgment against them in the aggregate, or without adjusting these equities, might lead to the most mischievous results. Now a court of law cannot shape its judgments according to interfering equities of this sort. It cannot mould them, so as to impose conditions and exceptions on the rights of one party, and give effectual aid to the interests of the other. It can only pronounce, whether the plaintiff has, or has not, a legal cause of action, and sustain the suit, or dismiss it, accordingly. Further, a court of law cannot grant specific relief. It can, with few exceptions, award damages only. These are, in many cases, utterly worthless, as a compensation or a remedy. If in some cases, as in ejectments, real actions, and replevins, it acts *in rem*, it touches only the gross and palpable interests of property; but it cannot, and does not pretend to reach the subtile rights growing out of incidental trusts, or equitable claims and liens. If we are still pursued by the inquiry, why courts of law may not do all these things? we answer, that they may; but it must be by a change of their organization and character; and by investing them in form and in fact with all the forms of a court of equity. While they remain with their present powers and distinctive character, they are prohibited by the cogent mandates of the law from such unhallowed usurpation. In short, such an inquiry might be at once stopped by a question of another sort: "Why may not courts of equity perform all the functions of a court of law? But the true answer is, that each is adapted to its own objects, and cannot accomplish the objects of the other, without breaking in upon all the settled analogies of the common law, and shaking its oldest and most venerable foundations. He who is bold enough for such an undertaking, may applaud himself as possessing the temerity of Phaëton, with the perfect certainty of not escaping his fate.

We have yet a few words to say as to the question of the general utility of courts of equity, which we the more readily offer at the present moment, because, if a convention should be called to revise the constitution of this State, it is not improbable that a proposition will be made to provide for the distinct and independent establishment of such a court. At all events, the subject will more and more engage the attention of the legislature, as well as of the profession of the law; and it is very desirable, whatever may be the result, to act on such subjects with all the light which experience or general reasoning may throw in our path.

And we think, in the first place, that, if a system of equity jurisprudence is to be introduced into this Commonwealth, its utility will principally depend upon the nature of the system, which we take for our guide. If, for instance, we take the equity jurisprudence of England, or, which is the same thing, of New York, so far as it is applicable to our situation, and adhere to it with a rigid and undeviating firmness, following closely its principles, and walking within its acknowledged limits, there can be no doubt that it would be a real blessing. But it cannot be disguised, that there is too strong a tendency, not merely in the legislative bodies, but in some of the courts of law, and still more in some of the courts of equity in the United States, to give a popular cast to our jurisprudence; to make it a sort of arbitration-law; or to decide cases upon their own peculiar circumstances, without reference to any general principles. Now, this is precisely the worst state of things, both for the profession and for the public; and yet, in popular governments, the mass of the community are most unaccountably wedded to it. The maxim of common sense, as well as of profound investigation is, *Misera est servitus, ubi jus est vagum aut incertum.* And yet, what can more tend to perpetuate this uncertainty, than to escape from exact and leading principles, and to plunge into decisions upon all the circumstances of cases? It is a very easy, but a very dangerous course, and often occasions apostasy from the law. Mr. Justice Buller has, somewhere, emphatically said, that he had a dread of hard cases; they were the shipwrecks of the law. The same observation applies quite as forcibly to the practice of mixing up all sorts of considerations and circumstances in judicial decisions. It confounds all clear distinctions of right and wrong, and bewilders and sometimes betrays us into unfrequented labyrinths, where there is not a single thread of the law to guide us onwards, and a thousand spectres prevent us from retracing our steps. In respect to equity jurisprudence, where so much is necessarily left to discretion, (we mean to judicial, not to arbitrary discretion,) it is of infinite moment that it be administered upon determinate principles. Lord Camden, on one occasion, protested in strong and indignant eloquence against the exercise of such discretion, which, he significantly observed, was the length of my Lord Chancellor's foot. Without meaning to become his followers in this protest, we have no hesitation in declaring our opinion, that the boundary cannot be too sedulously marked out, or too watchfully guarded. If a court of chancery be at liberty to deal in all sorts of inquiries, as to mere hardship, inconvenience, and conjectural imposition; if it may indulge in notional equities, upon its own views of what may be fair, and reasonable, and according to good morals between the parties; if it may remove the barriers and bars of the law, because there may not be much honor or honesty in a party's availing himself of their protection; if it may cover up deviations from settled rules, by encouraging lax practices, and aiming to cure all the blunders of unskilful or rash persons; — we have as little hesitation in declaring, that we think Massachusetts is better without such a court. We have now, at least, the security of settled rules to guide us to our claims of property. We are accustomed to considerable exactness and regularity in the transaction of our business. We know what our remedies are, if we pursue the usual forms of completing contracts; and, what is a still more powerful admonition, we know what they are not, if we neglect to give certainty and accuracy to our contracts. If we mean to be secure, we now take the proper steps to give that security a tangible shape, such as the law may grapple with and protect. We do not consider how little may be done, and just save us by its grace; but how much ought to be done, to make our sales and our purchases solid and safe. There is now a wholesome thrift and accuracy about our concerns that disciplines us to close attention, and gives us an almost instantaneous perception of what is proper. We have, at all times, and almost instinctively, the air, and character, and pride, of real business men, who look at their title-deeds before they lock them up, and, what is of quite as much consequence, look at them diligently afterwards. We do not slumber over our rights, but are instant in season and out of season; and we do not awaken from the dreams of indolence for the first time, after the lapse of twenty and thirty years, and then consult a solicitor as to the best mode of framing a bill that shall relieve us from all the ill effects of delay, and forgetfulness, and hardship, and folly. Our laws, hitherto, have secured only the vigilant, and not the sound sleepers. *Vigilantibus, non dormientibus, leges subveniunt.* Now, it is most desirable to perpetuate this course of things, to prevent litigation, and to encourage legal certainty. And all this, a good court of equity, sustained by a learned, intrepid, and discriminating chancellor, such as Lord Eldon, or Mr. Chancellor Kent, would accomplish; but all this would be lost under different auspices, as may be seen in some parts of the union. Without adverting to the learned judges of our State Bench, we could name a gentleman at the bar of Massachusetts, whose cautious, well-instructed, modest, powerful mind, would adorn such an equity bench, and create an equity bar.[1]

In the next place, we think, that the administration of equity should be by a distinct court, having no connection with, or dependence upon, any court of common law. There are many reasons, which urge us to this conclusion. The systems of equity and law are totally distinct in their relations and objects. The practice and proceedings have little or nothing in common. The principles of decision are, in most cases, exceedingly different. A life, devoted to either study, will not more than suffice to make an eminent judge; a life, devoted to either, will be filled up with constant employment. There is some danger, where both systems are administered by the same court, that the equity of a case will sometimes transfer itself to the law side of the court; or the law of a case narrow down the comprehensive liberality of equity. The mixture, whenever it takes place, is decidedly bad in flavor and in quality. *Tibi Doris amara suam non intermisceat undam.* Besides, we all know, that nothing is more distracting to the mind than a variety of pursuits. A steady devotion to one gives great accuracy and acuteness, and keeps the whole current of thought fresh and transparent. We do not say, that a judge may not be, with great advantage, transferred from one bench to the other; for this has been often done with splendid success. Witness the cases of Lord Hardwicke, and Lord Kenyon, and Lord Eldon. What we contend for is, that the same judge should not at the same time administer both systems. In this, as in many of the arts, the subdivision of labor gives greater perfection to the whole machinery. A man may be a great common law judge, but may have no relish for equity. The talents required for both stations are not necessarily the same; and

[1] It need not now (1835) be concealed, that this allusion is to the Hon. William Prescott, LL. D.

the cast of mind and course of study adapted to the one, may not insure success in the other.

There is another reason of no inconsiderable weight, founded upon the nature of the duties to be performed in equity. It is no small portion of the business of such a court to grant injunctions upon judgments obtained at law. This is a delicate duty, and should be intrusted to an independent court, which has as yet received no impressions of the cause, and to whom its previous merits are unknown.

We might suggest many other reasons, but we have not time for an ample discussion of such a subject. There is one objection, however, which we have heard repeatedly urged against these suggestions, which requires some answer. It is stated, that the courts of the United States are examples of the union of the powers of courts of law and equity, and that hitherto no inconvenience has been felt from this circumstance. Without stopping to inquire into the accuracy of this statement, we may be permitted to suggest, that there are some distinctions in reference to those courts, which deserve consideration. In the first place, those courts exercise but a limited jurisdiction in equity cases. This arises, not from any restriction of their powers upon the subject-matter, but from the qualified nature of their authority over persons. They can, in general, take cognizance of suits in equity, only where the United States, or aliens, or citizens of other states, are parties. Now it must be obvious, that the great mass of equity suits, in every state, must consist of controversies between citizens and inhabitants of that state; and that local laws will greatly swell that mass. Where there are few cases, a court either of law or equity may transact the whole business, without any serious inconvenience. But it is far otherwise, where suits mix up with all the concerns of society, and may have an indefinite multiplication. Besides, there is, or at least seems to be, under the constitution of the United States, an inherent difficulty in separating the supreme jurisdiction at law from that in equity. And precisely the same difficulty exists in the constitution of this state, and most urgently requires to be removed by an amendment. We hope that this subject will not escape the attention of the convention, which may be called to amend the constitution, whether it be thought best to create, or not to create, a court of equity, at the present time. If ever such a court be created, it should be capable of having a distinct and independent existence given to it. But to return. Another circumstance as to the courts of the United States is, that, in six out of the seven circuits, state courts of equity have an existence, either connected with the courts of law, or with an independent organization. So that the learned judges have the fullest opportunities of becoming familiarly acquainted with the practice and principles of equity through their whole professional career; and, thus, may readily transfer into the circuit courts the local practice of the states within their circuits. Such is not the case, in general, in New England. These are considerations which, in a combined view, ought very much to abate the strength of the objection raised from the example of the judicial legislation of Congress on this subject.

In the next place, if a court of equity is to be established, and appeals are to be allowed from its decrees, those appeals ought not to be to any court of law, but to a distinct tribunal created for the purpose. From causes, which will readily suggest themselves to every juridical mind, and to which we have, in some measure, already alluded, a court of law, as such, cannot be presumed to be thoroughly conversant with the doctrines and practice of equity. And, if it be intrusted with a superintendence over that subject, it must happen, that decrees will often be reversed without sufficient reasons, and the court of equity sink from its natural elevation to the level of the inferior courts in the state; and that the personal character of the Chancellor will settle the authority of decisions, and thus open the path to personal influence and judicial jealousies; or that the decrees will be affirmed without much consideration, leaving to the court of appeals little more effective power than that of registering the decrees. We are among those who believe, that the existence of rival coördinate courts has the most salutary influence upon all judicial proceedings. They act as checks and balances to each other; and, if their judgments are to be reviewed, it should be by a tribunal of a distinct organization, common, if you please, to both, but sufficient in independence and dignity to prevent any undue ascendency by either. England owes much of the perfection of her jurisprudence to this striking feature in the structure of her government. She has rival tribunals of law and equity, where the pride and learning of the profession and the bench are stimulated to the noblest purposes, the advancement of justice, and the redress of injuries, by that perpetual watchfulness, which keen intelligence and sincere devotion to the law never fail to stir up in ambitious minds.

While on this subject, we are disposed to recall the public attention to a Report made to the legislature of Massachusetts, and printed by its order, in the year 1808, recommending the establishment of an independent court of equity. We dare say this document is totally forgotten, as most of our unsuccessful legislative proceedings are, by the public at large, and perhaps by most of the committee who reported it. It has been consigned, as most other state papers are, to some dark and obscure corner of some lumber loft in the State House, there to await the dissolution of their mortal remains by the gradual operation of time, and moulds, and vermin, "unwept, unhonored, and unsung." Would it not be for the reputation and dignity of our state government, if, instead of leaving our public legislative documents to perish, some pains and some money were employed to preserve a number of copies bound and lettered in the state archives, that posterity may know the progress of our legislation, and find some public indexes to those subjects, which interested the public mind, and gave a new direction to public inquiry?

We doubt whether there exists, in the whole Commonwealth, at this moment, a single regular series of the reports, bills, and other proceedings of our legislature, which have been printed at the expense of the government, even within the last twenty years. Surely, this is a most wanton indifference to our public concerns; and it will be regretted, deeply regretted, when it can no longer be within the reach of common diligence to collect them. It should be made the special duty of our Secretary of State, to have bound, and kept in his office, at least twenty copies of all documents printed by order of the legislature; and to have a transcript in bound volumes of all manuscript proceedings, reports, bills, &c., acted upon in any shape by the legislature at every session, with a suitable index for reference. In this way the next generation would not be in utter and irretrievable ignorance of our domestic legislative history, full of instruction, as it must be, both as to what we ought to avoid, and what we ought to cherish.

But to return to the Report,[1] to which we have alluded, and which we accidentally found in searching our papers for another purpose. It contains a summary of the practice and principles of courts of equity, in some of the points most applicable to our jurisprudence. Since the period in which it was made the legislature has by law cured some of the defects enumerated in the Report; but the substance of it is just as true now, as it was at that time. We transcribe from it the following paragraphs, which we commend to the careful perusal of our statesmen and jurists.

"Courts of equity, as contradistinguished from courts of law, have jurisdiction in cases where the latter, from their manner of proceeding, either cannot decide at all upon the subject or cannot decide conformably with the principles of substantial justice. Whenever a *complete*, *certain*, and *adequate* remedy exists at law, courts of equity have generally

[1] This Report was made by a committee, of which the writer of this article was chairman.

no jurisdiction. Their peculiar province is to supply the defects of law in cases of *frauds, accidents, mistakes,* or TRUSTS. In cases of fraud, where an instrument is fraudulently suppressed or withheld from the party claiming under it; where an unconscientious advantage has been taken of the situation of a party; where a beneficial property is injuriously misappropriated; equity interferes and compels complete restitution. In cases of accident or mistake where a contract has been made respecting real or personal estate, and by reason of death cannot be completed; or where, by subsequent events, a strict performance has become impossible; where, in consequence of a defective instrument the intention of the parties is in danger of being defeated; or where a want of specific performance cannot be compensated in damages; equity administers the proper and effectual relief. In cases of trust, where real or personal estate by deed, will, or otherwise, is confided to one person for the benefit of another; where creditors are improperly preferred or excluded; where numerous or discordant interests are created in the same subject-matter; where testamentary dispositions for want of a proper trustee are not fulfilled; and where fiduciary estates are by connivance or obstinacy directed to partial or unjust purposes; equity applies the principles of conscience, and enforces the express or implied trusts according to good faith.

"Sometimes by fraud or accident a party has an advantage in proceeding in a court of ordinary jurisdiction, which must necessarily make that court an instrument of injustice, if the suit be suffered; and equity, to prevent such a manifest wrong, will interpose and restrain the party from using his unfair advantage. Sometimes one party holds completely at his mercy the rights of another, because there is no witness to the transaction, or it lies in the privity of an adverse interest; equity in such cases will compel a discovery of the facts and measure substantial justice to all. Sometimes the administration of justice is obstructed by certain impediments to a fair decision of the case in a court of law; equity in such cases as auxiliary to the law removes the impediments. Sometimes property is in danger of being lost or injured, pending a litigation; equity there interposes to preserve it. Sometimes oppressive and vexatious suits are wantonly pursued and repeated by litigious parties; for the preservation of peace and of justice, equity imposes in such cases an injunction of forbearance.

"These are a few only of the numerous cases in which universal justice requires a more effectual remedy than the courts of common law can give. In proportion as our commerce and manufactures flourish and our population increases, subjects of this nature must constantly accumulate; and, unless the legislature interpose, dishonest and obstinate men may evade the law and intrench themselves within its forms in security. One or two striking instances applicable to our present situation will illustrate these positions. In this Commonwealth no adequate remedy exists at law to unravel long and intricate *accounts between merchants in general;* and *between partners* the remedy is still less efficacious to adjust the partnership accounts. A refractory or fraudulent partner may seize the books, papers, and effects of the firm and cannot by any process be compelled to disclose or produce them. In many instances, therefore, neither debts can be recovered, nor accounts be adjusted by them unless both parties are equally honest and equally willing. Great evils have already arisen from this cause; and still greater must arise unless equity be brought in aid of law. In cases of *pecuniary and specific legacies*, no complete remedy lies to compel a marshalling of the assets, or an appropriation of them according to the intention of the testator; and where the interests of the parties are complicated, great injustice must often ensue. In cases of *trusts*, created by last wills and testaments, which are already numerous, no remedy whatsoever exists to compel the person on whom the fiduciary estate devolves to carry them into operation. He may take the devised property, and, if his conscience will permit, may defy all the ingenuity and all the terror of the law. *Mortgages* afford a great variety of questions of conflicting rights, which, when complicated, are beyond the redress of the ordinary courts; nay, more, may often be the instruments of iniquity under their judgments. A discovery on oath seems the only effectual means of breaking down the barriers with which the cunning and the fraudulent protect their injustice. The process by which the goods, effects, and credits of debtors are attached in the hands of their trustees, is often inefficient, and sometimes made the cove of crafty chicanery. Perhaps, too, in *assignments of dower* and *partition of estates*, where the titles of the parties are questionable and intricate, or the tenants in possession are seized of particular estates only; it will be found that courts of equity can administer the only safe and permanent relief.

"The Committee are not aware of any solid objection to the establishment of a court of equity in this Commonwealth. The right of trial by jury is preserved inviolate; and the decisions of the court must be governed as much by settled principles as courts of law. Precedents govern in each, and establish rules of proceeding. The relief granted is precisely what a court of law would grant if it could; *for equity follows the law*. The leading characteristics of a court of equity are the power to eviscerate the real truth by a discovery of facts upon the oath of the party charged; the power to call all parties concerned in interest, however remote, before it; and the power to adapt the form of its judgments to the various rights of the parties as justice and conscience may require."

We have yet many things more to say on this subject, but time fails us, and we have wearied ourselves, and we fear that our readers also are wearied with the length of this discussion. Perhaps at some future time we may resume it. At present we are willing to pass the short remainder of our journey in such good company as Mr. Chancellor Kent and his excellent Reporter.

Mr. Johnson, if we do not mistake, began the business of reporting in February, 1806. Since that period he has published, in an uninterrupted series, all the decisions of the Supreme Court of New York, down to the present time, in sixteen volumes. He has also published three volumes of reports of the cases in the period immediately preceding Mr. Caines's Reports in the same court. Unwearied in his labors, he has now added to our obligations to him, by presenting us the three volumes of chancery cases, whose title is prefixed to this article.[1] He has been so long before the public in this most respectable and useful character, that perhaps it may be thought almost superfluous to say a word upon the merits of his Reports. We will venture, however, to give them a passing notice, at the hazard of repeating what almost every body knows, and none would incline to disbelieve. He is a gentleman, as we have the pleasure to know, of great literary accomplishments, well-instructed in the law, and of most comprehensive research. He loves, too, — and it is no inconsiderable praise in what are called these degenerate days, — he loves the law with all his heart, and has a sincere and unaffected enthusiasm for its advancement. His Reports are distinguished by the most scrupulous accuracy, good sense, and good taste. He gives the arguments of counsel with force, precision, and fluency; transfusing the spirit, rather than the letter, of their remarks into his pages. One is never puzzled by unintelligible sentences, impertinent sallies, or disproportionate reasoning in his volumes. There is an exactness and symmetry about them that satisfies the judgment. His notes, too, are all good; so good, that we wish we had a great many more of them. He leaves little causes to take care of themselves, and assigns them a brief space. But when he comes to great arguments, where research and talent are brought out with vast power and authority, he pours their whole strength before the reader, giving him all

[1] The Reports of Mr. Johnson are now (1835) completed, and embrace thirty volumes, including those stated in the text.

the materials of an independent judgment. He can, if he pleases, repeat such cases for himself, by the aid of the reporter. As to the opinions of the court, we have not any necessity to say much. It is, and always has been, a very able court, whose decisions any man might be proud to report; and the highly commendable diligence of the judges, in committing all their important opinions to writing, while it gives the impress of authority, at the same time secures the court from the inaccuracies and mistakes of oral opinions. It gives dignity to the Bench, and certainty to the law. Who, but must read with delight and instruction the opinions of such men as Mr. Chief Justice Spencer, to say nothing of his learned coadjutors and predecessors? For ourselves, we have no hesitation in avowing the opinion, that the New York Reports, for the last twenty years, will bear comparison with those of an equal period in the best age of the English law, begin the selection where you may; and this, whether we examine the well-considered and ingenious arguments of the bar, or the deep reasoning and learning of the bench, or the accuracy and ability of the reporter. And as to the chancery decisions of Mr. Chancellor Kent, they are as full of learning, and painstaking research, and vivid discrimination, as those of any man that ever sat on the English woolsack.

Enough has been said, and more than enough, to attract the attention of our professional readers to the volumes, referred to at the beginning of this article. If we had room, we might be tempted to extract a case or two for perusal, on account either of its general interest, or the acute and learned discussion it contains. There may be some few cases in which jurists might venture to hesitate, as to the extent of the Chancellor's decision; at least where there might be a measuring cast in mooting the law. But these cases (if any such exist) are so few and so unimportant, that they are lost in the bulk of the volumes; and criticism is never employed to so little advantage as in attempting to revise the sentences pronounced by courts of justice. The only fit and efficient tribunal, except in very gross cases, seems to be that provided by the law itself, an appeal to a higher tribunal to review the sentence, or to the same court to reconsider, to another time, its own judgments. We cannot quit these volumes, however, without expressing our gratitude to Mr. Johnson for presenting them to the public. No lawyer can ever express a better wish for his country's jurisprudence, than that it may possess such a Chancellor and such a Reporter.

SPEECH ON THE APPORTIONMENT OF SENATORS,

DELIVERED IN THE CONVENTION OF MASSACHUSETTS, ASSEMBLED TO AMEND THE CONSTITUTION, IN NOVEMBER, 1820.[1]

We are at length arrived at the discussion of those questions, which it was easy to foresee would be attended with the most serious interest and difficulty—questions, which, indeed, were the principal causes of assembling this convention. Nor do I regret it. The great powers of eloquence and argumentation, which have already been displayed in the debate, I trust will do good here, and ultimately reach the homes of our constituents. I cannot hope, after the very ample discussion, which the subject has undergone, to add much to the arguments, and shall content myself with such illustrations of my own views, as have not been completely presented by others.

If it were necessary for my purpose, I might say with the gentleman from Worcester, that I come here pledged to no man or set of men, or to any settled course of measures. I come merely as the delegate of one town, to coöperate with other gentlemen, the delegates of other towns, in such measures, as the public good may require; and in their wisdom and discretion I place entire confidence. I might add, also, what my eloquent colleague has already remarked, that, upon this particular topic, and upon the grounds which we take, we are not in a situation even to be suspected of interested

1 This is a mere sketch, taken principally by the reporter, and was not written out at large by the speaker.

motives. The county of Essex is safe at present, and would have a fair and equal representation in the senate, whether the principle of population or that of valuation were adopted as a basis. If population were assumed as a basis, and no restriction were interposed, it is highly probable, that the county of Essex might hereafter be a loser; but upon the principle of valuation it could never be a gainer, since it would now have the whole number, to which it could ever be entitled. But I throw away all narrow considerations of this kind, and consider myself as a delegate of the Commonwealth, bound to consult for the interests of the whole, and to form such a constitution as shall best promote the interests of our children and of all posterity.

It is necessary for us, for a moment, to look at what is the true state of the question now before us. The proposition of my friend from Roxbury is, to make population the basis for apportioning the senate; and this proposition is to be followed up, as the gentleman with the candor and frankness which have always marked his character has intimated, by another to apportion the house of representatives in the same manner. The plan is certainly entitled to the praise of consistency and uniformity. It does not assume in one house a principle which it deserts in another. Those who contend on the other hand for the basis of valuation, propose nothing new; but they stand upon the letter and spirit of the present constitution.

Here, then, there is no attempt to introduce a new principle in favor of wealth into the constitution. There is no attempt to discriminate between the poor and the rich. There is no attempt to raise the pecuniary qualifications of the electors, or the elected; to give to the rich man two votes, and to the poor man but one. The qualifications are to remain as before; and the rich and the poor, and the high and the low, are to meet at the polls upon the same level of equality. And yet, much has been introduced into the debate about the rights of the rich and the poor, and the oppression of the one by the elevation of the other. This distinction between the rich and poor, I must be permitted to say, is an odious distinction, and not founded in the merits of the case before us. I agree, that the poor man is not to be deprived of his rights, any more than the rich man; nor have I as yet heard of any proposition to that effect; and if it should come, I should feel myself bound to resist it. The poor man ought to be protected in his rights, not merely of life and liberty, but of his scanty and hard earnings. I do not deny, that the poor man may possess as much patriotism as the rich; but it is unjust to suppose that he necessarily possesses more. Patriotism and poverty do not necessarily march hand in hand; nor is wealth that monster, which some imaginations have depicted, with a heart of adamant and a sceptre of iron, surrounded with scorpions, stinging every one within its reach, and planting its feet of oppression upon the needy and the dependent. Such a representation is not just with reference to our country. There is no class of very rich men in this happy land, whose wealth is fenced in by hereditary titles, by entails, and by permanent elevation to the highest offices. Here, there is a gradation of property from the highest to the lowest, and all feel an equal interest in its preservation. If, upon the principle of valuation, the rich man, in a district which pays a high tax, votes for a larger number of senators, the poor man in the same district enjoys the same distinction. There is not, then, a conflict, but a harmony of interests between them. Nor under the present constitution has any discontent or grievance been seriously felt from this source.

When I look round, and consider the blessings which property bestows, I cannot persuade myself, that gentlemen are serious in their views that it does not deserve our utmost protection. I do not here speak of your opulent and munificent citizens, whose wealth has spread itself into a thousand channels of charity and public benevolence. I speak not of those who rear temples to the service of the Most High

God. I speak not of those who build your hospitals, where want, and misery, and sickness, the lame, the halt, and the blind, the afflicted in body and in spirit, may find a refuge from their evils, and the voice of solace and consolation, and food, and medicine, and kindness. I speak not of those who build asylums for the insane; for the ruins of noble minds; for the broken-hearted and the melancholy; for those whom Providence has afflicted with the greatest of calamities, the loss of reason, and too often the loss of happiness; within whose walls the screams of the maniac may die away in peace, and the sighs of the wretched be soothed into tranquillity. I speak not of these; not because they are not worthy of all praise; but because I would dwell rather on those general blessings, which property diffuses through the whole mass of the community. Who is there, that has not a friend or a relative in distress, looking up to him for assistance? Who is there, that is not called upon to administer to the sick and the suffering; to those who are in the depth of poverty and distress; to those of his own household, or the stranger beside the gate? The circle of kindness commences with the humblest, and extends wider and wider, as we rise to the highest in society; each person administering in his own way to the wants of those around him. It is thus, that property becomes the source of comforts of every kind, and dispenses its blessings in every form. In this way it conduces to the public good by promoting private happiness; and every man, from the humblest, possessing property, to the highest in the state, contributes his proportion to the general mass of comfort. The man without any property may desire to do the same; but he is necessarily shut out from this most interesting charity. It is in this view, that I consider property as the souree of all the comforts and advantages we enjoy; and every man, from him who possesses but a single dollar, up to him who possesses the greatest fortune, is equally interested in its security and its preservation.

Government, indeed, stands on a combination of interests and circumstances. It must always be a question of the highest moment, how the property-holding part of the community may be sustained against the inroads of poverty and vice. Poverty leads to temptation, and temptation often leads to vice, and vice to military despotism. The rights of man are never heard in a despot's palace. The very rich man, whose estate consists in personal property, may escape from such evils, by flying for refuge to some foreign land. But the hardy yeoman, the owner of a few acres of the soil, and supported by it, cannot leave his home without becoming a wanderer on the face of the earth. In the preservation of property and virtue, he has, therefore, the deepest and most permanent interest.

Gentlemen have argued, as if personal rights only were the proper objects of government. But what, I would ask, is life worth, if a man cannot eat in security the bread earned by his own industry? if he is not permitted to transmit to his children the little inheritance which his affection has destined for their use? What enables us to diffuse education among all the classes of society, but property? Are not our public schools, the distinguishing blessing of our land, sustained by its patronage?

I will say no more about the rich and the poor. There is no parallel to be run between them founded on permanent constitutional distinctions. The rich help the poor, and the poor in turn administer to the rich. In our country, the highest man is not above the people; the humblest is not below the people. If the rich may be said to have additional protection, they have not additional power. Nor does wealth here form a permanent distinction of families. Those, who are wealthy to-day, pass to the tomb, and their children divide their estates. Property is thus divided quite as fast as it accumulates. No family can, without its own exertions, stand erect for a long time under our statute of descents and distributions, the only true and legitimate agrarian law. It silently and quietly dissolves the mass heaped up by the toil and diligence of a long life of enterprise and industry. Property is continually changing like the waves of the sea. One wave rises, and is soon swallowed up in the vast abyss and seen no more. Another rises, and having reached its destined limits, falls gently away, and is succeeded by yet another, which in its turn, breaks and dies away silently on the shore. The richest man among us may be brought down to the humblest level; and the child, with scarcely clothes to cover his nakedness, may rise to the highest office in our government. And the poor man, while he rocks his infant on his knees, may justly indulge the consolation, that, if he possess talents and virtue, there is no office beyond the reach of his honorable ambition. It is a mistaken theory, that government is founded for one object only. It is organized for the protection of life, liberty, and property, and all the comforts of society; to enable us to indulge in our domestic affections, and quietly to enjoy our homes and our firesides.

It has been said that the senate, under the present constitution, is founded on the basis of property. This I take to be incorrect. It is founded on the basis of taxation. It gives no particular privileges to the rich; all have equal rights secured by it. The gentleman from Worcester, to show the injustice and inequality of the present system, has alarmed us with a reference to the town of Hull. Suppose, said he, five of the richest men in Boston should remove to Hull, that removal would enable Hull to have six senators. Is this the case? Is Hull a county? Does it constitute a senatorial district? No; the property, thus carried from Suffolk, would be transferred to the county of Plymouth, and would increase the representation of that county proportionately in the Senate under a new valuation. If, instead of going to Hull, the same persons should remove to Salem, their property would not produce the slightest effect; for Essex, without it, possesses a right to as many senators as the constitution allows to any district. The case supposed by the gentleman is so extreme, that it could scarcely be supposed to exist; and, if it did, no such consequences could arise as have been stated.

It has been also suggested, that great property, of itself, gives great influence; and that it is unnecessary that the constitution should secure to it more. I have already stated what I conceive to be the true answer; that a representation in the senate, founded on a valuation of property, is not a representation of property in the abstract. It gives no greater power in any district to the rich than to the poor. The poor voters in Suffolk may, if they please, elect six senators into the senate; and so, throughout the Commonwealth, the senators of every other district may, in like manner, be chosen by the same class of voters. The basis of valuation was undoubtedly adopted by the framers of our constitution, with reference to a just system of checks and balances, and the principles of rational liberty. Representation and taxation should go hand in hand, was the doctrine of those days; a doctrine for which our fathers fought and bled in the battles of the Revolution. Upon the basis of valuation, property is not directly represented; but property in the aggregate, combined with personal rights. Where the greatest burden of taxation falls there the largest representation is apportioned. But still the choice depends upon the will of the majority of voters, and not upon that of the wealthier class within the district. There is a peculiar beauty in our system of taxation, and equalizing the public burdens. Our governor, counsellors, senators, judges, and other public officers are paid out of the public treasury; our representatives by their respective towns. The former are officers for the benefit of the whole Commonwealth. But the right of sending representatives is a privilege granted to corporations; and, as the more immediate agents of such corporations, they are paid by them. The travel, however, of the representatives is paid out of the public treasury; with the view, that no unjust advantage should arise to any part of the Commonwealth from its greater proximity to the capital. Thus, the principle of equalizing burdens is exemplified. But even if it were true, that the representation in the senate is founded on property, I would respectfully ask, gentlemen, if its natural influence would be weakened or destroyed by assuming the basis of population? I presume not. It would still be left to exert that influence over friends and dependents, in the same manner, that it now does. So that the change would not in the slightest degree aid the asserted object; I mean the suppression of the supposed predominating authority of wealth.

Gentlemen have argued, as though it was universally conceded, as a political axiom, that population is, in all cases and under all circumstances, the safest and best basis of representation. I beg leave to doubt the proposition. Cases may be easily supposed, in which, from the peculiar state of society, such a basis would be universally deemed unsafe and injurious. Take a State where the population is such as that of Manchester, in England, (and some States in our Union have not so large a population,) where there are five or ten thousand wealthy persons, and ninety or one hundred thousand artisans, reduced to a state of vice, and poverty, and wretchedness, which leave them exposed to the most dangerous political excitement. I speak of them, not as I know, but as the language of British statesmen and parliamentary proceedings exhibit them. Who would found a representation on such a population, unless he intended, that all property should be a booty to be divided among plunderers? A different state of things exists in our happy Commonwealth; and no such dangers will here arise from assuming population as the basis of representation. But still the doctrine, in the latitude now contended for, is not well founded. What should be the basis on which representation should be founded, is not an abstract theoretical question; but it depends upon the habits, manners, character, and institutions of the people who are to be represented. It is a question of political policy, which every nation must decide for itself, with reference to its own wants and circumstances.

The gentleman from Worcester has asserted, that intelligence is the foundation of government. Are not virtue and morality equally so? Intelligence without virtue is the enemy most to be dreaded by every government. It might make men despots, or bandits, or murderers, if their interests pointed in such directions. While, therefore, it may be admitted that intelligence is necessary for a free people, it is not less true, that sound morals and religion are also necessary. Where there is not private virtue, there cannot be public security and happiness.

The proposition of the gentleman from Roxbury is, to assume population for the basis of both houses. That of the gentleman from Worcester is to assume population for the senate, and corporate representation for the house. The latter gentleman wishes his last proposition to be considered distinctly from the first. It might suit the purposes of the gentleman's argument so to separate them. But in the nature of things, with reference to the doctrine of checks and balances, avowed and supported by the gentleman himself, they are inseparable. I feel myself constrained so to consider them, as parts of a system, the value of which must be ascertained by examining the effects of the whole combination. I am not opposed in principle to population as a basis of representation. There is much to recommend it. It has simplicity, and uniformity, and exemption from fraud in its application; circumstances of vast importance in every practical system of government. In the Select Committee, I was in favor of a plan of representation in the House founded on population, as the most just and equal in its operation. I still retain that opinion. There were serious objections against this system, and it was believed by others, that the towns could not be brought to consent to yield up the corporate privileges of representation, which had been enjoyed so ong, and was so intimately connected with their pride and their interests. I felt constrained, therefore, with great reluctance to yield up a favorite plan. I had lived long enough to know that, in any question of government, something is to be yielded up on all sides. Conciliation and compromise lie at the origin of every free government; and the question never was, and never can be, What is absolutely best? but, What is relatively wise, just, and expedient? I have not hesitated, therefore, to support the plan of the Select Committee, as one that, on the whole, was the best, that, under existing circumstances, could be obtained.

To the plan of the gentleman from Roxbury two objections exist. The first is, that it destroys the system of checks and balances in the government; a system which has been approved by the wisdom of ages. The value of this system has been forcibly illustrated by the gentleman from Boston, in the extract, which he read from the remarks of Mr. Jefferson on the constitution of Virginia. I will not, therefore, dwell on this objection. The next objection is, that it destroys all county lines and distinctions; and breaks up all habits and associations connected with them. They might thus be broken up; but it would be by tearing asunder some of the strongest bonds of society. The people of each county are drawn together by their necessary attendance upon the county courts, and by their county interests and associations. There is a common feeling diffused among the mass of the population, which extends to, but never passes, the boundary of each county; and thus these communities become minor States. These are valuable associations; and I am not prepared to say, that they ought to be given up altogether. The system of the gentleman from Roxbury, however, not only obliterates them; but, at the same time, is supposed to affect the interests and corporate representation of the towns; a representation which, with all its inconveniences, possesses intrinsic value. It appears to me, that the system of the Select Committee, combining valuation of property, as the basis of the senate, with corporate representation of the towns, as the basis of the house, has, both as a system of checks and balances, and convenient and practical distribution of powers, some advantages over that now under discussion.

It has been said that the system of valuation is novel, and cannot be traced beyond the era of the formation of our present constitution. It may be so; though the venerable gentleman from Quincy has endeavored to show that it is in principle as old as the republics of Greece and Rome. But be it novel; it is no objection to it. Our whole system of government is novel. It is a great experiment in the science of politics. The very principle of representation, and the theory of a division of powers are of modern origin, as are many of our dearest and most valuable institutions.

It is asked, too, why, if the principle of valuation be a just one, there is a restriction, that no district shall send more than six senators. A sufficient reason has been already given; that it was a compromise to silence any jealousy of an undue exercise of power by any particular district abounding in wealth. My answer is, that it is also for the purpose of equalizing the fractions of the smaller districts with the great districts. The same principle of equalization was provided for in forming the house of representatives, and is now more completely observed in the system of the Select Committee.

After all, what will be the effect of changing the basis of the senate from valuation to that of population? It will take three senators from Suffolk, give two more senators to the old county of Hampshire, leave Berkshire and Plymouth to struggle for one more, and Norfolk and Bristol to contend for another, the disposition of which may be doubtful. All the rest of the Commonwealth will remain precisely in the same situation as at present, whether we adopt the one basis or the other. Yet even this change will not produce any serious practical result, if we look forward twenty years. Suffolk has increased, within the last ten years, ten thousand in the number of its inhabitants, that is to say, one quarter part of its population; a much greater ratio of increase than the rest of the State. Population will probably, from the like causes, continue to increase on the seaboard, or at least in the capital, from its great attractions, in a ratio quite as great beyond that of the interior. So that in a short time, the difference of the two systems will be greatly diminished; and perhaps finally, the inland counties will gain more by the restriction of the districts to six senators, than they will now gain by the basis of population. In fifty years, Suffolk, upon this basis, may entitle itself not to six only, but to eight senators.

Now I would beg gentlemen to consider, if, in this view of the subject, a change in the basis of the senate can be useful? The constitution has gone through a trial of forty years in times of great difficulty and danger. It has passed through the embarrassments of the revolutionary war; through the troubles and discontents of 1787 and 1788; through collisions of parties unexampled in our history for violence and zeal; through a second war, marked with no ordinary scenes of division and danger; and it has come out of these trials, pure, and bright, and spotless. No practical inconvenience has been felt, or attempted to be pointed out by any gentleman, in the present system, during this long period. Is it, then, wise, or just, or politic to exchange the results of our own experience for any theory, however plausible, that stands opposed to that experience? for a theory, that possibly may do as well?

A few words as to the proposition of the gentleman from Worcester for representation in the house. It seems to me, I hope the gentleman will pardon the expression, inconsistent, not only with his own doctrine, as to the basis of population; but inconsistent with the reasoning by which he has endeavored to sustain that doctrine. The gentleman considers population as the only just basis of representation in the senate. Why, then, I ask, is it not as just as the basis for the house? Here, the gentleman deserts his favorite principle; and insists on representation of towns, as corporations. He alleges, that in this way the system of checks and balances (which the gentleman approves) is supported. But it seems to me, that it has not any merit as a check; for the aggregate population of the county will express generally the same voice as the aggregate representatives of the towns. The gentleman has said, that the poor man in Berkshire votes only for two senators, while the poor man in Suffolk votes for six. Is there not the same objection against the system of representation now existing as to the house; and against that proposed by the gentleman himself? A voter in Chelsea now votes for but one representative, while his neighbor, a voter in Charlestown, votes for six. Upon the gentleman's own plan there would be a like inequality. He presses us also, in reference to his plan of representation in the house, with the argument, that it is not unequal, because we are represented, if we have a single representative; and, he says, he distinguishes between the right to send one, and to send many representatives. The former is vital to a free government, the latter not. One representative in the British Parliament would probably have prevented the American Revolution. Be it so. But if the doctrine be sound, does it not plainly apply as well to the senate as to the house? If it be not unequal or unjust in the House, how can it be so in the Senate? Is not Berkshire with its two senators, or Barnstable with its one senator, or Worcester with its four senators, upon this principle just as fully represented in the senate, as Suffolk with its six senators? The argument of the gentleman may therefore be thrown back upon himself.

The gentleman from Worcester has illustrated his views, by a reference to the structure of the two houses under the constitution of the United States; and he conceives the Senate of the United States as analogous to his system of representation in our house, a presentation of corporations.

It certainly bears no analogy to his basis of representation for the senate. I take it, that the Senate of the United States is a representation of sovereignties, coördinate and coequal, and in no respect like our system, either of the house or senate; for neither towns nor districts have an equal representation here, for the reason that they are not independent sovereignties. But when we come to the House of Representatives of the United States, which is founded on the basis of population, we find, that it is accompanied with another principle, that representation and direct taxation shall be apportioned according to population. Not that population alone shall be the basis; but that they who enjoy the right shall also bear the burden. I have no objection to adopting this principle here. Let Worcester send her six senators, and Berkshire three; and let them consent, also, to bear a proportionable share of the public taxes; and then, and then only, will there be a well-founded analogy to the constitution of the United States. I thank the gentleman for his illustration; an argument more pertinent to my purpose could not have been found.

I beg, however, for a moment to ask the attention of the committee to the gross inequalities of the plan of the gentleman from Worcester, respecting the house of representatives. There are two hundred and ninety-eight towns in the state, each of which is to send one representative. And upon this plan the whole number of representatives will be three hundred and thirty-four. There are but twenty-four towns, which would be entitled to send more than one representative. These twenty-four towns, with a population of one hundred and forty-six thousand, would send fifty-eight representatives, or only one, upon an average, for every two thousand five hundred and twenty-six inhabitants; while the remaining two hundred and seventy-four towns, with a population of three hundred and thirteen thousand, would send two hundred and seventy-four representatives, or one for every one thousand one hundred and forty-four inhabitants.

I lay not the *venue* here or there in the Commonwealth, in the county of Worcester, or the county of Essex; but such would be the result throughout the whole Commonwealth, taken in the aggregate of its population. Salem would send one representative for every three thousand one hundred and thirty inhabitants; and Boston one for every four thousand two hundred inhabitants; while every town but the twenty-four largest would send one for every one thousand one hundred and forty-four inhabitants. What then becomes of the favorite doctrine of the basis of population? I would ask the gentleman, in his own emphatic language, Is not this system unjust, unequal, and cruel? If it be equal, it is so by some political arithmetic, which I have never learned, and am incapable of comprehending.

A few words upon the plan of the Select Committee, and I have done. Sir, I am not entitled to any of the merit, if there be any, in that plan. My own plan was to preserve the present basis of the senate, not because I placed any peculiar stress on the basis of valuation; but because I deemed it all-important to retain some element that might maintain a salutary check between the two houses. My own plan for the house of representatives was representation, founded on the basis of population in districts, according to the system proposed by the gentleman from Northampton. Finding that this plan was not acceptable to a majority of the committee, I acquiesced in the plan reported by it. I have learned, that we must not, in questions of government, stand upon abstract principles; but must content ourselves with practicable good. I do not pretend to think, nor do any of its advocates think, that the system of the Select Committee is perfect; but it will cure some defects in our present system, which are of great and increasing importance. I have always viewed the representation in the house under the present constitution, as a most serious evil, and alarming to the future peace and happiness of the state. My dread has never been of the senate; but of that multitudinous assembly, which has been seen within these walls, and may again be seen, if times of political excitement should occur. The more numerous the body, the greater the danger from its movements, in times when it cannot or will not deliberate. I came here, therefore, willing and ready to make sacrifices to accomplish an essential reduction in that body. It was the only subject relative to the constitution, on which I have always had a decided and earnest opinion. It was my fortune for some years to have a seat in our house of representatives; and for a short time to preside over its sittings, at a period when it was most numerous, and under the most powerful excitements. I am sorry to say it, but such is my opinion, that in no proper sense could it be called a deliberative assembly. From the excess of numbers deliberation became almost impossible; and, but for the good sense and discretion of those, who usually led in the debates, it would have been impracticable to have transacted business with any thing like accuracy or safety. That serious public mischiefs did not arise, from the necessary hurry and difficulty of the legislative business, is to be accounted for, only from the mutual forbearance and kindness of those who enjoyed the confidence of the respective parties. If the state should go on, increasing in its population, we might hereafter have eight hundred or nine hundred representatives according to the present system; and, in times of public discontent all the barriers of legislation may be broken down, and the government itself be subverted. I wish most deeply and earnestly to preserve to my native state a deliberative legislature, where the sound judgment, and discretion, and sagacity of its best citizens may be felt, and heard, and understood, at all times, and under all circumstances. I should feel the liberties of the state secure if this point were once fairly gained. I would yield up the little privileges of my own town, and of any others, that our children may enjoy civil, religious, and political liberty, as perfectly, nay, more perfectly than their fathers. With these views I am ready to support the report of the Select Committee, not in part, but as a whole, as a system; and if part is to be rejected, I do not feel myself bound to sustain the rest. Indeed, upon no other ground than a great diminution of the house of representatives, can I ever consent to pay the members out of the public treasury. For this is now the only efficient check against an overwhelming representation. By the plan of the Select Committee the small towns are great gainers; a sacrifice is made by the large towns, and by them only. They will bear a heavier portion of the pay of the representatives, and they will have a less proportionate representation than they now possess. And what do they gain in return? I may say, Nothing. All that is gained is public gain; a really deliberative legislature; and a representation in the senate, which is in fact a popular representation, emanating from and returning to the people; but so constructed, that it operates a useful check upon undue legislation, and as a security to property.

I hope that this system will be adopted by a large majority, because it can scarcely otherwise receive the approbation of the people. I do not know that it is even desirable, that the people should, nay, I might go further and say, that the people ought not to adopt any amendment which comes recommended by a bare majority of this Convention. If we are so little agreed among ourselves as to what will be for the future public good, we had much better live under the present constitution, which has all our experience in its favor. Is any gentleman bold enough to hazard the assertion, that any new measure we may adopt can be more successful? I beg gentlemen to consider, too, what will be the effect, if the amendments we now propose should be rejected by the people, having passed by a scanty majority. We shall then revert to the old constitution; and new parties, embittered by new feuds, or elated by victory, will be formed in the state, and distinguished as Constitutionalists, and Anti-constitutionalists; and thus new discontents and struggles for a new convention will agitate the Commonwealth. The revival of party animosities, in any shape, is most deeply to be deprecated. Who does not recollect with regret the violence, with which party spirit in times past raged in this state, breaking asunder the ties of friendship and consanguinity? I was myself called upon to take an active part in the public scenes of those days. I do not regret the course which my judgment then led me to adopt. But I never can recollect, without the most profound melancholy, how often I have been compelled to meet, I will not say the evil, but averted eyes, and the hostile opposition of men, with whom, under other circumstances, I should have rejoiced to have met in the warmth of friendship. If new parties are to arise, new animosities will grow up, and stimulate new resentments. To the aged in this Convention, who are now bowed down under the weight of years, this can of course be of but little consequence; for they must soon pass into the tranquillity of the tomb. To those in middle life it will not be of great importance; for they are far on their way to their final repose; they have little to hope of future eminence, and are fast approaching the period when the things of this world will fade away. But we have youth who are just springing into life; we have children whom we love; and families in whose welfare we feel the deepest interest. In the name of Heaven let us not leave to them the bitter inheritance of our contentions. Let us not transmit to them enmities which may sadden the whole of their lives. Let us not, like him of old, blind, and smitten of his strength, in our anger seize upon the pillars of the constitution, that we and our enemies may perish in their downfall. I would rather approach the altar of the constitution, and pay my devotions there; and, if our liberties must be destroyed, I, for one, would be ready to perish there in defending them.

PROGRESS OF JURISPRUDENCE.

AN ADDRESS DELIVERED BEFORE THE MEMBERS OF THE SUFFOLK BAR, AT THEIR ANNIVERSARY, SEPTEMBER 4, 1821, AT BOSTON.

In comparing the present state of jurisprudence with that of former times, we have much reason for congratulation. In governments purely despotic, the laws rarely undergo any considerable changes through a long series of ages. The fundamental institutions, (for such there must be in all civilized societies,) whether modelled at first by accident or by design, by caprice or by wisdom, assume a settled course, which is broken in upon only by the positive edicts of the sovereign, suited to some temporary exigency. These edicts rarely touch any general regulation of the state, and still more rarely attempt any general melioration of the laws. For the most part they affect only to express the arbitrary will of the monarch, stimulated by some pressing private interest, or gratifying some temporary passion, or some fleeting state policy. There is in such governments, what may be called a desolating calm, a universal indisposition to changes, and a fearfulness of reform on all sides; on the part of the people, lest it should generate some new oppression; and on the part of the ruler, lest it should introduce some jealousy or check of his arbitrary power. In such countries the Law can scarcely be said to have existence as a science. It slumbers on in a heavy and drowsy sleep, diseased and palsied. It breathes only at the beck of the sovereign. It assumes no general rules, by which rights or actions are to be governed. Causes are decided summarily, and more with reference to the condition and character of the parties than with reference to principles; and judges are ministers of state to execute the policy of the cabinet, rather than jurists to interpret rational doctrines.

Under such circumstances the lapse of centuries scarcely disturbs the repose of the laws, and men find themselves standing in the same crippled posture which was forced upon their ancestors long after their sepulchres have mouldered into dust, and the names of the oppressor and the oppressed are sunk into doubtful traditions.

The laws of the Medes and Persians were proverbially immutable. The institutions of China have undergone no sensible change since the discovery and doubling of the Cape of Good Hope; and the pyramids of Egypt, lost as their origin is in remote antiquity, are not perhaps of a higher age than some of its customary laws and institutions. And it may be affirmed of some of the Eastern nations, that through all the revolutions of their dynasties, it is difficult to point out any fundamental changes in the powers of the government, the rights of the subject, or the laws that regulate the succession to property, since the Christian era.

In free governments, and in those where the popular interests have obtained some representation or power, however limited, the case has been far otherwise. We can here trace a regular progress from age to age in their laws, a gradual adaptation of them to the increasing wants and employments of society, and a substantial improvement, corresponding with their advancement in the refinements and elegancies of life. In the heroic and barbarous ages, the laws are few and simple, administered by the prince in person, assisted by his compeers and council. But, as civilization advances, the judicial powers are gradually separated from the executive and legislative authorities, and transferred to men whose sole duty it is to administer justice and correct abuses. The punishment of crimes, at first arbitrary, is gradually moulded into a system, and moderated in its severity; and property, which is at first held at the mere pleasure of the chief, acquires a permanency in its tenure, and soon becomes transmissible to the descendants of those, whose enterprise or good fortune has accumulated it. Whoever examines the history of Grecian, or Roman, or Gothic, or Feudal jurisprudence, will perceive in the strong lines, which may every where be traced, the truth of these remarks. And it is a matter of curious reflection, that, while the laws and customs of the East seem in a great measure to have been stationary since the Christian era, those of Euiope have undergone the most extraordinary revolutions; attaining, at one period, great refinement and equity; then sinking from that elevation into deep obscurity and barbarism, under the northern invaders; and rising again from the ruins of ancient grandeur to assume a new perfection and beauty, which first softened the features, and then extinguished the spirit of the feudal system.

It is not, however, upon topics of this sort, suggested by a broad and general survey of the past, however interesting to the philosophical inquirer, that I propose to dwell at this time. My purpose, rather, is to offer some considerations touching the past and present state of the common law, and to suggest some hints as to its future prospects in our own country, and the sources from which any probable improvements must be derived. In doing this, I shall attempt nothing more than a few plain sketches, contenting myself with the hope of being useful, and leaving to others, of higher talents and attainments, the more ambitious path of eloquence and learning.

The history of the common law may be divided into three great epochs; the first extending from the reign of William the Conqueror to the Reformation; the second from the reign of Elizabeth to the Revolution, which placed the house of Brunswick on the throne; and the third including the period, which has since elapsed, down to our own time.

The first of these epochs embraces the origin and complete

establishment of the feudal system, with all its curious burdens and appendages; its primer seisins, its aids, its reliefs, its escheats, its wardships, its fines upon marriages and alienations, and its chivalric and soccage services. Connected with these were the distinct establishment of tribunals of justice, administered first by Judges in Eyre, and afterwards by the Courts at Westminster; the introduction of assizes, and writs of entry; and the perfecting of all those forms of remedies, by which rights are enforced, and wrongs redressed. Some of the most venerable sages of the law belong to this period; the methodical and almost classical Bracton; the neat and perspicuous Glanville; the exact and unknown author of Fleta; the criminal treatise of Britton; the ponderous collections of Statham, Fitzherbert, and Brooke; and, above all, the venerable Year Books themselves, the grand depositories of the ancient common law, whence the Littletons and the Cokes, the Hobarts and the Hales, of later times, drew their precious and almost inexhaustible learning. Of these black-lettered volumes few in our days can boast the mastery. Even in England they are suffered to repose on dusty and neglected shelves, rarely disturbed, except when some nice question upon an appeal of death, upon the nature of seizin, or upon proceedings in writs of right, calls them up, like the spirits of a departed age, to bear their testimony in the strife. This, too, was the age of scholastic refinements, and metaphysical subtilties, and potent quibbles, and mysterious conceits; when special pleading pored over its midnight lamp, and conjured up its phantoms to perplex, to bewilder, and sometimes to betray. This, too, was the age of strained and quaint argumentation, when the discussions of the bar were perilously acute and cunning. And yet, though much of the law of these times is grown obsolete, and the task of attempting a general revival of it hopeless, it cannot be denied, that it abounds with treasures of knowledge. It affords the only sure foundation in many cases, on which to build a solid fabric of argument; and no one ever explored its depths, rough and difficult as they are, without bringing back instruction fully proportioned to his labor.

The commencement of the second period is rendered remarkable by the enactment of two statutes, which have probably conduced more than any others to change the condition of real property; and at the same time that they have facilitated its application to the business and the wants of real life, they have in no small degree rendered its titles intricate. I allude to the great statutes of Wills and of Uses, in the reign of Henry VIII. The former statute has crowded our books of reports with cases, more numerous and more difficult in construction than any other single branch of the law. The latter, followed up by the statute of Elizabeth of Charitable Uses, is thought by many to have laid the foundation of that broad and comprehensive judicature, in which equity administers, through its searching interrogatories, addressed to the consciences of men, the most beneficent and wholesome principles of justice. The whole modern structure of Trusts, infinitely diversified as it is, by marriage settlements, terms to raise portions or to pay debts, contingent and springing appointments, resulting uses and implied trusts, grew out of this statute, and the constructions put upon it. And it is scarcely figurative language to assert, that the *scintilla juris* of Chudleigh's case is the spark which kindled the flame, which has burned so brightly and benignantly in the courts of equity in modern times.

Two statutes, equally remarkable, adorned the close of this second period; the one, the statute securing the writ of Habeas Corpus, the great bulwark of personal liberty; the other, the statute abolishing the burdensome tenures of the Feudal Law. These were the triumphs of sound reason and free inquiry over the dictates of oppression and ignorance. They were the harbinger of better days, and gave lustre to an age, which was scarcely redeemed from profligacy by the purity of Lord Hale, and was deeply disgraced by the harsh and vindictive judgments of Lord Jeffries. Yet through the whole of this period we may trace a steady improvement in the great departments of the law. Under the guidance of Lord Bacon, the business of chancery assumed a regular course; and, at the distance of two centuries his celebrated Ordinances continue to be the pole-star, which directs the practice of that court. A more noble homage to his memory, or a more striking proof of the profoundness of his genius, and of the wisdom and comprehensiveness of his views can scarcely be imagined. And it may be truly affirmed, that his *Novum Organum* scarcely introduced a more salutary change in the study of physics and experimental philosophy than his Ordinances did in the practical administration of equity. The common law, too, partaking of the spirit and enterprise of the times, gradually shifted and widened its channels. Courts of justice were no longer engaged in settling ecclesiastical or feudal rights and services. The intricacies of real actions were laid aside for the more convenient and expeditious trial of titles by ejectment. Assizes and writs of entry fell into neglect, and the subtilties of logic were exchanged for the more useful inductions of common sense. Arguments were no longer buried under a mass of learning; and reports, instead of overwhelming the profession, as in the pages of the venerable Plowden, with a flood of ancient authorities and curious analogies, began to be directed to the points in controversy with brevity and exactness. Philosophy, too, lent its aid to illustrate the science; and the criminal law, though occasionally disgraced by abuses, was softened by the humanity, illustrated by the genius, and methodized by the labors of the great luminaries of the law.

The third period may not inaptly be termed the Golden Age of the law; since it embraces the introduction of the principles of commercial law, and the application of them with wonderful success to the exposition of the then comparatively novel contracts of bills of exchange, promissory notes, bills of lading, charter-parties, and, above all, policies of insurance. Lord Holt, with great sagacity and boldness, led the way to some of the most important improvements, by his celebrated judgment in Coggs *v.* Barnard, in which the law of bailments is expounded with philosophical precision and fulness. It is true, that the leading maxims are borrowed from the Roman law, as the beautiful treatise of Sir William Jones sufficiently explains to the humblest student. But the merit of Lord Holt is scarcely lessened by this consideration, since he had the talent to discern their value, and the judgment to transfer them into the English code. The modest close of his opinion in this case shows, how little the law on this subject was at that time settled, and how much we owe to the achievements of a single mind. "I have said thus much" (is his language) "on this case, because it is of great consequence, that the law should be settled on this point. But I don't know, whether I may have settled it, or may not rather have unsettled it. But however that may happen, I have stirred these points, which wiser heads in time may settle." Wiser heads have not settled these points. This branch of the law stands now, at the distance of more than a century, on the immovable foundation, where this great man placed it, the foundation of reason and justice. And, if he had left no other judgment on record, this alone would justify the eulogy of an eminent modern judge, that "he was as great a lawyer as ever sat in Westminster Hall."

The doctrines of the courts of equity during this last period have attained a high degree of perfection, though the origin of them must in many cases be admitted to belong to the preceding age. Lord Nottingham brought to the subject a strong and cultivated mind, and pronounced his decrees after the most cautious and painstaking study. Lord Cowper and Lord Talbot pursued the same career with the genuine spirit of jurists. But it was reserved for Lord Hardwicke, by his deep learning, his extensive researches, and his powerful genius, to combine the scattered fragments into a scientific system; to define with a broader line the boundaries between the departments of the common law and chancery; and to give certainty and vigor to the principles, as well as the jurisdiction, of the latter. Henceforth, equity began to acquire the same exactness as the common law; and at this moment there is scarcely a branch of its jurisprudence, that is not reduced to method, and does not in the harmony of its parts rival the best examples of the common law. Our own age has witnessed, in the labors of Lord Eldon, through a series of more than twenty-five volumes of reports, a diligence, sagacity, caution, and force of judgment, which have seldom been equalled, and can scarcely be surpassed; which have given dignity, as well as finish, to that curious moral machinery, which, dealing in an artificial system, yet contrives to administer the most perfect of human inventions, the doctrines of conscience *ex æquo et bono.*

There is another great name which adorns this period, respecting whom it is difficult to speak in terms of moderated praise, and still more difficult to preserve silence. England, and America, and the civilized world lie under the deepest obligations to him. Wherever commerce shall extend its social influences; wherever justice shall be administered by enlightened and liberal rules; wherever contracts shall be expounded upon the eternal principles of right and wrong; wherever moral delicacy and juridical refinement shall be infused into the municipal code, at once to persuade men to be honest and to keep them so; wherever the intercourse of mankind shall aim at something more elevated than that grovelling spirit of barter, in which meanness, and avarice, and fraud strive for the mastery over ignorance, credulity, and folly; — the name of Lord Mansfield will be held in reverence by the good and the wise, by the honest merchant, the enlightened lawyer, the just statesman, and the conscientious judge. The maxims of maritime jurisprudence, which he ingrafted into the stock of the common law, are not the exclusive property of a single age or nation; but the common property of all times and all countries. They are built upon the most comprehensive principles, and the most enlightened experience of mankind. He designed them to be of universal application; considering, as he himself has declared, the maritime law to be, not the law of a particular country, but the general law of nations. And such under his administration it became, as his prophetic spirit, in citing a passage from the most eloquent and polished orator of antiquity, seems gently to insinuate. "Non erit alia lex Romæ, alia Athenis; alia nunc, alia posthac; sed, et apud omnes gentes et omni tempore, una eademque lex obtinebit." He was ambitious of this noble fame, and studied deeply, and diligently, and honestly to acquire it. He surveyed the commercial law of the continent, drawing from thence what was most just, useful, and rational; and left to the world, as the fruit of his researches, a collection of general principles, unexampled in extent and unequalled in excellence. The law of insurance was almost created by him; and it would be difficult to find a single leading principle in the beautiful system, that surrounds and protects the commerce of our times, which may not be traced back to the judgments of this surprising man. Of him it cannot be said, "*Stat magni nominis umbra.*" His character as a statesman and an orator, as the rival, and the equal, of Chatham and Camden, would immortalize him. But the proudest monument of his fame is in the volumes of Burrow, and Cowper, and Douglas, which we may fondly hope will endure as long as the language, in which they are written, shall continue to instruct mankind.

I have been drawn into these remarks on the character of Lord Mansfield, beyond the scope of my original intention, by my extreme solicitude to impress the younger members of the profession with a due sense of his learning and his labors. It appears to me, that his judgments should not be merely referred to and read, on the spur of particular occasions, but should be studied, as models of juridical reasoning and eloquence. I know not where a student can learn so much, or so well, as in the reports which I have named; and there is scarcely a sentence which dropped from his lips, which may not prove of permanent utility to the profession. Our young men of the present day are apt to confine their reading too much to elementary treatises. The utility of these cannot be doubted. But the reports are the true repositories of the law; and of these none are more interesting and convincing, than those which are graced by the persuasive judgments of Lord Mansfield.

The principal improvements in the law, during the period which has last passed under review, may be summed up under the following heads. 1. A more enlarged and liberal interpretation of contracts. 2. The adoption of the great principles of commercial law, borrowed from the usages of merchants, the dissertations and commentaries of foreign jurists, and the inductions of philosophical inquiry. 3. The enlargement of the remedy by assumpsit, moulding it, as in the action for money had and received, to the most important purposes of a bill in equity. 4. The reduction of many doctrines of the law to systematical accuracy by rejecting anomalies, and defining and limiting their application by the test of general reasoning.

Without doubt, many of these changes were brought about by the enterprise of commerce and the philosophizing spirit of the times. The former rendered indispensable the introduction of many general principles to regulate the complicated business of trade, and to protect and encourage navigation. The latter, by accustoming the profession to more comprehensive argumentations and more perfect generalizations, gradually wore away that exclusive devotion to technical rules and ancient practices, and the narrow policy of the old law, which had been for ages the reproach of the benchers of Westminster Hall. The common law had its origin in ignorant and barbarous ages; it abounded with artificial distinctions and crafty subtilties, partly from the scholastic habits of its early clerical professors, and partly from its subserviency to the narrow purposes of feudal polity. When this polity began to decline, the mass of its principles was so interwoven into the texture of the law, and so consecrated by authority, that it became dangerous, if not impracticable, to disentangle it. There was, therefore, a natural jealousy of changes, lest they should work mischiefs in the venerable fabric. It was not until the current of society had taken a new direction, and commerce had worn its channels wide and deep through the whole country, that the necessities of trade compelled the profession to look abroad for doctrines of more general application. Yet it cannot be denied, that the progress of improvement was slow, and that the genius of Lord Mansfield, by outstripping that of the age at least half a century, accomplished with brilliant success what a few may have ventured to hope for, but no one before him was bold enough to execute. The remarks of Mr. Justice Buller, a proud name in the English law, in the case of Lickbarrow *v.* Mason, fully confirm the views that I have attempted to unfold. "Before that period," says he, "we find, that in courts of law all the evidence in mercantile cases was thrown together; they were left generally to the jury, and they produced no established principle. From that time, we all know, the great study has been to find some certain general principles, which shall be known to all mankind, not only to rule the particular case, but to serve as a guide for the future. Most of us have heard these principles stated, reasoned upon, enlarged, and explained, till we have been lost in admiration of the strength and stretch of the human understanding."

Although the causes, to which I have alluded, contributed in a high degree to the advancement of the law; yet there is another, which, in my judgment, had a decided, though silent, operation in its favor. I refer to the change in the tenure of office, by which the judges, instead of being dependent on the pleasure of the Crown, enjoyed their offices during good behavior. This measure of consummate wisdom forms a part of the solemn act of settlement which fixed the succession of the throne of England in the house of Hanover, and was adopted, not merely to secure the personal independence of the judges, but the purity and independence of the law. The first effect was to check the undue influence of the Crown, through its judicial patronage; the next, and not least important, was to restrain the tumultuary excitements of the people. Men, for the most part, are willing to submit to the laws, when faithfully and impartially administered. If they are satisfied, that the judges are incorruptible, they acquiesce in their decisions, even when they may suspect them to be erroneous, as the necessary homage, by which their own rights and liberties are permanently secured. But if the fountain of justice is impure, and sends forth bitter waters, stained by influences which are not avowed, and yet are scarcely covered; if judges are removed at pleasure and appointed at pleasure, to gratify a favorite or a faction, an arrogant minister or a violent House of Commons; it is easy to foresee, that jealousy will lead to distrust, and distrust to hatred, and hatred to disobedience, and disobedience to resistance, which, if it stops short of treason, will yet utter itself in deep complaints, until public confidence is universally shaken, and armies become necessary to support the execution of the laws. Considerations of this sort have always impressed me with the belief, from the first moment that I ventured into the deeper studies of the law, that the independence of the judges is the great bulwark of public liberty, and the great security of property; and that the Revolution of 1688 would have been but a vain and passing pageant, a noble but ineffectual struggle against prerogative, if the triumph of its principles had not been secured by this practical means of enforcing them. Throughout the reigns of both the Charleses and both the Jameses, it is melancholy to remark the perpetual changes on the bench, induced by favoritism, or discontent, or an attempt to overawe the courts. The noble answer of Lord Coke to the inquiry of the king, in the dispute about commendams, what he would do, if the Crown in any case before him required the judges to stay proceedings, "that he would do that, which would befit a judge to do," is worthy of everlasting remembrance. But it was his solitary answer. To the disgrace of the age, all the other judges, intimidated by the king and his haughty chancellor, "the wisest, brightest, meanest of mankind," promised implicit submission to the commands of the Crown. And even Lord Coke, for his conduct on other occasions, drew from the king the bitter, though perhaps unjust, rebuke, "that he was the fittest instrument for a tyrant, that ever was in England." In the reign of Charles II. the conduct of the Crown was more openly profligate, and its influence was exerted to affect the judgments of the courts, even in private suits. It is matter of history, that Sir Edmund Saunders, after having advised the proceedings in the Quo Warranto against the city of London was promoted to the chief justiceship of the King's Bench, not on account of his talents, his learning, or his virtues, (though great) but on account of his known devotion to the interests of the Crown.

Such are some of the more offensive forms, under which the tenure of offices during pleasure will sometimes exhibit men, from whose elevation of character better things might be expected. But the more silent and unobtrusive influence of *popular* dependence, though less striking to the vulgar eye, is not less subversive of the great purposes of justice. It is, indeed, more dangerous to the liberty and property of the people; since it assumes the attractive appearance of obedience to the will of the majority; and thus, without exciting jealousy or alarm, it tramples under foot all those who refuse to obey the idol of the day. How can it be reasonably expected, that the law should flourish as a science, when the judges are doomed to resist the humors of the prince, or the clamors of the populace, at the peril of those stations, which may constitute their only refuge from pecuniary distress? If the old tenure of office had remained, we might still have possessed many valuable judgments of the later common-law judges. But we should have searched in vain for those bright displays of independence and virtue, for those beautiful arguments in defence of private rights, for those finished illustrations of pure and exalted equity, and for those comprehensive commentaries upon commercial law, which have immortalized their memories. If their places were of any value, they must have resigned them, or remained the timid followers of the old law, without the ambition to improve its doctrines, or the hardihood to encounter the alarm of innovation. Lord Mansfield would scarcely have sustained himself on the bench, in the midst of so many political and professional foes, to utter the thrilling declaration, "I wish for popularity; but it is that popularity which follows, not that which is run after. It is that popularity which, sooner or later, never fails to do justice to the pursuit of noble ends by noble means. I will not do that which my conscience tells me is wrong upon this occasion, to gain the huzzas of thousands, or the daily praise of all the papers which come from the press. I will not avoid doing that which I think is right, though it should draw on me the whole artillery of libels, all that falsehood and malice can invent, or the credulity of a deluded populace can swallow. I can say, with another great magistrate, upon an occasion and under circumstances not unlike, '*Ego hoc animo semper fui, ut invidiam virtute partam, gloriam, non invidiam, putarem.*'"

The review, which has been hitherto sketched, of the history of the common law, however imperfectly, is confined altogether to British jurisprudence. Before the American Revolution, from a variety of causes, which it is not difficult to enumerate, our progress in the law was slow, though not slower, perhaps, than in the other departments of science. The resources of the country were small, the population was scattered, the business of the courts was limited, the compensation for professional services was moderate, and the judges were not generally selected from those who were learned in the law. The colonial system restrained our foreign commerce; and, as the principal trade was to or through the mother country, our most important contracts began or ended there. That there were learned men in the profession in those times, it is not necessary to deny. But the number was small. And from the nature of the business which occupied the courts, the knowledge required for common use was neither very ample nor very difficult. The very moderate law libraries then to be found in the country, would completely establish this fact, if it could be seriously controverted. Our land titles were simple. Our contracts principally sprung up from the ordinary relations of debtor and creditor. Our torts were cast in the common mould of trespasses on lands or to goods, or personal injuries; and the most important discussions grew out of our provincial statutes. Great lawyers do not usually flourish under such auspices, and great judges still more rarely. Why should one accomplish himself in that learning which is more of curiosity than use? which neither adds to fame nor wealth? which is not publicly sought for or admired? which devotes life to pursuits and refinements not belonging to our own age or country? The few manuscripts of adjudged cases which now remain, confirm these remarks. If, here and there, a learned argument appears, it strikes us with surprise, rather from its rarity than its extraordinary authority. In the whole series of our reports, there are very few cases in which the ante-revolutionary law has either illustrated or settled an adjudication.

The progress of jurisprudence since the termination of the War of Independence, and especially within the last twenty years, has been remarkable throughout all America. More than one hundred and fifty volumes of reports are already published, containing a mass of decisions, which evince uncommon ambition to acquire the highest professional character. The best of our reports scarcely shrink from a comparison with those of England in the corresponding period; and even those of a more provincial cast exhibit researches of no mean extent, and presage future excellence. The danger, indeed, seems to be, not that we shall hereafter want able reports, but that we shall be overwhelmed by their number and variety.

In this respect our country presents a subject of very serious contemplation and interest to the profession. There are now twenty-four states in the Union, in all of which, except Louisiana, the common law is the acknowledged basis of their jurisprudence. Yet this jurisprudence, partly by statute, partly by judicial interpretations, and partly by local usages and peculiarities, is perpetually receding farther and farther from the common standard. While the states retain their independent sovereignties, as they must continue to do under our federative system, it is hopeless to expect that any greater uniformity will exist in the future than in the past. Nor do I know that, so far as domestic happiness and political convenience are concerned, a greater uniformity would in most respects be desirable. The task, however, of administering justice in the state as well as national courts, from the new and peculiar relations of our system, must be very laborious and perplexing; and the conflict of opinion upon general questions of law, in the rival jurisdictions of the different states, will not be less distressing to the philosophical jurist, than to the practical lawyer.

It may not be without utility to glance, for a few moments, at some of those circumstances, in which the coincidences and differences are most striking and instructive.

1. And first, as to the regulation of the transfers of property. These are either by the descent and distribution of estates, by conveyances *inter vivos*, or by testamentary dispositions. As to the first, so far as my knowledge extends, the canons of descent in the direct line are the same in all the states. In all the states the children and lineal descendants inherit in coparceny, without any distinction as to primogeniture or sex. In descents in the collateral line, there are some peculiar modifications in almost all the states. In some states there is a difference between the half and the whole blood; in others, a difference between inheritances *ex*

parte paternâ and *ex parte maternâ;* in others, a difference in the order of succession and representation. From the genius of our political institutions, as well as the habits of the people, there is every probability that inheritances will continue to descend substantially in the same manner, as long as our free governments endure. An attempt to establish the English canons of descent could hardly succeed, but upon the ruins of all those institutions, which are considered the best protection of a republican government. Then, as to conveyances *inter vivos.* Lands are universally conveyed by a deed, acknowledged by the parties before some competent magistrate, and recorded in some public records kept for the registry of conveyances of this nature. The ceremony of livery of seizin is obsolete, if, indeed, it have any where a legal entity. The common law forms of conveyance are in general use, and the statute of uses being recognized as a part of the common or statute law of the states, the English doctrines on these subjects are generally adopted. As to testamentary dispositions. Lands are universally disposable by will. The ceremonies by which solemn testaments are evidenced in most of the states, do not materially differ from the English statute on this subject. In Virginia and Kentucky, however, a will wholly written and signed by the testator is good, although there is no subscribing witness. In Louisiana the like provision exists; and it is to be observed, that the preceding remarks are in general inapplicable to this latter state, whose jurisprudence being founded on the civil law, the forms of conveyances, whether they be donations *inter vivos*, or donations *causâ mortis*, are regulated in general conformity to the rule of that law.

2. As to commercial law. From mutual comity, from the natural tendency of maritime usages to assimilation, and from mutual convenience, if not necessity, it may reasonably be expected, that the maritime law will gradually approximate to a high degree of uniformity throughout the commercial world. This is, indeed, in every view exceedingly desira-

ble. Europe is already, by a silent but steady course, fast approaching to that state, in which the same commercial principles will constitute a part of the public law of all its sovereignties. The unwritten commercial law of England at this moment differs in no very important particulars from the positive codes of France and Holland. Spain, Portugal, and the Italian States, the Hanseatic Confederacy, and the Powers of the North, have adopted a considerable part of the same system. And the general disposition in the maritime states, to acknowledge the superiority of the courts and code of England, leaves little doubt that their own local usages will soon yield to her more enlightened doctrines. What a magnificent spectacle will it be, to witness the establishment of such a beautiful system of juridical ethics; to realize, not the oppressive schemes of holy alliances in a general conspiracy against the rights of mankind, but the universal empire of juridical reason, mingling with the concerns of commerce throughout the world, and imparting its beneficent light to the dark regions of the poles, and the soft and luxurious climates of the tropics! Then, indeed, would be realized the splendid visions of Cicero, dreaming over the majestic fragments of his perfect republic; and Hooker's sublime personification of the law would stand forth almost as embodied truth, for "all things in heaven and earth would do her homage, the very least as feeling her care, and the greatest as not exempted from her power."

The commercial law of the Atlantic states has, indeed, already attained to a very striking similarity in its elements. Upon the subject of insurance there is no known difference founded on local usages or statutes. If the law be differently administered, it is not because there is any intention to deviate from the general doctrines of that law, but because the nature and extent of those doctrines have been differently understood. In all the states the same law prevails as to contracts of shipping and affreightment. In most of the states bills of exchange and promissory notes are negotiable, and rest upon the principles, which since the statute of Anne have won their way into the common law. Virginia affords the most striking exception to this remark; for, there, a limited negotiability only is recognized by law, and parties, who are remote indorsers, have no remedy against remote indorsers, except by a suit in equity. Massachusetts, as far as I know, stands alone in her local usage of denying days of grace to promissory notes, unless expressed on the face of the contract. And it is seriously wished, that by a legislative act we might fairly get rid of this anomaly, which has not a single ground, either of convenience, or policy, or antiquity, to recommend it.[1] There are some few other dissonances from the general commercial law, which have existence in some of the states; but it would serve no important purpose to explain them at this time.

3. As to remedies, it would be endless to point out the coincidences and differences between the various states. Remedies are necessarily modified by the wants and manners of the community; and processes, which from habit are thought useful and convenient in one state of society, are rejected as burdensome and injurious in another. In several of the New England States the attachment of real and personal property is allowed upon *mesne* process, not merely to coerce the appearance of the defendant, but to secure a final satisfaction of the judgment, if the plaintiff recovers in the suit. This process, except so far as it belongs to foreign attachments, (analogous to our trustee process,) is utterly unknown elsewhere; and the existence of it among ourselves is contemplated with surprise and regret by those who are accustomed to the general processes of the common law. It is thought a hardship that any person should be liable to be stripped of his property, before it is ascertained judicially,

1 Since this address was delivered, a statute has been passed in Massachusetts, providing that grace shall be allowed on all promissory notes, orders, and drafts, payable at a future day certain, in which there is not an express stipulation to the contrary. St. Mass. 1824, c. 130.

that a good cause of action exists against him; and the danger of abuse has been dwelt upon with much emphasis and force. And yet, perhaps, the annals of no country present fewer instances of abuse than those of the New England States, which allow this mode of proceeding. Personal arrests are rare here, even when property is not to be found; and it is not perhaps hazarding too much to assert, that the writ of capias has subjected more persons to wrongful imprisonment than the unjust attachment of property has to serious loss and inconvenience. Yet it cannot be denied that the latter process is liable to great abuses, and that our exemption from them has resulted principally from the sound discretion and integrity of the Bar. And it is most desirable that some summary practice, analogous to that of discharging on common bail, should be authorized by the legislature, so that fraud, and circumvention, and oppression, may find it more difficult to obtain undue advantages, and compel undue compromises under the influence of this dreaded process.

The remedy for trying land titles in all the states in the Union, except Louisiana and some of the New England States, is the English action of ejectment. It is scarcely modified even in its slightest forms; and John Doe and Richard Roe are the familiar guests, *hospites antiqui et constantes*, of the courts on the picturesque banks of the Hudson, the broad expanse of the Delaware and Chesapeake, the sunny regions of the South, and the fertile vales and majestic rivers of the West. In Louisiana the civil law governs all judicial proceedings, and administers all remedies *in personam* and *in rem*. And I cannot help paying my humble homage to the excellence of this code, which, adapting its remedies to the exigency of the case, gives complete relief without trammelling itself with prescribed forms, which often perplex, and sometimes defeat the ends of justice. In one or two of the adjoining states the old anomalous proceeding, known as a plea in ejectment, still prevails. The use of writs of entry for the trial of land titles is, I believe, unknown, except in Massachusetts, Maine, and New Hampshire. Whether we have derived any important benefit from the revival of the old forms of proceeding in real actions, is a question upon which wise men and sound lawyers may probably disagree. If we have disembarrassed them of some troublesome appendages and some artificial niceties, and rendered them more attractive by the simplicity of their structure; still it must be confessed, that they are not easily moulded to all the uses which modern conveyances and devises render convenient and necessary. The abandonment of these forms in England, from a general sense of their inadequacy to the purposes of justice, and the adoption there, as well as in most of the American States, of the action of ejectment, which has been ascertained by experience to be a perfect and convenient remedy, do certainly carry a weight of authority against our own practice, which if it be not difficult to resist, it would at least be safe to follow.

4. As to the structure of land titles, there is a considerable diversity in the states, and in several of them a great departure from the simplicity and certainty of those derived under the common law. I am not aware that in any part of New England any serious difficulties are to be found on this subject, all titles having had their origin in separate grants, derived directly from the government or confirmed by it, and having the usual formalities and certainty of grants of the crown at common law, or of grants by private legislative acts. The only questions which have been much litigated, are those of boundary which may and do ordinarily arise under grants between private persons; and of these there have been few of any considerable magnitude.

Far different has been the course of proceeding in some other parts of the Union. Titles there have originated in general laws, under which any person might appropriate the property of the state, by following the regulations pointed out by certain statutable provisions. These provisions are very complex, and embrace a variety of stages of title, in each of which the purchaser is obliged to observe great precision, or his rights may be postponed to a puisne holder or claimant. As, therefore, the titles stand upon general laws, and by taking steps to acquire them inchoate rights are obtained, or priorities secured, before the titles are consummated by grants from the government, many very difficult questions have grown up as to the nature, extent, validity, and priority of conflicting titles. A regular grant or patent from the government is no security against other claimants, although it should happen to be prior in point of date to all others. It is liable to be overreached and defeated, sometimes at law and sometimes in equity, according to the local jurisprudence by prior inchoate rights or equitable claims, whether arising under preëmptions, or settlements, or entries, or other matters, which have been held to confer upon an adverse claimant a legal preference.

These remarks apply with considerable force to the land laws of Pennsylvania, Maryland, North Carolina, and Tennessee. But it is in Virginia, and more especially in Kentucky, which derives its titles under the Virginia land laws, that they are realized in their fullest extent. The system of land titles in Kentucky is, indeed, one of the most abstruse branches of local jurisprudence, built up on artificial principles, singularly acute and metaphysical, and quite as curious and intricate as some of the higher doctrines of contingent remainders and executory devises. It affords an illustrious example of human infirmity and human ingenuity: of human infirmity in the legislative supposition, that the great statute on which it rests, was so certain as in a great measure to preclude future litigation; of human ingenuity, in overcoming obstacles apparently insurmountable, by devising approximations to certainty in descriptions strangely vague and inaccurate, thus preserving the legislative intention, and yet promoting the great purposes of justice. The vice of the original system consisted in enabling any persons to appropriate the lands of the state by entries and descriptions of their own, without any previous survey under public authority, and without any such boundaries as were precise, permanent, and unquestionable; and the issuing of grants upon such entries, without any inquiry as to the true nature, description, and survey of the lands, and without any attempt to prevent duplicate grants of the same property. If we consider that Kentucky was at this time a wilderness, traversed principally by hunters; that many places must have been but very imperfectly known even to them, and must have received different appellations from occasional and disconnected visitants; if we consider that the lands were rich, and the spirit of speculation was pushed to a most extravagant extent, and that the spirit of fraud, as is but too common, followed close upon the heels of speculation; if we consider the infinite diversity, which, under such circumstances, must unavoidably exist in the descriptions of the appropriated tracts of land, arising from ignorance, or carelessness, or innocent mistake, or fraud, or personal rashness; — we ought not to be surprised at the fact, that the best part of Kentucky is oppressed by conflicting titles, and that in many instances there are three layers of them lapping on or covering each other. The statute to which I have alluded, required, that the description in the original entry should be so certain, that other purchasers might be able to appropriate the adjacent residuum. The description of the tract might fail in two particulars. 1. It might be bounded by known objects or boundaries, but yet so general and imperfect, that the description might equally well suit different tracts of land, and thus want what has been technically called "identity." 2. Or the boundaries might refer to objects so universal as to defy all certainty, or to objects not generally known at the time by the particular names given to them, or known generally by another name; and then the description would be fatally defective for want of what is technically called "notoriety." Time would fail me to enumerate the doctrines which have started from this origin, or to go over other peculiarities of the system. Perhaps human genius has been rarely more severely tasked, or more fairly rewarded, than in its labors on this occasion. The land law of Kentucky, while it stands alone in its subtile and refined distinctions, has attained a symmetry which at this moment enables it to be studied almost with scientific precision. But ages will probably elapse, before the litigations founded on it will be closed. And so little assistance can be gained from the lights of the common law for its comprehension, that, to the lawyers of other states, it will forever remain an unknown code with a peculiar dialect, to be explored and studied, like the jurisprudence of some foreign nation.

In order to avoid such serious evils, the government of the United States, with a wisdom and foresight which entitle it to the highest praise, has, in the system of land laws which regulate the sales of its own territorial demesnes, given great certainty, simplicity, and uniformity, to the titles derived under it. With a few unimportant exceptions, all lands are surveyed before they are offered for sale. They are surveyed in ranges, and are divided into townships, each six miles square, and these are subdivided into thirty-six sections, each one mile square, containing six hundred and forty acres. All the dividing lines run to the cardinal points, and of course intersect each other at right angles, except where fractional sections are formed by navigable rivers, or by an Indian boundary line. The subdividing lines of quarter sections are not actually surveyed, but the corners, boundaries, and contents of these, are designated and ascertained by fixed rules prescribed by law; and regular maps of all the surveys are lodged in the proper departments of the government. In this manner, with some few exceptions, the public lands in Alabama, Mississippi, Louisiana, Ohio, Indiana, and Illinois, have been sold; and the system applies universally to all our remaining territorial possessions. The common law doctrines have, in respect to these titles, taken deep root and flourished; and the waters, which divide the states on the opposite banks of the Ohio, do not form a more permanent boundary of their respective territorial possessions, than the different origin of their land titles does in the character of their local jurisprudence.

5. Another circumstance, which will probably continue to form a leading diversity in the jurisprudence of the states, is the existence of slavery. This condition of society must necessarily involve a great variety of peculiar provisions, as to domestic policy and foreign intercourse, and as to crimes, rights, and duties, to which no parallel can be furnished in states, whose constitutions or laws prohibit its introduction and existence. The property in slaves, partaking as it does of the double aspects of real and personal estate, being transmissible by descent, and being sold as personalty; being perpetually in demand and marketable, and of course affording solid revenue and wealth; giving value to lands by increasing the culture of agricultural products; being also of intrinsic value and general necessity in climates where little or nothing is accomplished by other labor;—it follows that slavery and its appendages must sink deep into the mass of jurisprudence of the slaveholding states, and furnish much litigation in the shape of contracts, conveyances, torts, or crimes, which other states are happily exempt from, and need not study, either for admonition or instruction.

6. Another diversity which deserves attention is the equity jurisdiction, which exists in complete operation in some states, in partial operation in others, and in others again is obsolete, or totally prohibited. In New England no such establishment is known, as a separate, independent court of equity. In Connecticut and Vermont, general equity powers are exercised by the judges of their superior courts. But in all the other New England States equity powers are confined to a few cases, which are specified and limited by legislative acts. In Pennsylvania a mixed system exists. No court of

chancery, or court exercising chancery powers according to the forms and proceedings of that jurisdiction, is known. But in cases where the parties possess rights, which a court of equity would recognize and enforce, courts of law, following equity in this particular, endeavor to give efficacy to these rights through the instrumentality of remedies at law. Thus, a title to land merely equitable, or resting in a contract of which a court of equity would compel a specific performance, is sufficient to sustain an ejectment at law. On the other hand, in New York, New Jersey, Maryland, Virginia, and South Carolina, courts of equity have a distinct existence and organization, independent of courts of common law; and, as far as I have been enabled to learn, in the remaining states the equity jurisdiction is generally administered by the courts of common law. Wherever the equity jurisdiction is exercised, its admitted basis is the general doctrines of the English chancery. But it is so modified by local statutes, usages, and decisions, that it would be somewhat hazardous for a lawyer at the chancery bar of Westminster to form an opinion as to the authority to give, or to deny relief, however unequivocally those guides might speak, whom he was accustomed to consult. If I were obliged to speak from my own very imperfect knowledge and experience, I should be compelled to declare, that the deviations in America from the established principles of equity are far more considerable than from those of the common law. A more broad and undefined discretion has been assumed, and a less stringent obedience to the dictates of authority. Much is left to the habits of thinking of the particular judge, and more to that undefined notion of right and wrong, of hardship and inconvenience, which popular opinions alternately create and justify. There are, indeed, illustrious exceptions to these remarks, which it would be invidious to point out, though it would be of great importance to follow.

The slight sketches which I have thus ventured to draw of some of the prominent features of state jurisprudence, do, as

I think, justify the suggestion already made, that American jurisprudence can never acquire a homogeneous character; and that we must look to the future rather for increasing discrepancies than coincidences in the law, and the administration of the law. This is a consideration of no small moment to us all; lest, by being split up into distinct provincial Bars, the profession should become devoted to mere state jurisprudence, and abandon those more enlightened and extensive researches, which form the accomplished scholar, and elevate the refined jurist; which ennoble the patriot, and shed a never-dying lustre round the statesman. The establishment of the National Government, and of courts to exercise its constitutional jurisdiction, will, it is to be hoped, in this respect, operate with a salutary influence. Dealing, as such courts must, in questions of a public nature; such as concern the law of nations, and the general rights and duties of foreign nations; such as respect the domestic relations of the states with each other, and with the General Government; such as treat of the great doctrines of prize and maritime law; such as involve the discussion of grave constitutional powers and authorities;—it is natural to expect that these courts will attract the ambition of some of the ablest lawyers in the different states, with a view both to fame and fortune. And thus, perhaps, if I do not indulge in an idle dream, the foundations may be laid for a character of excellence and professional ability, more various and exalted than has hitherto belonged to any bar under the auspices of the common law;—a character, in which minute knowledge of local law will be combined with the most profound attainments in general jurisprudence, and with that instructive eloquence which never soars so high, or touches so potently, as when it grasps principles which fix the destiny of nations, or strike down to the very roots of civil polity.

In comparing the extent of American jurisprudence with that of England, we shall find, that, if in some respects it is more narrow, in others it is more comprehensive. The whole ecclesiastical law of England, unless so far as it may operate on past cases, is obsolete. The genius of our institutions has universally prohibited any religious establishment, state or national. Nor is there the slightest reason to presume, that the imposition of tithes could ever be successfully introduced here except by the strong arm of martial law, forcing its way by conquest. It was always resisted during our colonial dependency; and would now be thought at war with all that we prize in religion, or civil freedom. The numerous questions respecting tithes and moduses, quare impedits, and advowsons, and presentations, the fruitful progeny of that establishment, are gone to the same tomb where the feudal tenures repose in their robes of state, in dim and ancient majesty. In the next place, the right of primogeniture being abolished, and all estates descending in coparceny, and entails being practically changed into fee simple estates, there is no necessity for those intricate conveyances, settlements, and devises, with which the anxiety of parents and friends to provide against the inconveniences of the law has filled all the courts of England. Of this troubled stream of controversy we may indeed say, "It flows, and flows, and flows, and ever will flow on." In the next place, we are rid, not only of the feudal services and tenures, but of all the customary law, of our parent country, the ancient demesnes, the copyholds, the manorial customs and rights, and the customs of gavelkind, and borough English. The cases in which prerogative or privilege can arise are few, and limited by law. Long terms, and leases, and annuities, charged on land, are rare among us; and the complicated questions of contract and of rent, which fill the books, are of course scarcely heard of in our courts. We have no game laws to harass our peasantry, or to form an odious distinction for our gentlemen; and the melancholy inventions of later times connected with them, the spring-guns, and the concealed spears, and the man-traps, never cross our paths, or disturb our fancies. The penalties of a præmunire cannot be incurred; for we neither court nor fear papal bulls or excommunications. Outlawry, as a civil process, if it have a legal entity, is almost unknown in practice. An appeal of death or robbery never drew its breath among us; nor can it now be brought forth to battle in its dark array of armor, to astonish and confuse us, as it recently did all Westminster Hall. These are no small departments of the common law. A few of them, indeed, are almost obsolete in England; but the residue form a body of principles so artificial, and so difficult, that they leave behind them few which can in these respects justly claim precedency.

With all these abridgments, however, our law is still sufficiently extensive to occupy all the time, and employ all the talents, and exhaust all the learning of our ablest lawyers and judges. The studies of twenty years leave much behind that is yet to be grappled with and mastered. And if the law of a single state is enough for a long life of labor and ambition, the task falls still heavier on those who frequent the national courts and are obliged to learn other branches of law, which are almost exclusively cognizable there. When it is considered, that the equity jurisprudence of the courts of the United States is like that of England, with the occasional adoption of the peculiar equities of local law; and that their admiralty jurisdiction takes within its circuit not merely the prize and maritime law, but seizures also for the breach of municipal regulations; when to these are added the interpretation of the treaties and statutes of the United States, and the still more grave discussion of constitutional questions, and the relative rights of states and their citizens in respect to other states;—it cannot well be doubted, that the administration of justice is there filled with perplexities, that strain the human mind to its utmost bearings.

The most delicate, and at the same time the proudest attribute of American jurisprudence, is the right of its judicial tribunals to decide questions of constitutional law. In other governments these questions cannot be entertained or decided by courts of justice; and, therefore, whatever may be the theory of the constitution, the legislative authority is practically omnipotent, and there is no means of contesting the legality or justice of a law but by an appeal to arms. This can be done only when oppression weighs heavily and grievously on the whole people, and is then resisted by all because it is felt by all. But the oppression that strikes at a humble individual, though it robs him of character, or fortune, or life, is remediless; and, if it becomes the subject of judicial inquiry, judges may lament, but cannot resist, the mandates of the legislature.

Far different is the case in our country; and the privilege of bringing every law to the test of the constitution belongs to the humblest citizen, who owes no obedience to any legislative act which transcends the constitutional limits. Some visionary statesmen, indeed, who affect to believe that the legislature can do no wrong, and some zealous leaders, who affect to believe that popular opinion is the voice of unerring wisdom, have, at times, questioned this authority of courts of justice. If they were correct in their doctrine, we might as well be without a written constitution of government, since the minority would always be in complete subjection to the majority; and it is to be feared, that the experience of mankind has never shown, that the despotism of numbers has been more mild or equitable than that swayed by a single hand. This heresy, as questionable in point of sound policy as it is unconstitutional in its language, has hitherto made but little progress among us. The wise, and the learned, and the virtuous, have been nearly unanimous in supporting that doctrine, which courts of justice have uniformly asserted, that the constitution is not the law for the legislature only, but is the law, and the supreme law, which is to direct and control all judicial proceedings.

The discussion of constitutional questions throws a lustre round the bar, and gives a dignity to its functions, which can rarely belong to the profession in any other country.

Lawyers are here emphatically placed as sentinels upon the outposts of the constitution; and no nobler end can be proposed for their ambition or patriotism, than to stand as faithful guardians of the constitution, ready to defend its legitimate powers, and to stay the arm of legislative, executive, or popular oppression. If their eloquence can charm, when it vindicates the innocent, and the suffering under private wrongs; if their learning and genius can, with almost superhuman witchery, unfold the mazes and intricacies by which the minute links of title are chained to the adamantine pillars of the law;—how much more glory belongs to them, when this eloquence, this learning, and this genius, are employed in defence of their country; when they breathe forth the purest spirit of morality and virtue in support of the rights of mankind; when they expound the lofty doctrines which sustain, and connect, and guide the destinies of nations; when they combat popular delusions at the expense of fame, and friendship, and political honors; when they triumph by arresting the progress of error and the march of power, and drive back the torrent that threatens destruction equally to public liberty and to private property, to all that delights us in private life, and all that gives grace and authority in public office.

This is a subject, which cannot too deeply engage the most solemn reflections of the profession. Our danger lies in the facility, with which, under the popular cast of our institutions, honest but visionary legislators and artful leaders may approach to sap the foundations of our government. Other nations have their security against sudden changes, good or bad, in the habits of the people, or the nature of their institutions. They have a monarchy gifted with high prerogatives; or a nobility graced with wealth and knowledge and hereditary honors; or a stubborn national spirit, proud of ancient institutions, and obstinate against all reforms. These are obstacles, which resist the progress even of salutary changes; and ages sometimes elapse before such reforms are introduced, and yet more ages before they are sanctioned by public reverence. The youthful vigor of our constitutions of government, and the strong encouragements, held out by free discussion to new inquiries and experiments, expose us to the opposite inconvenience of too little regard for what is established, and too warm a zeal for untried theories. This is our weak point of defence; and it will always be assailed by those, who pant for public favor, and hope for advancement in political struggles.

Under the pressure of temporary evils, or the misguided impulses of party, or plausible alarms for public liberty, it is not difficult to persuade ourselves, that what is established is wrong; that what bounds the popular wishes is oppressive; and that what is untried will give permanent relief and safety. Frame constitutions of government with what wisdom and foresight we may, they must be imperfect, and leave something to discretion, and much to public virtue. It is in vain, that we insert bills of rights in our constitutions, as checks upon legislative power, unless there be firmness in courts, in the hour of trial, to resist the fashionable opinions of the day. The judiciary in itself has little power, except that of protection for others. It operates mainly by an appeal to the understandings of the wise and good; and its chief support is the integrity and independence of an enlightened bar. It possesses no control over the purse or arms of the government. It can neither enact laws, nor raise armies, nor levy taxes. It stands alone in its functions, without the countenance either of the executive or the legislature to cheer or support it. Nay, its duty sometimes arrays it in hostility to the acts of both. But while, though few, our judges shall be fearless and firm in the discharge of their functions, popular leaders cannot possess a wide range of oppression, but must stand rebuked in their ambitious career for power. And it requires no uncommon spirit of prophecy to foresee, that, whenever the liberties of this country are to be destroyed, the first step in the conspiracy will be to bring courts of justice into odium; and, by overawing the timid and removing the incorruptible, to break down the last barrier between the people and universal anarchy or despotism.

These are dangers common to all the states of the Union; but there are others, again, not less formidable to the National Government. State jealousies and state excitements, arising from accidental causes, or stimulated by local feelings or political disappointments, will continually create a pressure on the Constitution of the United States, or shake those provisions, which are destined to hold the state sovereignties in check. We have lived to see the pointed prohibitions, that no state shall coin money, emit bills of credit, make any thing but gold and silver a tender in payment of debt, pass ex post facto laws, or laws impairing the obligation of contracts, receive, under the guidance of a spirit of over-refined speculation, or the pressure of public calamities, a construction, which, if correct, will annihilate their supposed importance; which will make them an unreal mockery; a false and hollow sound; a dead and polluting letter; a letter which killeth, when the spirit would make alive. We have lived to see this constitution, the great bond and bulwark of the Union, subjected to a minute and verbal criticism, which the common law repudiated even in its most rigorous construction of the grants of kings; a criticism, which scarcely belonged to the stinted charter of a petty municipality. Attempts have been made, honestly if you please, but in the spirit of over curious jealousy, to cripple its general powers, by denying the means, when the end is required; to interpret a form of government, necessarily dealing in general expressions, if it mean to deal with any thing except legal entities and metaphysical notions, like the grant of a free fishery, or an easement, or franchise against common right; instead of interpreting it as a constitution to regulate great national concerns, and to protect and sustain the citizens against domestic misrule, as well as foreign aggression. Even its enumerated powers have been strained into a forced and unnatural posture, and tied down upon the uneasy bed of

Procrustes. And what, let me ask, with becoming solemnity, what would be the consequence, if these attempts, repudiating the old and settled doctrines of the constitution, should succeed? What but to subject it to the independent and uncontrollable interpretation of twenty-four sovereign states; to give it in no two states the same power and efficiency; to weaken its salutary influences, and subdue its spirit; to increase the discords and rivalries of contending states; to surrender its supreme judicial functions into the hands of those, who feel no permanent interest to exercise or support them; in short, to drive us back to the old times, and the old practices under the confederation, when the national powers died away in recommendations, and solemn compacts and pledges were forgotten and contemned, if it did not suit the convenience of states to remember or to redeem them? If the union of the states is to be preserved, (and most earnestly must we all hope, that it may be perpetual,) it can only be by sustaining the powers of the National Government in their full vigor, and holding the judicial jurisdiction, as the constitution holds it, coextensive with the legislative authority. If, by an adherence to some false and glossy theories of the day, we yield up its powers, as victims on the altar of public favor, or public necessity, the constitution will sink into a premature and hopeless decline. It will add another, and probably the last, to the long list of experiments to establish a free government, which have alternately illuminated and darkened the annals of other nations, as renowned in arts and arms, as they were for their advancement in literature and jurisprudence.

Something more I would say on this subject; but time fails me, and I feel, that I am entering on topics far too grave, and solemn, and delicate, for occasions like the present. May I be permitted, however, to say, that the duty devolved upon the profession in these times is of deep responsibility and interest. It depends upon the present age, whether the national constitution shall descend to our children in its masculine majesty, to protect and unite the country; or whether, shorn of its strength, it shall become an idle mockery, and perish before the grave has closed upon the last of its illustrious founders.

In looking to the future prospects of the jurisprudence of our country, it appears to me, that the principal improvements must arise from a more thorough and deep-laid juridical education, a more exact preparatory discipline, and a more methodical and extensive range of studies.

In the first place, it cannot be disguised, that we are far behind the English Bar in our knowledge of the practice, and of the elementary forms and doctrines of special pleading. I do not speak here of the technical refinements of the old law in special pleading, which the good sense of modern times has suppressed; but of those general principles, which constitute the foundation of actions, and of those forms, by which alone rights and remedies are successfully pursued. There is a looseness and inartificial structure in our declarations and other pleadings, which betray an imperfect knowledge both of principles and forms, an aberration from settled and technical phraseology, and a neglect of appropriate averments, which not only deprive our pleadings of just pretension to elegance and symmetry, but subject them to the coarser imputation of slovenliness. The forms of pleading are not, as some may rashly suppose, mere trivial forms; they not unfrequently involve the essence of the defence; and the discipline, which is acquired by a minute attention to their structure, is so far from being lost labor, that it, probably more than all other employments, leads the student to that close and systematical logic, by which success in the profession is almost always secured. Of the great lawyers and judges of the English forum one can scarcely be named, who was not distinguished by uncommon depth of learning in this branch of the law; and many have risen to celebrity solely by their attainments in it. We should blush to be accused of perpetual mistakes in grammatical construction, or of a gross and unclassical style of composition. Yet these are venial errors, compared with those, with which the law is sometimes reproached. Diffuse and tedious as are the modern English pleadings, it cannot be denied, that they exhibit a thorough mastery of the science. We miss, indeed, the close, lucid, and concentrated vigor of the pleadings in the days of Rastall, and Coke, and Plowden, and even of Saunders and Raymond. But our taste is not offended by loose and careless phraseology, nor our understanding distressed by omissions, which betray the genuine "*crassa negligentia*" of the law, or by surplusage so vicious and irrelevant, that one is at a loss to know at what point the pleadings aim, or whether they aim at any. We ought not to rest satisfied with mediocrity, when excellence is within our reach. The time is arrived when gentlemen should be scrupulously precise in their drafts of pleadings, and when the records of our courts should not be deformed by proceedings which could not stand the most rigorous scrutiny of the common law, in form as well as in substance. Exemplifications of our judgments may pass, nay, do already pass, to England; and it ought to be our pride to know, that they will not be disgraced under the inspection of the sober benchers of any Inn of Court. We should study ancient forms and cases, as we study the old English writers in general literature; because we may extract from them, not only solid sense, but the best examples of pure and undefiled language. There is a better reason still, and that is, that special pleading contains the quintessence of the law, and no man ever mastered it, who was not by that very means made a profound lawyer.

Another source of improvement is in the more general study of the doctrines of courts of equity. I do not here address myself to those who expect to practise in such courts, for to them it is almost unnecessary to say, that the study is indispensable. But I address the remark to those who are conversant only with courts of common law. The principles of equity jurisprudence are of a very enlarged and elevated nature. They are essentially rational, and moulded into a degree of moral perfection which the law has rarely aspired to. The arguments in courts of this sort abound with new views and elementary discussions. They present strong and brilliant contrasts to some of the perplexed notions of the old common law; and not unfrequently confirm and illustrate doctrines strictly legal, by unfolding new analogies, and expounding the nature and limits of principles, in a manner full of instruction and interest. It is a great mistake to confine our juridical researches to the narrow path, in which we mean to tread. There is no great mind but feels itself cramped and fettered by such a course; and no moderate mind but becomes thereby ground up into the most dusty professional pedantry. The great branches of jurisprudence mutually illustrate and support each other. The principles of one may often be employed with the most captivating felicity in aid of another; and in proportion as the common law becomes familiar with the lights of equity, its own code will become more useful and more enlightened. In our country, the study of equity jurisprudence has not, until within a few years, attracted general attention; and in New England, from causes which have been already alluded to, it has fallen into more neglect than our advances in other branches of the law would justify or excuse.

Connected with this, and, as a mine abounding with the most precious materials, to adorn the edifice of our jurisprudence, is the study of the foreign maritime law, and, above all, of the civil law. Where shall we find more full and masterly discussions of maritime doctrines, coming home to our own bosoms and business, than in the celebrated Commentaries of Valin? Where shall we find so complete and practical a treatise on insurance as in the mature labors of Emérigon? Where shall we find the law of contracts so extensively, so philosophically, and so persuasively expounded, as in the pure, moral, and classical treatises of Pothier? Where shall we find the general doctrines of commercial law so briefly, yet beautifully, laid down, as in the modern commercial code of France? Where shall we find such ample general principles to guide us in new and difficult cases, as in that venerable deposit of the learning and labors of the jurists of the ancient world, the Institutes and Pandects of Justinian? The whole continental jurisprudence rests upon this broad foundation of Roman wisdom; and the English common law, churlish and harsh as was its feudal education, has condescended silently to borrow many of its best principles from this enlightened code.[1] The law of contracts and personalty, of trusts, and legacies, and charities, in England, has been formed into life by the soft solicitudes and devotion of her own neglected professors of the civil law.

There is no country on earth which has more to gain than ours by the thorough study of foreign jurisprudence. We can have no difficulty in adopting, in new cases, such principles of the maritime and civil law, as are adapted to our own wants, and commend themselves by their intrinsic convenience and equity. Let us not vainly imagine that we have unlocked and exhausted all the stores of juridical wisdom and policy. Our jurisprudence is young and flexible; but it has withal a masculine character, which may be refined and exalted by the study of the best models of antiquity. And the structure of our state and national governments, while it easily admits of the incorporation of foreign maritime principles, at the same time makes it safe, useful, and commendable.

There is yet another study which may well engage the attention of American lawyers, and be, in the language of Lord Coke, both honorable and profitable to them. I mean the study of the law of nations. This is at all times the duty, and ought to be the pride of all, who aspire to be statesmen; and, as many of our lawyers become legislators, it seems to be the study to which, of all others, they should

[1] See 12 Mod. 482, by Lord Holt.

most seriously devote themselves. Independently of these considerations, there is nothing that can give so high a finish, or so brilliant an ornament, or so extensive an instruction, as this pursuit, to a professional education. What, indeed, can tend more to exalt and purify the mind, than speculations upon the origin and extent of moral obligations; upon the great truths and dictates of natural law; upon the immutable principles that regulate right and wrong in social and private life; and upon the just applications of these to the intercourse, and duties, and contentions of independent nations? What can be of more transcendent dignity, or better fitted to employ the highest faculties of genius, than the development of those important truths, which teach the duties of magistrates and people; the rights of peace and war; the limits of lawful hostility; the mutual duties of belligerent and neutral powers; and which aim at the introduction into national affairs of that benign spirit of Christian virtue, which tempers the exercise even of acknowledged rights with mercy, humanity, and delicacy? If the science of jurisprudence be, as it has been eloquently described to be, "the pride of the human intellect," and "the collected reason of ages, combining the principles of original justice with the infinite variety of human concerns," where can we find more striking proofs of its true excellence, than in the study of those maxims, which address themselves to the best interests and the most profound reflections of nations, and call upon them, as the instruments of Providence, to administer to each other's wants, to check inordinate ambition, to support the weak, and to fence in human infirmity, so that it can scarcely transcend the bounds of established rules, without drawing after it universal indignation and resistance? Yet, how few have mastered the elementary treatises on this subject, the labors of Albericus Gentilis, and Zouch, and Grotius, and Puffendorf, and Bynkershoek, and Wolfius, and Vattel? How few have read with becoming reverence and zeal the decisions of that splendid jurist, the ornament, I will not say of his own age or country, but of all ages and all countries; the intrepid supporter equally of neutral and belligerent rights; the pure and spotless magistrate of nations, who has administered the dictates of universal jurisprudence with so much dignity and discretion in the Prize and Instance Courts of England? Need I pronounce the name of Sir William Scott? How few have aspired, even in vision, after those comprehensive researches into the law of nations, which the Introductory Discourse of Sir James Mackintosh has opened and explained with such attractive elegance and truth?

Such are some of the studies from which American jurisprudence may, in my humble judgment, derive essential improvements; and I cannot but indulge the belief that they will be eagerly sought and thoroughly examined by the good and the wise of succeeding ages.

The mass of the law is, to be sure, accumulating with an almost incredible rapidity, and with this accumulation, the labor of students, as well as of professors, is seriously augmenting. It is impossible not to look without some discouragement upon the ponderous volumes, which the next half century will add to the groaning shelves of our jurists. The habits of generalization, which will be acquired and perfected by the liberal studies, which I have ventured to recommend, will do something to avert the fearful calamity, which threatens us, of being buried alive, not in the catacombs, but in the labyrinths of the law. I know, indeed, of but one adequate remedy, and that is by a gradual digest, under legislative authority, of those portions of our jurisprudence, which, under the forming hand of the judiciary, shall from time to time acquire scientific accuracy. By thus reducing to a text the exact principles of the law, we shall, in a great measure, get rid of the necessity of appealing to volumes which contain jarring and discordant opinions; and thus we may pave the way to a general code, which will present, in its positive and authoritative text, the most material rules, to guide the lawyer, the statesman, and the private citizen. It is obvious that such a digest can apply only to the law, as it has been applied to human concerns in past times. But by revisions at distant periods it may be made to reflect all the light which intermediate decisions may have thrown upon our jurisprudence. To attempt more than this would be a hopeless labor, if not an absurd project. We ought not to permit ourselves to indulge in the theoretical extravagances of some well-meaning philosophical jurists, who believe that all human concerns for the future can be provided for in a code, speaking a definite language. Sufficient for us will be the achievement, to reduce the past to order and certainty; and that this is within our reach cannot be matter of doubtful speculation. It has been already accomplished in a manner so triumphant, that no cavil has been able to lessen the fame of the authors. The Pandects of Justinian, imperfect as they are, from the haste in which they were compiled, are a monument of imperishable glory to the wisdom of the age; and they gave to Rome, and to the civilized world, a system of civil maxims, which has not been excelled in usefulness and equity. They superseded at once the immense collections of former times, and left them to perish in oblivion; so that, of all the ante-Justinianean jurisprudence, little more remains than a few fragments, which are now and then recovered from the dust and rubbish of antiquity, in the Codices Rescripti of some venerable libraries. The modern code of France, — embracing, as it does, the entire elements of her jurisprudence in the rights, duties, relations, and obligations of civil life; the exposition of the rules of contracts of every sort, including commercial contracts; the descent, distribution, and regulation of property; the definition and punishment of crimes; the ordinary and extraordinary police of the country; and the enumeration of the whole detail of civil and criminal practice and process, — is perhaps the most finished and methodical treatise of law, that the world ever saw. This code forms also the law of Holland, and, with comparatively few alterations, has been solemnly adopted as its fundamental law by the State of Louisiana. The materials of it were to be sought for among an almost infinite variety of provincial usages and customary laws; and were far more difficult to reduce into system than any which belong to the common law. It is left to the future jurists of our country and England to accomplish for the common law, what has thus been so successfully demonstrated to be a practical problem in the jurisprudence of other nations; a task which the modest but wonderful genius of Sir William Jones did not scruple to believe to be within the reach of a single mind successfully to accomplish.

Gentlemen,—I have thus endeavored, not as I could wish, but as I have been able, amidst the cares of private life, and the distractions of official business, to lay before you some imperfect sketches of the past history of the law, of its future prospects, and of the sources, whence we may derive improvement. May I add, in the language of the eminent living jurist (Sir James Mackintosh)[1] whom I have already cited, that "there is not, in my opinion, in the whole compass of human affairs, so noble a spectacle as that which is displayed in the progress of jurisprudence; where we may contemplate the cautious and unwearied exertions of a succession of wise men through a long course of ages, withdrawing every case, as it arises, from the dangerous power of discretion, and subjecting it to inflexible rules; extending the dominion of justice and reason; and gradually contracting, within the narrowest possible limits, the domain of brutal force and of arbitrary will."

If, in the discussion of these topics, I have suggested a single hint, that may cheer the student in his laborious devotion to the elements of the law; or have awakened in the mind of a single advocate another motive to quicken his eloquence or zeal, my humble labor will not be without its consolations. We are all bound by the strong ties of civil obli-

[1] Introd. Disc. 62.

gation, by professional character, by patriotic pride, and by moral feelings, to cultivate and extend this interesting science. No bar in America is more justly entitled to public confidence than that of my native state; and none may more justly claim respect for its moral, literary, and juridical elevation, than that which I have now the honor to address. Much, however, remains to be done, to satisfy a just ambition for excellence; and every day's experience admonishes us, that life is short, and art is long, furnishing motives at once to excite our diligence, and to restrain an undue ardor in any human pursuit.

When, indeed, I look round, and contemplate the ravages which death has made during my own brief career, not only among the sages of the law, but among those in the fresh bloom of youth, just struggling for distinction,—the consideration fills me with the most profound melancholy. Since we were convened here on the last anniversary, the modest and accomplished Gallison has closed his useful life, and buried with him many a brilliant hope of his parents, friends, and country. I will not dwell upon his distinguished talents and virtues, his blameless innocence of life, his elevated piety, his unwearied diligence, his extensive learning, his ardent devotion to literature, his active benevolence, exhausting itself in good deeds, and "blushing to find it fame." You knew him well, and your sympathies have mingled with the tears and sorrows that embalm his memory. But I may propose him as an example, polished, if not perfect, of that excellence, which the studies I have this day ventured to recommend, are calculated to produce. Tacitus has recorded with affectionate solicitude the life and character of Agricola. May I be permitted to borrow from his admirable page a single passage, to grace the memory of my lamented friend and pupil? "Placide quiescas, nosque, domum tuam, ab infirmo desiderio et muliebribus lamentis ad contemplationem virtutum tuarum voces, quas neque lugeri, neque plangi fas est; admiratione te potius quam temporalibus laudibus, et si natura suppeditet, æmulatione decoremus. Is verus honos, ea conjunctissimi cujusque pietas."

We, too, must soon pass away to the tomb, where our friends and instructors, the Ameses, the Sullivans, and the Dexters, the Lowells, the Danas, the Parsonses, and the Sewalls, are gone before us. We cannot be indifferent to the fate of our children, or our country; and the happiness, as well as the honor of both, is indissolubly connected with the faithful administration of justice. Nor ought we to disguise, that that science which has been the choice of our youth, and the ambition of our manhood, has much in its milder studies to soothe and cheer us in the infirmities of old age. Nor can it be deemed a human frailty, if, when we take our last farewell of the law, we "cast one longing, lingering look behind," and bless those rising lights, which are destined to adorn our juridical tribunals, however dimly they may be descried by our fading vision.

May our successors in the profession look back upon our times, not without some kind regrets, and some tender recollections. May they cherish our memories with that gentle reverence which belongs to those who have labored earnestly, though it may be humbly, for the advancement of the law. May they catch a holy enthusiasm from the review of our attainments, however limited they may be, which shall make them aspire after the loftiest possessions of human learning. And thus may they be enabled to advance our jurisprudence to that degree of perfection, which shall make it a blessing and protection to our own country, and excite the just admiration of mankind.

MEMORIAL AGAINST RESTRICTIONS ON COMMERCE,

ADDRESSED TO THE CONGRESS OF THE UNITED STATES, JUNE, 1820, IN BEHALF OF THE MERCHANTS AND OTHERS, INTERESTED IN COMMERCE IN SALEM AND ITS VICINITY, ON THE DISCONTINUANCE OF CREDITS ON REVENUE BONDS, THE ABOLITION OF DRAWBACKS, AND OTHER RESTRICTIONS ON COMMERCE PROPOSED IN CONGRESS.

The undersigned Memorialists, Merchants and Inhabitants of Salem, in the Commonwealth of Massachusetts, and of the towns in its vicinity, beg leave most respectfully to represent: — That they have seen, with unfeigned regret and surprise, some propositions recently brought forward in Congress, and others advocated by respectable portions of the community, which, in their humble opinion, are calculated seriously and certainly to injure, if not eventually to destroy, some of the most important branches of the commerce and navigation of the United States.

The Memorialists have not the slightest intention of casting any imputation of unworthy motives upon those, from whom, on this occasion, they feel themselves compelled to differ in the most decided manner. They are ready to admit, that many of those who are inclined to revive commercial prohibitions and restrictions, and to change some of the fundamental rules of our financial policy, are governed by motives solely suggested by their own views of the national interests. They are free also to admit, that the manufacturing interests of the country deserve to receive the fostering care and patronage of the government. But, while they make these admissions, they also beg leave to suggest, that the interests of commerce are not less vital to the welfare and prosperity of the Union, than manufactures; and that it never can be a sound or safe policy to build up the one upon the ruins of the other. Under a wise and enlightened revenue system, the commerce of our country has hitherto advanced with a rapidity and force which have exceeded the most sanguine expectations of its friends. This commerce has contributed largely to the employment of the capital, the industry, and the enterprise of our citizens. It has quickened the march of agriculture; and by increasing the value, as well as amount, of its products, has given to the planters and husbandmen a reward in solid profit for their toils. It has also materially sustained the credit and finances of the nation, by insuring a regular and growing revenue, through a taxation scarcely felt, and cheerfully borne by all classes of our citizens. It has also given birth to our naval power, by fostering a hardy race of seamen, and patronizing those arts, which are essential to the building, preservation, and equipment of our ships. It has greatly enlarged, and, the Memorialists had almost said, created, the moneyed capital of the country. And the Memorialists believe, that it cannot be too frequently or deeply inculcated as an axiom in political economy, that productive capital, in whatever manner added to the stock of the country, is equally beneficial to its best interests. Its real value can never be ascertained by the sources, from whence it flows; but from the blessings which it dispenses. A million of dollars added to the productive capital by commerce, is at least as useful as the same sum added by manufactures.

The benefits of the commerce of the United States which have been enumerated are not deduced from theoretical reasoning; they are established by thirty years' experience, since the constitution was adopted. At that time our capital was small, and had suffered for a series of years a continual diminution. Our agriculture was depressed, and our finances were embarrassed. The changes, which a thrifty commerce during this period has contributed to produce, are so striking, that they scarcely require to be stated. There is not a single portion of the country, that has not felt its beneficial influence. On the seaboard, we have everywhere flourishing towns and cities, the busy haunts of industry, where the products of our soil are accumulated on their transit to foreign countries. In the interior, hundreds of towns have arisen in places, which but a few years since were desolate wastes or dreary forests. The agriculture of the old states has grown up, and spread itself in a thousand new directions; and our cotton and our wheat, our tobacco and our provisions, are administering to the wants of millions, to whom even our very name was but a short time ago utterly unknown.

The Memorialists would respectfully ask, if it be not a part of the duty of a wise nation to profit by the lessons of experience? Is it just, is it salutary, is it politic, to abandon a course, which has so eminently conduced to our welfare, for the purpose of trying experiments, the effect of which cannot be fully ascertained, which are founded upon merely theoretical doctrines, at best complex and questionable, and, it may be, in practice, ruinous as well to morals as to property? Suppose it were practicable to arrest the present course of commerce, to narrow its limits, and even to reduce it to the mere coasting trade of the nation, is it clear, that the capital thus withdrawn from commercial pursuits could be as usefully or as profitably employed in any other branch of business? It is perfectly certain, that such a change must be attended with severe losses to the merchants, and with ruin to numerous classes of our citizens, to our seamen, and shipwrights, and other artisans, whose business depends on, or is connected with, commerce. Cases may possibly arise, in which the interests of a respectable portion of the community may be justly sacrificed; but they are cases of extreme public necessity; not cases, where the rivalry and the interests of one class of men seek to sustain themselves by the destruction of another. In a free country, too, it may well be asked, if it be a legitimate end of government to control the ordinary occupations of men, and to compel them to confine themselves to pursuits, in which their habits, their feelings, or their enterprise, forbid them to engage. While the manufacturers are left free to engage in their own peculiar pursuits, enjoying in common with others a reasonable protection from the government, the Memorialists trust, that it is no undue claim on their own part to plead for the freedom of commerce also, as the natural ally of agriculture and naval greatness. Nothing, however, can be more obvious, than that many of the maufacturers and their friends are attempting, by fallacious statements, founded on an interested policy or a misguided zeal, or very short-sighted views, to uproot some of the fundamental principles of our revenue policy, and to compel our merchants to abandon some of the most lucrative branches of commerce,—branches, which alone enable us to contend with success against the monopoly and the competition of foreign nations.

It is not a little remarkable, too, that these attempts, to which the Memorialists allude, are not only repugnant to those maxims of free trade, which the United States have hitherto so forcibly and perseveringly contended for, as the sure foundation of national prosperity; but they are pressed upon us at a moment, when the statesmen of the Old World, in admiration of the success of our policy, are relaxing the rigor of their own systems, and yielding themselves to the rational doctrine, that national wealth is best promoted by a free interchange of commodities upon principles of perfect reciprocity. May the Memorialists be permitted to say, that it would be a strange anomaly in America to adopt a system which sound philosophy is exploding in Europe; to attempt a monopoly of the home market, and yet claim an entire freedom of commerce abroad; to stimulate our own manufactures to an unnatural growth by the exclusion of foreign manufactures, and yet to expect that no retaliatory measures would be pursued by other nations. If we are unwilling to receive foreign manufactures we cannot reasonably suppose that foreign nations will receive our raw materials. We may force other nations to seek an inferior market for their productions; but we cannot force them to become buyers when they are not sellers, or to consume our cottons when they cannot pay the price in their own fabrics. We may compel them to use the cotton of the West Indies, or of the Brazils, or of the East Indies, or the wheat of the Mediterranean, an experiment in itself sufficiently dangerous to some of our most vital interests; but we cannot expect them to carry on with us a ruinous trade when the profit is all on one side. Nations, like individuals, will pursue their own interests, and sooner or later abandon a trade, however fixed may be its habits, where there is no reciprocity of benefit.

There is another consideration which the Memorialists would respectfully suggest, that is entitled, in their opinion, to great weight on questions of this nature, and that is, the dangers and inconveniences which fluctuations in the commercial policy of a nation unavoidably produce. The trade of a nation is of gradual growth, and forms its channels by slow and almost imperceptible degrees. Time, and confidence, and protection, and experience, are necessary to give it a settled course. It insinuates itself into the general commerce of the world with difficulty; and when incorporated into the mass, its ramifications are so numerous and intricate that they cannot be suddenly withdrawn without immense losses and injuries. Even the temporary stoppage of but a single branch of trade throws thousands out of employment; and by pressing the mass of capital and shipping which it held engaged in its service, into other branches, it is sure to produce embarrassment and depression, and not unfrequently ruin to the ship-holders and the merchants. Besides all this, men are slow to engage their capital in new pursuits. They have a natural timidity in embarking in enterprises to which they are not accustomed; and, if the commercial policy of the nation is fluctuating, they feel so much insecurity in it that they are unwilling to yield themselves up even to prospects apparently inviting. No nation ever prospered in commerce until its own policy became settled, and the channels of its trade were worn deep and clear. It is to this state of things that the capitalist looks with confidence; because he may conclude, that if his profits are but small, they are subject to a reasonable certainty of calculation. Another state of things may suit the young and enterprising speculators; but it can never be safe for a nation to found its revenue upon a trade that is not uniform in its operations. The Memorialists most sincerely believe that it is a sound political maxim, that the more free trade is, and the more widely it circulates, the more sure will be its prosperity, and that of the nation. Every restriction which is not indispensable for purposes of revenue, is a shoal which will impede its progress, and not unfrequently jeopard its security.

Having made these preliminary observations, which they cannot deem unworthy of the serious attention of the national legislature, the Memorialists now beg leave more particularly to call the attention of Congress to the measures which have been recently proposed and apparently approved, for the purpose of prohibiting the introduction of foreign woollen and cotton goods, and, as auxiliary thereto, the abolition of drawbacks and credits upon the duties due upon goods imported into the United States; measures, which, if adopted, will, in the opinion of the Memorialists, bring a premature decay and a general distress upon the whole commercial and agricultural interests of the nation.

It has been suggested, both in and out of Congress, when measures have been heretofore proposed, having a direct bearing upon commercial interests, that the silence of merchants ought justly to be considered as an acquiescence in the justice and policy of such measures. Truth compels the Memorialists to say, that the reverse has generally been the case. The merchants of our country have had a deep, and, it is hoped, not an ill-founded confidence in the firmness, the wisdom, and enlightened policy of Congress. They have not been prepared to suppose that old and well-tried and successful systems would be abandoned merely because they were assailed by those whose interests or whose mistaken zeal led them to plan their overthrow. They have believed, (nor is it an idle or vain credulity,) that our statesmen, selected from the whole community, would watch with anxiety and diligence over the interests of all; and that they would distinguish the natural biases of those whose judgments were blinded by a partial view of their own interests, from the just influences of superior political foresight, aided by the most comprehensive knowledge. On many occasions, therefore, in which their interests have been assailed, and, as the Memorialists think, injuriously assailed, the merchants have been silent, not from indifference, but from confidence; not from a sense of propriety and justice, but from a proud belief, that their interests were safe when they were understood; and that the national legislature could not be presumed to want knowledge or inclination to protect them. On the present occasion, however, so wide have been the exertions of the manufacturers, so plausible some of their statements, and so popular, though delusive, some of their doctrines, that the Memorialists feel themselves called upon to resist them in the most serious manner, as injurious to the country, and to throw themselves upon the intelligence and firmness of the representatives of the nation to vindicate their rights.

The subjects of drawbacks, and of credit upon duties, are intimately connected in their general aspects; but at the same time admit of some distinct views, which may well entitle them to separate consideration. Both of them originated at the earliest period of our government, and were incorporated into our first revenue laws. Both of them had the unequivocal approbation of our most enlightened statesmen of that day; and both of them have the sanction of nearly thirty years of experience in their favor. At no period of our political history, until the present, has any doubt been publicly breathed, at least to the knowledge of the Memorialists, of their practical advantages; and during this whole period, our commerce has been progressively increasing. Almost all commercial nations, too, have a system, analogous to ours, ingrafted into their revenue regulations. In all, it is believed, a discrimination is made between goods imported for home consumption, and those designed for exportation; and the duties on the latter are very trifling, especially when compared with the duties usually paid on the former. In respect to credit for duties, the known equivalent is the deposit of the goods in *entrepot;* and the duties are paid only after a limited period, or upon an eventual sale in the domestic market. In Great Britain, to whose system of revenue ours bears the strongest resemblance, imported goods are warehoused under the joint direction and keys of the government and the owner, and the duties are in general paid when they are disposed of in the market. This system of deposit is exceedingly expensive, and onerous, and complicated, and requires large stores in every commercial city, and numerous officers, and is attended with injurious delay. Its object is to give the benefit of credit to the merchant, and it has that effect; but it is at a heavy expense to the government. In this country the same object is obtained at a very small expense, in a much more simple way; and where the officers of the customs act with prudence and vigilance, the risk of loss to the government from the non-payment of the bonds given with sureties for the duties is small, very small indeed, compared with the expense of the other system. In the district of Salem and Beverly, the whole amount remaining unpaid on bonds for goods imported, from the origin of the government to the present time, deducting the debentures due and unpaid on the same goods, is but $1562.46; yet that district alone has furnished many millions to the revenue of the United States.

The fact, however, that in all foreign commercial nations, a credit is allowed for duties upon goods imported, and a drawback is allowed directly or indirectly upon exportation, seems to justify in an eminent degree the opinion, that the system is useful to the public and salutary to commerce. And the experience of this country is entirely in its favor. It may then with some confidence be asked, Why should it be changed? Why should we leave fact for conjecture, and hazard new experiments in cases where the great objects of the government have been already attained? Why should we involve the immense manufacturing, agricultural, and other interests, connected directly with commerce, in distress or ruin, for the purpose of speculating in new schemes, ill adapted to the state of our country, and whose success is yet to be ascertained? It appears to the Memorialists, that it is incumbent on those who would lead the nation into such schemes, to demonstrate their wisdom and policy before they are adopted; and not by arithmetical calculations bottomed on visionary notions, to call upon the nation to reject the lights already furnished by its own experience.

But it may perhaps be inquired, what are the benefits derived to commerce from a credit upon duties? The Memorialists are perfectly willing to state some of the leading benefits, public as well as private; for in this as in almost all the like cases, public and private interest go hand in hand.

It will not be denied that the United States, even at the present time, does not, when compared with the great nations in Europe, abound in moneyed capital. This is in almost every nation a subject of slow accumulation, even under circumstances peculiarly favorable to its growth. But in a young nation, the obstacles are generally great, from the character and various pursuits of the inhabitants, the extent of their wants, and the rivalry and superior advantages for its employment presented by flourishing nations. At the time when the United States adopted its system of credits and drawbacks on duties, its moneyed capital was very small; and the great policy of the government was to give every facility for its full employment. It is obvious, that the more capital is employed in commerce the more extensive will be its reach, and the more revenue will be acquired by the government. Whatever of capital, naturally flowing in this channel, is withdrawn from it, and remains unemployed, is so much lost to the commerce of the country. The duties upon the importation of goods is on an average at least twenty-five per cent. of the value of those goods, or of the capital employed. It follows, that, if this is immediately withdrawn from the funds of the merchant, it is so much loss of his commercial capital. A little detail will render this apparent. Whenever a voyage is undertaken, the merchant invests as much capital as he thinks necessary for the purchase of the goods to be imported, and also as much more as will be necessary to meet all the disbursements and expenses of the voyage. All this is paid in advance. When the goods are imported, they are not immediately sold. The market may be depressed, or the goods be of slow consumption, or not be adapted to the wants of this country, or be ultimately destined for a foreign market. In these cases, and these are common cases, it is obvious, that no immediate sale can be made without great sacrifices, which are wholly inconsistent with any profitable commerce. Even when sales are effected, they are rarely made for cash. A credit is almost universally allowed to the purchaser, varying according to the nature of the commodity and the demand in the market, from four to eight, and even twelve months. Under such circumstances, if a cash payment is required for the duties, it is obvious, that the merchant must either, in anticipation of this demand gradually withdraw from his other business a portion of his capital equal to the duties; or he must divert an equal portion ready to be employed in another voyage; or he must procure money upon credit from other sources, loaded with the payment of interest; or he must consent to make enormous sacrifices by an immediate, forced sale. If he be a prudent, cautious merchant, this very circumstance will operate to prevent him from employing his whole capital in commerce, lest he should be compelled to make ruinous sacrifices; or, by a mere temporary depression of the market, be exposed to the most painful embarrassments. It is with the express view of preventing this palsy upon commercial operations, that a credit upon duties has been allowed by the wise and great men who have hitherto governed our country; and this credit is carefully adjusted to the different portions of our trade, so as to form a credit equal in a general view to the time consumed and credit allowed before the merchant receives his money upon the sales of the goods upon which the specific duties have accrued.

In confirmation of this general statement, the Memorialists would respectfully call the attention of Congress to the East India trade, a trade in which Salem has been long, and deeply, and successfully engaged, a trade too which, however decried by the misguided zeal of some, and the interested suggestions of others, has largely contributed to the revenue of the United States, and yields not in importance to any other branch of commerce. Voyages to the East Indies are undertaken at very heavy expense, and with proportionably large capitals. The goods which are brought home consist of articles either of such high prices, or such slow consumption, or of such bulk and quantity, as require a considerable length of time before they can be sold at a reasonable profit, and the money actually realized upon the sale. The home market, too, for many of these goods is so limited, that ultimately a reëxportation to Europe becomes indispensable; and after a second voyage thus undertaken, the proceeds find their way by a circuitous remittance to England; and then again, before the merchant can realize his funds he must have notice of the remittance, and be able to sell his exchange at a reasonable rate in the market. It is not uncommon for cargoes designed for home consumption, to remain on hand for six months, and sometimes a twelvemonth; and, when sales are effected, the usual credit is from four to eight and twelve months. So that, even with the credit for duties allowed in this trade, it usually happens, that the first and second instalments become due before the proceeds of the sales have been realized, and not unfrequently before the cargoes have been finally disposed of. Yet the duties on these voyages are exceedingly heavy, amounting in some cases to $100,000,—a sum, which even our wealthiest merchants could not readily advance, and which would materially check even their commercial expeditions. It is not too much to declare, that in all probability an abolition of the credit on duties would immediately occasion a diminution of the East India trade one quarter part; and, of course, it would occasion a proportionate diminution of our revenue, and of employment to those whose bread is as hardly earned, and whose lives are as dear, and whose welfare is as important to the country as those of the manufacturers, who seek to found their own fortunes upon the ruins of this commerce.

Some of the ill effects which would result from the abolition of this credit will be obvious to the most careless observer. There is no pretence to say, that there is a superabundance of moneyed capital in our country. The universal opinion proclaims in a manner too audible and too distinct to be misunderstood, that much of the public distress arises from a deficiency of capital. The first effect, therefore, of the abolition of this credit would be a diminution of active capital engaged in trade and yielding a profit. It would be hoarded up to meet the anticipated demands of the government for accruing duties. The revenue would, as has been already intimated, immediately suffer. But other evils of a still graver cast would ensue. Men of small capitals could no longer engage in trade; and, least of all in trade, where the voyages are long and the returns slow. Capitalists, and they alone, could successfully carry on the great branches of commerce; and in their hands it would become a monopoly, which they might wield and manage at their own pleasure.

The young and enterprising merchants would be crushed in their attempts at competition, and would be compelled to navigate only in those narrow channels where trade almost stagnates or yields a scanty subsistence. Another necessary result would be the enhancement of the prices of all foreign articles of domestic consumption. The merchant would charge an interest and profit upon every advance made to the government in the shape of duties; and thus the consumer, upon whom all such charges ultimately fall, would pay these additional charges, together with the enhanced price, which a smaller importation, with an equal demand would necessarily produce. These are evils of no ordinary magnitude; and it is confidently believed, that no wise legislature would introduce them upon mere speculations, thus taxing the whole for the conjectural benefit of the few.

In respect to drawbacks, some additional considerations seem necessary to be stated, inasmuch as the subject has been greatly misunderstood by some of those, who advocate their abolition. The drawback of duties is allowed upon importations of goods into the country, which are reëxported within a year from the time of their entry. The object of the system is to increase the navigation and commerce of the country, by securing to our citizens a carrying trade between distant and foreign nations, in commodities, which are either unsuitable to our market, or of which a great surplus is imported. In every such case, the government derives a direct revenue of two and one half per cent. on the duties of the reëxported goods, this amount being always retained. This is a positive benefit to the government. It is obvious that, if no drawback were allowed upon such reëxportation, no surplus beyond the consumption would ever be imported. For, upon such reëxportation, the goods would be loaded with the whole duty, and the merchant could not afford to sell them so cheap in the foreign market by the full amount of that duty, which would much exceed the whole profit reasonably to be expected upon the goods. Under such circumstances, the shipping and capital of foreign merchants would be exclusively engaged in the carrying trade, and all the benefits of an increased employment for our seamen, our shipwrights, and our ships, including freight and profits, would be entirely lost. This is stated upon the supposition that such a trade could not be carried on, except circuitously, and after an actual importation into the United States. And this is regularly true in respect to the whole trade with the British East Indies, from which we are not permitted to carry on any trade direct to Europe, but are compelled by treaty to land the goods first in the United States.

In respect to the other portions of the carrying trade, the abolition of drawbacks would immediately lead to a direct trade between foreign ports, whenever foreign nations would permit our merchants to engage in it. This would compel them to equip, repair, and man their ships in Europe, and thus to give all their disbursements in this great trade to foreigners. No goods would be imported into the United States either from Europe or India, which were not indispensable for our consumption; and this diminished supply of the home market would increase speculation, and tend to produce, in a very great degree, alternating fluctuations from a depressed to a high market. Commercial adventures would be thereby rendered more hazardous and precarious, since the foreign market would be ordinarily cut off after an importation into the United States; and if at any moment the foreign market should happen to be so high, as to justify an exportation, an artificial scarcity, far beyond what can now ever arise, would immediately ensue in the United States. The abolition of drawbacks would, in this view, operate as a direct tax upon the consumers in this country. It would diminish the productive revenue, and give a foreign character to our seamen and commerce, instead of concentrating both, as their home, in the bosom of the country. Nor should it be forgotten how highly important the carrying trade has hitherto been, and how much it has increased our moneyed capital. During the years 1802, 1803, and 1804, the drawbacks allowed on an average of these years considerably exceeded a quarter part of the duties secured to the government. In the succeeding years 1805, 1806, and 1807, they constituted more than a third of the whole duties. So that on an average of these six years, the last three of which were the most prosperous years of our commerce, the carrying trade constituted nearly one third of our whole foreign commerce. And although this carrying trade be now, from the general state of the world, somewhat diminished, yet it still remains one of the most lucrative branches of our commerce, and yields a steady revenue to the government.

Under this aspect of the subject, the Memorialists would respectfully inquire whether the abolition of drawbacks would not be disastrous to the most important interests of our country, and dry up some of the best sources of our national glory, as well as of our national wealth. Let it be considered, also, that the policy of all commercial nations has uniformly dictated the same course; and that drawbacks, or their equivalent, are uniformly held out as an encouragement to importations; and thus the supply is always kept considerably above the domestic consumption, and enterprise and industry are protected and rewarded. Will America be the first to abandon a policy by which she has so greatly profited? At the very moment when her commerce is gasping for life, from the accumulated competitions of foreign nations, zealous for their own interests, will she aid the blows aimed at its existence, and consign it to a premature destruction?

The next subject to which the Memorialists would respectfully ask the attention of Congress, is a measure very pertinaciously and zealously advocated by manufacturers and their friends — they mean, the entire prohibition, either directly or by duties equivalent to a prohibition, of the importation of cotton and woollen goods. That the tariff of duties now existing is singularly favorable to manufacturers, the Memorialists had supposed would have been freely admitted.

Whatever articles are useful for domestic manufactures pay but a trivial duty; whatever articles can be wrought here are loaded with a heavy duty, varying from fifteen to thirty per cent. ad valorem. The duty upon East India cottons is indeed enormous, and practically amounts to a total probibition. The coarser fabrics of cotton in the British East Indies cost about six cents a square yard, and were formerly imported in large quantities into the United States, and supplied the poorer classes of citizens with necessary though humble clothing. The tariff directs all such cottons to be estimated at the cost of twenty-five cents per square yard, and levies upon them, therefore, a duty of one hundred per cent., or a sum equal to their original cost. During the years 1802, 1803, and 1804, the average imports from the British East Indies were about $3,500,000, of which a little short of $3,000,000 were goods paying ad valorem duties, being principally white cotton goods. In 1807 the goods paying ad valorem duties, imported from the same places, had increased to upwards of $4,000,000. In the same year fifteen ships were employed in this trade from the town of Salem alone. In the past year two ships only have been so employed; and for the four years last past, no cotton piece goods have been imported into this town for home consumption, the duty alone amounting to a prohibition. The sacrifice of this branch of our trade alone has very seriously affected the whole mercantile community engaged in East India commerce, and has nowhere been more sensibly or injuriously felt than in Salem. It has operated, too, as an excessive tax upon the poorer classes of the community, who have been compelled to buy domestic fabrics, to supply their wants at higher prices, which their narrow means could ill afford. It has also annually struck off from the revenue of the government the whole duty upon seven eighths of the importations of East India cotton; that proportion having been absorbed by the domestic consumption. The loss to our ship-owners, and seamen, and commercial artisans, has been proportionately great. And the Memorialists cannot refrain from expressing their decided conviction that this sacrifice was not called for by the public interests; but was a liberal indulgence granted for the exclusive benefit of the manufacturers, and pressed upon the nation by their importunate solicitations. However painful this measure was, it was borne in silence, under the hope, that experience would one day establish the propriety of its repeal; and that the zeal of the manufacturers would be satisfied with the destruction of one branch of commerce, and the heavy duties imposed upon all others. These expectations, however, have not been realized; and the Memorialists now learn with regret that one sacrifice is to be demanded after another, and one prohibition heaped upon another, by the friends of manufactures, until all the sources of foreign commerce are dried up, and domestic manufactures, sustained by enormous bounties, absorb the whole moneyed capital of the nation. The Memorialists would most respectfully, but most solemnly, protest against the policy and the justice of such measures.

And what are the claims, the Memorialists beg leave respectfully to ask, of any one class of our citizens, to throw such enormous burdens upon the other classes of the community? Is the agricultural interest nothing? Is the commercial interest nothing? Is the interest of the public in its revenues nothing? The cotton and woollen trade is already loaded with twenty and twenty-five per cent. duties; and if there be added the freight and charges upon importation, the domestic manufacturers have now an encouragement of a profit of from thirty to thirty-five per cent. more than the European manufacturers possess, if the same articles can be manufactured as cheap at home as they are abroad. In respect to the East india cotton trade, the encouragement is still more striking, the duties upon the coarsest fabrics in that trade amounting, as has been already seen, to one hundred per cent. upon the original cost. And if cotton and woollen goods cannot be manufactured here, and sold as cheap, with all these differences of duty in their favor, does it not establish the conclusion, that such manufactures are not the natural growth of our present situation, and are not adapted to the physical, and moral, and happy condition of the people? Why should the farmer, and the planter, and the merchant, and the mechanic, and the laboring classes of the community, be taxed for the necessaries of life a sum equal to more than one quarter part of their whole expenditures on these objects, that the manufacturers may put this sum into their own pockets?

The Memorialists are no enemies to manufactures; but they most sincerely express it as their deliberate judgment that no manufactures ought to be patronized in the country which will not grow up and support themselves, in every competition in the market, under the ordinary protecting duty; that the only manufactures which can ultimately flourish here, are those which are of slow growth and moderate profit; such as can be carried on by capitalists with economy and steadiness; and that a change of system, which should suddenly introduce great profits, by encouraging undue speculation, and the expectation of inordinate gain would end in the deepest injuries even to manufacturing establishments. The history of the cotton manufactories in New England completely demonstrates the truth of these positions. They grew up gradually under the protection of our ordinary duties in a time of peace, and were profitable to those engaged in them. But when the embargo and non-importation systems produced a deficiency in the foreign supply, a feverish excitement was produced; manufactories were established without sufficient capital; extravagant expenditures in buildings and machinery followed. For a while the demand was great and the profits high; but, upon the return of the ordinary state of things, many of these establishments sunk, one after another, and involved their owners in ruin. And such, in the opinion of the Memorialists, would be the scene acted over again in a few years if the manufacturers could now succeed in accomplishing their present objects. For a short time their establishments would flourish. But in a free country like ours, there would be a reaction of the other great interests of the community; and the national distress and national policy would soon require a repeal of the monopolizing system. A moderate protecting duty is the best support of domestic manufactures, for the very reason that it may be safely calculated on as permanent. It may not encourage speculation; but it will encourage the employment of capital, as fast as there is safety and a reasonable profit connected with it.

Nor will the high prices and eventual insecurity to domestic manufactures be the only evils attendant upon this prohibitory system. It will encourage smuggling and frauds to an extent truly formidable, and never yet practised in our country; and the same effect will arise, though in a more limited degree, from the abolition of drawbacks and credit on duties. The utter impossibility of suppressing frauds and smuggling, where the markets are very high, and the prohibitions very extensive, has been demonstrated by the experience of all Europe. During the most rigorous enforcement of the continental exclusion of British manufactures, aided by civil vigilance, and military bayonets, and despotic power, these manufactures found their way into every part of Europe, from the cottage to the throne. Great Britain herself, insulated as she is, and with a naval force adequate to every object, has not been able to suppress smuggling. Prohibited goods find their way into the United Kingdom, notwithstanding the vigilance of her custom-houses, and the unwearied jealousy of her manufacturers. In the United States, with a thousand miles of seacoast, indented with innumerable bays and harbors, how can it be reasonably expected that the temptations to illicit traffic will not soon outweigh the habits of obedience to the laws, especially when those laws shall become odious, as the supposed instruments of one class to oppress another? Hitherto our country has exhibited a spectacle not unworthy of a free people. Frauds upon the revenue have been comparatively few; and smuggling has been repressed by the general sense of the mercantile community. What system could be more disastrous than that which should hold out permanent temptations to smuggling, connected with a sense of the impolicy and injustice of the laws? The Memorialists believe that one of the first objects of legislation ought to be to make laws auxiliary to the preservation of the morals of the people, by interfering as little as possible with pursuits consonant with their habits and feelings, useful in their objects, and adapted to their wants.

Upon the whole, the Memorialists would respectfully state their unequivocal opinion that all the measures to which they have alluded, are calculated to impair our naval strength and glory; to injure our most profitable commerce; to diminish, in an alarming degree, the public revenue; to promote unjustifiable speculation; to enhance the prices of manufactures; to throw the great business and trade of the nation into the hands of a few capitalists, to the exclusion of the industrious and enterprising of other classes; to introduce general distress among commercial artisans and agriculturists; to aggravate the present distress of the other classes of the community; to provoke and extend an undue appetite for fraud and smuggling; and, in fine, to destroy many of the great objects for which the constitution of the United States was originally framed and adopted.

The Memorialists, therefore, most respectfully ask the interposition of Congress to prevent these great evils, and to promote the general good by a perseverance in that system, under the protection of which our commerce, and navigation, and agriculture have flourished, — a system conceived in political wisdom, justified by experience, and approved by the soundest maxims of national economy.

GROWTH OF THE COMMERCIAL LAW.

AN ARTICLE WRITTEN FOR THE NORTH AMERICAN REVIEW, IN 1825, ON "A TREATISE ON THE LAW OF INSURANCE, BY WILLARD PHILLIPS."

The progress of commerce in modern times will appear more surprising, the more minutely it is examined. It steadily advanced among the nations of Europe during the whole of the eighteenth century; and in the latter half, notwithstanding occasional interruptions by war, it was probably double in extent and value, what it had ever attained in any other equal period. Holland had, indeed, lost her maritime superiority by the destruction of her carrying trade. But the Northern Powers, and particularly Russia, assumed a highly commercial character. Italy was compelled to mourn the departure of the times, when Venice, and Genoa, and Leghorn, covered the Mediterranean with their wealth. But France felt the invigorating influence of trade, and began to court with respect what she had previously cherished only as a source of revenue. Above all, British commerce during this period enjoyed the most signal triumph. Her merchants and mariners were familiar with the whole globe, with the Baltic and the Levant, the Black and the White Sea, the Atlantic and the Pacific, with the Americas and the Indies, with the fisheries of Newfoundland and Greenland, with the fur-trade of the Indians, the timber, hemp, and manufactures of the North, the cottons, spices, and teas of the East, and with the gums, drugs, ivory, and flesh of Africa. It is probably short of the real state of the case to assert, that the commercial capital of Great Britain was quadrupled during the reign of George the Third. Of the causes of this vast increase it is beside our present purpose to enter into an examination. But there can be doubt that her navigation has been essentially aided by the improved state of her manufactures, arising as well from superior skill and workmanship, as from her wonderful inventions in cotton machinery. She now exports to the East Indies and China cotton goods of her own manufacture, to an immense value, which she formerly imported from those countries. And the unrivalled beauty and excellence of fabrics have not only suspended the use of those of foreign origin within her own dominions, but have enabled her in a great measure, to command all the open markets of the world.

Under such circumstances it would be a natural inference that there had been a corresponding advancement of her commercial law. The conclusion would seem natural, if not irresistible, that a people distinguished for centuries by their commercial activity and enterprise must have been under the protection of a well-settled system of commercial jurisprudence. Philosophers and practical jurists would ask how it would be possible for the infinite variety of business, growing out of an extensive foreign trade, to be adjusted, without resort to some well-known rules and general principles. Strange however, as it may seem, it is undeniable that England had made very little progress in commercial law, at so late a period as the commencement of the reign of George the Third. Yet she had been a commercial nation to a considerable extent, from the reign of Elizabeth; and for more than a century had possessed plantations and colonies whose population and trade perpetually invigorated her navigation.

A slight historical review will put this matter beyond any reasonable controversy. One of the earliest English works on maritime law is Malynes's Lex Mercatoria, published in 1622, in the reign of James the First. Welwood had a few years before printed his Abridgment of the Sea Laws; but it is principally a collection of the rules and ordinances of foreign countries. It is remarkable that Malynes refers to no antecedent English writer on the subject of his treatise, and, except in a very few unimportant instances, to no English adjudications. His work is principally a compendium of commercial usages not confined to England, but supposed by him to be common to all the maritime states of Europe. It is quite a meagre and loose performance, and contains few principles that are now of any practical importance. He has two or three short chapters upon bills of exchange, which show that the doctrines upon that subject, then familiar on the Continent, were not much known in England except as usages among merchants. He laments, that negotiable promissory notes, which then circulated among all the commercial cities of the neighboring nations, were strangers to the jurisprudence of England. In fact, they were not introduced into general use, until near the close of the reign of Charles the Second. Lord Holt, in the case of Buller *v.* Crisp, (6 Mod. Rep. 29,) decided in the second year of Queen Anne's reign, said, "I remember when actions upon *inland* bills did first begin; and there they laid a *particular* custom between London and Bristol, and it was an action against the accepter. The defendant's counsel would put them to prove the custom; at which Hale, Chief Justice, laughed and said, *they had a hopeful case of it.*" Lord Holt himself stubbornly denied the negotiability of promissory notes; and, in this very case of Buller *v.* Crisp, it was proved that these notes had been "used for a matter of *thirty* years." It is familiar to the profession that an Act of Parliament was found necessary to put promissory notes upon the same footing as inland bills of exchange, although "this laudable custom," as Malynes calls it, had been long established on the Continent. Malynes devoted five chapters, containing in all about *fifteen* folio pages, to the subject of insurance. We do not recollect, that in the whole of the discussion, a single reference is made to any English adjudication. It is, indeed, sufficiently apparent, that the author drew almost all his materials from foreign sources. The earliest case, indeed, that is to be found on a policy of insurance, is cited by Lord Coke in Dowdale's case, (6 Co. 48,) as having been decided in 30th and 31st Elizabeth; and from the manner in which he refers to it, as well as from the point in judgment, it is manifest that the action was then a novelty.

In 1651, Mr. Marius, a notary public, published his book, entitled, "Advice concerning Bills of Exchange," which went through several editions, and was the only work of much reputation that appeared on this subject in England until after the lapse of a century. It is altogether a practical treatise, referring for authority to the common usages of merchants, and pretending to no aid from any acknowledged doctrines of the English law. At the distance of fifty years after Malynes, Mr. Molloy, a barrister-at-law, published his work, De Jure Maritimo et Navali. The subject of insurance is despatched in one short chapter; and, though here and there a few short notes of English cases are interspersed, the substance is essentially what is found in Malynes. So that it may be fairly inferred, that, during the intermediate period little progress had been made in the true understanding of this branch of the law. Indeed, its real importance was so imperfectly estimated by the common lawyers, that Molloy triumphantly observes, "The policies now-a-days are so large, that almost all those curious questions that former ages and the civilians, according to the law marine, nay, and the common lawyers too, have controverted, are now out of debate. Scarce any misfortune that can happen, or provision to be made, but the same is taken care for in the policies that are now used; for they insure against heaven and earth, stress of weather, storms, enemies, pirates, rovers, &c., or whatever detriment shall happen or come to the thing insured, &c., is provided for." This would be strong language to use even in our days, when the legal construction of the terms and the risks of policies has been settled, after very numerous and expensive litigations. But for that day, and from a lawyer too, the language is most extraordinary; and could arise only from gross ignorance of the vast extent and variety of the subject.

In respect to navigation and shipping, which now form so large heads of commercial law, the information given by these treatises is miserably defective. It is given in three or four chapters containing little more than abstracts from the laws of Oleron, and from the short maritime titles in the civil law and its commentators. And yet these treatises, for we need hardly advert to Mr. Magens's Essay on Insurances, published so late as 1755, contain the substance of all English elementary collections of maritime jurisprudence, down to the period when Lord Mansfield succeeded Sir Dudley Ryder, as Chief Justice of the King's Bench. Nor was this deficiency owing to the want of talents or industry on the part of the compilers. They accumulated most of the valuable English materials within their reach. The reports furnished very few principles, and still fewer illustrations of general application. It is true, that Lord Holt, in his famous decision in the case of Coggs *v.* Barnard, in which *per saltum* he incorporated the whole civil law of bailments into the common law, led the way to a more exact understanding of the law of shipping; but the actual application of his principles belongs to a later age.

That there is no exaggeration in this statement of the uncertainty and defects of the English law on maritime subjects, will be still more fully evinced by reference to some of the best authors. Mr. Justice Blackstone, in his very elegant and classical Commentaries, a work professing to contain a summary of the principles of English law, treats the subject of insurance in a single paragraph; and, after defining the contract, and showing it not to be usurious, briefly adds, "The learning relating to these insurances hath, of *late years*, been greatly improved by a series of judicial decisions, which have now established the law in such a variety of cases, that, if well and judiciously collected, they would form a very complete title in a code of commercial jurisprudence. But being founded on equitable principles, which chiefly result from the special circumstances of the case, it is not easy to reduce them to any *general heads* in mere elementary treatises." Such was the view of a very competent judge on the state of the law in the year 1765. Mr. Park, in the introduction to his system, after adverting to the history of the establishment of the court of policies of assurance in the reign of Queen Elizabeth, and its having subsequently fallen into disuse, and probably into disrepute, observes, "But, though the court of policies of assurance has been long disused, though it is near a century since questions of this nature became chiefly the subject of common law jurisdiction; yet, I am sure I rather go beyond bounds, if I assert, that in all our reporters, from the reign of Queen Elizabeth to the year 1756, when Lord Mansfield became Chief Justice of the King's Bench, there are *sixty* cases upon matters of insurance. Even those cases which are reported are such loose notes mostly of trials at *nisi prius*, containing a short opinion of a single judge, and *very often no opinion at all*, but merely a general verdict. From hence it must necessarily follow, that as there have been but few positive regulations upon insurances, the principles on which they were founded could never have been widely diffused, nor very generally known." Mr. Marshall in general terms confirms these observations. After referring to the establishment of the two great English insurance companies by the statute of 6th George I., ch. 18, he proceeds to say, "From this time it may reasonably be supposed that all suits on policies of insurance were brought in the courts of common law; and yet but few questions on this subject appear to have been determined in the courts of Westminster, before the middle of the last [eighteenth] century. Whether this arose from the number of insurances in England being inconsiderable compared to what it has since become, or from the parties being still in the habit of settling their difference by arbitration, or from both these causes united, it is not now easy to determine." Mr. Miller gives a similar view of the English law, and in marked terms attributes its great improvement to Lord Mansfield; and then, speaking of his own country in 1787, adds the following remarks: "In Scotland the improvements of this branch of law have been still later than in England, as might be expected from the slower growth of its commerce. Although the decisions of the principal court of justice have been pretty regularly collected, for more than a century; yet the first decisions, which, strictly speaking, relate to insurance, are all, except one, within the course of the last ten years. During this period, however, the trade of insuring has risen to a very great height; and the decisions of the Court of Session upon that subject have become proportionably comprehensive and systematic."

What renders this state of the English law the more extraordinary, is the fact, that almost all the important general principles of commercial jurisprudence had, for more than three quarters of a century, been reduced to a very clear and practical code in France. The very early treatise on insurance, called Le Guidon, was republished by Cleirac, in his Us et Coutumes de la Mer, in 1671. In 1673, Louis the Fourteenth published his Ordinance upon Commerce, which, among other things deals largely upon the doctrines of bills of exchange and promissory notes and orders. This was followed by the truly admirable Ordinance of 1681, in which the whole law of navigation, shipping, insurance, and bottomry is collected in a most systematic and masterly manner. It would be a very narrow and unjust view of these ordinances, to consider them as mere collections of the municipal regulations of France. They are more properly collections of those commercial principles and usages, which the experience of merchants had found most wise and convenient in their intercourse, and which the habits of business and the necessities of trade, had gradually introduced into favor among all modern maritime nations. Yet the English common lawyers, if not profoundly ignorant of the value of this code, then passed it by with obstinate indifference, and contented themselves with a proud reliance on the old doctrines of Westminster Hall, as adequate to all the exigencies of modern society.

It seems to have been thought somewhat difficult to account in a satisfactory manner for this state of things, especially as Mr. Magens, referring to the period when he wrote, states, " It must be allowed, that the business of insurance is carried to a much greater extent in London than in any other country in Europe. Insurances are daily made here on adventures by foreign ships, as well as others, whose risks are wholly determinable in foreign dominions." Mr. Park and Mr. Marshall obviously consider the subject as involved in much obscurity, and prudently, if not warily, abandon it to the conjectures of the reader.

To us it appears to admit of a very simple solution, although one which the pride of the profession might not choose to point out, without confessing the fallibility of the system. It is, that the common law was an *utter stranger* to the principles of commercial jurisprudence, and slowly and reluctantly admitted them into its bosom; so that the age was always greatly in advance of the doctrines of the judicial tribunals. The ancient law dealt altogether in feudal tenures and doctrines, abounding in scholastic subtilties and refinements, and nice and curious distinctions, much better fitted for the times of chivalry and feudal burdens, than for the manhood of commerce. It had a narrow and technical mode of expounding contracts, and a still more narrow and unsatisfactory mode of enforcing them. Instead of widening its channels to accommodate the active business of life, the whole was compelled to pass, as it might, within the ancient boundaries. The subtilties of pleading, the difficulty of enforcing various defences, and the inconveniences of screwing down general merits into established forms, embarrassed every remedy upon contracts of a special nature, and drove the parties to seek redress in the then infant, and of course very imperfect, administration of equity.

When the spirit of English commerce had embarked vast interests in trade, it found itself without any encouragement from the law, and endeavored to work its way to its rights and its duties, by the aid of lights reflected from other countries. English merchants became familiar with foreign usages, and soon adopted them into the habits of their business, for want of a more certain guide. These usages soon became general; and, first, as a matter of honor, and, then as a customary law they fastened themselves upon all the transactions of trade. But it was very gradually that the common law recognized them in any shape, and always with a cold, hesitating, and jealous caution. Slade's Case, in 4th Coke's Reports, shows how unwilling the courts of common law were to entertain the action of assumpsit in the plainest cases. They clung with obstinate reverence to the old forms of the action of debt, and found the Benchers of the Inns of Court always ready to sound the alarm against innovations. But the doctrine now universally admitted of giving equitable defences in evidence, and sustaining equitable claims in the action of assumpsit, would have astonished Westminster Hall, almost down to the period of the Revolution of 1688, and encountered adversaries even in the days of Lord Mansfield. What would one say if he were now told, that, upon a bargain to deliver, at a certain price, twenty quarters of wheat every year, during the life of the party, no action could lie for any breach of the annual delivery until the party was dead? And yet this was certainly the law, while the action of debt was the sole remedy, (as it was for ages,) for debt did not lie for any breach, until all the days were incurred, that is, until the agreement was ended by the death of the party, however inconsistent it might be with the intention of the contract. Nay, even now, the action of debt stands on the same nicety, and cannot be brought upon a note for money payable by instalments, until all the days of payment are past. The sagacity of the old law discovered, that a single action only ought to be brought upon a single contract; and to support an action for each instalment would be to make the contract divisible. Such a conclusion, though readily reconcilable with common sense and the intention of the parties, was abhorrent to the settled forms in the Register. Such were the narrow views of the old lawyers; and the judges at length tasked their wits in supporting the new device of the action of general assumpsit, the history of which has been given with great ability by Lord Loughborough, in the case of Rudder *v.* Price, in Henry Blackstone's Reports. How utterly inadequate must such a system have been for the infinite diversity of contracts in our day!

If the difficulties which have been adverted to applied to contracts generally, they must have applied with far greater force to commercial contracts, which are so mixed up with usages and negotiations, unknown to the common law, and are so loose in their terms and general in their obligations. In fact, the Admiralty was the only court in which maritime law was much understood or studied; and this court had the misfortune to labor under the heavy displeasure of the courts at Westminster. The civilians were always looked upon with forbidding jealousy, and every effort was made to undervalue their learning, and depress the popularity of the civil law. We know well, what were the causes of this conduct; and do not mean to insinuate, that it was without a very strong apology. But it is, nevertheless, true, that from this very source, this disparaged civil law — this great fountain of rational jurisprudence — the common law has borrowed, without acknowledgment, all that is most useful and important in its own doctrines of contract.

It were easy to multiply these observations, and to demonstrate their correctness, by exhibiting in detail the manner, in which the remedies upon commercial contracts were hampered by technical proceedings under the old law. But such a detail would be very dry, and, though matter of curiosity, would scarcely repay the labor of perusal, even to a professional reader. It has, indeed, often been said, that the law-merchant is a part of the common law of England; and my Lord Coke has spoken of it in this manner in his Institutes; though it would be somewhat difficult to find out, what part of the law-merchant, as we now understand it, existed at that period. If the expression, that the *lex mercatoria* is a part of the common law, be any thing more than an idle boast, it can mean only, that the general structure of the common law is such, that, without any positive act of the legislature, it perpetually admits of an incorporation of those principles and practices, which are from time to time established among merchants, and which, from their convenience, policy, and consonance with the general system, are proper to be recognized by judicial tribunals. In this sense, the expression is perfectly correct; in any other sense, it has a tendency to mislead.

Almost all the principles, that regulate our commercial concerns, are of modern growth, and have been ingrafted into the old stock of the law by the skill of philosophical, as well as practical, jurists. One of the leading cases, in which there is some flourish made about this maxim, that the law-merchant is part of the common law, is Vanheath *v.* Turner, in the nineteenth year of the reign of King James the First. It is reported in Winch's Reports; and, as it happens now to lie open before us, we will extract the substance of it, to show how commercial contracts were dealt with at that period. It was a special action, and Winch states it thus: "Peter Vanheath brought an action against Turner, and declared upon the *custom of merchants*, that, if any merchant, over the sea, deliver money to a factor, and make a bill of exchange under his seal, and this is subscribed by the merchant, or by any of the company of such merchants, that the merchant himself, or all the company, or any one in particular, may be charged to pay that; and he showed, that one merchant was factor of the company, of which the defendant was one, and that merchant did substitute one G., to whom the plaintiff delivered £100 upon a bill of exchange, to which bill one B., being one of the company, set his hand in England, and so the action accrued to the plaintiff. The defendant pleaded, *nil debet per legem;* and upon that the plaintiff demurred in law, and the question was, whether the defendant might wage his law." This is Winch's statement of the case, very imperfect to be sure, but by which it appears to have been the case of a bill of exchange, drawn for money received of the payee, by the agent of a factor of an English partnership on the company, and accepted by one of the partners, and, upon that acceptance, the suit was brought against the defendant, who was one of the partners. Now the first thing that strikes us, is, that so little did the common law recognize the custom of merchants, that it was necessary to set it forth specially in the declaration, so that it might appear, how the custom bound the party; and the court might decide, whether it was good or not. After the argument, Lord Chief Justice Hobart is reported to have delivered his opinion as follows: "If the bailiff at the common law make a substitute, the substitute is not chargeable, but here the custom will bind the law. Secondly, he said, two or three merchants trade over the sea, who made a factor there, who takes money there, and gives a bill, and this is subscribed by one of the company; that this should bind all or any of the company *is not a good custom;* and the custom of merchants is part of the common law of this realm, of which the judges ought to take notice; and if any doubt arise to them about their custom, they may send for the merchants to know their custom, as they may send for the civilians to know their law; and he thought the defendant ought to be admitted to wage his law." Now, independently of the objection, that, if the defendant were admitted to wage his law, that is to say, discharge himself from the debt by taking his oath, that he did not owe it, which of itself would almost extinguish the negotiability of bills, it would sound very odd at this day to hear any such doctrine assumed, as that respecting the badness of the custom. It is now the plain mercantile law, as it always was common sense, that the acts of a factor within the scope of his authority, whether done by himself or his substitute, bind the partnership, for which he acts; and the acts of a partner in the partnership business in like manner bind the whole. Such was at that period, as it should seem, the custom of merchants; but it was strange to the common lawyers, and seems to have harmonized very little with the notions of the court. Yet Lord Hobart was an eminent judge; and we are to attribute his views, not to a want of sagacity, but to a steady adherence to the rigid doctrines of the common law as to bailiffs and customs, to which the old lawyers clung with a pertinacious idolatry. The truth is, that these gentlemen were, from habit and professional feeling, wedded to the artificial notions of the old system, and strenuously resisted almost every innovation upon it, both in Parliament and out; and every advance made in adopting the custom of merchants, until the days of Lord Mansfield, was a victory gained, by the spirit of the age and the influence of commerce, over professional prejudices.

And this leads us to say a few words upon the actual administration of insurance law, during the days of Lord Mansfield, and of the improvements made by him. We do not know, that it can be done with more brevity than by quoting an extract from Mr. Park.

"In former times," says he, "the whole of the case was left generally to the jury,[1] without any minute statement from the bench of the principles of law, on which insurances were established; and, as the verdicts were general, it was almost impossible to determine from the reports we now see,

[1] Very much as it used to be within our early recollection in the courts of Massachusetts.

upon what grounds the case was decided. Nay, even if a doubt arose in point of law, and a case was reserved upon that doubt, *it was afterwards argued in private, at the chambers of the judge who tried the cause, and by his single decision the parties were bound.* Thus, whatever his opinion might be, it was never promulgated to the world, and could never be the rule of decision in any future case. Lord Mansfield introduced a different mode of proceeding; for, in his statement of the case to the jury, he enlarged upon the rules and principles of law, as applicable to that case, and left it to them to make the application of those principles to the facts in evidence before them. So that, if a general verdict were given, the ground on which the jury proceeded, might be more easily ascertained. Besides if any real difficulty occurred in point of law, his lordship advised the counsel to consent to a special case, &c. &c. These cases are afterwards argued, *not before the judge in private*, but in *open court*, before *all the judges* of the bench, from which the record comes. Thus, nice and important questions are now not hastily and unadvisedly decided; but the parties have their case seriously considered and debated by the whole court; the decision becomes notorious to the world; it is recorded for a precedent of law, arising from the facts found; and serves as a rule to guide the opinion of future judges."

The commendation of Lord Mansfield, which this extract implies, falls very far short of his real merits. The change in the course of proceedings did much; but the genius, liberality, and extensive learning of this extraordinary man gave a new and enduring vigor to the system itself. He may be truly said to have created the commercial law of England; and during his long, active, and splendid life, it attained a maturity and perfection which, perhaps, no other nation can boast, and which will transmit his name to posterity as one of the greatest benefactors of jurisprudence. The achievement was not, indeed, the result of his own unassisted mind. He read extensively the maritime laws of foreign countries, and with an admirable mixture of boldness, discretion, and sagacity, infused all their most valuable principles into the municipal code of England. At the distance of half a century, one looks back with wonder upon the labors of this single judge. His successors have here and there added some pillars to the edifice; but the plan, the proportions, the ornaments, the substructions, all that is solid, and fundamental, and attractive belong to him as the original architect. Standing in the temple of commercial law, the most sober jurist, while contemplating Lord Mansfield's labors, might with enthusiasm exclaim, *Si monumentum quæris, circumspice.* Dropping, however, figurative language, we may with plain gravity venture to suggest a doubt, whether the deviations from his doctrines, introduced by his successors, have not been inconvenient in practice, and mischievous in principle. They partake too much of the subtilties and technical refinements of the common law, and stand little upon general reasoning, and those analogies, which equity and a comprehensive view of the business of commerce would commend for adoption. Lord Kenyon was an honest, intelligent, and learned magistrate; but from habit, and education, and perhaps original cast of mind, he does not seem ever to have entered into the true spirit of commercial jurisprudence. He took no comprehensive principles in his range, and contented himself by administering the maritime law as he found it, without any ambition to extend its boundaries. Lord Ellenborough possessed a more powerful and vigorous mind. But his early reading beyond the walks of the common law, does not seem to have been very extensive; and he manifested on many occasions a desire to bring down the maritime doctrines to the standard of the common law, rather than to give to the latter the expansion of universal jurisprudence. He was certainly a great judge, of a clear, decisive, and rapid mind, but devoted to England, and feeling little enthusiasm and less curiosity to embark in foreign studies. The times, too, in which he lived were not propitious to any extensive researches into continental jurisprudence. They were times of deep political and national struggles, when the spirit of war and conquest attempted to overturn the established doctrines of public law; and those who clung to old institutions felt, that resistance to innovation was safety, and that dangers lurked in ambush under the cover of general principles. Fortunate will it be, however, for England, if in the present peaceful times there shall be found a successor of Lord Mansfield who breathes his liberal spirit, and fills up his splendid outline of principles.

It cannot, however, be disguised that there are a national pride and loftiness of pretension occasionally mixed up in the character of Englishmen which lead them, especially as public men, to look down, sometimes with contempt, but more generally with indifference upon the usages, laws, and institutions of other countries. *Nil admirari* is not always a safe or useful national motto. The English bar is not exempt from this infirmity, and betrays it sometimes when it would be more honorable to seek instruction from foreign sources. It is curious to observe how little of foreign jurisprudence is brought into the discussions of their courts of common law (for it is far otherwise in their admiralty and civil law courts) upon topics which seem most powerfully to demand its introduction. Even upon questions of the operation of the Lex Loci, how rarely has continental or even Scottish jurisprudence been cited with effect in these tribunals! Ireland is separated but by a narrow strait. Her jurisprudence is in substance that of England. Her most distinguished lawyers and judges have been bred in the English Inns of Court. In eloquence, in learning, in general ability, they are inferior to few in the united kingdom. Yet, who ever heard the citation in an English court of an Irish decision? With the exception of a few of Lord Redesdale's, which probably owe their admittance into English society to his elevated rank in the House of Lords, we scarcely recollect any in the course of our reading. Why should they not be cited? Was Sir

John Mitford, when he wrote his excellent Treatise on Equity Pleadings, or held the office of Attorney-General of England, superior to Lord Redesdale, when he held the seals of Ireland? Is Lord Manners less distinguished as an Irish chancellor than when he filled the office of a Baron of the English Exchequer?

Perhaps it may be suggested, as an apology, that the English law is of itself so vast a field that it can scarcely be mastered, and it is unnecessary to attempt any foreign conquests; that the decisions of English judges are alone of authority; and it is unwise and impolitic to open wider inquiries, which would perplex and obstruct the already darkened and crowded avenues of professional studies. There is something plausible in such a suggestion; but it vanishes on a close examination of the subject. If the English common law were perfect in itself, and were susceptible of no improvement, it might justly refuse any foreign admixture. But no one will be so rash as to advance a pretension of this sort. The common law is gradually changing its old channels and wearing new. It has continual accessions on some sides; and on others leaves behind vast accumulations which now serve little other purpose than to show what were its former boundaries. What has become of the feudal tenures, and the thousand questions of right and might which formerly came home not merely to the lords of the manors but to every thatched cottage of the kingdom? What has become of real actions, with all the complicated apparatus of proceedings with which they so much perplexed, not to say confounded and overwhelmed the profession? More than sixty years ago we were told, in the celebrated judgment of Taylor *v.* Horde, that the precise definition of what constituted a disseisin was not then known, and could not be traced in the books. And yet almost all the contests of the old law were upon questions in which the law of disseisins was a material ingredient. What has become of the nice and curious distinctions in respect to uses and trusts, which, in Lord Coke's time, and in earlier periods, exercised all the ingenuity of the profession? In a *practical* sense they have almost disappeared, or are felt to be of little value since the courts of equity have exerted their most salutary jurisdiction over this vast field of litigation. Where in the old law shall we find principles to adjust the innumerable questions arising in bankruptcy? Where shall we look for the doctrine of liens, of stoppage in transitu, of marshalling assets, of the execution of charities, in short, of the mass of business in which modern legal and equitable jurisdiction is employed? It is obvious, that the law must fashion itself to the wants, and in some sort to the spirit of the age. Its stubborn rules, if they are not broken down, must bend to the demands of society. A merely written code must forever be inadequate to the business of a nation increasing in wealth and commerce, and connecting itself with the interests of all the world. A customary law, adopted in rude and barbarous times, must melt away or mix itself with the new materials of more refined ages. Human transactions are dividing and subdividing themselves into such innumerable varieties that they cannot be adjusted or bounded by any written or positive legislation. The law, to be rational and practicable, must, as was finely said by Lord Ellenborough of the rules of evidence, expand with the exigencies of society. As new cases arise, they must be governed by new principles; and though we may not remove ancient landmarks, we must put down new ones when the old are not safe guides and no longer indicate the travelled road, or mark the busy, shifting channels of commerce.

It is most manifest, therefore, that the English law, working as it does, into the business of a nation crowded with commerce and manufactures, must forever be in search of equitable principles to be applied to the new combinations of circumstances, which are daily springing up to perplex its courts. In adopting new rules it is indispensable to look to public convenience, mutual equities, the course of trade, and even foreign intercourse. It is plain, that in such inquiries the customary and positive law of foreign countries as the result of extensive experience, must be of great utility. No nation can be so vain as to imagine that she possesses all wisdom and all excellence. No civilized nation is so humble that her usages, laws, and regulations do not present many things for instruction, and some for imitation. In respect to the general principles of jurisprudence, those which are applicable to the ordinary concerns of human life in all countries, and ought to be law in all, because they are founded in common sense and common justice, it is undeniable that much light may arise from the investigations of foreign jurists. Genius and learning can never fail to illustrate the principles of universal law, even when the primary object is merely to expound municipal institutions. The Dutch, the German, the Italian, the Spanish, or the French civilian is not less a master of equity and rational jurisprudence, when he deals with the Roman law, colored, and it may be shaded by his own local customs and ordinances, than the Lord Chancellor on the woolsack, enforcing trusts in *foro conscientiæ*, or the Lord Chief Justice when expounding commercial contracts at the Guildhall of London. The truth is, that the common law, however reluctant it may be to make the acknowledgment, and however boastful it may be of its own perfection, owes to the civil law, and its elegant and indefatigable commentators, (as has been already hinted,) almost all its valuable doctrines and expositions of the law of contract. The very action of assumpsit, in its modern refinements, breathes the spirit of its origin. It is altogether Roman and Prætorian. And there never has been a period in which the common lawyers, with all their hostility to the civil law, have not been compelled to borrow its precepts. The early work of Bracton shows how solicitous some of the sages were, even in that rude age, to infuse into their own code some of that masculine sense which found favor in the days of Justinian.

What, indeed, should we think, in the present times, of men, who affect to be indifferent to the writings of such authors as D'Aguesseau, Domat, Valin, Pothier, and Emérigon? Mr. Duponceau, in his late excellent Dissertation on the Jurisdiction of the Courts of the United States, — a work that should be profoundly studied by all American lawyers, — has said, that the works of Pothier were warmly recommended by Sir William Jones to his countrymen, "*but without success.*" We hope his language is too strong. That such a writer as Pothier should be neglected by Englishmen, would be a disgrace to the learning and literature of the nation. Who has written with so much purity of principle, such sound sense, such exact judgment, such practical propriety, on all the leading divisions of contracts? Who has treated the whole subject of maritime law so fully, so profoundly, so truly with a view to its equity and advancement, as Valin? Who has equalled Emérigon, as a theoretical and practical writer on the law of insurance? He has exhausted every topic, so far as materials were within his reach; and upon all new questions his work, for illustration, and authorities, and usages, is still unrivalled.

We think, indeed, that we perceive the dawn of a brighter age in the English law, when the foreign lights, which have been, slowly and by stealth, admitted into Westminster Hall, will be hailed with a liberal spirit, and will irradiate its bar and benches. Mr. Joy, in the case of M'Iver *v.* Henderson, (4 M. and S. 576,) and Mr. Campbell and Mr. Bosanquet, in the case of Bush *v.* the Royal Exchange Insurance Company, (2 Barn. and Ald. 72,) showed a familiar acquaintance with the foreign maritime jurists, and argued with great effect from their authority; and on a comparatively recent occasion, (5 M. and S. 436,) when Emérigon was cited, Lord Ellenborough said, "Emérigon, whose name has been so frequently mentioned in the course of the argument, is entitled to all the respect which is due to a very learned writer, discussing a subject with great ability, diligence, and learning, and adverting to all the authorities relating to it." Mr. Justice Bailey and Mr. Justice Best, who are judges of uncommon ability, have repeatedly, of late, adverted to the French maritime authors with discriminating accuracy, and in terms of the most unreserved respect. We consider these indications of a liberal study of foreign jurisprudence as extremely creditable to this age of the common law; and we augur from them, for the future, a far more expanded view of commercial questions than has usually been encouraged since the days of Lord Mansfield.

If we were disposed to recommend the study of public and foreign law to common lawyers, we do not know how we could better do it than by pointing out some illustrious examples of its successful accomplishment in our own age. Sir James Mackintosh, of late years so distinguished in Parliament, as a friend to liberty, to science, and liberal institutions, and who is, at the same time, a most humane and philosophical jurist, has, in his incomparable Introductory Discourse to his Lectures on the Law of Nations, given us a finished specimen of the advantages resulting from the mastery of foreign public writers. It would, perhaps, be difficult to select from the whole mass of modern literature a discourse of equal length which is so just and beautiful, so accurate and profound, so captivating and enlightening, so enriched with the refinements of modern learning, and the simple grandeur of ancient principles. It should be read by every student, for instruction and purity of sentiment; and by lawyers of graver years, to refresh their souls with inquiries which may elevate them above the narrow influences of a dry and hardening practice.

But a still more striking example is Lord Stowell, (better known in this country as Sir William Scott,) the present venerable Judge of the High Court of Admiralty, of whom it may be justly said, in the language of Cicero, that he is *jurisperitorum eloquentissimus.* This great man has presided in the Court of Admiralty since the year 1798; and during this period he has commanded the admiration of all Europe, by the learning, acuteness, and finished elegance of his judgments. There was a time when it was somewhat the fashion in this country to undervalue the solid excellence of his opinions. Our commerce was brought so directly in conflict with his administration of prize law, that it was difficult to avoid prejudices on a subject in which, as neutrals, we had so deep an interest, and were so liable to indulge strong animosities. But time has dissipated many delusions on this subject; and we have had, in the late war, ample opportunity to try the accuracy of his principles, when we changed the character of neutrals for that of belligerents. We can now look back upon his decisions with somewhat of the calmness and sobriety of a philosophical historian. With the exception of the doctrines respecting the colonial trade, in which it is but common justice to admit, that he either acted upon public Orders in Council which he was bound to obey, or upon the Rule of 1756, which his government had previously chosen to consider, as an established part of its prize code, the differences between his decisions upon prize law, and those promulgated by the Supreme Court of the United States, are so few, as to be almost evanescent. After the most powerful arguments under the highest political excitements, and with the aid of the most striking eloquence, there has been but a single principle adopted by him, which has been deliberately overruled by the Supreme Court; and on that occasion there was a serious difference of opinion among the judges.

But it is not in respect to prize law that we intend to speak of Lord Stowell, though he everywhere exhibits the most profound and accurate knowledge of all the publicists of continental Europe; but as a maritime judge, deciding, in what is called the Instance Court, the great principles of commercial jurisprudence. His superiority in this department over the technical reasoning of the common lawyers is most signal. He discusses every question with a persuasive and comprehensive liberality, with a tone of general equity, a knowledge of maritime usages, and a disposition to consider maritime jurisprudence as the unwritten law of the world, rather than the municipal monopoly of a single nation; and he draws from all sources, ancient and modern, the best and purest principles, to aid, to illustrate, and to confirm his own judgment. With him the grave learning of Grotius, the acute, bold, and somewhat vehement discussions of Bynkershoek, the reverend testimonies of the Consolato del Mare, the collections of Cleirac, the busy, practical sense of Roccus, the brief but clear text of Heineccius, the various and exhausting labors of Casaregis, the argumentative commentaries and luminous treatises of the French jurists, appear as perfectly familiar as the writers of his own age and country. He evidently reposes upon them, even when he does not cite them; and transfuses into his own eloquent and impressive judgments whatever they afford of general doctrine, or just interpretation, upon all the doubtful questions of maritime law. One scarcely knows which most to admire, the simplicity of his principles, the classical beauty of his diction, the calm and dispassionate spirit of his inquiries, his critical but candid estimate of evidence, his strong love of equity, his deep indignation against fraud, chastened by habitual moderation, or that pervading common sense which looks into, and feels, and acts upon the business of life with a discriminating but indulgent eye, content to administer practical good without ostentation, and wasting nothing upon speculations, whose origin is enthusiasm, and whose end is uncertainty or mischief. Even when he deals with subjects of another class, as in ecclesiastical causes in the Consistory Court, one is surprised to see with what admirable propriety he uses his knowledge of general jurisprudence and the civil law, to give vigor to his decrees. And upon questions involving the *lex loci*, he has triumphantly shown that he can master the results of foreign jurisprudence; and, as in the very interesting case of Dalrymple *v.* Dalrymple, compose the strifes of the learned advocates of the Scottish bar, and fix forever upon an immovable basis a question which had vexed the domestic forum of Scotland for a long period with its doubts and difficulties. We say, without hesitation, that the character of this eminent judge, whatever may have been his original genius and ability, owes its present elevation, in a great measure, to his enlarged studies, and his cultivation of universal jurisprudence. Take, for instance, his celebrated judgment in the case of the Gratitudine, in 1801, on the right of the master to hypothecate the cargo, as well as the ship and freight, for the necessities of the voyage; or the case of the Julianna, in 1822, on the invalidity of a stipulation in the shipping-paper to cut off the seamen from wages, unless the voyage should be performed to the final port of destination; where shall we find in the annals of the common law, except among the judgments of Lord Mansfield, cases argued out upon such rational and enlightened principles, aided by sober and various learning, and ending in conclusions so irresistible? One seems in them to be reading, not the law of England merely, but the law of the world — the results of human reason and human learning, acting on human concerns, with reference to principles absolutely universal in their justice and convenience of application. We wish American lawyers would study the fine models of this sagacious judge with a diligence proportionate to their importance and utility.

We cannot quit this subject without recommending to our brethren of the English Bar, if, perchance, these pages should attract their notice, the study of American jurisprudence. Of course we do not mean of our local laws and peculiar systems; for we should as little advise this, as we should to our own lawyers the study of the English law of tithes, and moduses, and copyholds, from which we are separated *toto cœlo.* What we do recommend is, the study of our commercial adjudications. This is not said, we hope they will believe, from vanity under a false estimate of our own attainments. American lawyers are in the constant habit of reading all the English Reports; and it would be worse than affectation to attempt to disguise, that we are greatly instructed and improved by them. They present to us the fruits of great experience, industry, intelligence, and ability. But we "also are painters." The American Courts collectively considered, embrace a large proportion of talent and learning, and they are perpetually engaged in many of the discussions which perplex the English tribunals. Of course there is a great diversity in the attainments of the judges and lawyers in the different states composing the Union, arising from local circumstances. But in the principal Atlantic States the system of maritime law is of daily application to business, and is studied with earnest diligence.

In one respect there is a striking contrast between the state of the English and that of the American Bar. In England, the profession is broken up into distinct classes. The civilians engross exclusively the admiralty and ecclesiastical courts, and even these are separated into proctors and advocates. The chancery courts have their own solicitors and counsellors. The barristers and sergeants of the common law generally confine themselves to the practice of their own particular courts. The attorney is a being who deals with processes and proceedings in suits, but is shut out from the rights of arguing counsel. The conveyancer pores over his own peculiar studies for chamber-practice; and the special pleader, if he wins his way to a lucrative practice, sits under the bar a quiet spectator of forensic disputations, unless the niceties of his own craft come into play. In America all this is different. The same gentleman acts, or may act, (with scarcely an exception,) in all these different capacities; and in the course of a single term of a court may assume many of the functions of all of them. He is, or may be, at once, proctor, advocate, solicitor, attorney, conveyancer, and pleader; he may draw libels and bills, frame pleas and answers, direct process, prepare briefs, sketch drafts of conveyances, argue questions of fact to the jury, and questions of law to the court; and find himself quite at home in all these various employments. If it should be thought that this singleness of occupation and subdivision of labor give to the English lawyer more accuracy, minute knowledge, and perfect facility in the use of his materials, they carry with them, on the other hand, some disadvantages. The general tendency of such close pursuits is to narrow down the mind to mere technical rules; to exhaust its powers upon subtile distinctions and dull details; to make professional life an affair of collections and recollections; to create an acute and nice discrimination, rather than a solid and comprehensive understanding. What is gained by skill in the manipulation is lost in the vigor of the blow.

The course of the American lawyer does not, it must be confessed, generally lead to such exact inquiries, and such perfect finish, although there have been eminent examples to the contrary. But a survey of the whole structure of the law conducts him to large and elevated views, to brilliant and successful illustrations, to reasonings from various contrasts and analogies of the law, and to those generalizations which invigorate eloquence, and shadow out the finer forms of thought. His learning must be deep and various, even if it is not in all respects exact; and will be tinctured with the hues of all his studies. His law silently acquires the tone and spirit of equity; and his commercial discussions urge him to search for, and adopt in argument, whatever of excellence the genius and erudition of foreign jurists have brought to his notice. He knows, too, that in the American courts there is no disposition to discourage the study of foreign jurisprudence. There is a freedom from restraint, and an habitual eagerness to expand our law, which favor every attempt to build up commercial doctrines upon the most liberal foundation. We do not mean to affirm, that American lawyers in general cultivate such extensive studies, or are distinguished by such elevated attainments. What we mean to assert is, that the general tendency of our system is to excite an ambition for such studies and attainments, and that the genius of the profession is perpetually attracted in its researches and reasonings to those general principles which constitute the philosophy of the law. We could point out living models who exemplify all that we have suggested in commendation of the American system; and among the illustrious dead, within our own brief career, we fear no rebuke in naming Hamilton, Dexter, Pinkney, and Wells. But it is unnecessary to trust to assertion. The records are before us, and can be searched. Look to the judgments of the supreme courts in the states of Pennsylvania, New York, and Massachusetts, upon questions of maritime and commercial law, as they stand in the Reports of Messrs. Tyng, Binney, Johnson, and Sergeant and Rawle. It is impossible not to feel, that the arguments in these causes, and the judgments which followed them, would do credit to the tribunals of any country. They are full of learning, fine reasoning, acute distinctions, and solid principles, such as might well guide the sober sense of Westminster Hall, and cast a strong light upon its oracles. Look to the chancery decisions of New York. Where shall we find in our times a more thorough mastery of the civil and maritime, of the common and equity law, where a more untiring research, a more critical exactness, a more philosophical spirit than is displayed in the elaborate arguments of her late chancellor?

We think, therefore, that, in recommending the labors of the American lawyers and judges to the attention of English lawyers, we do them a service, by which they may greatly profit; and in this manner we may make a suitable return for the many aids which America received from the parent country, when her own jurisprudence was loose, unformed, and provincial.

The progress, indeed, that has been made in America, in the knowledge and administration of commercial law, since the Revolution, is very extraordinary; and in no branch more striking than in that of Insurance. Before that event policies of insurance were of rare use among us. Our intercourse with the mother country was so direct and so dependent, that most of the important risks were underwritten in London, through the instrumentality of agents. Our printed reports do not reach far back beyond the revolutionary period; but the manuscripts we have seen, and the absence of references to cases, in the arguments even of ante-revolutionary lawyers, establish, to the satisfaction of all accurate observers, that the subject was new to the studies of the bar. The earliest, and, indeed, the only case we recollect in any of our books, before the Declaration of Independence, is that of Story and Wharton *v.* Strettell, in 1764, reported by Mr. Dallas in the first volume of his Reports. It was not until the French revolution, by opening new and extensive sources of profitable trade, gave an impulse to our maritime enterprise, that the contract struggled into notice from a state of languor, and became common in our commercial cities. It immediately advanced with almost inconceivable rapidity, and became so profitable that it may truly be said to have laid the foundation of many fortunes in our country. The profession soon felt the necessity of an entire mastery of the subject, and applied itself with a most commendable diligence to the study of all the English and other foreign authorities. And within the last thirty years, probably as large a number of cases of insurance have been contested and decided in the American courts, upon points of difficulty and extensive application, as in the courts of England in the same period. We do not hesitate to assert, that these cases have been argued with as much learning and ability, and with as comprehensive a view of the true principles of the contract, as any in the brightest days of the English law. And we are greatly deceived, if, upon a general examination, they will not be found by English lawyers and judges to be full of useful instruction, and worthy of their deliberate study. Many of them discuss questions arising from the complicated state of our commerce as a neutral nation, which have not, as yet undergone any adjudication in the English courts.

We will close this topic with a very short historical sketch of the principal modern English treatises on insurance. We pass over at once without any particular notice, the remarks on the subject contained in the work on Bills of Exchange and Insurance, ascribed to Mr. Cunningham, and in Mr. Parker's Laws of Shipping and Insurance, as they were so imperfect as to have sunk into obscurity. Mr. Weskett's book is a mere collection in the form of a dictionary, of all the heads of maritime law, and contains little more than an index to foreign ordinances and usages. The title, Insurance, in the collections of Postlethwayte and Beawes are of the same character. The first treatises, correctly speaking, are those of Mr. Millar, a Scotch advocate, and Mr. Park, (now Mr. Justice Park of the common pleas,) both published in the year 1787. Mr. Millar's work is certainly creditable to his talents and industry, and exhibits considerable research and habits of observation. It has not, however, received a great share of public favor, nor, as we believe, reached a second edition, probably, because it has been superseded in practice by the very superior treatise of his rival, both in method and materials. Mr. Park, indeed, deserves much praise for the judgment, accuracy, and general excellence of his System of the Law of Insurance. The best testimony to its value is the continued approbation of the profession, which has already carried it through seven large editions. As a collection of authentic cases in the fullest and most accurate form, it still remains unrivalled. Although it professes to be principally "a collection of cases and judicial opinions," the learned author occasionally discusses general principles with a good deal of ability. In 1802 Mr. Sergeant Marshall published his Treatise on the Law of Insurance, and again in 1808 published a second and improved edition. His work professes to be, not, like Mr. Park's, a collection of cases, but an examination and collection of principles. It is certainly a work of high merit, analyzing and criticizing the cases with great acuteness and vigor; and citing the foreign authorities with which the learned author appears familiar, with a creditable liberality. Whenever he ventures to give his own comments, they indicate perspicacity and closeness of observation. But, after all, the work seems to promise more than it performs. It contains little of doctrine or discussion, beyond what the English decisions exact or furnish. We look in vain for any attempt to extend the boundaries of the law beyond actual adjudications, and for any satisfactory argument upon topics which yet remain unsettled by the courts. And a great defect in the work, as indeed in all others — a defect, which has been but imperfectly supplied by the late treatise of Mr. Stevens — is the want of a *practical* treatise upon averages and the adjustment of losses. We believe, that the learned author is now dead, so that there is little probability that the work will be rendered more complete.

But, whatever may be the value of the English treatises on insurance, it is most obvious, that they are inadequate to supply the necessities of the American Bar. They embrace no cisatlantic decisions; and every work for our use, which does not contain them, is infected with a fatal infirmity. From what has been already suggested, it is clear, that the actual administration of commercial jurisprudence in our own courts must, for argument, for authority, and for practice, be far more important to us than any foreign opinions ever can be. In respect to insurance, although the law in most commercial states rests on the same basis of general principles, these principles admit of considerable diversity of judgment in their application, and are often controlled by the known policy or ordinances of each particular government. This is so true, that there are probably no two civilized nations, in which the law of insurance is exactly the same in all its outlines and details. Although our own law of insurance professes to be, and in fact is, the same in its general structure and principles, as that of England; yet, without any statutable provisions, we already find many conclusions embodied in it, which are at variance with those of Westminster Hall. In some of these cases the English decisions may be more just and satisfactory than our own. In others we have no hesitation in declaring the American more solid, rational, and convenient. If it would not lead us into too prolix a discussion, we should incline to enter on the task of enumerating the leading differences, in order to enable the profession to form an exact judgment on the subject. But we must pass from these topics, and hasten to the close of an article already extended far beyond the limits, which we had originally intended. We will just mention, however, the point, that the right of abandonment depends upon the state of the fact at the time when it is actually made, and when once legally exercised, it is not divested by any subsequent change of the facts, as one, in which we differ from English courts; and we are entirely satisfied, that our rule has the justest foundation in principle, as well as in policy. The same conclusion has been more than once intimated by the great mind of Lord Chancellor Eldon.

From what has been said, our opinion may be readily conjectured, as to the indispensable necessity of a new treatise on insurance, for the use of American lawyers; and Mr. Phillips has done a most acceptable service to the profession by the publication of that, the title of which stands at the head of this article. One of two courses only could be pursued; either to republish the best English work, and append the American decisions in the shape of perpetual notes, which would have formed a very inconvenient and bulky commentary, not easily reducible to specific heads; or to recast the whole materials, and produce a new work, which should contain in one text the mass of English and American authority. Mr. Phillips has chosen the latter course, and in our opinion, with great sagacity and sound judgment; and he has executed his task in a manner, which will obtain the general confidence and respect of the profession. His work is arranged in a very lucid method, and embodies in an accurate form the whole system of the law of insurance, as it is actually administered in the courts of England and America. It is eminently practical and compendious, at the same time that it is full of information. Wherever he has introduced any comments of his own, of which he has been somewhat too sparing, he has shown sound sense, and a liberal juridical spirit. In respect to America, his work will probably supersede altogether the use of Mr. Marshall's; but Mr. Park's, as the fullest repertory of all the cases, will continue to retain the public favor. The labor of such a compilation must unavoidably have been great, and required the most patient research and various study. The author, as a scholar, a gentleman, and a lawyer, has put himself before the public and the profession, for their patronage of his labors; and we are satisfied, that he will not be disappointed in the result. He need not blush for his authorship, nor fear the scrutiny of dispassionate criticism. His work has a solid character, and will sustain itself the better, the more it is examined.

. . . .

Of a work confessedly professional, it cannot be expected, that we should enter upon a minute review, for the purpose of detecting slight faults, or contesting particular opinions. The task would be irksome to ourselves, and so heavy and technical, as to afford very little satisfaction to our readers. It is impossible to include in a single volume the opposite qualities of brevity and copiousness, a condensed summary of principles, and an elaborate discussion of the minute details and distinctions of cases. Whoever writes a merely practical treatise, must leave much matter worthy of observation to more exhausting authors. In this age, books, to be read, must be succinct, and direct to their purpose. The business of commercial life will not stop, while lawyers plunge into folios of a thousand pages, to ascertain a possible shade of distinction in the construction of contracts. If, therefore, there should be any persons disposed to think, that cases and comments should have been given more at large, the true answer is, that such was not Mr. Phillips's plan; and that his work is to be judged of, not by its adaptation to other purposes, but by its actual execution of his own design. In this respect it has our hearty approbation, and we sincerely recommend it to all, who are interested in commercial jurisprudence, as merchants, lawyers, and judges. We think, however, that in a future edition, Mr. Phillips will do well to enrich his work with extracts from Valin, Emérigon, and Pothier, upon points, which have not yet received any adjudication, and occasionally to introduce some of their speculative reasonings. We should be glad, also, to have more full practical information upon the adjustment of averages and losses, and the items, which are to be admitted or rejected; having had occasion to know, that nothing is more various, uncertain, and anomalous, than the modes of settling losses in different insurance offices. Even in the same office, a departure from the principle assumed as to one subject of insurance is not uncommon as to another, upon some fanciful notion of its inapplicability. The form of Mr. Phillips's Index also might be advantageously changed, so as to make it more easy for consultation, by the use of a larger type, and breaking it up into more paragraphs, with short subordinate titles.

RIGHTS OF THE FELLOWS OF HARVARD UNIVERSITY.

AN ARGUMENT DELIVERED BEFORE THE BOARD OF OVERSEERS OF HARVARD COLLEGE, IN JANUARY, 1825, UPON THE DISCUSSION OF THE MEMORIAL OF THE PROFESSORS AND TUTORS OF THE COLLEGE, CLAIMING A RIGHT THAT NONE BUT RESIDENT INSTRUCTORS IN THE COLLEGE SHOULD BE CHOSEN OR DEEMED "FELLOWS" OF THE CORPORATION.

[The following statements, on the subject of the claim of the resident Instructors, are chiefly borrowed from a pamphlet published in 1825, entitled "Remarks on Changes lately proposed or adopted in Harvard University. By George Ticknor, Smith Professor," &c.

"The management of the College at Cambridge has been heretofore in the hands of three bodies of men, who hold their authority under an Act of the General Court, passed in 1642; a Charter given in 1650, with an Appendix, dated in 1657; the fifth chapter of the Constitution of the Commonwealth, made in 1780, and revised, but not altered in relation to the College, in 1821; and an Act passed in February, 1814, by the Legislature of the Commonwealth.

"The first of the bodies, who, under the provisions of these acts, or by powers mediately derived from them, have had the management of the College, is, the Faculty or Immediate Government, consisting of the President, and a part of the resident Instructors, amounting in all to from ten to thirteen persons, who have the entire discipline of the students in their hands, and have been obliged to meet together as an executive body, to decide on every punishment above a small fine; a body, which, both in Cambridge and in other colleges, is too large for the prompt, consistent, and efficient discipline of such a collection of young men.

"Over the Faculty is the Corporation, which derives its powers from the Charter of 1650, the Appendix of 1657, and the Constitution of 1780, and consists of the President, the Treasurer, and five 'Fellows,' as they are technically called; and of the gentlemen, who now [1825] compose that body, three, namely, Mr. W. Prescott, Judge Jackson, and the Rev. W. E. Channing, reside in Boston; one, Mr. Justice Story, resides in Salem; and one, Rev. E. Porter, resides in Roxbury. The Corporation have the management of the funds and revenues of the College: appoint its instructors and other officers, and assign them their duties and pay; make laws for the government of the instructors and the students; and fill vacancies in their own body; but are restricted in their powers, and can do almost nothing without the expressed assent of the Overseers.

"The Overseers are the last and highest body for the government of the College. They hold their power by virtue of the Act of 1642, the Constitution of 1780, and the Statutes of 1810 [&] 1814, and consist of the Governor of the Commonwealth, the Lieutenant-Governor, the Council, the Senate, . . and the Speaker of the House of Representatives; in all fifty-three persons; together with the President of the College, and fifteen laymen and fifteen clergymen, elected, and to be elected, from the community at large, by the whole Board; so that out of eighty-four members of the upper Board for the government of the College, fifty-three are annually elected by the people, and, therefore, completely and truly represent the public interest in the institution." . . .

"On the 2d of April, 1824, eleven of the resident teachers, namely, five Professors engaged in the instruction of undergraduates, two engaged in the instruction of graduates, and four Tutors, offered a memorial to the Corporation," containing certain 'statements and considerations relative to *the mode in which, according to the charter of the institution, the Corporation of the same ought of right to be constituted,*' (Memorial, p. 1,) and preferring to the Corporation as 'matter of chartered right,' 'the claim of the resident Instructors to be elected to vacancies in the Board of the President and Fellows.' (Mem. p. 31.)

"To this memorial the Corporation returned no formal answer, on the ground, as has been stated by the memorialists, that, if the claim were well founded, the members of the Corporation, to whom it was sent, not being rightfully 'Fellows' of the College, were not competent to perform any act in its government; and could only resign their seats. On the 1st of June, nine of the same memorialists presented the same claim and memorial to the Overseers; giving, as one reason for presenting it at that particular juncture, that they understood the Overseers were then engaged in considering important measures relative to the organization of the College. This memorial was by the Overseers referred to a committee, and so the matter rested for some months." — *Remarks*, pp. 11, 12, 13.

"After this memorial had been presented to the Overseers, a report on it was made, January 6, 1825, by Mr. Hill, of the Council, on behalf of the committee appointed to consider the subject, in which report it is maintained, that it is *not* necessary, by the charter or otherwise, that the Fellows of Harvard College be either resident in Cambridge, Instructors, or Stipendiaries. The memorialists desired to be heard in reply. They were so heard on the 4th of February; Professor Everett and Professor Norton appearing on their behalf. The discussion was very interesting, and one of the most thorough ever witnessed among us. It lasted three days. At the end of this time, the following resolutions were *unanimously* adopted, at a remarkably full meeting of the Overseers: 'Resolved, That it does not appear in this Board, that the resident Instructors in Harvard University have any exclusive right to be elected members of the Corporation. Resolved, That it does not appear to the members of this Board, that the members of the Corporation forfeit their offices by not residing at College.'

"It may be added to this, that, as a legal question, few have ever been examined among us with more laborious care, or by persons better qualified to decide what is the law. In the Corporation, at the time, were Mr. W. Prescott, Mr. H. G. Otis, and Mr. J. Davis, District Judge of the United States. In the Board of Overseers, Mr. Justice Story, of the Supreme Court of the United States, delivered his opinion against the memorial in a long argument. He was succeeded, on the same side, by Chief Justice Parker, of the Supreme Court of Massachusetts, Mr. Justice Jackson, Mr. F. C. Gray, and some other persons of distinguished talent. On the final question, not a voice was raised in the Board, or elsewhere, I believe, in favor of the memorial. The profession, in particular, seemed unanimous on all the points; and many years will probably elapse before any important question will be decided with such a great weight of legal talent and learning, after so long, so patient, and so interesting a discussion." — *Remarks*, pp. 25, 26.

"The charter of 1650, under which chiefly the Corporation hold their powers, and the memorialists make their claim," (*Remarks*, p. 13,) commences as follows: —

"Whereas, through the good hand of God, many well devoted persons have been, and daily are, moved and stirred up, to give and bestow sundry gifts, legacies, lands, and revenues, for the advancement of all good literature, arts, and sciences, in Harvard College, in Cambridge, in the County of Middlesex, and to the maintenance of the President and Fellows, and for all accommodations of buildings, and all other necessary provisions, that may conduce to the education of the English and Indian youth of this country, in knowledge and godliness; —

"It is therefore ordered and enacted by this Court, and the authority thereof, for the furthering of so good a work, and for the purpose aforesaid, from henceforth, that the said College in Cambridge, in Middlesex, in New England, shall be a Corporation, consisting of seven persons, namely, a President, five Fellows, and a Treasurer or Bursar; and that Henry Dunster shall be the first President, Samuel Mather, Samuel Danford, Masters of Arts, Jonathan Mitchell, Comfort Starr, and Samuel Eaton, shall be the five Fellows, and Thomas Danford to be present Treasurer, all of them being inhabitants in the Bay, and shall be the first seven persons, of which the said Corporation shall consist; and that the said seven persons, or the greater number of them, procuring the presence of the Overseers [rendered unnecessary by the Appendix of 1657] of the College, and by their counsel and consent, shall have power, and are hereby authorized, at any time or times, to elect a new President, Fellows, or Treasurer, so oft, and from time to time, as any of the said persons shall die or be removed; which said President and Fellows, for the time being, shall for ever hereafter, in name and in fact, be one body politic and corporate in law, to all intents and purposes; and shall have perpetual succession; and shall be called by the name of the President and Fellows of Harvard College, and shall from time to time be eligible as aforesaid." — *Mass. Col. Laws*, *&c.* 78, 79.

Besides the Memorial, and the Remarks of Mr. Ticknor, several other pamphlets have been published in relation to the claim of the resident Instructors, namely, "Remarks on a Pamphlet printed by the Professors and Tutors of Harvard University, touching their Right to the exclusive Government of that Seminary." "A Letter to John Lowell, Esq., in Reply to a Publication entitled, Remarks on a Pamphlet," &c. This letter is from the Hon. Edward Everett, then a Professor in the College. "Speech delivered before the Overseers of Harvard College, February 3, 1825, in behalf of the Resident Instructors of the College; with an Introduction. By Andrews Norton." "Report of a Committee of the Overseers of Harvard College on the Memorial of the Resident Instructors."

It will be at once perceived, that the argument is strictly confined to the mere question of legal right. The author, in opening his speech, expressly disclaimed any intention to inquire into the expediency of such a choice, supposing it not a matter of right; considering that to be a topic of a very large and comprehensive nature, and that no case was then before the Board, which required or invited such a discussion.]

I REGRET that I am compelled, by a sense of duty, to enter upon the discussion of the question presented by the Memorial, at the distance of more than a century and a half after the foundation and charter of the college. I entertain a very great respect for the Memorialists. Some of them were the instructors of my youth, while I was a student at the university, and for them I feel much of filial reverence; others of them I have the pleasure of being well acquainted with by their literary and scientific acquirements; and others of them I feel myself at liberty to name among the friends whom I most honor. Under such circumstances, I should be glad, if I could, to escape from the embarrassment and responsibility of a public discussion, in which my judgment requires me to dissent from claims, which, whatever may be my personal respect for the Memorialists, I am convinced are utterly unfounded in law.

Considerations of this nature have pressed upon my feelings; but I have yielded them up to a sense of duty. This Board has a right to demand from the members of it, who have been bred to the profession of the law, a clear view of their own opinions upon the question as a matter of law; and the suggestions of my friends have led me to believe, that upon such an occasion, silence on my part would not be deemed excusable.

But there is another matter of regret which I am bound to acknowledge, and which I trust will be accepted as an apology for any imperfections and infirmities in my argument. The question is one quite remote from the ordinary occupations and studies of lawyers in this country. It has not, as far as I know, been stirred here for a century; and, unfortunately little or nothing of the grounds of the opinions and reasonings of that distant period can be now gathered up to aid or enlighten the present inquiry. It would have been desirable on my own part to have consulted at large the charters, foundations, and statutes of the colleges in the English Universities; and to have fortified myself by an intimate study of all the peculiarities as well of their language and legal construction as of the usages under them, so that I might have been better prepared to meet any objections. But the best works on such subjects are not generally within my reach or within that of my friends. I am obliged, therefore, to rely upon books and authorities, which, though perfectly satisfactory upon the leading principles, are less full and exact in details than I could have wished. I have in some instances been obliged to gather up fragments of facts, and put them together in order to illustrate positions, which appear to me in a legal view absolutely irresistible. Few controversies of a nature like the present have ever come before the English courts of justice; and where they have been settled by the visitors of a college or their assessors upon legal principles, they are either locked up in works not generally accessible, or left merely upon the manuscript records of the colleges to which we have no access.

Notwithstanding these disadvantages, I have an entire confidence, that the conclusions to which I have arrived are perfectly well founded in point of law. They rest upon principles which, as a lawyer, I think either do not admit of serious controversy, or, if controverted, can be satisfactorily maintained. And I trust in many instances I shall be able to establish, by suitable illustrations, that they are justified by the highest authority.

I will now, after these prefatory remarks, beg the indulgence of the Board while I invite their attention, and particularly that of my legal friends who are members of it, to my argument. Some of its details may be dry and uninteresting; some of them may be thought superfluous; and some of them such as lawyers, at the first presentation of them, would not deem necessary to be farther expounded. My excuse must be sought in the great deference I feel for the Memorialists themselves. I am unwilling to have it thought, for a moment, that any thing which they deem in any degree important as bearing upon their case, should not be met and answered with directness and in a spirit of candor, whatever may be the value which others may attribute to it.

I shall have occasion, in the course of the discussion, to allude to a pamphlet containing a vindication of the doctrines of the Memorial, which has been attributed to one of the learned professors, and which I shall the more freely allude to because it purports to invite public discussion, and its authorship is not attempted to be concealed. In so doing I trust I shall not be suspected of feeling towards the learned author any thing but respect and friendship.

The object of the Memorial is to show, that the Corporation of Harvard College, as at present organized, is not conformable to the charter of 1650. The proposition maintained is, that, by "Fellows," in the charter, is meant a particular description of persons, known in English colleges, and, at the time of the charter, existing in Harvard College, and having known rights and duties. The Memorial then asserts and endeavors to prove, that "Fellow" imports a person resident at the college, and actually engaged there in carrying on the duties of instruction or government, and receiving a stipend from its revenues."[1] In the view of the Memorial, each of these facts, *residence*, *instruction* or *government*, and *receiving a stipend*, constitutes a necessary part of the definition of a "Fellow." And it is contended by the Memorialists, that this is the meaning attached to the word in the charters of the English colleges; that it was so actually applied in Harvard College before 1650; and that, consequently, it is the true and only sense of the term in the charter of 1650. The Memorial seems to maintain, that no persons but such as have the necessary qualifications at the time of the choice, are eligible as Fellows.[2] But if it does not go to this extent it maintains, that, after the choice, the party must be a *resident*, an *instructor* or *governor*, and a *stipendiary*.

[1] Page 2.

[2] Pages 2, 4, 7, 30.

My first object will be to ascertain whether the above definition of "Fellow" be true and correct, as applied to English colleges; for on this definition the whole argument rests. I shall contend, and endeavor to show: 1. That the term, "Fellow," when used in the charters of English colleges, has no peculiar meaning, distinct from its ordinary meaning of *associate* or *socius:* 2. That the qualifications of Fellows are not the same in all the colleges; but vary according to the requisitions of the charters, and the successive statutes of the particular foundations: 3. That, as an enumeration of the particular qualifications of Fellows in the colleges generally, the above definition is incomplete: 4. That the objects of these Fellowships are very various; and generally, if not universally, of a nature wholly distinct from any, which the Memorial itself supposes to be the principal object of the charter.

I. The *meaning* of the word, "FELLOW." — This word is by no means confined to college charters. It occurs in charters of a very different description. Thus the Royal Society is incorporated by the name of the "President and Fellows." So the College of Physicians. So the American Academy of Arts and Sciences. So the Medical Society of Massachusetts. In these and like cases, no person supposes, that the word imports any thing more than member or associate. Johnson, among his definitions of "Fellow," enumerates as one, "a *member* of a college, that shares its revenues, *or of any incorporated society.*" We also speak of the Chief Justice of a court and his Fellows; of the Foreman of the Grand Jury and his Fellows. The oath of the Grand Jury declares, "The United States' counsel, your *Fellows'*, and your own, you shall keep secret."

In all these cases, the word companion, associate, or *confrere*, might be substituted indifferently for Fellow. If there be any peculiar force in the term, it is, that it imports *equality* in general rights. Why, then, should it be supposed to be used in any other sense in a college charter? It cannot be from the nature of the objects to be attained, for these might be attained by persons under any other denomination; nor from any peculiar structure of college institutions, for these exist under very various charters at home and abroad. The corporate name of Dartmouth College is, "The Trustees of Dartmouth College." The ends can be obtained as well without Fellows as with; as well by incorporating a distinct body as by incorporating the college instructors. Many of the trustees of Dartmouth College, in the original charter were non-residents, and so described in the charter. Many, who have been since elected, were non-residents, and continued such.

The sole ground of the memorialists must be, that the word has a fixed meaning as to English colleges; and is, as it were, so appropriated by art, as necessarily to import in a college charter something more than associate. If so, then the word would naturally be used in all English college charters; and "Fellows" could not exist where the charter did not create them *eo nomine*. But how is the fact? Let us take a few of the colleges at Oxford.

Brazen Nose College; founded in 1509. Name — "Principal and *Scholars* of King's Hall and Brazen Nose College in Oxford."[1] Yet there are in this college twenty *fellows*, thirty-two scholarships, and fifteen exhibitions, *on the foundation.*

Trinity College; founded in 1554, by name of the "Master, *Fellows*, and *Scholars* of the College," &c. &c.[2] There are on the foundation, a president, twelve *fellows*, twelve *scholars*, and four *exhibitions*.

St. John's College; founded in 1557. The charter is for a president, and fifty *fellows* OR *scholars*.[3]

Christ Church College; founded by Cardinal Wolsey and Henry VIII., 1532: a collegiate church. Name — "*Dean*

[1] Oxford Guide, ed. 1822, p. 67.
[2] Oxf. Guide, 119. 2 Bro. Par. Cas. 221. 1 Ayliffe, Hist. Oxf. 40.
[3] 1 Ayl. 418, 419.

and *Chapter* of the Cathedral Church, &c. in Oxford," &c.[1] On the foundation are the dean, eight canons, eight chaplains, one organist, eight clerks, one hundred and one students, and a schoolmaster, and usher. This is a very material case. No Fellows are named. What says the Oxford Guide? In college phrase, "A *student* is one of the *one hundred and one members* of that name at Christ Church, whose rank is similar to that of '*Fellow*' of other colleges." "The number of members on the books is about seven hundred, amongst whom are *three hundred and forty-five members of convocation*."[2] This college is governed solely by the laws of the *Dean* and *Chapter* of the Cathedral Church.[3]

Corpus Christi College; founded 1516. Name — "Collegium Corpus Christi Oxonii." It originally had on its foundation a president, twenty *scholars*, and two chaplains: it now has a president, twelve *fellows*, twenty *scholars*, four exhibitions, two chaplains.[4]

Merton College; founded 1274. Its name originally, "Custos et *Scholares* Domus de Merton;"[5] and also, "Guardiani et *Scholarium* Domus, sive Collegii *Scholarium* de Merton in Universitate Oxonii."[6] The old colleges sometimes used more than one name. This college has now a *warden*, twenty-four fellows, fourteen *postmasters* (postrinistæ), four scholars, two chaplains, two clerks.

Peter House College, founded Cambridge, 1284. Name — "The *scholars* of the Bishop of Ely." "The number of persons on the foundation, being the number mentioned in the statutes, consisted of a master and fourteen *fellows*, sometimes called perpetual scholars, eight poor scholars, and two bibliotists. There had been *other fellowships and scholarships* annexed at different times and by different benefactors; *but these had never been considered as conferring on those who held them, any privileges as members of the so-*

[1] 2 Ayl. 47. Oxf. Guide, 159.
[2] Page 179, 180.
[3] 1 Ayl. 246.
[4] 1 Ayl. 394. Oxf. Guide, 169.
[5] 1 Ayl. 273, 275.
[6] 2 Ayl.

ciety."[1] The statutes given by Simon de Montacute, Bishop of Ely, 1344, are addressed "Magistro et *Scholaribus* domus nostræ Sancti Petri. Cantab."; and he directs that these fourteen "*Scholares* essent *perpetui* et studiosi," &c.[2] The statutes constantly designate what are now called "Fellows" as *scholares*.[3]

From these citations it is apparent that there is nothing technical in the word "Fellow," as applied to colleges; that it is sometimes not found in the words of the charters, and yet exists in the foundation; that it is sometimes used as synonymous with *student* (*studens*), sometimes with *scholar* (*scholaris*); while at other times it imports something different, depending upon the usages and statutes of the foundation.

Mr. Kyd views the word exactly in this light. He says, "In the colleges of the Universities, there are, in general, beside the head of the college,[4] two classes, the *scholars* and the *fellows*, each class having some rights and privileges distinct from the other; and where there are either only *scholars* or only *fellows*, or where the terms *scholars* and *fellows* are *synonymous, which is sometimes the case*, there is generally a distinction between junior and senior *fellows*, and junior and senior *scholars*. Independent members, usually called '*fellow-commoners*,' are mere *boarders*, and have no corporate rights."[5]

In corroboration of these remarks I may add, that the Universities both of Oxford and Cambridge, which embrace all the colleges, and in convocation all the members of the government of the respective colleges are incorporated by the name of "The Chancellor, Masters, and *Scholars* of the University" of Oxford and Cambridge, respectively.[6]

1 Rex *v*. Bishop of Ely, 2 T. R. 290, 291. 2 Id. 296.
3 Id. 299, 302–305.
4 The head has different names in different colleges — Dean, Rector, Provost, Warden, President, Master, Principal. — *Oxf. Guide*, 179.
5 1 Kyd, Corp. 329, 330.
6 Stat. 13 Eliz. Prynne, Animad. 166; 1 Ayl. 197.

We may deceive ourselves by affixing to the words used in English colleges the sense in which we are accustomed to use them. Thus, *scholar* with us means an undergraduate, who is taught; so does *student*. But in Oxford, "*scholars*," in some few colleges, are *probationary fellows;* in others, they are mere *beneficiaries*, having an annual sum allowed towards their education. The Oxford Guide says, (p. 180) "Strangers are often perplexed with the terms *scholar* and *student*, and sometimes apply them indiscriminately *to all members* of the University. By a *scholar* of a college is meant the person who holds the rank above-mentioned, and that of a *student* is one of the *one hundred and one* members of that name at Christ Church, whose rank is similar to that of *fellow* of other colleges." It is plain, therefore, that *scholar* and *student* do not import there, as with us, all undergraduates, who resort there for education; but fellows and scholars on the foundation.

From the facts which I have stated, I derive the conclusion that, for all the purposes of a college charter, the terms Fellow, Scholar, Socius, Associate, Student, may be used, nay, are used, to indicate the same general thing; and that the rights depend, not on the name, but *singly* and *solely* on the *government* provided by the *charter*, and by the *statutes* of the foundation. If so, the term "Fellow" imports no more in a college charter, than in any other act of incorporation. This, however, will be more clear as we advance in our discussion of some other points. Lord Mansfield, in Rex *v.* Dr. Askew, 4 Burr. 2195, says, "I consider the words *Socii*, *Communitas*, *Collegium*, *Societas*, *Collega*, and *Fellows*, as synonymous; and every *socius* or *collega* as a member of the society, or corporation, or college." So Plowden says, (p. 103,) Master and Fellows "is the usual recital of a corporation." The case turned on the point.

II. The *qualifications* of Fellows are not the same in all the colleges, but vary, being entirely governed by the charter and statutes of the foundation.

The Oxford Guide says, (p. 180,) "The qualifications for fellowships vary in almost every society. The Fellows are, according to the statutes of the college, elected from *certain public schools*, and admitted on their arrival in Oxford; or they are *young men* who, having studied and distinguished themselves in other colleges, offer themselves as candidates, and are selected by the votes of the Fellows. In some societies they are confined to the natives of particular counties, or elected from the scholars; and in others the kindred of the founder have peculiar privileges." It adds, (p. 180) "The Fellows, in conjunction with the head of the college are, *in all cases*, the directors of the internal regulations of their society, and the managers of its property and estates." In this passage there is a slight mistake; it should be, in *most* cases.

Thus, in All-Souls College, Oxford, founded in 1437. The college is composed of a warden and forty fellows, two chaplains, six clerks, of kin to the founder, or born in the province of Canterbury.[1] — New College, founded in 1379. The foundation is seventy fellows from Winchester College, ten chaplains, &c.[2] — Wadham College, founded in 1613. The fellows are chosen from the scholars of the college.[3] — Corpus Christi College. The fellowships must be distributed among natives of different counties.[4] So, the Bishop of Durham in 1403 gave a manor to University College, for the maintenance of three fellows born in York or Durham, without respect to degrees, and though *undergraduates.*[5]

It is remarkable that in no instance is *previous residence* required, as a distinct qualification; though in some instances it may be inferred, in connection with other qualifications; as where the qualification is that the party, to be a Fellow, must be elected from the scholars of the same college. There are many other qualifications and limitations as to Fellows. These will more properly fall under the subsequent heads.

III. The enumeration of qualifications in the Memorial is

1 Oxf. Guide, p. 58.
2 Id. 95.
3 Id. 101.
4 1 Ayl. 394.
5 Id. 152.

incorrect and incomplete. It refers to three things, as constituting necessary qualifications, viz.: Residence, Instruction, and Government, in the college.

1. As to *Residence.* — This is often required; not by the terms of the charter; not *ex vi termini* Fellow; but from the statutes of the foundation.

But residence is not universally required. This may be inferred from several authorities. Thus, in Rex *v.* Grundon,[1] where a fellow-commoner was excluded from the college gardens of Queen's College, Cambridge, on an indictment, one question was whether he was legally expelled, it having been done by the Master and less than a majority of the Fellows. The statute was, that it should be done, " de consensu Presidentis et majoris partis sociorum." It was said, that this had already been considered in construction as meaning, of the Fellows *resident* in the college.[2] Lord Mansfield and the Court thought the construction right. Now, the question could not have arisen if there had not been *non-resident* Fellows.

So Dr. Radcliffe's foundation in University College.[3] It is expressly for the support of two persons, elected out of the physic line, for their maintenance for ten years in the study of physic, and to *travel half the time.* Lord Hardwicke considered these as Fellows and members of the college, though not required to be residents.

But what is decisive, as coming from the highest authority, is what Lord Camden says, in Hayes *v.* Long.[4] It was a case against a non-resident Fellow of Christ Church College. It is to be remembered, that there are no Fellows, *eo nomine*, in that college; but they are called *Students.* The University of Oxford claimed cognizance of the law under its charter. The Court denied it, holding that the party, being a curate at Benson, (twelve miles south of Oxford,) was a non-resident Fellow; and none but resident Fellows

[1] Cowper, 315.
[2] Id. 322.
[3] Atty. Gen. *v.* Stephens, 1 Atk. 358, 360.
[4] 2 Wils. 310.

were entitled to the benefit. Lord Camden said, "Great numbers of persons remain on the books, *long after they have left* the University, on purpose to vote for members, &c.; many who are Fellows of colleges *never go thither at all.* I myself was one for a long time *and never went there at all.*" So Sir William Jones, (Oxford,)[1] Mr. Justice Blackstone, (All-Souls College,)[2] were Fellows long after they ceased to reside at college; Mr. Blackstone from 1743 to 1761; Sir William Jones from 1766 to 1783. Johnson, in his Lives of the Poets, states that Prior, the poet, at fifty-three years of age had no resource but his fellowship (p. 340); yet Prior was not a resident. It is clear, therefore, that *residence* is not a universal qualification of a Fellow, though probably by the statutes of a particular college it very often is made so.

2. As to *Instruction.*—I have no doubt, that the Fellows are not *ipso facto* required to be Instructors or Tutors. In none of the statutes or charters (summarily stated) that I have seen, is such a qualification spoken of, as attaching to Fellows necessarily. Can the *one hundred and one* Fellows of Christ Church College be all Tutors in that college, when the greatest number of members of all sorts are not more than seven hundred, half of whom are not residents? I think I shall by-and-by show, that, as Fellows, they never or rarely are Tutors.

It is stated in the Oxford Guide generally, that "The *Tutors* [not the Fellows] undertake the direction of the classical, mathematical, and other studies of the *junior members* [that is, of the college.] Many of the undergraduates have also private tutors." (p. 180.) This paragraph occurs in a general description of the officers, &c., and after the description of Fellows as a distinct class.

Trinity College, or Hall, Cambridge, has a foundation of a Master and twelve Fellows. "Ten of the Fellows were usually laymen; and *two* were in holy orders, who performed

1 See Lord Teignmouth's Life, 36, 93, 113, 142, 221.

2 Preface to W. Blackstone's Rep. 7, 9, 10, 13, 16.

the duty in the chapel, and *were usually the college tutors*."[1] This shows, that the other ten were not.

Ayliffe, in his History of Oxford, says,[2] that scholars in every college are to have their tutors, till promoted to a degree; and no one may be a tutor, unless a graduate of some faculty, of learning, and probity, and religion, *to be approved of by the head* of the house wherein he lives. How can this be, if the Fellows are *ex officio* "Tutors?"

The very case cited in page third of the Memorial, as to Dr. E. Calamy, as *Tanquam Socius* of Pembroke Hall, is in our favor. He was entitled to the society of the Fellows, and had additional privileges, one of which was *pupillos, leave to take pupils.* From which I should infer, that this was a peculiar privilege of some, instead of a common duty of all Fellows.

3. As to the *government* of the college.— This, probably, more generally than any other thing, attaches to the Fellows. But it attaches to them, not as Fellows, but as corporators, where the charter gives the authority.

But all Fellows do not participate in the powers or authorities of the college. It is manifest, that, whether they do or do not, must depend upon the charter and statutes of the founder. So Ayliffe says.[3]

The Oxford Guide says, "The members of the University may be divided into two classes; those on the foundation, commonly called *dependent members;* and those not on the foundation, termed *independent members.*

"*The independent members* consist of such persons as repair to the University for their education and degrees; but who, as they have no claim on the estate of the society to which they belong, so they possess no voice or authority in its management; and during their residence in a college or hall, they are supported at their own expense."[4]

"The *dependent members*, or members on the foundation,

[1] Ex parte Wrangham, 2 Ves. jr. 609.
[2] 2 Ayliffe, 115.
[3] Ib. 29.
[4] Oxf. Guide, p. 179.

are as follows: — The *head* of the college, the *fellows*, (called *students* at Christ Church,) the *scholars*, (called *demies*[1] at Magdalen,) *chaplains*, and *Bible clerks*.

"The dependent members derive emolument from the revenues of their societies; and *on some of them the management and discipline of the whole body devolve*."[2]

"The independent members are *noblemen*, *gentlemen-commoners*, (at Worcester called *fellow-commoners*,) and *commoners*."[3]

In Christ Church College we have already seen that there are Fellows on the foundation; but the government of the college belongs exclusively to the *Dean* and *Chapter*.[4]

In many of the colleges the original foundation provided for a limited number of fellowships only. Where the charter admitted of an increase of the number without violating its provisions, new fellowships have from time to time been ingrafted on the college; and in such cases the new ingrafted Fellows enjoy the same privileges as the old, the corporators only being increased.

The doctrine of law is, that, if the charter does not restrict the number of Fellows, all new ones partake of the original privileges and duties. So, in St. John's College *v*. Todington,[5] it was held. So, in Attorney-General *v*. Talbot, 1 Ves. 78, 475; S. C. 3 Atk. 662.

But where the charter restricts the Fellows to a particular number, there, though there may be new ingrafted fellowships, yet *the latter have no privileges in the government, like the old*, but only partake of the bounty of their own founder. They are no part of the collegiate body. It is so said by the Attorney-General, in Attorney-General *v*. Talbot, 3 Atk. 662, 670, and admitted by the Court, Id. 674. The same doctrine was held in Rex *v*. Bishop of Ely, 2 Term Rep. 290.

1 So called originally on account of their being entitled to *half* commons only.

2 Oxf. Guide, 179.

3 Id. 183.

4 1 Ayliffe, 240.

5 1 Burr, 158.

Therefore, in Peter-House College, where the number of Fellows is by the statutes of the foundation restricted to fourteen, and other fellowships have been since ingrafted; these latter, though called Fellows, have no corporate rights or authorities.[1]

It seems clear, from the foregoing statements, that in the English colleges the Fellows are not necessarily either *residents*, *tutors*, or *governors*. I imagine the only thing common to all (and that I only conjecture) is, that they are all *stipendiaries*, or members on the foundation. And here I might advert to some other circumstances respecting English Fellows, which will show that other adjuncts, as well as residence, &c., attach to them. But I reserve them for the fourth head.

IV. The original intention and objects of the English Fellowship are very materially different from those, which the Memorial supposes to be the main objects of the same office in our college.

I need not advert to the known fact, that all colleges are eleemosynary corporations. Lord Holt says, "There is no difference between a college and an hospital, except only in degree. A hospital is for those that are poor, and mean, and low, and sickly. A college is for another sort of indigent persons; but it hath another intent, *to study in, and breed up persons in the world that have not otherwise to live.*"[2] What I mean to assert is, that the sole scope and design of the English colleges were to provide maintenance and funds to *educate persons;* that the Fellows (by whatever name they were called, whether Fellows, Scholars, Students, or otherwise,) were not intended to be *instructors*, but to be themselves *instructed;* that the object was to enable the Fellows to go to the colleges to learn, and not to give learning to others. If this be established, how will it be possible to affirm, that the charter of Harvard College of 1650 could

[1] 2 T. R. 291.

[2] Phillips *v.* Bury, 2 T. R. 291.

intend the same sort of persons? The whole Memorial disavows it.

Colleges were founded *ad orandum et studendum*, says Ayliffe,[1] for prayer and study. This is true; but it is also true that the *Fellows* themselves were to *pray* and to *study*. Let us recur to some of the foundations of the principal colleges.

In All-Souls College, the statutes of the founder direct, that *twenty-four* of the *Fellows* (the whole number being forty) shall apply themselves to the *study* of *philosophy* and *divinity*, and *sixteen* to the science of *the civil and canon law*. The latter are called *lawyers*, the former *artists*.[2]

In Magdalen College some of the Fellows are expressly required to be of a particular diocese, and educated in the study of divinity only; as Mr. Ingledon's. The original foundation was for *poor* and *indigent clerks* in the University, *studying* the arts and sciences.[3]

In Brazen-Nose College, the original statutes confine the Fellows to the study of divinity and philosophy: "For a principal and sixty scholars *to receive an education in philosophy and divinity here*."[4]

In University College, the Bishop of Durham founded three fellowships, for the maintenance of three *Fellows*, though *undergraduates*.[5]

In New College the founder divided his Fellows into *artists* and *lawyers;* namely, ten civil law, ten canon law, and the remaining fifty *to study* the arts and divinity.[6]

In Exeter College the original statutes direct, that the persons to live on this charity shall not exceed thirteen; namely, one student in divinity, one in law, the other in philosophy.[7]

In Trinity College, (Oxford,) the original statutes direct the college to be for *poor and indigent scholars* in the University; *twelve* are styled *Fellows*, *to be educated* in the study

1 2 Ayl. 3. 2 1 Ayl. 338. 3 Id. 347. 4 Id. 378.
5 Id. 152. 6 Id. 315, 319. 7 Id. 207.

of philosophy and divinity; eight called *scholars*, to be educated in logic, rhetoric, &c.[1]

In St. John's College the charter is for a president and fifty Fellows or scholars; twelve to be lawyers, three chaplain priests, three lay clerks, to live unmarried, and sixty choristers.[2]

In Pembroke College seven of the fourteen Fellows are *to be in holy orders.*

In Christ Church College, originally, of the one hundred students or Fellows, forty were required to be *grammar scholars;* and Queen Elizabeth converted these forty into *students.*[3]

And I believe it will be found that the object uniformly was to *educate the Fellows*, so as to fit them for the learned professions, and principally for the church. In 4 Mod. 84, it was said by counsel, *arguendo*, "A fellowship of a college is for a private design only, *to study.*"

Dr. Radcliffe's fellowships, already referred to, were of this nature. They were for the maintenance of two persons, for *ten years*, in the *study of physic*, to travel half the time.[4]

This leads me to another topic, the *duration of fellowships.* The English fellowships are not all *perpetual*, that is, during life, if the party behaves well. Some undoubtedly are; as in Peter-House, Cambridge; for the statutes of the foundation are, that they shall be scholares *perpetui* et studiosi, *insistentes studio literarum.*[5] But this is far from being universal. We see Dr. Radcliffe's are only for *ten years.*

In Wadham College, founded in 1613, by the statutes, the Fellows are *superannuated*, and resign their fellowships, on the completion of eighteen years from the expiration of their regency.[6]

In Baliol College, founded in 1263, at first each Fellow

[1] 1 Ayl. 412.
[2] Id. 418, 419.
[3] Id. 440.
[4] 1 Atk. R. 358.
[5] 2 T. R. 296, 297.
[6] 1 Ayl. 434.

received only 8*d.* per week, and was under an obligation of leaving the college, *as soon as he had taken a master's degree.*[1]

Probably most fellowships were not looked upon as permanencies, but merely as places before preferment. I observe that Mr. Brown, in arguing in 3 Atk. R. 669, says, that the fellowships in the Universities, one with another, are not of great value, perhaps not above £24 or £25 a year.

I believe it is agreed on all sides that the Fellows of Harvard College, under the charter of 1650, hold their offices during good behavior. So Mr. Everett agrees in his pamphlet.

There are some other circumstances attached to fellowships in England which deserve notice.

Ayliffe says, that the founders of the colleges have *generally* provided, not only, that the heads should be divines; but that the *Fellows also should* in a competent time *enter into holy orders.* This shows that *Fellows* were there to *learn* and to *qualify* themselves for the church.

So "the Fellows cannot marry, nor succeed to a college living, nor indeed to another, beyond a certain value, without relinquishing their fellowships."[2]

Probably there are many other peculiarities attached to them, which a minute inspection of the charters and statutes (which I regret are not within my reach) would exhibit.

To conclude this summary. From these remarks, we perceive that it cannot be maintained for a moment, that the term "Fellow" necessarily imports a resident, an instructor, a governor of a college, or a corporator, in England. Nor is there any identity in the *rights*, *duties*, *powers*, *privileges*, *tenure of office*, or *qualifications* of *English Fellows.* The name itself is often away, when the party is still *deemed*, though not *styled*, a *Fellow.* How, then, can it be correctly

[1] Id. 263, 268.

[2] Oxf. Guide, 190.

said, that a "Fellow" means in the charter of 1650 a certain personage, whose duties and qualifications are well known and fixed?

If it be said that Fellows must be *residents;* many of the English Fellows are *non-residents.*

If it be said that they must be *instructors;* many (I presume most) of the English Fellows are *not instructors.* So far from it, the object in the original creation of most, if not all, of the foundations, is charity, — to support the Fellows in their own studies, and not in teaching others. They may now teach; but it is a distinct business from their fellowships, for which, I doubt not, they receive a distinct compensation.

If it be said, that they must be *Corporators*, or members of the Corporation, entitled to exercise the government, and conduct the revenues of the government; there are many English Fellows, who have no such authority, and are *not corporators.* Even a part of the body named in the charter may not have a title to such government. Some colleges are incorporated as *Master*, *Fellows*, and *Scholars.* Now, though "scholars," as here used, does not mean, what we call "scholars," but beneficiaries of a certain grade; yet I do not doubt, that in some cases the "scholars" are altogether excluded from the government by the statutes or charters. Traces are to be found in our books leading to this conjecture; but I affirm nothing positively, because I have not yet seen a direct case. Where "scholars" are, or may be, *undergraduates*, or *grammar scholars*, (as some foundations are,) it is presumable that they are not *governors.* Certain it is, that such statutes may be made, and such charters granted.

So, many English Fellows are required to study particular branches of science, as divinity, law, philosophy, the civil law, the canon law; to be clerks; to be artists; to be medical students; to be poor and indigent; to be in holy orders; as qualifications for the office.

Many English Fellows hold their places for life; some for

years; some merely until they graduate as masters. Acceptance of church livings, or possession of church livings of a certain value, vacates some fellowships, and constitutes ineligibility. Livings of a less value constitute no vacancy or ineligibility. Absence for six months vacates some fellowships.[1] Travelling for five years is indispensable as a qualification in others, (Dr. Radcliffe's Fellowships.)

Some English Fellows are chosen from particular schools; some from particular colleges, counties, dioceses; some from inferior grades of persons in their own college, as scholars, probationary Fellows; some from the University at large; some must be graduates; some must be undergraduates.

It is said, "*All* fellows are bound not to marry." Celibacy is, therefore, it seems, a universal qualification.

What qualifications, then, are we to take, or reject? Shall we say, that all must be residents, because some are? that all must be tutors, though all originally were pupils or students? that all must be corporators, or collegiate governors, when a part only are, or were? Why not take the opposite course; and say, that all may be non-residents, because some are, &c.?

If universality of qualification be the ground of adoption of a similar qualification here, then all our Fellows ought to be in *celibacy*. Who in *America* ever contended for that, from the charter of 1650 downwards?

The truth is, the word "Fellow" has not, as to colleges, any peculiar meaning. The *students* at Christ Church; the *demies* at Magdalen; the *scholars* in some other colleges, are Fellows in fact, though not in name. Why? Because they are known admitted *members* on the foundation. Ingrafted Fellows are not the less Fellows, because they constitute no part of the original or present college Corporation. Why? Because "Fellow" imports no particular powers, authorities, or duties; but simply Socius, Associate,

[1] 2 Term Rep. 291.

or Member of the foundation, entitled to such privileges, and such only as the charter or statutes define or admit.

When, therefore, we construe the charter of 1650, we must construe it upon its own terms, and apply to the persons named therein such powers, and authorities, and qualifications, as the charter itself provides, and no other. Where the charter is silent, we are not at liberty to insert any limitations.

If I am right in this view of the case, the ground proposed by the Memorial must be surrendered. If the main argument fail, there is an end of all that follows.

If there be not an identity between our Fellows and the English Fellows, or between all of the latter, as to rights, duties, and privileges, I do not see how any argument can be bottomed on it. Conjectural similarity is of no importance. Until we can definitely affirm, what ours are, and theirs are, we cannot proceed; for until that is done we can institute no process of comparison, as to similarity or dissimilarity. In the order of things, therefore, the first point is to ascertain what our Fellows are.

But I propose to notice some of the auxiliary grounds stated to fortify the principal one.

V. It is said, that there were persons in the College at the time of the charter, and previously, known by the denomination of "Fellows." This I freely admit. The preamble of the charter states it; the form of admission states it; and other college records recognize it. The Memorial does not pretend that there is any thing in the college records before the formula of admitting Fellows, that recognizes it. When that formula was first adopted is not stated, or exactly known. But it appears in the college records immediately after "certain orders by the scholars and officers of the college to be observed," under date of 28th March, 1650. The next preceding entry in the book is the 26th of March, 1650. President Leverett, in his Journal, states, that it was written by the Rev. Jonathan Mitchell, one of the members of the

Corporation. There is no evidence that it was ever, after the charter of 1650, used upon the admission of any Fellow of the Corporation under the charter.

There is reason to believe, that the word "Fellow" was not used, or the person known in the College, in 1646. There is an entry in the book entitled, "The laws, liberties, and orders of the College, confirmed by the Overseers and President in the years 1642, 1643, 1644, 1645, 1646." In this collection, consisting of nineteen articles, "Tutors" are frequently mentioned; "Fellows" are never mentioned. Yet in some instances, if they then existed, there would be a propriety in naming them; as in the 7th article, which requires of the scholars, that "they shall honor, as their parents, magistrates, elders, *tutors*, and aged persons."

In January 13, 1647, there is an agreement on the books for a lease for years to Richard Taylor of a shop in Boston belonging to the College, in which he covenants to leave it in good repair, &c., "to Harvard College, the President and *Fellows* thereof."

In an entry on 6th May, 1650, there is an order of the Overseers directing that no scholar, "without the fore-acquaintance and leave of the president and his *tutor*, or, in the absence of either of them, of *two* of the *senior Fellows*," should be present at any public meeting or concourse of people, "in the time or hours of the College exercise, public or private." It is added, in the same orders, "Neither shall any scholar exercise himself in any military band, unless of known gravity, and of approved sober and virtuous conversation, and that with the leave of the president and his *tutor*." These orders clearly show, that at this time *Tutor* and *Fellow* were not identical in the College; and that there were "*Senior Fellows*," who were not *Tutors*. How, then, can we say, that "*Fellows*" in the charter meant *Instructors?* So, in the "Formula admittendi scholares ædiles," the scholar is, by one article, to show reverence to the *President* "una *cum sociis* singulis," and, in the next article, to *obey his tutor*.

In such obscure transactions of so early a period, with so few materials to give certainty, I may mistake in the view that I take of these facts. But I feel great confidence in the conjecture, that the "*Fellows*," here referred to, were graduates of the College, then resident there and pursuing their studies, to qualify them for some profession, and probably they were beneficiaries. It would be natural, that there should not be any such Fellows there until 1646, because there were so few graduates, (the first being only four years before,) who were not in fact tutors.

In respect to the words in Taylor's lease, either the word, "Fellows," there used, is loosely used to designate the Immediate Government of the College; or, what is possible, the shop may have been a donation for the benefit of the President and Fellows; and so the lease conformed to the words of the grant, however inartificially drawn.

In respect to the Formula.[1] It does not show, who the *socii* were, or what was their occupation. The third article requires them to *instruct* all the students committed to their charge. But it does not prove, that they were the general tutors. If they were beneficiaries, they might properly be required, in the then infant state of the College, to perform *some duty* there. But the preceding entry shows, that they were not identical with *tutors*, whose duty it was to give general instruction.

The 4th article proves nothing, as to these "*Fellows*" having any particular office or government over the College, or being the actual administrators of its funds. For, in another article, a similar engagement is required of the *scholars*, in the form entitled "In *scholaribus* admittendis," or, according to the record in Lib. 3, p. 9, "Formula admittendi *scholares œdiles*." The words in the 4th article are, "Sedulo prospicies ne quid detrimenti collegium capiat, quantum in te situm est, sive in ejus *sumptibus*, sive in edi-

[1] Memo. p. 4.

ficiis et structura, fundis, *proventibus*, fenestris, ceterisque omnibus, quæ nunc ad collegium pertinent, aut dum egeris, pertinere possint."[1] Besides; the article itself contains but a very imperfect enumeration of the duties of *Fellows of the Corporation*. Their duties extend to making laws, elections, removals, investing funds, &c. The words may be construed, as merely an engagement to prevent any wanton dilapidations or mischiefs.

It is also perfectly clear, that "Fellows" and "Tutors," or general Instructors, were not used after the charter as identical terms; because, though there were five Fellows, there never were but two tutors until 1703. One Tutor was added in 1703, and another in 1720; and up to the year 1800 there were not more than four tutors.

But further. There could not, in the English sense of the term, "Fellow," (if by that is to be understood a collegiate corporator,) be any such persons as Fellows in Harvard College before 1650; for the charter of 1642 did not authorize any such officers to be created. That act (for it is a subsisting part of the chartered authority of the College) gives to the governor, deputy governor, magistrates, and teaching elders of the six neighboring towns, the powers of governing, regulating, and managing the College and its members, its revenues and concerns. And by implication they are created a corporation, for they are made capable of taking bequests, donations, revenues, &c., that had been, or might be, given to the College; and they were to manage the same "to the use and behoof of the College and the members thereof."

By *Members* of the College must have been meant all persons connected with the institution; namely, the president, instructors, and other officers, and the students. But they could not delegate their corporate powers to other persons. Nor could they make the president and instructors corporators. Nor could the president, or instructors, or per-

[1] College Records, under date December 10th, 1646.

sons called *Fellows*, take in *succession* by any bequest to them as a corporate body; for they were not so incorporated. The gifts and donations, given to the College, must have been given, in legal construction, to the governor and magistrates and elders. *They* must comply with the wills of the donors; and *they* only could take the donation. If any donor gave a fund to support any poor persons in their studies at the College, or any Fellows in the College, the words could import no more than this, that persons residing there, and, in a sense, members of the College, that is, beneficiaries upon the foundation, should be so maintained. But tutors in no exact sense could be considered as Fellows, *ipso facto;* but, as beneficiaries, they might be both Tutors and Fellows, that is, members on the foundation.

But I understand, that in point of fact the College records do not show, that before the time of the charter of 1650[1] any donations had been made for the maintenance of persons at the College, answering the description of Fellows at the English colleges, in the sense of the Memorial.[2] Some indigent students were provided for; and probably also some resident graduates, who received stipends. But as to Fellows on *permanent foundations*, I am not aware, that there now are, or ever have been, any in Harvard College correspondent to English Fellows. The only persons on permanent foundations are, as I believe, our *Professors.* The gifts of Glover, Keyne, and Pennoyer, might have authorized such foundations; but none have been established.

To be sure, in a loose and general sense, almost all persons, who are officers of the College, might be called Fellows, if by that word we are to understand, not English Fellows, but merely persons "resident at the College, and actually engaged there in carrying on the duties of instruction or government, and receiving a stipend for their services." Thus, Proctors and Regents fall within the description, as well as Tutors

[1] See as to Tutor's Pasture, *post.*

[2] Memo. p. 2.

and Professors. And the definition would apply as well to any resident graduate at the College, who should be casually intrusted with any instruction or government, however small, as to any tutor or professor. But though such a definition may exemplify what the Memorial now means by Fellows, it would in no respect help us to an understanding of what the charter meant by Fellows; for that is expressly argued in the Memorial to be what is meant in English colleges by Fellows.

It is incumbent on the Memorialists to show, that there were in Harvard College, before 1650, fellowships on foundations, like the English, before we are called upon to admit, that the charter used the word *Fellows* in that sense. They have not shown that by any direct or positive evidence.

But it is said, that the preamble of the charter shows, that there were such Fellows in the College previously. It may be admitted, that whatever is recited in the preamble should be assumed as facts at this period. What, then, are the facts stated in the preamble? It recites, that many well-disposed persons, &c., have given sundry gifts, &c., for the advancement of all good literature, arts, and sciences in Harvard College, &c., "and to the maintenance of the *President* and *Fellows*, and for all accommodations of buildings, and all other necessary provisions, that may conduce to the education of the English and Indian youth of this country in knowledge and godliness."

Now the sole question is, In what sense is the word "Fellows" here used?

The College charter was doubtless drawn under the direction of the college officers, as I shall show from a document by-and-by. At that time there were persons known in the college by the name of "Fellows." What were they? We are certain they were not Fellows on any foundation like those in English colleges, because none such then existed. We have strong proof that they were not tutors, for they are contradistinguished from tutors. They must, therefore, have been some persons resident at the college, and beneficiaries there; or graduates studying for the professions; or the term must have been used in a general sense, as importing the *Associates* of the President in the immediate business of the college. It cannot be presumed that the word meant to designate mere beneficiaries; for that would exclude tutors; and yet, I presume, the main grants must have been for instructors. I conclude, then, the sense is general, that grants had been made for the maintenance of the President and his Associates, that is, the other officers in the college, without designating them by any permanent or fixed character. The charter referred to the fact, and not to any particular quality in the parties.

The charter, then, declares that "the said college, &c., shall be a corporation consisting of *seven persons*, to wit: a President, *five Fellows*, and a Treasurer, or Bursar." Now, pausing here, if the corporation were any other than a college, could there be a doubt what the charter intended? If it had been a charter of the American Academy, or of the Royal Academy, or of a Bank, or of an Insurance Company, could any one doubt that by "Fellows" was meant a mere *designatio personarum* as equals, and associates, and members of the corporation? If the word, Trustees, or Directors, or Governors, or Members, had been inserted, would not the sense have been complete, and the same?

If the charter meant to incorporate persons, who were then acting officers, would it not have recited the fact? Were there *five Fellows* at the college at the time? Was there a Treasurer or Bursar? We know there was a President; but beyond that there is no certainty.

If the charter meant to incorporate certain persons then in office, as the Memorial seems in some parts to suppose, there was no need to designate any particular persons by name afterwards.

If it meant to *select* from the "Fellows," &c., then existing, then it created the select few a corporation, and ascertained them to be the present incumbents, without providing who should be the future incumbents.

If it is supposed, that the *existing collegiate officers* were incorporated, because it is said, that "the college shall be a corporation," the argument proves too much; for then it means the aggregate of the institution, *scholars* and *pupils*, as well as instructors and officers.

But the truth is, that the phrase is a very common one, though not a very exact one. It is only saying, that thereafter the college shall be under a corporate government. All-Souls College in Oxford, 1437, was incorporated by the name of "Collegium Animarum omnium defunctorum Oxonii." No one, however, supposes that the dead were incorporated. We well know that it is under the government of a Warden and forty Fellows. These were appointed by or after the act of incorporation.

The charter proceeds to name the persons who shall constitute the first corporation. This shows that they were not incorporated *ex officio*. The words are, "And that Henry Dunster shall be the first President, Samuel Mather, Samuel Danforth, *Masters of Arts*, Jonathan Mitchell, Comfort Starr, and Samuel Eaton, *Bachelors of Arts*, shall be the five Fellows, and Thomas Danforth to be present Treasurer; all of them being inhabitants of the Bay." Now, why are not these persons designated, instead of Masters and Bachelors of Arts, as existing Instructors or Fellows of the college? Why is it not said that they *are, and shall continue to be, Fellows*, instead of, *shall be Fellows?* Why are they described as "all of them being inhabitants of the Bay," instead of all of them being Fellows of the college?

The corporation are further by the charter "authorized, at any time or times, to elect a *new* President, *Fellows*, or Treasurer, so oft, from time to time, as any of the said persons shall die or be removed." They are to elect "*new Fellows;*" then the persons, who are to be successors, are not Fellows until elected. And there is no restriction as to the persons from whom they shall be chosen; of course they may be chosen at large. Even in the English colleges new Fellows may be chosen at large, unless the charter or statutes of the foundation prohibit it.

No duties are prescribed to the Fellows, as distinct from the duties of the corporation itself. It is not said they shall be, before or after the choice, residents or instructors. But, doubtless, they have authority as corporators to regulate the college, because the charter confers it on the corporation.

The charter adds, "Which said President and Fellows for the time being shall forever hereafter, in name and in fact, be one body politic and corporate in law to all intents and purposes, and shall have perpetual succession, and shall be called by the name of *President and Fellows of Harvard College*, and shall from time to time be eligible as aforesaid." As the corporation is designated as "President and Fellows," the Treasurer, though not so called, is properly, and in fact, a Fellow, in the sense of law; but he is also something more, namely, Bursar.

The President and Fellows are further authorized to "meet and choose such *officers* and servants for the college, and make such allowance to them, &c., as they shall think fit." It seems to me clear, that this part of the charter contemplates, that the *Officers* may be different from the Corporators. There are other clauses to the same purpose.

There was an order of the General Court in May, 1650, a few days only before the grant of the charter, which illustrates this subject. It is in these words: "In answer to the petition of Henry Dunster, President of Harvard College, in Cambridge, with relation to his desire in few particulars, namely, for the grant of a corporation for the well ordering and managing the affairs belonging to the college, the Court is ready to grant a corporation to the college, so as meet persons be presented to the Court, with a draft of their power and ability, neither *magistrates*, who are to be judges in point of difference, that shall or may fall out, nor *ministers*, who are *unwilling to accept* thereof," &c.

Now this appears to me to show that the legislature did not contemplate that none should be in the corporation, except *residents* and *instructors*. Why otherwise should the exception be confined to *magistrates*, and to such *ministers* as would not accept? Why not exclude all ministers not resident in the college? Why not exclude all persons not then in office at the college?

Further. If there were Fellows in the college at the time of the charter, they were then *Fellows of the House* or *Academical Fellows;* but they were certainly not *corporate Fellows*, that is, not Fellows of the existing corporation, for that was by law composed only of the governor, &c., magistrates, and elders. If there were more than *five*, then those not appointed of the corporation by the charter, remained simply *Academical Fellows*. Whether there were any such, I know not.

The Memorial lays stress on the supposed incongruity of saying, that *Fellow* means only *member* or *associate;* because it is said, that then the corporation consists of *seven* and not of *five Fellows*.

To me it is clear, from the words of the charter, that the Treasurer is necessarily a *Fellow*. The Treasurer is declared one of the corporation; the corporate name is "President and Fellows;" and it is said that the "President and Fellows" shall be a corporate body. How can this be, unless under the term "Fellows," is here included the *Treasurer?* If he is one of the corporation, and yet the corporation is composed of the President and Fellows, he must be a Fellow, or nothing.

The Memorial, too, supposes that it would be absurd to say a *Fellow* of the *Corporation*.

This is an extraordinary assertion. The words of the charter expressly declare that "The said college shall be a corporation consisting of seven persons, to wit, a President, five Fellows, and a Treasurer or Bursar." Observe, it does not say *the* President, *the* five Fellows, *the* Treasurer, now in office. Now of what were these five persons the Fellows? — Of the college, says the Memorial. The words of the charter are not so; they are Fellows of the corporation; for that is what the charter creates them. The President is President of the corporation; the Treasurer is Treasurer of the corporation; the Fellows are Fellows of the corporation. In common parlance we call them President, Fellows, and Treasurer of the college; but, strictly speaking, they are Fellows of the corporation. The Memorial confounds the corporate name of "President and Fellows of Havard College," with the character of the parties as resident members.

Nor is there any thing unusual or incorrect in the phrase. In the English colleges there are fellows who are not corporators, in other words, who are not Fellows of the corporation; and there are others, who are corporators. Thus, in Christ Church College, the Dean and Chapter constitute the sole corporation. The Fellows of the college (one hundred and one in number) are not members of the corporation. They are, therefore, strictly, only Fellows of the House, or Academical Fellows. So, in all those colleges, where the corporation consists of a limited number of Fellows by the original statutes, those Fellows, and those only, are Fellows of the corporation, that is, corporators. And all the ingrafted Fellows, who are very numerous, are only Fellows of the House, or Academical Fellows. In St. John's College, Cambridge, there are thirty-two original Fellows, and twenty-seven Fellows upon ingrafted foundations.[1] So, in Peter House College, Cambridge, the original Fellows are restricted to fourteen. There are many ingrafted Fellows. The former are Fellows of the corporation; the latter Fellows of the House only. It is a real distinction; and the words are accurate in

[1] 1 Burr. R. 202.

indicating the thing meant. Nay, more; if by "Fellows" were meant resident instructors or governors, &c., as the Memorial asserts, there would now be many Fellows in Harvard College, (supposing the five Fellows were all resident instructors,) who would be Fellows of the House, or Academical Fellows, and the five only would be Fellows of the corporation. There are many traces in the public proceedings in relation to the college, showing this distinction. The pretence of incongruity or absurdity, therefore, vanishes.

There must be some phrase to distinguish Members on the foundation and Corporators, from resident students, whether graduates or not. In many of the English colleges they are called *commoners*, in some cases *fellow-commoners*, &c.

In this connection, I advert again to the formula for the admission of Fellows. I think I have shown what these Fellows were; at all events, that they were not Corporators. This formula never was used for the induction of fellows after the charter. It really, therefore, has no bearing to prove what sort of Fellows the Corporation was to be composed of

It is said, however, that this formula has not been repealed; and, therefore, that it ought still to be considered as a subsisting regulation of the College. But it is a clear rule of law, that a statute for the government of a college may be presumed to be repealed from long disuse.[1] A disuse from the period of the charter would be decisive on this head, that it was then repealed. But it was in fact repealed by operation of law from the time the charter was granted; for, as the Corporation had the sole power under the charter to make laws and regulations, and the old regulations were not confirmed, either by the charter of 1650, or by any subsequent order, they fell with the old establishment.[2] This accounts, and satisfactorily, why nothing was done about or under them.

[1] Attorney-General *v.* Middleton, 2 Ves. 330.

[2] President Dunster, in his letter of 10th June, 1654, resigning his office, states the fact, "that our former laws and orders, by which we have managed our place, be *declared illegal and null.*" *College Charters, Ap.* 17.

But, in point of fact, were the Fellows first named all resident instructors at the time of the charter? It seems almost incredible, that they should all have been so; for the College had not more than thirty scholars, and to have employed five tutors at that time, or before, would seem utterly inconsistent with the acknowledged poverty of the College. It is probable, that Samuel Mather was an instructor; Mitchell may have been an instructor; Samuel Danforth was, probably, an instructor, or one of those, who were denominated Fellows. Whether Eaton and Starr were, I have no means of knowing. The probability is, that they were not. It is asked, why persons so young were selected. The answer is, that at that time the Colony was small, the charge burdensome, and the order of the General Court, in May, 1650, agreeing to give a charter, shows, that there was a difficulty in getting *ministers* to accept. They probably took men, though young, who were disposed to be *zealous* in the College affairs. If they were all Fellows, why were they not so designated in the charter? It was the peculiar and appropriate name. Why are they designated as *Masters*, and *Bachelors*, and *Inhabitants of the Bay*, and not as *Fellows?*

As to Samuel Danforth, there are some facts worthy of notice. The charter was granted on the 31st of May, 1650. The Roxbury records, under date of 12th May, 1650, have the following clause: "Samuel Danforth recommended and dismissed from Cambridge church, and *admitted here*." This shows, that he either had then removed, or contemplated a removal, from Cambridge. On the 24th September, 1650, Samuel Danforth was ordained pastor of the church in Roxbury. Now, it must be inferred from these facts, that his intention to remove from Cambridge and settle at Roxbury was known to the College officers. If residence and instruction were indispensable for a Fellow of the Corporation, would his name, under these circumstances, have been inserted originally in the charter? He accepted the office. There is no proof, that he ever resigned it, or was removed. If not, then the legal presumption is, that he remained in office until his death, which was on the 19th day of the 8th month, 1674. In the charter of 1672, in which Samuel Danforth is named as a Corporator, he is described as " Fellow of the said College," which certainly was meant to state his present designation; for the present designation of all the other Fellows is given; as, " Minister of the church," " Teacher of the church," " Master of Arts," &c. In a note in the College Records, (No. 3, p. 63,) stating his death, it is said, " This day died Samuel Danforth, *Senior Fellow of the College.*"

These facts would, probably, be thought decisive proof, that, notwithstanding Danforth's non-residence, he remained a member of the Corporation until his death. But there are some circumstances, brought to discredit this conclusion by the learned Professor, Mr. Everett, in the Pamphlet alluded to, pp. 30 and 34. Thus, Dr. Hoar, writing to his nephew, in a letter of 27th March, 1661, and speaking of Richardson's Tables, says, " I know no way to recover them, but of some, that were of *that society in former times;* I suppose *Mr. Danforth*, Mr. Mitchell, and others have them."[1]

Now when was this letter written? Mr. Everett does not give the date; but it was in 1661. Mr. Danforth had been a student and a *tutor* at the College. What Dr. Hoar refers to is, that when Danforth was there as a student or tutor, he had these Tables transcribed. But this does not show, that he was not a corporate Fellow at the time; but only not then a resident of the *society*. It is common, but it is loose language.

Another circumstance relied on is, what is stated in Johnson's Wonder-working Providence, in a passage of a letter in 1651. He writes, " Also the godly *Mr. Samuel Danforth*, &c. He put forth many almanacs, and is now called to the office of a teaching elder in the church of Christ at Roxbury, who *was* one of the *Fellows* of this College." The only question

[1] Hist. Collect. vi. 103.

is, what the writer means by "Fellow." If he meant a Fellow in the sense of *Tutor*, or resident instructor, and as a mere synonyme, there is no difficulty; and if the Memorial is right, that the instructors were so called, the writer is correct. But the question is, did he mean to assert, that Danforth had then resigned his seat as a Fellow of *the Corporation*, or only that he had left the College? Surely, this language cannot overturn the strong presumption of law arising from the other facts already mentioned.

But, for the purpose of argument, I am willing to concede, (what has not been proved,) that all the persons named in the charter were at the time *Tutors* and *Fellows*, in the sense of the Memorial, in the College. What then? It proves, that they were *eligible* as Fellows of the Corporation, not that, *ipso facto*, they were under the charter the Corporators. Much less does it prove, that they, and *they alone*, were eligible as members of the Corporation.

Mr. Everett now surrenders this point. He admits, that *any person* may be elected as a Fellow into the Corporation, whether a resident or non-resident instructor, or not. All he now contends for is, that, after their election the Fellows ought to be residents, and assist in the instruction or government of the College. This certainly surrenders much of the original argument; for if prior residence and instruction were not indispensable qualifications for the office, the charter did not refer to the existing Fellows. It did not designate them; it did not make it a condition precedent, that they should be resident and instructors. But at most, *ex vi termini*, "Fellow" imported a subsequent obligation to reside and instruct.

This point has been already fully considered; and I leave it, and proceed to notice some other documents, introduced by the friends of the Memorial.

First. In August, 1652, two years after the charter, a collection was directed to be made for the maintenance of the President and Fellows of the College. The Memorial and the Argument of Mr. Everett suppose that by such a gift *after the charter* the maintenance should be for the individual Fellows of the College. I apprehend in law, that such a gift, generally made, would be construed, as a mere gift to the *Corporation* by its *corporate name*, and the maintenance to be the general maintenance of the institution. The words of this order are, "for the maintenance of the President, *certain Fellows*, and poor scholars," and therefore may be construed justly to apply to individuals. But what does this prove? that all the Fellows were to be maintained? No; "*certain* Fellows" only. At this very time, some of the Fellows, named in the charter, were doubtless instructors; all of them probably were not. This accounts for the distinction.[1]

The like remarks are generally applicable to the donation of the General Court, in June, 1653, "for the more comfortable maintenance of the President, Fellows, and Students" of the College.[2] And the grant is made, in terms, "unto the said *Society* and *Corporation*." The charter then had an existence, and the Corporation was recognized, as a subsisting body, governing the College. It might be proper to give stipends even to the students at that time.

In August, 1653, the General Court ordered, that the Cambridge rate should be paid to the College, for the discharge of any debt from the country to the College; and if any surplus, it was "to be and remain for the College stock, and for further clearing and settling all matters in the College, in reference to the yearly maintenance of the President, Fellows, and necessary officers thereof, and repairing the houses."[3] Now this only shows, that there were Fellows at the College at that time, who needed support. But the document goes further. It shows that a committee was appointed for certain objects of inquiry, as to the expenditures of the College; among them, to "consider what number of Fellows may be necessary for carrying on the work in the College, and what yearly allowance they shall have, and how to be paid." Now,

1 Letter to John Lowell, Esq., p. 62. 2 Ib. 3 Ibid. p. 63, 64.

this shows, that the General Court contemplated, that all the Fellows would not be required for the purpose; that all might not be resident, or maintained; leaving it, not on the charter, but as a matter of policy and expediency.

The committee made a report. We have not that report. But in August, 1653, the General Court passed an order, that the donations should be continued "to the care and trust of the Overseers of the College;" and the produce was "to be for the maintenance of the President, *Fellows*, and other necessary charges of the College, and the several yearly allowances of the President and Fellows; to be proportioned as the said Overseers shall determine."[1] Now, this proves no more than the fact, that there were then "Fellows" at the College, who ought to be maintained; not that *all* the Fellows ought to reside there, or that all were maintained, and did reside there.

I observe, that, in President Dunster's resignation, on the 10th June, 1654, he speaks not only of new regulations having been imposed on the College, and the former laws annulled; [by whom?] but he says, "that, whatever we do is to myself and *the Fellows* unwarrantable, and not secure." Now, he cannot be supposed to speak of himself and the Fellows of the Corporation; for the charter gave them express warrant to make by-laws, &c., the Overseers consenting thereto. He probably, therefore, alludes to the Fellows of the House, who had no authority at all, unless so far as the Corporation gave them authority. But if he refers to the Fellows of the Corporation, he then alludes solely to the negative of the Overseers. It appears to me, therefore, that the charter was really acted upon from its original grant, though feebly.

The grant of Charlestown ferry, in 1654, &c., is to the same effect.[2]

In respect to the Fellows' or Tutors' Lot, I can say but

[1] Letter, p. 65.

[2] Colony Laws, 1672, p. 30; Letter, p. 66.

little, as I have not seen the deed, which is said to be in Latin.[1] I know not the terms of the grant, or the persons to whom granted. It is said by Mr. Everett, in his Pamphlet, that it was granted in 1645 (five years before the charter); and from the Memorial and the Pamphlet I gather, that it was given to the "Fellows" of the College, *eo nomine*.[2] If so, it was a void grant; for they were not at that time a Corporation, capable of taking in succession by that or any other name. If given to the existing Body or Corporation, that is, to the governor, &c., for the use of the Fellows, doubtless it referred to that class of persons known there at that time by the name of Fellows, whether they were instructors or not. We have already seen, that in 1650, "Tutors" and "Fellows" were contradistinguished in the College orders. But I am given to understand, by those who are acquainted with the terms of this deed, that they have been totally misconceived by the writer of the Pamphlet; and that the deed is a legal grant to the College itself by its corporate name. I dismiss this point, therefore, as one upon which I am not sufficiently informed to risk an argument.

[Mr. John Lowell (one of the Overseers) here rose, and stated, that the Pamphlet of Professor Everett had totally mistaken the grant of the Tutors' Lot; that it was in fact a grant to the College by its corporate name, and passed a good title to it.]

As to Coggan's grant, in 1652, for the use of the President and Fellows of Harvard College,[3] I apprehend it is a grant to the Corporation in its corporate character.

Glover's legacy, in 1653, to Harvard College, "for and towards the maintenance of a *Fellow* there five pounds forever,"[4] must be understood as referring not to the *Fellows of the Corporation*, but to a person approaching somewhat to the description of an English Fellow; that is, to a person to be *taught*, and not to *teach*.

[1] Memo. 5. [2] Letter 25, 39, 69. [3] Id. 69. [4] Id. 70.

So, Keyne's legacy of £320, in 1653, "for poor and hopeful scholars, and for some addition yearly to the poorer sort of *Fellows*."[1] This surely refers to a class of Fellows resident at the College and not of the Corporation.

Pennoyer's fund, in 1670, is given, "that *two Fellows* and *two Scholars* for ever should be *educated*, *brought up*, and *maintained* in the College at Cambridge."[2] This answers exactly to the description of English Fellows. The gift was, not to support *teachers*, but to *educate* persons. It is impossible to believe, that *the Fellows of the Corporation* were to be *educated*.

But that after the charter there were Fellows not receiving salaries, as well as Fellows who did receive them, is apparent from an order of the Overseers, anno 1666. "It is ordered by the Overseers, that such as are *Fellows of the College and have salaries paid them* out of the treasury shall have their *constant residence* in the College, and shall lodge therein, and be present with the scholars at all times in the hall, and have their studies in the College; so that they may be better enabled to inspect the manners of the scholars, and prevent all unnecessary damage to the society."

After the charter of 1672, there is no question that there were *non-resident* Fellows as well as *resident* Fellows.

The passage cited from Randolph's Narrative, addressed to the Privy Council, 12th October, 1676, contains this clause:—"The allowance of the President is £100 a year, and a good house. There are but *four* fellowships; the *two Seniors* have each £30 per annum; the *two Juniors* £15; but no diet allowed. *These are tutors* to all such as are admitted students."[3]

Now, if Randolph is accurate at all, it is clear, that all the Fellows of the Corporation were not residents at that time; for the Corporation consisted of *five* Fellows. In point of fact we know, that *three* of the then existing Corporation, to

[1] Letter, p. 70. [2] Id. 170.
[3] Id. 70. Hutch. Collect. of Papers, 477, 502.

wit, Mr. Shepard, Mr. Mather, and Mr. Oakes, were not tutors, and two of them were non-residents.

This leads me to another consideration.

VI. The point of usage. — I agree to the doctrine stated by Lord Mansfield, that, where the words of a charter are doubtful, the usage is of great force. "Not," (as he says,) "that usage can overturn the clear words of a charter; but, if they are doubtful, the usage under the charter will tend to explain the meaning of them." [1]

But what was the case to which his remarks applied? It was one respecting the borough of Portsmouth, a corporation by presumption, and also by a charter of Charles I. The corporation consisted of a Mayor, twelve Aldermen, and an indefinite number of Burgesses. The charter declared, that the election of Mayor should be thus: that the Mayor, Aldermen, and Burgesses, *or the greater part of them*, should assemble and should there continue till they, *or the greater part of them then there assembled*, should elect a Mayor. The sole question was, whether the charter meant, that a major part of *the whole corporate body*, or only a major part of *those assembled*, were to choose the Mayor. The usage had been for the latter to choose, and that usage was for one hundred and seventy years. The court thought the usage decisive; but they thought it also a right construction of the charter.

But it is material to consider the effect of usage in cases of this nature. A long uninterrupted usage in the affirmative establishes nothing but its being rightful. For instance, if, in the present case, there had been a long usage to elect the tutors into the Corporation, that would certainly prove that tutors were not ineligible. But if, from the first institution of the College to this time, none but tutors had been chosen Fellows, it would not prove, that no other persons were eligible. Why? Because the charter has not in terms confined

[1] 1 Cowper, R. 250.

the choice to tutors; and, therefore, all that can be affirmed is, that there is no pretence to exclude them as a matter of right or duty. On the other hand, if a tutor had never been elected a Fellow to this day, it could afford no proof that the charter excluded them; for it contains no disqualification of tutors; and the exclusion might be merely from policy. Suppose every president of the College had been to our day a minister of the Gospel, there would be no pretence to say, that by the charter all other persons were ineligible. Why? For the plain reason, that such an appointment is not required by the charter; and the usage could affirm no more than that it was not inconsistent with the charter.

Now, take the case in the most favorable view, which the Memorial states, that for the space of twenty-two years (namely, from 1650 to 1672,) the Fellows were residents and instructors. A usage for twenty-two years is very short to establish any construction of words of a doubtful nature in a charter. But upon the words of the charter the construction could not be doubtful; for, I repeat it, tutors, on our construction, are clearly eligible. The usage, then, establishes only its own correctness.

But the Memorial contends that the charter excludes all persons, if not from election at least from acting as Fellows after election, unless they are or become residents and instructors. Now, what are the admitted facts on this point? That the usage has been without interruption, from 1672 to the present time, a period of one hundred and fifty-two years, to have non-resident Fellows, and for a great length of time a majority of the Fellows have been non-residents and not instructors. Now, this usage, if usage is of any avail, is a flat negative to the exclusion or qualification. It directly contradicts it. If the words of the charter were doubtful on this point it would settle it. An early usage for twenty-two years cannot be permitted to prevail against a subsequent usage of one hundred and fifty-two years. If the former asserts an exclusive right in residents, the latter denies it, and proves it founded in mistake, and becomes itself conclusive the other way.

But it may be said, that the very point was contested in 1722. I admit it, and do not mean to enter into any consideration of the respectability, talents, or virtues of the different parties. It is clear, that there was a difference of opinion among men of high standing. Upon full argument, and after much excitement, the point was settled against the exclusive right of the resident instructors; and for a century past the Corporation has remained organized with *non-residents* in the Board. The usage of a century, after such a controversy so ended, must be decisive, if any can be. If it be not, then surely a short usage, not negativing any other right for twenty-two years, can be of no weight.

VII. Then, let us consider, in the next place, the confirmation of the charter by the State constitution of 1780. It must be deemed to act upon the *known* and *settled* state of things then existing, as to the Corporation. Four of the Fellows were then non-residents. The Constitution declares, that "The President and *Fellows* of Harvard College in their corporate capacity, and *their successors* in that capacity, &c., shall have, &c., all the powers, &c., *which they now have*, or are entitled to have, &c., and the same are hereby ratified and confirmed unto them, the said President and *Fellows* of Harvard College, and to their *successors*, &c., forever."

Now, for myself, I should be willing to rest the whole case upon this single solemn act of ratification. It is the highest sovereign sanction of the charter, and of the Corporation *de facto*, as being then rightfully organized.

VIII. An argument, now greatly relied on in behalf of the Memorialists, is, that as the College is by the charter required to be at Cambridge, the Corporation must be local, and the Corporators or Fellows must therefore be local residents.

This argument has no foundation in law. In general, Corporations may be said to have no locality; though the Corporators may be local, and entitled to be such only by locality; as, for instance, the inhabitants of a town or parish are Corporators only during their residence. But the Corporation itself is not local. It exists only in intendment of law. It is a mere legal entity, and can have no *habitation*, though it has a *name*. It is itself but a shadow, though it necessarily acts, and is brought into operation by living beings. A Corporation may be required to do its business at a particular place, and there only; but this is a limitation of its objects, and it does not give the Corporation locality. This is frequently the case with regard to banks, insurance companies, bridge and turnpike corporations, academies, manufactories, &c. In Sutton's Hospital, 10 Co. 32 b., the Court say, "A Corporation aggregate of many is *invisible*, immortal, and rests only in intendment of law." So, in Inhabitants of Lincoln County *v.* Prince, 2 Mass. R. 544, Chief Justice Parsons said, "A Corporation aggregate has in law no place of commorancy, although the Corporators may have." There is the same point in Taunton and South Boston Turnpike Corporation *v.* Whiting, 9 Mass. R. 321. And, in general, when Corporations are created for local objects, the Corporators are not to be deemed such, so long only as they reside in the place, unless the charter expressly makes such a qualification. The proprietors of a bank, insurance company, bridge, turnpike, or manufactory, may reside anywhere, unless expressly prohibited by the charter. The law never imputes locality to Corporators, simply because the objects of the Corporatien are local.

Upon the whole, after examining all the grounds of legal right assumed by the Memorialists, it appears to me, that their case is wholly unsupported by any legal principles. And I advise that the Overseers reject the Memorial accordingly.

CHARACTERISTICS OF THE AGE.

A DISCOURSE PRONOUNCED AT CAMBRIDGE, BEFORE THE PHI BETA KAPPA SOCIETY OF HARVARD UNIVERSITY, AUGUST 31, 1826.

GENTLEMEN:

IF I had consulted my own wishes, I should not have presumed to address you on the present occasion. The habits of professional employment rarely admit of leisure for the indulgence of literary taste. And in a science, whose mastery demands a whole life of laborious diligence, whose details are inexhaustible, and whose intricacies task the most acute intellects, it would be matter of surprise, if every hour withdrawn from its concerns did not somewhat put at hazard the success of its votary. Nor can it escape observation, how much the technical doctrines of a jurisprudence, drawn from remote antiquity, and expanding itself over the business of many ages, must have a tendency to chill that enthusiasm which lends encouragement to every enterprise, and to obscure those finer forms of thought, which give to literature its lovelier, I may say, its inexpressible graces. The consciousness of difficulties of this sort may well be supposed to press upon every professional mind. They can be overlooked by those only, whose youth has not been tried in the hard school of experience, or whose genius gives no credit to impossibilities.

I have not hesitated, however, to yield to your invitation, trusting to that indulgence, which has not hitherto been withheld from well-meant efforts, and not unwilling to add the testimony of my own example, however humble, in favor of the claims of this society to the services of all its members.

We live in an extraordinary age. It has been marked by events, which will leave a durable impression upon the pages of history by their own intrinsic importance. But they will be read with far deeper emotions in their effects upon future ages; in their consequences upon the happiness of whole communities; in the direct or silent changes forced by them into the very structure of society; in the establishment of a new and mighty empire, the empire of public opinion; in the operation of what Lord Bacon has characterized almost as supreme power, the power of knowledge, working its way to universality, and interposing checks upon government and people, by means gentle and decisive, which have never before been fully felt, and are even now, perhaps, incapable of being perfectly comprehended.

Other ages have been marked by brilliant feats in arms. Wars have been waged for the best and for the worst of purposes. The ambitious conqueror has trodden whole nations under his feet, to satisfy the lust of power; and the eagles of his victories have stood on either extreme of the civilized world. The barbarian has broken loose from his northern fastnesses, and overwhelmed in his progress temples and thrones, the adorers of the true God, and the worshippers of idols. Heroes and patriots have successfully resisted the invaders of their country, or perished in its defence; and in each way have given immortality to their exploits. Kingdoms have been rent asunder by intestine broils, or by struggles for freedom. Bigotry has traced out the march of its persecutions in footsteps of blood; and superstition employed its terrors to nerve the arm of the tyrant, or immolate his victims. There have been ancient leagues for the partition of empires, for the support of thrones, for the fencing out of human improvement, and for the consolidation of arbitrary power. There have, too, been bright spots on the earth, where the cheering light of liberty shone in peace; where learning unlocked its stores in various profusion; where the arts unfolded themselves in every form of beauty and grandeur; where literature loved to linger in academic shades, or enjoy the public sunshine; where song lent new inspiration to the temple; where eloquence alternately consecrated the hall of legislation, and astonished the forum with its appeals.

We may not assert, that the present age can lay claim to the production of any one of the mightiest efforts of human genius. Homer and Virgil, and Shakspeare and Milton were of other days, and yet stand unrivalled in song. Time has not inscribed upon the sepulchre of the dead any nobler names in eloquence than Demosthenes and Cicero. Who has outdone the chisel of Phidias, or the pencil of Michael Angelo, and Raffaelle? Where are the monuments of our day, whose architecture dares to contend with the Doric, Ionic, or Corinthian of Greece, or even with the Composite or Gothic of later times? History yet points to the pregnant though brief text of Tacitus, and acknowledges no finer models than those of antiquity. The stream of a century has swept by the works of Locke and Newton; yet they still stand alone in unapproached, in unapproachable majesty.

Nor may we pronounce, that the present age by its *collective* splendor in arts and arms casts into shade all former epochs. The era of Pericles witnessed a combination of talents and acquirements, of celebrated deeds and celebrated works, which the lapse of twenty-two centuries has left unobscured. Augustus, surveying his mighty empire, could scarcely contemplate with more satisfaction the triumph of his arms, than the triumph of the philosophy and literature of Rome. France yet delights to dwell on the times of Louis the Fourteenth, as the proudest in her annals; and England, with far less propriety, looks back upon the reign of Queen Anne for the best models of her literary excellence.

But, though we may not arrogate to ourselves the possession of the first genius, or the first era in human history, let it not be imagined, that we do not live in an extraordinary age. It is impossible to look around us without alternate emotions of exultation and astonishment. What shall we say of one revolution, which created a nation out of thirteen feeble colonies, and founded the empire of liberty upon the basis of the perfect equality in rights and representation of all its citizens? which commenced in a struggle by enlightened men for principles, and not for places; and in its progress and conclusion exhibited examples of heroism, patriotic sacrifices, and disinterested virtue, which have never been surpassed in the most favored regions? What shall we say of this nation, which has in fifty years quadrupled its population, and spread itself from the Atlantic to the Rocky Mountains, not by the desolations of successful war, but by the triumphant march of industry and enterprise? What shall we say of another revolution, which shook Europe to its centre, overturned principalities and thrones, demolished oppressions, whose iron had for ages entered into the souls of their subjects; and, after various fortunes of victory and defeat, of military despotism and popular commotion, ended at last in the planting of free institutions, free tenures, and representative government in the very soil of absolute monarchy? What shall we say of another revolution, or rather series of revolutions, which has restored to South America the independence, torn from her three centuries ago by the force or by the fraud of those nations, whose present visitations bespeak a Providence, which superintends and measures out at awful distances its rewards and its retributions? She has risen, as it were, from the depths of the ocean, where she had been buried for ages. Her shores no longer murmur with the hoarse surges of her unnavigated waters, or echo the jealous footsteps of her armed oppressors. Her forests and her table lands, her mountains and her valleys gladden with the voices of the free. She welcomes to her ports the whitening sails of commerce. She feels, that the treasures of her mines, the broad expanse of her rivers, the beauty of her lakes, the grandeur of her scenery, the products of her fertile and inexhaustible soil, are no longer the close domain of a distant sovereign, but the free inheritance of her own children. She sees, that these are to bind her to other nations by ties, which outlive all compacts and all dynasties, by ties of mutual sympathy, mutual equality, and mutual interest.

But such events sink into nothing, compared with the great moral, political, and literary revolutions, by which they have been accompanied. Upon some of these topics, I may not indulge myself even for a moment. They have been discussed here, and in other places, in a manner, which forbids all hope of more comprehensive illustration. They may, indeed, be still followed out; but whoever dares the difficulties of such a task, will falter with unequal footsteps.

What I propose to myself on the present occasion is of a far more limited and humble nature. It is, to trace out some of the circumstances of our age, which connect themselves closely with the cause of science and letters; to sketch here and there a light and shadow of our days; to look somewhat at our own prospects and attainments; and thus to lay before you something for reflection, for encouragement, and for admonition.

One of the most striking characteristics of our age, and that, indeed, which has worked deepest in all the changes of its fortunes and pursuits, is the general diffusion of knowledge. This is emphatically the age of reading. In other times this was the privilege of the few; in ours, it is the possession of the many. Learning once constituted the accomplishment of those in the higher orders of society, who had no relish for active employment, and of those, whose monastic lives and religious profession sought to escape from the weariness of their common duties. Its progress may be said to have been gradually downwards from the higher to the middle classes of society. It scarcely reached at all, in its joys or its sorrows, in its instructions or its fantasies, the home of the peasant and artisan. It now radiates in all directions; and exerts its central force more in the middle than in any other class of society. The means of education were formerly within the reach of few. It required wealth to accumulate knowledge. The possession of a library was no ordinary achievement. The learned leisure of a fellowship in some university seemed almost indispensable for any successful studies; and the patronage of princes and courtiers was the narrow avenue to public favor. I speak of a period at little more than the distance of two centuries; not of particular instances, but of the general cast and complexion of life.

The principal cause of this change is to be found in the freedom of the press, or rather in this, coöperating with the cheapness of the press. It has been aided also by the system of free schools, wherever it has been established; by that liberal commerce, which connects by golden chains the interests of mankind; by that spirit of inquiry, which Protestantism awakened throughout Christian Europe; and above all by those necessities, which have compelled even absolute monarchs to appeal to the patriotism and common sentiments of their subjects. Little more than a century has elapsed since the press in England was under the control of a licenser; and within our own days only has it ceased to be a contempt, punishable by imprisonment, to print the debates of Parliament. We all know how it still is on the continent of Europe. It either speaks in timid under-tones, or echoes back the prescribed formularies of the government. The moment publicity is given to affairs of state, they excite every where an irresistible interest. If discussion be permitted, it will soon be necessary to enlist talents to defend, as well as talents to devise measures. The daily press first instructed men in their wants, and soon found, that the eagerness of curiosity outstripped the power of gratifying it. No man can now doubt the fact, that wherever the press is free, it will emancipate the people; wherever knowledge circulates unrestrained, it is no longer safe to oppress; wherever public opinion is enlightened, it nourishes an independent, masculine, and healthful spirit. If Faustus were now living, he might exclaim with all the enthusiasm of Archimedes, and with a far nearer approach to the truth, Give me, where I may place a free press, and I will shake the world.

One interesting effect, which owes its origin to this universal love and power of reading, is felt in the altered condition of authors themselves. They no longer depend upon the smiles of a favored few. The patronage of the great is no longer submissively entreated, or exultingly proclaimed. Their patrons are the public; their readers are the civilized world. They address themselves, not to the present generation alone, but aspire to instruct posterity. No blushing dedications seek an easy passport to fame, or flatter the perilous condescension of pride. No illuminated letters flourish on the silky page, asking admission to the courtly drawing-room. Authors are no longer the humble companions or dependants of the nobility: but they constitute the chosen ornaments of society, and are welcomed to the gay circles of fashion and the palaces of princes. Theirs is no longer an unthrifty vocation, closely allied to penury; but an elevated profession, maintaining its thousands in lucrative pursuits. It is not with them, as it was in the days of Milton, whose immortal "Paradise Lost" drew five sterling pounds, with a contingent of five more, from the reluctant bookseller.

My Lord Coke would hardly find good authority in our day for his provoking commentary on the memorable statute of the fourth Henry, which declares that "none henceforth shall use to multiply gold or silver, or use the craft of multiplication," in which he gravely enumerates five classes of beggars, ending the catalogue in his own quaint phraseology with "poetasters," and repeating, for the benefit of young apprentices of the law, the sad admonition,

> "Sæpe pater dixit, Studium quid inutile tentas?
> Mæonidas nullas ipse reliquit opes."

There are certainly among us those, who are within the penalty of this prohibition, if my Lord Coke's account of the matter is to believed; for they are in possession of what he defines to be "a certain subtil and spiritual substance extracted out of things," whereby they transmute many things into gold. I am indeed afraid, that the Magician of Abbotsford is accustomed to "use the craft of multiplication;" and most of us know, to our cost, that he has changed many strange substances into the very gold and very silver. Yet, even if he be an old offender in this way, as is shrewdly suspected, there is little danger of his conviction in this liberal age; since, though he gains by every thing he parts with, we are never willing to part with any thing we receive from him.

The rewards of authorship are now almost as sure and regular as those of any other profession. There are, indeed, instances of wonderful success and sad failure; of genius pining in neglect; of labor bringing nothing but sickness of the heart; of fruitless enterprise baffled in every adventure; of learning, waiting its appointed time to die in patient suffering. But this is the lot of some in all times. Disappointment crowds fast upon human footsteps, in whatever paths they tread. Eminent good fortune is a prize rarely given even to the foremost in the race. And, after all, he who has read human life most closely, knows that happiness is not the constant attendant of the highest public favor; and that it rather belongs to those who, if they seldom soar, seldom fall.

Scarcely is a work of real merit dry from the English press before it wings its way to both the Indies and Americas. It is found in the most distant climates, and the most sequestered retreats. It charms the traveller, as he sails over rivers and oceans. It visits our lakes and our forests. It kindles the curiosity of the thick-breathing city, and cheers the log hut of the mountaineer. The Lake of the Woods resounds with the minstrelsy of our mother tongue, and the plains of Hindoostan are tributary to its praise. Nay more, what is the peculiar pride of our age, the Bible may now circulate its consolations and instructions among the poor and forlorn of every land, in their native dialect. Such is the triumph of letters; such is the triumph of Christian benevolence.

With such a demand for books, with such facilities of intercourse, it is no wonder that reading should cease to be a mere luxury, and should be classed among the necessaries of life. Authors may now, with a steady confidence, boast that they possess a hold on the human mind, which grapples closer and mightier than all others. They may feel sure that every just sentiment, every enlightened opinion, every earnest breathing after excellence, will awaken kindred sympathies, from the rising to the setting sun.

Nor should it be overlooked what a beneficial impulse has been thus communicated to education among the female sex. If Christianity may be said to have given a permanent elevation to woman, as an intellectual and moral being, it is as true that the present age, above all others, has given play to her genius, and taught us to reverence its influence. It was the fashion of other times to treat the literary acquirements of the sex as starched pedantry, or vain pretensions; to stigmatize them as inconsistent with those domestic affections and virtues, which constitute the charm of society. We had abundant homilies read upon their amiable weaknesses and sentimental delicacy, upon their timid gentleness and submissive dependence; as if to taste the fruit of knowledge were a deadly sin, and ignorance were the sole guardian of innocence. Their whole lives were "sicklied o'er with the pale cast of thought;" and concealment of intellectual power was often resorted to, to escape the dangerous imputation of masculine strength. In the higher walks of life, the satirist was not without color for the suggestion, that it was

> "A youth of folly, an old age of cards;"

and that elsewhere, "most women had no character at all," beyond that of purity and devotion to their families. Admirable as are these qualities, it seemed an abuse of the gifts of Providence to deny to mothers the power of instructing their children, to wives the privilege of sharing the intellectual pursuits of their husbands, to sisters and daughters the delight of ministering knowledge in the fireside circle, to youth and beauty the charm of refined sense, to age and infirmity the consolation of studies, which elevate the soul and gladden the listless hours of despondency.

These things have in a great measure passed away. The prejudices which dishonored the sex have yielded to the influence of truth. By slow but sure advances education has extended itself through all ranks of female society. There is no longer any dread, lest the culture of science should foster that masculine boldness or restless independence, which alarms by its sallies, or wounds by its inconsistencies. We have seen that here, as everywhere else, knowledge is favorable to human virtue and human happiness; that the refinement of literature adds lustre to the devotion of piety; that true learning, like true taste, is modest and unostentatious; that grace of manners receives a higher polish from the discipline of the schools; that cultivated genius sheds a cheering light over domestic duties, and its very sparkles, like those of the diamond, attest at once its power and its purity. There is not a rank of female society, however high, which does not now pay homage to literature, or that would not blush even at the suspicion of that ignorance which a half century ago was neither uncommon nor discreditable. There is not a parent whose pride may not glow at the thought that his daughter's happiness is in a great measure within

30

her own command, whether she keeps the cool sequestered vale of life, or visits the busy walks of fashion.

A new path is thus open for female exertion, to alleviate the pressure of misfortune, without any supposed sacrifice of dignity or modesty. Man no longer aspires to an exclusive dominion in authorship. He has rivals or allies in almost every department of knowledge; and they are to be found among those whose elegance of manners and blamelessness of life command his respect, as much as their talents excite his admiration. Who is there that does not contemplate with enthusiasm the precious Fragments of Elizabeth Smith, the venerable learning of Elizabeth Carter, the elevated piety of Hannah More, the persuasive sense of Mrs. Barbauld, the elegant Memoirs of her accomplished niece, the bewitching fictions of Madame D'Arblay, the vivid, picturesque, and terrific imagery of Mrs. Radcliffe, the glowing poetry of Mrs. Hemans, the matchless wit, the inexhaustible conversations, the fine character painting, the practical instructions of Miss Edgeworth, THE GREAT KNOWN, standing, in her own department, by the side of THE GREAT UNKNOWN?

Another circumstance, illustrative of the character of our age is the bold and fearless spirit of its speculations. Nothing is more common, in the history of mankind, than a servile adoption of received opinions, and a timid acquiescence in whatever is established. It matters not, whether a doctrine or institution owes its existence to accident or design, to wisdom or ignorance, or folly, there is a natural tendency to give it an undue value in proportion to its antiquity. What is obscure in its origin warms and gratifies the imagination. What in its progress has insinuated itself into the general habits and manners of a nation becomes imbedded in the solid mass of society. It is only at distant intervals, from an aggregation of causes, that some stirring revolution breaks up the old foundations, or some mighty genius storms and overthrows the intrenchments of error. Who would believe, if history did not record the fact, that the metaphysics of Aristotle, or rather the misuse of his metaphysics, held the human mind in bondage for two thousand years? that Galileo was imprisoned for proclaiming the true theory of the solar system? that the magnificent discoveries of Sir Isaac Newton encountered strong opposition from philosophers? that Locke's Essay on the Human Understanding found its way with infinite difficulty into the studies of the English Universities? that Lord Bacon's method of induction never reached its splendid triumphs until our day? that the doctrine of the divine right of kings, and the absolute allegiance of subjects, constituted nearly the whole theory of government, from the fall of the Roman Republic to the seventeenth century? that Christianity itself was overlaid, and almost buried, for many centuries, by the dreamy comments of monks, the superstitions of fanatics, and the traditions of the Church? that it was an execrable sin, throughout Christendom, to read and circulate the Holy Scriptures in the vulgar tongue? Nay, that it is still a crime in some nations, of which the Inquisition would take no very indulgent notice, even if the Head of the Catholic Church should not feel that Bible Societies deserve his denunciation? Even the great reformers of the Protestant Church left their work but half done, or rather came to it with notions far too limited for its successful accomplishment. They combated errors and abuses, and laid the broad foundations of a more rational faith. But they were themselves insensible to the just rights and obligations of religious inquiry. They thought all error intolerable; but they forgot, in their zeal, that the question, what was truth, was open to all for discussion. They assumed to themselves the very infallibility which they rebuked in the Romish Church; and as unrelentingly persecuted heresies of opinion, as those who had sat for ages in the judgment-seat of St. Peter. They allowed, indeed, that all men had a right to inquire; but they thought that all must, if honest, come to the same conclusion with themselves; that the full extent of Christian liberty was the liberty of adopting those opinions which they promulgated as true. The unrestrained right of private judgment, the glorious privilege of a free conscience, as now established in this favored land, was farther from their thoughts even than Popery itself. I would not be unjust to these great men· The fault was less theirs than that of the age in which they lived. They partook only of that spirit of infirmity which religion itself may not wholly extinguish in its sincere, but over zealous votaries. It is their glory to have laid the deep, and, I trust, the imperishable foundations of Protestantism. May it be ours to finish the work, as they would have done it, if they had been permitted to enjoy the blessed light of these latter times. But let not Protestants boast of their justice, or their charity, while they continue to deny an equality of rights to the Catholics.

The progress of the spirit of free inquiry cannot escape the observation of the most superficial examiner of history. The press, by slow but firm steps, first felt its way, and began its attacks upon the outworks of received opinions. One error after another silently crumbled into the dust, until success seemed to justify the boldest experiments. Opinions in science, in physic, in philosophy, in morals, in religion, in literature, have been subjected to the severest scrutiny; and many, which had grown hoary under the authority of ages, have been quietly conveyed to their last home, with scarcely a solitary mourner to grace their obsequies. The contest, indeed, between old and new opinions has been, and continues to be, maintained with great obstinacy and ability on all sides, and has forced even the sluggish into the necessity of thinking for themselves. Scholars have been driven to arm themselves for attack, as well as for defence; and in a literary warfare, nearly universal, have been obliged to make their appeals to the living judgment of the public for protection, as well as for encouragement.

The effects of this animated and free discussion have, in general, been very salutary. There is not a single department of life, which has not been invigorated by its influence, nor a single profession, which has not partaken of its success.

In jurisprudence, which reluctantly admits any new adjunct, and counts in its train a thousand champions ready to rise in defence of its formularies and technical rules, the victory has been brilliant and decisive. The civil and the common law have yielded to the pressure of the times, and have adopted much, which philosophy and experience have recommended, although it stood upon no text of the Pandects, and claimed no support from the feudal polity. Commercial law, at least so far as England and America are concerned, is the creation of the eighteenth century. It started into life with the genius of Lord Mansfield, and gathering in its course whatever was valuable in the earlier institutes of foreign countries, has reflected back upon them its own superior lights, so as to become the guide and oracle of the commercial world. If my own feelings do not mislead me, the profession itself has also acquired a liberality of opinion, a comprehensiveness of argumentation, a sympathy with the other pursuits of life, and a lofty eloquence, which, if ever before, belonged to it only in the best days of the best orators of antiquity. It was the bitter scoff of other times, approaching to the sententiousness of a proverb, that to be a good lawyer was to be an indifferent statesman. The profession has outlived the truth of the sarcasm. At the present moment England may count lawyers among her most gifted statesmen; and in America, I need but appeal to those who hear me for the fact, our most eminent statesmen have been, nay, still are, the brightest ornaments of our bar.

The same improving spirit has infused itself into the body of legislation and political economy. I may not adventure upon this extensive topic. But I would for a moment advert to the more benignant character manifested in the criminal law. Harsh and vindictive punishments have been discountenanced or abolished. The sanguinary codes, over which humanity wept and philosophy shuddered, have felt the potent energy of reform, and substituted for agonizing terror the gentle spirit of mercy. America has taken the lead in this glorious march of philanthropy, under the banners of that meek sect, which does good by stealth, and blushes to find it fame. There are not in the code of the Union, and probably not in that of any single State, more than ten crimes, to which the sober judgment of legislation now affixes the punishment of death. England, indeed, counts in her bloody catalogue more than one hundred and sixty capital offences; but the dawn of a brighter day is opening upon her. After years of doubtful struggle, the meliorations suggested by the lamented Sir Samuel Romilly have forced their way through Parliament to the throne; and an enlightened ministry is redeeming her from this reproach upon her national character.

In medicine, throughout all its branches, more extraordinary changes have taken place. Here, indeed, inductive philosophy looks for some of its fairest trophies. In anatomy, in physiology, in pharmacy, in therapeutics, instructed skill, patient observation, and accurate deduction have been substituted for vague conjecture and bold pretension. Instead of mystical compounds, and nostrums, and panaceas, science has introduced its powerful simples, and thus given energy and certainty to practice. We dream no longer over the favorite theories of the art, succeeding each other in endless progression. We are content to adopt a truer course; to read nature in her operations; to compel her to give up her secrets to the expostulations of her ministers; and to answer the persevering interrogatories of her worshippers. Chemistry, by its brilliant discoveries and careful analysis, has unfolded laws, which surprise us by their simplicity, as well as by the extent of their operations. By its magic touch the very elements of things seem decomposed, and to stand in disembodied essences before us.

In theology a new era has commenced. From the days of Grotius almost to our own, a sluggish indifference to critical learning fastened upon most of those who administered the high solemnities of religion. Here and there, indeed, a noble spirit was seen, like Old Mortality, wiping away the ancient dust and retracing the fading lines, and in his zeal for truth, undergoing almost a moral martyrdom. But the mass of professed theologians slumbered over the received text in easy security, or poured the distillations of one commentary into another, giving little improvement to the flavor, and none to the substance. They were at length roused by a spirit of another sort, which by ridicule, or argument, or denunciation of abuses, was attempting to sap the very foundations of Christianity. It made its approaches in silence, until it had attained strength enough for an open assault; and at last, in a moment of political revolution, it erected the standard of infidelity in the very centre of Christendom. Fortunately, the critical studies of the scholars of the old world enabled them to meet the difficulties of the occasion. The immense collations of manuscripts and various readings by such men as Mill, and Wetstein, and Kennicott, prepared the way for a more profound investigation of the genuineness and authenticity of the Scriptures. And the sober sense and unwearied diligence of our age have given to the principles of interpretation an accuracy and authority, to biblical researches a dignity and certainty, to practical as well as doctrinal theology a logic and illustration, unparalleled in the annals of the Church. If Christianity has been assailed in our day with uncommon ability, it has never been defended with more various learning. If it has surrendered here and there an interpolated passage, it has placed almost beyond the reach of doubt the general integrity of the text. If it has ceased in some favored lands to claim the civil arm for its protection, it has established itself in the hearts of men, by all, which genius could bring to illumine, or eloquence to grace its sublime truths.

In pure mathematics and physical science there has been a correspondent advancement. The discoveries of Newton have been followed out and demonstrated by new methods and analyses, to an extent, which would surprise that great philosopher himself, if he were now living. I need but name such men as La Grange and La Place. By means of observatories, the heavens have been, if I may so say, circumnavigated, and every irregularity and perturbation of the motions of the heavenly bodies ascertained to depend upon the same eternal law of gravitation, and to result in the harmonious balance of forces. But it is in physical science, and especially in its adaptation to the arts of life, that the present age may claim precedence of all others. I have already alluded to chemistry, which has enabled us to fix and discharge colors with equal certainty; now to imitate the whiteness of the driven snow, and now the loveliness of the Tyrian dyes. But who can measure the extent of the changes in agriculture, manufactures, and commerce, produced by the steam-engine of Watt, by the cotton-machinery of Arkwright, by the power-looms of a later period, by the cotton-gin of Whitney, and though last, not least, by the steam-boat of Fulton? When I name these, I select but a few among the inventions of our age, in which nature and art minister alternately to the wants and the triumphs of man.

If in metaphysics no brilliant discoveries have rewarded the industry of its votaries, it may nevertheless be said, that the laws of the mind have been investigated with no common success. They have been illustrated by a fuller display of the doctrine of association of Hartley, by the common sense of Reid, by the acute discrimination of Brown, and by the incomparable elegance of Dugald Stewart. If, indeed, in this direction any new discoveries are to be expected, it appears to me, with great deference, that they must be sought through more exact researches into that branch of physiology, which respects the structure and functions of those organs, which are immediately connected with the operations of the mind.

I have but glanced at most of the preceding subjects, many of which are remote from the studies, which have engaged my life, and to all of which I am conscious, that I am unable to do even moderate justice.

But it is to the department of general and miscellaneous literature, and above all, of English literature, that we may look with pride and confidence. Here the genius of the age has displayed itself in innumerable varieties of form and beauty, from the humble page, which presumes to teach the infant mind the first lines of thought, to the lofty works, which discourse of history, and philosophy, and ethics, and government; from the voyager, who collects his budget of wonders for the amusement of the idle, to the gallant adventurer to the Pole, and the scientific traveller on the Andes. Poetry, too, has dealt out its enchantments with profuse liberality, now startling us with its visionary horrors and superhuman pageants, now scorching us with its fierce and caustic satire, now lapping us in Elysium by the side of sunny shores, or lovely lakes, or haunted groves, or consecrated ruins. It is, indeed, no exaggeration of the truth to declare, that polite literature, from the light essay to the most profound disquisition, can enumerate more excellent works, as the production of the last fifty years, than of all former ages since the revival of letters.

Periodical literature has elevated itself from an amusement of cultivated minds, or a last resort of impoverished authors, to the first rank of composition, in which the proudest are not ashamed to labor, and the highest may gain fame and consequence. A half century ago a single magazine and a single review almost sufficed the whole reading public of England and America. At present a host crowd round us, from the gossamery repository, which adorns the toilet to the grave review, which discusses the fate of empires, arraigns the counsels of statesmen, expounds all mysteries in policy and science, or, stooping from such pursuits, condescends like other absolute powers, sometimes to crush an author to death, and sometimes to elevate him to a height where he faints from the mere sense of giddiness. We have our journals of science and journals of arts; the New Monthly, with the refreshing genius of Campbell, and the Old Monthly, with the companionable qualities of a familiar friend. We have the Quarterly Reviewers, the loyal defenders of Church and State, the *laudatores temporis acti*, the champions, ay, and exemplars too of classical learning, the admirers of ancient establishments and ancient opinions. We have, on the other hand, the Edinburgh, the bold advocates of reform, and still bolder political economists, hunting out public abuses, and alarming idle gentlemen pensioners with tales of misapplied charities; now deriding, with bitter taunts the dull but busy gleaners in literature; now brightening their pages with the sunshine of wit; and now paying homage to genius by expounding its labors in language of transcendent felicity. One might approach nearer home, and, if it were not dangerous to arouse the attention of critics, might tell of a certain North American, which has done as much to give a solid cast to our literature, and a national feeling to our authors as any single event since the peace of 1783.

Another interesting accompaniment of the literature of the age, is its superior moral purity over former productions. The obscene jests, the low ribaldry, and the coarse allusions which shed a disastrous light on so many pages of misguided genius in former times find no sympathy in ours. He who would now command respect must write with pure sentiments and elevated feelings; he who would now please must be chaste as well as witty, and moral as well as brilliant. Fiction itself is restrained to the decencies of life; and whether in the drama, or the novel, or the song, with a few melancholy exceptions, it seeks no longer to kindle fires which would consume the youthful enthusiast, or to instil precepts which would blast the loveliness of the innocent.

But let it not be imagined, that in the present state of things there is nothing for regret, and nothing for admonition. The picture of the age, when truly drawn, is not wholly composed of lights. There are shades which disturb the beauty of the coloring and points of reflection, where there is no longer harmony in the proportions.

The unavoidable tendency of free speculation is to lead to occasional extravagances. When once the reverence for authority is shaken, there is apt to grow up in its stead a cold skepticism respecting established opinions. Their very antiquity, under such circumstances, betrays us into suspicion of their truth. The overthrow of error itself urges on a feverish excitement for discussion, and a restless desire for novelty, which blind, if they do not confound, the judgment. Thus the human mind not unfrequently passes from one extreme to another; from one of implicit faith to one of absolute incredulity.

There is not a remark deducible from the history of mankind more important than that advanced by Mr. Burke, that "to innovate is not to reform." That is, if I may venture to follow out the sense of this great man, that innovation is not necessarily improvement; that novelty is not necessarily excellence; that what was deemed wisdom in former times, is not necessarily folly in ours; that the course of the human mind has not been to present a multitude of truths in one great step of its glory, but to gather them up insensibly in its progress, and to place them at distances, sometimes at vast distances, as guides or warnings to succeeding ages. If Greece and Rome did not solve all the problems of civil government, or enunciate the admirable theorem of representative legislation, it should never be forgotten, that from them we have learned those principles of liberty, which, in the worst of times, have consoled the patriot for all his sufferings. If they cannot boast of the various attainments of our days, they may point out to us the lessons of wisdom, the noble discoveries, and the imperishable labors of their mighty dead. It is not necessarily error to follow the footsteps of ancient philosophy, to reverence the precepts of ancient criticism, to meditate over the pages of ancient exploits, or to listen to the admonitions of ancient oratory.

We may even gather instruction from periods of another sort, in which there was a darkness which might be felt as well as seen. Where is to be found a nobler institution than the trial by jury, that impregnable bulwark of civil liberty? Yet it belongs to ages of Gothic darkness or Saxon barbarism. Where is there a more enduring monument of political wisdom than the separation of the judicial from the legislative power? Yet it was the slow production of ages which are obscured by the mists of time. Where shall we point out an invention whose effects have been more wide, or more splendid than those of the mariner's compass? Yet five centuries have rolled over the grave of its celebrated discoverer. Where shall we find the true logic of physical science so admirably stated, as in the Novum Organum of him, who, more than two centuries ago, saw, as in vision, and foretold, as in prophecy, the sublime discoveries of these latter days?

This is a topic which may not wholly be passed over, since it presents some of the dangers to which we are exposed, and calls upon us to watch the progress of opinion and guard against the seductive influence of novelties. The busy character of the age is perpetually pressing forward all sorts of objections to established truths in politics, and morals, and literature. In order to escape from the imputation of triteness some authors tax their ingenuity to surprise us with bold paradoxes, or run down with wit and ridicule the doctrines of common sense, appealing sometimes to the ignorance and sometimes to the pride of their readers. Their object is not so much to produce what is true as what is striking; what is profound, as what is interesting; what will endure the test of future criticism as what will buoy itself up on the current of a shallow popularity. In the rage for originality the old standards of taste are deserted or treated with cold indifference; and thus, false and glittering thoughts, and hurried and flippant fantasies are substituted for exact and philosophical reasoning.

There is, too, a growing propensity to disparage the importance of classical learning. Many causes, especially in England and America, have conduced to this result. The signal success which has followed the enterprises in physical science, in mechanics, in chemistry, in civil engineering, and the ample rewards both of fortune and fame attendant upon that success, have had a very powerful influence upon the best talents of both countries. There is, too, in the public mind a strong disposition to turn every thing to a practical account; to deal less with learning and more with experiment; to seek the solid comforts of opulence rather than the indulgence of mere intellectual luxury. On the other hand, from the increase of materials as well as of critical skill, high scholarship is a prize of no easy attainment; and, when attained, it slowly receives public favor, and still more slowly reaches the certainty of wealth. Indeed, it is often combined with a contemplative shyness and sense of personal independence, which yield little to policy, and with difficulty brook opposition. The honors of the world rarely cluster round it; and it cherishes with most enthusiasm those feelings which the active pursuits of life necessarily impair, if they do not wholly extinguish. The devotion to it, therefore, where it exists, often becomes an exclusive passion; and thus the gratification of it becomes the end instead of the means of life. Instances of extraordinary success by mere scholarship are more rare than in other professions. It is not then to be wondered at that the prudence of some minds and the ambition of others, should shrink from labors which demand days and nights of study, and hold out rewards which are distant, or pleasures which are, for the most part, purely intellectual.

Causes like these, in an age which scrutinizes and questions the pretensions of every department of literature, have contributed to bring into discussion the use and the value of classical learning. I do not stand up on this occasion to vindicate its claims or extol its merits. That would be a fit theme for one of our most distinguished scholars in a large discourse. But I may not withhold my willing testimony to its excellence, nor forget the fond regret with which I left its enticing studies for the discipline of more severe instructors.

The importance of classical learning to professional education is so obvious, that the surprise is, that it could ever have become matter of disputation. I speak not of its power in refining the taste, in disciplining the judgment, in invigorating the understanding, or in warming the heart with elevated sentiments; but of its power of direct, positive, necessary instruction. Until the eighteenth century, the mass of science, in its principal branches, was deposited in the dead languages, and much of it still reposes there. To be ignorant of these languages is to shut out the lights of former times, or to examine them only through the glimmerings of inadequate translations. What should we say of the jurist, who never aspired to learn the maxims of law and equity which adorn the Roman codes? What of the physician who could deliberately surrender all the knowledge heaped up for so many centuries in the Latinity of continental Europe? What of the minister of religion, who should choose not to study the Scriptures in the original tongue, and should be content to trust his faith and his hopes for time and for eternity to the dimness of translations, which may reflect the literal import, but rarely can reflect with unbroken force the beautiful spirit of the text? Shall he whose vocation it is "to allure to brighter worlds, and lead the way," be himself the blind leader of the blind? Shall he follow the commentaries of fallible man, instead of gathering the true sense from the Gospels themselves? Shall he venture upon the exposition of divine truths, whose studies have never aimed at the first principles of interpretation? Shall he proclaim the doctrines of salvation, who knows not, and cares not, whether he preaches an idle gloss or the genuine text of revelation? If a theologian may not pass his life in collating the various readings, he may and ought to aspire to that criticism which illustrates religion by all the resources of human learning; which studies the manners and institutions of the age and country in which Christianity was first promulgated; which kindles an enthusiasm for its precepts by familiarity with the persuasive language of Him who poured out his blessings on the Mount, and of him at whose impressive appeal Felix trembled.

I pass over all consideration of the written treasures of antiquity, which have survived the wreck of empires and dynasties, of monumental trophies and triumphal arches, of palaces of princes and temples of the gods. I pass over all consideration of those admired compositions, in which wisdom speaks, as with a voice from heaven; of those sublime efforts of poetical genius, which still freshen, as they pass from age to age, in undying vigor; of those finished histories, which still enlighten and instruct governments in their duty and their destiny; of those matchless orations, which roused nations to arms, and chained senates to the chariot wheels of all-conquering eloquence. These all may now be read in our vernacular tongue. Ay, as one remembers the face of a dead friend by gathering up the broken fragments of his image — as one listens to the tale of a dream twice told — as one catches the roar of the ocean in the ripple of a rivulet — as one sees the blaze of noon in the first glimmer of twilight.

There is one objection, however, on which I would for a moment dwell, because it has a commanding influence over many minds, and is clothed with a specious importance. It is often said, that there have been eminent men and eminent writers, to whom the ancient languages were unknown; men, who have risen by the force of their talents, and writers, who have written with a purity and ease which hold them up as models for imitation. On the other hand, it is as often said, that scholars do not always compose either with elegance or chasteness; that their diction is sometimes loose and harsh, and sometimes ponderous and affected. Be it so. I am not disposed to call in question the accuracy of either statement. But I would nevertheless say, that the presence of classical learning was not the cause of the faults of the one class, nor the absence of it the cause of the excellence of the other. And I would put this fact, as an answer to all such reasonings, that there is not a single language of modern Europe, in which literature has made any considerable advances, which is not directly of Roman origin, or has not incorporated into its very structure many, very many, of the idioms and peculiarities of the ancient tongues. The English language affords a strong illustration of the truth of this remark. It abounds with words and meanings drawn from classical sources. Innumerable phrases retain the symmetry of their ancient dress. Innumerable expressions have received their vivid tints from the beautiful dyes of Roman and Grecian roots. If scholars, therefore, do not write our language with ease, or purity, or elegance, the cause must lie somewhat deeper than a conjectural ignorance of its true diction.

But I am prepared to yield still more to the force of the objection. I do not deny, that a language may be built up without the aid of any foreign materials, and be at once flexible for speech and graceful for composition; that the literature of a nation may be splendid and instructive, full of interest and beauty in thought and in diction, which has no kindred with classical learning; that in the vast stream of time it may run its own current unstained by the admixture of surrounding languages; that it may realize the ancient fable, *Doris amara suam non intermisceat undam;* that it may retain its own flavor, and its own bitter saltness too. But I do deny, that such a national literature does in fact exist in modern Europe, in that community of nations of which we form a part, and to whose fortunes and pursuits in literature and arts we are bound by all our habits, and feelings, and interests. There is not a single nation, from the

North to the South of Europe, from the bleak shores of the Baltic to the bright plains of immortal Italy, whose literature is not imbedded in the very elements of classical learning. The literature of England is, in an emphatic sense, the production of her scholars; of men, who have cultivated letters in her universities, and colleges, and grammar schools; of men, who thought any life too short, chiefly, because it left some relic of antiquity unmastered, and any other fame humble, because it faded in the presence of Roman and Grecian genius. He, who studies English literature without the lights of classical learning, loses half the charms of its sentiments and style, of its force and feelings, of its delicate touches, of its delightful allusions, of its illustrative associations. Who, that reads the poetry of Gray, does not feel, that it is the refinement of classical taste, which gives such inexpressible vividness and transparency to his diction? Who, that reads the concentrated sense and melodious versification of Dryden and Pope, does not perceive in them the disciples of the old school, whose genius was inflamed by the heroic verse, the terse satire, and the playful wit of antiquity? Who, that meditates over the strains of Milton, does not feel, that he drank deep at

> "Siloa's brook, that flowed
> Fast by the oracle of God" —

that the fires of his magnificent mind were lighted by coals from ancient altars?

It is no exaggeration to declare, that he, who proposes to abolish classical studies, proposes to render, in a great measure, inert and unedifying the mass of English literature for three centuries; to rob us of much of the glory of the past, and much of the instruction of future ages; to blind us to excellences, which few may hope to equal, and none to surpass; to annihilate associations, which are interwoven with our best sentiments, and give to distant times and countries a presence and reality, as if they were in fact our own.

There are dangers of another sort, which beset the literature of the age. The constant demand for new works, and the impatience for fame, not only stimulate authors to an undue eagerness for strange incidents, singular opinions, and vain sentimentalities, but their style and diction are infected with the faults of extravagance and affectation. The old models of fine writing and good taste are departed from, not because they can be excelled, but because they are known, and want freshness; because, if they have a finished coloring, they have no strong contrasts to produce effect. The consequence is, that opposite extremes in the manner of composition prevail at the same moment, or succeed each other with a fearful rapidity. On one side are to be found authors, who profess to admire the easy flow and simplicity of the old style, the naturalness of familiar prose, and the tranquil dignity of higher compositions. But in their desire to be simple, they become extravagantly loose and inartificial; in their familiarity, feeble and drivelling; and in their more aspiring efforts, cold, abstract, and harsh. On the other side, there are those, who have no love for polished perfection of style, for sustained and unimpassioned accuracy, for persuasive, but equable diction. They require more hurried tones, more stirring spirit, more glowing and irregular sentences. There must be intensity of thought and intensity of phrase at every turn. There must be bold and abrupt transitions, strong relief, vivid coloring, forcible expression. If these are present, all other faults are forgiven, or forgotten. Excitement is produced, and taste may slumber.

Examples of each sort may be easily found in our miscellaneous literature among minds of no ordinary cast. Our poetry deals less than formerly with the sentiments and feelings belonging to ordinary life. It has almost ceased to be didactic; and in its scenery and descriptions reflects too much the peculiarities and morbid visions of eccentric minds. How little do we see of the simple beauty, the chaste painting, the unconscious moral grandeur of Crabbe and Cowper! We have, indeed, successfully dethroned the heathen deities. The Muses are no longer invoked by every unhappy inditer of verse. The Naiads no longer inhabit our fountains, nor the Dryads our woods. The River gods no longer rise, like old father Thames,

> "And the hushed waves glide softly to the shore."

In these respects our poetry is more true to nature, and more conformable to just taste. But it still insists too much on extravagant events, characters, and passions, far removed from common life, and farther removed from general sympathy. It seeks to be wild, and fiery, and startling; and sometimes, in its caprices, low and childish. It portrays natural scenery, as if it were always in violent commotion. It describes human emotions, as if man were always in ecstasies or horrors. Whoever writes for future ages, must found himself upon feelings and sentiments belonging to the mass of mankind. Whoever paints from nature, will rarely depart from the general character of repose impressed upon her scenery, and will prefer truth to the ideal sketches of the imagination.

Our prose, too, has a tendency to become somewhat too ambitious and intense. Even in newspaper discussions of the merits or misdeeds of rulers, there is a secret dread of neglect, unless the page gives out the sententious pungency or sarcastic scorn of Junius. Familiar, idiomatic prose seems less attractive than in former times. Yet one would suppose, that we might follow with safety the unaffected purity of Addison in criticism, and the graceful ease of Goldsmith in narrative. The neat and lively style of Swift loses nothing of its force by the simplicity with which it aims to put "proper words in proper places." The correspondence of Cowper is not less engaging, because it utters no cant phrases, no sparkling conceits, and no pointed repartees.

But these faults may be considered as temporary, and are far from universal. There is another, however, which is more serious and important in its character, and is the common accompaniment of success. It is the strong temptation of distinguished authors to premature publication of their labors, to hasty and unfinished sketches, to fervid, but unequal efforts. He who writes for immortality, must write slowly, and correct freely. It is not the applause of the present day, or the deep interest of a temporary topic, or the consciousness of great powers, or the striking-off of a vigorous discourse, which will ensure a favorable verdict from posterity. It was a beautiful remark of Sir Joshua Reynolds, that "Great works, which are to live, and stand the criticism of posterity, are not performed at a heat." "I remember," said he, "when I was at Rome, looking at the fighting gladiator, in company with an eminent sculptor, and I expressed my admiration of the skill with which the whole is composed, and the minute attention of the artist to the change of every muscle in that momentary exertion of strength. He was of opinion, that a work so perfect required nearly the whole life of man to perform." What an admonition! What a melancholy reflection to those who deem the literary fame of the present age the best gift to posterity! How many of our proudest geniuses have written, and continue to write, with a swiftness which almost rivals the operations of the press! How many are urged on to the ruin of their immortal hopes by that public favor which receives with acclamations every new offspring of their pen! If Milton had written thus, we should have found no scholar of our day, no "Christian Examiner," portraying the glory of his character with the enthusiasm of a kindred spirit. If Pope had written thus, we should have had no fierce contests respecting his genius and poetical attainments, by our Byrons, and Bowleses, and Roscoes. If Virgil had written thus, he might have chanted his verses to the courtly Augustus; but Marcellus and his story would have perished. If Horace had written thus, he might have enchanted gay friends and social parties; but it would never have been said of his composition, *Decies repetita placebit.*

Such are some of the considerations, which have appeared to me fit to be addressed to you on the present occasion. It may be, that I have overrated their importance, and I am not unconscious of the imperfections of my own execution of the task.

To us, Americans, nothing, indeed, can, or ought to be indifferent, that respects the cause of science and literature. We have taken a stand among the nations of the earth, and have successfully asserted our claim to political equality. We possess an enviable elevation, so far as concerns the structure of our government, our political policy, and the moral energy of our institutions. If we are not without rivals in these respects, we are scarcely behind any, even in the general estimate of foreign nations themselves. But our claims are far more extensive. We assert an equality of voice and vote in the republic of letters, and assume for ourselves the right to decide on the merits of others, as well as to vindicate our own. These are lofty pretensions, which are never conceded without proofs, and are severely scrutinized and slowly admitted by the grave judges in the tribunal of letters. We have not placed ourselves as humble aspirants, seeking our way to higher rewards under the guardianship of experienced guides. We ask admission into the temple of fame, as joint heirs of the inheritance, capable, in the manhood of our strength, of maintaining our title. We contend for prizes with nations whose intellectual glory has received the homage of centuries. France, Italy, Germany, England can point to the past for monuments of their genius and skill, and to the present, with the undismayed confidence of veterans. It is not for us to retire from the ground which we have chosen to occupy, nor to shut our eyes against the difficulties of maintaining it. It is not by a few vain boasts, or vainer self-complacency, or rash daring, that we are to win our way to the first literary distinction. We must do as others have done before us. We must serve in the hard school of discipline; we must invigorate our powers by the studies of other times. We must guide our footsteps by those stars which have shone, and still continue to shine, with inextinguishable light in the firmament of learning.

Nor have we any reason for despondency. There is that in American character, which has never yet been found unequal to its purpose. There is that in American enterprise, which shrinks not, and faints not, and fails not in its labors. We may say, with honest pride,

> "*Man* is the nobler growth our realms supply,
> And *souls* are ripened in our Northern sky."

We may not, then, shrink from a rigorous examination of our own deficiencies in science and literature. If we have but a just sense of our wants, we have gained half the victory. If we but face our difficulties, they will fly before us. Let us not discredit our just honors by exaggerating little attainments. There are those in other countries, who can keenly search out, and boldly expose every false pretension. There are those in our own country, who would scorn a reputation ill-founded in fact, and ill-sustained by examples. We have solid claims upon the affection and respect of mankind. Let us not jeopard them by a false shame, or an ostentatious pride. The growth of two hundred years is healthy, lofty, expansive. The roots have shot deep and far; the branches are strong and broad. I trust that many, many centuries to come, will witness the increase and vigor of the stock. Never, never, may any of our posterity have just occasion to speak of our country in the expressiveness of Indian rhetoric, "It is an aged hemlock; it is dead at the top."

I repeat it, we have no reason to blush for what we have been, or what we are. But we shall have much to blush for, if, when the highest attainments of the human intellect are within our reach, we surrender ourselves to an obstinate indifference, or shallow mediocrity; if, in our literary career, we are content to rank behind the meanest principality of

Europe. Let us not waste our time in seeking for apologies for our ignorance, where it exists, or in framing excuses to conceal it. Let our short reply to all such suggestions be, like the answer of a noble youth on another occasion, that we know the fact, and are every day getting the better of it.

What, then, may I be permitted to ask, are our attainments in science and literature, in comparison with those of other nations in our age? I do not ask, if we have fine scholars, accomplished divines, and skilful physicians. I do not ask, if we have lawyers who might excite a generous rivalry in Westminster Hall. I do not ask, if we have statesmen, who would stand side by side with those of the old world, in foresight, in political wisdom, in effective debate. I do not ask, if we have mathematicians, who may claim kindred with the distinguished of Europe. I do not ask, if we have historians, who have told with fidelity and force, the story of our deeds and our sufferings. I do not ask, if we have critics, and poets, and philologists, whose compositions add lustre to the age. I know full well, that there are such. But they stand as light-houses on the coasts of our literature, shining with a cheering brightness, it is true, but too often at distressing distances.

In almost every department of knowledge, the land of our ancestors annually pours forth from its press many volumes, the results of deep research, of refined taste, and of rich and various learning. The continent of Europe, too, burns with a generous zeal for science, even in countries, where the free exercise of thought is prohibited, and a stinted poverty presses heavily on the soul of enterprise. Our own contributions to literature are useful and creditable; but it can rarely be said, that they belong to the highest class of intellectual effort. We have but recently entered upon classical learning, for the purpose of cultivating its most profound studies, while Europe may boast of thousands of scholars engaged in this pursuit. The Universities of Cambridge and Oxford count more than eight thousand students, trimming their classical lamps, while we have not a single university, whose studies profess to be extensive enough to educate a Heyne, a Bentley, a Porson, or a Parr. There is not, perhaps, a single library in America sufficiently copious to have enabled Gibbon to verify the authorities for his immortal History of the Decline and Fall of the Roman Empire. Our advances in divinity and law are probably as great as in any branch of knowledge. Yet, until a late period, we never aspired to a deep and critical exposition of the Scriptures. We borrowed from Germany and England nearly all our materials, and are just struggling for the higher rewards of biblical learning. And in law, where our eminence is least of all questionable, there are those among us, who feel that sufficient of its learning, and argument, and philosophy remains unmastered to excite the ambition of the foremost advocates.

Let me not be misunderstood. I advert to these considerations, not to disparage our country, or its institutions, or its means of extensive, I had almost said, of universal education. But we should not deceive ourselves with the notion, that, because education is liberally provided for, the highest learning is within the scope of that education. Our schools neither aim at, nor accomplish such objects. There is not a more dangerous error than that, which would soothe us into indolence, by encouraging the belief, that our literature is all it can, or ought to be; that all beyond is shadowy and unsubstantial, the vain theories of the scientific, or the reveries of mere scholars. The admonition, which addresses itself to my countrymen respecting their deficiencies, ought to awaken new energy to overcome them. They are accustomed to grapple with difficulties. They should hold nothing, which human genius or human enterprise has yet attained, as beyond their reach. The motto on their literary banner should be, *Nec timeo, nec sperno.* I have no fears for the future. It may not be our lot to see our celebrity in letters rival that of our public polity and free institutions. But the time cannot be far distant. It is scarcely prophecy to declare, that our children must and will enjoy it. They will see, not merely the breathing marble and the speaking picture among their arts, but science and learning everywhere paying a voluntary homage to American genius.

There is, indeed, enough in our past history to flatter our pride and encourage our exertions. We are of the lineage of the Saxons, the countrymen of Bacon, Locke, and Newton, as well as of Washington, Franklin, and Fulton. We have read the history of our forefathers. They were men full of piety, and zeal, and an unconquerable love of liberty. They also loved human learning, and deemed it second only to divine. Here, on this very spot, in the bosom of the wilderness, within ten short years after their voluntary exile, in the midst of cares, and privations, and sufferings, they found time to rear a little school, and dedicate it to God and the church. It has grown; it has flourished; it is the venerable University, to whose walls her grateful children annually come, with more than filial affection. The sons of such ancestors can never dishonor their memories; the pupils of such schools can never be indifferent to the cause of letters.

There is yet more in our present circumstances, to inspire us with a wholesome consciousness of our powers and our destiny. We have just passed the jubilee of our independence, and witnessed the prayers and gratitude of millions, ascending to heaven, for our public and private blessings. That independence was the achievement, not of faction and ignorance, but of hearts as pure, and minds as enlightened, and judgments as sound, as ever graced the annals of mankind. Among the leaders, were statesmen and scholars, as well as heroes and patriots. We have followed many of them to the tomb, blessed with the honors of their country. We have been privileged yet more; we have lived to witness an almost miraculous event in the departure of two great authors of our independence on that memorable and blessed day of jubilee.

I may not, in this place, presume to pronounce the funeral panegyric of these extraordinary men. It has been already done by some of the master spirits of our country, by men worthy of the task, worthy as Pericles to pronounce the honors of the Athenian dead. It was the beautiful saying of the Grecian Orator, that "This whole earth is the sepulchre of illustrious men. Nor is it the inscriptions on the columns in their native soil alone, that show their merit; but the memorial of them, better than all inscriptions, in every foreign nation, reposited more durably in universal remembrance than on their own tomb."

Such is the lot of Adams and Jefferson. They have lived, not for themselves, but for their country; not for their country alone, but for the world. They belong to history, as furnishing some of the best examples of disinterested and successful patriotism. They belong to posterity, as the instructors of all future ages in the principles of rational liberty and the rights of the people. They belong to us of the present age, by their glory, by their virtues, and by their achievements. These are memorials, which can never perish. They will brighten with the lapse of time, and, as they loom on the ocean of eternity, will seem present to the most distant generations of men. That voice of more than Roman eloquence, which urged and sustained the Declaration of Independence, that voice, whose first and whose last accents were for his country, is indeed, mute. It will never again rise in defence of the weak against popular excitement, and vindicate the majesty of law and justice. It will never again awaken a nation to arms to assert its liberties. It will never again instruct the public councils by its wisdom. It will never again utter its almost oracular thoughts in philosophical retirement. It will never again pour out its strains of parental affection, and, in the domestic circle, give new force and fervor to the consolations of religion. The hand, too, which inscribed the Declaration of Independence is indeed laid low. The weary head reposes on its mother earth. The mountain winds sweep by the narrow tomb, and all around has the loneliness of desolation. The stranger guest may no longer visit that hospitable home, and find him there, whose classical taste and various conversation lent a charm to every leisure hour; whose bland manners and social simplicity made every welcome doubly dear; whose expansive mind commanded the range of almost every art and science; whose political sagacity, like that of his illustrious coadjutor, read the fate and interests of nations, as with a second sight, and scented the first breath of tyranny in the passing gale; whose love of liberty, like his, was inflexible, universal, supreme; whose devotion to their common country, like his, never faltered in the worst, and never wearied in the best of times; whose public services ended but with life, carrying the long line of their illumination over sixty years; whose last thoughts exhibited the ruling passion of his heart, enthusiasm in the cause of education; whose last breathing committed his soul to God, and his offspring to his country.

Yes, Adams and Jefferson are gone from us for ever — gone, as a sunbeam to revisit its native skies — gone, as this mortal to put on immortality. Of them, of each of them, every American may exclaim,

> "Ne'er to the chambers, where the mighty rest,
> Since their foundation, came a nobler guest;
> Nor e'er was to the bowers of bliss conveyed
> A fairer spirit, or more welcome shade."

We may not mourn over the departure of such men. We should rather hail it as a kind dispensation of Providence, to affect our hearts with new and livelier gratitude. They were not cut off in the blossom of their days, while yet the vigor of manhood flushed their cheeks, and the harvest of glory was ungathered. They fell not, as martyrs fall, seeing only in dim perspective the salvation of their country. They lived to enjoy the blessings, earned by their labors, and to realize all, which their fondest hopes had desired. The infirmities of life stole slowly and silently upon them, leaving still behind a cheerful serenity of mind. In peace, in the bosom of domestic affection, in the hallowed reverence of their countrymen, in the full possession of their faculties, they wore out the last remains of life, without a fear to cloud, with scarcely a sorrow to disturb its close. The joyful day of our jubilee came over them with its refreshing influence. To them, indeed, it was "a great and good day." The morning sun shone with softened lustre on their closing eyes. Its evening beams played lightly on their brows, calm in all the dignity of death. Their spirits escaped from these frail tenements without a struggle or a groan. Their death was gentle as an infant's sleep. It was a long, lingering twilight, melting into the softest shade.

Fortunate men, so to have lived, and so to have died! Fortunate, to have gone hand in hand in the deeds of the revolution! Fortunate, in the generous rivalry of middle life! Fortunate, in deserving and receiving the highest honors of their country! Fortunate, in old age to have rekindled their ancient friendship with a holier flame! Fortunate, to have passed through the dark valley of the shadow of death together! Fortunate, to be indissolubly united in the memory and affections of their countrymen! Fortunate, above all, in an immortality of virtuous fame, on which history may, with severe simplicity, write the dying encomium of Pericles, "No citizen, through their means, ever put on mourning."

I may not dwell on this theme. It has come over my thoughts, and I could not wholly suppress the utterance of them. It was my principal intention to hold them up to my countrymen, not as statesmen and patriots, but as scholars, as lovers of literature, as eminent examples of the excellence of the union of ancient learning with modern philosophy. Their youth was disciplined in classical studies; their active life was instructed by the prescriptive wisdom of antiquity; their old age was cheered by its delightful reminiscences. To them belongs the fine panegyric of Cicero, "Erant in *eis* plurimæ litteræ, nec eæ vulgares, sed interiores quædam, et reconditæ; divina memoria, summa verborum et gravitas et elegantia; atque hæc omnia vitæ decorabat dignitas et integritas."

I will ask your indulgence only for a moment longer. Since our last anniversary, death has been annually busy in thinning our numbers. I may not look on the right, or on the left, without missing some of those, who stood by my side in my academic course, in the happy days spent within yonder venerable walls.

"These are counsellors, that feelingly persuade us, what *we are*," and what we must be. Shaw and Salisbury are no more. The one, whose modest worth and ingenuous virtue adorned a spotless life; the other, whose social kindness and love of letters made him welcome in every circle. But what shall I say of Haven, with whom died a thousand hopes, not of his friends and family alone, but of his country? Nature had given him a strong and brilliant genius, and it was chastened and invigorated by grave, as well as elegant studies. Whatever belonged to human manners and pursuits, to human interests and feelings, to government, or science, or literature, he endeavored to master with a scholar's diligence and taste. Few men have read so much, or so well. Few have united such manly sense with such attractive modesty. His thoughts and his style, his writings and his actions, were governed by a judgment, in which energy was combined with candor, and benevolence with deep unobtrusive, and fervid piety. His character may be summed up in a single line, for there

"was given
To Haven every virtue under Heaven."

He had just arrived at the point of his professional career, in which skill and learning begin to reap their proper reward. He was in possession of the principal blessings of life, of fortune, of domestic love, of universal respect. There are those, who had fondly hoped, when they should have passed away, he might be found here to pay a humble tribute to their memory. To Providence it has seemed fit to order otherwise, that it might teach us "what shadows we are, and what shadows we pursue." We may not mourn over such a loss, as those who are without hope. That life is not too short which has accomplished its highest destiny; that spirit may not linger here, which is purified for immortality.

DIGESTS OF THE COMMON LAW.

AN ARTICLE WRITTEN FOR THE NORTH AMERICAN REVIEW, IN 1826, ON A GENERAL ABRIDGMENT AND DIGEST OF AMERICAN LAW, WITH OCCASIONAL NOTES AND COMMENTS, BY NATHAN DANE, LL. D., COUNSELLOR AT LAW.

The utility of abridgments, in all departments of learning, will scarcely be doubted by any person, who is accustomed to due reflection on the subject. The vast extent and intricacy of some branches of knowledge, the minute distinctions and details of others, and the perpetual accumulations of all, present obstacles to a thorough mastery of them, which are not easily overcome by the most powerful genius, or the most retentive memory. Those who are to learn must be assisted by steps, by general principles, by succinct elucidation, and by compendious abstracts, before they are able to engage in the task of comprehensive analogies; and those who are themselves instructed, find that memory is often treacherous, and that the constant demand for knowledge compels them to use many helps, in order to facilitate their recurrence to exact principles, or exact facts. The details of a whole science, at least in our day, are probably beyond the immediate grasp of any single mind, however gigantic. Recollections must be constantly refreshed, and the obscure traces of past acquirements carefully retraced, if we aspire to any thing like a vigorous command of that department of knowledge to which we are most devoted. Dr. Priestley, whose various scientific, as well as general knowledge, will scarcely be questioned, has somewhere stated, that he made use of many mechanical aids in the course of his own studies, some of which might be thought so humble as to excite a smile, or even a doubt of the abilities of the author. Indeed, the general auxiliary of most students used to be a common-place book, in which the various readings and accumulations of their learned hours were collected, sometimes with, and sometimes without method. In whatever shape these were preserved, they had the good effect of fixing the impressions of many important truths, and of saving many hours of fruitless research, to regain what was lost from the memory. Before the invention of printing, this labor must have been very great among the learned; and it has been gradually lessening, only because the press has, in the principal departments of learning, by means of indexes, digests, compends, concordances, dictionaries, and other abridgments, supplied their place, and brought within a reasonable compass the mass of those references, which are most useful to the scholar, the professional gentleman, and the scientific student. It is true, therefore, what of old was said, *Qui compendiariam alicujus artis sive scientiæ viam indicat, is gemino beneficio juvat studiosum; primum, ut maturius quo tendit pertingat, deinde ut minori labore sumptuque quod sequitur assequatur.*

But, whatever may be thought of other cases, it is certain that, in the department of law, abridgments are indispensable. Before reports of adjudged cases were published, no other adequate means existed of acquiring the science of jurisprudence, except what were furnished by a faithful attendance upon the courts, and a diligent collection of the substance of their decisions. The early professors of the common law were compelled to resort to common-place books, and personal reports of cases, falling under their own observation. Many manuscripts of this description are still extant, exhibiting a patient industry, care, and accuracy, worthy of all praise. The labor, indeed, of these venerable jurists almost transcends the belief of students of the present day. They noted every case in all its points and principles. They abstracted from records, and general treatises, and private manuscripts, often obscure and crabbed, every thing that could be found to aid them in study or in practice. They gathered voluminous collections of special pleadings, and unusual writs and judgments, to suit the exigencies of their possible avocations; and thought no labor too great which brought any solid addition to their knowledge, or any increased facilities to their clients.

The necessity was the more pressing in those days, from the subtilties, and quibbles, and scholastic logic, which characterized every department of learning. The law then dealt with forms, even more than with substances. The slightest variance from the *Registrum Brevium*, the neglect of any precise technical order, the most insignificant error in words, the smallest mistake in the description of persons or things, nay, the omission of a single letter was perilous, and brought in its train an abatement of the suit, and sometimes, by consequence, an extinction of the remedy. The strictness observed in England, in the present times, to discourage the use of the writ of right, affords some feeble illustration of this misplaced ingenuity, in hunting up and sustaining objections. The curious refinements, the nice distinctions, the quaint conceits, the arbitrary formularies, and the stiff, unbending roughness of the bar and bench in those days, made every thing important, from the first rudiment of principle, to the last ramification of practice. There were no public repositories, in which principles or practices could be ascertained by a glance of the eye. They were to be learned from the oral explanations of the ancient sages of the law, or the conversational debates of the judges, or the close lecture rooms of the benchers, or the dry expositions of the titular readers of the Inns of Court.

When Reports began to be published, the labor was not materially diminished. The decisions were not uniformly reported at stated times; and many cases were not reported at all. The early Reports contain no indexes. The Year

Books have not a single line to direct the student to their contents, and leave their bulky and abbreviated text without title or comment, so mixed up in one common mass that it requires no small share of historical knowledge to ascertain who, at any given period, speak as judges or as counsel. When tables of contents came subsequently into fashion, they were so incomplete and incorrect, that they were comparatively of little assistance. Ashe's Repertory, or Table to the Year Books, large as it seems, in two ponderous folios, does nothing more than put one upon inquiry, and condescends not to select a single proposition asserted by the cases. Indeed, the original indexes to the old reporters are almost useless, and, in some instances, serve only the bad purpose of misleading the inquirer, by holding out hopes, which vanish when he touches the adjudication.

The practice of keeping common-place books, which was thus begun from absolute necessity by the old lawyers, was afterwards continued from a sense of its convenience. Nor was it generally discontinued by the profession until a late period; and it is not, perhaps, without some examples, even in the present age. In America, the ante-revolutionary lawyers were in the habit of compiling manuscript abridgments for their private use, some of which have reached our times. They also left behind them many notes of adjudications, which are yet to be found in the hands of the curious and the learned. And, probably, in most of the states the practice of preserving short notes of new cases was common among the leaders at the bar, until the legislature provided for the regular publication of reports.

It is to sources like those already adverted to, that we owe the early, and perhaps all the abridgments hitherto made of the common law. What was introduced originally, from the mere scantiness of public materials, in process of time obtained a continued favor, from the unwieldy bulk of adjudications. Lord Coke poured the contents of his common-place book into his Commentary upon Littleton, and his superabundant Reports. Plowden may well be suspected of the same overlearned zeal; and Lord Hale has attested his own unwearied diligence and antiquarian researches, by manuscript collections, which yet surprise us by their variety and comprehensiveness.

The earliest printed abridgment of the law is that of Statham, (Nicholas,) who was appointed a baron of the exchequer in the eighth year of the reign of Edward the Fourth (1468.) It is a very curious book, printed, as it would seem, before title-pages were in use, for it is without any title-page, or imprint, or date; and the only notice we have of the printer is the following brief and modest remark, at the end of a short table of contents: "Per me, R. Pynson." It has been conjectured from the type that it was printed at Rouen, by William Le Tailleur, who printed Littleton's Tenures, for Pynson. The latter was bred in the service of Caxton, the first printer with metal types in England, and he succeeded his master in the business. Statham's Abridgment was published between the years 1470 and 1490, and is a remarkable specimen of the typography of the age. It shows that there has been little substantial improvement in the art, during the three last centuries. The art appears, indeed, to have reached perfection within the first half century after its invention. The copy now before us seems to have formerly belonged to Sir Heneage Finch, afterwards the celebrated Earl of Nottingham. The paper is of a very firm, silky texture, forming a strong contrast to the sleazy linen and cotton of our day; the ink is of a bright jetty and unfaded black; the type, though small, and partly composed of abbreviated characters, has a sharp and distinct face; and the mechanical execution is so exact, that scarcely a letter exhibits a blur, and the surface of every page presents a uniform appearance, putting to shame many of the standard volumes of our times. The work itself contains, under appropriate heads, brief abstracts of the cases in the Year Books, to the end of the reign of Henry the Sixth, as well as some cases not elsewhere to be found. It has now very little value, except occasionally to verify a quotation, or to gratify the curiosity of a professed antiquary.

The next abridgment, in the order of time, is that of Sir Anthony Fitzherbert, first printed by Pynson about 1516, and afterwards reprinted in 1565 and 1577. The edition of 1565 is far the best, for size of type and general accuracy. Besides many cases not reported at large, it contains an abstract of all the cases in the Year Books, down to the twenty-first year of the reign of Henry the Seventh. It has always been deemed of very high authority, where the author states cases solely on his own responsibility. The marginal titles and numbers, in the common editions of the Year Books, refer to the titles and numbers of this abridgment. The learned author died in 1538, leaving behind him the reputation of a very laborious and upright judge.

At the distance of half a century afterwards, followed the Abridgment of Sir Robert Brooke, of which there have been several reprints; but the best is that on royal paper by Tottell, in 1573. It contains the substance of Fitzherbert, together with a collection of the later authorities, some of which are nowhere else extant.

The character of the Abridgments of Fitzherbert and Brooke may be summed up in a few words. They are mere indexes, under general heads, of the principal adjudged cases up to their own times, in which the points are accurately stated, but without any attention to order, or any attempt at classification. As repositories of the old law, they now maintain a very considerable value, and may be consulted with advantage. Whoever examines them (for a thorough perusal of them will be a mere waste of time) will probably feel inclined, when he can, to ascend to the original sources; but if these should not be within his reach, he may rely with confidence, that these learned judges have not indulged themselves in a careless transcription, or a loose statement, of the law. In our own practice we have frequently found them the safest guides to the old law, and particularly to the contents of the Year Books. At the times, when these Abridgments were originally published, they must have been very acceptable presents to the profession. But many of the titles are now obsolete; and the works lie on the dusty shelves of our libraries, rarely disturbed, except upon some extraordinary inquiry, touching the feudal tenures, or the doctrine of *seizin*. The modest motto prefixed to both of them deserves to be remembered: *Ne moy reproves sauns cause, car mon entent est de bon amour.*

We pass over, without observation, Hughes's Abridgment, printed in 1660, because it embraces but a short period, and is a mere supplement to the earlier works; and also Sheppard's Abridgment, printed in 1675, because, though not disreputable in its execution, it scarcely struggled into existence against the superior work of Lord Chief Justice Rolle, which was published under the auspices of Sir Matthew Hale, in 1668. Lord Hale contributed to it a very able and learned preface, in which he bestows just commendation on its execution; and of the author he says, "He was a man of very great natural abilities, of a ready and clear understanding, strong memory, sound, deliberate, and steady judgment; of a fixed attention of mind to all business, that came before him; of great freedom from passions and perturbations, of great temperance and moderation, of a strong and healthy constitution of body, which rendered him fit for study and business, and indefatigable in it." The Abridgment itself is a posthumous work, intended by the author for his own private use, and not for the public; and Lord Hale says, "Though it is of excellent use and worth, yet it comes far short of the worth and abilities of him, that compiled it, and therefore is an unequal monument of him." The chief advantage, that it possesses over the earlier compilations, is in a more scientific arrangement of the materials, and a greater subdivision of the general heads, so as to bring together matters of the same nature or relative to the same branch, instead of heaping them up in one undistinguishing mass. Mr. Hargrave, in his edition of Coke on Littleton (note 1 to page 9,) speaks of it, as a "work most excellent in its kind; and, in point of method, succinctness, legal precision, and many other respects, fit to be proposed as an example for other abridgments of law." In practice, however, it has been in a great measure superseded by the later works, and is resorted to, principally, to verify quotations, when the original authorities are not to be found reported at large, or when Lord Rolle has stated circumstances, which are omitted by other authors.

D'Anvers's Abridgment, printed early in the eighteenth century, which Mr. Viner informs us was eighteen years in passing through the press,[1] is a mere translation of Rolle, with the addition of more modern cases, and is incomplete, extending only to the title "Extinguishment." Nelson's is chiefly borrowed from Hughes; and though the author was a very harsh and unsparing critic on the labors of others, his own have a general character of incorrectness stamped upon them, and have fallen into utter neglect.

Bacon's Abridgment, so well known to the profession, was first published in 1736, and has passed through six large editions. The contents of the work owe very little to the nominal author, (Matthew Bacon, Esq., of the Middle Temple,) and were chiefly extracted from the manuscript collections of Lord Chief Baron Gilbert. Mr. Gwillim has well observed, that "It was the hard fate of his excellent writings to lose their author before they had received his last corrections and improvements, and in that unfinished state, to be thrust into the world without even the common care of an ordinary editor. Those invaluable tracts were, for the most part, published, not only with their original imperfections, without any attempt to supply their defects, or explain, or correct what seemed in them perplexed or erroneous, but

[1] Preface to the eighteenth volume of his Abridgment.

with all the improprieties and inaccuracies, which the ignorance and neglect of the amanuenses, whom the author's infirmities compelled him to employ, could accumulate upon them." Mr. Bacon deserves very little credit, in any view; because he seems to have been willing to appropriate to himself the labors of another, without due acknowledgment, and to have employed no diligence in correcting errors, and no learning in supplying deficiencies. He died before the work was completed; and the remainder, from the title, "Sheriff," was furnished by Mr. Sergeant Sayer, and Mr. Ruffhead.

Of this collection, which has been almost for a century before the public, it seems scarcely necessary, at the present time, to express any opinion. It consists of a series of tracts, or dissertations, upon various topics of the law, generally illustrated by adjudications, and, though incomplete, exhibiting a rare union of sagacity and industry. As a text-book for students, it has long maintained an unrivalled reputation; and, as the expositions of a very able and learned judge upon a large survey of the law, dealing with its history and its reasons, it must for ever hold a high rank among the treasures of the profession. Mr. Gwillim's edition is far the best, which has appeared in England, and is entitled to much praise for the manner in which the duties of the editor have been performed. This edition has been republished in America, under the superintendence of Bird Wilson, Esquire, who has enriched it with many valuable additions. Still it must be admitted, that there is great awkwardness and inconvenience in ingrafting such an abundance of marginal notes upon the original text, threatening, in every new edition, to overlay, if they do not bury it beneath their weight.

Mr. Viner's Abridgment was published between the years 1741 and 1751, and extending, as it does, over the space of twenty-four folio volumes, may be thought by some not to have a very apt title. The learned author passed a whole life in compiling the work, and superintending the printing of it, which, by the consent of the law patentees, was done at his own house, in Aldershot in Hampshire. The basis of the work is Rolle's Abridgment, with the addition of all the materials, which had accumulated in the intermediate period. In the preface, (which appears in the thirteenth volume,[1] occasioned by the author's having begun with the title "Factor," where D'Anvers ended his Abridgment,) he states, that he commenced the undertaking with the eighteenth century, and it was, of course, for nearly fifty years under his revising hand. Mr. Hargrave (Co. Litt. 9, a, note 3,) calls it an immense body of law and equity, which, notwithstanding all its defects and inaccuracies, must be allowed to be a necessary part of every lawyer's library. He adds, that it is a most useful compilation, and would have been infinitely more so, if the author had been less singular and more nice in his arrangement and method, and more studious in avoiding repetitions. This praise, qualified as it is, seems to us rather to go beyond, than to fall short of the real merits of the work. It is a cumbrous compilation, by no means accurate or complete in its citations, and difficult to use, from the irregularity with which the matter is distributed, and from the inadequacy, and sometimes the inaptness, of the subdivisions. Indeed, every thing appears to have been thrown into it, without any successful attempt at method or exactness. Almost every thing valuable in the older abridgments is, indeed, to be found in it; but sometimes so ill arranged, that the search is almost as troublesome, as it would be to run over the whole title in Fitzherbert or Brooke. The author has observed, in the preface to his thirteenth volume, that "The study of the law is a very long journey, and the roads not the plainest; in which they [abridgments] may serve as posts and Mercuries to direct the students in their way, but ought not by any means to be considered as their journey's end, or place of their last resort and residence." What a pity, that the author had not more diligently followed the directions,

[1] There is a second preface in the eighteenth volume.

which he seems to approve by the above allusion! He has, by no means, made the roads very plain or smooth; and the sign-posts, which he has put up, do not always indicate either the truest way, or the shortest distance, to the striking point of the traveller's journey. Nor has he the satisfactory apology, *Dum brevis esse laboro, obscurus fio;* for his work is both long and confused. It may, and, indeed, ought, to constitute a part of every law library, which aims to be tolerably complete; for it embraces the body of the law antecedent to the reign of George the Third. Its principal merit is its extent; and though in some parts it is redundant, in others defective, and in all irregular, it is a vast index of the law, which time and patience can master; and it often rewards the labor, when all other resources have failed the diligent searcher for authorities.

It is impossible, however, not to feel, that we owe to this work a deep debt of gratitude, which should disarm criticism, and almost extinguish every recollection of its infirmities. To the establishment of the Vinerian professorship, at Oxford University, we are indebted for one of the most elegant and classical works in our language, "The Commentaries on the Laws of England," by Sir William Blackstone. From a zeal for the study of the law, for "the benefit of posterity, and the perpetual service of his country," Mr. Viner devoted his property, and the proceeds of the sale of his great Abridgment, to the noble purpose of founding a professorship of the common law. And we are informed, that the fund proved sufficiently productive to enable the University, also, to establish some fellowships and scholarships for the study of the law there.[1]

A work of a very different character, and almost perfect in its kind, is the Digest of Lord Chief Baron Comyns. Though a posthumous publication, it has been justly observed, that, unlike most publications of that nature, it was left by its

[1] 1 Blackstone's Commentaries, 28.

learned author in a state very fit to meet the eye of the public. Lord Chief Baron Comyns died sometime between the years 1740 and 1743; the exact period, Mr. Rose, his late editor, does not seem to have been able to ascertain. It is a melancholy fact, that very few particulars of the lives even of the most eminent lawyers reach posterity. Great as their fame may be, and extensive as may be their professional labors, while living, they rarely leave a permanent impression upon the public mind; and after the lapse of a few years, the most diligent search enables us to collect little more than the facts of their birth, death, and parentage. This distinguished judge is a very striking illustration of the remark. It was said by the late Lord Kenyon, that "Comyns's opinion alone is of great authority, since he was considered by his contemporaries as the most able lawyer in Westminster Hall." (3 T. R. 64.) There is no reason to doubt the truth of this assertion; and yet, of such a man, nothing more can now be gathered, than a few short dates of his appointments to public stations. Mr. Rose says, "It was the editor's wish, for the purpose of satisfying a laudable curiosity in respect to so eminent a man, to have stated some particulars of the life of Sir John Comyns; but, after several inquiries, the following dates are all he has been able to collect." He then introduces the dates of his appointment as a Baron of the Exchequer, and a Judge of the Common Pleas.

Of the plan of this incomparable Digest, it is difficult to speak in terms, which will do it justice, without seeming to be extravagant. Mr. Hargrave (Co. Litt. 17, note 96,) says, "The whole of Lord Chief Baron Comyns's work is equally remarkable for its great variety of matter, its compendious and accurate expression, and the excellence of its methodical distribution." Our own opinion is, that, for the purpose it proposes to accomplish, no plan could be more judicious, and no execution more singularly successful. It does not, like Bacon's Abridgment, affect to enter into disquisitions upon the various doctrines of the law, or to explain the reasons, on which it is built. But, as the preface to the first edition states, "The general plan of this Digest is, that the author lays down principles or positions of law, and illustrates them by instances, which he supports by authorities; and these are trenched out and divided into consequential positions or points of doctrine, illustrated and supported in the same manner. By this means, each head or title exhibits a progressive argument upon the subject, and one paragraph, &c. follows another in a natural and successful order, till the subject is exhausted." It is a curious fact, that the original text was composed in Law French, which it is conjectured, the author chose on account of its apt expression and singular brevity.

The editors of the first edition translated the whole work into English, which was, of itself, a prodigious undertaking, and they declare that "The translation of the book has been carefully compared with, and corrected by, the original, and with very great labor *has also been compared with, and corrected by, the several books cited.*" Who the gentlemen were, to whose patient industry and accuracy we are indebted for the publication of so choice a work, we have never been able to ascertain. They have modestly withdrawn their names from the titlepage and preface, leaving the latter to speak the extent and credit of their labors. We regret this concealment; for never did a posthumous work fall into more able hands, and never was the duty of an editor more faithfully discharged. It is this consideration which gives to the original edition so very distinguished a value, even in our days. It was published between the years 1762 and 1767, in five folio volumes, on excellent paper, with a large type, and it stands unrivalled for the accuracy and beauty, with which it came from the press. In 1776, a supplemental folio volume was added, containing a digest of the recent cases, upon the same plan as the original work.

Of the later editions, in octavo, we can say little by way

of commendation. They have the gross fault of a total departure from the style, brevity, accuracy, and simplicity of Comyns; a departure which is utterly without apology; as it exhibits, on the part of the editor, either an incapacity for the task, or an indifference to the manner of executing it. If, indeed, other authors have suffered from the posthumous publication of their unfinished works, it has been the hard fate of Comyns to have the symmetry and excellence of his work essentially impaired by the unmerciful interpolations of his later editors. Without any regard to the dependencies of the original text, or the sequence of principles and illustrations, they have thrust in between the different paragraphs their new matter, in a crude state, and often so little sifted, that it is a mere copy of the marginal abstracts of the later reports. The consequence is, that passages, which are connected in sense in the original text, are often separated by these misshapen adjuncts; and sometimes a half page is to be run over by the reader, before he can gather up the *disjecta membra*, the scattered fragments, of the author.

In the art of bookmaking, there is scarcely any thing more reprehensible than this practice, by which an author, singularly clear, exact, and methodical, is presented in the habiliments of a slovenly common-place man. The only rational course to be pursued, in any new edition of Comyns, would be to leave the text untouched, with all the authority belonging to it from the author's venerable character; and, by supplementary volumes, drawn up in the same method, to add the new matter, which has accumulated from the litigation of later times. The good example of the editors of the Supplement, in 1776, seems, however, to have suited ill with the notions of our age; and, from the rage for innovation, or from the pitiful prevalence of a bookselling interest, every successive edition, instead of being of a higher value, has constantly diminished the real utility of the work. Mr. Kyd's edition has the negative merit of having done but little injury; Mr. Rose's, in 1800, has interwoven a miserable patchwork; and Mr. Hammond's, in 1824, has even less merit, containing the substance of his indexes to the common law and chancery reports, thrown together with a strange neglect of the symmetry of the original work. Indeed, this last edition deserves the severe rebuke of the profession, as its main object seems to be to swell the work to ten ponderous volumes. If the new matter had been properly abridged, and reduced to simple principles and brief illustrations, in the manner of Comyns, it might easily have been compressed into two supplementary volumes. But the last Supplement equals the original in size, and wants every excellence, that characterizes it.

We hope to live long enough to see Comyns rescued from the hands of such editors, and restored to his just value, by an edition worthy of his labors. We are confident, that the task of collecting and digesting the modern matter, however operose it may seem, is within the power of any one learned and diligent lawyer, and that its accomplishment would receive an ample reward from the profession. Such an achievement would lay the foundation of a most honorable fame. As the case now is, he is the most fortunate jurist, who possesses the earliest edition of the work. We have been more emphatic in our remarks on this subjects, because we perceive an increasing propensity, in our own country, to load and overload new editions of professional works with notes of little intrinsic value, or at most, with notes whose value is materially diminished by the loose and unskilful manner, in which they are introduced. There are, however, some exceptions to this remark; and none are entitled to more praise than the learned comments of Mr. Metcalf.

But we hasten from this digression to resume the subject to which the work named at the head of this article immediately conducts us. Upon the appearance of a new abridgment of the law, the question naturally occurs, whether it be necessary; and if necessary, what is the best plan, with a view to comprehensiveness and convenience, on which it can be formed?

In respect to England, there may perhaps be some doubt whether such a work would be of any extensive utility. A continuation of Comyns's Digest seems all that is necessary for lawyers of advanced standing; and Bacon's Abridgment, however imperfect, is perhaps sufficient, with Blackstone's Commentaries and Cruise's Digest, as a general outline for students. Indeed, most of the branches of law of great practical importance have in modern times been discussed in independent treatises with much ability, and sometimes in so masterly a manner as to exhaust the subject. What could be added to Fearne's Essay on Contingent Remainders and Executory Devises? But we think the subject admits of a very different consideration in relation to America. The learned author of the "General Abridgment and Digest of American Law" has stated the reasoning in favor of it with so much force and correctness that we transcribe his remarks in the Introduction to his work rather than hazard our own.

"At the close of the American revolutionary war, when the United States became an independent nation, it was very material to inquire and to know what was law in them, collectively and individually; also to examine, trace, and ascertain what were the political principles on which their system was founded; and their *moral* character, so essential to be attended to in the support and administration of this system; especially in selecting from the English laws in force in a monarchy once feudal, those parts of them adopted here, and remaining in force in our republic. With such impressions the author early turned his attention to these subjects, and in good earnest engaged in collecting materials upon them: and the more readily, as such a pursuit perfectly accorded with his professional and political employments in which he engaged in the spring of 1782. He early found there was in the United States nothing like *one collected body of American law, or one collected system of American politics;* but all was found in scattered fragments. Scarcely any native American law was in print, but the colony statutes, charters, and some of the constitutions. No judicial decisions made in America, of any importance, had been published, and but very few forms. The laws enacted here were found separately published in many states, in colony, province, and state statutes. Our law labored under another material disadvantage; most of it was found only in English books. These were written and published to be used in England, not in America; a a large part of which was of no real use here.

"No measures had ever been taken to ascertain with any accuracy what part of English law our ancestors had adopted in the colonies or provinces. The result was, our ablest lawyers were often unable to decide what parts of the English laws were in use here; and our students at law often studied as laboriously the useless as the useful parts of those laws. No one had attempted to embody our laws or political principles, dispersed in numerous local charters, constitutions, statutes, and also English books; many of which laws and principles were to be traced to the free parts of the British system, and even to the ancient Germans, in several cases; and in some to the Hebrews, several of whose laws some of our ancestors early adopted in America.

"In this state of things a very important object naturally presented itself to one who for several years had been in a situation highly to appreciate American principles, especially those of the American Revolution; which was a *collected body of American law*, formed with a constant reference to those principles, and to our character and situation. Forty years ago the materials for such a work were but few in comparison with what they now are; and then it was very useful and even necessary to collect them for the lawyer's private use; and to such purpose was the undertaking commenced and pursued many years. The title, 'A General Abridgment and Digest of American Law, with occasional Notes and Comments,' is intended to give a clear and concise view of the nature of the work. Formerly the word,

Digest, in law-books, meant much more than an alphabetical arrangement of marginal notes, or of several indexes. But, as this seems to be nearly its modern meaning, it applies but to an inconsiderable part of this work, the principal parts of which are described by the other words in the title, to wit, 'Abridgment, Notes, and Comments.' The first object has been to abridge and compress cases within narrow limits, but not so as to lose or obscure the law, decided or settled in them. Next, on proper occasions, by remarks, notes, and comments, to examine and explain a few obscure points of law, and sometimes to show the law is not as it has been in some decisions stated to be.

"The work is calculated to consist of eight royal octavo volumes, of about seven hundred pages each, to be purely American, and, among other things, to supply the place generally of the English abridgments and digests now read, especially by students, very disadvantageously, because in many respects inapplicable to our practice. As every lawyer of experience must have found a common life too short to be well read in the immense mass of law and equity, federal, state, and territorial, really applicable to our affairs, it must be in some degree a waste of time, especially for students and some others, to spend a large part of their time in reading English law as to tithes, forest, game prerogatives, ancient demesne, advowsons, boroughs, English copyhold estates, many parts of feudal tenures, most kinds of English courts and customs, modes of punishments and forfeitures, laws as to English religion, privileges, revenue, stamps, modes of conveying and assuring property, and a vast many other matters peculiar to England. In fact, near half the English and Irish law we buy at a heavy expense, and read often to the exclusion of reading our own laws, so useful, is as inapplicable to our concerns as the laws of Germany or Spain; and more so than the civil code of France, since it is adopted in substance by Louisiana, one of our States." *Introd.* pp. 3 – 5.

Now we entirely agree with the author in his conclusion, that an American abridgment is indispensable both for lawyers and students, at the present day. We can hardly conceive of any thing more preposterous than to engraft on such a work those titles of the English law which have nothing correspondent with them in our country to which they can be applied. It is true, that decisions in those branches of English law may sometimes furnish an illustration of a doubtful point, or an analogy to direct our researches. But these occasions must be of rare occurrence; and the same inducements might be as well urged in favor of the incorporation of the law of other foreign countries. Abridgments can embrace only those portions of law which are of most frequent and general use. English sources will always be open to the curious who desire to explore the more obscure doctrines; and the practising lawyer must, in extraordinary cases, task his diligence to master what is unknown, and to bring to light what is buried in dark and remote antiquity.

In regard to the plan most proper for an American abridgment, various opinions will probably be entertained by the profession. It is not, indeed, easy to say what plan would, abstractedly speaking, be best. Much must depend upon the extent and object of the work; and even here there is sufficient room for diversity of judgment, without in the slightest degree indulging in dogmatism. Whoever selects must omit something; and what is proper to be omitted, and what to be retained, is, of course, a matter for the exercise of much delicate discretion. If the object of the author be to present to the learned in the profession a mere dry abstract of principles, with cases to illustrate them, a more perfect model than Comyns's Digest can scarcely be devised; and an order, if not strictly alphabetical, at least nearly approaching to it, will be naturally resorted to. If, on the other hand, he wishes to expound the reasons of the law, or to comment on cases with a view to try their accuracy, and to deal with all parts of the same general subject in the mode of dissertation, he will bring together all the incidental topics: and then, of course, to some extent, he must desert an alphabetical arrangement. Again, if his object be to present matter of direct and positive authority only to assist experienced advocates in their consultations, he may spare many explanations which are indispensable for students. If, on the other hand, his main object be to instruct students, and give collateral aids to the profession at large, he will begin with the easier branches of the law, and gradually open upon those which require more thought, sagacity, and experience. He will, for instance, begin with the law of contracts, rather than with the intricate distinctions of real estates. He will initiate the student in matters of general observation and practice before he deals with the more recondite portions of jurisprudence. He will embody, in some degree, the general principles with the remedies which accompany a violation of them; so that the student may perceive that he is to practise, at the very outset, whatever he is taught.

It is manifest, that, under such circumstances, the whole plan and method of a work must essentially deviate from an alphabetical order; and that materials must often be separated, where, upon another plan, they would be joined, and joined where they would otherwise stand at great distances. The only rule then that can be laid down in cases of this nature, is to judge of the work from the design of the author; or, as Pope expresses it,

> "In every work regard the writer's end,
> Since none can compass more than they intend."

Mr. Dane, in his Introduction, has given very much at large the plan and objects of his work. Its objects may be summarily stated to be, to frame an abridgment "to be useful to American lawyers, especially to students, and those of the profession, who cannot possess many books;" "to make our American charters and constitutions, statutes and adjudged cases, the groundwork of each subject, and therewith to incorporate that portion of the English law, recognized in the United States, beginning with Magna Charta, and the first charters and statutes in our colonies;" "to examine such cases as are binding on all parts of the Union, and to cite some of the most important *verbatim*, and abridge the others;" to include as much of the local law of the different states as is practicable; and to incorporate manuscript reports of adjudications, not in print.

Thus far, as to the objects of the work. It appears to us, that these objects are sufficiently comprehensive, and that the principle of selection, which pervades the whole, is highly creditable to the judgment of the learned author. In regard to one point only will there probably be much difference of opinion with the profession; and that is, whether local law ought to find a place in the work; and if it ought, how far the selection of the local law of Massachusetts, as a basis, is judicious. On this point let Mr. Dane speak for himself; and we think no one will deny, that his suggestions are of very great weight. In enumerating the objects of the work, he says, one is, —

"To examine the charters, constitutions, and statutes of the several colonies and states, of a public nature, and the judicial decisions made in the highest courts in them, and published, so far as to acquire correct ideas of such state law; but so voluminous is it, and so much of it merely local, in small portions of the nation, that it has been deemed not practicable or useful to include large portions of it in this work, except in regard to a few of the states; and it has been considered, that the judges and lawyers of any state best understand its local laws; and it will be found, that the courts in one state have not often noticed the laws and decisions in other states.

"This being the case in regard to state law, it was found best to select the state law of some one state, to be included much at large in this work. Accordingly, the laws of Massachusetts, in substance including Maine, have been selected for the purpose, and for the following reasons. 1. These laws are, in fact, the laws of two large states. 2. With these the author has long been well acquainted. 3. As the other New England states were at first peopled from Massachusetts, her laws were the root of theirs. 4. Her laws, as to the rights of persons, property, &c., were made the root or germ of nearly all our territorial law east of the Mississippi, by being made the material parts of the ordinance of Congress, passed July 13, 1787, for the government of the United States' territories northwest of the Ohio, and from time to time extended to their other territories, as will appear on examining the ordinance itself. 5. Much the largest part of the judicial decisions made in Massachusetts (and Maine) have been made on those principles of law, which are common to all the states, except Louisiana. 6. Many of the statutes of Massachusetts having been copied or formed in substance from English statutes, and many others of our colonies and states having done the same, her statutes in these respects are substantially theirs; for instance, Massachusetts, Virginia, &c., nearly copied their statutes of limitations from the statutes of limitations of the 32d Henry VIII., ch. 2, and hence, so far, the statutes of one are those of all.

"However, there is embraced in this work much of the local law of the other states in the Union in different ways, especially of New York, Virginia, and Kentucky. The State of Louisiana having, by statute, adopted the new French civil code, with some variations, and made it, of course, a part of our American system, many parts of this code have been taken into this work. In fact, on a careful examination it will be found, that more than four fifths of the decisions made in Massachusetts, New York, and Virginia, stated in this work, have been made on principles and authorities common to twenty-three states, and so practised on in all. Though in the statutes of the several states there is a sameness in principle, yet there is a vast variety in words and detail, when not formed from one source, as above; but not a tenth part of the law in a state is found in its statute-books. Owing to this variety, the statutes of each state must be used somewhat at large, in order to practise on them safely." pp. 5, 6.

We would refer the reader to the fourteenth page of the Introduction, for a more full exposition of the author's reasons for not inserting in his work more of the local law of the several states. These reasons are, certainly, not without considerable weight. Besides, such an enlargement of the plan of the work would have occasioned an increase of its cost, without conferring an equal value upon the work; for it can hardly be supposed, that the profession, generally, would find much local law of so many states useful to them.

We are next to consider the plan of the work.

[The author's plan was here stated in his own words.]

Now it seems to us, that, with reference to the leading objects of the work, nothing could be more judicious than to give a view of the general principles of each branch of the law, and to illustrate them with cases, and then to proceed to the more minute and subordinate particulars. The remarks and comments, which accompany the leading doctrines and cases, cannot fail to be useful to all the profession; for they are the result of a half century's steady devotion to the law, by one, whose diligence has never been weary, whose caution has been disciplined by very patient investigations, and whose learning has been matured by very extensive studies.

The plan has several peculiarities; but the principal distinction between this and other abridgments is, that in many instances it treats the rights and remedies of parties in the same connection, and consequently introduces, in no inconsiderable degree, in the discussions of remedies, the most important rules of property. In this respect it pursues a method, not unlike that of Mr. Espinasse in his valuable Digest of the Law of Actions at Nisi Prius.

That there are many advantages in this system of arrangement, especially for students, will be denied by few; that it has some disadvantages ought not to be concealed. One advantage is, that it keeps up in the student's mind a close affinity between the right and remedy, and compels him to make a practical application of his knowledge, as he advances in his studies. On the other hand, one disadvantage is, that it sometimes separates into distinct heads matters of the same nature, which require different remedies in different stages of title; and leads to extensive researches into collateral questions, which do not strictly touch the remedy. Whichever way we look, there is some ground, on which the advocates of different systems may rest plausible arguments. The system, however, adopted by Mr. Dane, is not a rash innovation; and, in our judgment, has much in it entitled to commendation. If it do not unite the whole profession in its favor, it will always count among its advocates many enlightened jurists. The principal disadvantage, in a practical view, to which this method of arranging subjects is liable, is, that it is not of so easy reference in the hurry of consultation. But in Mr. Dane's work this disadvantage is entirely overcome by a general Index to the whole work, occupying, with the names of cases, a volume. This Index we venture to pronounce absolutely unrivalled in fulness and accuracy, bringing within the reach of the most ordinary diligence all the leading positions and doctrines of this extensive compilation.

As to the execution of the plan, the nature of which we have endeavored to explain in a succinct manner, it is difficult to give any but a very general sketch. It is obviously impracticable to go into the details of a work, extending through eight octavo volumes, with a crowded type and margin, and embracing nearly six thousand pages. We have no room to indulge in criticisms on particular passages.

Even to examine the divisions and subdivisions of a single title would be a most exhausting process, and occupy more pages than belong to the review of any single work. In general, it may be said, that the learned author has executed his task with becoming diligence and ability. He has bestowed forty years of a most studious life in the labor; and has here given the results of all his juridical reading in a compendious and accurate form. His comments exhibit various learning and close reflection; and his illustrations cannot fail to assist such as seek for aid in those obscurer parts of the law, which perplex by their intricacy and equivocal direction. We choose rather to subjoin extracts exhibiting the actual execution of the work, from which the reader will be able to form a fair judgment, than, by mere general expressions of approbation, to hazard in any respect the just reputation of the author.

Upon one or two topics, however, we wish to be indulged in saying a few words, because they give a distinguishing value to this Abridgment.

In the first place, it contains a full view of the doctrines, which belong to subjects principally within the cognizance of the Federal courts. Such are matters of admiralty jurisdiction and revenue seizures; the law of prize; the rights and duties of neutral nations; the claims of foreign sovereignties to immunities in our courts, and other topics connected with the administration of public law; the equity system administered in the courts of the United States, in some respects, necessarily varying from that, constituting a part of the local law of the states; and, lastly, this local law itself, so far as in these courts it regulates the rights and remedies of parties, and is brought into discussion in cases between citizens of different states. The complicated relations of the states with each other make the administration of this branch of jurisprudence (which may, not unfitly, be denominated *international private law*) a task of no inconsiderable delicacy and difficulty. Above all, it embraces the discussions of those questions of constitutional law, which have, on various occasions, engaged the earnest attention of the different states in the Union, and which have been so ably argued at the bar of the Supreme Court of the United States.

In the next place, it devotes a whole chapter to the collection and arrangement of the laws of the several states respecting titles to real estate, by grant, by devise, and by descent and distribution. This, of course, must bring together a very important mass of matters, not easily found in any single private or public library, and furnish ample means not only for professional instruction, but for the exercise of legislative discretion. The harmonies and discrepancies of the different systems are thus presented in a single view; and the best opportunity afforded of correcting errors, and introducing gradually homogeneous and consistent regulations on these vital interests of the Union.

Moreover, it embraces a large collection of decisions, many of which have never before appeared in print, and are valuable, from their general applicability, as well as the fidelity, with which they are reported. Before the publication of regular Reports in our country, many questions of the highest moment were litigated and decided in our courts, which form rules of property; and it is no inconsiderable present to the profession to embody these in an authentic form, as well as to add to some of the cases now in print, reports more full, exact, and satisfactory.

Again, large extracts are introduced from the civil, the French, and other foreign law. The utility of this part of the work cannot escape the observation of the profession. The civil law, modified by French and Spanish ordinances and usages, constitutes the basis of the law of Louisiana and the territory of the Floridas. These portions of the Union are daily becoming more and more interesting, in a commercial view, to all the states. The law, which there regulates civil and commercial rights and remedies, is of great practical importance to emigrants, to merchants, and to relatives residing in distant regions. Unlike the other states, in which a common jurisprudence, that of the common law, prevails, these territories are perpetually presenting unsuspected differences, not only in rights, but in the administration of remedies, which require to be accurately known, in order to avoid embarrassing and often fatal mistakes. Lawyers, therefore, in every part of the Union, will gladly accept any means of assisting their inquiries on these subjects, and will find ready answers to many questions. Fortunately for Louisiana, no inconsiderable portion of her civil jurisprudence has been reduced into a systematic code, whose basis is that admirable performance, the Napoleon Code. Mr. Livingston is now executing, under her patronage, a Digest of her Criminal Jurisprudence; and from the portions which we have been permitted to inspect, we have no difficulty in saying that it is a work of singular acuteness and philosophical precision, and in the highest degree creditable to his genius and industry. Such works have been occasionally disparaged by the exclusive admirers of the common law, and still more so by the overheated zeal and extravagance of some of the advocates of codes; but we feel a confidence that they are so useful and convenient, that they will, at no distant period, attract the attention of the legislatures of other states, and gradually lead to great improvements in the science of legislation, as well as in the actual administration of the law.

But it is not in this view alone that the civil and foreign law have claims upon those, whose province it is to cultivate the study of the common law. The civil law itself is an inexhaustible treasury of general principles, solid distinctions, and just doctrines, applicable to the concerns of a busy commercial age, and especially to every species of commercial contracts. The common law has, indeed, appropriated to itself, without a fair acknowledgment, many principles of this admired jurisprudence. Our law of contracts rests on this basis, and has become equitable only so far as it has ceased to be feudal, and liberal so far as it has been drawn from

Roman fountains. The splendid panegyric of Gibbon, in the forty-fourth chapter of his Decline and Fall of the Roman Empire, is not a mere vainglorious boast, but is supported by facts. "The vain titles of the victories of Justinian," says the historian, "are crumbled into dust; but the name of the legislator is inscribed on a fair and everlasting monument. Under his reign, and by his care, the civil jurisprudence was digested in the immortal works of the Code, the Pandects, and the Institutes. The public reason of the Romans has been silently or studiously transfused into the domestic institutions of Europe; and the laws of Justinian still command the respect or obedience of independent nations." Dr. Brown, a very competent judge, in one of the notes to his Brief Sketch of the Civil Law, says, "I scarcely ever yet have met with a point, not connected with the feudal law, in which, if English books did not satisfy the doubt, I have failed to find its resolution in the civil law." Can it, then, be doubted that an incorporation of such of the civil law principles, as are illustrative of the common law, into an abridgment, is of great value to students, and especially to those who wish to acquire philosophical views of jurisprudence, and aspire to something beyond the reach of an ordinary attorney? The author well remarks that,—

"A complete system of law and equity, best calculated to preserve the power of the magistrate and the rights of the people, is the last thing men attain to in society. Peter the Great soon understood every thing in the civilized parts of Europe, but the laws; and because he could not understand them, he never ceased to prefer the despotism of Turkey, , where the judges are not restrained by any methods, forms, or laws.' Ancient Greece, though eminent in other sciences, never had such a system. The reason is seen in the almost infinite variety, extent, and combination of ideas, founded in nature, experience, and cultivated morality, so essential in forming and completing such a system. It is very clear that a great republic, in which there is room for talents; in which thoughts and actions are not restrained by religious or political despotism; in which education is encouraged, and moral character is esteemed; in which the law rules, and not the sword; in which each one asserts his rights by law, and not by force; and in which there is representation, jury-trial, and a free press, is the natural field of law and equity; but to produce these in perfection, there must be a *national* character. The rules of law and equity, in important matters, must be uniform, and pervade the whole nation." *Introd.* pp. 14, 15.

HISTORY AND INFLUENCE OF THE PURITANS.

A DISCOURSE PRONOUNCED AT THE REQUEST OF THE ESSEX HISTORICAL SOCIETY, SEPTEMBER 18, 1828, IN COMMEMORATION OF THE FIRST SETTLEMENT OF SALEM, MASS.

THERE are certain epochs in the history of nations, which always attract to themselves a lasting interest. They constitute steps in the progress or decline of empire, at which we involuntarily pause to look back upon the past, or to spell out the fortunes of the future. They become associated with our inmost feelings and profoundest reflections. Our imaginations embody the time, the place, and the circumstances. We drop the intermediate distances of space and years which divide us from them. We breathe the very air and spirit of the age itself. We gather up the fragments of broken facts, as history or tradition has scattered them around us. We arrange them with a fond solicitude; and having dressed them out in all the pride and pomp of fair array, our hearts kindle at the contemplation; and we exult or mourn, glow with confidence or bow with humiliation, as they pass before us, and we realize their connection with ourselves, the glory of our country, or the fate of the world.

Of memorable events, few awaken a more lively curiosity than the origin of nations. Whence we sprung, at what period, from what race, by what causes, under what circumstances, for what objects, are inquiries so natural, that they rise almost spontaneously in our minds; and scarcely less so in the humblest than in the most exalted of society. They are intimately connected with our pride, our character, our hopes, and our destiny. He, who may look back upon a long line of illustrious ancestors, cannot forget that the blood, stirring in his own veins, is drawn from a common source; and that the light, reflected by their virtues, casts upon his own path a cheering, even though it may be a distant, radiance. And he, who may not claim kindred with the mighty dead, feels that they are the common inheritance of his country, and that he has a right to share in their fame, and triumph in their achievements.

Nor let it be supposed, that this strong propensity of our nature is attributable to the indulgence of mere personal or national vanity. It has a higher and better origin. It is closely interwoven with that reverence and affection with which we regard our parents, and the patriarchs of our own times; with that gratitude, with which we follow the benefactors of our race; with that piety, which reads in every event the superintendence of a wise and benevolent Providence; with that charity, which binds up our interests in those of mankind at large; with that sympathy, which links our fate with that of all past and future generations; and with that sense of duty, which the consciousness of trusts of unmeasured extent never fails to elevate and strengthen. Above all, we are thus enabled to extract from remote events that instruction, which the vicissitudes of human life should press home to our own business and bosoms. The toils and misfortunes incident to infant settlements; the slow progress even of successful effort; the patience, fortitude, and sagacity, by which evils are overcome or diminished; the fundamental causes, which quicken or retard their growth; these all furnish lessons, which improve the wise, correct the rash, and alarm the improvident.

Two hundred years have just elapsed, since our forefathers landed on these shores for the permanent plantation of New England. I say, emphatically, for the permanent plantation of New England. There had been, before that period, various adventurers, who, from curiosity, or necessity, or hope of gain, explored the coast; but their purposes were transient, or their stay short. There had been here and there little establishments for fishery or trade, successively taken up and abandoned, from the rigors of the climate, the unprofitableness of the employment, or the disappointments naturally following upon such novel enterprises. Few persons, comparatively speaking, had turned their thoughts to this, as a land favorable for the cultivation of the soil, or the arts of social life. It promised little to the European, who should leave his native country with a fancy warm with descriptions of the luxuriance of this western world, and hoping to pass the residue of his life, as "one long summer day of indolence" and ease. It offered no mines, glittering with gold and silver, to tempt the avarice of the selfish, or to stimulate the hopes of the ambitious. It presented an irregular and rocky front, lashed by the waves of a stormy ocean, and frowning with dark forests and bleak promontories. Its rough and stubborn soil yielded with reluctance to the labors of the husbandman; and the severities of a northern winter, for almost half the year, stripped the earth of its vegetation by its bitter blasts or drifting snows. It required stout hands and stouter hearts to encounter such discouragements; to subdue the ruggedness of nature, and to wait the slow returns, which perseverance and industry alone could reasonably hope to obtain. Men must have strong motives to lead them, under such circumstances, to such a choice. It was not an enterprise, which, being conceived in a moment of rashness, might by its quick success plead its own justification. It had none of the allurements of power, or the indulgences of pleasure, or the offerings of fame, to give it attractions. Higher motives and deeper thoughts, such as engross the passions and the souls of men, and sink into comparative insignificance the comforts of social life, are alone adequate to produce such results. One might well say, as Tacitus did of the Germany of his own times,[1] "Quis porro, præter periculum horridi et ignoti maris, Asiâ aut Africâ aut Italiâ relictâ, Germaniam peteret, informem terris, asperam cœlo, tristem cultu aspectuque, nisi si patria sit?" Who, independently of the perils of a terrific and unknown sea, would leave the soft climates of Asia, Africa, or Europe, and fix his abode in a land rough and uncultivated, with an inclement sky and a dreary aspect, unless indeed it were his mother country?

It should excite no surprise, therefore, that a century had passed away after the Cabots discovered the southern part of this continent, and yet the Aborigines remained there in undisturbed security. Even the neighboring colony of Plymouth, where the renowned Pilgrims, under Carver, Bradford, and Winslow, had already raised the standard of liberty and the cross, was encountering the severest trials, and struggling almost for existence. There were not a few friends, who began to entertain fears, that unless succors came in from other quarters, this noble band of worthies, worn down by hardships and discouragements, might be destined, at no distant period, to follow the fate of other adventurers, or be reduced to a narrow factory.[2] Their original scheme of colonization involved in it some fatal defects, which were afterwards corrected by their own wisdom and experience. The notion of a community of property and profits was utterly incompatible with the growth of a state. It cut off, at a blow, every excitement to individual enterprise; and, by its unequal distribution of burthens and benefits, sowed far and wide the elements of discord. The followers of the excellent Robinson might, indeed, comfort themselves with the present possession of a refuge from religious oppression; but the possibility of a dissolution of their connection at any period, however remote, must, whenever it was suggested, have filled their

1 Hutchinson, in his History, (vol. i. p. 2,) cites this passage. It is from Tacitus, *De Germaniâ*, c. 2.

2 2 Hutch. Hist. 468, 469, 470, 472, 476; Prince's Annals, 268; Robertson's America, book 10; 3 Hist. Collect. 417.

hearts with sorrow, and, even when least indulged, sometimes have disturbed their peace. Their own language, in defence of their settlement at Hartford, affords a striking picture of their situation. "They lived upon a barren place, where they were by necessity cast; and neither they, nor theirs, could long continue upon the same; and why should they be deprived of that, which they had provided, and intended to remove to, as soon as they were able?"[1] At the distance of ten years from their first landing, the colony could scarcely number three hundred inhabitants;[2] a proof, at once, of the magnitude of their difficulties, and of the heroic zeal and perseverance, which met them without shrinking or dismay.

By the blessing of God, however, our Fathers also came hither, and, in connection with the good "Old Colony," fixed henceforth, and as we fondly trust, for ever, the settlement and destiny of New England. And we are met, on the very spot first trodden by their footsteps, on the very day first welcoming their arrival, to celebrate this memorable event. It is fit, that we should so do. What occasion could occur more worthy of our homage? What recollections could rise up, better adapted to awaken our gratitude, cheer our hearts, and elevate our thoughts? Who is he that can survey this goodly land, and not feel a present sense of its various blessings? Let him cast his eyes over our mountains, or our valleys, our deep forests, or our cultivated plains. Let him visit our villages, and hamlets, and towns, thickening on every side, and listen to the sounds of busy, contented, thrifty industry. Let him view the green meadows, and the waving fields, and the rich orchards, rising under his eyes in alternate order, yielding their products in profusion, and quickened into fertility by the labors of man. Let him hold communion with the inhabitants of these peaceful abodes, with the mountaineers, and

[1] 2 Hutch. Hist. 469, &c.

[2] Robertson's America, book x. p. 267; Chalmers's Annals, p. 97. See also the Commissioners' Report in 1665 (3 Hutch. Collect.) 417.

peasants, and yeomen, the lords of the soil, the reapers of their harvests, who look proudly down upon their own inheritance. Let him learn from them the resolute spirit, the manly virtues, the intelligence and piety, which pervade New England. Let him glance at the neighboring metropolis; its splendid spires glittering in the sun; its noble hospitals and public charities; its crowded and well-built streets; its beautiful harbor, floating on its bosom the commerce of the world, and reflecting on its surface islands, and islets, and shores of ever-varying magnificence; its amphitheatre of hills, whose gentle slopes whiten with neat mansions, or soften into shade, under the joint ministry of nature and art; its lofty halls, where eloquence has burst forth in strains of patriotism, which have made captive the souls of thousands; its visible industry, and enterprise, and public spirit, gathering into the lap of a common mother the products of all climates, and spreading out a generous hospitality. Let him catch, in the distant reach, the walls of our venerable University, cemented by the solid strength of centuries, where learning and religion obtained their early glory, and will, we trust, receive their latest praise. Let him, I say, contemplate these scenes, and survey this goodly heritage; and who is he, even though a stranger to us and ours, whose voice shall not eagerly ask our lineage, our ancestry, our age? Who is he, that here inhales his natal air, and embraces his mother earth, and does not rejoice, that he was born for this day, and is privileged to pour out his thanks, and offer up his prayers at the home of his forefathers?

To us, indeed, who own the local genius, and feel the inspirations of the place, the day may well be presumed to be crowded with thick-coming fancies and joyance. We may not turn our eyes on any side, without meeting objects to revive the images of the primitive times. We can still realize the fidelity of the description of the voyager of 1629, who said, "We passed the curious and difficult entrance into the large, spacious harbor of Naimkeake; and, as we passed along, it was wonderful to behold so many islands replenished with thick wood, and high trees, and many fair green pastures." The woods have disappeared; but the islands and the fair green pastures remain with more than native beauty; and the rivers still meander in their early channels. This "city of peace," so called by our fathers, as significant of their enjoyment of civil and religious freedom, still boasts its ancient name; still justifies the original allusion to the Scriptures, "In Salem also is *God's* tabernacle, and his dwelling-place in Zion."[1] The thin and scattered settlements can no longer be traced. But in their stead, are found spacious streets, and neat dwellings, and lively schools, and numerous churches, and busy marts, and all the fair accompaniments of opulence and knowledge, simplicity of life and manners, unobtrusive refinement, and social kindness. Yet, in the midst of these blessed changes, we can point out the very spot, where the first flock was gathered, and the first church consecrated to the service of the living God; where the meek and learned Higginson (alas, how soon to perish!) first raised his voice in prayer, and with trembling lips, and pale cheeks, where sorrow and sickness had worn many an early furrow, discoursed most eloquently of life, and death, and immortality, the triumphs of faith, and the rewards of obedience. Yes, it is still devoted to the same holy purpose. There, the voice of praise, and thanksgiving, and prayer still ascends from pious hearts; there, the doctrines of salvation are still preached with enlightened zeal and charity; there, the humble, the contrite, and the pure still assemble in sweet communion, and worship God in spirit and in truth.[2] The sepulchres of our forefathers are also among us. We can trace them through all their various labors to their last appointed home; *sedes ubi fata quietas ostendunt.* Time has not yet levelled the incumbent sod, nor the moss overgrown the frail memorials erected to their worth. But their noblest monument is around us,

[1] Historical Collections, 117; Psalm lxxvi.

[2] See the excellent dedication sermon of the Rev. Mr. Upham, one of the pastors of this church, in November, 1826.

and before us. Their deeds speak their eulogy in a manner, which it requires no aid of language to heighten. They live in their works; not, indeed, in the perishable structure of human skill, in marble domes or triumphal arches, in temples or in palaces, the wonders of art; but in the enduring institutions which they created, in the principles which they taught, and by which they sought to live, and for which they were ready to die. On these they laid the solid foundations of our strength and glory; and on these, if on any thing human, may be written the words of immortality. Our graveyards offer no better epitaph for them than that, Here lie the Founders of New England; and brief though it be, and of simple phrase, it has a pregnant meaning, the extent of which no human mind has yet grasped. It can be unfolded only with the destiny of our latest posterity.

May I venture on some allusions not unbecoming this occasion, and yet of a nature somewhat personal, though not, I trust, obtrusive? I speak in the presence of the descendants of these men. Their names sound with familiar welcome in our streets, and greet us on every side, as we pass along. They seem to live again in their offspring. Their images grace our processions, and throng our churches, and enliven our festivals. We feel almost as in their conscious presence, and listen to the voices of other days. When, in the enthusiasm of poetry, we are asked, "And the pilgrims, where are they?" Where are Winthrop, and Endicott, and Higginson, and Dudley, and Saltonstall, and Bradstreet, and Pickering, and Sprague, and Pynchon, and Hathorne, and Conant, and Woodbury, and Palfrey, and Balch, and the other worthies? we are ready to exclaim, — They are here. This is their home. These are their children.

There is yet among us one, who brings their revered forms before us with peculiar dignity, and is at once the representative of their age and our own. Generation after generation has passed away, and yet he survives, the model, and the monument of a century. His early youth almost clasped the knees of the pilgrims. He was familiar with their sons, and listened to their story from the lips of those, who painted with the vividness of contemporaries and with the feelings of Puritans. Standing upon the very verge of the first century, he seems the living herald of the first settlers, breathing into our souls their very words and sentiments, as one, who speaks not for the dead, but for those, who yet sojourn on the earth. Time in his favor has relaxed his wonted course, and touched even the faded graces of the past with a kind and mellowing charm. If one were to task his imagination to portray a patriarch of primitive simplicity, warmed with the refinements of these latter days, he could scarcely clothe the being of his own creation with other qualities than we have seen. He could not fail to point out to us a form, venerable for wisdom, learning, and modesty, in which the spirit of philosophy and benevolence was sustained by meekness and piety; in which blamelessness of life, cheerfulness of heart, and gratitude for past blessings, imparted solid lustre to a faith and hope, and joy, resting upon immortality. Well may it be asked of such a being, in the tender language of Scripture, "And the old man, of whom ye spake, is he yet alive?" Your own hearts have already answered the question. We have seen this centennial patriarch; and we count it among the triumphs of this day, that he yet lives, the delight of his friends, the crown of his profession, and the ornament of human nature.

Such are some of the circumstances and associations belonging to the festival, which has assembled us together. I am but too sensible how utterly inadequate my own powers are, to meet the exigencies of such a day. I have not been unconscious of the difficulties of the task; and I now stand here with sincere self-distrust, having yielded to a sense of duty, what I should gladly have declined if left to my own choice. After all, however, the occasion carries along with it its own means of gratification, in the thoughts of home, and kindred, and ancestry, and country, which rise in every heart, and hang on every tongue. If I falter in the course, I may well share this consolation, since a common sympathy must disarm the severity of criticism.

Many topics, appropriate to this celebration, have already been discussed by others, in a manner which does not require, even if it should admit of, farther illustration. The genius of New England has employed some of its best efforts to add dignity to the scene. History and tradition have been laid under contribution to adorn the narrative; and philosophy itself, while studying the events, has unfolded speculations, as profound and engrossing as any which can engage the human mind. I profess not the rashness to follow in the high course thus marked out; content to walk in the ancient paths, and to gather, as I may, the gleanings of a harvest, which has so amply rewarded the labors of my predecessors.

My object is to furnish you with a brief sketch of the origin of the colony; of the motives which led to the enterprise; of the characters of the men who conducted it; of the principles upon which it was established; and of the grand results which it has hitherto developed. I shall also adventure upon some topics where the conduct of our ancestors has been severely put to question; and, without attempting to disguise their mistakes, I trust that something may be said to rescue their memory from unmerited reproach.

If the origin of nations be, as it confessedly is, a source of deep interest, there are circumstances connected with the first settlement of New England peculiarly to gratify a national pride. We do not trace ourselves back to times of traditionary darkness, where truth and fiction are blended at every step, and what remains, after the closest investigation, is but conjecture, or shadowy fact. We do not rely upon the arts of the poet to give dignity to the narrative, and invest it with the colorings of his imagination. Greece might delight to trace her origin up to the high renown and antiquity of Egypt; and Rome soothe herself with her rise from the smouldering ruins of Troy. We have no legends which genius may fashion into its own forms, and crowd with imaginary personages. Such as it is, our history lies far within the reach of the authentic annals of mankind. It has been written by contemporaries with a simplicity which admits of no embellishment, and a fidelity which invites scrutiny. The records are before us, sketched by the first adventurers; and there we may learn all their wanderings, and cares, and sufferings, and hopes, their secret thoughts, and their absorbing motives. We can ask of the world no credit for modern statements of old events. We can conceal nothing; and our true glory is, that there is nothing which we wish to conceal. And yet, I think, whoever shall read these annals in their minute details; whoever shall bring home to his thoughts the causes and consequences of these events; whoever shall watch the struggles of conscience against the seductions of affection, and the pressure of dangers; will feel his soul touched with a moral sublimity, which poetry itself could not surpass. So mighty is truth; so irresistible is the voice of nature.

Take but a single passage in their lives, the opening scene of that drama, on which we seem but just to have entered. Go back and meet the first detachment, the little band, which, under the guidance of the worthy, intelligent, and intrepid Endicott, landed on the neighboring shore. It was then, as it is now, the early advance of autumn. What can be more beautiful or more attractive than this season in New England? The sultry heat of summer has passed away; and a delicious coolness at evening succeeds the genial warmth of the day. The labors of the husbandman approach their natural termination; and he gladdens with the near prospect of his promised reward. The earth swells with the increase of vegetation. The fields wave with their yellow and luxuriant harvests. The trees put forth their darkest foliage, half shading and half revealing their ripened fruits, to tempt the appetite of man, and proclaim the goodness of his Creator. Even in scenes of another sort, where nature reigns alone in her own majesty, there is much to awaken religious enthusiasm. As yet, the forests stand clothed in their dress of undecayed magnificence. The winds that rustle through their tops scarcely disturb the silence of the shades below. The mountains and the valleys glow in warm green, or lively russet. The rivulets flow on with a noiseless current, reflecting back the images of many a glossy insect, that dips his wings in their cooling waters. The mornings and evenings are still vocal with the notes of a thousand warblers, which plume their wings for a later flight. Above all, the clear blue sky, the long and sunny calms, the scarcely whispering breezes, the brilliant sunsets, lit up with all the wondrous magnificence of light, and shade, and color, and slowly settling down into a pure and transparent twilight. These, these are days and scenes which even the cold cannot behold without emotion; but on which the meditative and pious gaze with profound admiration; for they breathe of holier and happier regions beyond the grave.

But lovely as is this autumn, so finely characterized as the Indian Summer of New England, and so favorably contrasting itself with the chills and moisture of the British Isles, let us not imagine that it appeared to these Pilgrims, as it does to us, clothed in smiles. Their first steps on this continent were doubtless with that buoyancy of spirit, which relief from the tediousness and dangers of a sea voyage naturally excites. But, think you, that their first hasty glances around them did not bring some anxieties for the future, and some regrets for the past? They were in the midst of a wilderness untrodden by civilized man. The native forests spread around them, with only here and there a detached glade, which the Indian tomahawk had levelled or the fisherman cleared for his temporary hut. There were no houses inviting to repose; no fields ripening with corn; no cheerful hearths; no welcoming friends; no common altars. The heavens, indeed, shone fair over their heads; and the earth beneath was rich in its beauties. But where was their home? Where were those comforts and endearments, which that little word crowds into our hearts in the midst of the keenest sufferings? Where were the objects to which they might cling to relieve their thoughts from the sense of present desolation? If there were some who could say, with an exile of the succeeding year, "We rested that night with glad and thankful hearts, that God had put an end to our long and tedious journey through the greatest sea in the world;"[1] there were many whose pillows were wet with bitter though not repentant tears. Many a father offered his evening prayer with trembling accents; many a mother clasped her children to her bosom in speechless agony. The morrow came; but it brought no abatement of anxiety. It was rather a renewal of cares, of sad reminiscences, of fearful forebodings.

This is no idle picture of the fancy, tricked out for effect, to move our sympathies, or blind us to the real facts. How could their situation be otherwise? They were not fugitives from justice, seeking to bury themselves and their crimes in some remote corner of the earth. They were not prodigals, endeavoring to retrieve their wrecked fortunes in distant adventures. They were not idle and luxurious wanderers, weary of society, and panting for unexplored novelties. They had left a country full of the refinements of social life, and dear to them by every human tie. There were the tombs of their ancestors; there the abodes of their friends; of mothers, who kissed their pale cheeks on the seashore; of sisters, who wrung their hands in sharp distress; of children, who dropped upon their knees and asked a blessing at parting, ay, at parting for ever. There was the last, lingering embrace; there the last sight of the white cliffs of England, which had faded from their straining gaze, for time, and for eternity. There, for the last time, were uttered from their broken voices, "Farewell, dear England; farewell, the church of God in England; farewell, all Christian friends there."[2]

[1] 3 Hutch. Collect. 44. [2] Eliot's Dictionary, Art. *Higginson*, 252.

They were now landed on other shores. The excitements of the voyage were gone. Three thousand miles of ocean rolled between them and the country they had left; and every illusion of hope had vanished before the sober realities of a wilderness. They had now full leisure for reflection,

> "While busy, meddling memory,
> In barbarous succession mustered up
> The past endearments of their softer hours,
> Tenacious of its theme."

There is nothing so depressing in exile as that sickness of the heart, which comes over us with the thoughts of a lost, distant home. There is nothing which softens the harsh features of nature like the feeling that this is our country. The exiles of New England saw not before them either a home, or a country. Both were to be created.

If the past could bring few consolations, the future was not without its embarrassments. The season was passed, in which any addition could be made to their scanty stock of provisions from the produce of the soil. No succors could reach them until the ensuing spring; and even then, they were subject to many contingencies. The winter must soon approach, with its bleak winds and desolating storms. The wild beasts were in the woods; and the scarcely less savage Indians lurked in the ravines, or accosted them with questionable friendship. Trees were to be felled, and houses built, and fortifications arranged, as well for shelter as for safety; and brief was the space, and feeble the means, to accomplish these necessary defences. Beyond these, were the unknown dangers of change of climate, and new habits of life, and scanty food; of the pestilence, that walketh in darkness, and the famine, that wasteth at noonday. These were discouragements, which might well appall the timid, and subdue the rash. It is not, then, too much to affirm, again, that it required stout hands, and stouter hearts, to overcome such difficulties. But

> "If misfortune comes, she brings along
> The bravest virtues."

The men, who landed here, were no ordinary men; the motive for their emigration was no ordinary motive; and the glory of their achievement has few parallels in the history of the world. Their perseverance in the midst of hardships, their firmness in the midst of dangers, their patience in the midst of sufferings, their courage in the midst of disasters, their unconquerable spirit, their unbending adherence to their principles, their steady resistance of all encroachments, surprise us even more than the wisdom of their plans, and the success of their operations.

If we trace on the colony during the two or three next succeeding years, in which it received an accession of almost two thousand persons, we shall find abundant reason to distrust those early descriptions, of which the just complaint was, that "honest men, out of a desire to draw over others to them, wrote somewhat hyperbolically of many things here," and "by their too large commendations of the country, and the commodities thereof, so strongly invited *others* to go on;"[1] and to express our astonishment, that the enterprise was not instantly abandoned. Many of those, who accompanied Endicott, died, in the ensuing winter, by disease from exposure, and want of food and suitable medical assistance. They were reinforced, the next summer, by new colonists with fresh supplies; and again in the succeeding year, when the Corporation itself was also removed, under the auspices of Winthrop, Dudley, Johnson, Saltonstall, and others. What was then the state of the Colony? We are told by a friend and eye-witness[2]—"We found the Colony," says he, "in a sad and unexpected condition; above eighty of them" (that is, more than one quarter of the whole number) "being dead the winter before; and many of those alive, weak and sick; all the corn and bread amongst them all, hardly sufficient to feed them a fortnight." He adds, "If any come hither to

[1] Governor Dudley's Letter, 3 Hist. Coll. 36, 38, 43.

[2] Governor Dudley's Letter, 3 Hist. Coll. 38.

plant for worldly ends, that can live well at home, he commits an error, of which he will soon repent him." — "In a word, we have little to be envied; but endure much to be pitied, in the sickness and mortality of our people." And then, in the conclusion of this memorable letter, he breaks out with the unconquerable spirit of Puritanism — "We are left, a people poor and contemptible, yet such as trust in God; and are contented with our own condition, being well assured, that he will not fail us, nor forsake us." Men, who were thus prepared to encounter such distresses, were prepared for every thing. The stake had no terrors for them; and earth had no rewards, which could, for a moment, withdraw them from the dictates of conscience and duty.

This year was, indeed, still more disastrous than the preceding, and robbed them of some of their brightest ornaments. Before December, the grave had closed upon two hundred of their number; and among these were some of the most accomplished of both sexes. It is impossible, even at this distance of time, to contemplate their character and fate, without the deepest sympathy. Higginson, the reverend and beloved teacher of the first flock, fell, an early victim, in the forty-third year of his age, and the first of his ministry. Let me pause, for a moment, to pay a passing tribute to his worth. He received his education at Emanuel College in Cambridge, where he was so much distinguished by his talents, acquirements, and scholarship, that he gained an early introduction into a benefice of the church. The arguments of Hildersham and Hooker, however, soon infused scruples into his mind respecting the doctrines and discipline of the establishment, and he was ejected for nonconformity. He then taught a few pupils, for the maintenance of his family; and having received an invitation to remove to New England, in the hope of restoring his health, and animated by the glorious prospect of a free enjoyment as he expresses it, "of the true religion and holy ordinances of Almighty God," he embarked, with his family, in the Talbot, in 1629. In the course of the voyage he had the misfortune to lose one of his daughters, of whose death he gives us an account in his journal, drawn up with a simplicity beautifully illustrative of his own character. "And so," says he, "it was God's will the child died about five o'clock at night, being the first in our ship that was buried in the bowels of the great Atlantic sea; which, as it was a great grief to us, her parents, and a terror to all the rest, as being the beginning of a contagious disease and mortality, so in the same judgment it pleased God to remember mercy in the child, in forcing it from a world of misery, wherein she had lived all her days." And, after an allusion to her personal infirmities, he concludes, "So that in respect of her, we had cause to take her death as a blessing from the Lord to shorten her misery."[1] Alas! he was destined too soon to follow her. Not many months elapsed before a consumption settled on his cheeks, and by its hectic flushes betrayed an irretrievable decline. He died with the composure, resignation, and Christian confidence of a saint; leaving behind him a character, in which learning, benignity of manners, purity of life, fervent piety, and unaffected charity, were blended with most attractive grace; and his name is enrolled among the earliest and truest benefactors of New England.

A death scarcely less regretted, and which followed with a fearful rapidity, was that of a lady of noble birth, elegant accomplishments, and exemplary virtues. I speak of the Lady Arabella Johnson,[2] a daughter of the Earl of Lincoln who accompanied her husband in the embarkation under Winthrop, and in honor of whom, the admiral ship on that occasion was called by her name. She died in a very short time after her arrival; and lies buried near the neighboring shore. No stone or other memorial indicates the exact place; but tradition has preserved it with a holy reverence. The

[1] 3 Hutch. Collect. 32, 36.

[2] Her name is commonly spelt in the records of that day, possibly as an abbreviation, "Arbella."

remembrance of her excellence is yet fresh in all our thoughts; and many a heart still kindles with admiration of her virtues; and many a bosom heaves with sighs at her untimely end. What, indeed, could be more touching than the fate of such a woman? What example more striking than hers, of uncompromising affection and piety? Born in the lap of ease, and surrounded by affluence; with every prospect which could make hope gay, and fortune desirable; accustomed to the splendors of a court, and the scarcely less splendid hospitalities of her ancestral home; she was yet content to quit, what has not inaptly been termed "this paradise of plenty and pleasure," for "a wilderness of wants," and, with a fortitude superior to the delicacies of her rank and sex, to trust herself to an unknown ocean and a distant climate, that she might partake, with her husband, the pure and spiritual worship of God. To the honor, to the eternal honor of her sex, be it said, that in the path of duty no sacrifice is with them too high, or too dear. Nothing is with them impossible, but to shrink from what love, honor, innocence, religion, requires. The voice of pleasure or of power may pass by unheeded; but the voice of affliction never. The chamber of the sick, the pillow of the dying, the vigils of the dead, the altars of religion, never missed the presence or the sympathies of woman. Timid though she be, and so delicate, that the winds of heaven may not too roughly visit her; on such occasions she loses all sense of danger, and assumes a preternatural courage, which knows not, and fears not consequences. Then she displays that undaunted spirit, which neither courts difficulties, nor evades them; that resignation, which utters neither murmur nor regret; and that patience in suffering, which seems victorious even over death itself.

The Lady Arabella perished in this noble undertaking, of which she seemed the ministering angel; and her death spread universal gloom throughout the colony. Her husband was overwhelmed with grief at the unexpected event, and survived her but a single month. Governor Winthrop has pronounced his eulogy in one short sentence. "He was a holy man, and wise, and died in sweet peace." He was truly the idol of the people; and the spot selected by himself for his own sepulture became consecrated in their eyes; so that many left it as a dying request, that they might be buried by his side. Their request prevailed; and the Chapel Burying-ground in Boston, which contains his remains, became, from that time, appropriated to the repose of the dead.[1] Perhaps the best tribute to this excellent pair is, that time, which, with so unsparing a hand, consigns statesmen and heroes, and even sages to oblivion, has embalmed the memory of their worth, and preserved it among the choicest of New England relics. It can scarcely be forgotten, but with the annals of our country.

I have dwelt with some particularity, perhaps with undue solicitude, upon some of the circumstances attending the emigration of our forefathers. They are necessary to a full comprehension of the difficulties of the enterprise, and of the sufferings, which they bore, I will not say with fortitude merely, but with cheerful, unrepining resolution. It is not by a few set phrases, or a few strong touches, that we can paint their sorrows, or their struggles; their calmness, when their friends were falling around them, and themselves were placed at the

> "dreadful post
> Of observation, darker every hour;"

or their courage, at the approach of dangers of another sort. Many of them went down to an early grave, without the consolation, even in vision, of an ultimate triumph; and many, who lived to partake it, grappled with hardships, the plain recital of which would appall more than the most studied exaggerations of rhetoric. But, let me repeat it, thanks be to God, their efforts were successful. They laid

[1] 1 Hutch. Hist. 16; 1 Winthrop's Journal, 34; Eliot's Dictionary, Art. ohnson.

the foundations of empire in these northern regions with slow and thoughtful labor. Our reverence for their services should rest, not upon the fictions of fancy, but upon a close survey of their means and their ends, their motives and their lives, their characters and their actions. And I am much mistaken, if that close survey does not invigorate our patriotism, confirm our principles, and deepen and widen the channels of our gratitude.

The history of colonies, both in ancient and modern times, may be generally traced back to the ambition of princes, the love of adventure or gain, the pressure of poverty, or the necessity of a refuge from political oppressions. The ancient nations, for the most part, transplanted colonies to distant regions, to extend the boundaries of their power, and consolidate their strength. They were sometimes outposts of the empire, to hold in check a conquered province; and sometimes military stations, to overawe and watch a formidable rival. The beautiful regions of Asia Minor were peopled with Grecian tribes, by the attractions of a fertile soil and delicious climate, by the passion for conquest, by the temptations of eastern luxury, and by the ostracisms of successive factions. Rome gathered them within the folds of her ample domain, as the booty of her arms; and pushed her own colonies only where tribute was to be exacted, or distant conquests secured. The whole line of her colonies in Gaul, Germany, and the North, was but a chain of military communications, to intercept the inroads of the barbarians, and furnish employment for leaders and legions, too restless and too ambitious for civil life. They were at once the sources of her power, and her weakness. To them Rome was every thing; and the colonies they occupied, nothing, except as resources and depots to command the republic, or dictate the succession to the imperial purple. The Capitol was but too often obedient to the will of a provincial commander, and a licentious soldiery.

The colonies of modern nations owe their origin almost exclusively to the spirit of commerce. If power has mixed itself among the objects of their governments, it has rather been, as a consequence of commerce, than an independent motive. Ships, commerce, and colonies were so long associated in the minds of European statesmen, that they seemed inseparable accompaniments. Hence arose that system of monopoly, which narrowed down all trade to the mother country, and stinted the growth and crippled the resources of the colonies to the measure of the wants of the former. All Europe, as if by a general conspiracy, acted up to the very letter of this system for centuries. The general practice was, like that attributed to the Dutch in respect to the Spice Islands, to destroy all the surplus, beyond that which would yield the established rate of profits. The South American colonies of France, Spain, and Portugal were hermetically sealed against the approach of foreign ships, until the mighty revolutions of our day crumbled the whole system into dust, and opened, almost like an earthquake, a pathway through their interior. Even England relaxed her grasp with a slow and reluctant caution, yielding little, except to necessity, indifferent to the colonial interests, and solicitous only that the home market should gather up and distribute all the profits and products of the Indies. Her famous navigation acts, the boast of her statesmen from the times of Cromwell down to ours, are an undisguised appropriation of the means of the colonies to the policy of the mother country. She generally left the plantations to the private enterprise of her subjects, until their trade was worthy of her interference; and she then assumed the government and regulation of them for her own, and not for their benefit. Protection became a duty only at the time when it seemed no longer a burden. Her vast empire in the East, the wonder of our day, whose fate furnishes a problem, not to be solved by any former experience, is but the ill-managed contrivance of a private corporation for trade. It affords a curious example of the spirit of conquest ingrafted on the spirit of commerce; of a government founded on calculations of profit; of a legislation acting on the industry of sixty millions of subjects, wholly without representation; of a judicial establishment seeking to administer justice by appeals to an unknown code, with entire good faith, but wholly inadequate means; of a political superintendence, which guards against external violence, but which sits down contented, while provinces are plundered, and thrones are overturned, in wars brought on by the encroachments of commerce.

The colonies, planted on the continent of North America, were in a great measure the offspring of private adventure and enterprise, and, with a single exception, of the spirit of commerce. That exception is New England; and it is an exception as extraordinary as it is honorable. We owe our existence to the love of religion; and, I may say, exclusively to the love of religion. I am aware, that the council of Plymouth had profitable objects in view, and that capital was first embarked, and a charter obtained, to accomplish these ends. But the scheme had little chance of success, and was in fact suspended, if not entirely abandoned. The first settlement at Plymouth was made solely from motives of religion, without any charter, and even without any title to the land. And it was not until the charter of 1628 was obtained, by men whose whole hearts were devoted to religion, that the same impulse effected the colonization of Massachusetts. This is not left to tradition; but it is the sober truth of history, unquestioned, because unquestionable. It has the highest record evidence in its support. It has, if possible, even weightier proofs, in the public acts of the colony; in our past and existing institutions; in the very errors, as well as the virtues, of our forefathers. They were Christians; they were Puritans; they were Christians persecuted by Christians; they were Puritans driven into exile by the priesthood.

The influence of religion upon the human character is one of the most interesting studies in the history of our race. But the influence of Christianity, whether viewed in respect to the extent of its reach, or the nature of its operations, is the most instructive of all speculations, which can employ the intellect of man. Paganism was indulgent in its general policy; for it taught little of duty, and claimed no exclusive possession of the oracles, or even of the favor of its divinities. In truth, it floated round the mind with a loose and indeterminate credit, and easily admitted into its temples the worship of strange gods; sometimes because their favor might be propitiated, or their vengeance averted; sometimes, perhaps, because the relative power, superiority, and office of each might not be well adjusted in their mythology. Quarrels and divisions about faith and doctrines were of very rare occurrence, in the heathen world; for their religion dealt more in rites and ceremonies than in fixed belief.[1] There would be little inclination for public struggles, where rewards and punishments were supposed to be administered, not according to desert, but according to the favor, to the passions, and even to the animosities of their divinities. There could be little responsibility cherished, where acts, offensive to some, might on that very account be grateful to others of their gods. Gibbon's splendid description of the Roman religion is true of nearly the whole ancient world. "The various modes of worship, which prevailed in the Roman world, were all considered by the people, as equally true; by the philosopher, as equally false; and by the magistrate, as equally useful. And thus toleration produced, not only mutual indulgence, but even religious concord."[2]

Far different is the case with Christianity. It propounds no equivocal doctrines. It recognizes no false or foreign gods. It allows no idolatrous worship. It presents to all men one Supreme Being the only proper object of worship, unchangeable, infinite, omniscient, all-wise, all-good, all-powerful, all-merciful, the God of all, and the Father of all. It develops one complete system of duties, fit for all times, and all sta-

[1] Bacon's Essays; 2 Bacon's Works, 257.

[2] 1 Gibbon's Hist. ch. 2, p. 46; Montesquieu's Spirit of Laws, b. 25, ch. 15.

tions; for the monarch on his throne, and the peasant in his cottage. It brings all men to the same level, and measures all by the same standard. It humbles in the dust the proud and the arrogant; it gives no heed to the glory of princes, or conquerors, or nobles. It exalts the lowly virtues, the love of peace, charity, humility, forgiveness, resignation, patience, purity, holiness. It teaches a moral and final accountability for every action. It proposes sanctions for its precepts of no earthly reach; but such as are infinite, unchangeable, and eternal. Its rewards are the promises of immortal bliss; its punishments a fearful and overwhelming retribution. It excuses no compromises of principle, and no paltering with sin. It acknowledges no sacrifices, but of a broken and contrite spirit; no pardon, but by repentance of heart and reformation of life. In its view, this life is but the entrance upon existence; a transitory state of probation and trial; and the grave is the portal to that better world, where "God shall wipe away all tears from our eyes; and there shall be no more death, neither sorrow, nor crying, neither shall there be any more pain."

To minds engrossed by such thoughts, and fixed in such belief, what could there be seducing, or satisfying, in the things of this world? It would be impossible for them, for a moment, to put in competition the affairs of time with the dazzling splendors and awful judgments of eternity. We need not wonder, therefore, that Christianity has had, in all ages, and in all sects, its devotees and martyrs, men who would endure every evil, rather than renounce it, whether it were exile, or forfeiture, or torture, or death; that persecution should have been at no loss for victims, whenever she had lighted her fires; and that in the very moment of her imagined triumph, while her hands were yet reeking with blood, she should have felt her own doom sealed, and her own power withered.

The Reformation was the natural result of causes, which had been silently working their way from the first dawn of the revival of letters. Learning stimulated inquiry; inquiry created doubt; and doubt brought on a feverish restlessness for knowledge, which must sooner or later have corrected abuses and errors, even if political causes had not hastened the event. Fortunately for England, fortunately for the cause of religion, in its most catholic sense, the passions of a sanguinary and sensual monarch effected, at a single blow, what perhaps it would otherwise have required ages to accomplish. The controversy of Henry the Eighth with the Papal See arrested the attention of all Europe, and produced in England a deep conviction of the necessity of some reformation in the Church. It was of course, that parties should, upon such an occasion, rally under different banners. Many of the dignitaries, both of the Church and state, resisted every innovation, as fraught with evil; not merely from a blind reverence for antiquity, but also from that sympathetic dread of change, which belongs to the habits of mankind in all ages. Many were ardently devoted to the cause of reform; but wished to touch gross abuses only, and thus to pave the way for gradual, but solid improvements. Many, of deeper thought, and warmer zeal, and bolder purposes, deemed it matter of conscience to root out every error, and to bring back Christianity at once to what they esteemed the simplicity of the Gospel. To this last class belonged the body of the Puritans, a class as distinguished for learning, talents, probity, and disinterestedness, as any which adorned their own times. It is a mistake, commonly enough entertained, that they were, in the modern sense, Dissenters; that they were hostile to episcopacy in every shape; and that they pushed their aims to the overthrow of all church government. The truth was far otherwise. Many of the most distinguished among them were reared in the bosom of the Church, and sincerely loved its venerable forms. Their object was to reform such of its rites and ceremonies only, as they deemed inconsistent with the Scriptures. If, in the course of events, they arrived at different conclusions, it was because prerogative pressed on them with a heavy hand; because prelacy became the instrument of persecution; because the laws respecting uniformity, under the famous High Commission Court, trampled upon their rights and consciences, and drove them to examine into the scriptural foundations of the hierarchy. In all their struggles, from the reign of Henry the Eighth, to that of James the First, the Puritans clung to the Establishment with a sincerity of affection, which, considering their sufferings from papacy and prelacy, is marvellous. In the farewell address of our forefathers, at the very moment of their departure for America, it breaks out into expressions of warm and filial attachment. We "esteem it our honor," say they, "to call the Church of England, from whence we rise, our dear mother; and cannot part from our native country, where she specially resideth, without much sadness of heart, and many tears in our eyes, ever acknowledging, that such hope and part, as we have obtained in the common salvation, we have received in her bosom, and sucked it from her breasts. We leave it not, therefore, as loathing that milk, wherewith we were nourished there; but, blessing God for the parentage and education, as members of the same body, shall always rejoice in her good, and unfeignedly grieve for any sorrow, that shall ever betide her; and, while we have breath, sincerely desire and endeavor the continuance and abundance of her welfare, with the enlargement of her bounds in the kingdom of Christ Jesus."[1]

The Puritans have been divided by an accomplished historian into three parties; the political Puritans, who maintained the highest principles of civil liberty; the Puritans in discipline, who were averse to the ceremonies and episcopal government of the church; and the doctrinal Puritans, who rigidly defended the speculative opinions of the first reformers.[2] The remark, such as it is, is applicable to a later period; for at the emigration of our ancestors, scarcely any divisions in doctrine existed among the Protestants of England. The

1 Hutch. Hist. Appendix, 487, 488,
2 6 Hume's Hist. ch. li. p. 272.

great controversies touched the rites and ceremonies, and the fasts and feasts of the church, the vestments of the priesthood, kneeling at the altar, the sign of the cross, and the manner of celebrating the ordinances. The usages of the church, in some of these respects, were deemed by the Puritans unscriptural, the remnants of popery, and gross corruptions of religion. In the sincerity of their hearts they could not practise them; in the scruples of their conscience they felt bound to reject them. For this sincerity, for these scruples, they were expelled from their benefices; they were subjected to spiritual censures; they were loaded with temporal punishments. They were even compelled, by penalties, to attend upon a public worship which they abhorred, from the time of Elizabeth down to the Revolution of 1688.[1] The language of the haughty James to them was, "I will have but one doctrine and one discipline, one religion in substance and in ceremony."[2] And he denounced them as "a sect unable to be suffered in any well governed commonwealth."[3] As if to ensnare their consciences, or to deride their scruples, Archbishop Laud enjoined the introduction of sports on Sunday, a day which he knew they held consecrated solely to the solemn services of religion. For nonconformity to these, and other canonical injunctions of a like nature, four hundred clergymen were ejected, suspended, or silenced, in one single year of this reign.[4] With an ill-omened perseverance in the same bigoted system, Charles the Second, soon after his restoration, compelled two thousand clergymen, in a single day, to relinquish their cures, presenting to a licentious court the noble spectacle of men who resigned all earthly preferments to their religious tenets.[5] Yet Mr. Hume, in his eager apologies for royalty, could survey such scenes with philosophical indifference, and intimate a doubt whether they deserved the appellation of persecution, because the victims were Puritans[6]

1 6 Hume's Hist. 163; 7 Hume's Hist. 41, 516.
2 Prince's Annals, 105. 3 Ibid. 107. 4 Ibid. 111.
5 6 Hume's Hist. 164. 6 Hume's Hist. 384.

After all, it is not in the power of the scoffer, or the skeptic; of the parasite, who fawns on courts, or the proselyte, who doats on the infallibility of his own sect, to obscure the real dignity of the character of the Puritans. We may lament their errors; we may regret their prejudices; we may pity their infirmities; we may smile at the stress laid by them on petty observances and trifling forms. We may believe that their piety was mixed up with too much gloom and severity; that it was sometimes darkened by superstition, and sometimes degraded by fanaticism; that it shut out too much the innocent pleasures of life, and enforced too strictly a discipline, irksome, cheerless, and oppressive; that it was sometimes over rigid, when it might have been indulgent; stern, when it might have been affectionate; pertinacious, when concession would have been just as well as graceful; and flashing with fiery zeal, when charity demanded moderation and ensured peace. All this, and much more, may be admitted, for they were but men; frail, fallible men; and yet leave behind solid claims upon the reverence and admiration of mankind. Of them it may be said, with as much truth as of any men that have ever lived, that they acted up to their principles, and followed them out with an unfaltering firmness. They displayed, at all times, a downright honesty of heart and purpose. In simplicity of life, in godly sincerity, in temperance, in humility, and in patience, as well as in zeal, they seemed to belong to the apostolical age. Their wisdom, while it looked on this world, reached far beyond it in its aim and objects. They valued earthly pursuits no farther than they were consistent with religion. Amidst the temptations of human grandeur they stood unmoved, unshaken, unseduced. Their scruples of conscience, if they sometimes betrayed them into difficulty, never betrayed them into voluntary sin. They possessed a moral courage which looked present dangers in the face, as though they were distant or doubtful, seeking no escape, and indulging no terror. When, in defence of their faith, of what they deemed pure and undefiled religion, we see them resign their property, their preferments, their friends, and their homes; when we see them submitting to banishment, and ignominy, and even to death; when we see them in foreign lands, on inhospitable shores, in the midst of sickness and famine, in desolation and disaster, still true to themselves, still confident in God's providence, still submissive to his chastisements, still thankful for his blessings, still ready to exclaim, in the language of Scripture — "We are troubled on every side, yet not distressed; we are perplexed, but not in despair; persecuted, but not forsaken; cast down, but not destroyed;" when we see such things, where is the man whose soul does not melt within him at the sight? Where shall examples be sought or found, more full, to point out what Christianity is, and what it ought to accomplish?

What better origin could we desire than from men of characters like these? Men, to whom conscience was every thing, and worldly prosperity nothing. Men, whose thoughts belonged to eternity rather than to time. Men who, in the near prospect of their sacrifices, could say, as our forefathers did say, "When we are in our graves it will be all one whether we have lived in plenty or in penury; whether we have died in a bed of down, or locks of straw. Only this is the advantage of the mean condition, THAT IT IS A MORE FREEDOM TO DIE. And the less comfort any have in the things of this world, the more liberty they have to lay up treasure in heaven."[1] Men who, in answer to the objection, urged by the anxiety of friendship, that they might perish by the way, or by hunger, or the sword, could answer, as our forefathers did, "We may trust God's providence for these things. Either he will keep these evils from us; or will dispose them for our good, and enable us to bear them."[2] Men who, in still later days, in their appeal for protection to the throne, could say with pathetic truth and simplicity, as our fore-

[1] 3 Hutch. Collect. p. 29.

[2] Ibid. 29, 30.

fathers did, "That we might enjoy divine worship without human mixtures, without offence to God, man, our own consciences, with leave, *but not without tears*, we departed from our country, kindred, and fathers' houses into this Patmos; in relation whereunto we do not say, 'Our garments are become old by reason of the very long journey,' but that ourselves, who came away in our strength, are, by reason of long absence, many of us become grey-headed, and some of us stooping for age."[1]

If these be not the sentiments of lofty virtue; if they breathe not the genuine spirit of Christianity; if they speak not high approaches towards moral perfection; if they possess not an enduring sublimity; then, indeed, have I ill read the human heart; then, indeed, have I strangely mistaken the inspirations of religion. If men, like these, can be passed by with indifference, because they wore not the princely robes, or the sacred lawn, because they shone not in courts, or feasted in fashionable circles, then, indeed, is Christian glory a vain shadow, and human virtue a dream, about which we disquiet ourselves in vain.

But it is not so — it is not so. There are those around me whose hearts beat high, and whose lips grow eloquent, when the remembrance of such ancestors comes over their thoughts; when they read in their deeds, not the empty forms, but the essence of holy living and holy dying. Time was when the exploits of war, the heroes of many battles, the conquerors of millions, the men who waded through slaughter to thrones, the kings whose footsteps were darkened with blood, and the sceptred oppressors of the earth were alone deemed worthy themes for the poet, and the orator, for the song of the minstrel and the hosannas of the multitude. Time was when feats of arms, and tournaments, and crusades, and the high array of chivalry, and the pride of royal banners waving for victory, engrossed all minds. Time was

[1] Hutch. Collect. p. 328.

when the ministers of the altar sat down by the side of the tyrant and numbered his victims, and stimulated his persecutions, and screened the instruments of his crimes, — and there was praise, and glory, and revelry for these things. Murder and rapine, burning cities, and desolated plains, if so be they were at the bidding of royal or baronial feuds, led on by the courtier or the clan, were matters of public boast, the delight of courts, and the treasured pleasure of the fireside tales. But these times have passed away. Christianity has resumed her meek and holy reign. The Puritans have not lived in vain. The simple piety of the pilgrims of New England casts into shade this false glitter, which dazzled and betrayed men into the worship of their destroyers.

It has been said, in the wantonness of folly, or the presumptuousness of ignorance, that America was peopled much in the same way as Botany Bay, with outcasts and convicts. So far as respects New England, there could not be a more flagrant violation of the truth of history. The poor, the friendless, and the oppressed came, indeed, hither. But their sole crime was, that they loved God more than they feared man. They came, too, under the guidance of men elevated by their rank, their fortune, and their learning, in their own country. Some of them were allied to noble families, whose graceful honors have descended to our days. Many of them were gentry of the realm, and possessed public respect from their known virtues and opulence. Many were distinguished for high attainments in literature and science, and could trace back their matriculations to the Universities of Oxford and Cambridge. Many of them were ripe for public honors at home, if they had chosen to remain there. Many of them were the friends and compeers of Cromwell, and Pym, and Hampden, and Milton, and other illustrious men, who in the midst of all the changes of party and all the studied disparagements of royalty, still continue to attract the reverence of mankind. Need I name Winthrop,

Dudley, Endicott, Humphrey, Saltonstall, Johnson, Nowel, Bradstreet, and Pynchon? Or, among the clergy, Higginson, Skelton, Cotton, Eliot, Davenport, Williams, Wilson, Norton, Rogers, and Hooker; to many of whom we may, with the honest enthusiasm of Mather, apply the praise of Salmasius, *Vir nunquam satis laudatus, nec temere sine laude nominandus.*[1]

But to us it would not be matter of regret, much less of reproach, if the case were far otherwise; if we could count among our ancestors only the humble, the poor and the forlorn. Rank, station, talents, and learning did indeed add lustre to their acts, and impart a more striking dignity to their sufferings, by giving them a bolder relief. But it was the purity of their principles, their integrity, and devout piety, which constituted the solid fabric of their fame. It was Christianity, which cast over their character its warm and glorious light, and gave it an everlasting freshness. It was their faith in God, which shed such beauty over their lives, and clothed this mortal with the form of immortality. In comparison with these, the distinctions of this world, however high or various they may be, are but evanescent points, a drop to the ocean, an instant to eternity, a ray of light to the innumerous fires, which blaze on unconsumed in the skies. This is not the poor estimate of man, the being of a day; it is the voice of that Revelation, which has spoken to our hopes and fears with an authority, which rebukes, while it convinces, our reason.

Let us rejoice, then, at our origin, with an honest joy. Let us exultingly hail this day as one of glorious memory. Let us proudly survey this land, the land of our fathers. It is our precious inheritance. It was watered by their tears; it was subdued by their hands; it was defended by their valor; it was consecrated by their virtues. Where is the

1 See Eliot's Biog. Dictionary, Art. *Davenport;* 2 Hist. Collect. (2d series) p. 260.

empire, which has been won with so much innocence? Where is the empire, which has been maintained with so much moderation?

I pass to other topics, where the task of vindication or apology becomes a duty of the day; a task, which, I trust, may be performed with due reverence to our forefathers, and with a still greater reverence for truth.

It has been said, that our forefathers were bigoted, intolerant, and persecuting; that while they demanded religious freedom for themselves, they denied it to all others; that in their eyes even error in ceremony or mode of worship was equally reprehensible with error in doctrine; and, if persisted in, deserved the temporal punishments denounced upon heresy. Mr. Hume[1] has dwelt with no small complacency upon the fact, that the Puritans "maintained that they themselves were the only pure Church; that their principles and practices ought to be established by law; and that no others ought to be tolerated."

I am not disposed to deny the truth of the charge, or to conceal, or to extenuate the facts. I stand not up here the apologist for persecution, whether it be by Catholic or Protestant, by Puritan or Prelate, by Congregationalist or Covenanter, by Church or State, by the monarch or the people. Wherever, and by whomsoever, it is promulgated or supported, under whatever disguises, for whatever purposes, at all times, and under all circumstances, it is a gross violation of the rights of conscience, and utterly inconsistent with the spirit of Christianity. I care not, whether it goes to life, or property, or office, or reputation, or mere private comfort, it is equally an outrage upon religion and the unalienable rights of man. If there is any right, sacred beyond all others, because it imports everlasting consequences, it is the right to worship God according to the dictates of our own consciences. Whoever attempts to narrow it down in any de-

[1] 6 Hume's Hist. 164.

gree, to limit it by the creed of any sect, to bound the exercise of private judgment, or free inquiry, by the standard of his own faith, be he priest or layman, ruler or subject, dishonors, so far, the profession of Christianity, and wounds it in its vital virtues. The doctrine, on which such attempts are founded, goes to the destruction of all free institutions of government. There is not a truth to be gathered from history, more certain, or more momentous, than this, that civil liberty cannot long be separated from religious liberty without danger, and ultimately without destruction to both. Wherever religious liberty exists, it will, first or last, bring in, and establish political liberty. Wherever it is suppressed, the Church establishment will, first or last, become the engine of despotism; and overthrow, unless it be itself overthrown, every vestige of political right. How it is possible to imagine, that a religion, breathing the spirit of mercy and benevolence, teaching the forgiveness of injuries, the exercise of charity, and the return of good for evil; how it is possible, I say, for such a religion to be so perverted, as to breathe the spirit of slaughter and persecution, of discord and vengeance, for differences of opinion, is a most unaccountable and extraordinary moral phenomenon. Still more extraordinary, that it should be the doctrine, not of base and wicked men merely, seeking to cover up their own misdeeds; but of good men seeking the way of salvation with uprightness of heart and purpose. It affords a melancholy proof of the infirmity of human judgment; and teaches a lesson of humility, from which spiritual pride may learn meekness, and spiritual zeal a moderating wisdom.

Let us not then, in examining the deeds of our fathers, shrink from our proper duty to ourselves. Let us not be untrue to the lights of our own days, to the religious privileges which we enjoy, to those constitutions of government which proclaim Christian equality to all sects, and deny the power of persecution to all. Our fathers had not arrived at the great truth, that *action*, not *opinion*, is the proper object of human legislation; that religious freedom is the birthright of man; that governments have no authority to inflict punishment for conscientious differences of opinion; and that to worship God according to our own belief is not only our privilege, but is our duty, our absolute duty, from which no human tribunal can absolve us. We should be unworthy of our fathers, if we should persist in error, when it is known to us. Their precept, like their example, speaking, as it were, from their sepulchres, is, to follow truth, not as they saw it, but as we see it, fearlessly and faithfully.

Let us meet the charge against them of bigotry, intolerance, and persecution, and gather from it instruction and admonition for our own conduct. Were our forefathers singular in this respect? Does the reproach, if reproach it be, that men do not live up to truths which they do not comprehend, rest upon them alone? So far from this being true, there was not, at that time, in all Christendom, a single spot, however remote, in which the freedom of religious opinion was supported by prince or people. Throughout all Europe, if we except Holland, the practice of burning heretics still prevailed, not only in Catholic but in Protestant countries. And even in Holland, banishment was not an uncommon punishment for those, who obstinately persisted in heresies of doctrine.[1] What is it, then, that is required of our forefathers? That they should have possessed a wisdom and liberality far superior to their own age; — that they should have acted upon truths as clear and settled, of which faint glimmerings only, or at least a brief and dubious twilight, had then shot up in unsteady streams to direct their course; — that, learned as they were, and wide as were their researches, and painful as was their diligence, they should have outstripped all others in the race, and surmounted the prejudices and prescriptions of twelve centuries. It would be dealing out a hard measure of justice to require perfect conformity under all circum-

[1] 6 Hume's Hist. 57, 163; 7 Hume's Hist. 20, 41, 515.

stances to our own sense of duty. It would be dealing out a still harder measure to press upon one poor, persecuted sect the sins of all Christendom; to make them alone responsible for opinions, which had become sacred by their antiquity, as well as their supposed coincidence with Scripture. Uniformity of faith and intolerance of error had been so long the favorite dogmas of all schools of theology and government, that they had ceased to be examined. They were deemed texts for the preacher, and not inquiries for the critic.

I am aware that in the writings of some of the early reformers there may be found, here and there, passages, which recognize the principles of religious liberty. But, we must remember, that they were uttered in the heat of controversy, to beat down the authority of the Romish Church; and so little were they sustained by public opinion, that they were lamentably forgotten in the first moments of Protestant victory. They were mere outworks in the system of theological opinions, which might form a defence against Catholic attacks; and were treated with contempt or indifference, when heresies sprung up in the bosom of the new faith. My Lord Bacon, in his discourse upon the unity of religion, written with a moderation becoming his great mind, and with a spirit of indulgence far beyond the age, has nevertheless contended strenuously for the unity of faith, and declared, that "heresies and schisms are of all others the greatest scandals." At the same time, he boldly warns us not "to propagate religion by wars, or by sanguinary persecutions to force consciences."[1] At the distance of a century, the enlightened author of "The Spirit of Laws" avowed the doctrine, that it is sound policy, when the state is already satisfied with the established religion, not to suffer the establishment of another. And while he declares, that penal laws, in respect to religion, ought to be avoided, he paradoxically maintains the doctrine, as a fundamental principle, that, when the state

[1] 2 Bacon's Works, 259.

is at liberty to receive or reject a new religion, it ought to be rejected; when it is received, it ought to be tolerated.[1] So slowly does truth make its way, even among the most gifted minds, in opposition to preconceived opinions and prejudices.

Nay, we need not go back to other times for illustrative examples. Is it even now true, that the doctrine of religious liberty is received with entire approbation in Christendom? Where it is received with most favor, is it not recognized more as matter of toleration and policy, than of right? suffered, rather than supported? connived at from fear, rather than vindicated upon principle? Even in England, free and enlightened as she is, how slow and reluctant has been the progress towards a generous toleration! It is scarcely twelve years since it ceased to be a crime, punishable with fine and imprisonment, to deny the doctrine of the Trinity. The Universities of Oxford and Cambridge are still, by their statutes, closed against the admission of Dissenters from the established Church. For more than a century and a half, Protestant Dissenters of every description were excluded by law from the possession of offices of trust or profit in the kingdom. The repeal of the odious corporation and test acts, by which this exclusion was guarded, was, after much resistance, accomplished only at the last session of Parliament; and the celebrations of this event, of this emancipation from thraldom of *one third* of her whole population, are just reaching our ears from the other side of the Atlantic. The Catholic yet groans under the weight of disabilities imposed upon him by the unrelenting arm of power, and sickens at the annual visitation of that hope of relief, which mocks him at every approach, and recedes at the very moment when it seems within his grasp. Even in our own country, can we lay our hands upon our hearts, and say with sincerity, that this universal freedom of religion is watched by none with jealousy and discontent? that there are none, who would

[1] Montesquieu's Spirit of Laws, book 25, ch. 10, 12.

employ the civil arm to suppress heresy, or to crush the weaker sects?

With what justice, then, shall we require from the Puritans of James's reign, lessons of Christian liberality, which, even in the nineteenth century, are rejected by statesmen and patriots, by laity and clergy, in regions adorned with all the refinements of letters, and the lights of science? If they had continued in the mother country, it is more than probable, that persecution would have taught them, what reason and revelation had failed to teach them. They would have reached the point, at which the Independents arrived in the next reign, whose true glory it is, that, "of all Christian sects, this was the first, which, during its prosperity as well as its adversity, always adopted the principle of toleration."[1]

But our forefathers acted far otherwise. The truth of history compels us to admit, that, from the first settlement down to the charter of William and Mary, in 1692, in proportion as they gathered internal power, they were less and less disposed to share it with any other Christian sect. That charter contained an express provision, that there should be "a liberty of conscience allowed in the worship of God to all Christians, *except Papists*." Objectionable as this clause would have been under other circumstances, the recent attempts of James the Second to introduce Popery, and the dread which they entertained of being themselves the subjects of political, as well as religious persecution, reconciled them to it, and they hailed it almost as another *magna charta* of liberty."[2] So true it is, that accident or interest frequently forces men to the adoption of correct principles, when a sense of justice has totally failed to effect it. In the intermediate period, the Quakers and Anabaptists, and, in short, all other Dissenters from their creed, had been unrelentingly persecuted by fine, imprisonment, banishment, and sometimes even by death itself. Episcopalians, too, fell under their special displeasure;

[1] 7 Hume's Hist. 20.

[2] 1 Hutch. Hist. 75, and note.

and, notwithstanding every effort of the Crown, by threats and remonstrance, they studiously excluded them from every office, and even from the right of suffrage. No person but a freeman was permitted to vote in any public affairs, or to hold any office; and no person could become a freeman but by being a member of their own church, and recommended by their own clergy.[1] In truth the clergy possessed a power and influence in the state, as great as ever was exercised under any church establishment whatsoever. There was not, until after the repeal of the first charter, in 1676, a single Episcopal society in the whole colony;[2] and even the celebration of Christmas was punished as a public offence.[3] In this exclusive policy our ancestors obstinately persevered, against every remonstrance at home and abroad. When Sir Richard Saltonstall wrote to them his admirable letter, which pleads with such a catholic enthusiasm for toleration, the harsh and brief reply was, "God forbid our love for the truth should be grown so cold, that we should tolerate errors."[4] And Cotton himself, "whose praise is in all our churches," the man, who could, with a noble independence, address himself to the bishop of Lincoln in language like this: "However much I do highly prize, and much prefer other men's judgment, and learning, and wisdom, and piety; yet in things pertaining to God and his worship, *still I must* (as I ought) *live by my own faith, not theirs;*" such a man, I say, could meanly stoop, in the defence of persecution, to arguments not unworthy of the worst ages of bigotry.[5] They went farther, imitating in this respect the famous act of uniformity of Elizabeth, and compelled an attendance upon their own mode of worship under a penalty. Yes, the very men did this, who thought that paying one shilling for not coming to prayers in England was an unsupportable tyranny.[6] Yes,

[1] 3 Hutch. Collect. 478, 484, 520, note. [2] 3 Hutch. Hist. 430, 431.
[3] 3 Hutch. Collect. 419, 482; Colony and Province Laws, edit. 1814, p. 119, ch. 50.
[4] 3 Hutch. Collect. 401, 402. [5] Ibid. 403.
[6] Ibid. 418, 419, 422; 1 Hutch. Hist. 75.

the very men, who asked from Charles the Second, after his restoration, liberty of conscience and worship for themselves, were deaf, and dumb, and blind, when it was demanded by his commissioners for Episcopalians and others. They silently evaded the claim, or resolutely refused it, as the temper of the times enabled them to act."[1]

The very efforts, made in the colony to establish this uniformity of faith, afford striking proofs of the utter hopelessness, as well as injustice of such attempts. Within ten years after their first landing, the whole colony was thrown into confusion by religious dissensions, by controversies about faith, and about forms of church government; about the covenant of grace, and the covenant of works; about liberty of conscience, and exclusiveness of worship; about doctrines so mysterious and subtle, as seem past all human comprehension, and customs so trifling and vain, as seem beyond the reach of ecclesiastical censure. Who could imagine, that the reveries of Mrs. Hutchinson, and the question, whether ladies should wear veils, and the legality of bearing the cross in a military standard, should have shaken the colony to its foundations? So thickly sown were the seeds of spiritual discord, that more than *fourscore* opinions were pronounced heresies, by an ecclesiastical Synod convened in 1637.[2] Yet were the difficulties far from being removed, although fines and imprisonment and banishment followed in the train of the excommunications of the Church. The struggle for toleration was still maintained; the discontent with the laws which confined political privileges to church members, constantly increased; and diversities of faith at last grew up, so numerous and so formidable, that persecution became less frequent, because it was less safe. The single fact, that, under this exclusive system, not more than one sixth of the qualified inhabitants were freemen in 1676, affords an ample

1 3 Hutch. Collect. 188, 191, 192, 193, 194, 418, 419, 422; 8 Hist. Collect. (second series) pp. 76, 78; 1 Hutch. Hist. Appendix, 537; 3 Hutch. Collect. 478, 482, 484, 519, 520.

2 1 Hutch. Hist. 37, 55, 67, 73, 75, 430.

commentary upon its injustice and folly. Five sixths of the colony were disfranchised by the influence of the ecclesiastical power.[1]

The fundamental error of our ancestors, an error which began with the very settlement of the colony, was a doctrine which has since been happily exploded; I mean the necessity of a union between church and state. To this they clung, as the ark of their safety. They thought it the only sure way of founding a Christian commonwealth. They maintained, that "church government and civil government may very well stand together; it being the duty of the magistrate to take care of matters of religion, and to *improve* his civil authority for observing the duties commanded by it."[2] They not only tolerated the civil power in the suppression of heresy, but they demanded and enjoined it. They preached it in the pulpit and the synod. It was in their closet prayers, and in their public legislation. The arm of the civil government was constantly employed in support of the denunciations of the Church; and, without its forms, the Inquisition existed in substance, with a full share of its terrors and its violence. There was, indeed, far more caution in shedding human blood; but there was scarcely less indulgence for human error. For such proceedings there was not the poor apology, which has been sometimes suggested, that every religion, which is persecuted, becomes itself persecuting, because it attacks the religion which persecuted it, not as a *religion*, but as a *tyranny*.[3] Our ancestors could not frame such an apology for themselves; for no ecclesiastical tyranny attempted to usurp authority over them within the colony. It had a deeper origin, in that wretched doctrine of the union of Church and state, by which Christianity has been made the minister of almost every wrong in the catalogue of crimes. It has been said, with as much truth as force, by one of the most eloquent of modern divines, that "The boasted alliance

[1] 3 Hutch. Collect. 484. [2] 1 Hutch. Hist. 434.

[3] Montesquieu's Spirit of Laws, book 25, ch. 9.

between church and state, on which so many encomiums have been lavished, seems to have been little more than a compact between the priest and the magistrate to betray the liberties of mankind, both civil and religious."[1]

To the honor of New England be it said, that if here persecution obtained an early triumph, here also, for the first time since the Reformation, was simultaneously proclaimed the doctrine of liberty of conscience, — a doctrine which, I trust, will, by the blessing of God, be maintained by us and our posterity at all hazards, and against all encroachments. Here, on this very spot, in Naumkeag, in this "bosom of consolation,"[2] it was proclaimed by Roger Williams, in 1635; and for this, among other grave offences, he was sentenced to banishment. He fled to Rhode Island; and there, in the code of laws for the colony, planted by his energy and sagacity, we read for the first time since Christianity ascended the throne of the Cæsars, the declaration that "conscience should be free, and men should not be punished for worshipping God in the way they were persuaded he required," — a declaration which, to the honor of Rhode Island, she has never departed from, — a declaration which puts to shame many a realm of wider domains and loftier pretensions. It still shines among her laws, with an argument in its support in the shape of a preamble, which has rarely been surpassed in power of thought or felicity of expression.[3] Massachusetts may blush, that the Catholic colony of Lord Baltimore, and the Quaker, the blameless Quaker colony of Penn, were originally founded on the same generous principles of Christian right, long before she felt or acknowledged them.[4]

1 Robert Hall; "Christianity Consistent with a Love of Freedom."

2 In "The Planter's Plea," published in London, in 1630, the writer says that Nahum Keike is perfect Hebrew, and by interpretation means "The bosom of consolation."

3 It is almost *in totidem verbis* with the act of Virginia, of 1785, which has been attributed to Mr. Madison. To which state the merit of the original draft belongs, I am unable to say, as I have not the means of tracing it in Rhode Island acts earlier than in the Digest of 1798.

4 1 Pitkin's Hist. 56, 67; Chalmers, p. 218; 2 Proud's Hist. Append.

While, then, we joyfully celebrate this anniversary, let us remember that our forefathers had their faults as well as virtues; that their example is not always a safe pattern for our imitation, but sometimes a beacon of solemn warning. Let us do, not what they did, but what with our lights and advantages, they would have done, must have done, from the love of country, and the love of truth. Is there any one who would now, for a moment, justify the exclusion of every person from political rights and privileges who is not a Congregationalist of the straitest sect in doctrine and discipline? Is there any one who would exclude the Episcopalian, the Baptist, the Methodist, the Quaker, or the Universalist, not merely from power and Christian fellowship, but from breathing the same air, and enjoying the same sunshine, and reaping the same harvest, because he walks not in the same faith, and kneels not at the same altar with himself? Is there any one who would bring back the bygone penalties, and goad on tender consciences to hypocrisy or self-destruction? Is there any one who would light the fagot to burn the innocent? who would stain the temples of God with the blood of martyrdom? who would cut off all the charities of human life, and, in a religious warfare, arm the father against the son, the mother against the daughter, the wife against the husband? who would bind all posterity in the fetters of his own creed, and shipwreck their consciences? If any such there be, whatever badge they may wear, they are enemies to us and our institutions. They would sap the foundations of our civil, as well as religious liberties. They would betray us into worse than Egyptian bondage. Of the doctrines of such men, if any such there be, I would say, with the earnestness of the apostolical exhortation, "Touch not, taste not, handle not." If ever there could be a case in which intolerance would rise almost into the dignity of a virtue, it would be when its object was to put down intolerance. No — let us cling with a holy zeal to the Bible, and the Bible only, as the religion of Protestants. Let us proclaim, with

Milton, that "Neither traditions, nor councils, nor canons of any visible church, much less edicts of any civil magistrate, or civil session, but the Scripture only, can be the final judge or rule in matters of religion, and *that only in the conscience of every Christian to himself*." Let us inscribe on the walls of our dwelling-houses, in our temples, in our halls of legislation, in our courts of justice, the admirable declaration of Queen Mary, the consort of William the Third,—than which a nobler precept of wisdom never fell from uninspired lips,—"It is not in the power of men to believe what they please; and therefore they should not be forced in matters of religion contrary to their persuasions and their consciences."[1]

I pass, with unmixed pleasure, to other and more grateful topics, where approbation need not be slow, or praise parsimonious. If, in laying the foundations of this Christian commonwealth, our forefathers were governed, in respect to religion, by a spirit unworthy of Protestantism, it was far otherwise in respect to their civil institutions. Here, a wise forecast and sound policy directed all their operations; so wise and so sound, that the lapse of two hundred years has left unchanged the body of their legislation, and, in a general sense, added little to their securities for public or private rights. There is no reason to suppose that they were opposed to monarchy, as a suitable form of government for the mother country, or that opposition to the civil establishments mingled in the slightest degree with the motives of their emigration.[2] There is just as little reason to suppose that they desired or would have acquiesced in the establishment of a colonial monarchy or aristocracy. On the contrary, we know that they refused to confer the magistracy for life; and that they repelled every notion of an hereditary nobility, in their celebrated answer to the propositions of Lord Say and Seale.[3] This attachment to the form of government of the mother country was not only sincere, but continued down to

1 9 Hist. Collect. 251.

2 3 Hutch. Collect. 326.

3 1 Hutch. Hist. 490, 493, 494.

the Revolution. Their descendants took many opportunities to evince it; and some of the most powerful appeals made by the patriots of the revolution to the British Crown are filled with eloquent professions of loyalty. The formation of a Republic was the necessary result of the final separation from England. The controversy was then narrowed down to the consideration of what form of government they might properly adopt. All their habits, principles, and institutions prohibited the existence of a real to titular peerage. They had no materials for a king. They were, as they had been from the beginning, essentially republicans. They followed the lead of their existing institutions; and the most striking change introduced by them was the choice of a governor by themselves, as a substitute for the like choice by the Crown.

Their connection with and dependence upon the mother country grew up from their national allegiance, and was confirmed by the sense of their own weakness and the desire of protection. In return for this protection, they were ready to admit a sovereign right in Parliament to regulate, to some, though to an undefined extent, their foreign intercourse, and in the Crown to supervise their colonial legislation. But they never did admit the right of Parliament or the Crown to legislate generally for them, or to interfere with their domestic polity. On the contrary, from the first they resisted it, as an encroachment upon their liberties. This was more emphatically true of Massachusetts than of any other of the colonies. The commissioners of Charles the Second, in 1665, reported that "she was the last and hardliest persuaded to use his majesty's name in the forms of justice;" — that her inhabitants "proclaimed by sound of trumpet, that the General Court was the supremest judicatory in all that province;" "that the commissioners' pretending to hear appeals was a breach of their privileges;" "and that they should not permit it."[1] In short, the commissioners well

[1] 3 Hutch. Collect. 417, 418.

described "their way of government as *commonwealth like*."[1] Even in relation to foreign commerce their strong sense of independence was illustrated by the complaint that "no notice was taken of the act of navigation, plantation, or any other laws made in England for the regulation of trade; all nations having free liberty to come into their ports, and vend their commodities without any restraint."[2] These acts of navigation and trade were never recognized as in force in the colony, until their own legislature required their observance.[3] So strenuous were our ancestors, even at this early period, in maintaining the doctrine, that Parliament could not bind them, because they were not represented there. So jealous were they to guard against every usurpation of the Crown. He, indeed, must have read our annals with a very careless eye, who does not perceive, at every turn, a constant struggle for substantial independence.

The basis of their institutions was, from the first settlement, republican. The people were the admitted source of all power. They chose the magistrates and the executive. They established a representative government; they created a colonial legislature, whose power to enact laws was, until the overthrow of the first charter, deemed for most purposes absolute and supreme. Their earliest legislation recognized the great rights secured by the Magna Charta of England: the trial by jury; the free administration of justice; the equality of freemen; the abolition of all slavish and feudal tenures; and, above all, the distribution of intestate estates among all the descendants of the deceased. This was indeed a signal triumph over the prejudices in favor of primogeniture. It constituted a fundamental principle in their policy; and, by its silent, but irresistible influence, prevented the undue accumulation of estates in a few hands, so that the introduction of a colonial nobility became absolutely impracticable.

1 3 Hutch. Collect. 422.
2 Randolph's Letter in 1676; 3 Hutch. Collect. 496.
3 1 Hutch. Hist. 322; 3 Hutch. Collect. 521.

Henceforth, the partible nature of estates was so fixed in public opinion, that it broke down every attempt to perpetuate entails; and left the mass of our landed interests, as we now find them, in the possession of the yeomanry in fee simple. While this great law of descents exists, it will forever prevent the establishment of any arbitrary power. The government, that once admits it into its code, may remain in form a monarchy, or an aristocracy; but it will follow the impulses of public opinion, and find its surest protection in the advancement of popular principles.

Thus broad, thus elevated, was the early legislation of our forefathers. If we except from it that portion, which was tinged by the bigotry and superstition of the times, we shall find it singular for its wisdom, humanity, and public spirit; and admirably adapted to the wants of a free, simple, and intelligent people.

Among the most striking acts of their legislation are those, which respect the cause of learning and education. Within ten short years after their first settlement, they founded the University at Cambridge, and endowed it with the sum of four hundred pounds; a sum, which, considering their means and their wants, was a most generous benefaction. Perhaps no language could more significantly express the dignity of their design, than their own words. "After God had carried us safe to New England," said they, "and we had builded our houses, provided necessaries for our livelihood, reared convenient places for God's worship, and settled the civil government; one of the next things we longed for, and looked after, was *to advance learning and perpetuate it to posterity*, dreading to leave an illiterate ministry to the churches, when our present ministers shall lie in the dust."[1] They were not disappointed in their hopes. By the blessing of Providence, this little College, planted by their hands, and nursed by their care, has flourished. Already she counts nearly six thousand

[1] 1 Hist. Collect. 240.

in her matriculations. She still stands erect, in the midst of her offspring, clothed with her ancient glory and matron dignity, and lovelier by her age. Our hearts still yearn towards her; our thoughts still kindle at her praise; our prayers still rise for her prosperity. We may smile at the early charge made by the royal commissioners, that "it may be feared this College may afford us many schismatics to the Church."[1] But we proudly proclaim their reluctant confession, that by her means there was "a scholar to their minister in every town or village" in Massachusetts.[2]

But the truest glory of our forefathers is in that system of public instruction, which they instituted by law, and to which New England owes more of its character, its distinction, and its prosperity, than to all other causes. If this system be not altogether without example in the history of other nations (as I suspect it to be, in its structure and extent,) it is, considering the age and means of the projectors, an extraordinary instance of wise legislation, and worthy of the most profound statesmen of any times. At the distance of centuries it stands alone and unrivalled. Europe has not ventured as yet to copy its outlines; nor could they be copied in a despotism, without undermining its foundations. England herself, where letters and learning have so long held the highest rank, is but just beginning to think seriously of a system of national instruction; and her statesmen are now gathering admiration at home from schemes of public education far, very far short of what her own poor, feeble, neglected colony established at the starting point of its political existence. Yes, it was in this system of public instruction that our fathers laid the foundation for the perpetuity of our institutions, and for that growth of sound morals, industry, and public spirit, which has never yet been wanting in New England, and, we may fondly hope, will forever remain her appropriate praise. Yes, in the year 1647, they ordered every

[1] 3 Hutch. Collect. 421. [2] Ibid. 413.

township of fifty householders to maintain a public school at public expense; and every township of one hundred householders to maintain in like manner a grammar school, to instruct youth, and fit them for the University, "to the end," say they, in this memorable law, "to the end, that learning may not be buried in the graves of our forefathers, in church and commonwealth." And this was done by them, when they had just made their first lodgment in the wilderness; when they had scarcely found leisure to build, I do not say fair dwellings, but humble cottages for their own shelter and safety. When they were poor and unprotected, persecuted and in peril — they could then look forward with a noble disregard of present enjoyments, and forgetting themselves, provide the bread of life for their posterity. This system has never been broken in upon: it still stands, in its substance, on the pages of our statute book, an enduring record of wisdom and patriotism. Under its blessed influence our youth have grown up. They have received early instruction in their rights and liberties, and, as the law itself requires, "not only in sound literature, but in sound doctrine." It is here that industry has learned the value of its own labors; that genius has triumphed over the discouragements of property; that skill has given polish, as well as strength, to talent; that a lofty spirit of independence has been nourished and sustained; that the first great lesson of human improvement has been taught, that knowledge is power; and the last great lesson of human experience felt, that without virtue there is neither happiness nor safety.

I know not what more munificent donation any government can bestow, than by providing instruction at the public expense, not as a scheme of charity, but of municipal policy. If a private person deserves the applause of all good men, who founds a single hospital or college, how much more are they entitled to the appellation of public benefactors who, by the side of every church in every village, plant a school of letters. Other monuments of the art and genius of man may perish; but these, from their very nature, seem, as far as human foresight can go, absolutely immortal. The triumphal arches of other days have fallen; the sculptured columns have crumbled into dust; the temples of taste and religion have sunk into decay; the pyramids themselves seem but mighty sepulchres, hastening to the same oblivion to which the dead they cover have long since passed. But here every successive generation becomes a living memorial of our public schools, and a living example of their excellence. Never, never may this glorious institution be abandoned or betrayed by the weakness of its friends, or the power of its adversaries. It can scarcely be abandoned or betrayed, while New England remains free, and her representatives are true to their trust. It must for ever count in its defence a majority of all those who ought to influence public affairs by their virtues or their talents; for it must be that here they first felt the divinity of knowledge stir within them. What consolation can be higher, what reflection prouder, than the thought, that in weal and in woe our children are under the public guardianship, and may here gather the fruits of that learning, which ripens for eternity?

There is another topic connected with the settlement of this country which may not be passed over upon this occasion. At the very threshold of the enterprise a nice question, both in morals and public law, must have presented itself to the consideration of conscientious minds. How far was it lawful to people this Western world, and deprive the Indians of that exclusive sovereignty over the soil which they had exercised for ages beyond the reach of human tradition? Men of deep reflection, and especially men who felt a serious, religious accountability for their conduct, could not be presumed to pass over such a subject without weighing it with scrupulous delicacy. It did not escape the attention of our forefathers. They met it, and discussed it with a manly freedom. They sought neither to disguise their own opinions, nor to conceal the real difficulties of the inquiry.

In ascending to the great principles upon which all human society rests, it must be admitted that there are some which are of eternal obligation, and arise from our relations to each other, and our common dependence upon our Creator. Among these are the duty to do justice, to love mercy, and to walk humbly before God. There are others again which are merely founded in general convenience, and presuppose some regulations of society, or conventional law. The rights belonging to this latter class are coextensive only with the nations which recognize them; and, in a general sense, cannot be deemed obligatory upon the rest of the world. The plain reason is, that no portion of mankind has any authority delegated to it by the Creator, to legislate for, or bind all the rest. The very equality of original rights, which every argument presupposes, excludes the notion of any authority to control those rights, unless it is derived by grant or surrender, so as to bind others in conscience and abstract justice.

We are told in the Scriptures, that in the beginning God gave man dominion over the earth, and commanded him to replenish and subdue it; and this has been justly said to be the true and solid foundation of man's dominion over it.[1] But this principle does not lead to the conclusion that any particular person may acquire to himself a permanent and exclusive interest in the soil; much less, that any single nation may appropriate to itself as much of the surface as it shall choose, and thus narrow down the common inheritance, and exclude all others from any participation in its products for the supply of their own wants. If any right can be deduced from this general grant of dominion to man, it is of a far more limited nature; the right to occupy what we possess during the time of possession, the right of mere present enjoyment; which seems to flow as much from the consideration that no one can show a better right to displace us, as from the consideration, that it affords the only means of any

[1] 2 Bl. Com. 2.

enjoyment. But where shall we find, independently of maxims derived from society, the right of any nation to exclude others from cultivating the soil, which it does not itself choose to cultivate, but which may be indispensable to supply the necessities of others? Where is the principle which withdraws from the common inheritance, and gives to a few what the bounty of God has provided for all? The truth is, (though it is a truth rarely brought into discussion among civilized nations,) that exclusive sovereignty or ownership of the soil is a derivative right, resting upon municipal regulations and the public law of society; and obtaining its whole validity from the recognitions of the communities, which it binds, and the arm of power, which encircles and protects it. It is a right founded upon the soundest policy; and has conduced, more than almost any human achievement, to create the virtues which strengthen, and the refinements which grace civilized life. But if general consent should abolish it to-morrow, it would be difficult to say that a return to the patriarchal or pastoral state of nations, and the community of property, would be any departure from natural right.

When this continent was first discovered, it became an object of cupidity to the ambition of many of the nations of Europe. Each eagerly sought to appropriate it to itself. But it was obvious, that, in a mutual struggle for power, contests of the most sanguinary nature would soon intervene, if some general principle were not adopted, by the consent of all, for the government of them all. The most flexible and convenient principle, which occurred, was, that the first discovery should confer upon the nation of the discoverer an exclusive right to the soil, for the purposes of sovereignty and settlement. This principle was accordingly adopted, and became a fundamental doctrine in the code of legal ethics, by which the European governments regulated their acquisitions. No European subject was permitted to interfere with it; and the possession acquired under it was deemed absolute and unquestionable. In respect to desert places, the principle, as one of peace and equality of benefits, is not, perhaps, obnoxious to censure. But in respect to countries already inhabited, neither its general justice, nor its conformity to public law, entitles it to commendation. If, abstractly considered, mere discovery could confer any title, the natives already possessed it by such prior discovery. If this were put aside, and mere possession could confer sovereignty, they had that possession, and were entitled to the sovereignty. In short, it is clear, that, upon the principles generally recognized by European nations, as between themselves, the natives could not be rightfully displaced. And if they were not entitled to the benefit of those principles, they might still stand upon the eternal laws of natural justice, and maintain their right to share in the common inheritance. Such a conclusion could not escape the sagacity of the statesmen and princes of the old world; but it was quite too refined to satisfy their ambition and lust of dominion. It was easy to found an argument for the expulsion of the natives upon their infidelity and barbarism, which allowed them to be treated as the enemies of God. It was still more plausible to hold out the prospect of converting them to the Christian faith, and thus to secure a new triumph to civilization and the cross. If their territory was invaded, and their governments were overthrown, if they were compelled to yield to the superior genius and power of Europe, they would still receive an ample compensation, in their admission into the bosom of European society, with its privileges and improvements. Such were some of the suggestions by which royal ambition sought to disguise its real objects, and to reconcile to religion itself the spirit of conquest. It is but justice, however, to add, that there was no public avowal, that the natives possessed no right whatsoever. On the contrary, it was conceded, that they possessed a present right of occupancy; temporary, indeed, and limited; which might be surrendered to the discovering nation, and in the mean time was entitled to respect.

Our forefathers did not attempt to justify their own emigration and settlement, upon the European doctrine of the right of discovery. Their patent from the Crown contained a grant of this right; but they felt that there was a more general question behind, "What warrant have we to take that land, which is, and hath been of long time, possessed by others, the sons of Adam?" Their answer is memorable for its clearness, strength, and bold assertion of principles. That which is common to all, say they, is proper to none. This savage people ruleth over many lands without title or property. Why may not Christians have liberty to go and dwell amongst them in their waste lands? God hath given to the sons of men a twofold right to the earth. There is a natural right and a civil right. The first right was natural, when men held the earth in common. When, afterwards, they appropriated some parcels of ground, by enclosing and peculiar manurance, this, in time, got them a civil right. There is more than enough land for us and them. God hath consumed them with a miraculous plague, whereby the greater part of the country is left void of inhabitants. Besides, we shall come in with the good leave of the natives.[1] Such arguments were certainly not unworthy of men of scrupulous virtue. They were aided by higher considerations, by the desire to propagate Christianity among the Indians; a desire, which is breathed forth in their confidential papers, in their domestic letters, in their private prayers, and in their public devotions. In this object they were not only sincere, but constant. So sincere and so constant, that one of the grave accusations against them has been, that, in their religious zeal, they compelled the Indians, by penalties, to attend public worship, and allured them by presents, to abandon their infidelity.[2] In truth, the propagation of Christianity was a leading motive with many of the early promoters of the settlement; and we need no better proof of it, than the esta-

[1] 3 Hutch. Collect. 30, 31. [2] 3 Hutch. Collect. 28, 32, 420, 490.

blishment of an Indian school at Harvard College, to teach them the rudiments of the Christian faith.

Whatever, then, may have been the case in other parts of the continent, it is a fact, and it should not be forgotten, that our forefathers never attempted to displace the Indians by force upon any pretence of European right. They occupied and cultivated what was obtained by grant, or was found vacant. They constantly respected the Indians in their settlements and claims of soil. They protected them from their enemies, when they sought refuge among them. They stimulated no wars for their extermination. During the space of fifty years, but a single case of serious warfare occurred; and, though we cannot but lament the cruelties then perpetrated, there is no pretence, that they were the aggressors in the contest. Whatever complaints, therefore, may be justly urged by philosophy, or humanity, or religion, in our day, respecting the wrongs and injuries of the Indians, they scarcely touch the Pilgrims of New England. Their hands were not imbrued in innocent blood. Their hearts were not heavy with crimes and oppressions engendered by avarice. If they were not wholly without blame, they were not deep in guilt. They might mistake the time, or the mode, of christianizing and civilizing the Indians; but they did not seek pretences to extirpate them. Private hostilities and butcheries there might be; but they were not encouraged or justified by the government. It is not, then, a just reproach, sometimes cast on their memories, that their religion narrowed down its charities to Christians only; and forgot, and despised, and oppressed these forlorn children of the forest.

There is, indeed, in the fate of these unfortunate beings, much to awaken our sympathy, and much to disturb the sobriety of our judgment; much, which may be urged to excuse their own atrocities; much in their characters, which betrays us into an involuntary admiration. What can be more melancholy than their history? By a law of their nature, they seem destined to a slow, but sure extinction.

Everywhere, at the approach of the white man, they fade away. We hear the rustling of their footsteps, like that of the withered leaves of autumn, and they are gone forever. They pass mournfully by us, and they return no more. Two centuries ago, the smoke of their wigwams and the fires of their councils rose in every valley, from Hudson's Bay to the farthest Florida, from the ocean to the Mississippi and the lakes. The shouts of victory and the war-dance rang through the mountains and the glades. The thick arrows and the deadly tomahawk whistled through the forests; and the hunter's trace and the dark encampment startled the wild beasts in their lairs. The warriors stood forth in their glory. The young listened to the songs of other days. The mothers played with their infants, and gazed on the scene with warm hopes of the future. The aged sat down; but they wept not. They should soon be at rest in fairer regions, where the Great Spirit dwelt, in a home prepared for the brave, beyond the western skies. Braver men never lived; truer men never drew the bow. They had courage, and fortitude, and sagacity, and perseverance, beyond most of the human race. They shrank from no dangers, and they feared no hardships. If they had the vices of savage life, they had the virtues also. They were true to their country, their friends, and their homes. If they forgave not injury, neither did they forget kindness. If their vengeance was terrible, their fidelity and generosity were unconquerable also. Their love, like their hate, stopped not on this side of the grave.

But where are they? Where are the villages, and warriors, and youth; the sachems and the tribes; the hunters and their families? They have perished. They are consumed. The wasting pestilence has not alone done the mighty work. No, — nor famine, nor war. There has been a mightier power, a moral canker, which hath eaten into their heart-cores — a plague, which the touch of the white man communicated — a poison which betrayed them into a lingering ruin. The winds of the Atlantic fan not a single region, which they may now call their own. Already the last feeble remnants of the race are preparing for their journey beyond the Mississippi. I see them leave their miserable homes, the aged, the helpless, the women and the warriors, "few and faint, yet fearless still." The ashes are cold on their native hearths. The smoke no longer curls round their lowly cabins. They move on with a slow, unsteady step. The white man is upon their heels, for terror or despatch; but they heed him not. They turn to take a last look of their deserted villages. They cast a last glance upon the graves of their fathers. They shed no tears; they utter no cries; they heave no groans. There is something in their hearts, which passes speech. There is something in their looks, not of vengeance or submission; but of hard necessity, which stifles both; which chokes all utterance; which has no aim or method. It is courage absorbed in despair. They linger but for a moment. Their look is onward. They have passed the fatal stream. It shall never be repassed by them, — no, never. Yet there lies not between us and them an impassable gulf. They know and feel, that there is for them still one remove farther, not distant nor unseen. It is to the general burial-ground of their race.

Reason as we may, it is impossible not to read in such a fate much, that we know not how to interpret; much of provocation to cruel deeds and deep resentments; much of apology for wrong and perfidy; much of pity, mingling with indignation; much of doubt and misgiving as to the past; much of painful recollections; much of dark forebodings.

Philosophy may tell us, that conquest in other cases has adopted the conquered into its own bosom; and thus, at no distant period, given them the common privileges of subjects; — but that the red men are incapable of such an assimilation. By their very nature and character, they can neither unite themselves with civil institutions, nor with safety be allowed to remain as distinct communities. Policy may suggest, that their ferocious passions, their independent spirit, and their wandering life disdain the restraints of society; that they will submit to superior force only, while it chains them to the earth by its pressure. A wilderness is essential to their habits and pursuits. They can neither be tamed, nor overawed. They subsist by war or hunting; and the game of the forest is relinquished only for the nobler game of man. The question, therefore, is necessarily reduced to the consideration, whether the country itself shall be abandoned by civilized man, or maintained by his sword, as the right of the strongest.

It may be so; perhaps, in the wisdom of Providence, it must be so. I pretend not to comprehend, or solve, such weighty difficulties. But neither philosophy nor policy can shut out the feelings of nature. Humanity must continue to sigh at the constant sacrifices of this bold, but wasting race. And Religion, if she may not blush at the deed, must, as she sees the successive victims depart, cling to the altar with a drooping heart, and mourn over a destiny without hope and without example. Let our consolation be, that our forefathers did not precipitate the evil days. Their aim was peace; their object was the propagation of Christianity.

There is one other circumstance in the history of the Colony, which deserves attention, because it has afforded a theme for bitter sarcasm and harsh reproach; and, as the principal scenes of the tragedy took place on this very spot, this seems a fit occasion to rescue the character of our forefathers from the wanton attacks of the scoffer and the satirist. I allude to the memorable trials for witchcraft in this town, in 1692, which terminated in the death of many innocent persons, partly from blind credulity, and partly from overwhelming fraud. The whole of these proceedings exhibit melancholy proofs of the effect of superstition in darkening the mind, and steeling the heart against the dictates of humanity. Indeed, nothing has ever been found more vindictive and cruel than fanaticism, acting under the influence of preternatural terror, and assuming to punish offences created by its own gloomy reveries. Under such circumstances it becomes itself the very demon, whose agency it seeks to destroy. It loses sight of all the common principles of reason and evidence. It sees nothing around it but victims for sacrifice. It hears nothing but the voice of its own vengeance. It believes nothing but what is monstrous and incredible. It conjures up every phantom of superstition, and shapes it to the living form of its own passions and frenzies. In short, insanity could hardly devise more refinements in barbarity, or profligacy execute them with more malignant coolness. In the wretched butcheries of these times, (for so they in fact were,) in which law and reason were equally set at defiance, we have shocking instances of unnatural conduct. We find parents accusing their children, children their parents, and wives their husbands, of a crime, which must bring them to the scaffold. We find innocent persons, misled by the hope of pardon, or wrought up to frenzy by the pretended sufferings of others, freely accusing themselves of the same crime. We find gross perjury practised to procure condemnations, sometimes for self-protection, and sometimes from utter recklessness of consequences. We find even religion itself made an instrument of vengeance. We find ministers of the gospel and judges of the land stimulating the work of persecution, until, at last, in its progress, its desolations reached their own firesides.[1]

And yet, dark and sad as is this picture, it furnishes no just reproach upon this ancient town, beyond what belongs to it in common with all New England, and, indeed, with all Christendom. Thirty years before this period there had been executions for witchcraft in this and other colonies, in Charlestown, Boston, Springfield, and Hartford. It has been justly observed, by an intelligent historian,[2] that the importance given to the New England trials proceeded more from the general panic than from the number executed; "more having been put to death in a single county in England, in a short

[1] 2 Hutch. Hist. 16 to 60, &c.

[2] 2 Hutch. Hist. 15, 16.

space of time, than have suffered in all New England, from the first settlement to the present time."

Our forefathers were sincere believers in the reality of witchcraft; and the same opinion then prevailed throughout all Europe. The possibility, nay, the actual existence of a commerce with evil spirits, has had in its support the belief of many enlightened nations of the world. Mr. Justice Blackstone has not scrupled to declare, that to deny it "is at once flatly to contradict the revealed word of God in various passages both of the Old and New Testament."[1] I meddle not with this matter of controversial divinity. But it is certain, that, from the earliest times, it has been punished as a crime in all Christian countries, and generally, as a mark of peculiar horror and detestation, with death. Such was its punishment in England at the time of the emigration of our ancestors; and such it continued to be until the reign of George the Second. Surely, when we read of convictions before so mild and enlightened a judge as Sir Matthew Hale, it should excite no surprise, that our own judges were not superior to the delusion; that they possessed not a wisdom beyond the law, nor a power to resist the general credulity. My Lord Coke, in the simplicity of his own belief, loads witches with the most opprobrious epithets, as "horrible, devilish, and wicked offenders;"[2] and the Parliament of King James the First has enumerated, in studied detail, divers modes of conjuration and enchantment, upon which it has inflicted the punishment of death.[3] Lord Bacon has lent the credit of his own great name to preserve some of the wonders and ointments of witchcraft, with sundry wholesome restrictions upon our belief in their efficacy.[4] And we have high authority for saying, that "it became a science, everywhere much studied and cultivated, to distinguish a true witch by proper trials and symptoms."[5]

1 4 Bl. Com. 60; 3 Inst. 43. 2 3 Inst. 44. 3 Ibid. 44, 45.
4 2 Bacon's Works, 27, 45, 69. 5 7 Hume's Hist. 186.

We may lament, then, the errors of the times, which led to these persecutions. But surely our ancestors had no special reasons for shame in a belief, which had the universal sanction of their own and all former ages; which counted in its train philosophers, as well as enthusiasts; which was graced by the learning of prelates, as well as the countenance of kings; which the law supported by its mandates, and the purest judges felt no compunctions in enforcing. Let Witch Hill remain forever memorable by this sad catastrophe, not to perpetuate our dishonor, but as an affecting, enduring proof of human infirmity; a proof, that perfect justice belongs to one judgment-seat only, that which is linked to the throne of God.

Time would fail me to go at large into the history of New England, and my own strength, as well as your patience, is far spent. Yet it should not be concealed, that we have a proud consciousness of the spirit and principles of our fathers throughout every period of their colonial existence. At no time were they the advocates of passive obedience and non-resistance to rulers, at home or abroad. At all times they insisted, that the right of taxation and the right of representation were inseparable in a free government; and that on that account the power of taxation was vested exclusively in their own colonial legislature. At all times they connected themselves, with a generous fidelity, to the fortunes of the mother country, and shared the common burdens, and bore the common hardships, with cheerfulness. The sons of New England were found in her ranks in battle, foremost in danger; but, as is not unusual in colonial service, latest in the rewards of victory. An ante-revolutionary historian, of unquestionable accuracy, has said, that, "in the course of sixty years, the Province of Massachusetts hath been at a greater expense, and hath lost more of its inhabitants, than all the other colonies upon the continent taken together." In the Indian wars, in the successive attacks upon the French colonies, and in the capture of Quebec and the Canadas, they bore an honorable and important part. Even when their first charter was vacated, their resistance to the arbitrary measures of Sir Edmund Andros was but a prelude to the principles and practice of the Revolution.

Of the memorable events of a later period; of the resistance to British oppression; of the glorious war of Independence; of the subsequent establishment of the national government, I need not speak. They are familiar to all of us; but though repeated for the thousandth time, they still possess an animating freshness. In the struggle for independence, in which all the colonies embarked in a common cause, and all exhibited examples of heroism and public spirit, in which all seemed to forget themselves, and remember only their country, it would be invidious to draw comparisons of relative merit, since the true glory of each is in the aggregate achievements of all. Throughout the contest, the citizens of various states fought side by side, and shared the common toils. Their sufferings and their fame were blended at every step in the hour of peril, and in the hour of triumph. Let not those be separated in death, who in life were not divided.

But I may say, that New England was not behind the other states in zeal, in public sacrifices, in contributions of men and money, in firmness of resolve, or in promptitude of action. The blood of her children was freely poured out, not only on her own soil, but in every field, where armies met in hostile array. It flowed not on the land alone; the ocean received it into its swelling bosom. Wherever the battle raged, they were found; and many a gallant spirit breathed his last breath on the deck, with his thoughts still warm with the love of his native New England. Let a single fact concerning Massachusetts suffice to establish no mean claim to respect. Upon the final adjustment of the accounts of the revolutionary war, although her own soil had been but for a short period occupied by the enemy, she had expended eighteen millions of dollars, and the balance then due to her exceeded one million. One state only in the Union surpassed her in expenditures, and none in the balance in her favor.[1] But this would give a very inadequate view of her real efforts. Her voluntary bounties upon enlistments, her town and county contributions, are almost incredible, when we consider the general poverty and distress. But I forbear. Much might be urged in her favor, much in favor of her New England sisters, which has been sometimes remembered, only to be forgotten. Much might be said of the long array of statesmen and divines and lawyers and physicians, of the literature and science, which have adorned our annals. Let it pass — let it pass. Their works shall praise them. They cannot be concealed, whenever the deeds of our country are recited. The writer of the Declaration of Independence is not ours; but the author of the act itself reposes among us. He, who was "first in war, first in peace, and first in the hearts of his countrymen," sleeps in his native soil by the side of the beautiful Potomac. But the colony of Roger Williams, of narrow territory, yet of ample enterprise, may boast of one, second in excellence only to Washington.

But while we review our past history, and recollect what we have been, and are, the duties of this day were but ill performed, if we stopped here; if, turning from the past, and entering on the third century of our political existence, we gave no heed to the voice of experience, and dwelt not with thoughts of earnest, busy solicitude upon the future. What is to be the destiny of this Republic? In proposing this question, I drop all thought of New England. She has bound herself to the fate of the Union. May she be true to it, now, and for ever; true to it, because true to herself, true to her own principles, true to the cause of religion and liberty throughout the world. I speak, then, of our common country, of that blessed mother, that has nursed us in her lap, and led us up to manhood. What is her destiny? Whither does the finger of fate point? Is the career, on which we have

[1] 2 Pitkin's Hist. of United States, p. 538.

entered, to be bright with ages of onward and upward glory? Or is our doom already recorded in the past history of the earth, in the past lessons of the decline and fall of other republics? If we are to flourish with a vigorous growth, it must be, I think, by cherishing principles, institutions, pursuits, and morals, such as planted and have hitherto supported New England. If we are to fall, may she still possess the melancholy consolation of the Trojan patriot:

> " Sat patriæ Priamoque datum ; si Pergama dextrâ
> Defendi possent, etiam hâc defensa fuissent."

I would not willingly cloud the pleasures of such a day, even with a transient shade. I would not, that a single care should flit across the polished brow of hope, if considerations of the highest moment did not demand our thoughts, and give us counsel of our duties. Who, indeed, can look around him upon the attractions of this scene, upon the faces of the happy and the free, the smiles of youthful beauty, the graces of matron virtue, the strong intellect of manhood, and the dignity of age, and hail these as the accompaniments of peace and independence; — who can look around him, and not at the same time feel, that change is written on all the works of man; that the breath of a tyrant, or the fury of a corrupt populace, may destroy, in one hour, what centuries have slowly consolidated? It is the privilege of great minds, that to them "coming events cast their shadows before." We may not possess this privilege; but it is true wisdom, not to blind ourselves to dangers, which are in full view; and true prudence, to guard against those, of which experience has already admonished us.

When we reflect on what has been, and is, how is it possible not to feel a profound sense of the responsibleness of this Republic to all future ages? What vast motives press upon us for lofty efforts! What brilliant prospects invite our enthusiasm! What solemn warnings at once demand our vigilance, and moderate our confidence!

The old world has already revealed to us, in its unsealed books, the beginning and end of all its own marvellous struggles in the cause of liberty. Greece, lovely Greece, "the land of scholars and the nurse of arms," where sister republics, in fair processions, chanted the praises of liberty and the gods; where, and what is she? For two thousand years, the oppressor has bound her to the earth. Her arts are no more. The last sad relics of her temples are but the barracks of a ruthless soldiery; the fragments of her columns and her palaces are in the dust, yet beautiful in ruin. She fell not, when the mighty were upon her. Her sons were united at Thermopylæ and Marathon; and the tide of her triumph rolled back upon the Hellespont. She was conquered by her own factions. She fell by the hands of her own people. The Man of Macedonia did not the work of destruction. It was already done, by her own corruptions, banishments, and dissensions. Rome, republican Rome, whose eagles glanced in the rising and setting sun, where, and what is she? The Eternal City yet remains, proud even in her desolation, noble in her decline, venerable in the majesty of religion, and calm as in the composure of death. The *malaria* has but travelled in the paths worn by her destroyers. More than eighteen centuries have mourned over the loss of her empire. A mortal disease was upon her vitals before Cæsar had crossed the Rubicon; and Brutus did not restore her health by the deep probings of the senate chamber. The Goths and Vandals and Huns, the swarms of the North, completed only what was already begun at home. Romans betrayed Rome. The legions were bought and sold; but the people offered the tribute money.

And where are the republics of modern times, which clustered round immortal Italy? Venice and Genoa exist but in name. The Alps, indeed, look down upon the brave and peaceful Swiss in their native fastnesses; but the guaranty of their freedom is in their weakness, and not in their strength. The mountains are not easily crossed, and the valleys are not easily retained. When the invader comes, he moves like an avalanche, carrying destruction in his path. The peasantry sinks before him. The country is too poor for plunder; and too rough for valuable conquest. Nature presents her eternal barriers on every side to check the wantonness of ambition; and Switzerland remains, with her simple institutions, a military road to fairer climates, scarcely worth a permanent possession, and protected by the jealousy of her neighbors.

We stand, the latest, and, if we fail, probably the last experiment of self-government by the people. We have begun it under circumstances of the most auspicious nature. We are in the vigor of youth. Our growth has never been checked by the oppressions of tyranny. Our constitutions have never been enfeebled by the vices or luxuries of the old world. Such as we are, we have been from the beginning; simple, hardy, intelligent, accustomed to self-government and self-respect. The Atlantic rolls between us and any formidable foe. Within our own territory, stretching through many degrees of latitude and longitude, we have the choice of many products, and many means of independence. The government is mild. The press is free. Religion is free. Knowledge reaches, or may reach every home. What fairer prospect of success could be presented? What means more adequate to accomplish the sublime end? What more is necessary than for the people to preserve what they themselves have created?

Already has the age caught the spirit of our institutions. It has already ascended the Andes, and snuffed the breezes of both oceans. It has infused itself into the life-blood of Europe, and warmed the sunny plains of France, and the low lands of Holland. It has touched the philosophy of Germany and the North; and, moving onward to the South, has opened to Greece the lessons of her better days.

Can it be that America, under such circumstances, can betray herself? that she is to be added to the catalogue of republics, the inscription upon whose ruins is, "They were, but they are not"? Forbid it, my countrymen; forbid it, Heaven.

I call upon you, Fathers, by the shades of your ancestors, by the dear ashes which repose in this precious soil, by all you are, and all you hope to be; resist every project of disunion, resist every encroachment upon your liberties, resist every attempt to fetter your consciences, or smother your public schools, or extinguish your system of public instruction.

I call upon you, Mothers, by that which never fails in woman, the love of your offspring; teach them, as they climb your knees, or lean on your bosoms, the blessings of liberty. Swear them at the altar, as with their baptismal vows, to be true to their country, and never to forget or forsake her.

I call upon you, Young Men, to remember whose sons you are; whose inheritance you possess. Life can never be too short, which brings nothing but disgrace and oppression. Death never comes too soon, if necessary in defence of the liberties of your country.

I call upon you, Old Men, for your counsels, and your prayers, and your benedictions. May not your gray hairs go down in sorrow to the grave, with the recollection, that you have lived in vain. May not your last sun sink in the west upon a nation of slaves.

No — I read in the destiny of my country far better hopes, far brighter visions. We, who are now assembled here, must soon be gathered to the congregation of other days. The time of our departure is at hand, to make way for our children upon the theatre of life. May God speed them and theirs. May he, who, at the distance of another century, shall stand here to celebrate this day, still look round upon a free, happy, and virtuous people. May he have reason to exult, as we do. May he, with all the enthusiasm of truth, as well as of poetry, exclaim, that here is still his country,

> "Zealous, yet modest; innocent though free;
> Patient of toil; serene amidst alarms;
> Inflexible in faith; invincible in arms."

DEVELOPMENTS OF SCIENCE AND MECHANIC ART.

A DISCOURSE DELIVERED BEFORE THE BOSTON MECHANICS' INSTITUTE, AT THE OPENING OF THEIR ANNUAL COURSE OF LECTURES, NOVEMBER, 1829.

MUCH has been said respecting the spirit of our age, and the improvements by which it is characterized. Many learned discussions have been presented to the public, with a view to illustrate this topic; to open the nature and extent of our attainments; to contrast them with those of former times; and thus to vindicate, nay more, to demonstrate our superiority over all our predecessors, if not in genius, at least in the perfection and variety of its fruits. There is, doubtless, much in such a review to gratify our pride, national, professional, and personal. But its value in this respect, if we stop here, is but of doubtful, or, at most, of subordinate importance. It is not the sum of our attainments, but the actual augmentation of human happiness and human virtue thereby, of which we may justly be proud. If every new acquisition operates as a moving spirit upon the still depths of our minds, to awaken new enterprise and activity, to warm our hearts to new affection and kindness to our race, and to enable us to add something to the capital stock of human enjoyment, we may well indulge in self-congratulation. It has been said that he who makes two blades of grass grow where only one grew before, deserves to be reckoned among the benefactors of mankind. And it has been justly said; because he has added so much means to the support of life, and thus promoted the effective power and prosperity of the whole community. The true test of the value of all attainments is their real utility.

I do not mean by this remark to suggest that nothing is to be esteemed valuable except its utility can be traced directly home to some immediate benefit, in visible operation, as an effect from a cause. Far otherwise. There are many employments whose chief object seems little connected with any great ultimate benefit, which yet administer widely, though indirectly, to the substantial good of society. There are many studies which seem remote from any direct utility, which yet, like the thousand hidden springs which form the sources and streams of rivers, pour in their contributions to augment the constantly increasing current of public wealth and happiness. We must not, therefore, when we examine an art, or an invention, a book, or a building, a study, or a curiosity, measure its value by a narrow rule. We must not ask ourselves, whether we could do without it; whether it be indispensable to our wants; or whether, though missed, it could yet be spared. But the true question in such cases ought to be whether, in the actual structure of society, it gratifies a reasonable desire, imparts an innocent pleasure, strengthens a moral feeling, elevates a single virtue, or chastens or refines the varied intercourse of life. If it does, it is still useful in the truest sense of the term, although it may not seem directly to feed the hungry, cure the sick, administer consolation to the afflicted, or even remove the irksome doubt of a poor litigant, groping blindfold through the dark passages of the law.

It is not easy, indeed, to name many pursuits of which the inutility is so clearly made out that they may be parted with without regret, or without disturbing the good order and arrangements of society. Some that at a short sight seem, if not frivolous, at least unnecessary, to men of narrow capacities, will be found, on a larger survey, to be connected with the most important interests. The fine arts, for instance, painting, music, poetry, sculpture, architecture, seem almost the necessary accompaniments of a state of high civilization. They are not only the grace and ornament of society, but they are intimately connected with its solid comforts. If they did no more than gratify our taste, increase our circle of innocent enjoyment, warm our imaginations, or refine our feelings, they might fairly be deemed public blessings. But who is so careless as not to perceive that they not only give encouragement to men of genius, but employment to whole classes in the subordinate arts? They not only create a demand for labor; but make that very labor a means of subsistence to many, who must otherwise be idle and indolent, or, by pressing upon other business, sink the compensation for labor by a ruinous competition to its minimum price. How many thousands are employed upon a single block of marble before, under the forming hand of the artist, it breathes in sculptured life! before it meets us in the surpassing beauty of a Venus, or the startling indignation of an Apollo! Our granite would have slumbered forever in its quarries if architecture had not, under the guidance of taste, taught us to rear the dome, and the temple, the church of religion, and the hall of legislation, the column of triumph, and the obelisk of sorrow. To what an amazing extent are the daily operations of the press! With how many arts, with how much commerce, with what various manufactures, is it combined! The paper may be made of the linen of Italy, and the cotton of Carolina, or Egypt, or the Indies; the type and ink of the products of various climes; and the text must be composed, and the sheets worked off, by the care and diligence of many minds. And yet, if no books were to be printed, or no newspaper or pamphlet were to be struck off, but what were indispensable; if we were to deem all classical learning useless; and all poetry, and fiction, and dissertation, and essay, and history, a sad abuse of time and labor and ingenuity, because we could do without them, and because they did not plant our fields, or turn our mills, or sail our ships; I fear that the race of authors would soon become extinct; and the press, busy as it now is, with its myriads, would sink back into the silence of the days of Faustus, and require no aid from the supernatural arts of his suspected coadjutor. Sure I am, that the power-press of your own Treadwell, that beautiful specimen of skill and ingenuity, would be powerless, and no longer in its magical works delight us in our morning search, or in our evening lucubrations.

I have made these suggestions, not so much as appropriate to the objects which I have in view in this address, as to guard against the supposition in what follows, that the liberal arts are not worthy of our most intense admiration and respect.

If I were called upon to state that which, upon the whole, is the most striking characteristic of our age, that which in the largest extent exemplifies its spirit, I should unhesitatingly answer, that it is the superior attachment to practical science over merely speculative science. Into whatever department of knowledge we may search, we shall find that the almost uniform tendency of the last fifty years has been to deal less and less with theory, and to confine the attention more and more to practical results. There was a period when metaphysical inquiries constituted the principal delight of scholars and philosophers; and endless were the controversies and the subtleties about which they distracted themselves and their followers. The works of Aristotle, one of the greatest geniuses of all antiquity, were studied with a diligence which will hardly be believed in our day; and exerted an influence over the minds of men almost down to the close of the seventeenth century, as wonderful as it was universal. He was read, not in what would now be deemed most important in his researches into natural history, and the phenomena of the external world, or in his dissertations on politics, and government, and literature; but in his metaphysics, and endless inquiries into mind, and spirit, and essences, and forms, and categories, and syllogisms.

Lord Bacon, two centuries ago, in some most profound

discourses, exposed the absurdity of the existing system of study, and of its unsatisfactory aims and results. He vindicated the necessity of inquiring into mental, as well as natural phenomena, by other means; by what is called the method of induction, that is, by a minute examination of facts, or what may properly be called experimental philosophy. This, in his judgment, was the only safe and sure road to the attainment of science; and, by subjecting every theory to the severe test of facts, would save a useless consumption of time and thought upon vague and visionary projects.

It may seem strange, that such wise counsels should not have been listened to with immediate, if not universal approbation. The progress, however, even of the most salutary truths is slow, when there are no artificial obstacles in the way. But when men's minds are preoccupied by systems and pursuits, which have received the sanction of many generations, every effort to overcome errors, is like the effort to carry an enemy's fortress. It can rarely be accomplished by storm. It must be subdued by patient mining, by a gradual destruction of outposts, and by advances under cover of powerful batteries. Lord Bacon's admonitions can scarcely be said to have gained any general credence until the close of the seventeenth century; and their triumphant adoption was reserved as the peculiar glory of our own day.

It is to this cause, that we are mainly to attribute the comparatively slight attention first paid to discoveries, which have since become some of the most productive sources, not only of individual opulence, but, in a large sense, of national wealth. The history of the steam engine is full of instruction upon this subject. The Marquis of Worcester, early in the reign of Charles II. (1655), first directed the attention of the public to the expansive power of steam, when used in a close vessel; and of its capacity to be employed as a moving power in machinery. The suggestion slept almost without notice, until about the year 1698, when Captain Savary, a man of singular ingenuity, constructed an apparatus, for which he obtained a patent, to apply it to practical purposes. The invention of a safety-valve soon afterwards followed; and that again was succeeded by the use of a close-fitted piston, working in a cylinder. Still, however, the engine was comparatively of little use, until Mr. Watt, a half century afterwards, effected the grand improvement of condensing the steam in a separate vessel, communicating by a pipe with the cylinder; and Mr. Washbrough, in 1778, by the application of it to produce a rotatory motion, opened the most extensive use of it for mechanical purposes.

It was in reference to the astonishing impulse thus given to mechanical pursuits, that Dr. Darwin, more than forty years ago, broke out in strains equally remarkable for their poetical enthusiasm, and prophetic truth, and predicted the future triumph of the steam engine.

> "Soon shall thy arm, unconquered steam, afar
> Drag the slow barge, or drive the rapid car;
> Or on wide waving wings expanded bear
> The flying chariot through the fields of air;—
> Fair crews triumphant, leaning from above,
> Shall wave their fluttering kerchiefs, as they move,
> Or warrior bands alarm the gaping crowd,
> And armies shrink beneath the shadowy cloud."

What would he have said if he had but lived to witness the immortal invention of Fulton, which seems almost to move in the air, and to fly on the wings of the wind? And yet how slowly did this enterprise obtain the public favor! I myself have heard the illustrious inventor relate, in an animated and affecting manner, the history of his labors and discouragements. When (said he) I was building my first steamboat at New York, the project was viewed by the public either with indifference, or with contempt, as a visionary scheme. My friends, indeed, were civil, but they were shy. They listened with patience to my explanations, but with a settled cast of incredulity on their countenances. I felt the full force of the lamentation of the poet,

> "Truths would you teach, or save a sinking land?
> All fear, none aid you, and few understand."

As I had occasion to pass daily to and from the building-yard, while my boat was in progress, I have often loitered unknown near the idle groups of strangers, gathering in little circles, and heard various inquiries as to the object of this new vehicle. The language was uniformly that of scorn, or sneer, or ridicule. The loud laugh often rose at my expense; the dry jest; the wise calculation of losses and expenditures; the dull, but endless, repetition of the Fulton Folly. Never did a single encouraging remark, a bright hope, or a warm wish, cross my path. Silence itself was but politeness, veiling its doubts, or hiding its reproaches. At length the day arrived, when the experiment was to be put into operation. To me it was a most trying and interesting occasion. I invited many friends to go on board to witness the first successful trip. Many of them did me the favor to attend, as a matter of personal respect; but it was manifest, that they did it with reluctance, fearing to be the partners of my mortification, and not of my triumph. I was well aware, that in my case there were many reasons to doubt of my own success. The machinery was new and ill made; many parts of it were constructed by mechanics unaccustomed to such work; and unexpected difficulties might reasonably be presumed to present themselves from other causes. The moment arrived, in which the word was to be given for the vessel to move. My friends were in groups on the deck. There was anxiety, mixed with fear, among them. They were silent, and sad, and weary. I read in their looks nothing but disaster, and almost repented of my efforts. The signal was given, and the boat moved on a short distance, and then stopped, and became immovable. To the silence of the preceding moment now succeeded murmurs of discontent, and agitations, and whispers, and shrugs. I could hear distinctly repeated, "I told you it would be so — it is a foolish scheme — I wish we were well out of it." I elevated myself upon a platform, and addressed the assembly. I stated, that I knew not what was the matter; but if they would be quiet, and indulge me for a half hour, I would either go on, or abandon the voyage for that time. This short respite was conceded without objection. I went below, examined the machinery, and discovered that the cause was a slight mal-adjustment of some of the work. In a short period it was obviated. The boat was again put in motion. She continued to move on. All were still incredulous. None seemed willing to trust the evidence of their own senses. We left the fair city of New York; we passed through the romantic and ever-varying scenery of the highlands; we descried the clustering houses of Albany; we reached its shores; and then, even then, when all seemed achieved, I was the victim of disappointment. Imagination superseded the influence of fact. It was then doubted, if it could be done again; or if done, it was doubted if it could be made of any great value.

Such was the history of the first experiment, as it fell, not in the very language which I have used, but in its substance, from the lips of the inventor. He did not live, indeed, to enjoy the full glory of his invention. It is mournful to say, that attempts were made to rob him, in the first place, of the merit of his invention, and, next, of its fruits. He fell a victim to his efforts to sustain his title to both. When already his invention had covered the waters of the Hudson, he seemed little satisfied with the results, and looked forward to far more extensive operations. My ultimate triumph, he used to say, my ultimate triumph will be on the Mississippi. I know, indeed, that, even now, it is deemed impossible by many, that the difficulties of its navigation can be overcome. But I am confident of success. I may not live to see it; but the Mississippi will yet be covered by steamboats; and thus an entire change be wrought in the course of the internal navigation and commerce of our country.

And it has been wrought. And the steamboat, looking to its effects upon commerce and navigation, to the combined influences of facilities of travelling and facilities of trade, of rapid circulation of news, and still more rapid circulation of pleasures and products, seems destined to be numbered among the noblest benefactions to the human race.

I have passed aside from my principal purpose, to give, in this history of the steamboat, a slight illustration of the slow progress of inventions. It may not be unacceptable, as a tribute to the memory of a man, who united in himself a great love of science with an inextinguishable desire to render it subservient to the practical business of life.

But, perhaps, the science of chemistry affords as striking an instance as any which can be adduced, of the value of Lord Bacon's maxims, and of the paramount importance of facts over mere speculative philosophy. It was formerly an occult science, full of mysteries and unedifying processes, abounding in theories, and scarcely reducible to any rational principles. It is now in the highest sense entitled to the appellation of a science. The laws of chemical action have been examined and ascertained with great accuracy, and can now be demonstrated with as much clearness and facility, as any of the laws which belong to mechanical philosophy. It has become eminently a practical science; and its beneficial effects are felt in almost every department of life. The apothecary's shop no longer abounds with villanous compounds and nostrums, the disgrace of the art. Chemistry has largely administered to the convenience as well as the efficacy, of medicines, by ascertaining their qualities and component parts, by removing nauseous substances, simplifying processes, and purifying the raw materials. It has secured the lives of thousands by its wonderful safety-lamps, which prevent explosions from the invisible, but fatal fire-damps of mines. It lights our streets and theatres by its beautiful gas, extracted from coal. It enters our dye-houses, and teaches us how to fix and discharge colors, to combine and to separate them; to bleach the brown fibre, and impart the never-fading tint. It discloses the nature and properties of light and heat, of air and water, of the products of the vegetable and animal kingdoms, of earths, and alkalies, and acids, and minerals, and metals. And, though we have not as yet discovered by it the philosopher's stone, or learned how to transmute all other substances into gold; we have gained by it a much more valuable secret, the art of improving our agriculture, perfecting our manufactures, and multiplying all our comforts, by giving new power to all the arts of life, and adding new vigor to home-bred industry. It has indeed conferred benefits, where they have been least expected. By expounding the origin and causes of *ignes fatui*, it has put to flight the whole host of goblins, and imps, and fairies, and sprites, that inhabited our low grounds and wastes, and required some holy incantation to lay them, in the good old days of superstition, and omens, and death-watches, and ghosts, that vanished at the crowing of the cock. It may not, indeed, be said to have given much aid to the law, except when some luckless inventor has been driven into a tedious lawsuit by an infringement of his patent, and has found his money melt away under its dissolving power.

Half a century ago the composition of the atmosphere and ocean were unknown to philosophy. The identity of the electric fluid and lightning was scarcely established. The wonders disclosed by the galvanic battery had not even entered into the imagination of man.

It is unnecessary for me to trace the causes, which gradually led to these changes in the objects and pursuits of science. For a long period after the revival of letters, the minds of educated men were almost wholly engrossed by classical learning, and philology, and criticism, and dogmatical theology, and endless commentaries upon scanty texts, both in law and divinity. The study of pure and mixed mathematics succeeded; and astronomy, as it deserved, absorbed all the attention and genius which were not devoted to literature. But scholars of all sorts, by general consent, looked with indifference or disdain upon the common arts of life, and felt it to be a reproach to mingle in the business of the artisan. One would suppose, that the alliance between science and the arts was so natural and immediate, that little influence would be necessary to bring about their union. But the laboratory and the workshop, the study of the gometrician and the shed of the machinist, were for ages at almost immeasurable distances from each other; and the pathways between them were few, and little frequented.

It was not until some fortunate discoveries in the arts had led to opulence, that scientific men began to surrender their pride, and to devote themselves practically to the improvement of the arts. The first great step in modern science was to enter the workshop, and superintend its operations, and analyze and explain its principles. And the benefits derived from this connection have already been incalculable both to art and science. Each has been astonishingly improved by the other; and a hint derived from one has often led on to a train of inventions and discoveries, the future results of which are beyond all human power to measure. Thus, dignity and importance have been added to both. The manufacturer, the machinist, the chemist, the engineer, who is eminent in his art, may now place himself by the side of the scholar, and the mathematician, and the philosopher, and find no churlish claim for precedency put in. His rank in society, with reference either to the value of the products of his skill, or the depth of his genius, sinks him not behind the foremost of those, who strive for the first literary distinctions. This fortunate change in the public opinion, which has made it not only profitable, but honorable, to pursue the mechanical arts, is already working deeply into all the elements of modern society. It has already accomplished, what it is scarcely a figure of speech to call, miracles in the arts. Who is there, that would not desire to rival, if he does not envy, the inventions of Watt, of Arkwright, and Fulton? Who would ask for a fairer reputation, or loftier or more enduring fame, than belongs to them? And yet we have but just entered on the threshold of the results, to which their labors must lead future generations. We can scarcely imagine the number of minds, which have been already stimulated to the pursuit of practical science by their successful example. Whichever way we turn, we may see minds of the first class diverted from the established professions of law, physic, and divinity, to become the votaries, nay, the enthusiastic votaries, of the arts. And we are beginning to realize the first effects of this intense application and appropriation of the genius of our age, in simultaneous and elegant inventions in various arts.

It is true, in the general progress of society, that art commonly precedes science. The savage first constructs his hut, prepares his food, fashions his weapons of defence, and multiplies his power, by the application of the rudest materials. His wants being supplied, he may next dream of luxuries. But the road lies open to him, not by the investigation of principles, but by the application of manual dexterity and steady labor to acquire them. And this, for the most part, continues, or rather has continued, to be the order of things, until very late stages of civilization and refinement. At present, this order is almost entirely reversed. It may now be said with truth, that, in a general view, science precedes art; that is, the improvements which are made in art, arise more often from an exact investigation of principles, than from bare experiments, or accidental combinations. Principles suggest the experiment, rather than experiment the principles. In the most important branches of manufactures, where skill is so constantly in demand, and economy in operation is so indispensable, and competition is universal, there is now a perpetual tasking of the wit of man to invent some cheaper, thriftier, or neater combination. Something to increase the velocity and uniformity of motion, the delicacy and certainty of spinning, the beauty or fineness of fabrics, the simplicity or directness in the application of power, or something to ascertain and separate the worthless from the valuable in materials, is the ambition of a thousand minds at the same instant; and the project holds out ample rewards to the fortunate discoverer. The result is, that the discovery is often simultaneously made by different minds at great distances, and without the slightest communication with each other. At other times, different inventions are at the same moment employed, and work out with rival skill the same purposes by opposite means. In this way, and especially in manufactures, the most perfect existing machinery is perpetually in danger of becoming useless, or at least unprofitable, by the introduction of a single improvement, which gives it a superiority of one per centum upon the capital employed. An instance, illustrative of these remarks, occurred in the course of my own official duties, in a suit for the infringement of a patent right. A beautiful improvement had been made in the double-speeder of the cotton-spinning machine, by one of our ingenious countrymen. The originality of the invention was established by the most satisfactory evidence. The defendant, however, called an Englishman, as a witness, who had been but a short time in the country, and who testified most explicitly to the existence of a like invention in the improved machinery in England. Against such positive proof there was much difficulty in proceeding. The testimony, though doubted, could not be discredited; and the trial was postponed to another term, for the purpose of procuring evidence to rebut it. An agent was despatched to England, for this and other objects; and, upon his return, the plaintiff was content to become nonsuited. There was no doubt that the invention here was without any suspicion of its existence elsewhere; but the genius of each country, almost at the same moment, accomplished independently the same achievement.

I have introduced these considerations to the view of those who are engaged in the arts, and especially of those, whose studies this society is designed to patronize, for the purpose of leading them to the reflection, that, in the present state of things, it is no longer safe to be ignorant; and that mere dexterity and mechanical adroitness, expertness of hand, or steadiness of labor, are not alone sufficient to guarantee to the individual a successful issue in his business. Science is becoming almost indispensable, in order to master improvements as they occur, and to keep up, in some measure, with the skill of the age. It will otherwise happen, that a mechanic, by the time he has arrived midway in life, will find himself superseded by those, who, though much younger, have begun life under more favorable auspices. But upon this I may have occasion to enlarge a little more hereafter.

I have already spoken of the advantages resulting from scientific men's becoming familiar with the workshop, and the operations of art. But a far more important object, and the second great step in improvement, is to elevate mechanics and artisans to the rank of scientific inquirers.

It is singular, that no attempt was ever made to provide systematically for such an object, until a period so recent, that it seems but an affair of yesterday. The truth is so obvious, that he, who is engaged in the practice of an art, must, with equal advantages, be far better qualified to improve and perfect its operations, than he, who merely theorizes, without any knowledge of practical difficulties, that it is matter of surprise, that it should have been so long overlooked. The origin and history of Mechanics' Institutions were brought before you, on the first opening of your own Institution, with so much fulness and accuracy, by the learned gentleman who addressed you on that occasion, that I may well be spared any effort to retouch, what he has so faithfully delineated. Until the nineteenth century, no one thought of a system of scientific instruction, much less of mutual instruction, for those who were to be bred in the arts. These institutions began, as you know, under the auspices of Professor Anderson, at Glasgow, and so slowly worked their way into public favor, that, ten years ago, they were unknown in that city, which boasts herself the modern Athens; and, seven years ago, all the influence and reputation of Dr. Birkbeck were requisite to introduce them into the reluctant circles of London.

I look upon this, as a new era in the history of science; and it may be safely predicted, that these establishments are destined hereafter to work more important changes in the structure of society, and in the improvement of the arts, than any single event, which has occurred since the invention of printing.

What I propose in the residue of this discourse is, to offer some considerations in vindication of this opinion, and also some considerations by way of encouragement to those, who, as mechanics and artisans, are invited to devote themselves to the pursuit of liberal science.

And, in the first place, I might remark that genius and talent are limited to no rank or condition of life. They have been distributed by the bounty of Providence, with an equal hand through every class of society. They are among those gifts, which poverty cannot destroy, or wealth confer; which spring up in the midst of discouragements and difficulties, and, like the power of steam, acquire new elasticity by pressure; which ripen in the silence of solitude, as well as in the crowded walks of society; which the cottage may nourish into a more healthy strength, than even the palace or the throne. The most formidable enemy to genius is not labor, but indolence; want of interest and excitement; want of motive to warm, and of object to accomplish; ignorance of means, leading to indifference to ends. Hence it is, that the very highest and the very lowest orders of society often present the same mental phenomena — a fixed and languishing disease of the intellectual powers, where curiosity wastes itself in trifles, and a cold listlessness, brooding over the thoughts, lets fall a preternatural stupor. Their misfortune is that, so beautifully touched by the poet,

> "But knowledge to their eyes her ample age,
> Rich with the spoils of time, did ne'er unroll."

I might remark, in the next place, that the rewards of science are most ample, whether they be viewed in reference to personal enjoyment, to rank in society, or to substantial wealth. It is one of the wise dispensations of Providence, that knowledge should not only confer power, but should also confer happiness. Every new attainment is a new source of pleasure; and thus the desire for it increases as fast as it is gratified. It not only widens the sphere of our thoughts, but it elevates them, and thus gives them a livelier moral action. When one has seen an apple fall from a tree, and is told, for the first time, that its fall is regulated by the law of gravitation, the simplicity of the truth may scarcely awaken his curiosity. When he is told, that the same law regulates the plumb line, and enables him unerringly to erect his house in the true perpendicular, he perceives, with pleasure, a new application of it. When he is further told, that there is a constantly increasing rapidity in every descending body, by the same law, so that it falls in the second instant double the space it does in the first; and that the whole doctrine of projectiles, both in nature and art, depends upon it; that it governs the flow of rivers, and the fall of cataracts, and the gentle rains, and the gentler dews, and the invisible air; that it guides the motion of the water-mill, the aim of gunnery, and the operations of the steam engine;—he cannot but awaken to some emotions of admiration. But when he has been taught, that the same law regulates the ebb and flow of the tide, the motions of the earth, and the planets, and the sun, and the stars, and holds them in their orbits, and binds them in an eternally revolving harmony; that to this he owes the return of day and night, the changes of the seasons, seed-time and harvest, summer and winter; if he be any thing, but a clod of the valley, how can he but exclaim, in wonder and amazement,

> "These, as they change, Almighty Father, these
> Are but the varied God. The rolling year
> Is full of thee."

What can tend more to exalt the dignity of our nature, than the consideration, that the mind of man has not only been able to grasp and demonstrate this law, but to apply it to the solution of an infinite number of questions, apparently beyond the reach of his boldest efforts? He has been able to ascertain the motions and size of the whole planetary system; to calculate every perturbation, arising from the constant, but changeful influence of mutual gravitation; to ascertain the paths of comets; to calculate eclipses with unerring certainty; and to foretell the very minute, nay, the very instant, of occultation of the most distant satellites. He can thus read, through the past, as well as the future, all the various states of the heavens for thousands of years. He has been able to apply this knowledge to the noblest purposes; and the mariner, by its aid, descries his home port with the same ease, on the dark bosom of the ocean, as he points it out from the little hill-top, that overlooks his native village.

If we pass from the contemplation of this sublime law of nature to others, which belong to animal or vegetable life, to those, which form and preserve the treasures of the earth, and of the sea, even down to those, which regulate the minutest particles of matter, the light of science will enable us every where to behold new and increasing wonders, and to remark the operations of infinite power, forever varied, and yet forever the same. It is impossible, that the mere perception of such laws should not afford pleasure to every rational mind. But when we further learn, that these very laws are made continually subservient to the use of man; that, by the knowledge of them, he is enabled to create power, and perfect mechanical operations; that he can make the winds and the waves, the earth and the air, heat and cold, the ductile metals and the solid rocks, the fragile flower and the towering forest, minister to his wants, his refinements, and his enterprise; we are compelled to admit, that the capacity to trace back such effects to their causes must elevate, and enlarge, and invigorate the understanding.

There is also real dignity, as well as delight, in such studies; and whenever they shall become the general accompaniment of mechanical employments, they must work a most beneficial change in the general structure of society. The arts of life are now so various and important, so intimately connected with national prosperity and individual comfort, that, for the future, a very large proportion of the population of every civilized country must be engaged in them. The time is not far distant, when the mechanic and manufacturing interest will form the great balancing power, between the conflicting interests of commerce and agriculture; between the learned professions and the mere proprietors of capital; between the day laborer and the unoccupied man of ease. In proportion to the degree of the knowledge, which shall belong to this collective interest, in proportion as its industry shall be combined with science, will be its influence on the wellbeing and safety of society. It is of the first importance, therefore, that education should here exert its most extensive power; and, by elevating the morals, as well as stimulating the enterprise of artisans, give a triumph to intellect over mere physical force; and thus secure one of the most dangerous passes of social life against the irruptions of ignorance and popular fury. It is a truth not always sufficiently felt, that science, while it elevates the objects of desire, has, in the same proportion, a tendency to restrain the outbreakings of the bad passions of mankind.

I might remark, in the next place, that the pursuit of practical science is not only a source of inexhaustible pleasure, opening new avenues to rank and reputation; but it is, at the same time, one of the surest foundations of opulence. Mere mechanical labor, from the perpetual competition arising from an increasing population, has a natural tendency to descend in the scale of compensation. But this effect is astonishingly increased by the constant application of machinery, as a substitute for the labor of man. The perfection of machinery has, in this manner, at times, thrown whole classes of artisans out of employment, and compelled them to resort to new pursuits for support. Mere manual skill and dexterity are nothing, when put in competition with the regularity, rapidity, and economy of machinery, working under the guidance of science. Now, it must be obvious, that in proportion as an artisan possesses science, will be his facility in passing from one branch of an art to another; and his ability to command a higher price for his services. His capacity, too, for adopting improvements, and keeping pace with the genius of the age, will (as has been already hinted) be thus immeasurably increased. So that, in the narrowest and most limited view, there is a positive certainty of gain, by understanding the scientific principles of the art, which we profess.

But this would be a very inadequate view of the benefits arising from this source. It is the power of science, in awakening the dormant energy of genius; in pointing out to it the true means to arrive at great ends; in preventing it from being wasted in visionary schemes, or retarded by clumsy processes; in short, it is the power of science, in suggesting the first hint, or striking out the first spark, or directing the unsteady aim, or removing the intermediate obstacles, that constitutes its true value, and perhaps its noblest excellence. Even after the first step is taken, and the first development of inventive genius assumes shape and body, how many obstacles are to be overcome; how many unexpected difficulties are to be met; how many toilsome days and nights are to be consumed, in nice adjustments and minute alterations! It is here, that science may be said to foster and nourish genius; to administer to its wants, and soothe its disquietudes, and animate its inquiries. What logarithms are to the mathematician, knowledge of principles is to the mechanic. It not only abridges the processes of computation, and thus diminishes labor, but it puts him in possession of means and computations, otherwise absolutely beyond the reach of human calculation. After Fulton had securely achieved, in his own opinion, the invention of the steamboat, months were consumed by him, as I learned from his own lips, in making the necessary calculations upon the resistance of fluids, in order to ascertain what was the best form for the boat, to ensure a successful issue to his experiment. I myself, in the course of my judicial life, have had occasion to learn from witnesses the origin, and history, and gradual formation, of two of the most elegant inventions in our own country; and, in both instances, the original machine, rude, and unsightly, and cumbrous enough, was brought into court, as the best proof of the first sketch, compared with the last labors of the admirable inventors. I have not the least hesitation in saying, that, if either of those extraordinary minds had been originally instructed in the principles of mechanical science, half their labors would have been saved. Sure I am, that one of them would not, with his later acquirements in science, have laid aside, for a long time, the creation of his own genius, as if in despair, that it could ever attain maturity.

I allude to the card machine of Whittemore, and the nail machine of Perkins. Of the former it would not become me to speak in terms of confident praise, from my own want of the proper knowledge of machinery. But I must confess, that, when I first saw it, it seemed to me to be almost an intelligent being, and to do every thing but speak; and whether considered with reference to the simplicity of its means, the accuracy and variety of its operations, or its almost universal capacity for common use, it deserves the highest commendation. Other inventions have since somewhat narrowed the sphere of its operations, and made its celebrity less felt. But I may quote the remark of one of our most ingenious countrymen, who, to a question put to him, what, after two months' examination of the patent office at Washington, and his own surveys elsewhere, appeared to him the most interesting of American inventions, unhesitatingly answered, Whittemore's card machine. The remark was made by Perkins; and perhaps no person, but himself, would have thought, that his own nail machine, which with its toggle-joint consumes bars of iron, and returns them in nails, with the tranquil grandeur of a giant, conscious of superior power, might not have borne the most strenuous rivalry.

And this leads me to remark, in the next place, as matter of pride, as well as of encouragement, that to mechanics themselves we are indebted for some of the most useful and profitable inventions of the age. I have already adverted to the perfection of the steam engine by Watt. The cotton-machine of Arkwright constitutes an era in inventions, and has already thrown back upon Asia all her various fabrics, and compelled her to yield up to European skill the cheapest labor of her cheapest population. The inventions of Wedgewood have led to almost as striking a rivalry of the pottery and wares of the East. The cotton-gin, which has given to the cotton-growing States of the south their present great staple, is the production of the genius of Whitney. In the year 1794, the Carolinas and Georgia were scarcely known to our ablest diplomatists, as cultivators of the plant; so obscure and unimportant were its results. The invention of Whitney at once gave it the highest value; and laid the broad foundation of their present wealth and prosperity. At this very moment, New England annually consumes, in her manufactories, more than one fifth part of the eight hundred and fifty thousand bales of cotton, the annual produce of their soil; which, but for him, would have had no existence. What wonders were accomplished by the self-taught architect, Brindley, himself a humble mill-wright; and yet of such vast compass of thought, that to him rivers seemed of no use, but to feed navigable canals, and the ocean itself but a large reservoir for water-works! What effects is our own Perkins producing, by one only of his numerous inventions, — the art of softening steel, so as to admit of engraving, and then hardening it again, so as to retain the fine point and polish of copper-plate, without the constant wear of the latter, and its consequent tendency to depreciation! He has enabled us, as it were to stereotype, and multiply, to an almost incalculable extent, the most beautiful specimens of some of the fine arts; and cheapen them, so as to bring them within the reach of the most moderate fortunes. Many other illustrious instances of genius, successfully applied to the improvement of the arts, might be selected from the workshops and common trades of life. But in most of these instances it will be found, that the discovery was not the mere result of accident, but arose from the patient study of principles, or from hints gathered from a scientific observation of nice and curious facts. And it may be added, that, in all these instances, in proportion as the inventors acquired a knowledge of the principles of the arts, their genius assumed a wider play, and accomplished its designs with more familiar power and certainty. It is a subject of most profound interest, to observe to what grand results a common principle in mechanics, or an apparently insulated fact, may conduct us, under the guidance of a man of genius. The rule, for instance, in geometry, that the circumferences of circles are in proportion to their diameters, lies at the foundation of most of the operations of practical mechanics, and has led to the means of increasing mechanical power to an almost incalculable extent. The lever, the pulley, and the wheel, are but illustrations of it. So, too, the habit of nice observation of facts (the almost constant attendant upon scientific acquirements) has led to surprising conjectures, which have ended in the demonstration of equally surprising truths. Let me avail myself of one or two illustrations, which have been already noticed by others, as better to my purpose than any which my own memory could furnish. In the course of Sir Isaac Newton's experiments to ascertain the laws of optics, he was led, from the peculiar action of the diamond upon light, to express an opinion that it was carbon, and capable of ignition, and not belonging to the class of crystals. That conjecture has in our day been established, by chemical experiments, to be a fact. He made the discovery, also, of the compound nature of light, and that its white color arises from a mixture of all the various colors. This has led to various ingenious improvements in the formation of the lenses of telescopes, by which modern astronomy has been able to display the heavens in new beauty and order. When Franklin, by close observation, had established the identity of lightning with the electric spark, he was immediately led to the practical application of his discovery, by ascertaining the relative conducting power of various substances, so as to guard our dwellings from its tremendous agency. The galvanic battery, to which we are indebted for so many discoveries in chemistry, owes its origin to an apparently trivial circumstance. The discoverer's attention was drawn to an investigation of the cause of the twitching of a dead frog's leg; and by patient and laborious experiments, he was at length conducted to the discovery of animal electricity. The polarization of light, as it is called, — that is, the fact, that rays of light have different sides, which have different properties of reflection, — is a discovery in optics of very recent date, which, it is said, "is so fertile in the views it lays open of the constitution of natural bodies, and the minuter mechanism of the universe, as to place it in the very first rank of physical and mathematical science." It was discovered by the French philosopher, Malus, as late as in 1810, by various minute and delicate experiments, and has already led to very extraordinary results.

Indeed, such is the quickening power of science, that it is scarcely possible that its simplest germ should be planted in the human mind, without expanding into a healthy growth. It generates, as it moves on, new thoughts, and new inquiries, and is forever gathering, without exhaustion and without satiety. The curiosity which is once awakened by it never sleeps; the genius which is once kindled at its altar, burns on with an inextinguishable flame.

It has been remarked that such was the progress of astronomical science, and the number of minds engaged in it, towards the close of the seventeenth century, that if Sir Isaac Newton had never lived his splendid and invaluable discoveries must have been in the possession of the succeeding age. The approaches had been so near that they almost touched the very verge of the paths which his genius explored, and demonstrated with such matchless ability. If this be true in respect to that branch of physical science, it is far more strikingly true in respect to mechanics. The struggle here, in respect to priority of inventions, is often so very close that a single day sometimes decides the controversy.

It is from considerations of this nature; that what has been must continue to be; that art is never perfect, and nature is inexhaustible; that science, while it is the master of art, is itself ultimately dependent upon it; that the intellectual power grows up in all stations, and in all soils; that, all other circumstances equal, he who knows and practises must for ever take the lead of him who merely knows, and has none of the skill to apply power, or the practical sagacity to overcome difficulties; that he whose interest is indissolubly connected with his science, and who feels at every turn the animating impulse of reward, as well as the pleasure of speculation, and the desire of fame, has more enduring and instant motives for exertion, than he who merely indulges his leisure or his curiosity; — it is, I say, from these considerations that I deduce the conclusion that when artisans and mechanics shall have become instructed in science, the inventions of this class will be more numerous, more useful, more profitable, and more ingenious, than those of any other class, and even perhaps of all other classes of society.

What an animating prospect does this afford! What noble ends to poor, neglected, suffering genius! What constant comfort, to cheer the hard hours of labor, and the heavier hours of despondency! Much less of success in life is in reality dependent upon accident, or what is called luck, than is commonly supposed. Far more depends upon the objects which a man proposes to himself; what attainments he aspires to; what is the circle which bounds his vision and his thoughts; what he chooses, not *to be educated for*, but to *educate himself for;* whether he looks to the end and aim of the whole of life, or only to the present day or hour; whether he listens to the voice of indolence or vulgar pleasure, or to the stirring voice in his own soul, urging his ambition on to the highest objects. If his views are low and grovelling; if the workshop, in its cold routine of duties, bounds all his wishes and his hopes, his destiny is already fixed; and the history of his whole life may be read, though the blush of youth still lingers on his cheeks. It is not a tale merely twice told; it has been told for millions. If, on the other hand, he aspires to be a man, in dignity, independence, spirit, and character, and to give his talents their full scope and vigor; if, to a steady devotion to the practice of his art, he adds a scientific study of its processes and principles, his success is as sure as any thing on this side of the grave can be. He may even go farther and dream of fame; and, if he possess the sagacity of genius, may build a solid immortality upon the foundation of his own inventions.

And why should it not be so? Why should not our youth, engaged in the mechanic arts, under the auspices of institutions like this, reach such a noble elevation of purpose? America has hitherto given her full proportion of genius to the cultivation of the arts. She has never been behind the most intelligent portions of the world, in her contribution of useful inventions for the common good. There are some circumstances in the situation and character of her population, which afford a wider range for talent and inquiry, than in any other country. The very equality of condition; the natural structure of society; the total demolition of all barriers against the advancement of talent from one department of life to another; the non-existence of the almost infinite subdivisions of labor by which, though more perfection in the result is sometimes obtained, the process has an almost uniform tendency to reduce human beings to mere machines; the mildness of the government; the general facility of subsistence; the absence of all laws regulating trades, and obstructing local competition; — these, and many other causes, and especially our free schools, and our cheap means of education, offer to ingenuous youth the most inviting prospects to expand and cultivate their intellectual powers. Under such circumstances is it too much to prophesy, that hereafter America may take the lead in mechanical improvements, and give another bright example to the world, by the demonstration of the truth, that free governments are as well adapted to perfect the arts of life, and foster inventive genius, as they are to promote the happiness and independence of mankind?

There are no real obstacles in the way, which may not be overcome by ordinary diligence and perseverance. A few hours saved every week from those devoted to idle pleasure, or listless indolence, would enable every artisan to master, in a comparatively short time, the elementary principles of the arts. He would have the constant benefit of refreshing his recollection by the practical application of them, and receive the demonstration at the same time that he was taught the truth. He would find that the acquisitions of every day added a new facility for future improvement; and that his own mind, quickened and fertilized by various stores of thought, would soon turn that into the truest source of enjoyment, which at first was the minister of toil and anxiety. Consider, for a moment, what must be the immediate effects of the general adoption of a system of mutual instruction. How powerfully would it work by way of encouragement to laudable ambition; how irresistibly to an increase of skill and sagacity in the most common employments of life! Ask yourselves what would be the result of one hundred thousand minds engaged at the same moment in the study of mechanical science, and urged on by the daily motives of interest, to acquire new skill, or invent new improvements. It seems to me utterly beyond the reach of human imagination to embody the results to which such a constant discipline of the intellect, strengthened by the daily experience of the workshop, would conduct us. The slightest spark of intelligence (if I may borrow a figure from the arts) would be blown into a steady flame, and the raw material of genius be kindled by a spontaneous combustion into the most intense light.

Gentlemen, I will detain you no longer. The remarks which I have addressed to you have been unavoidably of a loose and desultory nature. They have been thrown together not in the abundance of my leisure, but of my labors; in the midst of private cares and many pressing public duties. Such as they are, I trust they may receive your indulgence, if not for their intrinsic value, at least as my small tribute to the merit of this Institution. If I had possessed more leisure I should have preferred to have given you, as a more suitable topic for an introductory discourse, some account of the rise and progress of the more important arts and inventions in modern times. A close survey of the difficulties overcome, and of the triumphs achieved by mechanical genius, would, after all, constitute the most valuable commentary upon the powers of the human mind, and the most encouraging lesson in the study of science.

I conclude with the reflection naturally arising from the subject, that as the true end of philosophy is to render us wiser and happier, so its tendency is to warm our hearts, and elevate our affections, and make us, in the highest sense, religious beings. When we contemplate the physical creation, and observe, from the minutest atom up to the highest intelligence, continual displays of infinite wisdom, power, and goodness; when we trace out by the light of science the laws which govern the material world, and observe the order, and harmony, and wonderful adaptation of all, from those which form the sparkling diamond in the mine, or prepare the volleyed lightning, or generate the terrific earthquake, or direct the motions of the ocean, up to those which hold the planets in their spheres; when we turn our thoughts within us, and endeavor to learn what we ourselves are, and consider the nature and capacities of our minds, and feel the divinity, as it were, stir within us; when we look abroad at the curious displays of human invention in the arts and arrangements of life, and see how man has acquired dominion over the earth, and the sea, and the air, and the water; how is it possible, I say, when we contemplate such things, not to look up with awe, and admiration, and gratitude, to the First Great Cause of all these blessings? How is it possible not to feel that we are an emanation of that eternal Spirit which formed and fashioned us, and breathed into us a rational soul? How is it possible not to read for ourselves a higher destiny, where our powers shall be permitted to expand in endless progression, and continually witness new wonders of the divine perfection? Surely, in the contemplation of such things, we may well exclaim,

"Great and marvellous are thy works, Lord God Almighty; in wisdom hast thou made them all."

VALUE AND IMPORTANCE OF LEGAL STUDIES.

A DISCOURSE PRONOUNCED AT THE INAUGURATION OF THE AUTHOR AS DANE PROFESSOR OF LAW IN HARVARD UNIVERSITY, AUGUST 25, 1829.

It has been customary in this University for professors, upon their induction into office, to deliver a public discourse upon some topics suitable to the occasion. Upon the establishment of a new professorship it may also be expected that he, who for the first time fills the chair, should give some account of the foundation, and of the studies which it proposes to encourage. I shall endeavor not wholly to disappoint the just expectations of my audience in both respects; premising, however, that much reliance must be placed upon their indulgence, since the subject affords little scope for elegant disquisition, and almost forbids those ornaments, which gratify the taste, and warm the imagination of the scholar.

My plan is, in the first place, to lay before you some considerations touching the general utility of the study of the law; and to address them with more pointed application to those who propose to make it the business of their lives. In the next place, I shall briefly unfold the nature and objects of the professorship, which I have now the honor to occupy, and the particular studies which it comprehends; so that the noble design of the founder may be amply vindicated, and receive, as it deserves, the public approbation. In proportion, however, to the value and importance of these studies, I cannot but feel a diffidence, lest they should fail under my care of becoming as attractive and interesting as they ought to be; and lest my own imperfect execution of duty should cast a shade upon the bright prospects, which the founder is opening to our view.

In the present state of knowledge, such a diffidence might well become the teacher of any science; but the remark applies with augmented force to a science so vast, so intricate, and so comprehensive, as that of jurisprudence. In its widest extent it may be said almost to compass every human action; and in its minute details, to measure every human duty. If we contemplate it in the highest order of subjects, which it embraces, it can scarcely be surpassed in dignity. It searches into and expounds the elements of morals and ethics, and the eternal law of nature, illustrated and supported by the eternal law of revelation. It is in this sense, that it has constituted the panegyric of philosophers and sages in almost every age. It is in this sense that Cicero has spoken of it, in a passage, which is upon the lips of every scholar: "Est quidem vera lex recta ratio, naturæ congruens, diffusa in omnes, constans, sempiterna, quæ vocet ad officium jubendo, vetando a fraude deterreat, quæ tamen neque probos frustra jubet aut vetat, nec improbos jubendo aut vetando movet. Huic legi nec obrogari fas est, neque derogari ex hac aliquid licet, neque tota abrogari potest. Nec vero, aut per senatum aut per populum, solvi hac lege possumus."[1] It is in this sense, also, that the genius of Sir William Jones, rising into poetical enthusiasm, has proclaimed, that

"Sovereign law, the state's collected will,
O'er thrones and globes elate
Sits empress, crowning good, repressing ill."

But if we contemplate it in a narrower view, as a mere system of regulations for the safety and harmony of civil society; as the instrument of administering public and private justice; as the code, by which rights are ascertained,

[1] Cic. de Repub. Lib. iii. § 22. See also, Cic. de Legg. Lib. i. § 6.

and wrongs redressed; by which contracts are interpreted, and property is secured, and the institutions, which add strength to government, and solid happiness to domestic life, are firmly guarded; — if, I say, we contemplate it in this narrower view, its dignity may in some measure be lessened, but its design will yet appear sufficiently grand, and its execution sufficiently difficult, to have strong claims upon the gratitude and admiration of mankind.

The common law purports to be such a system of jurisprudence. By the *common* law is sometimes understood that collection of principles, which constitutes the basis of the administration of justice in England, in contradistinction to the maxims of the Roman code, which has universally received the appellation of the *civil* law. The latter has been adopted, or, if I may say so, inosculated, into the juridical polity of all continental Europe, as a fundamental rule. The former is emphatically the custom of the realm of England, and has no authority beyond her own territory, and the colonies, which she has planted in various parts of the world. It is no small proof of its excellence, however, that where it has once taken root, it has never been superseded; and that its direct progress, or silent sway, has never failed to obliterate the attachment to other codes, whenever the accidents of conquest or cession have brought it within the reach of popular opinion. But there is another sense, (which is the most usual sense,) in which it is called the *common* law, to distinguish it from the *statute* law, or the positive enactments of the legislature. In this sense, the common law is the *lex non scripta*, that is, the unwritten law, which cannot now be traced back to any positive text; but is composed of customs, and usages, and maxims, deriving their authority from immemorial practice, and the recognitions of courts of justice. Thus, the right of primogeniture, which is a fundamental rule of inheritances in England, does not depend upon any known statute, but upon the simple custom of the realm, of such high antiquity, that history does not reach its exact origin. Much, indeed, of this unwritten law may now be found in books, in elementary treatises, and in judicial decisions. But it does not derive its force from these circumstances. On the contrary, even judicial decisions are deemed but the formal promulgation of rules antecedently existing, and obtain all their value from their supposed conformity to those rules.

When our ancestors emigrated to America, they brought this common law with them, as their birthright and inheritance; and they put into operation so much of it, as was applicable to their situation. It became the basis of the jurisprudence of all the English colonies; and, except so far as it has been abrogated or modified by our local legislation, it remains to this very hour the guide, the instructor, the protector, and the ornament of every state within this republic, whose territory lies within our boundaries settled by the treaty of peace of 1783. May it ever continue to flourish here; for it is the law of liberty, and the watchful and inflexible guardian of private property and public rights.

It is of this common law, in its largest extent, that the Law Institution in this University proposes to expound the doctrines and diversities; and thus to furnish the means of a better juridical education to those, who are destined for the profession, as well as to those, who, as scholars and gentlemen, desire to learn its general principles.

Nor let any scholar or gentleman imagine, that the study is little worthy his attention, unless he is to engage in it for professional objects. I do not exaggerate its value, when I express the deliberate opinion, that there is not within the compass of human attainment any science, which has so direct a tendency as this, to strengthen the understanding, to enlarge its powers, to sharpen its sagacity, and to form habits of nice and accurate discrimination. Sir James Mackintosh, an elegant scholar, as well as a very competent judge, has said,[1] that "More understanding has, perhaps, been in this manner exerted to fix the rules of life, than in any other science; and it is certainly the most honorable occupation of the understanding, because it is the most immediately subservient to general safety and comfort." If this were a question dependent upon mere authority, perhaps testimony more unexceptionable to the general scholar might be drawn from other sources. Dr. Johnson, with his accustomed vigor of expression has stated, that "Law is the science, in which the greatest powers of the understanding are applied to the greatest number of facts." And Mr. Burke, himself an orator and statesman of the most enlarged research, has not hesitated to declare, that it is "One of the first and noblest of human sciences; a science, which does more to quicken and invigorate the understanding than all other kinds of learning put together."[2]

But there is little need to appeal to the testimonies of the living or the dead upon such a topic. Whoever will take the trouble to reflect upon the vast variety of subjects, with which it is conversant, and the almost infinite diversity of human transactions, to which it applies; whoever will consider, how much astuteness and ingenuity are required to unravel or guard against the contrivances of fraud and the indiscretions of folly, the caprices of the wise and the errors of the rash, the mistakes of pride, the confidence of ignorance, and the sallies of enterprise; will be at no loss to understand, that there will be ample employment for the highest faculties. If he will but add to the account, that law is a science, which must be gradually formed by the successive efforts of many minds in many ages; that its rudiments sink deep into remote antiquity, and branch wider and wider with every new generation; that it seeks to measure the future by approximations to certainty, derived solely from the experience

1 Introductory Discourse on the Study of the Law of Nature and Nations, p. 62, (3d edition.)

2 Speech on American Taxation, 1774.

of the past; that it must forever be in a state of progress, or change, to adapt itself to the exigencies and changes of society; that, even when the old foundations remain firm, the shifting channels of business must often leave their wonted beds deserted, and require new and broader substructions to accommodate and support new interests;[1] if, I say, he will but add these things to the account, it will soon become matter of surprise, that even the mightiest efforts of genius can keep pace with such incessant demands; and that the powers of reasoning, tasked and subtilized, as they must be, to an immeasurable extent, should not be absolutely overwhelmed in the attempt to administer justice.

From its nature and objects, the common law, above all others, employs a most severe and scrutinizing logic. In some of its branches it is compelled to deal with metaphysical subtilties and abstractions, belonging to the depths of intellectual philosophy. From this cause it has sometimes been in danger of being enslaved by scholastic refinements, by the jargon of the old dialectics, and the sophisms of over-curious minds. It narrowly escaped shipwreck in the hands of the schoolmen of the middle ages; and for a while was almost swallowed up in the quicksands of the feudal system. If it had not been, that the common law necessarily dealt with substances, instead of shadows, with men's business, and rights, and inheritances, and not with entities and notions, it would have shared the fate, or justified the satire pronounced upon metaphysical inquiries, that those, who have attempted to sound its depths,

"In that unfathomable gulf were drowned."

But common sense has at all times powerfully counteracted the tendency to undue speculation in the common law, and silently brought back its votaries to that, which is the end of all true logic, the just application of principles to the actual

[1] See Lord Hale's noble Discourse on the Amendment of the Law, ch. 3.

concerns of human life. One cannot but smile, in the present times, at some of the reasoning, and some of the fictions, which spread themselves, here and there, in small veins in the system. We are gravely told, for instance, by Bracton, in which he is followed by Lord Coke, that the true reason, why by the common law a father cannot inherit real estate by descent from his son, is, that inheritances are heavy, and descend, as it were, by the laws of gravitation, and cannot reascend.[1] We are again told, that, when the title to an estate is suspended upon future contingencies, the inheritance is in the mean time in abeyance, that is, (as we are taught by the accompanying explanations,) the inheritance is *in gremio legis*, or *in nubibus*, in the bosom of the law, or in the clouds, which seems to mend the matter exceedingly in point of plainness. And, again, when an estate is conveyed to trustees to serve existing uses, and future contingent uses also, we are told, that though a seisin is necessary to feed them, and it be now exhausted; yet, happily for us, there remains a possibility of seisin, a *scintilla juris*, which kindles at the very moment the new uses spring into being, and by its vital power executes at once the possession of the estate to those uses, by some sort of legal legerdemain.[2] Shakspeare has immortalized by his genius the report of a case in that book of painful learning, Plowden's Commentaries,[3] in which Lady Margaret Hales, by the suicide of her husband, lost an estate by forfeiture to the crown, which she held jointly with him. One of the learned judges upon that occasion, in order to establish the legal conclusion, that the party killed himself in his lifetime, reasoned in this manner: "The felony is attributed to the act, which act is always done by a living man, and in his lifetime; for Sir James Hales was dead, and how

1 "Descendit itaque jus, quasi ponderosum quid cadens deorsum rectâ lineâ, vel transversali, et nunquam reascendit eâ viâ quâ descendit." Bracton, lib. 2, ch. 29; Co. Litt. 11; 2 Bl. Com. 212.

2 Chudleigh's case (1 Co. Rep. 120) contains some curious reasoning on this subject.

3 Plowden's Com. 258, 262.

came he to his death? It may be answered, By drowning. And who drowned him? Sir James Hales. And when did he drown him? In his lifetime. So that Sir James Hales, being alive, caused Sir James Hales to die; and the act of the living man was the death of the dead man. And then for this offence it is reasonable to punish the living man, who committed the offence, and not the dead man. But how can he be said to be punished alive, when the punishment comes after his death?" &c. &c.

But, apart from a few blemishes of this sort, which belong, indeed, rather to the studies of the age than to the law, and are now so harmless, that they serve little more than to give point to some sarcasm upon the profession, it is certain, that the common law follows out its principles with a closeness and simplicity of reasoning, which approach, as near as any artificial or moral deductions can, to the rigor of demonstration.

How, indeed, can it be otherwise? It is not employed in closet speculations, in the silence of the monastery, or in the seclusion of private life. Every cause is heard in the presence of men, whom practice and study have made singularly acute and discriminating. The advocate is stimulated, not merely by the hope of reward, and devotion to his client, but by the love of fame, to exert all his talents in order to detect fallacies and answer objections. He is not at liberty, from mere courtesy or kindness, from private respect, or popular feeling, to gloss over the mistakes, or conceal the blunders, or suppress the inconsistencies of the argument of his adversary. In such places, and on such occasions, the law expects every man to do his duty, and his whole duty. He must search the dark, explore the weak, clear the doubtful, or confirm the strong points of his cause, as its exigencies may require. In such contests, victory is rarely to be won, victory I had almost said, is never won, without an arduous struggle. Mere fanciful analogies, and set phrases, and fine turns of expression, and plausible statements will not do. They are but shadows or mists, which hover over the pathways to truth, but do not impede them. They may blind the novice, or betray the ignorant; but they do not deceive the wary and experienced traveller. There must be a firmer and closer grapple with realities. The contest is fit for men of strong sinews, and deep thoughts; and such men, in all ages, have been found foremost in the ranks of the bar, and eager for its distinctions. To the inquisitive scholar and gentleman, therefore, the law will be found a study full of instruction, and admirably adapted to brace his mind to a wholesome discipline. He will thus avoid what Lord Bacon considers some of the greatest obstacles to knowledge. For, says he, "Facility to believe, impatience to doubt, temerity to answer, glory to know, doubt to contradict, end to gain, sloth to search, seeking things in words, resting in part of nature; these, and the like, have been the things, which have forbidden the happy match between the mind of man, and the nature of things."[1]

I might commend the study of the law to American citizens generally upon considerations of a broader cast. From the structure of our institutions, there is much to provoke the vigilance, and invite the leisure of all, and especially of educated men. Our government is emphatically a government of the people, in all its departments. It purports to be a government of laws, and not of men; and yet, beyond all others, it is subject to the control and influence of public opinion. Its whole security and efficiency depend upon the intelligence, virtue, independence, and moderation of the people. It can be preserved no longer than a reverence for settled, uniform laws constitutes the habit, I had almost said the passion, of the community. There can be no freedom, where there is no safety to property, or personal rights. Whenever legislation renders the possession or enjoyment of property precarious; whenever it cuts down the obligation and security of contracts; whenever it breaks in upon personal

[1] Praise of Knowledge, 2 Bacon's Works, 125.

liberty, or compels a surrender of personal privileges, upon any pretext, plausible or otherwise, it matters little, whether it be the act of the many, or the few, of the solitary despot, or the assembled multitude; it is still in its essence tyranny. It matters still less, what are the causes of the change; whether urged on by a spirit of innovation, or popular delusion, or state necessity, (as it is falsely called,) it is still power, irresponsible power, against right; and the more to be dreaded, when it has the sanction of numbers, because it is then less capable of being resisted or evaded. Unfortunately, at such times the majority prevail by mere numbers, and not by force of judgment; *numerantur, non ponderantur.* I do not, therefore, overestimate its value, when I say, that a knowledge of the law and a devotion to its principles are vital to a republic, and lie at the very foundation of its strength.

An American citizen has many political duties to perform; and his activity is constantly demanded for the preservation of the public interests. He must watch the exercise of power in every department of government; and ascertain, whether it is within the prescribed limits of the constitution. He is to study deeply and thoroughly the elements, which compose that constitution; elements, which were the slow results of genius and patriotism, acting upon the largest views of human experience. The reasons, on which every part of this beautiful system is built, (may it be as durable as it is beautiful!) are to be examined and weighed. Slight inconveniences are not to overturn them; slight objections are not to undermine them. Whatever is human is necessarily imperfect; whatever is practical necessarily deviates from theory; whatever works by human agency works with some inequality of movement and result. It is easier to point out defects than to devise remedies; to touch blemishes than to extract them; to demolish an edifice than to erect a convenient substitute. We may not say of forms of government, "Whate'er is best administered is best." But we may say, that that, which generally works well, should rarely be hazarded upon the chances of a better. It has been observed by a profound statesman, that the abstract perfection of a government, with reference to natural rights, may be its practical defect. By having a right to do every thing, men may want every thing.[1] Great vigilance and great jealousy are therefore necessary in republics, to guard against the captivations of theory, as well as the approaches of more insidious foes. Governments are not always overthrown by direct and open assaults. They are not always battered down by the arms of conquerors, or the successful daring of usurpers. There is often concealed the dry rot, which eats into the vitals, when all is fair and stately on the outside. And to republics this has been the more common and fatal disease. The continual drippings of corruption may wear away the solid rock, when the tempest has failed to overturn it. In a monarchy, the subjects may be content to trust to the hereditary sovereign and the hereditary nobility the general superintendence of legislation and property. But in a republic, every citizen is himself in some measure intrusted with the public safety, and acts an important part for its weal or woe.

Our government also opens the widest field for talents and exertion to every rank of life. Few men, comparatively speaking, may not indulge the hope, if they covet the distinction, at some time to have a seat in the public councils, and assist in the public legislation. What can be more important or useful in such a station, than a knowledge of those laws, which the legislator is called upon to modify, amend or repeal? How much doubt may a single injudicious amendment introduce! One would hardly trust to an unskilful artisan the repairs of any delicate machine. There would be an universal exclamation against the indiscretion of such an attempt. Yet it would seem, that we are apt to think, that men are

[1] Burke on the French Revolution. The whole passage is worthy of commendation. It begins thus: "Government is not made in virtue of natural rights, which may and do exist in total independence of it, and exist in much greater clearness, and in a much greater degree of abstract perfection. But their abstract perfection is their practical defect."

born legislators; that no qualifications beyond plain sense and common honesty are necessary for the management of the intricate machine of government; and, above all, of that most delicate and interesting of all machines, a republican government. To adjust its various parts requires the skill of the wisest, and often baffles the judgment of the best. The least perturbation at the centre may transmit itself through every line of its movements; as the dip of a pebble on the calm surface of a lake sends its circling vibrations to the distant shore.

It is a fact well known, to professional gentlemen, that more doubts arise in the administration of justice from the imperfections of positive legislation, than from any other source. The mistakes in the language of a deed, or a will, rarely extend far beyond the immediate parties to the contract or bounty. And yet innumerable questions of interpretation have arisen from these comparatively private sources of litigation, to perplex the minds, and exhaust the diligence of the ablest judges. But what is this to the sweeping result of an act of the legislature, which declares a new rule for a whole state, which may vary the rights, or touch the interests, or control the operations, of thousands of its citizens? If the legislation is designedly universal in its terms, infinite caution is necessary, to prevent its working greater mischiefs than it purports to cure. If, on the other hand, it aims only at a single class of mischiefs, to amend an existing defect, or provide for a new interest, there is still great danger, that its provisions may reach beyond the intent, and embrace what would have been most sedulously excluded if it had been foreseen or suspected. An anecdote of Lord Coke may serve as an appropriate illustration. A statesman told him that he meant to consult him on a point of law. "If it be common law," said Lord Coke, "I should be ashamed if I could not give you a ready answer; but if it be statute law I should be equally ashamed if I answered you immediately." [1]

[1] Teignmouth's Life of Sir W. Jones, 268.

What an admonition is this! And how forcibly does it teach us the utility of a knowledge of the general principles of law to persons who are called upon to perform the functions of legislation!

But to gentlemen who contemplate public life with higher objects, who indulge the ambition of being not silent voters, but leaders in debate, and framers of laws, and guides in the public councils, every consideration already urged applies with tenfold force. I will not speak of the disgrace and defeat which must in such stations follow upon the exposure of ignorance; nor of the easy victory achieved by those who bring to the controversy a ready knowledge over those who grope in the dark and rely on their own rashness for success; nor of the intrinsic difficulty, in times like the present, of commanding public confidence without bringing solid wisdom in aid of popular declamation. But I would speak to the consciences of honorable men, and ask how they can venture, without any knowledge of existing laws, to recommend changes which may cut deep into the quick of remedial justice, or bring into peril all that is valuable in jurisprudence by its certainty, its policy, or its antiquity. Surely, they need not be told, how slow every good system of laws must be in consolidating; and how easily the rashness of an hour may destroy what ages have scarcely cemented in a solid form. The oak, which requires centuries to rear its trunk, and stretch its branches, and strengthen its fibres, and fix its roots, may yet be levelled in an hour. It may breast the tempest of a hundred years, and survive the scathing of the lightning. It may even acquire vigor from its struggles with the elements, and strike its roots deeper and wider as it rises in its majesty; and yet a child, in the very wantonness of folly, may in an instant destroy it by removing a girdle of its bark.

It has been said, that a spirit of innovation is generally the result of a selfish temper and confined views.[1] Perhaps this is pressing the reasoning too far. It is more often the

[1] Burke on the French Revolution.

result of a strong imagination and ardent temperament, working upon the materials of the closet. But it is well in all cases to remember the wise recommendation of Lord Bacon, "that men in their innovations would follow the example of time itself; which, indeed, innovateth greatly, but quietly, and by degrees scarce to be perceived."[1] And nothing can introduce more sobriety of judgment than the experience derived from the history of jurisprudence; and thus check what has been so happily termed too great a fluidness, lubricity, and unsteadiness in the laws.[2]

It is not, therefore, from mere professional pride or enthusiasm, that I would urgently recommend to gentlemen, ambitious of public life, some devotion to the study of the law; or suggest to scholars that their education still wants perfection and polish, unless they have mastered its elements. In doing so, I do little more than adopt the precept of Mr. Locke, who says it is so requisite, that he knows of no place, from a justice of the peace to a minister of state, that can be well filled without it.[3] And in the days of Fortescue it was esteemed almost a necessary accomplishment for a gentleman of rank.[4]

But my principal object in this discourse is, to address myself to those who intend to make the law a profession for life. To them it seems almost unnecessary to recommend the study, or press the ancient precept,

> "Versate diu, quid ferre recusent,
> Quid valeant humeri."

To them the law is not a mere pursuit of pleasure or curiosity, but of transcendent dignity, as it opens the brightest rewards of human ambition, opulence, fame, public influence, and political honors. I may add, too, that if the student of the law entertains but a just reverence for its precepts, it will

[1] Essay, 24.
[2] Lord Hale in Harg. Tracts, 255.
[3] Locke on Education, p. 84.
[4] Fortescue De Legg. ch. 49.

teach him to build his reputation upon the soundest morals, the deepest principles, and the most exalted purity of life and character. One of the beautiful boasts of our municipal jurisprudence is, that Christianity is a part of the common law, from which it seeks the sanction of its rights, and by which it endeavors to regulate its doctrines. And, notwithstanding the specious objection of one of our distinguished statesmen, the boast is as true as it is beautiful. There never has been a period in which the common law did not recognize Christianity as lying at its foundations.[1] For many ages it was almost exclusively administered by those who held its ecclesiastical dignities. It now repudiates every act done in violation of its duties of perfect obligation. It pronounces illegal every contract offensive to its morals. It recognizes with profound humility its holidays and festivals, and obeys them as *dies non juridici.* It still attaches to persons believing in its divine authority the highest degree of competency as witnesses; and, until a comparatively recent period, infidels and pagans were banished from the halls of justice, as unworthy of credit. The error of the common law was, in reality, of a very different character. It tolerated nothing but Christianity, as taught by its own established church, either Protestant or Catholic; and with unrelenting severity consigned the conscientious heretic to the stake, regarding his very scruples as proofs of incorrigible wickedness. Thus, justice was debased, and religion itself made the minister of crimes, by calling in the aid of the secular power to enforce that conformity of belief, whose rewards and punishments belong exclusively to God.

But, apart from this defect, the morals of the law are of the purest and most irreproachable character. And notwithstanding the sneers of ignorance and the gibes of wit, no men are so constantly called upon in their practice to exemplify the duties of good faith, incorruptible virtue, and chivalric honor,

1 See the remarks of Mr. Justice Park, in Smith *v.* Sparrow, 4 Bing. R. 84, 88.

as lawyers. To them is often intrusted the peace and repose as well as the property of whole families; and the slightest departure from professional secrecy, or professional integrity, might involve their clients in ruin. The law itself imposes upon them the severest injunctions never to do injustice, and never to violate confidence. It not only protects them from disclosing the secrets of their clients, but it punishes the offenders by disqualifying them from practice. The rebuke of public opinion, also, follows close upon every offence; and the frown of the profession consigns to infamy the traitor and his moral treason. Memorable instances of this sort have occurred in other ages as well as in our own. Even the lips of eloquence breathe nothing but an empty voice in the halls of justice, if the ear listens with distrust or suspicion. The very hypocrite is there compelled to wear the livery of virtue, and to pay her homage. If he secretly cherishes a grovelling vice, he must there speak the language and assume the port of innocence. He must feign, if he does not feel, the spirit and inspiration of the place.

I would exhort the student, therefore, at the very outset of his career, to acquire a just conception of the dignity and importance of his vocation. Let him not debase it by a low and narrow estimate of its requisites or its duties. Let him consider it not as a mere means of subsistence, an affair of petty traffic and barter, a little round of manœuvres and contrivances to arrest some runaway contract, to disinter some buried relic of title, or let loose some imprisoned wrong from the vengeance of the law. Let him not dream that all is well if he can weave an intricate net of special pleadings to catch the unwary in its meshes; or hang a doubt upon a subtile distinction; or quibble through the whole alphabet of sophisms. Let him not imagine that it is sufficient if he be the thing described by Cicero in his scorn; — "jurisconsultus ipse per se nihil, nisi leguleius quidam cautus et acutus, præco actionum, cantor formularum, auceps syllabarum;" [1]

[1] Cicero, De Orat. Lib. i. § 55.

"a sharp and cunning pettifogger; a retailer of lawsuits; a canter about forms, and a caviller upon words;" — or one of the tribe defined by a master-spirit of the last age, as the ministers of municipal litigation, and the fomenters of the war of village vexation.[1] God forbid that any man standing in the temple and in the presence of the law, should imagine that her ministers are called to such unworthy offices. No. The profession has far higher aims and nobler purposes.[2] In the ordinary course of business, it is true, that sound learning, industry, and fidelity are the principal requisites, and may reap a fair reward, as they may in any other employment of life. But there are some, and in the lives of most lawyers many occasions, which demand qualities of a higher, nay, of the highest order. Upon the actual administration of justice in all governments, and especially in free governments, must depend the welfare of the whole community. The sacred rights of property are to be guarded at every point. I call them sacred, because, if they are unprotected, all other rights become worthless or visionary. What is personal liberty, if it does not draw after it the right to enjoy the fruits of our own industry? What is political liberty, if it imparts only perpetual poverty to us and all our posterity? What is the privilege of a vote, if the majority of the hour may sweep away the earnings of our whole lives, to gratify the rapacity of the indolent, the cunning, or the profligate, who are borne into power upon the tide of a temporary popularity? What remains to nourish a spirit of independence, or a love of country, if the very soil, on which we tread, is ours only at the beck of the village tyrant? If the home of our parents, which nursed our infancy and protected our manhood, may be torn from us without recompense or remorse? If the very graveyards, which contain the memorials of our love and our

1 Burke's Reflections on the French Revolution.

2 I would commend to students the perusal of Mr. (now Judge) Hopkinson's Address before the Law Academy of Philadelphia, in 1826. It abounds with just remarks, chaste diction, and unpretending eloquence. Its matters and its style are excellent.

sorrow, are not secure against the hands of violence? If the church of yesterday may be the barrack of to-day, and become the gaol of to-morrow? If the practical text of civil procedure contains no better gloss than the Border maxim, that the right to plunder is only bounded by the power?

One of the glorious and not unfrequently perilous duties of the Bar is the protection of property; and not of property only, but of personal rights, and personal character; of domestic peace, and parental authority. The lawyer is placed, as it were, upon the outpost of defence, as a public sentinel, to watch the approach of danger, and to sound the alarm when oppression is at hand. It is a post not only full of observation but of difficulty. It is his duty to resist wrong, let it come in whatever form it may. The attack is rarely commenced in open daylight; but it makes its approaches by dark and insidious degrees. Some captivating delusion, some crafty pretext, some popular scheme, generally masks the real design. Public opinion has been already won in its favor, or drugged into a stupid indifference to its results, by the arts of intrigue. Nothing, perhaps, remains between the enterprise and victory, but the solitary citadel of public justice. It is then the time for the highest efforts of the genius, and learning, and eloquence, and moral courage of the Bar. The advocate not unfrequently finds himself, at such a moment, putting at hazard the popularity of a life devoted to the public service. It is then that the denunciations of the press may be employed to overawe or intimidate him. It is then that the shouts of the multitude drown the still, small voice of the unsheltered sufferer. It is then that the victim is already bound for immolation; and the advocate stands alone, to maintain the supremacy of the law against power, and numbers, and public applause, and private wealth. If he shrinks from his duty, he is branded as the betrayer of his trust. If he fails in his labor, he may be cut down by the same blow which levels his client. If he succeeds, he may, indeed, achieve a glorious triumph for truth, and justice, and the law. But that very triumph may be fatal to his future hopes, and bar up for ever the road to political honors. Yet what can be more interesting than ambition thus nobly directed? that sinks itself, but saves the state? What sacrifice more pure, than in such a cause? What martyrdom more worthy to be canonized in our hearts?

It may be, that his profession calls him to different duties. He may be required to defend against the arm of the government a party standing charged with some odious crime, real or imaginary. He is not at liberty to desert even the guilty wretch in his lowest estate; but he is bound to take care that even here the law shall not be bent or broken to bring him to punishment. He will, at such times, from love of the law, as well as from compassion, freely give his talents to the cause, and never surrender the victim until the judgment of his peers has convicted him upon legal evidence. A duty not less common, or less interesting, is the vindication of innocence against private injustice. Rank, and wealth, and patronage may be on one side; and poverty and distress on the other. The oppressor may belong to the very circle of society in which we love to move, and where many seductive influences may be employed to win our silence. The advocate may be called upon to require damages from the seducer for his violation of domestic peace; or to expose to public scorn the subtle contrivances of fraud. The ardor of youth may have been ensnared by cunningly devised counsels to the ruin of his estate. The drivelling of age may have been imposed on to procure a grant or a will, by which nature is outraged and villany rewarded. Religion itself may have been treacherously employed at the side of the death-bed to devour the widow's portion, or plunder the orphan. In these and many other like cases, the attempt to unravel the fraud, and expose the injury, is full of delicacy, and may incur severe displeasure among friends, and yield a triumph to enemies. But it is on such occasions that the advocate rises to a full sense of the dignity of his profession, and feels the power and the responsibility of its duties. He must then lift himself to thoughts of other days, and other times; to the great moral obligations of his profession; to the eternal precepts of religion; to the dictates of that voice which speaks within him from beyond the grave, and demands that the mind, given by God, shall be devoted to his service, without the fear, and without the frailty of man.

But, whatever may be the dignity and the brilliancy either of fame or fortune, which the profession holds out to those who strive for eminence in the law, the student should never imagine that the ascent is easy, or the labor light. There cannot be any delusion cherished more fatal to his ultimate success than this. Young men of gay and ardent temperaments are apt to imagine, that little more is necessary than to read a few elementary books with reasonable diligence, and the rewards are already within their grasp. They fondly indulge the belief that fluency of speech, a kindling imagination, ready wit, graceful action, and steady self-confidence will carry them through every struggle. If they can but address a court or jury without perturbation, and state their points with clearness and order, the rest may fairly be left to the workings of their own minds upon the excitements of the occasion. That, because the hour is come, and the trial is come, the inspiration for the cause will come also.

Whoever shall indulge in such visionary views will find his career end in grievous disappointment, if not in disgrace. I know not if among human sciences there is any one which requires such various qualifications and extensive attainments as the law. While it demands the first order of talents, genius alone never did, and never can, win its highest elevations. There is not only no royal road to smoothe the way to the summit, but the passes, like those of Alpine regions, are sometimes dark and narrow; sometimes bold and precipitous; sometimes dazzling from the reflected light of their naked fronts; and sometimes bewildering from the shadows projecting from their dizzy heights. Whoever advances for safety must advance slowly. He must cautiously follow the old guides, and toil on with steady footsteps; for the old paths, though well beaten, are rugged; and the new paths, though broad, are still perplexed. To drop all metaphor, the law is a science, in which there is no substitute for diligence and labor. It is a fine remark of one who is himself a brilliant example of all he teaches, that "It appears to be the general order of Providence, manifested in the constitution of our nature, that every thing valuable in human acquisition should be the result of toil and labor." [1] But this truth is nowhere more forcibly manifested than in the law. Here, moderate talents with unbroken industry have often obtained a victory over superior genius, and cast into shade the brightest natural parts.

The student, therefore, should, at his first entrance upon the study, weigh well the difficulties of his task, not merely to guard himself against despondency on account of expectations too sanguinely indulged, but also to stimulate his zeal by a proper estimate of the value of perseverance. He who has learned to survey the labor without dismay, has achieved half the victory. I will not say, with Lord Hale, that "The law will admit of no rival, and nothing to go even with it;" but I will say, that it is a jealous mistress, and requires a long and constant courtship. It is not to be won by trifling favors, but by lavish homage.

Many causes combine to make the study of the common law, at the present day, a laborious undertaking. In the first place, it necessarily embraces the reasoning and doctrines of very remote ages. It is, as has been elegantly said, "The gathered wisdom of a thousand years;" [2] or, in the language of one of the greatest of English judges, it is not "the product of the wisdom of some one man, or society of men, in any

1 Chancellor Kent's Introductory Discourse, p. 8. Why has this finished Discourse been withdrawn from his Commentaries?

2 Teignmouth's Life of Sir W. Jones, 100.

one age; but of the wisdom, counsel, experience, and observation of many ages of wise and observing men."[1] It is a system having its foundations in natural reason; but, at the same time, built up and perfected by artificial doctrines, adapted and moulded to the artificial structure of society. The law, for instance, which governs the titles to real estate, is principally derived from the feudal polity and usages, and is in a great measure unintelligible without an intimate acquaintance with the peculiarities of that system. This knowledge is not, even now, in all cases easily attainable; but must sometimes be searched out amidst the dusty ruins of antiquity, or traced back through black-lettered pages of a most forbidding aspect both in language and matter. The old law, too, is not only of an uncouth and uninviting appearance; but it abounds with nice distinctions, and subtile refinements, which enter deeply into the modern structure of titles. No man, even in our day, can venture safely upon the exposition of an intricate devise, or of the effect of a power of appointment, or of a deed to lead uses and trusts, who has not, in some good degree, mastered its learning. More than two centuries ago, Sir Henry Spelman[2] depicted his own distress on entering upon such studies, when at the very vestibule he was met by a foreign language, a barbarous dialect, an inelegant method, and a mass of learning, which could be borne only upon the shoulders of Atlas; and frankly admitted, that his heart sunk within him at the prospect. The defects of a foreign tongue, and barbarous dialect, and inelegant method, have almost entirely disappeared, and no longer vex the student in his midnight vigils. But the materials for his labor have in other respects greatly accumulated in the intermediate period. He may, perchance, escape from the dry severity of the Year-Books, and the painful digestion of the Abridgments of Statham, Fitzherbert, and Brooke. He may even venture to glide

[1] Lord Hale in Preface to Rolle's Abridgment, 1 Coll. Jurid. 266.

[2] Preface to his Glossary. The passage is partially quoted in 1 Blackstone's Com. 31, note. See, also, p. 227, *supra*.

by the exhausting arguments of Plowden. But Lord Coke, with his ponderous Commentaries, will arrest his course; and, faint and disheartened with the view, he must plunge into the labyrinths of contingent remainders, and executory devises, and springing uses; and he may deem himself fortunate, if, after many years' devotion to Fearne, he may venture upon the interpretation of that darkest of all mysteries, a last will and testament. So true it is, that no man knows his own will so ill, as the testator; and that over-solicitude to be brief and simple ends in being profoundly enigmatical, "*Dum brevis esse laboro, obscurus fio.*"

In the next place, as has been already hinted, every successive age brings its own additions to the general mass of antecedent principles. If something is gained by clearing out the old channels, much is added by new increments and deposits. If here and there a spring of litigation is dried up, many new ones break out in unsuspected places. In fact, there is scarcely a single branch of the law, which belonged to the age of Queen Elizabeth, which does not now come within the daily contemplation of a lawyer of extensive practice. And all these branches have been spreading to an incalculable extent since that period, by the changes in society, wrought by commerce, agriculture, and manufactures, and other efforts of human ingenuity and enterprise.

We are, therefore, called upon at this moment to encounter, ay, and to master, the judicial learning of the three last centuries, during which the talents of the Bar, and the researches of the Bench are embodied in solid and enduring volumes. Fortescue[1] has told us, that in his age the judges did not sit in court but three hours in the day; and that, when they had taken their refreshments, they spent the rest of the day in the study of the law, reading of the Holy Scriptures, and other innocent amusements, at their pleasure; so that it seemed rather a life of contemplation than of much action; and that

[1] Fortescue, De Laud. Legum Angliæ, cap. 51.

their time was spent in this manner, free from care and worldly avocations. The case was greatly changed in the succeeding century; and we need but examine the ample reports and commentaries of Lord Coke, to perceive what a prodigious influx of learning bore down the profession in his day. At the distance of another century, Lord Hale was compelled to admit the heavy and almost overwhelming burdens of the law. And we in the nineteenth century may well look with some apprehension upon the accumulations of our own times. It is not an overstatement to declare, that the labors of the profession now are ten times as great as they were in the days of Lord Coke; and that they have been quadrupled within the last century. The whole series of English reports, down to the Revolution of 1688, scarcely exceeds one hundred volumes; while those since that period fall little short of three hundred. To this goodly mass America has added, within the short space of twenty years, more than two hundred volumes. If to these we add the excellent elementary treatises, which have filled our libraries during these latter periods, we shall find, that not merely the lucubrations of twenty years, but a long life, will scarcely suffice to attain the requisite learning.

In truth, the common law, as a science, must be forever in progress; and no limits can be assigned to its principles or improvements. In this respect it resembles the natural sciences, where new discoveries continually lead the way to new, and sometimes to astonishing, results. To say, therefore, that the common law is never learned, is almost to utter a truism. It is no more than a declaration, that the human mind cannot compass all human transactions. It is its true glory, that it is flexible, and constantly expanding with the exigencies of society; that it daily presents new motives for new and loftier efforts; that it holds out forever an unapproached degree of excellence; that it moves onward in the path towards perfection, but never arrives at the ultimate point.

But the student should not imagine, that enough is done, if he has so far mastered the general doctrines of the common law, that he may enter with some confidence into practice. There are other studies, which demand his attention. He should addict himself to the study of philosophy, of rhetoric, of history, and of human nature. It is from the want of this enlarged view of duty, that the profession has sometimes been reproached with a sordid narrowness, with a low chicane, with a cunning avarice, and with a deficiency in liberal and enlightened policy. Mr. Burke has somewhat reluctantly admitted the fact, that the practice of the law is not apt, except in persons very happily born, to open and liberalize the mind exactly in the same proportion as it invigorates the understanding; and that men too much conversant in office are rarely minds of remarkable enlargement.[1] And Lord Bacon complains, that lawyers have never written as statesmen.[2] The reproach is in some measure deserved. It is, however, far less true in our age than in former times; and far less true in America than in England. Many of our most illustrious statesmen have been lawyers; but they have been lawyers liberalized by philosophy, and a large intercourse with the wisdom of ancient and modern times. The perfect lawyer, like the perfect orator, must accomplish himself for his duties by familiarity with every study. It may be truly said, that to him nothing, that concerns human nature or human art, is indifferent or useless. He should search the human heart, and explore to their sources the passions, and appetites, and feelings of mankind. He should watch the motions of the dark and malignant passions, as they silently approach the chambers of the soul in its first slumbers. He should catch the first warm rays of sympathy and benevolence, as they play around the character, and are reflected back from its varying lines. He should learn to detect the cunning arts

1 See Burke's Reflections on the French Revolution, and Speech on American Taxation.

2 Lord Bacon on the Advancement of Learning, 1 Bacon's Works, 218.

of the hypocrite, who pours into the credulous and unwary ear his leperous distilment. He should for this purpose make the master-spirits of all ages pay contribution to his labors. He should walk abroad through nature, and elevate his thoughts, and warm his virtues, by a contemplation of her beauty, and magnificence, and harmony. He should examine well the precepts of religion, as the only solid basis of civil society; and gather from them, not only his duty, but his hopes; not merely his consolations, but his discipline and his glory. He should unlock all the treasures of history for illustration, and instruction, and admonition. He will thus see man, as he has been, and thereby best know what he is. He will thus be taught to distrust theory, and cling to practical good; to rely more upon experience than reasoning; more upon institutions than laws; more upon checks to vice than upon motives to virtue. He will become more indulgent to human errors; more scrupulous in means, as well as in ends; more wise, more candid, more forgiving, more disinterested. If the melancholy infirmities of his race shall make him trust men less, he may yet learn to love man more.

Nor should he stop here. He must drink in the lessons and the spirit of philosophy. I do not mean that philosophy described by Milton, as

> " A perpetual feast of nectared sweets,
> Where no crude surfeit reigns; "

but that philosophy which is conversant with men's business and interests, with the policy and the welfare of nations; that philosophy, which dwells, not in vain imaginations, and Platonic dreams; but which stoops to life, and enlarges the boundaries of human happiness; that philosophy, which sits by us in the closet, cheers us by the fireside, walks with us in the fields and highways, kneels with us at the altars, and lights up the enduring flame of patriotism.

What has been already said rather presupposes than insists upon the importance of a full possession of the general literature of ancient and modern times. It is this classical learning alone, which can impart a solid and lasting polish to the mind, and give to diction that subtile elegance and grace which color the thoughts with almost transparent hues. It should be studied, not merely in its grave disquisitions, but in its glorious fictions, and in those graphical displays of the human heart, in the midst of which we wander as in the presence of familiar but disembodied spirits.

It is by such studies, and such accomplishments, that the means are to be prepared for excellence in the highest order of the profession. The student, whose ambition has measured them, if he can but add to them the power of eloquence, (that gift, which owes so much to nature, and so much to art,) may indeed aspire to be a perfect lawyer. It cannot be denied, indeed, that there have been great lawyers who were not orators; as there have been great orators who were not lawyers. But it must be admitted at the same time, that, when both characters are united in the same person, human genius has approached as near perfection as it may. They are kindred arts, and flourish best in the neighborhood of each other.[1]

The eloquence of the bar is far more various and difficult than that which is required in the pulpit, in the legislative hall, or in popular assemblies. It occasionally embraces all that belongs to each of these places, and it has, besides, many varieties of its own. In its general character it may be said to be grave, deliberative, and earnest, allowing little indulgence to fancy, and less to rhetoric. But, as it must necessarily change its tone, according to its subject, and the tribunal, to which it is addressed, whether the court or the jury, there is ample scope for the exercise of every sort of talent, and sometimes even for dramatic effect. On some occasions it throws aside all the little plays of phrase, the vivid touches of the pencil, and the pomp and parade of dic-

1 "Præclaras duas artes," says Cicero, "atque inter se pares, et ejusdem socias dignitatis." Cic. de Oratore, Lib. i. § 55.

tion. It is plain, direct, and authoritative. Its object is to convince the understanding, and captivate the judgment, by the strength and breadth of its reasoning. Its power is in the thought, and not in the expression; in the vigor of the blow from the hand of a giant; in the weight of the argument, which crushes, in its fall, what it has not levelled in its progress. At other times it is full of calm dignity and persuasiveness. It speaks with somewhat of the majesty of the law itself, in strains of deep, oracular import. It unfolds its results with an almost unconscious elegance, and its thoughts flash like the sparkles of the diamond. At other times it is earnest, impassioned, and electrifying; awing by its bold appeals, or blinding by its fiery zeal. At other times it is searching, and acute, and rigorous; now brilliant in point, now gay in allusion, now winning in insinuation. At other times it addresses the very souls of men in the most touching and pathetic admonitions. It then mingles with the close logic of the law those bewitching graces which soothe prejudice, disarm resentment, or fix attention. It utters language, as the occasion demands, which melts to pity, or fires with indignation, or exhorts to clemency.

But, whatever may be the variety of effort demanded of forensic eloquence, whether to convince, or captivate, or persuade, or inflame, or melt; still its main character must for ever be like the "grave rebuke," so finely sketched by our great epic poet, "severe in youthful beauty," that it may possess an "added grace invincible."[1] It may not stoop to ribaldry, or vulgar jests, or sickly sentimentality, or puerile conceits. It forbids declamation, and efflorescence of style. There is no room for the loquacity of ignorance, or the insolence of pride. If wit be allowable, it must be chaste and polished. The topics discussed in courts of justice are too grave for merriment, and too important for trifling. When life, or character, or fortune, hangs on the issue, they must be vindicated with dignity, as well as with force.

[1] Paradise Lost, Book iv. line 844.

But I forbear. I seem, indeed, when the recollection of the wonders wrought by eloquence comes over my thoughts, to live again in scenes long since past. The dead seem again summoned to their places in the halls of justice, and to utter forth voices of an unearthly and celestial harmony. The shades of Ames, and Dexter, and Pinkney, and Emmett pass and repass, not hush as the foot of night, but in all the splendor of their fame, fresh with the flush of recent victory. I may not even allude to the living. Long, long may they enjoy the privilege of being nameless here, whose names are everywhere else upon the lips of praise.

Enough has been said, perhaps more than enough, to satisfy the aspirant after juridical honors, that the path is arduous, and requires the vigor of a long and active life. Let him not, however, look back in despondency upon a survey of the labor. The triumph, if achieved, is worth the sacrifice. If not achieved, still he will have risen by the attempt, and will sustain a nobler rank in the profession. If he may not rival the sagacity of Hardwicke, the rich and lucid learning of Mansfield, the marvellous judicial eloquence of Stowell, the close judgment of Parsons, the comprehensive reasoning of Marshall, and the choice attainments of Kent; — yet he will, by the contemplation and study of such models, exalt his own sense of the dignity of the profession, and invigorate his own intellectual powers. He will learn that there is a generous rivalry at the bar; and that every one there has his proper station and fame assigned to him; and that, though one star differeth from another in glory, the light of each may yet be distinctly traced, as it moves on, until it is lost in that common distance, which buries all in a common darkness.

Having spoken thus much upon the dignity, the qualifications, and the duties of the profession, I trust it will not be supposed that we have the rashness to indulge the belief that the Law Institutions here, under the guidance of its present Professors, can fill up the outline which has thus been traced. My learned brother will, indeed, bring to the task of instruction, the ardor, the attainments, and the experience, which elsewhere have given him such an elevated reputation. Little, indeed, of what has been sketched out in this discourse, can be attained by any academical instruction during the usual period assigned for the preparatory studies for the bar. And of that little, we have not the presumption to believe, that our method or efforts can reach even our own wishes and opinions. What we propose is no more than plain, direct, familiar instruction; something to assist the student in the first steps of his studies; something to cheer him in his progress; something to disencumber him of difficulties by the wayside; and something to awaken a sincere ambition for professional excellence.

For myself, I am but too conscious how little I can bring to the task, worthy of the occasion. The perpetual round of judicial duties, full of anxious thoughts and anxious vigils, might, even at an earlier period of my life, have repressed the elasticity of hope. But in entering upon new duties at the present time, I confess myself more fearful of failure than ambitious of distinction. I may not say, with the enviable self-satisfaction of an eminent judge, now reposing in leisure sustained with dignity, that "Long absence from the bar, the consequent want of practice, age, the enjoyment of repose, and the indolence which that repose often produces, have increased my unwillingness to undertake a work of labor."[1] But I may say, in the language of a kindred mind to his, that, "After a certain age and portion of experience, the sense of duty becomes a stronger principle of action than the love of reputation."[2] I shall be content, therefore, if, able to meet the duties of the office, I shall not wholly disappoint the expectations of the founder, by whose kind solicitude I have been advanced to this chair. Indeed, I may say, that but from a desire to justify his early friendship, (as welcome as it was then unexpected,) and to express my own sense of his liberal donation, I should have declined a post

[1] Lord Resdesdale. [2] Chancellor Kent.

which others might fill with more undivided attention, though not, perhaps, with more sincere zeal. Under such circumstances, I hope that I may be permitted to occupy a few moments more, in expounding the objects of this professorship, and thus demonstrate the wisdom and munificence of the founder.

The duties assigned to the Dane Professorship are, in the first instance, to deliver lectures upon the Law of Nature, the Law of Nations, Maritime and Commercial Law, Equity Law, and, lastly, the Constitutional Law of the United States. No reflecting man can hesitate to admit the importance of these branches of jurisprudence, and their intimate connection with the best interests of civilized society. To comment on either of them fully and worthily might well employ the diligence of a long life, without exhaustion or repetition. A course of lectures, therefore, which embraces them all, must necessarily treat them in a brief, summary, and imperfect manner. It must suggest matter for inquiry, rather than expound principles with copiousness. It must excite, rather than satisfy, curiosity. It must illustrate by examples, rather than exhaust by analysis. It must display the foundations, rather than the size or exact proportions, of the edifice. It must, if I may venture upon such a metaphor, conduct the inquirer to the vestibule of the temple of jurisprudence; and leave to his future curiosity the survey of its magnificent halls, its decorated columns, its splendid porticos, its harmonized orders, its massive walls, its varied crypts, its lofty domes, its "ever-during gates, on golden hinges moving."

And first, the law of nature. This lies at the foundation of all other laws, and constitutes the first step in the science of jurisprudence. The law of nature is nothing more than those rules which human reason deduces from the various relations of man, to form his character, and regulate his conduct, and thereby insure his permanent happiness. It embraces a survey of his duties to God, his duties to himself, and his duties to his fellow men; deducing from those duties a corresponding obligation. It considers man, not merely in his private relations as a social being, but as a subject and magistrate, called upon to frame, administer, and obey laws; and owing allegiance to his country and government; and bound, from the protection he derives from the institutions of society, to uphold and protect them in return. It is, therefore, in the largest sense, the philosophy of morals; what Justinian has defined justice to be: "*Constans et perpetua voluntas jus suum cuique tribuendi;*" or what may be denominated national jurisprudence, as expounded by the same authority: "*Divinarum atque humanarum rerum notitia, justi atque injusti scientia.*" With us, indeed, who form a part of the Christian community of nations, the law of nature has a higher sanction, as it stands supported and illustrated by revelation. Christianity, while with many minds it acquires authority from its coincidences with the law of nature, as deduced from reason, has added strength and dignity to the latter by its positive declarations. It goes farther. It unfolds our duties with far more clearness and perfection than had been known before its promulgation; and has given a commanding force to those of imperfect obligation. It relieves the mind from many harassing doubts and disquietudes; and imparts a blessed influence to the peaceful and benevolent virtues, to mercy, charity, humility, and gratitude. It seems to concentrate all morality in the simple precept of love to God and love to man. It points out the original equality of all mankind in the eyes of the Supreme Being, and brings down the monarch to the level of his subjects. It thus endeavors to check the arrogance of power, and the oppression of prerogative; and becomes the teacher as well as the advocate of rational liberty. Above all, by unfolding, in a more authoritative manner, the doctrine of the immortality of the soul, it connects all the motives and actions of man in his present state with his future interminable destiny. It thus exhorts him to the practice of virtue by all that can awaken hope or secure happiness. It deters him from crimes, by all that can operate upon his fears, his sensibility, or his conscience. It teaches him that the present life is but the dawn of being; and that in the endless progress of things the slightest movement here may communicate an impulse which may be felt through eternity. Thus, Christianity becomes, not merely an auxiliary, but a guide, to the law of nature; establishing its conclusions, removing its doubts, and elevating its precepts.

In this manner it is that the law of nature involves a consideration of the nature, faculties, and responsibilities of man. From his intellectual powers, and the freedom of his will, it deduces his moral perceptions and accountability. From his love of happiness, as the end and aim of his being, it deduces the duty of preserving that happiness. From his dependence upon the Supreme Being, whose will has indissolubly connected virtue with happiness, it deduces the primary duty of obedience to that will. From these simple elements, it proceeds to consider him in the various relations of life, in which he may be placed, and ascertains in each his obligations and duties. It considers him as a solitary being, as a member of a family, as a parent, and lastly, as a member of the commonwealth.

The consideration of this last relation introduces us at once to the most interesting and important topics; the nature, objects, and end of government; the institution of marriage; the origin of the rights of property; the nature and limits of social liberty; the structure of civil and political rights; the authority and policy of laws; and, indeed, all those institutions which form the defence and the ornament of civilized society.[1]

Upon many of these topics, of which a very imperfect

[1] Mr. Hoffman's Legal Outlines, of which the first volume only is yet published, contains some very interesting and valuable disquisitions upon several of the topics belonging to this branch of law. I trust the learned author will soon favor the public with the residue of his work.

sketch can here be given, I shall speak with much brevity and reserve, for two reasons. In the first place, in the course of the academical instruction in this University already provided for, the subjects of ethics, natural law, and theology, are assigned to other professors. In the next place, in the elementary education, everywhere passed through before entering upon juridical studies, they are usually taught with sufficient fulness and accuracy.

In the second place, the Law of Nations. By this we are to understand, not merely that portion of public law which is generally recognized among nations (as seems to have been the prevailing sense of the phrase in the Roman code,) but that portion of public law which regulates the intercourse, adjusts the rights, and forms the basis, of the commercial and political relations of states with each other. Perhaps the most appropriate name would be, International Law, *jus inter gentes.* It has in this view been very correctly subdivided into three sorts; first, the natural or necessary law of nations, in which the principles of natural justice are applied to the intercourse between states; secondly, the customary law of nations, which embodies those usages which the continued habit of nations has sanctioned for their mutual interest and convenience; and thirdly, the conventional or diplomatic law of nations, which embraces positive compacts by treaties and conventions between nations, and derives its sole obligation from the same sources as other contracts. Under this last head many regulations will now be found which at first resulted from custom, or a general sense of justice, and are now made of positive obligation, for the purpose of preventing national disputes and collisions.

Upon the general theory of the law of nations, much has been written by authors of great ability and celebrity. At the head of the list stands that most extraordinary man Grotius, whose treatise, *de Jure Belli et Pacis,* was the first great effort in modern times to reduce into any order the principles belonging to this branch of jurisprudence, by deducing them from the history and practice of nations, and the incidental opinions of philosophers, orators, and poets. His eulogy has been already pronounced in terms of high commendation, but so just and so true that it were vain to follow or add to his praise.[1] Puffendorf, in a dry, didactic manner, has drawn out, in the language of the times, much to strengthen the conclusions of his master upon natural law; and the sagacity of Barbeyrac, in his luminous Commentaries, has cleared away many obscurities, and vindicated many positions. Wolfius, who is better known among us in his elegant abridger, Vattel, has more elaborately discussed the theory with the improved lights of modern days. And Ward, in his unpretending, but exact, Inquiry into the Foundation and History of the Law of Nations in Europe, from the time of the Greeks and Romans to the age of Grotius, has afforded ample materials for illustration and profound reflection. Bynkershoeck is a writer of a very different cast; and in a clear, bold, and uncompromising manner, lays down his principles, as practical results, with a brevity and vigor, which give them almost the authority of a text-book. He is not, however, a mere apologist, or collector of usages; but he insists, with an animated vehemence, that reason is the very soul of the law of nations. "*Ratio ipso, inquam, ratio juris gentium est anima.*"[2]

But I know not if there be in existence any treatise on this subject which, in point of fulness and accuracy of principles, or copiousness of detail, is adapted to the exigencies of modern society, or is calculated in any moderate degree to satisfy the expectations of a scholar or a publicist. There

[1] Sir James Mackintosh, in his Introductory Discourse on the Law of Nations.

[2] Bynker. Quest. Pub. Jur. ch. 2. Mr. Du Ponceau's Translation of this work is a most valuable present to the profession. Indeed, when one considers the liberal and acute spirit which pervades all the juridical publications of Mr. Du Ponceau, it is matter of universal regret that he has not exclusively devoted his life to the exposition of law, and particularly of the civil law.

is yet living a man[1] whose character, as a philosophical moralist, enlightened statesman, and liberal jurist, commands universal respect, who taught us in his early performances that to his genius we might thereafter owe such an invaluable donation. But the lapse of thirty years, and the seductive influence of other studies, lead us now to fear that our hopes will end in disappointment. Such a treatise should embrace, among other things, a general view of the sovereignty, equality, and independence of nations; the rights of public domain, and territorial jurisdiction in rivers, bays, lakes, and streams, and the ocean; the intercourse of nations in times of peace in respect to commerce and navigation; the immunities, and liabilities, and privileges of foreigners; the rights and duties of ambassadors and other ministers; the grounds of just war; the rights and duties of belligerents and neutrals, and the limits of just hostilities; the rights of conquest; the nature of piracy; the nature and effect of alliances, armistices, passports, and safe-conducts; and the negotiation, interpretation, and obligation of treaties of peace and other treaties.

My object will be, in the discussion of these topics, to expound the general theory with as much conciseness as the nature of the case will admit; and to devote my principal labor to the development of those practical results, which are of perpetual application in the common business of life, and regulate the daily concerns of individuals and nations, in peace and in war. For this purpose, I shall adventure far more than has been usual with publicists, into an examination of those general principles of jurisprudence, which affect the contracts, govern the titles, and limit the remedies of the subjects of independent powers, who acquire rights, or contract obligations, or succeed to property, or are in any measure subjected to the municipal law in a foreign country. This will include a variety of delicate and interesting topics

1 Sir James Mackintosh. [He is since dead.]

belonging to the operation of foreign jurisprudence, or, as it is sometimes called, the *lex fori et lex loci*. Among these are the law of foreign domicil and expatriation; of foreign marriages, divorces, and crimes; of foreign testaments, and successions *ab intestato;* of foreign grants and agreements; of foreign prescriptions, limitations, presumptions, discharges, and judgments; of foreign asylum to deserters and fugitives; and, as incidental, the nature and extent of the jurisdiction, exercised by courts of law in enforcing rights between foreigners, or giving effect to the municipal prohibitions of foreign countries. I shall also adventure upon an ample discussion of the law of prize, including therein the law of captures, and recaptures, and reprisal, the law of postliminy, and the law of contraband, and blockade, and illegal trade. And, as a fit conclusion of such a discussion, I shall give a summary view of the practice and jurisprudence of those tribunals, emphatically called courts of the law of nations, which in every country are ordained to administer this important branch of public law. In England and America, this jurisdiction is vested in the courts of admiralty. In this part of my labors I shall freely use the materials, which have been furnished by those distinguished civilians, who have from time to time adorned the English and American courts of admiralty. And, above all, I shall endeavor to avail myself of those masterly judgments, full of wisdom, and learning, and captivating eloquence, which have been pronounced within the last thirty years by a man[1] to whom, in my deliberate opinion, the world is more indebted for a practical exposition of the law of nations upon the eternal principles of justice and reason, than to all the jurists of all former ages.

In the next place, Equity Jurisprudence. This is a very comprehensive head of our municipal law, and in its actual administration probably embraces as great a variety and

[1] Lord Stowell, (late Sir William Scott.)

extent of learning, as the aggregate of all those, which now fall within the jurisdiction of the courts of common law, in the strict sense of the terms. The jurisdiction in equity is sometimes concurrent with courts of common law, as in matters of account, partition, and dower; and sometimes it is exclusive and paramount. Its exclusive jurisdiction covers an immense mass of doctrines, relative to truths, frauds, mistakes, and accidents, and other cases, which the remedial justice of the common law courts cannot reach. It is a common, but groundless notion, that equity consists in the administration of a sort of discretionary justice; and is not, like the common law, built upon exact principles and settled rules; that it is a transcendental power, acting above the law, and superseding and annulling its operations, and resting in an undefined and arbitrary judgment, at best the *arbitrium boni viri*, rather than *boni jurisconsulti*. There is, therefore, among those, who have not cultivated it as a science, a spectral dread of it, as if some unquiet spirit walked abroad to disturb the repose of titles, and revive forgotten and dormant claims. It is strange, that such a delusion should find countenance, even within the pale of the profession itself. There is not, at the present moment, a single department of the law, which is more completely fenced in by principle, or that is better limited by considerations of public convenience, both in doctrine and discipline, than equity. It is an intricate, but an exquisitely finished system, wrought up with infinite care, and almost uniformly rational and just in its conclusions. Indeed, that portion of the common law, which is now most admired for its sound policy, derives its principal attraction from its being founded in a large and liberal equity, and therefore is assumed as a rule equally at Paris and at London, at Rome and at Washington. If it would not occupy too much space in an introductory discourse, I might vindicate these assertions against every objection. But this is not the time, or the occasion.

In the next place, Commercial and Maritime Law. By

commercial law, we are accustomed to understand those branches of jurisprudence, which regulate the operations of trade at home and abroad; and by maritime law, those, which concern navigation, shipments, commerce, and other transactions on the sea. In truth, they are perpetually running into each other, as the streams of many rivers flow into the ocean, and form a part of its mass of waters, and are almost incapable of an absolute separation. There can be little need to descant upon the value and importance of this part of our jurisprudence. It is the golden chain, which connects the nations of the earth, and binds them together in the closest union. It comes home to every man's business and bosom; and is as captivating by the philosophy of its doctrines, as it is commendable for its sound morals, its flexible adaptations, and its enlightened policy. Much of its excellence, it must be admitted, is the growth of modern times. Its history may easily be traced back to the classical shores of the Mediterranean, where maritime enterprise, upon the revival of letters, spread itself with wonderful rapidity and success. It succeeded the age of chivalry; and, by blending the common interests of nations, it softened the manners, and subdued the barbarous spirit of rivals and adversaries. The customs of trade and navigation soon acquired the authority of law; and assisted by the persuasive equity of the Roman law of contract, (then much studied and admired, and still entitled to profound admiration,) it silently pervaded all Europe, from the farther Calabria to the frozen Baltic. The *Consolato del Mare*, which still instructs us by the wisdom of its precepts, is but a collection of the rules and maxims of this voluntary international code. The celebrated Ordinance of Louis the Fourteenth (which will be gratefully remembered, when his ambitious projects are lost in the dimness of tradition) is little more than a text gathered from the civilians, and the customs of commerce, by the genius of a minister, whose life seemed devoted to the interests of posterity. England was almost the last to receive into her bosom this beautiful effort of human reason. Little more than a century has elapsed, since she could scarcely be said to possess any commercial jurisprudence. The old common lawyers repelled it with a sullen inhospitality and indifference. And, though it cannot be doubted, that the spirit of commerce would, first or last, have forced it into the courts of England, and compelled them to protect the interests, which the enterprise of her subjects had created; it may be reasonably questioned, whether, but for the extraordinary genius of Lord Mansfield, she would not have been, at this very moment, a century behind continental Europe in adopting its doctrines. He was in a great measure the author of the law of insurance; and he gave to the other branches of commercial law a clearness and certainty, which surprise us more and more, as we examine and study his decisions. That he borrowed much from foreign jurisprudence is admitted; but he more than repaid every obligation to these sources. He naturalized the principles of commercial law, when he transplanted them into the soil of England, and they have flourished with new vigor in her genial climate. It is her just boast, that, having been once a tributary, she has now in turn laid the whole continent under contribution. Her commercial law has attained a perfection, order, and glory, which command the reverence of the whole world. It is almost universally followed and obeyed; not, indeed, as of positive institution; but as wisdom, practical wisdom, acting upon the results of a large experience, in a government, where opinion is free, and justice is administered without favor and without reproach.

A treatise upon this branch of law must necessarily comprehend a wide range of subjects. It must discuss, among other things, the law of principals and agents, brokers, factors, and consignees; of partnerships, and other joint ownerships; of negotiable instruments, such as bills of exchange, promissory notes, checks, and bills of lading; of contracts of bailment, shipments, and affreightment; and, as incidents, of charter-parties, freight, demurrage, and stoppage *in transitu;* of navigation and shipping, and, as incidents, the rights and duties of owners, masters, and mariners; and of insurance, bottomry, respondentia, salvage, and general average. My object will be to deal as fully with these topics, as may consist with the limits, by which every system of lectures must be circumscribed.

In the last place, the Constitutional law of the United States. In the correct exposition of this subject there is not a single American citizen, who has not deep stake and permanent interest. "In questions merely political," says Junius, an honest man may stand neuter. But the laws and constitution are the general property of the subject. Not to defend, is to relinquish; and who is so senseless as to renounce his share in a common benefit, unless he hopes to profit by a new division of the spoil?"[1] The existence of the union of these States does (as I think) mainly depend upon a just administration of the powers and duties of the national government; upon the preservation of that nice, but ever-changing influence, which balances the state and general governments, and tends, or should always tend, to bring them into a due equilibrium. There is no safety to our civil, religious, or political rights, except in this union. And it is scarcely too much to affirm, that the cause of liberty throughout the world is in no small measure suspended upon this great experiment of self-government by the people. I shall endeavor in my commentaries upon this important branch of political law, to discuss it with all the delicacy and reserve becoming my official station, and with all the sobriety appertaining to the fundamental law of organization of a free government. My object will be to unfold its divisions, and explain its principles, as far as practicable, by the lights of those great minds, which fostered into being, and nourished its infancy. I shall deal little with speculative discussions, and still less with my own

[1] Letter 41, to Lord Mansfield.

personal opinions. But I shall rely with undoubting confidence upon the early commentaries of its framers, upon the legislative recognitions of authority and duty, and the judicial decisions of the highest courts, as safe guides for interpretation. Above all, I shall freely use the doctrines of the admirable production [1] of Hamilton, Madison and Jay, (patriots as pure, and statesmen as wise as any, who have graced our country,) which has already acquired the weight of an authority throughout America. If by such means I shall contribute to fix in the minds of American youth a more devout enthusiasm for the constitution of their country, a more sincere love of its principles, and a more firm determination to adhere to its actual provisions against the clamors of faction, and the restlessness of innovation, my humble labors will not be without some reward in the consciousness of having contributed something to the common weal.

I have thus sketched a general outline of the course of lectures which the founder of the Dane Professorship has in the first instance assigned to this chair for the encouragement of juridical learning. Imperfect as this outline is, it must strike the most superficial observer, how rich and various are the topics which it proposes to examine; how extensive is the learning, and how exhausting the diligence, to accomplish the design. While it does honor to the public spirit, and the sagacity, and the enlightened zeal of the founder; while it testifies his enthusiasm for the science in which he has so deservedly attained eminence, it at the same time admonishes us, that he, who matured the plan, seems alone to possess the courage and ability to execute it with complete success. In truth, the venerable founder has measured the strength of others by his own; and scarcely seems to have suspected the difficulties of the task, from the consciousness of his own power to subdue them. The skilful guide in the Alps walks with fearless confidence in the midst of dangers

[1] The Federalist.

which appall the traveller who has never made trial of his strength. Lord Coke, himself a prodigy of professional learning, has somewhere laid down, for the benefit of students, the various employments for every day, and has assigned *six* hours for the pursuit of the law.[1] Lord Hale has limited his exactions to the same period;[2] and Sir Walter Jones, whose early ambition thought that all the departments of law might be mastered by a single mind in satisfactory commentaries, has not ventured upon a different assignment of labor.[3] I feel justified in saying, that for more than fifty years our generous patron has daily devoted to his favorite studies of politics and jurisprudence more than double that number of hours.

I trust it will not be deemed an intrusion, if upon this occasion I venture to speak somewhat of the public services of this distinguished lawyer, which are already matter of notoriety, and, considering his age and character, may almost be deemed matter of history.

It is now more than fifty years since Mr. Dane first came to the bar, and brought to its practice his varied stores of knowledge. He was almost immediately engaged in the duties of legislation in this, his native state; and to him we are chiefly indebted for the first general revisal of our Provincial Statutes, as well as for other improvements in our code of positive law. At the distance of thirty years, he was again called by the voice of the legislature to a similar duty; and to him, in a great measure, we owe the valuable collection of our Colonial and Provincial Statutes, which now adorns our libraries. In the intermediate period he served many years

1 Co. Litt. 64 b.

> "Sex horas somno, totidem des legibus æquis,
> Quatuor orabis, des epulis duas.
> Quod superest, ultro sacris largire camœnis."

2 Boswell's Life of Johnson, iii. 398.

3 Teignmouth's Life of Sir William Jones, p. 257.

> "Six hours to law, to soothing slumber seven,
> Ten to the world allot, and all to Heaven."

See also, Law of Bailments, pp. 122, 123.

in the Continental Congress, during some of its most difficult operations, and there maintained a high reputation for sound judgment, and an inflexible adherence to the best principles of political polity. His advancement to public life was always unsought for by himself; and his retirement from it has always been matter of public regret. To him belongs the glory of the formation of the celebrated Ordinance of 1787, which constitutes the fundamental law of the states northwest of the Ohio. It is a monument of political wisdom, and sententious skilfulness of expression. It was adopted unanimously by Congress, according to his original draft, with scarcely the alteration of a single word. After his retirement from public life he devoted himself with matchless assiduity to the duties of the bar; and gradually arriving at the first rank, he became the guide, the friend, and the father of the profession in his own county. In the midst of an extensive practice, he found leisure to compile his Digest and Abridgment of American Law, which, in eight large octavo volumes, comprehends a general survey of all our jurisprudence, and attests the depth of his learning, his unwearied industry, and his independent, but cautious, judgment. It is now some years since he bade farewell to the bar, but not to his favorite studies.[1] In contemplating his professional character, one is perpetually reminded of the fine portrait of Lord Chief Justice Rolle, drawn by Lord Hale, in his Preface to Rolle's Abridgment of the Law, which has so close a resemblance, that it seems another, and the same. "He argued frequently and pertinently," says Lord Hale; "his arguments were fitted to prove and evince, not for ostentation; plain, yet learned; short, if the nature of the business permitted, yet perspicuous. His words few, but significant and weighty. His skill, judgment, and advice, in points of law and pleading, were sound and excellent. In

[1] A supplementary volume (now constituting the ninth) of his Digest and Abridgment, was published by Mr. Dane a short time after this Discourse was delivered,— which contains an abstract of thirty volumes of reports.

short, he was a person of great learning and experience in the common law, profound judgment, singular prudence, great moderation, justice, and integrity." Mr. Dane has nobly dedicated the whole proceeds of his great work to the establishment of this professorship; and thus has become to our parent University, in the highest sense, the American Viner. I am but too sensible, that here the parallel must stop; and that to pursue it farther would cover him with humiliation, who now addresses you. To the liberal donation of Mr. Viner the world is indebted for the splendid Commentaries of Sir William Blackstone, a work of such singular exactness and perspicacity, of such finished purity and propriety of style, and of such varied research, and learned disquisition, and constitutional accuracy, that, as a text-book, it probably stands unrivalled in the literature of any other language, and is now studied as a classic in America, as well as in England. Perhaps when we are gathered in the dust, some future Blackstone, nursed and reared in this school, may arise; and by a similar achievement blend his own immortality with the fame of the founder. Would to God, that it may be so! Then would this fair seat of science become the pride of the law, as it now is the pride of the literature of our country.

When we look around us, and consider how much has been done by this University for the glory and safety of the Commonwealth; when we recollect how many distinguished men have been nourished in her bosom, and warmed by her bounty, and cheered by her praise;[1] it is impossible to sup-

[1] The members delegated from Massachusetts to serve in the Revolutionary Congress between 1774 and 1789, (when the new Constitution was adopted,) were in number twenty-one. Of these, seventeen were educated in Harvard University. Their names are as follows: Samuel Adams, Thomas Cushing, John Hancock, John Adams, Robert T. Paine, Francis Dana, Elbridge Gerry, John Lowell, Samuel Osgood, Jonathan Jackson, Artemas Ward, George Partridge, Rufus King, James Lovell, Samuel A. Otis, George Thacher, and Nathan Dane. Mr. Dane, at the time of the delivery of this Discourse, was the sole survivor. He is since deceased, having died on the 15th of February, 1835.

press the wish, the earnest wish, that this last triumph may yet crown her matron dignity. What consolation could be more affecting to her grateful children, than that in these academical shades there should arise a temple, sacred to the majesty of the law; where our future orators, and jurists, and judges, and statesmen, might mature their genius, and deepen their learning, and purify their ambition; where future generations may approach, and read the wisdom of the law, as it is personified in the glowing sketch of Algernon Sidney: "It is void of desire and fear, lust and anger. It is *mens sine affectu*, written reason, retaining some measure of the divine perfection. It does not enjoin that which pleases a weak, frail man; but, without any regard to persons, commands that which is good, and punishes evil in all, whether rich or poor, high or low. It is deaf, inexorable, inflexible."[1]

[1] Works of Algernon Sidney, sect. 15, p. 69.

INFLUENCE OF SCIENTIFIC STUDIES.

A DISCOURSE INTRODUCTORY TO A COURSE OF LECTURES BEFORE THE FAMILIES OF THE PROFESSORS IN HARVARD UNIVERSITY, DELIVERED IN HOLDEN CHAPEL, DECEMBER 23, 1830.

I SHOULD have hesitated to address you on the present occasion if it had been supposed to involve any peculiar or extraordinary duties. I have not the leisure to mature a discourse which should invite the attention of the learned by the extent of its views, or the depth of its investigations. The necessities arising from the constant pressure of professional engagements would alone be sufficient to induce me to decline the task, even if more obvious considerations did not lead me to the same result. He who would address himself to those who have cultivated literature with eminent success, or who have travelled, not merely through the broad ways, but the intricate mazes of science, must feel that he has many things to do, before he can suitably meet the just expectations of his audience. It is not for him, under such circumstances, to place entire reliance upon the resources of his own mind, however comprehensive they may seem to be. It is not for him, under such circumstances, to draw exclusively upon his own genius or imagination for views original or attractive. He may not rest even on the powers of eloquence (if he should happen to possess them) to adorn his topics with the beauties of an animated diction, or the graces of a vivid style. His thoughts may be brilliant, without being just; or just, without being striking; so as to lead to the bitter sarcasm, that his discourse contains many things new, and many things true; but the new is not true, and the true is not new. The least of his anxiety, however, should be, under such circumstances, to be original; for who can, without rashness, imagine that, after the lapse of so many ages, in which the lives of so many of the brightest of human minds have been devoted to the cause of science; who, I say, can, without rashness, imagine that little of truth has hitherto been gathered, and that her ample stores are, for the first time, about to be revealed to his sight? If he should indulge in such a vain and dreamy self-complacency, he would painfully learn that other minds had already anticipated almost all his peculiarities of opinion and comment; that antiquity had exhausted them in its captivating literature, never yet excelled, and perhaps never to be excelled; or that modern science, by its exact experiments, had put to flight whatever of theory might float round his own physical researches.

No — under such circumstances he could rely securely on nothing but the results of deep and various study. He would seek to fill his mind with the thoughts of others, and elevate his own conceptions by making them the familiar spirits of his hours. He would feel it necessary to invigorate his own powers, by giving his early and his later vigils to the profound meditations of the great men of other days. He would endeavor to comprehend the large conceptions of Lord Bacon, and, by following the method of induction pointed out by his wonderful mind, he would invite nature to disclose her mysteries, and aid him in the analysis of her inexhaustible stores. He would meditate — but it is unnecessary to dwell on such considerations. Enough has been said, and more than enough to teach us the difficulties of such a task; and to demonstrate that time as well as diligence, and patience as well as strength, are necessary to the successful accomplishment of such an achievement.

As I comprehend it, the design of our meetings involves no such complexity of effort or attainment. The lectures which belong to the brief course sketched out for these walls, belong to a humbler and more facile duty. It is our design, not to sound the depths of any portion of science or literature, but to bring together some of the truths which lie on the surface; not so much to seek for buried treasures, as to unfold those which are known and approachable; not so much to display rarities, as to bring together the useful and the simple; to present what may not be unworthy of the contemplations of manhood, but yet may lie within the reach of the playfulness of youth. In short, we are here to listen to thoughts which are so familiar to the wise that they come almost without bidding, and are dismissed without question or criticism. The poet has told us in two lines of the masculine brevity and strength of the best days of English verse, (borrowed indeed from classical sources,) the whole of our case: —

> " Content, if here the unlearn'd their wants may view,
> The learn'd reflect on what before they knew."

And narrow and humble as such a scheme may seem to those whose leisure can command the range of science, or whose ambition would soar to the boundaries of literature, there are some local considerations which render this not undesirable or unimportant in the circle of our families and friends. We live, indeed, in the midst of academical scenes, where learning has for ages secured the public reverence. We are encompassed with the means and the instruments of science on every side. A noble library, the gift of the munificence of the living as well as of the dead, looks down upon us with its ponderous and speaking volumes. A philosophical apparatus, which at once lifts our thoughts to the heavens, and busies us with the motions and the changes, the powers and the laws of the material universe, is within our apparent grasp. We need not call upon the earth to open upon us her minerals and geological treasures; for our cabinets are enriched with many of her most valuable, as well as most attractive specimens. We seem as if within the very purlieus of the laboratory, where chemistry, no longer dealing with occult arts and preternatural sorceries, contents herself with solving and resolving bodies, with combining and separating the elements and the gases, and unfolding the phenomena of light and heat, and, as it were, giving a local habitation and a name to her endless wonders. The very bell which so often rouses us in our morning slumbers, seems forever vocal with annunciations, inviting our presence to the rooms where learned professors pour forth their stores upon the interesting topics of divinity, and physics, and metaphysics, and rhetoric, and oratory, and botany, and anatomy, and the philosophy of nature, and the mysteries of art. And yet, in the midst of all this profusion, our families seem in some danger of starving for want of intellectual food. If they cannot count themselves among the matriculated; if their age, their sex, their pursuits, or even their retiring modesty, forbid them from entering upon these scenes; they are compelled to forego all that curiosity and taste would covet, to nourish their home resources; and they are left to consume their time in the monotonous round of common duties. In a larger society their very wants would soon work out a remedy to relieve them from such embarrassments. The evil felt in the family circle would extend to the head; and thus, as in large cities, public lectures would be multiplied, at once to stimulate and to satisfy the desire for knowledge. But here, if I may so say, the very evil has its origin in the ample employments and devotion to science of the heads of our families. They who labor abroad with so much success and ability, require all their domestic leisure to recruit their exhausted spirits, or to prepare themselves for ever-recurring labors. I speak, therefore, to the sober sense of those whom I address, when I say that there seems a peculiar duty on us to give those of our families and friends, who are necessarily precluded from the general cultivation of science, some chance of understanding its elements, and relishing its truths by the only adequate methods — the demonstrations of the laboratory, and the living examples of the lecture room. Truth from the lips is often felt with double sway; but truth, confirmed by experiment, is not only irresistible in its conviction, but in its permanent impression on the memory.

With reference, therefore, to our domestic circles, it is of no small importance for us to enlarge the sphere of innocent pleasure, to instruct the inquisitive mind, and to furnish new sources of thought and conversation, by observations drawn from the processes of nature, and the elegant demonstrations of art.

But I am far from considering this as the sole, though it may well be deemed a sufficient motive to warm our hearts and kindle our zeal. There are, to those professedly engaged in a particular science, many motives for seeking some acquaintance with other sciences, even if they should not seem, at first, of a kindred character. I do not here allude to those motives which may be drawn from the abstract value of learning, or the practical benefits of its cultivation. I do not address myself to the pride of scholars as such; or to the ambition of those minds which deem nothing attained while there yet remains any thing unattained; which, forgetting the past, press onward and upward for the prize of glory. I do not attempt to shadow forth, even in outline, the praises of knowledge as they have been vindicated in ancient or in modern times. There are some places and some circumstances, in which such topics, if not matters of impertinent detail, are, at least, matters of supererogation. The genius of the place, the literary atmosphere which we breathe, the very habits of our lives, presuppose that learning in its widest sense, human and divine, is at once our pride and our guide, the companion of our morning walks and of our evening meditations; the instructive friend of our youth; the support and glory of our old age; the light that beams cheerfully upon us in the noonday of hope and joy; and the polestar that sets not and changes not and deceives not in the midnight hours of adversity, or in the heavier darkness whose shadows brood over the valley of death. If I were called upon, indeed, to intermingle in the argument of such topics, I might well distrust my own resources; and I should repose myself upon the sententious wisdom of the greatest of modern philosophers. "Studies," says my Lord Bacon, "serve for delight, for ornament, and for ability. Their chief use for delight is in privateness and retiring; for ornament, is in discourse; and for ability, is in the judgment and disposition of business. Histories make men wise; poets, witty; the mathematics, subtile; natural philosophy, deep; morals, grave; logic and rhetoric, able to contend. '*Abeunt studia in mores.*'" To which he might have added, jurisprudence enlarges, invigorates, and chastens the judgment; and theology fills the soul with thoughts of time and eternity, and,

> "Letting down the golden chain from high,
> Draws every mortal upward to the sky."

But one motive, upon which I would venture to insist, is drawn from the very nature of academical studies, and the exclusive zeal which they are calculated to nourish. No one can fail to remark, that the subdivision of intellectual, as well as of manual labor, though it tends greatly to the perfection of the workmanship, has, in quite as striking a degree, a tendency, if not to narrow the mind, at least to close its vision to the value of surrounding objects. In proportion as our attainments rise in a favorite pursuit, it grows in importance, in intensity of attraction, and in variety of interest. We feel our own minds expanding under its influence, and our own curiosity enlivened and warmed by its developments. We have the gratifying consciousness of difficulties overcome, of intellectual wealth accumulated, and of honorable ambition rewarded. A spirit of exclusiveness is thus awakened and cherished; until, at last, the appetite increasing with what it feeds on, our imaginations exaggerate the value of our peculiar labors to an alarming extent; and, in the extravagance of our attachment, we look down with utter indifference upon every other department of learning, and deem all but our own, weary, stale, flat, and unprofitable. This dangerous delusion besets the scholar and the devotee of science in every walk of life. But it especially besets him in those academical scenes where he becomes at once the teacher and the taught; where he is perpetually pouring into other minds the streams of his own knowledge, and at the same time, is as perpetually compelled to widen and deepen the channels of his own thoughts to meet the constant demands of such an exhausting flow.

This error is not of a merely speculative nature, but is often attended with practical mischiefs. The mere scholar, intent upon the glorious products of classical literature, dwells with a fond and overweening delight upon the wisdom and the beauty, and the sublimity of the ancients, until modern learning seems to him but the pastework of imitative jewelry, compared with the pure sparkling of the diamond, or the pellucid crystallizations of the emerald. He is content, if I may so say, to dream with antiquity, and to live with past ages; forgetful of the sober realities of his own life, and that he yet walks this nether sphere. The devotee of physical science, absorbed in its splendid discoveries, and in its new and ever-varying details, compelling nature, as it were, to expound her hidden contrivances to him, and to answer his untiring interrogatories, delights in the consciousness of this exercise of power, and looks with amazement on him, who, with equal enthusiasm, traces out the laws of the mind, and gathers up its finer filaments and associations, and touches its secret springs, and unfolds its admirable faculties. The mathematician, dealing with facts of another kind, which rest on demonstrative evidence, and ascending by strict analysis to the most extraordinary results, lying apparently beyond the reach of human genius, acquires a preternatural love for certainties of this sort, and feels, at times, almost as if matter were made only to exercise his ingenuity in searching out the laws of gravitation, and in subjecting the motions of the earth and the heavens to his sublime calculus. On the other hand, the votary of jurisprudence, absorbed in the actual business of human life, and the administration of human laws, in which probabilities and presumptions are the principal instruments to arrive at his conclusions, is apt to place all other sciences at an immeasurable distance below his own, which deals with moral evidence, and to boast of his common sense, which, though no science, is, in his estimate, fairly worth the seven.

Thus each, in his turn, from the common fascination of his own peculiar profession or study, is but too apt to become generally insensible or indifferent to all others. Instead of gathering new strength from their invigorating truths, or storing his mind with their treasures for use or illustration, each is but too apt to walk in his own round of close and solitary pleasure. If, therefore, no other motive could be found for these lectures of mutual instruction, but the desire to draw the sciences, as it were, in open contact and contrast with each other, that alone, it seems to me, ought to furnish a sufficient inducement, and should stimulate us to a sincere encouragement of the design.

And this leads me to remark, in the next place, that the sciences are of a social nature, and flourish best in the neighborhood of each other. They furnish literature with some of its most engaging imagery, as well as with some of its most effective instruction. In return, they receive an infinite variety of aids from literature, not merely by way of ornament, but by profound reflection, and close and vigorous reasoning. There is not, within the compass of human learning, a single department which does not connect itself with every other; which does not derive illustrations of its own truths, and mingle its own results with every other. One of the admirable dispensations of Providence is, thus to make every human attainment pour in its tribute to the common stream of knowledge, so as to widen the common means of social intercourse and social happiness. Whatever be the science, it becomes cold and cheerless, when it casts around a sepulchral light, in its own solitary and noiseless cell. It is when it becomes connected with other sciences, reflecting its own radiance on other objects, and receiving again from them their own brilliant lights, that it warms and elevates, and enlarges the human soul. A truth is but half felt, when it stands alone. It is only when it belongs to a cluster, that it incites the intellectual appetite, and gives a keener relish to other food, by the richness as well as the delicacy of its flavor.

One of the most popular journals of our day has lately declared, in a bold and peremptory tone, that it had not "any hesitation in adding, that, within the last fifteen years, not a single discovery or invention of prominent interest has been made in our colleges, and that there is not one man in all the eight universities of Great Britain, who is at present known to be engaged in any train of original research."[1] Without yielding to the truth of this unqualified remark, it may be justly stated, that, if there be any color for it, it arises from the dissociation of science and literature, which is too apt to be nourished in those universities, by the single pursuits of their eminent professors. They are not compelled to think together, or to warm their genius by broad and comprehensive views of physical and intellectual science.

But there are other considerations, not of an academical nature, and belonging to us, in common with all our race, which ought not, on an occasion of this sort, to be wholly passed over. We live in an age full of intellectual excitement. It is not with us, as it was in former times, when science belonged to solitary studies, or philosophical ease, or antiquarian curiosity. It has escaped from the closet, and become an habitual accompaniment of every department of life. It comes, emphatically, home to men's business and bosoms. It accosts us equally in the highways and by-ways

[1] Quarterly Review, October, 1830, p. 327.

of life. We meet it in the idle walk, and in the crowded street; in the very atmosphere we breathe, in the earth we tread on, in the ocean we traverse, and on the rivers we navigate. It visits the workshop of the mechanic, the laboratory of the apothecary, the chambers of the engraver, the vats of the dyer, the noisy haunts of the spinning jenny, and the noiseless retreats of the bleachery. It seems a very spirit of all work, assuming all shapes, and figuring out all sorts of wonders, in that epitome of a world, a factory. It plays about us in the very smoke of the glasshouse, in the gas-lights of our shops and theatres, in the beautiful coruscations of nature, and the exquisite imitations of art. It crosses our paths in the long, winding canal, in the busy railroad, in the flying steamboat, and in the gay and gallant merchant ship, wafting its products to every clime. It enters our houses, and sits down at our firesides, and lights up our conversations, and revels at our banquets. Not an ice-cream meets our lips, which has not felt the freezing coldness of its hand; not a vapor ascends, which may not be perfumed by its cosmetics and essences. One is almost tempted to say, that the whole world seems in a blaze; and that the professors of science and the dealers in the arts surround us by their magical circles, and compel us to remain captives in the spells of their witchcraft.

Under such circumstances, we are scarcely permitted to remain ignorant of principles, while we are encircled by practical applications of them. If curiosity does not stimulate us to knowledge, we are almost compelled to ask it for safety. Our very ignorance, if it does not betray us into peril, meets us like a spectre, at every turn. We are liable to be questioned on every side, and are not permitted to play the part of mutes. In short, we are driven to the necessity of confessing our ignorance, and avoiding the censure, or manfully meeting the topic, we are obliged to redeem our credit by syllabling out the first outlines of science.

And yet, with the busy employments and crowded interests of society, how few can find leisure for collateral studies! There is not a single branch of science or literature, which is not, at the present day, so extensive in its reach, that to master it requires a long life of patient labor. Nay, when such a life is at its close, the student seems but just arrived on the threshold of learning. He has done little more than to climb up a hillock, and look to the far distant valley, beyond which lie the mountains he would ascend, that he may survey a wider scene, and inhale a purer atmosphere. We seem, therefore, to be surrounded on every side by difficulties. We must learn what belongs to our own vocation, in order to attain the comforts and the honors of life. We must learn enough of what belongs to other vocations, that we may mingle in the interests, and partake the triumphs, and relish the pleasures of society. We must read something of other literature, besides that which belongs to our own pursuits, that we may understand the daily, and the weekly, and the monthly, and the quarterly journals, which crowd our tables. We must gather up something of other sciences, that we may not seem to belong to the class of mummies, or the dead relics of former ages. We must learn how to thread some of the labyrinths of knowledge, in which we are compelled to wander, lest we should be buried alive in its artificial catacombs. In short, we must be content to be superficial in many things, if we would be wise in the ways of this world; and yet, without this wisdom, we shall scarcely find ourselves, in a temporal sense, in the ways of pleasantness, or the paths of peace.

It seems to me, that, under such circumstances, the delivery of public lectures, by concentrating what is most valuable in science, and most interesting in art and literature; by gathering what comes home most closely to our common wants, and illustrates our common pursuits, and varies our common enjoyments, by shortening the road, and clearing the obstructions, and smoothing the ruggedness of the journey, accomplishes a most valuable purpose. It has been very recently said, in the bitterness of sarcasm, that, "in this age of extended and diluted knowledge, popular science has become the staple of an extensive trade, in which charlatans are the principal dealers."[1] If this be true, in any, however qualified, sense, it only proves the intrinsic value of the genuine commodity; and the insatiable thirst for knowledge, which is abroad in the whole community. It is a fact honorable to the spirit of the age, and brings neither our taste nor our judgment into discredit. It is in vain to contend, that, because we cannot find time to master all science, therefore we should seek for none; that, because we cannot understand all the details, we should never learn the elements; that we should seek to know every thing, or know nothing; that one should stop short at the first step in knowledge, because he cannot compass the universe. The same line of argument would go to the utter prostration of all intellectual attainments. It would furnish to ignorance its best vindication, and to indolence its boldest excuse. We should not consult a library, because it were a vain attempt to read all the volumes; we should not hear a lecture, because it did not embrace and exhaust all the science; we should disdain to hear one, who taught important truths, because he had not himself travelled round the farthest limits of human knowledge.

A just estimate of human life and human wants will lead us to far different conclusions. We are perpetually admonished, that life is short, and art is long, and nature is inexhaustible. Our destiny allows us, at best, but a narrow choice of objects of pursuit; and our leisure, brief and transient as it is, admits of little variety of indulgence. We must content ourselves with getting knowledge by snatches; with gathering it up in fragments; with seizing on principles and results. We must welcome every mode, which abridges labor, and supersedes personal search. We must take the

[1] Quarterly Review, Oct. 1830, p. 326.

easiest demonstrations and the most simple enunciations. We must follow that, which is the ultimate object of all improved processes in the arts, to save labor, insure certainty, and husband time and resources. More than this can belong to the attainments of few, even of the most gifted minds. Less than this ought not to satisfy any one, who is conscious of the end and aim of his being; and who feels, that, in the proper pursuit of happiness here, he begins the race of immortality.

I have thus far spoken principally of the advantages of lectures upon the elements of science. But the same remarks apply with equal force to select disquisitions upon literary topics of general interest. In truth, literature is so abundant in its products of all sorts, whether for instruction, or pleasure, or ornament; whether to gratify the taste, or improve the morals, or enlarge the understanding; whether for the purpose of civil duties, or political education, or intellectual discipline; that the task of selection is of itself not unattended with difficulties, and requires talents of no ordinary character. The literature of a single language, ancient or modern, is perhaps beyond the grasp of any single mind; but the literature of all languages, or even of those within the pale of European fellowship, would require more than an Atlas to carry it on his shoulders. All that can be done, under such circumstances, is to follow Lord Bacon's advice, and "read by deputy."

But what strikes me of quite as much value, in such enlarged studies, as any which has been mentioned, is the delightful contemplation it affords us of the successful labors of other minds. We are brought into direct and active sympathy with men of genius in every age. We become witnesses of their toils, their disappointments, and their sufferings. We learn the slow and tedious steps, by which eminence has been acquired. We see the result of patient investigation and cautious sagacity. We trace the progress of discovery and invention, from the first clumsy process, or the first accidental guess, to the last glorious result. We see how the slightest incident leads gradually on to the most sublime truths; how facts, apparently the most remote, converge to the same ultimate point; how human ingenuity conquers obstacles apparently insurmountable; and how human enterprise gathers courage even from its very defeats. What can be more curious, or more affecting, than the history of many discoveries? In the midst of poverty and disappointment, the discoverer is sometimes condemned to pursue his solitary studies. He wastes his health and his resources in experiments, which seem ever on the point of success, and yet mock his toil and delude his hopes. At length the discovery comes. But does it always reward his toil? No—it but too often happens, that it is received by the public with a cold, reluctant indifference; or is put in operation, to his ruin, by some more thrifty competitor. Sometimes, indeed, as in the case of Galileo, it subjects him to a prison; sometimes it sends him, like Dolland, to his grave, "unwept, unhonored, and unsung;" sometimes it leaves him, like Fulton, to witness fortunes reared by others upon his labors, and yet, to find himself destined to fall a sacrifice to the vindication of his right to his own discovery. These are some of the misfortunes which affect us with lively sympathies for the benefactors of mankind. On the other hand, we are warmed, and sometimes dazzled, by the brilliant successes of genius. Who has not felt his soul melt within him, at the liberal ease and modest competence, which crowned the life of Newton? Who has not rejoiced in the opulence, which followed upon the labors of Watt, and Arkwright, and Franklin, and Davy?

But that, which fills us with the deepest admiration, is the wonderful workings of genius, in its own silent studies and inmost feelings. We see how it learns to thread the mazes of nature, and unfold her laws; at one time, tracing out the hidden causes, which link time to eternity, and earth to heaven; at another time, descending to the most minute operations of her power, in the dark mine, or the dripping cave, or the invisible air; and, at still another time, applying its subtile analysis to the decomposition of bodies, until at at last we seem in the very presence of the monads, whose miraculous vitality startles us into terror of our own delicate structure.

It is in the contemplation of such minds, and such discoveries, that we loose all grovelling thoughts and vulgar passions. We rise into a higher moral grandeur of desire. We relish holier views of our destiny. We see, that these are but the first fruits, or rather buds, of immortality. We enjoy the consciousness, that they are but emanations from that Almighty Being, who has formed and fashioned us from the dust, and breathed into us a portion of his own uncreated and eternal spirit.

And this leads me to remark, in the last place, that there is nothing so well adapted to make us feel a sincere and glowing devotion, such a lively sense of a present Deity, as a wide survey of the operations of nature. It is not by a few reflections alone, on the order and harmony of the visible universe, that we are brought to a just conception of the existence or attributes of God. It may even be doubtful, if the demonstrations of wisdom and design are more affecting, or more striking, in the power of the unsleeping ocean, or the rushing cataract, or the terrific earthquake, or the blazing volcano, than in the silent forms of crystallization, the infinite combinations of the gases, the microscopic perfection of the insect tribes, or the almost superhuman contrivances, by which the lowest order of beings builds up its coral continent for the dwelling-places of man. Who would imagine, if he were not told, that the very law which retains the planets in their spheres, enables the fly, by means of the pressure of the atmosphere, to walk securely on the ceiling over our heads, by an artificial vacuum instinctively made by its feet? that the very oxygen, which lights up and sustains the ignition of matter, is the same admirable principle which carries on the circulations of our own blood, and keeps up, in scarcely a figurative sense, the steady flame of life? The truth is, that, the farther our researches extend, the wider our philosophy explores, the deeper our discoveries penetrate, the more are we struck with the evidence of almighty contrivance, design and power. If we take but a drop of water, we find it crowded with myriads of beings, deriving life, and sustenance, and pleasure, from its uncounted particles. If we take the wing of the minutest insect, we know that its slender fibres and its glossy down are perforated by thousands of vessels, and nerves, and filaments, which convey its appropriate nutriment, and impart to it its beautiful colors. Not a single function is misplaced; not a single ligature is superfluous. Nay, perhaps it is not too bold an assertion, which has sometimes been made, that such are the mutual ties and dependencies of things, such as the laws of action and reaction, of attractive support and repulsive effort, that not a single atom could be struck out of existence, without involving the destruction of the universe.

If these humble efforts should answer no other purpose, than thus to draw us to a more enlarged and varied contemplation of our relations, to the first Almighty Cause, they would not be without their reward. They would awaken a livelier gratitude, and more cheerful confidence towards the Author of our being. They would create a new sense of the dignity of intellectual pursuits, and of the powers of human genius. They would increase our aspirations after that better world, where darkness shall no longer cover our paths, but the light of truth shall break upon our souls with unclouded glory and majesty.

CONSECRATION OF THE CEMETERY AT MOUNT AUBURN.

AN ADDRESS DELIVERED AT THE CONSECRATION OF MOUNT AUBURN, AS A CEMETERY, SEPTEMBER 24, 1831.

MY FRIENDS:

THE occasion which brings us together has much in it calculated to awaken our sensibilities, and cast a solemnity over our thoughts.

We are met to consecrate these grounds exclusively to the service and repose of the dead.

The duty is not new; for it has been performed for countless millions. The scenery is not new; for the hill and the valley, the dark, silent dell, and the deep forest, have often been devoted to the same pious purpose. But that which must always give it a peculiar interest is, that it can rarely occur, except at distant intervals; and whenever it does, it must address itself to feelings intelligible to all nations, and common to all hearts.

The patriarchal language of four thousand years ago is precisely that to which we would now give utterance. We are "strangers and sojourners" here. We have need of a "possession of a burying-place, that we may bury our dead out of our sight." Let us have "the field, and the cave, which is therein; and all the trees that are in the field, that are in all the borders round about;" and let them "be made sure for a possession of a burying-place."

It is the duty of the living thus to provide for the dead.

It is not a mere office of pious regard for others; but it comes home to our own bosoms, as those who are soon to enter upon the common inheritance.

If there are any feelings of our nature, not bounded by earth, and yet stopping short of the skies, which are more strong and more universal than all others, they will be found in our solicitude as to the time and place and manner of our death; in the desire to die in the arms of our friends; to have the last sad offices to our remains performed by their affection; to repose in the land of our nativity; to be gathered to the sepulchres of our fathers. It is almost impossible for us to feel, nay, even to feign, indifference on such a subject.

Poetry has told us this truth, in lines of transcendent beauty and force, which find a response in every breast:—

> "For who, to dumb forgetfulness a prey,
> This pleasing, anxious being e'er resigned,
> Left the warm precincts of the cheerful day,
> Nor cast one longing, lingering look behind?
>
> "On some fond breast the parting soul relies;
> Some pious drops the closing eye requires;
> E'en from the tomb the voice of nature cries;
> E'en in our ashes live their wonted fires."

It is in vain that philosophy has informed us that the whole earth is but a point in the eyes of its Creator,—nay, of his own creation; that, wherever we are,—abroad or at home, on the restless ocean or the solid land,—we are still under the protection of his providence, and safe, as it were, in the hollow of his hand. It is in vain that religion has instructed us that we are but dust, and to dust we shall return; that whether our remains are scattered to the corners of the earth, or gathered in sacred urns, there is a sure and certain hope of a resurrection of the body and a life everlasting. These truths, sublime and glorious as they are, leave untouched the feelings of which I have spoken, or rather they impart to them a more enduring reality. Dust as we are, the frail tenements which inclose our spirits but for a season are dear, are inexpressibly dear to us. We derive solace, nay, pleasure, from the reflection that when the hour of separation comes, these earthly remains will still retain the tender regard of those whom we leave behind; that the spot where they shall lie will be remembered with a fond and soothing reverence; that our children will visit it in the midst of their sorrows; and our kindred in remote generations, feel that a local inspiration hovers round it.

Let him speak who has been on a pilgrimage of health to a foreign land. Let him speak who has watched at the couch of a dying friend, far from his chosen home. Let him speak who has committed to the bosom of the deep, with a sudden, startling plunge, the narrow shroud of some relative or companion. Let such speak; and they will tell you that there is nothing which rings the heart of the dying — ay, and of the surviving — with sharper agony than the thought that they are to sleep their last sleep in the land of strangers, or in the unseen depths of the ocean.

"Bury me not, I pray thee," said the patriarch Jacob, "bury me not in Egypt: but I will lie with my fathers. And thou shalt carry me out of Egypt; and bury me in their burying-place." "There they buried Abraham, and Sarah his wife; there they buried Isaac, and Rebecca his wife; and there I buried Leah."

Such are the natural expressions of human feeling, as they fall from the lips of the dying. Such are the reminiscences that forever crowd on the confines of the passes to the grave. We seek again to have our home there with our friends, and to be blest by a communion with them. It is a matter of instinct, not of reasoning. It is a spiritual impulse which supersedes belief, and disdains question.

But it is not chiefly in regard to the feelings belonging to our own mortality, however sacred and natural, that we should contemplate the establishment of repositories of this sort. There are higher moral purposes, and more affecting considerations which belong to the subject. We should accustom ourselves to view them rather as means than as ends; rather as influences to govern human conduct, and to moderate human suffering, than as cares incident to a selfish foresight.

It is to the living mourner — to the parent, weeping over his dear dead child — to the husband, dwelling in his own solitary desolation — to the widow, whose heart is broken by untimely sorrow — to the friend, who misses at every turn the presence of some kindred spirit, — it is to these that the repositories of the dead bring home thoughts full of admonition, of instruction, and slowly, but surely, of consolation also. They admonish us, by their very silence, of our own frail and transitory being. They instruct us in the true value of life, and in its noble purposes, its duties, and its destination. They spread around us, in the reminiscences of the past, sources of pleasing though melancholy reflection.

We dwell with pious fondness on the characters and virtues of the departed; and, as time interposes its growing distances between us and them, we gather up with more solicitude the broken fragments of memory, and weave, as it were, into our very hearts the threads of their history. As we sit down by their graves, we seem to hear the tones of their affection whispering in our ears. We listen to the voice of their wisdom, speaking in the depths of our souls. We shed our tears; but they are no longer the burning tears of agony. They relieve our drooping spirits, and come no longer over us with a deathly faintness. We return to the world, and we feel ourselves purer, and better, and wiser, for this communion with the dead.

I have spoken but of feelings and associations common to all ages, and all generations of men — to the rude and the polished — to the barbarian and the civilized — to the bond and the free — to the inhabitant of the dreary forests of the north, and the sultry regions of the south — to the worshipper of the sun, and the worshipper of idols — to the heathen, dwelling in the darkness of his cold mythology, and to the Christian, rejoicing in the light of the true God. Everywhere we trace them, in the characteristic remains of the most distant ages and nations, and as far back as human history carries its traditionary outlines. They are found in the barrows, and cairns, and mounds of olden times, reared by the uninstructed affection of savage tribes; and everywhere the spots seem to have been selected with the same tender regard to the living and the dead; that the magnificence of nature might administer comfort to human sorrow, and incite human sympathy.

The aboriginal Germans buried their dead in groves consecrated by their priests. The Egyptians gratified their pride, and soothed their grief, by interring them in their Elysian fields, or embalming them in their vast catacombs, or inclosing them in their stupendous pyramids, the wonder of all succeeding ages. The Hebrews watched with religious care over their places of burial. They selected, for this purpose, ornamented gardens, and deep forests, and fertile valleys, and lofty mountains; and they still designate them, with a sad emphasis, as the "House of the Living." The ancient Asiatics lined the approaches to their cities with sculptured sarcophagi, and mausoleums, and other ornaments, embowered in shrubbery; traces of which may be seen among their magnificent ruins. The Greeks exhausted the resources of their exquisite art in adoring the habitations of the dead. They discouraged interments within the limits of their cities; and consigned their relics to shady groves, in the neighborhood of murmuring streams and mossy fountains, close by the favorite resorts of those, who were engaged in the study of philosophy and nature; and called them, with the elegant expressiveness of their own beautiful language, CEMETERIES,[1] or "Places of

[1] κοιμητήρια — literally, *places of sleep.*

Repose." The Romans, faithful to the example of Greece, erected the monuments to the dead in the suburbs of the Eternal City (as they proudly denominated it,) on the sides of their spacious roads, in the midst of trees, and ornamental walks, and ever-varying flowers. The Appian Way was crowded with columns, and obelisks, and cenotaphs, in memory of their heroes and sages; and, at every turn, the short, but touching inscription met the eye, — Siste, Viator, — Pause, Traveller, — inviting at once to sympathy and thoughtfulness. Even the humblest Roman could read on the humblest gravestone the kind offering — "May the earth lie lightly on these remains!"[1] And the Moslem successors of the emperors, indifferent as they may be to the ordinary exhibitions of the fine arts, place their burying-grounds in rural retreats, and embellish them with studious taste, as a religious duty. The cypress is planted at the head and foot of every grave, and waves with a mournful solemnity over it. These devoted grounds possess an inviolable sanctity. The ravages of war never reach them; and victory and defeat equally respect the limits of their domain. So that it has been remarked, with equal truth and beauty, that while the cities of the living are subject to all the desolations and vicissitudes incident to human affairs, the cities of the dead enjoy an undisturbed repose, without even the shadow of change.

But I will not dwell upon facts of this nature. They demonstrate, however, the truth, of which I have spoken. They do more; they furnish reflections suitable for our own thoughts on the present occasion.

If this tender regard for the dead be so absolutely universal, and so deeply founded in human affection, why is it not made to exert a more profound influence on our lives? Why do we not enlist it with more persuasive energy in the cause of human improvement? Why do we not enlarge it as a source of religious consolation? Why do we not make it a more

[1] "Sit tibi terra levis."

efficient instrument to elevate ambition, to stimulate genius, and to dignify learning? Why do we not connect it indissolubly with associations, which charm us in nature, and engross us in art? Why do we not dispel from it that unlovely gloom, from which our hearts turn, as from a darkness that ensnares, and a horror that appalls our thoughts?

To many, nay, to most of the heathen, the burying-place was the end of all things. They indulged no hope, at least, no solid hope, of any future intercourse or re-union with their friends. The farewell at the grave was a long, and an everlasting farewell. At the moment when they breathed it, it brought to their hearts a startling sense of their own wretchedness. Yet, when the first tumults of anguish were passed, they visited the spot, and strewed flowers, and garlands, and crowns around it, to assuage their grief, and nourish their piety. They delighted to make it the abode of the varying beauties of nature; to give it attractions, which should invite the busy and the thoughtful; and yet, at the same time, afford ample scope for the secret indulgence of sorrow.

Why should not Christians imitate such examples? They have far nobler motives to cultivate moral sentiments and sensibilities; to make cheerful the pathways to the grave; to combine with deep meditations on human mortality the sublime consolations of religion. We know, indeed, as they did of old, that "man goeth to his long home, and the mourners go about the streets." But that home is not an everlasting home; and the mourners may not weep, as those who are without hope. What is the grave to us, but a thin barrier, dividing time from eternity, and earth from heaven? What is it, but "the appointed place of rendezvous, where all the travellers on life's journey meet," for a single night of repose?

"'Tis but a night — a long and moonless night,
We make the grave our bed, and then are gone."

Know we not,

"The time draws on
When not a single spot of burial earth,

> Whether on land, or in the spacious sea,
> But must give up its long committed dust
> Inviolate?"

Why, then, should we darken, with systematic caution, all the avenues to these repositories? Why should we deposit the remains of our friends in loathsome vaults, or beneath the gloomy crypts and cells of our churches; where the human foot is never heard, save when the sickly taper lights some new guest to his appointed apartment, and "lets fall a supernumerary horror" on the passing procession? Why should we measure out a narrow portion of earth for our graveyards, in the midst of our cities; and heap the dead upon each other, with a cold, calculating parsimony, disturbing their ashes, and wounding the sensibilities of the living? Why should we expose our burying-grounds to the broad glare of day, to the unfeeling gaze of the idler, to the noisy press of business, to the discordant shouts of merriment, or to the baleful visitations of the dissolute? Why should we bar up their approaches against real mourners, whose delicacy would shrink from observation, but whose tenderness would be soothed by secret visits to the grave, and holding converse there with their departed joys? Why all this unnatural restraint upon our sympathies and sorrows, which confines the visit to the grave to the only time in which it must be utterly useless — when the heart is bleeding with fresh anguish, and is too weak to feel, and too desolate to desire consolation?

It is painful to reflect, that the cemeteries in our cities, crowded, on all sides, by the overhanging habitations of the living, are walled in only to preserve them from violation; and that in our country towns they are left in a sad, neglected state, exposed to every sort of intrusion, with scarcely a tree to shelter their barrenness, or a shrub to spread a grateful shade over the new-made hillock.

These things were not always so among Christians. They are not worthy of us. They are not worthy of Christianity in our day. There is much in these things, that casts a just reproach upon us in the past. There is much, that demands for the future a more spiritual discharge of our duties.

Our cemeteries, rightly selected, and properly arranged, may be made subservient to some of the highest purposes of religion and human duty. They may preach lessons, to which none may refuse to listen, and which all that live must hear. Truths may be there felt and taught, in the silence of our own meditations, more persuasive, and more enduring, than ever flowed from human lips. The grave hath a voice of eloquence, ay, of superhuman eloquence, which speaks at once to the thoughtlessness of the rash, and the devotion of the good; which addresses all times, and all ages, and all sexes; which tells of wisdom to the wise, and of comfort to the afflicted; which warns us of our follies and our dangers; which whispers to us in accents of peace, and alarms us in tones of terror; which steals with a healing balm into the stricken heart, and lifts up and supports the broken spirit; which awakens a new enthusiasm for virtue, and disciplines us for its severer trials and duties; which calls up the images of the illustrious dead, with an animating presence, for our example and glory; and which demands of us, as men, as patriots, as Christians, as immortals, that the powers given by God should be devoted to his service, and the minds created by his love, should return to him with larger capacities for virtuous enjoyment, and with more spiritual and intellectual brightness.

It should not be for the poor purpose of gratifying our vanity or pride that we erect columns, and obelisks, and monuments to the dead; but that we may read thereon much of our own destiny and duty. We know that man is the creature of associations and excitements. Experience may instruct, but habit, and appetite, and passion, and imagination, will exercise a strong dominion over him. These are the Fates which weave the thread of his character, and unravel the mysteries of his conduct. The truth, which strikes home, must not only have the approbation of his reason, but it must be embodied in a visible, tangible, practical form. It must be felt, as well as seen. It must warm, as well as convince.

It was a saying of Themistocles, that the trophies of Miltiades would not suffer him to sleep. The feeling thus expressed, has a deep foundation in the human mind; and, as it is well or ill directed, it will cover us with shame, or exalt us to glory. The deeds of the great attract but a cold and listless admiration, when they pass in historical order before us like moving shadows. It is the trophy and the monument which invest them with a substance of local reality. Who, that has stood by the tomb of Washington on the quiet Potomac, has not felt his heart more pure, his wishes more aspiring, his gratitude more warm, and his love of country touched by a holier flame? Who, that should see erected, in shades like these, even a cenotaph to the memory of a man like Buckminster, that prodigy of early genius, would not feel that there is an excellence, over which death hath no power, but which lives on through all time, still freshening with the lapse of ages?

But, passing from those who, by their talents and virtues, have shed lustre on the annals of mankind, to cases of mere private bereavement; who, that should deposit, in shades like these, the remains of a beloved friend, would not feel a secret pleasure in the thought that the simple inscription to his worth would receive the passing tribute of a sigh from thousands of kindred hearts? that the stranger and the traveller would linger on the spot with a feeling of reverence? that they, the very mourners themselves, when they should revisit it, would find there the verdant sod, and the fragrant flower, and the breezy shade? that they might there, unseen except of God, offer up their prayers, or indulge the luxury of grief? that they might there realize, in its full force, the affecting beatitude of the Scriptures: "Blessed are they that mourn, for they shall be comforted?"

Surely, surely, we have not done all our duty, if there yet remains a single incentive to human virtue, without its due play in the action of life, or a single stream of happiness which has not been made to flow in upon the waters of affliction.

Considerations like those which have been suggested have, for a long time, turned the thoughts of many distinguished citizens to the importance of some more appropriate places of sepulture. There is a growing sense in the community of the inconveniences and painful associations, not to speak of the unhealthiness, of interments beneath our churches. The tide which is flowing with such a steady and widening current into the narrow peninsula of our metropolis, not only forbids the enlargement of the common limits, but admonishes us of the increasing dangers to the ashes of the dead from its disturbing movements. Already, in other cities, the churchyards are closing against the admission of new incumbents, and begin to exhibit the sad spectacle of promiscuous ruins and intermingled graves.

We are therefore but anticipating at the present moment the desires, nay the necessities, of the next generation. We are but exercising a decent anxiety to secure an inviolable home for ourselves and our posterity. We are but inviting our children and their descendants to what the Moravian Brothers have, with such exquisite propriety, designated as "The Field of Peace."

A rural cemetery seems to combine in itself all the advantages which can be proposed to gratify human feelings, or tranquillize human fears; to secure the best religious influences, and to cherish all those associations which cast a cheerful light over the darkness of the grave.

And what spot can be more appropriate than this for such a purpose? Nature seems to point it out with significant energy as the favorite retirement for the dead. There are around us all the varied features of her beauty and grandeur — the forest-crowned height, the abrupt acclivity, the sheltered valley, the deep glen, the grassy glade, and the silent grove. Here are the lofty oak, the beach, that "wreaths its old fantastic roots so high," the rustling pine, and the drooping willow — the tree, that sheds its pale leaves with every autumn, a fit emblem of our own transitory bloom; and the evergreen, with its perennial shoots, instructing us that "the wintry blast of death kills not the buds of virtue." Here is the thick shrubbery, to protect and conceal the new-made grave; and there is the wild flower creeping along the narrow path, and planting its seeds in the upturned earth. All around us there breathes a solemn calm, as if we were in the bosom of a wilderness, broken only by the breeze, as it murmurs through the tops of the forest, or by the notes of the warbler pouring forth his matin or his evening song.

Ascend but a few steps, and what a change of scenery to surprise and delight us! We seem, as it were, in an instant to pass from the confines of death to the bright and balmy regions of life. Below us flows the winding Charles, with its rippling current, like the stream of time hastening to the ocean of eternity. In the distance the city — at once the object of our admiration and our love — rears its proud eminences, its glittering spires, its lofty towers, its graceful mansions, its curling smoke, its crowded haunts of business and pleasure, which speak to the eye and yet leave a noiseless loneliness on the ear. Again we turn, and the walls of our venerable University rise before us, with many a recollection of happy days passed there in the interchange of study and friendship, and many a grateful thought of the affluence of its learning, which has adorned and nourished the literature of our country. Again we turn, and the cultivated farm, the neat cottage, the village church, the sparkling lake, the rich valley, and the distant hills, are before us, through opening vistas; and we breathe amidst the fresh and varied labors of man.

There is, therefore, within our reach, every variety of natural and artificial scenery, which is fitted to awaken emotions of the highest and most affecting character. We stand, as it were, upon the borders of two worlds; and, as the mood of our minds may be, we may gather lessons of profound wisdom by contrasting the one with the other, or indulge in the dreams of hope and ambition, or solace our hearts by melancholy meditations.

Who is there that, in the contemplation of such a scene, is not ready to exclaim, with the enthusiasm of the poet,

> "Mine be the breezy hill, that skirts the down,
> Where a green, grassy turf is all I crave,
> With here and there a violet bestrewn,
> Fast by a brook, or fountain's murmuring wave;
> And many an evening sun shine sweetly on my grave?"

And we are met here to consecrate this spot, by these solemn ceremonies, to such a purpose. The legislature of this Commonwealth, with a parental foresight, has clothed the Horticultural Society with authority (if I may use its own language) to make a perpetual dedication of it as a Rural Cemetery, or Burying-Ground, and to plant and embellish it with shrubbery, and flowers, and trees, and walks, and other rural ornaments. And I stand here by the order and in behalf of this Society, to declare that by these services it is to be deemed, henceforth and forever, so dedicated. Mount Auburn, in the noblest sense, belongs no longer to the living, but to the dead. It is a sacred, it is an eternal trust. It is consecrated ground. May it remain forever inviolate!

What a multitude of thoughts crowd upon the mind in the contemplation of such a scene! How much of the future, even in its far distant reaches, rises before us with all its persuasive realities! Take but one little narrow space of time, and how affecting are its associations! Within the flight of one half century how many of the great, the good, and the wise will be gathered here! How many, in the loveliness of infancy, the beauty of youth, the vigor of manhood, and the maturity of age, will lie down here, and dwell in the bosom of their mother earth! The rich and the poor, the gay and the wretched, the favorites of thousands and the forsaken of the world, the stranger in his solitary grave, and the patriarch surrounded by the kindred of a long lineage! How many will here bury their brightest hopes or blasted expectations! How many bitter tears will here be shed! How many agonizing sighs will here be heaved! How many trembling feet will cross the pathways, and, returning, leave behind them the dearest objects of their reverence or their love!

And if this were all, sad indeed, and funereal would be our thoughts; gloomy, indeed, would be these shades, and desolate these prospects.

But, thanks be to God, the evils which he permits have their attendant mercies, and are blessings in disguise. The bruised reed will not be laid utterly prostrate. The wounded heart will not always bleed. The voice of consolation will spring up in the midst of the silence of these regions of death. The mourner will revisit these shades with a secret though melancholy pleasure. The hand of friendship will delight to cherish the flowers and the shrubs that fringe the lowly grave, or the sculptured monument. The earliest beams of the morning will play upon these summits with a refreshing cheerfulness; and the lingering tints of evening hover on them with a tranquillizing glow. Spring will invite hither the footsteps of the young by its opening foliage; and autumn detain the contemplative by its latest bloom. The votary of learning and science will here learn to elevate his genius by the holiest studies. The devout will here offer up the silent tribute of piety, or the prayer of gratitude. The rivalries of the world will here drop from the heart; the spirit of forgiveness will gather new impulses; the selfishness of avarice will be checked; the restlessness of ambition will be rebuked; vanity will let fall its plumes; and pride, as it sees "what shadows we are, and what shadows we pursue," will acknowledge the value of virtue as far, immeasurably far, beyond that of fame.

But that which will be ever present, pervading these shades like the noon-day sun, and shedding cheerfulness around, is the consciousness, the irrepressible consciousness, amidst all these lessons of human mortality, of the higher truth, that we are beings, not of time, but of eternity; that "this corruptible must put on incorruption, and this mortal must put on immortality;" that this is but the threshold and starting point of an existence compared with whose duration the ocean is but as a drop, nay, the whole creation an evanescent quantity.

Let us banish, then, the thought that this is to be the abode of a gloom, which will haunt the imagination by its terrors, or chill the heart by its solitude. Let us cultivate feelings and sentiments more worthy of ourselves, and more worthy of Christianity. Here let us erect the memorials of our love and our gratitude, and our glory. Here let the brave repose, who have died in the cause of their country. Here let the statesman rest who has achieved the victories of peace, not less renowned than war. Here let genius find a home, that has sung immortal strains, or has instructed with still diviner eloquence. Here let learning and science, the votaries of inventive art, and the teacher of the philosophy of nature come. Here let youth and beauty, blighted by premature decay, drop, like tender blossoms, into the virgin earth; and here let age retire ripened for the harvest. Above all, here let the benefactors of mankind, the good, the merciful, the meek, the pure in heart, be congregated; for to them belongs an undying praise. And let us take comfort, nay, let us rejoice, that in future ages, long after we are gathered to the generations of other days, thousands of kindling hearts will here repeat the sublime declaration, "Blessed are the dead that die in the Lord, for they rest from their labors; and their works do follow them."

LAW RELATING TO CAPTURE.

A MEMORIAL IN THE CASE OF THE SCHOONER REWARD, WILLIAM GOSS, MASTER, ADDRESSED TO THE COMMISSIONERS FOR THE SETTLEMENT OF CLAIMS, UNDER THE TREATY WITH FRANCE, RATIFIED ON FEBRUARY 2, A. D. 1832.

THE undersigned, claimant of the cargo of the Schooner Reward, on behalf of himself and his co-claimants, having learned, that the claim has been rejected by the Commissioners upon grounds which he deems incorrect and erroneous in point of law, respectfully submits the present Memorial to the Commissioners, as the grounds of his prayer, that they would review the award made by them rejecting his claim.

The facts of the case, as presented to the Commissioners, are: — That the said Schooner Reward, (William Goss, master,) being owned by American citizens, and belonging to Marblehead, in the State of Massachusetts, on the 6th day of December, 1807, sailed from that port on the same day with a cargo on board consisting of codfish, cod oil, potashes, and cotton, of the invoice value of $7487 81; and was then and there owned by the claimants, citizens of and residents in the United States, and bound on a voyage direct to the port of Rochelle, in France. That in the course of the voyage on the high seas near the coast of France, the said Schooner, with her cargo, being wholly neutral property, and neutral to both the belligerents, (France and Great Britain,) was on the 1st day of January, 1808, captured by His Britannic Majesty's armed Brig Conflict. That afterwards, on the 9th day of the same January, the said Schooner was recaptured from the British possession by a French Privateer, and carried into the port of Parros, in France. That the said Schooner and cargo were afterwards sold by order of the French authorities, and the proceeds deposited in the hands of the French government. That the claim of the French privateer to any share of the proceeds, was rejected by the Council of Prizes. That finally, about the 7th of November, 1810, the same proceeds were confiscated by the orders and authority of the then Emperor of France, Napoleon; and that the same have become thus totally lost to the owners of the same Schooner and her cargo.

Such are the facts of the case. And, upon this state of the facts, the Memorialist contends, that the original capture by the British cruiser was illegal and wrongful; that their capture was illegal, or at least conferred no title as prize upon the recaptors; that the subsequent confiscation of the property by the French government was a gross violation of the Law of Nations, and a wrong to the neutral rights of the claimants; and that, therefore, they are entitled to a full indemnity under the treaty with France.

The claim has been rejected by the Commissioners (as the Memorialist understands) upon the following grounds: —

First, That by the Law of France at the time of the recapture, the property, so recaptured, though neutral to all parties in the war, was not entitled to restitution; but was good prize to the recaptors.

Secondly, That the Milan decree made this the law of France in all cases of recapture from British cruisers, because every such capture included a visit by such cruisers.

Thirdly, That the law of France on this subject of recapture is in conformity to the Law of Nations; and consequently obligatory upon all neutrals.

Fourthly, That the Act of Congress of the third of March, 1800, respecting salvage on recaptures, by adopting towards all nations the rule of reciprocity on this subject, negatives all right on our part to complain of the law of France.

The Memorialist respectfully submits to the Commissioners, that the foregoing positions are essentially erroneous, both upon principle and authority; and he trusts he shall be able to satisfy the Commissioners of the truth of his statement. And he does so the more fully and freely, because he shall deem it his duty, in case his claim shall be finally rejected by the Commissioners, to make a solemn appeal to his country, and ask an indemnity from Congress for the losses sustained by such a rejection, which, with all deference to the Commissioners, he deems neither warrantable by the Law of France, nor the Law of Nations, nor the Laws of the United States. He feels, therefore, an anxiety to present his own views deliberately to the Commissioners, so that in no possible event there can be the least doubt, that the subject was fully brought under the review of the Commissioners.

Before proceeding to the direct points in controversy, it may be proper to state (and the Memorialist freely admits it) that the Schooner Reward and her cargo were without question captured by the British cruiser under the British Orders of Council of November, 1807; and that the final confiscation was made by the French government upon the principles of the Milan Decree of the 17th of December, 1807. It requires no argument, on the part of the Memorialist, to establish the doctrine, that the British Orders in Council and the Milan Decree above-mentioned, were gross violations of the Law of Nations; and as such could furnish no just ground of capture or condemnation of the Schooner or her cargo. This doctrine has been so uniformly and publicly maintained by the American government, under all circumstances, that it would be a mere waste of time to endeavor to establish it. It constituted the basis of all the hostile resistance and measures of the American government against both those Powers, from the moment of the first promulgation of those Orders and that Decree, to their final repeal or abandonment. So far, then, from the Milan Decree constituting any justification of the confiscation of the Reward and her cargo, it is an aggravation of the injustice of the French government; and so indeed, all the confiscations under that Decree have been treated by the American government. The British Orders in Council of November, 1807, could furnish as little justification for the original capture. And if the original British capture was (as it certainly was) unjustifiable according to the Law of Nations, it is impossible, that a wrongful capture of a neutral by one belligerent could furnish any just title of prize to the recaptors; for they could only succeed to the rights of the original captors. No principle of the Law of Nations countenances the idea, that a wrongful capture of an American vessel and cargo by a British cruiser can confer on the French recaptors any title of prize, which shall take away the original rights of American owners.

If, therefore, it could be shown, that by the laws of France, neutral property, recaptured by France from her enemy, became good prize to the recaptors, though the original capture of such neutral property was wrongful and unlawful; still, unless by the Law of Nations the neutral property would upon such recapture be good prize, the laws of France would be a violation of our neutral rights; and consequently the condemnation and confiscation of the neutral property would be as unjustifiable, as if it were made under any other infraction of the Law of Nations; such, for instance, as the Berlin and Milan Decrees. There is no pretence to say, that France, by her municipal laws, can change the Law of Nations; or that she has a right to confiscate neutral property, because her enemy has unjustly captured it. That would be to add oppression to oppression, and to make the injustice of one nation a foundation of similar injustice on the part of another nation. The United States have constantly and indignantly rejected any such doctrine.

But let us see, whether the French laws do authorize any such injustice, or have promulgated any such doctrine. The Memorialist most sincerely and deliberately contends, that the French laws nowhere assert any such doctrine. But the contrary has (as he will presently show) been constantly and openly declared to be the law of France and the Law of Nations, by the highest tribunals of France, upon all occasions, when the question has come before them. They have treated the opposite doctrine as founded in the grossest injustice, and as incompatible with the unquestionable rights of neutrals. The difficulty upon this subject has arisen from the very imperfect view which has been taken of the existing laws of France.

Before proceeding to state, what those laws are, it may be proper to say a few words by way of explanation. It is well known that it has been long a vexed question among nations, as well as among writers on the Law of Nations, when and at what time in cases of capture of property, confessedly belonging to an enemy, by one belligerent from another belligerent, the captured property ceases to be that of the original owners, and becomes the property of the captors by a "firm possession." Some writers and some nations hold, that the property is changed immediately upon the capture. Others hold, that twenty-four hours' possession after the capture is indispensable to change the property. Others hold, that the property is not changed until the property is carried into the ports of the capturing power, or, as it is technically expressed, *infra præsidia* of the ports of the captors. Others again hold that the property is not changed until a final sentence of condemnation as prize in a judicial tribunal. This last doctrine is understood to be maintained for many purposes in England and America. France, in common with most of the continental nations of Europe, holds the doctrine, that twenty-four hours' possession after capture constitutes a change of the property of the original owners, and vests the title in the captors. She applies this rule in all cases of capture of belligerent property by another belligerent; and she applies it (as we shall presently see) as well to the property of her own subjects, captured by her enemy, as to the property of her allies captured by their enemy, and to the property of neutrals to her captured by their enemy. In short, in all such cases, she treats the property of the original owners as gone; and of course upon a recapture, she treats it as to all intents and purposes that of her enemy. But this rule has never been applied to any property, except that of a *belligerent*, by France or any other Power. It has never been applied to any property of a *neutral* to all the belligerents.

In whatever manner this rule, as to the time necessary for "firm possession," or change of ownership, has been interpreted by different nations and different writers, it has never been supposed, by any nation or any writer, to apply to any cases, except where the capture is made by one belligerent of property belonging to his enemy. It has never been supposed, that the property of a party, neutral to all the belligerents, is changed by the mere capture by a belligerent, with whom he is at peace, until after a sentence of condemnation. For until such a sentence is passed, the capture is necessarily deemed to be merely made in order to bring the neutral in for adjudication, and to ascertain, whether the property is bonâ fide neutral or not. This doctrine has been often recognized by the Courts of the United States; and it was acted upon by the American High Court of Appeals during the American Revolution, as the clear result of the Law of Nations.[1] Let us, with these principles in view, examine the laws of France on the subject of recaptures.

The Ordinance of Louis XIV., in the Title on Prizes, (Book 3, tit. 9, art. 7,) enacts as follows: "If a vessel belonging to *one of our subjects* is recaptured from our enemies, after she has remained in the hands of the enemy twenty-four hours, she shall be good prize." This article is plainly inapplicable to *neutrals*. It is in terms confined to the property of French subjects. It is founded wholly upon the French doctrine already stated, that twenty-four hours' possession of

[1] Miller *v.* The Resolution, 2 Dallas, Rep. 1, 2, 4.

French property by a belligerent enemy devests the title of the French owners, and vests a title in the enemy captors; so that upon a recapture by a French cruiser, after that time, the property recaptured is deemed the property of the enemy; and the title of the original French owners is lost.

It seems to have been thought, by the Commissioners, that the French ordinance of 1779, cited by Azuni on Maritime Law, (Vol. II. Part 2, ch. 4, article 5, § 5, p. 276,) had applied the same rule to neutrals, that the Ordinance of Louis XIV. already cited, applied to French subjects. But the truth is, that the Ordinance of 1779 does not, in its terms or purport, apply to the capture of neutral property at all. This Ordinance is given by Azuni; and in the American translation of his work, (Vol. II. Part 2, ch. 4, art. 5, § 5, p. 277,) it is represented to be thus: "That vessels recaptured from privateers lawfully armed, after having been twenty-four hours in their possession, shall wholly belong to the recaptors." Now, the Ordinance is somewhat different in its terms; and purports on its face to be a mere continuance of the old Law. The words of the original will be here quoted, as they are given in the second volume of the "Code des Prises," published by authority of the king of France in 1784, (p. 723.) "Elle (sa Majesté) a ordonnè et ordonne; Que les Reglemens concernent la Recousse continueront d'étre observés suivant leur forme et teneur; En consequence, lorsque *los Navires de ses sujets* auront été repris par les corsaires armés en course contra les enemis de l'Etat, apres avoir été vingt-quatre heures en leurs mains, ils leur appartiéndront en totalité." The literal translation of which is, "His Majesty has ordained and does ordain, that the rules concerning recaptures shall continue to be observed according to their form and tenor; and accordingly, when the *vessels of his subjects* shall have been recaptured by privateers, armed for the cruise against the enemies of the State, after having been twenty-four hours in their hands, they shall entirely belong to them." This, it will be at once seen, is a mere renewal of the Ordinance of 1681. It applies, in terms only, to the property of French subjects, recaptured from the enemy by a French cruiser. It seems, however, to have been applied, in the tribunals of France, to the property of a co-belligerent ally of France, recaptured from the common enemy of both, as we are informed by the learned Editor of the Code des Prises. In such a case France has applied to her ally the same rule, which she applies to her own subjects. In such cases the Ordinance treats the property of the original owner as devested by the twenty-four hours' possession of the enemy captor. But the Ordinance never has been applied to cases of neutral property, captured by a belligerent, with whom the neutral was at peace, and recaptured by a French cruiser, with whom, also, the neutral was at peace. This is expressly declared by the learned Editor of the Code des Prises, in a note to the very Ordinance. "Sa Majesté," (says he,) "a jugé pendant la dernière guerre, que la Reprise d'une *navire Neutre* faite par un Corsaire Français (lorsque le Navire neutre n'etoit pas chargé de marchandises prohibees, ni dans le cas d'etre confisqué par l'Enemi) etoit ulle." (Code de Prises, Tom. II., p. 725, edit. 1784.) "His Majesty adjudged, during the last war, that a recapture of a neutral ship, (when the neutral ship was not laden with prohibited, (contraband) goods, or had not been confiscated (condemned) by the enemy) was void." And in proof of this, he states four cases, two of Swedish ships, one of a Portuguese ship, and one of an Imperial (Austrian) ship, decided upon that very point. The reason is obvious. No belligerent can acquire any title by a capture to bonâ fide neutral property. And, therefore, he cannot confer any title on the recaptors. The capture of such bonâ fide neutral property can be deemed no more than a possession for the purpose of ascertaining whether the neutral has been guilty of any violation of the law of nations, or not. And so the doctrine is understood by Azuni himself, who puts the very case of the recapture of neutral property, (neutral to both of the belligerents) from the possession of the enemy, by a French cruiser; and he declares, that in such case the original capture being unlawful, cannot confer on the recaptor any right of property whatsoever.[1] And he cites three decisions made by the French Council of Prizes, in the year 1779 and 1781, on the very point. "During the last American war," (says he) "when Portugal was neutral (to all the belligerents) a ship of that nation, the Nostra Senora d' Ovelle, captured by an English cruiser, and recaptured within twenty-four hours after by the French privateer Le Prince de Tingry, was restored by a decree of the 29th of December, 1781; the French privateer was condemed to pay 20,000 livres damages and costs to the Portuguese owners; and the captors were refused any salvage, upon the ground, that the law of recapture did not apply, so as to allow salvage to French cruisers for recapturing a neutral vessel, which, it was presumed, would not be condemned by the English. Besides, the vessel was captured and recaptured on the same day; and of course within the twenty-four hours."[2] Now, if the Ordinance of 1799 had had any application whatsoever to the case of neutral property recaptured from an enemy of France, this decree could not have been made. The truth is, that the doctrine of this case is the received doctrine of the Law of Nations everywhere. A belligerent, by recapturing neutral property, (neutral to all the belligerents,) has done no meritorious service; and is not entitled even to any salvage. Nay, the recaptors may be held responsible in damages for the act, unless there was a real danger of condemnation to the neutral by the original captors, from their lawless disregard of the laws of nations; and if there was such danger, then the recaptors are entitled to salvage only. So the doctrine has been uniformly held in England; and particularly by Sir William Scott, in the case of The War Onskan, (2 Robin. Adm. R.

[1] Azuni on Maritime Law, Part 2, ch. 4, art. 5, § 6, p. 277.

[2] Azuni, Vol. II. Part 2, ch. 4, art. 5, § 12, p. 284, 285. The same case is given at large in the Code des Prises, Tom. II. p. 1021.

299,)[1] and by the Supreme Court of the United States in the case of Talbot *v.* Seeman, (1 Cranch, Rep. 1.)

The other cases cited by Azuni were as follows: "Sweden being neutral (to all the belligerents) during the American war, a Swedish ship, the Mercury, laden with hemp, captured by an English cruiser, and recaptured by a French cruiser within twenty-four hours, was ordered to be restored by a decree of the Council of Prizes, the 14th of April, 1779, confirmed by an order of the King's Council, of the 27th December, 1779. A similar decree was made relative to the Swedish ship Argos, laden with bar iron, taken by an English cruiser, and recaptured *nine* days after by the French privateer Josephine." In this last case not only was a decree of restitution made, but the recaptors were decreed to pay damages, costs, and expenses, on account of the recapture.[2]

These cases are all reported at large in the Code des Prises; and the specific sentences therein rendered by the King in Council upon the final hearing thereof, are set forth verbatim; and they fully confirm the statement given by Azuni.[3] These cases do not stand alone. The same question occurred during the late war between England and France, (the war of 1793 to 1802) and it was decided in the same manner and upon the same principles by the highest Courts of Prize in France. And, what makes it a still more direct and important authority, the question arose in the cases of American ships captured by the English, and recaptured by the French; so that they are cases exactly in point with the present. The first case was that of the Statira, which was an American ship recaptured from an English cruiser by a French cruiser, (Le Hazard) and carried into the port of Parros, Guirec. The question was, whether the American ship so recaptured, being a neutral ship, (at peace both with France and England,) was good prize to the recaptors, she

[1] See also, The Carlotta, 5 Robinson, Rep. 54.
[2] 2 Azuni, Maritime Law, Part 2, ch. 4, art. 5, § 13, p. 285, 286.
[3] See Code des Prises, Tom. II. p. 787; Id. p. 1081; Id. p. 1044.

50

having been retaken from the enemy of France after having been in the possession of the latter more than twenty-four hours. It was expressly decided by the High Court of Prizes, that the vessel was to be restored; the cargo being condemned for other causes. The Court expressly declared, that there was no pretence to say, that, by the Ordinance of 1681, or any subsequent Ordinance of France, a neutral, who was neutral to all the belligerents, and recaptured from the enemy by a French cruiser, (whether the latter was a ship belonging to the government, or a privateer,) was good prize. The language of the Court on that occasion was, that upon general principles it was clearly otherwise. "A neutral ship was entitled to be respected by all nations. If she is oppressed by one of the belligerents, that furnishes no reason why the other belligerents should be accomplices in that oppression, or be authorized to turn that to their profit. Therefore, a neutral ship, recaptured by a French cruiser from the enemy, ought to be released, if her neutrality is established."[1] The same principles were adopted by the Council of Prizes in the case of the American ship Kitty, (neutral to all the belligerents,) which was recaptured from the enemy of France by a French cruiser; and the vessel and cargo were accordingly restored. The doctrine of these decisions has never been doubted, or denied in France, as matter of French law, or of the Law of Nations. And in confirmation of this assertion, the Memorialist would respectfully refer to the great Work of that great French Jurist, Merlin, in his Repertoire de Jurisprudence, (article, Prise Maritime, § 3, art. 4, n. 5, p. 107 to 111, edit. 1827,) where these cases, and the reasoning in support of them, are given at large by the learned author, from the decisions of the Court.

Upon this part of the case the Memorialist begs respectfully to state, that the established law of France is this.

[1] Merlin, Repertoire, tit. Prise Maritime, § 3, art. 4, n. 5, Tom. 25, p. 107, edit. 1827.

First, that upon a recapture of a *French vessel* from the enemy by a French cruiser, after she has been in the possession of the enemy more than twenty-four hours, the recaptors are entitled to the property, as good prize, by the express provisions of the Ordinances of France. Secondly, that upon a recapture of a ship belonging to an ally of France in the war, (that is, an ally who is equally with France at war with her enemy,) by a French cruiser, the same rule is, by the French Ordinances, applied to such property of the ally as is applied to the case of French property; that is, if it is recaptured, after it has been more than twenty-four hours in possession of the enemy, it is good prize. The reason is, that such property of an ally in the war, upon such capture by the enemy of the ally, becomes, after twenty-four hours' possession, the property of such enemy, upon the principles of the Law of Nations as understood by France. Thirdly, that a neutral ship, (that is, neutral to all the belligerents,) recaptured by a French cruiser from the enemy of France, is to be restored, because the neutral was not justly liable to capture by the enemy, and could not lawfully be condemned as prize; and therefore the recapture was unlawful.

These principles of the French law are in perfect consonance with the Law of Nations, and with the recognized law of America. They were formerly promulgated and acted upon by the American High Court of Appeals, in the case of Miller *v.* The Ship Resolution, (2 Dall. R. 1,) during the Revolution, and since that period by the Supreme Court of the United States, in the case of Talbot *v.* Seeman, in 1801, (1 Cranch, R. 1.) In both of these cases the very same question arose; and it was decided in the same manner and upon the same principles as it had been decided before by the French tribunals.

If the Memorialist is right in this view of the law of France, and of the Law of Nations, on the subject of the recapture of neutral property; it is manifest, that the Commissioners are in error, and that their former award ought to be reversed. Indeed, it is difficult to state the present case without perceiving that any different doctine would involve the grossest injustice, and abandonment of neutral rights. Here is a case of an American vessel and cargo wrongfully and unlawfully captured by a British cruiser under the British orders in Council, which have been uniformly held by the American government to be a gross violation of our neutral rights, and on account of which we entered into a war with Great Britain; and the original capture being thus wrongfully and unlawfully made, a French cruiser (with whose nation also we were at peace) recaptured the American vessel, and instead of restoring her to her lawful owners, she is confiscated, because she has been already captured by a British cruiser without any default of her own. Thus, the recaptors are permitted to assert in an American tribunal a claim to condemn neutral American property upon the mere ground, that it was found in the possession of a wrongdoer. The French government have never asserted any such right. They rejected the claim of the recaptors; and confiscated the property solely and wholly under the Milan Decree; because the vessel had been visited and searched by a British cruiser. Now, as the Memorialist has already remarked, that very decree (the Milan Decree) has always been treated by the American government as a gross violation of our neutral rights. How, then, can it be held in an American tribunal to be a just cause for denying damages to the injured American owners?

But the Memorialist understands, that the Commissioners have founded their award upon a construction supposed to have been put upon the act of Congress respecting recaptures, passed the 3d of March, 1800. If the views already suggested by the Memorialist as to the law of France are, as he humbly conceives them to be, irrefragably correct, it is perfectly clear, that the Act of Congress of 1800 can have no bearing on the cause; for the present case can in no just sense be deemed within the letter or spirit of that Act. It is not a case for the application of any rule of reciprocity; or, if it be, we must apply the rule which France ought to have applied according to the Law of Nations.

The Memorialist, however, wishes now in further explanation of his own views, as well as to show the true interpretation of the case of the Adeline (9 Cranch, 244,) which is founded on the Act of Congress of 1800, and has been erroneously supposed by the Commissioners to conflict with his claim, to make some remarks upon the Act of Congress of 1800. That Act is entitled, "An Act providing for Salvage in cases of Recapture." It must be presumed to apply to such cases, and to such only in which, consistently with the Law of Nations, salvage could be demanded upon a recapture. It would be utterly unjustifiable to presume, that Congress intended to provide a permanent law, applicable to all times and all nations, which should provide for a compensation by way of salvage in cases where such recapture would be unlawful, and a violation of neutral rights under the Law of Nations. That would be to presume that Congress meant deliberately to violate the Law of Nations in regard to all neutrals, and under all circumstances, in cases of recapture. Now, such a violation of the Law of Nations would be a good ground for neutral nations to claim indemnity from the American government; and if that should be refused, to declare war against us. Now, the Supreme Court of the United States, as has been already mentioned, have decided (in conformity to the prior decisions of the American Courts) in the case of Talbot *v.* Seeman, that the recapture of a neutral from our enemy is an unlawful act, unless the neutral be in real danger of condemnation from the habitual disregard of the Law of Nations by such enemy; and in such case the recaptors are entitled to salvage, and nothing more. Common sense, therefore, as well as the rules of interpretation, adopted by Courts of Justice, require, that such a construction should not be given to the Act of Congress of 1800, as shall violate the Law of Nations, unless that construction be inevitable. It is clear, that no such construction is necessary; and that the general language may well be restrained to the very class of cases, for which provisions of this sort are usually made by nations. The third section of the Act of 1800 in substance declares, that when any vessel or goods, taken as prize by an American cruiser from an enemy of the United States, shall belong to foreign subjects, the same shall be restored to such owners, upon the payment of such salvage, as by the law or usage of the foreign government, to which such owners belong, is required on the restoration of the property of American citizens upon a recapture, made by the authority of such foreign government; and if no such restoration would be made to American citizens by the laws or usage of such foreign government on payment of salvage, then none shall be made to such foreign owners on such recapture by American cruisers. The rule here prescribed in cases of recapture by American cruisers, is the rule of reciprocity; and it is the very rule laid down by the British Courts of Admiralty as the general Law of Nations. It was, without doubt, adopted by the Act of Congress as affirmative of the general Law of Nations. Now, to what cases has this rule of the Law of Nations been applied? We have already seen, that it has not been, and cannot be applied, consistently with the Law of Nations, to cases of recaptures of neutrals strictly so called, (that is, to neutrals to all the belligerents.) But, it has been applied constantly, as the rule of reciprocity, to cases of an ally in the same war, and to persons, who are neutrals in respect to the recaptors, and yet are at war with one or more of the belligerents. This will be apparent upon an examination of the cases decided in the English Courts of Admiralty, and especially in the cases of The Santa Cruz. (1 Robinson, Rep. 50 to 80.) The War Onskan, (2 Robin. R. 299.) The Eleanora Catharina, (4 Robin. R. 156.) The Carlotta, (5 Robin. R. 59.) The Huntress, (6 Robin. R. 108,) decided by Sir William Scott.

But it is to be understood that the Commissioners have supposed that the third section of the Act of Congress, 1800, had been construed by the Supreme Court of the United States, in the case of the Adeline, (9 Cranch, 244, &c.) to apply to, and include all cases of neutrals, as well cases where they are neutrals to all the belligerents, as cases where they are neutrals to some only of the belligerents, or allies in the war. A moment's consideration of the circumstances of that case will demonstrate that no such decision could have been made by the Supreme Court; for no such case was before the court as that of a party neutral to all the belligerents. And, in referring to the language of the court in any case, the universal rule is to consider that language with reference to the particular facts of the case. The Adeline was the case of an American letter of marque, sailing in March, 1814, (during the late war between England and the United States) from Bordeaux, in France, for the United States, with a cargo on board, belonging partly to citizens of the United States and partly to French subjects domiciled in France. At this time there was open war between Great Britain and France. The United States was not an *ally* in this war on the part of France; but was simply a belligerent, neutral to France, and carrying on the war against Great Britain without any coöperation with France. The Adeline was captured by a British squadron in the course of the voyage; and, after being six days in the possession of the British, she was recaptured by an American privateer, and brought into New York for adjudication. One of the questions arising in the case was, whether the property of the French subjects, domiciled in France, was good prize; or ought to be restored under the Act of Congress, upon payment of salvage to the recaptors. And that question depended upon another, whether France would, upon principles of reciprocity, restore under the like circumstances, upon the payment of salvage. The court decided that France would not restore under the like circumstances, and therefore that the property of the parties domiciled in France was good prize. On that occasion the court said, " By the Act of

Congress, as well as by the general law in cases of recapture the rule of reciprocity is to be applied." Now this language is plainly applicable only to the case of a co-belligerent, or an ally in the war; for, as we have seen, by the general principles of the Law of Nations, in cases of the recapture of property strictly neutral to all the parties in the war, no such rule exists; and the same court has held the recapture, under such circumstances, unlawful. The court go on to say, "If France would restore in a like case, then are we bound to restore. If otherwise, then the whole property must be condemned to the recaptors." Now what was the case before the court? It was the case of the capture of the property of the subjects of one belligerent (France) by her enemy (England.) It was not the case of the capture of neutral property by England from French subjects, with whom she was at peace. The court then proceed to say, "It appears that, by the law of France in cases of recapture, after the property has been twenty-four hours in possession of the enemy, the whole property is adjudged good prize to the recaptors, whether it belonged to her subjects, to her allies, or to neutrals." Now the only possible question which can arise, is from the word "neutrals" in this sentence. Does the word "neutrals" here refer to neutrals to all the belligerents in the war; or to neutrals to France, though belligerents in regard to other parties? Certainly, there can be no doubt that a nation may be engaged in a war against another nation, with which France is at the same time at war, without being an ally of France. In such a case, she is strictly neutral as to France, and a billigerent as to her enemy. That was in fact our situation in our late war with Great Britain. The United States were not allies of France in that war; but merely co-billigerents. Each nation acted without reference to, and independent of, the other in that war. That also was the very case of the Adeline before the Supreme Court. So that the language of the court, with reference to the facts of the case, was strictly correct and appropriate. The case of a party neutral to all the belligerents was not before the court, and could not have been intended to be decided. It is impossible that the court could have intended deliberately to overrule their own decision in Talbot *v.* Seeman, as to the Law of Nations on this very subject, without discussing the point, or alluding to that case. Now, as we have seen, France considers property captured by one belligerent from another, and in the possession of the captors, twenty-four hours, to be absolutely vested in the latter under the Law of Nations. She applies this rule indiscriminately to her own subjects, to her allies, and to all other belligerents, who are not her allies. But she does not apply this rule to parties neutral to all the belligerents; nor could she do so consistently with the Law of Nations, as administered and understood in France or in America. The language of the Supreme Court, then, interpreted in its genuine sense, does not in the slightest degree touch the present case. Nor could it be intended to touch it.

What confirms this view of the subject is, that the argument for the recaptors, in the case of the Adeline, did not pretend to state or contend for a broader doctrine. That argument relies wholly upon the fact that the original capture was of French *belligerent* property, of which the enemy of France had had more than twenty-four hours' possession, which devested the property. And those recaptors relied solely on the Ordinance of 1779, and the Commentaries of Azuni, in the places referred to in this memorial, to establish their conclusion. Now, as we have seen, Azuni points out and sustains the very distinction for which the Memorialist contends; and the argument of the recaptors, in the case of the Adeline, admitted that distinction. (See the Adeline, 9 Cranch, p. 247, and especially p. 248, 249, and p. 276, 277.) The argument for the French claimants did not attempt to impugn that distinction or conclusion. It is plain, then, that as neither the facts nor the arguments raised any doubt, as to the rights of neutrals to all the belligerents; and as the court took no notice of the exception, but decided the case upon the general principle, admitted by the argument, the court could not have intended to make the doctrine broader than that contended for by the recaptors.

All of which is respectfully submitted by the Memorialist for the consideration of the Commissioners.

WILLIAM FETTYPLACE,

In behalf of himself and the other Claimants.

BOSTON, December 16, 1835.

EULOGY ON PROFESSOR ASHMUN,

PRONOUNCED AT THE OBSEQUIES OF JOHN HOOKER ASHMUN, ROYALL PROFESSOR OF LAW IN HARVARD UNIVERSITY, APRIL 5, 1833.

THE occasion, which has brought us together, is full of melancholy interest. It is not, that it is new; for the annals of time are crowded with memorials of the dead; with repetitions of sorrows, which know no end; and with renewals of anguish, which continually find utterance upon the departure of the good, the wise and the great. It is not, that there is even any thing unusual in the present event, or beside the general course of human experience; for when has the time been, in which youth and manhood have not dropped into the grave, in all the pride of their power, and the affluence of their hopes? We have seen the aged linger on to the last syllable of their recorded time; and we have seen the bud of beauty nipped and withered, in the first faint blushes of its dawn. These are common events; so common, indeed, that they scarcely attract more than a transient notice; and, so that they strike not within our own immediate circle of friends, we gaze on them, for a moment, with subdued thoughtfulness, and then press on to our own accustomed duties; we return to our homes, and the sadness has passed away from our hearts.

Such is human life. I will not say, such is human infirmity. It is, doubtless, in the wisdom of Providence, that it should be so. If, with such constantly recurring scenes of death on every side, our sympathy should always hover round the mourners; if we should partake of all their agonized feelings, and dwell, as they dwell, on the vanity of all human pursuits, and the desolateness of all human hopes; if we should take counsel, like them, only from our own dark meditations upon the frail tenure of our existence, and the utter worthlessness of every thing on this side of the grave; who does not perceive, that we should be unfit for all the active duties of life; that we should be absorbed in one unchanging reverie; that our affections would soon be exhausted, or extinguished; that our families and friends would soon cease to be felt, as the exciting source of our highest enjoyments; and that we should fly to forests and caverns, to impenetrable shades, and secret recesses, that we might bury ourselves from every thing but our own thoughts, and become as unfit for this earth, as it would then seem unfit for us?

On the other hand, we are not permitted to be insensible to the dangers, that everywhere surround us. We become daily touched with the sense of human infirmity. We learn the salutary lesson, that Providence has allotted to each of us his own sufferings; that there is no exemption of age, or rank, or station; and that, however often we may have occasion to lift our souls in grateful prayer for past blessings, there is a common doom appointed for all. The stream of time has always flowed on, and ever will flow on, noiseless, but irresistible, to the ocean of eternity.

Thoughts, like these, if rightly improved, have a natural tendency to make us wiser, and holier, and better. They enable us to feel, as it were, the yet distant evils; to administer to the calamities of others with a soothing kindness; to warm, as well as to exalt, our own virtues; and to cherish habitually that compassionate tenderness, which, when the day of our own visitation shall arrive, will be found one of the surest sources of earthly comfort. They prepare us also for the higher consolations of religion; for those sublime views of another and a better world, which Christianity has unfolded with such inexpressible glory, — "When this corruptible shall put on incorruption, and this mortal shall put on immortality."

And the day of our own visitation is arrived. Death has entered into our little academical circle, and struck down one of its choicest ornaments and supports. His cold and lifeless remains are now before us. We are gathered, in this consecrated temple, to perform his obsequies; to devote a brief space to the recollection of his character and virtues; and then to consign these perishable relics to the home, where they shall rest, until that hour, when

> "The trumpet shall be heard on high;
> The dead shall live — the living die."

I feel, my friends, how utterly inadequate I am, under such circumstances, to the performance of the task assigned me. What can I say, that has not been said a thousand times before? What can I suggest, which has not already suggested itself to your own hearts in a more touching form, and with a more homefelt pathos? Alas! the language of bereavement has long since rung out all its melancholy changes. The mourners have daily woven anew the texture of their sorrows, that they might more diligently employ their nightly vigils in separating the threads, and moistening each with their tears.

It has been said, with great force and truth, that

> "Our dying friends come o'er us like a cloud,
> To damp our brainless ardors, and abate
> That glare of life, which often blinds the wise."

But they often subserve another, if it be not a holier purpose. By severing every earthly tie, they compel us to rely wholly on the past; to treasure up in our memories every little incident, that we may be enabled to preserve, however faintly, some faithful resemblance of our departed friends. We are thus driven back to trace out every striking feature of their minds and characters; to recall every fleeting association; and thus, by placing the lines in their due order, to draw out a softened image of every excellence, until, at length, it seems to breathe with the warmth and freshness of life. Painful as is the first effort, the very employment soon becomes the minister of good; and, like an angel of mercy, it comes with healing in its wings. It is one of the beautiful illustrations of the compensatory power of Providence, that sorrow is thus enabled to extract a secret cure from its own bitterest meditations.

And may I not say, how much there is in such a thought peculiarly appropriate to the present occasion? However deep may be our affliction in our present loss, the past is full of brightness, and the evening shuts not down in a settled and appalling gloom. We can look back upon the life of our departed friend with an approving consciousness. We can see much to love, admire, and reverence in his character; and nothing to awaken regret for error, or apology for frailty. Such as he was, we can bear him in our hearts and on our lips with a manly praise. We can hold him up as a fit example for youthful emulation and ambition; not dazzling, but elevated; not stately, but solid; not ostentatious, but pure.

Of his life there are but few incidents, and these may be briefly told; for in a life not long, but uniform and consistent, filled up in the regular discharge of duty, and in the quiet occupations of a profession, little will be found to attract notice, or invite curiosity. He, who has marked out for himself a course of habitual diligence and virtue; who has no ambition, except for wisdom, and no love of power, that he may reap the ordinary rewards of popular favor; even if he does not pass his days along the sequestered paths of life with a noiseless tenor, has little to engage the vulgar gaze, and can furnish no eccentricities to gratify the idle, and no follies to console the indolent. Such a man addresses himself to higher objects and more enduring aims. He seeks to be what he ought; and is not content to dream on through life, the shadow of greatness, or the finger-point of scorn.

Our departed friend, John Hooker Ashmun, was born in Blandford, in Massachusetts, on the third day of July, 1800. His father was the Honorable Eli P. Ashmun, a distinguished lawyer of the Hampshire bar, who for several years represented that county in our State Senate, and afterwards represented this Commonwealth in the Senate of the United States. It was my good fortune to know him in the latter station, which he filled with great dignity, ability, and public respect. He retired voluntarily from public life, either from a superior attachment to his profession or from ill health, and died about the year 1819. His mother was the daughter of the Reverend John Hooker, a distinguished clergyman of Northampton, from whom he derived his name. His mother died when he was quite young; so that he early lost that maternal care which is always deeply felt, and is so generally irreparable; though it was in his case fortunately supplied by another, towards whom he entertained during his whole life a very tender regard. At an early age he was put under the instruction of a Mr. Grosvenor, who kept a private school at Northampton, with whom he made such proficiency that at nine years of age he was deemed an extraordinary Latin scholar. He was afterwards removed to Blandford, and was there fitted for college by the Rev. Mr. Keep, of that town. At the age of twelve he was deemed well qualified to enter upon the usual collegiate studies; but he was kept back until the succeeding year by the prudence of his father. He was then matriculated, and remained three years at Williamstown College, and then joined the Junior Class in Harvard University, and took his first degree at the annual commencement in the year 1818. During his residence at this University he does not appear to have exerted himself with any uncommon ardor in his studies. His own account of the matter seems to have been, that, though the labors required of him would not have cost him much effort, he had little relish for them; and his extreme youth rendered them less attractive and less instructive than they would otherwise have been; so that much of his time passed without any correspondent improvement, except in the department of mathematics. It is not improbable, too, that entering at an advanced standing, he did not easily acquire that intimacy with his classmates which was calculated to nourish his ambition; and that he felt something of that estrangement which rarely fails to be the accompaniment of young persons engaging in new studies with those who have already caught, as it were, the genius and inspiration of the place by an earlier union in common pursuits.

As soon as he was graduated, he entered upon the study of the law in the office of his father, whom, however, he had the misfortune, soon afterwards, to lose; and he then completed his studies under the care of the Honorable Lewis Strong, of Northampton. It was about this period that he became intimately acquainted with the late Judge Howe, then a resident in the same town, whose very high professional attainments and untimely death are yet fresh in the memory of all of us. In due time he was admitted to the bar; and henceforth he devoted himself with intense zeal and strenuous industry to the noble science of the Law — his favorite, and, I had almost said, his all-absorbing study. His career was soon marked by deserved success; and before he left the bar at which he then was accustomed to practise, he stood in the very first rank of his profession without an acknowledged superior. It is well known that Judge Howe had established a Law School at Northampton of very high character; and, during the last year of his life, Mr. Ashmun, although quite young, was associated in his labors; and, on his decease, in connection with that accomplished statesman and jurist, the late Mr. Mills, he continued the establishment with unabated celebrity and success. In fact, from the ill health of Mr. Mills, the principal instruction in the School devolved almost entirely on Mr. Ashmun; and, with his characteristic vigor, he rose in energy, as the pressure demanded more various and exhausting labors.

Upon the reorganization of the Law Institution in this

University, in the year 1829, Mr. Ashmun was invited by the unanimous vote of the Corporation, to the chair of the Royall Professorship of Law. This tribute to his extraordinary merit occurred under circumstances as gratifying as any which could well attend any similar appointment. The office was not only unsought on his own part, but it was wholly unexpected. It was a spontaneous movement of the Corporation itself, acting on its own responsibility, upon a deliberate review of his qualifications, and after the most searching inquiry into the solidity of his reputation. The choice was fully justified by the event. The honors of the University were never more worthily bestowed, never more meekly worn, and never more steadily brightened. He remained in the conscientious discharge of the arduous duties of this station with an unfaltering fidelity to the last. He might almost be said to have died with his professional armor on him. Scarcely a fortnight is now elapsed since his voice was heard in the forum, mastering a case of no inconsiderable nicety and importance; and only on the day before his death he was meditating new labors, and laying before me the scheme of our future juridical instructions.

I need hardly say, in this place, with what distinguished ability he filled the professor's chair. His method of instruction was searching and exact. It disciplined, while it awakened the mind. It compelled the pupil to exert his own powers; but it brought with it the conscious rewards of the labor. His explanations were always clear, and forcible, and satisfactory. Although his learning was exceedingly various, as well as deep, he never assumed the air of authority. On the contrary, whenever a question occurred, which he was not ready to answer, he had no reserves and no concealments. With the modesty, as well as the tranquil confidence, of a great mind, he would candidly say, "I am not lawyer enough to answer that." In truth, his very doubts, like the doubts of Lord Eldon, and the queries of Plowden, let you at once into the vast reach of his inquiries and attainments. There is not, and there cannot be, a higher tribute to his memory than this, that, while his scrutiny was severely close, he was most cordially beloved by all his pupils. He lived with them upon terms of the most familiar intimacy; and he has sometimes, with a delightful modesty and elegance, said to me, "I am but the eldest boy upon the form."

He had for more than eight years been in a state of declining health, the victim of a constitutional disease, slow and silent in its approaches, which deluded our hopes, and lulled our fears, and was most insidious in the very hours, in which it moved the heart with unusual cheerfulness. It may be truly said, in the language of one of the most eloquent of modern statesmen on a similar occasion, that it pleased the Almighty "to make his shortened span one long disease."[1] No man could have resisted it with a more firm yet gentle spirit. He saw the danger without dismay, and struggled to meet and overcome it. Whatever medical skill could bring to his aid, to alleviate, or subdue it, was faithfully administered. Without being confident that he should triumph over this constitutional infirmity, he seemed constantly encouraged by the consciousness that it was worth the trial. No man ever bore himself, through every change of its aspect, with a more uncomplaining moderation, or more unshrinking fortitude. He sought concealment of his sufferings; and was even sensitive to inquiries on the subject. He buried in his own bosom both his hopes and his fears; and seemed, most of all, anxious to avoid giving trouble and inconvenience to others. There were periods when the disease seemed, in a great measure, to have lost its potency; and there were other periods in which it seemed to move on, with a hurried process, to an immediate catastrophe. Yet in every vicissitude the same imperturbable resolution and the same unrepining calmness marked his conduct. His intellectual energy seemed rather heightened, than impaired, by the gradual diminution

[1] The Right Honorable George Canning's Epitaph on his eldest son.

of his physical strength. Its activity seemed to furnish a salutary stimulus, if it did not administer a necessary aliment to his existence. I have sometimes been led to doubt whether, if he had had less professional excitement, he would not earlier have fallen a victim.

Although for the few last days it was obvious, to those of us who had most intercourse with him, that he could not live many weeks, or, at most, many months; yet the actual occurrence of his death was a calamity so sudden and startling that all his friends were awakened, as it were from a dreadful dream. He was himself without the slightest suspicion of the impending event. He sought repose at the usual hour on Sunday evening, being for the first time watched by the care of an interesting friend, without any wish expressed on his own part. He retained his senses almost to the last; and sank away in a gentle, childlike sleep, without the smallest struggle, and almost without observation. At the very moment when he was breathing his last breath, the first beams of the morning were beginning to blend their beautiful and softened lights. His spirit, as it bore itself away from the earth, seemed almost to whisper in our ears the affecting aspiration of the Psalmist, "O! that I had wings like a dove; for then would I flee away, and be at rest."[1]

Such is the simple narrative of the life of Mr. Ashmun, and such the enviable felicity of his death. Yet, brief as was his career, there was much in it calculated to awaken our admiration, as well as to engage our affections. Few men have impressed upon the memory of their friends a livelier sense of excellence and unsullied virtue. Fewer have left behind them a character so significant in its outlines, and so well fitted to sustain an enduring fame.

My own acquaintance with him commenced only with his residence in Cambridge. But ever since that period I have counted it among my chief pleasures to cultivate his friend-

[1] Mr. Ashmun died on Monday morning, the first day of April, 1833.

ship, and justify his confidence. Engaged, as we have been, in kindred pursuits and duties, it has been almost of course that our intercourse should be frank, as well as frequent; and I feel a pride in declaring, that we have worked hand in hand with the most cordial fellowship, and with a union of opinion, which nothing but the strongest mutual attachment could have successfully cherished. I can, therefore, with all sincerity of heart, join the general voice of his afflicted relatives and friends, in bearing testimony to his rare endowments and exalted merits.

In the private and domestic circle he was greatly beloved, as well as respected. He was confiding and affectionate; and, as an elder son, occupying the place of a parent, he indulged a truly paternal kindness towards the younger branches of the family, mixed up with the eager solicitude and sympathy of a brother. In his feelings he possessed an enlightened benevolence, and a warm sensibility; and was gratified by an opportunity to advance those, who were within the sphere of his influence. He was a man of the most inflexible honor and integrity, a devout lover of truth, conscientiously scrupulous in the discharge of his duties, and constantly elevating the standard of his own virtue. His candor was as marked, as his sense of justice was acute and vivid. He held in utter contempt that low and grovelling spirit, which contented itself with common observances, so as not to offend against the established decencies of life; which was sordid, as far as it dared; and mean, as far as it was safe. And yet the voice of censure rarely escaped from his lips; and he seemed solicitous to moderate the language of the sentence, even when truth demanded that he should not withhold it. He habitually softened the lineaments of the portraits, which he had no wish to gaze on, or to sketch.

He had also, as might easily be gathered from what has been already said, a deep sense of the value and importance of religion; though, from his ill health, he was of late years compelled to abstain a good deal from its public solemnities. In his opinions he was unequivocally a Unitarian, without the slightest propensity to proselytism or bigotry. His great aim was to be good, and not merely to seem so. He had a profound feeling of his responsibleness to God for all his actions, and clung with devout reverence to the doctrines of life and immortality, as revealed in the Gospel. His opinions on these subjects were not built upon transitory emotions; but they grew up and mingled with all his thoughts, and gave to them a peculiar transparency and force. They imparted a serenity and confidence, which may be truly enumerated, as among the choicest of human blessings.

In his general deportment, he was modest and reserved, less desirous to please than his high powers would have justified, and never eager either for contest or victory. On this account, as well as on account of his thoughtful aspect, he was often supposed, on the first approaches, to be cold or indifferent, having little relish for social scenes and the lighter pleasures of life. This was far from being true; for among those with whom he was intimate, no man was more social in his temper, more indulgent in playful and delicate humor, or more familiar in easy conversation. His abstinence from general society was partly from choice, and partly from duty. Besides ill health he felt another disadvantage from the infirmity of a slight deafness, with which he had been long afflicted. Time, also, was to him inestimable. It was a prize not to be thrown away, but to be employed in intellectual advancement, in widening and deepening the foundations of his constantly accumulating knowledge. Though he read much, he thought still more; and there was a freshness in all his views, which stamped them at once with the impress of originality.

But it is chiefly in a professional point of view, that he should be remembered in this place, as at once an ornament to be honored, and an example to be followed. If we look at his years, it seems almost incredible, that he should have attained so high a distinction in so short a period. Let it be recollected, that he died before he had attained the age of thirty-three; and that he had then gathered about him all the honors, which are usually the harvest of the ripest life.

The law is a science of such vast extent and intricacy, of such severe logic and nice dependencies, that it has always tasked the highest minds to reach even its ordinary boundaries. But eminence in it can never be attained without the most laborious study, united with talents of a superior order. There is no royal road to guide us through its labyrinths. They are to be penetrated by skill, and mastered by a frequent survey of landmarks. It has almost passed into a proverb, that the lucubrations of twenty years will do little more than conduct us to the vestibule of the temple; and an equal period may well be devoted to exploring the recesses. What, then, shall we think of a man, who in ten years had elevated himself to the foremost rank, and laid the foundations of deep, various, and accurate learning? What shall we think of a man, who, at that early period, was thought as worthy as any one in the profession to fill the chair just vacated by the highest judicial officer of the Commonwealth, in the full vigor of his own well-earned fame?

There were yet difficulties to be overcome in the case of Mr. Ashmun, which bring out in stronger relief the traits of his professional character, and invest it with a peculiar charm and dignity. He was defective in some of the most engaging and attractive accomplishments of the bar. Owing to ill health, he could not be said to have attained either grace of person, or ease of action. His voice was feeble; his utterance, though clear, was labored; and his manner, though appropriate, was not inviting. He could not be said to possess the higher attributes of oratory, copiousness and warmth of diction, persuasiveness of address, a kindling imagination, the scintillations of wit, or the thrilling pathos which appeals to the passions. Yet he was always listened to with the most profound respect and attention. He convinced, where others sought but to persuade; he bore along the court and jury by the force of his argument; he grappled with their minds, and bound them down with those strong ligaments of the law which may not be broken and cannot be loosened. In short, he often obtained a triumph where mere eloquence must have failed. His conscientious earnestness commanded confidence, and his powerful expostulations secured the passes to victory. It has been said, and I doubt not with entire correctness, that, in the three interior counties of the State, to which his practice extended, he was, during the last years of his professional residence, engaged on one side of every important cause. Certain it is, that no man of his years was ever listened to with more undivided attention by the court and bar, or received from them more unsolicited approbation. If, to the circumstances already alluded to, we add his ill health and deafness, his professional success seems truly marvellous. It is as proud an example of genius subduing to its own purposes every obstacle opposed to its career, and working out its own lofty destiny, as could well be presented to the notice of any ingenuous youth. It is as fine a demonstration as we could desire of that great moral truth, that man is far less what nature has originally made him, than what he chooses to make himself.

If I were called upon to declare what were the most characteristic features of his mind, I should say they were sagacity, perspicacity, and strength. His mind was rather solid than brilliant; rather active than imaginative; rather acute in comparing than fertile in invention. He was not a rapid, but a close, thinker; not an ardent, but an exact, reasoner; not a generalizing, but a concentrating speaker. He always studied brevity and significance of expression. And hence his remarks were peculiarly sententious terse, and pithy; and sometimes quite epigrammatic. He indulged little in metaphors; but when used, they were always direct, and full of meaning. Few persons have left upon the minds of those who have heard them so many striking thoughts, uttered with so much proverbial point, and such winning simplicity.

They adhered to the memory in spite of every effort to banish them. They were philosophy brought down to the business of human life, and disciplined for its daily purposes. He possessed, in a remarkable degree, the faculty of analyzing a complicated case into its elements, and of throwing out at once all its accidental and unimportant ingredients. He easily separated the gold from the dross, and refined and polished the former with an exquisite skill. He rarely amplified by illustrations; but poured at once on the points of his cause a steady and luminous stream of argument. In short, the prevailing character of his mind was judgment, arranging all his materials in a lucid order, moulding them with a masterly power, and closing the results with an impregnable array of logic.

I had almost forgotten to add, that when, about a year ago, the legislature of this Commonwealth authorized the formation of a new code of our laws, he was selected, in connection with two of our most distinguished jurists, to give it its appropriate form and body. To such a task, what rare qualifications must be brought! If I have but succeeded in impressing upon others my own deep sense of his capacity for the task, who is there that will not join me in lamenting his death as a public calamity?

I must close these hasty sketches, thrown together in the midst of various cares, and with the languor of a drooping spirit. And yet I would not close them in the language even of gloom, and far less of discontent. In the natural course of events, indeed, the thought might have been indulged, that our respective places would be changed; and that he might be called upon, at some future time, to perform a kindred office for one who had cherished his friendship and partaken of his labors. To Providence it has seemed fit to order otherwise. Nor can we justly mourn over the loss of such a man, as those who are without hope or consolation. Thanks be to God, in the midst of our sorrows there yet spring up in our hearts the most soothing recollections, and the most sublime contemplations. He is but removed before us to a more exalted state of being, immortal and unchangeable. We have nothing to regret but for ourselves. The tears that fall upon his grave are unstained by any mixture of bitterness for frailty, or for vice. The circle of his life was not large, but it was complete. If he had lived longer he might have reared more enduring monuments of fame for posterity; but his virtues could not have been more mature, or more endeared. They are now beyond the reach of accident, or question. They are treasured up among the records of eternity. He lived as a wise man would aspire to live. He died as a good man would desire to die. Well may we exclaim, "How beautiful is death, when earned by virtue!"

THE SCIENCE OF GOVERNMENT.

A LECTURE READ BEFORE THE AMERICAN INSTITUTE OF INSTRUCTION IN AUGUST, 1834.

The objects of the American Institute of Instruction are, as I understand them, in great measure, if not altogether, of a practical nature. Under such circumstances, the time passed here might well be deemed ill employed, if any attempt were now made merely to bring together topics for literary amusement and recreation; or an elaborate discourse, designed to gratify the taste of scholars, should be substituted for plain, direct, and grave discussion. I shall, therefore, proceed at once to the task, which has been assigned to me on the present occasion, and endeavor to bring before you such views as have occurred to me, touching "The Science of Government, as a Branch of popular Education."

The subject naturally divides itself into three principal heads of inquiry. In the first place, is the science of government of sufficient general importance and utility, to be taught, as a branch of popular education? In the next place, if it be of such importance and utility, is it capable of being so taught? And, in the third place, if capable of being so taught, what is the best or most appropriate method of instruction? My object is to lay before you some considerations on these topics, in the order in which they are stated; and I think, that I do not overvalue them, when I assert, that there are few questions of a wider or deeper interest, and few of a more comprehensive and enlarged philosophy, so far as philosophy bears upon the general concerns of human life.

First, then, as to the importance and utility of the science of government. Of course, I do not intend here to speak of the necessity of government in the abstract, as the only social bond of human society. There are few men in our age, who are disposed to engage in the vindication of what some are pleased to call natural society, as contradistinguished from political society; or to pour forth elaborate praises in favor of savage life, as superior to, and more attractive than, social life. There is little occasion now to address visionaries of this sort; and if there were, this is not the time or the place to meet their vague and declamatory asseverations. It is to the *science* of government that our attention is to be drawn. The question is not, whether any government ought to be established; but what form of government is best adapted to promote the happiness, and secure the rights and interests, of the people, upon whom it is to act. The science of government, therefore involves the consideration of the true ends of government, and the means, by which those ends can be best achieved or promoted. And in this view it may be truly said to be the most intricate and abstruse of all human inquiries; since it draws within its scope all the various concerns and relations of man, and must perpetually reason from the imperfect experience of the past, for the boundless contingencies of the future. The most that we can hope to do under such circumstances, is, to make nearer and nearer approximations to truth, without our ever being certain of having arrived at it in a positive form.

This view of the matter is not very soothing to human pride, or human ambition. And yet the history of human experience, for four thousand years, has done little more than to teach us the melancholy truth, that we are as yet but in the infancy of the science; and that most of its great problems remain as yet unsolved; or have been thus far solved, only to mortify human vanity, and disappoint the spirit of political prophecy. Aristotle and Cicero, the great masters of antiquity in political philosophy, exhausted their own ample resources, rather in the suggestion of hints, than in the formation of systems. They pointed out what had been, or then were, the forms and principles of existing governments, rather to check our ardor, than to encourage our hopes; rather to instruct us in our duties and difficulties, than to inflame our zeal, or confirm our theories. They took as little courage from the speculations of Plato, pouring out his fine genius upon his own imaginary republic, as modern times have from examining the Utopia of Sir Thomas More, or the cold and impracticable reveries of one of the most accomplished men of the last age, David Hume.

The truth is, that the study of the principles of government is the most profound and exhausting of any, which can engage the human mind. It admits of very few fixed and inflexible rules; it is open to perplexing doubts and questions, in most of its elements; and it rarely admits of annunciations of universal application. The principles, best adapted to the wants and interests of one age or country, can scarcely be applied to another age or country, without essential modifications, and perhaps even without strong infusions of opposite principles. The different habits, manners, institutions, climates, employments, characters, passions, and even prejudices and propensities, of different nations, present almost insurmountable obstacles to any uniform system, independently of the large grounds of diversity, from their relative intelligence, relative local position, and relative moral advancement. Any attempt to force upon all nations the same modifications and forms of government, would be founded in just as little wisdom and sound policy, as to force upon all persons the same food, and the same pursuits; to compel the Greenlanders to cultivate vineyards, the Asiatics to fish in the Arctic seas, or the polished inhabitants of the south of Europe to clothe themselves in bear skins, and live upon Iceland moss and whale oil.

Government, therefore, in a just sense, is, if one may so say, the *science of adaptations* — variable in its elements, dependent upon circumstances, and incapable of a rigid mathematical demonstration. The question, then, What form of government is best? can never be satisfactorily answered, until we have ascertained, for what people it is designed; and then it can be answered only by the closest survey of all the peculiarities of their condition, moral, intellectual, and physical. And when we have mastered all these, (if they are capable of any absolute mastery,) we have then but arrived at the threshold of our inquiries. For, as government is not a thing for an hour or a day, but is, or ought to be, arranged for permanence, as well as for convenience of action, the future must be foreseen and provided for, as well as the present. The changes in society, which are forever silently, but irresistibly, going on; the ever diversified employments of industry; the relative advancement and decline of commerce, manufactures, agriculture, and the liberal arts; the gradual alterations of habits, manners, and tastes; the dangers, in one age, from restless enterprise and military ambition, in another age, from popular excitements and an oppressive poverty, and in another age, from the corrupting influence of wealth and the degrading fascinations of luxury; — all these are to be examined and guarded against, with a wisdom so comprehensive, that it must task the greatest minds and the most mature experience.

Struck with considerations of this sort, and with the difficulties inherent in the subject, there are not a few men among those, who aim to guide the opinions of others, who have adopted the erroneous and alarming doctrine, so forcibly expressed by Pope in a single couplet:

> "For forms of government let fools contest;
> What e'er is best administered is best."

As if every thing were to be left to the arbitrary will and caprice of rulers; and the whole interests of society were to be put at risk upon the personal character of those, who constitute the existing government. According to this theory, there is no difference between an absolute despotism, and a well-organized republic; between the securities of a government of checks and balances, and a division of powers, and those of a sovereignty, irresistible and unresisted; between the summary justice of a Turkish sultan, and the moderated councils of a representative assembly.

Nay, the doctrine has been pressed to a farther extent, not merely by those who constitute, at all times, the regular advocates of public abuses, and the flatterers of power; but by men of higher characters, whose morals have graced, and whose philosophy has instructed the age in which they lived. The combined genius of Goldsmith and Johnson arrived at the calm conclusion, that the mass of the people could have little reason to complain of any exercises of tyranny, since the latter rarely reached the obscurity and retirement of private life. They have taught us this great conservative lesson, so deadening to all reforms and all improvements, with all the persuasive eloquence of poetry.

> "In every government, though terrors reign,
> Though tyrant kings and tyrant laws restrain,
> How small, of all, that human hearts endure,
> That part, which laws or kings can cause or cure!"

If this were true, it would, indeed, be of very little consequence to busy ourselves about the forms or objects of government. The subject might amuse our leisure hours, but could scarcely touch our practical interests. But the truth is far otherwise. The great mass of human calamities, in all ages, has been the result of bad government, or ill-adjusted government; of a capricious exercise of power, a fluctuating public policy, a degrading tyranny, or a desolating ambition. Bad laws and bad institutions have gradually sunk the peasantry and artisans of most countries to a harsh and abject poverty; and involved them in sufferings, as varied and overwhelming, as any inflicted by the desolating march of a conqueror, or the sudden devastations of a flood.

But an error of an opposite character, and quite as mischievous in its tendency, is, the common notion, that government is a matter of great simplicity; that its principles are so clear, that they are little liable to mistake; that the fabric can be erected by persons of ordinary skill; and that, when once erected upon correct principles, it will stand without assistance,

"By its own weight made steadfast and immovable."

This is the besetting delusion (I had almost said the besetting sin) in all popular governments. It sometimes takes its rise in that enthusiasm, which ingenuous minds are apt to indulge in regard to human perfectibility. But it is more generally propagated by demagogues, as the easiest method of winning popular favor, by appeals, which flatter popular prejudices, and thus enable them better to accomplish their own sinister designs. If there be any truth, which a large survey of human experience justifies us in asserting, it is, that, in proportion as a government is free, it must be complicated. Simplicity belongs to those only, where one will governs all; where one mind directs, and all others obey; where few arrangements are required, because no checks to power are allowed; where law is not a science, but a mandate to be followed, and not to be discussed; where it is not a rule for permanent action, but a capricious and arbitrary dictate of the hour.

But passing from these general considerations, (upon which it is, at present, unnecessary to enlarge,) I propose to bring the subject immediately home to our own business and bosoms, by examining the importance and utility of the science of government to Americans, with reference to their own political institutions. And I do not hesitate to affirm, not only that a knowledge of the true principles of government is important and useful to Americans, but that it is absolutely indispensable, to carry on the government of their choice, and to transmit it to their posterity.

In the first place, what are the great objects of all free

governments? They are, the protection and preservation of the personal rights, the private property, and the public liberties of the whole people. Without accomplishing these ends, the government may, indeed, be called free, but it is a mere mockery, and a vain, fantastic shadow. If the person of any individual is not secure from assaults and injuries; if his reputation is not preserved from gross and malicious calumny; if he may not speak his own opinions with a manly frankness; if he may be imprisoned without just cause, and deprived of all freedom in his choice of occupations and pursuits;—it will be idle to talk of his liberty to breathe the air, or to bathe in the public stream, or to give utterance to articulate language. If the earnings of his industry may be appropriated, and his property may be taken away, at the mere will of rulers, or the clamors of a mob, it can afford little consolation to him, that he has already derived happiness from the accumulation of wealth, or that he has the present pride of an ample inheritance; that his farm is not yet confiscated, his house has not yet ceased to be his castle, and his children are not yet reduced to beggary. If his public liberties, as a man and a citizen, his right to vote, his right to hold office, his right to worship God according to the dictates of his own conscience, his equality with all others, who are his fellow-citizens; if these are at the mercy of the neighboring demagogue, or the popular idol of the day;—of what consequence is it to him, that he is permitted to taste of sweets, which may be wantonly dashed from his lips at the next moment, or to possess privileges, which are felt more in their loss, even, than in their possession? Life, liberty, and property stand upon equal grounds in the just estimate of freemen; and one becomes almost worthless without the security of the others. How, then, are these rights to be established and preserved? The answer is, by constitutions of government, wisely framed and vigilantly enforced; by laws and institutions, deliberately examined and steadily administered; by tribunals of justice above fear, and beyond reproach, whose duty it shall be to protect the weak against the strong, to guard the unwary against the cunning, and to punish the insolence of office, and the spirit of encroachment and wanton injury. It needs scarcely be said, how much wisdom, talents, discretion, and virtue, are indispensable for such great purposes.

In the next place, the people have taken upon themselves, in our free form of government, the responsibility of accomplishing all these ends; the protection and preservation of personal rights, of property, and public liberty. Is it quite certain, that we shall successfully accomplish such a vast undertaking? Is any considerate man bold enough to venture such an assertion? Is not our government itself a new experiment in the history of the world? Has not every other republic, with all the wisdom, and splendor, and wealth, and power, with which it has been favored, perished, and perished by its own hands, through the might of its own factions? These are inquiries, which may not be suppressed or evaded. They must be met, and deliberately weighed. They press upon the minds of thousands, who are most interested in our destiny, as patriots and statesmen. They are not disposed of by a few fine flourishes of rhetoric, or by a blind and boasting confidence. They involve the hopes and happiness of our whole posterity; and we must meditate on them, if we would save either ourselves or them. One of the first lessons of wisdom is to understand our dangers; and, when we understand them, we may then be prepared to meet the duties and difficulties of our position.

In the next place, we have chosen for ourselves the most complicated frame of republican government, which was ever offered to the world. We have endeavored to reconcile the apparent anomaly of distinct sovereignties, each independent of the other in its own operations, and yet each in full action within the same territory. The national government, within the scope of its delegated powers, is, beyond all doubt, supreme and uncontrollable; and the state governments are equally so, within the scope of their exclusive powers. But there is a vast variety of cases, in which the powers of each are concurrent with those of the other; and it is almost impossible to ascertain with precision, where the lines of separation between them begin and end. No rulers on earth are called to a more difficult and delicate task than our own, in attempting to define and limit them. If any collision shall happen, it can scarcely be at a single point only. It will touch, or it will trench, upon jealousies, interests, prejudices, and political arrangements, infinitely ramified throughout the whole extent of the Union. The adjustments, therefore, to be made from time to time, to avoid such collisions, and to carry on the general system of movements, require a degree of forecast, caution, skill, and patient investigation, which nothing but long habits of reflection, and the most mature experience, can supply.

In the interpretation of constitutional questions alone, a vast field is open for discussion and argument. The text, indeed, is singularly brief and expressive. But that very brevity becomes of itself a source of obscurity; and that very expressiveness, while it gives prominence to the leading objects, leaves an ample space of debatable ground, upon which the champions of all opinions may contend, with alternate victory and defeat. Nay, the very habits of free inquiry, to which all our institutions conduct us, if they do not urge us, at least incite us, to a perpetual renewal of the contest. So that many minds are unwilling to admit any thing to be settled; and the text remains with them a doubtful oracle, speaking with a double meaning, and open to glosses of the most contradictory character. How much sobriety of judgment, solid learning, historical research, and political sagacity are required for such critical inquiries! Party leaders may, indeed, despatch the matter in a few short and pointed sentences, in popular appeals to the passions and prejudices of the day, or in harangues, in which eloquence may exhaust itself in studied alarms, or in bold denunciations. But statesmen will approach it with a reverent regard. They will meditate upon consequences with a slow and hesitating assent. They will weigh well their own responsibility, when they decide for all posterity. They will feel that a wound inflicted upon the constitution, if it does not bring on an immediate gangrene, may yet introduce a lingering disease, which will weaken its vital organs, and ultimately destroy them.

But it is not in the examination and solution of constitutional questions alone, that great abilities, and a thorough mastery of the principles of government, are required of American statesmen. The ordinary course of legislation, in the national councils, is full of intricate and perplexing duties. It is not every man, who can make an animated address at a popular meeting, or run through the common places of party declamation at the hustings, with a fluent elocution and a steady presence, who is qualified for a seat in the national legislature. The interests of four-and-twenty states are there represented, and are there to be scrupulously weighed and protected.

Look, but for a moment, over the vast extent of our country; the varieties of its climates, productions, and pursuits; its local peculiarities and institutions; its untiring enterprise, and inexhaustible industry. Look to the ever-changing character of agriculture; the sugar, cotton, and rice of the South; the wheat, corn, and tobacco of the Middle States; and the stubborn, but thrifty growth of the North, yielding to culture what seems almost denied to climate. Look to the busy haunts of our manufactures, rising on a thousand hills, and sheltered in a thousand valleys, and fed by a thousand streams. Everywhere they are instinct with life, and noisy or noiseless industry, and pouring forth their products to every market with an unceasing flow, which gathers as it goes. Look to the reaches of our foreign commerce through every region of the globe. It floats on the burning breezes of Africa; it braves the stormy seas of the Arctic regions. It glides with a bounding speed on the weary coasts and broad streams of Southern America. It doubles the Capes of the Indies, and meets the trade-winds and monsoons in the very regions of their birth. It gathers its treasures from the deep soundings of the Banks of Newfoundland. It follows the seal in his secret visits to the lonely islands of the Southern Pacific. It startles the whale on his majestic march through every latitude, from the hither Atlantic to the seas of Japan. The sun shines not on the region where its flag has not saluted the first beams of the morning. It sets not, where its last lingering rays have not played on the caps of its masts. And then, again, look to the reaches of our internal commerce along the various inlets, and bays, and ports of the seaboard, through the vast and almost interminable rivers and valleys of the West; on the broad and restless lakes, through the deep prairies, and up the steeps of the Rocky Mountains, and onward to the far ocean which washes the darkened shores of two continents. Look, I say, to these extensive yet connected interests, and who but must admit that to understand their intricate relations and dependencies, to gather up even the fragments of that knowledge which it is necessary to possess in order (I will not say to guide and direct them, but) not to mar and destroy them, there must be years of patient, thorough, and laborious research into the true principles, and policy, and objects of government.

But it is not to rulers and statesmen alone that the science of government is important and useful. It is equally indispensable for every American citizen to enable him to exercise his own rights, to protect his own interests, and to secure the public liberties and the just operations of public authority. A republic, by the very constitution of its government, requires, on the part of the people, more vigilance and constant exertion than all others. The American republic above all others demands from every citizen unceasing vigilance and exertion; since we have deliberately dispensed with every guard against danger or ruin, except the intelligence and virtue of the people themselves. It is founded on the basis, that the people have wisdom enough to frame their own system of government, and public spirit enough to preserve it; that they cannot be cheated out of their liberties; and that they will not submit to have them taken from them by force. We have silently assumed the fundamental truth, that, as it never can be the interest of the majority of the people to prostrate their own political equality and happiness, so they never can be seduced by flattery or corruption, by the intrigues of faction, or the arts of ambition, to adopt any measures which shall subvert them. If this confidence in ourselves be justified, (and who among Americans does not feel a just pride in endeavoring to maintain it?) let us never forget that it can be justified only by a watchfulness and zeal proportionate to our confidence. Let us never forget that we must prove ourselves wiser, and better, and purer, than any other nation ever yet has been, if we are to count upon success. Every other republic has fallen by the discords and treachery of its own citizens. It has been said, by one of our departed statesmen, himself a devout admirer of popular government, that power is perpetually stealing from the many to the few. It has been said, by one of the greatest orators of antiquity, whose life was devoted to the republic with a zealous but unsuccessful patriotism, that the bad will always attack with far more spirit than the good will defend sound principles. The republic, said he, with a melancholy eloquence, the republic is assailed with far more force and contrivances than it is defended, because bold and profligate men are impelled by a nod, and move of their own accord against it. But I know not how it happens, the good are always tardy. They neglect the beginning of things, and are roused only in the last necessity. So that sometimes, by their delay and tardiness, while they wish to retain ease, even without dignity, they lose both. Those who are willing to be the defenders of the republic, if they are of the lighter sort, desert; if they are of the more timid sort they fly. Those alone remain and stand by the republic whom no power, no threats, no malice can shake in their resolution.[1] Such is the lesson of ancient wisdom, admonishing us as from the grave; and it was pronounced, as it were, at the very funeral of Roman liberty.

Besides, in other countries, there are many artificial barriers against sudden changes and innovations which retard, if they do not wholly obstruct them. There are ecclesiastical and civil establishments, venerable from their antiquity, and engrafted into the very habits, and feelings, and prejudices of the people. There are hereditary honors and privileges, the claims of aristocracy, and the influences of wealth, accumulated and perpetuated in a few families. We have none of these to embarrass or overawe us. Our statutes regulating the descent of estates have entirely broken down all the ordinary means of undue accumulation; and our just pride is, that the humblest and highest citizens are upon a footing of equality. Nothing here can resist the will of the people; and nothing certainly ought to resist their deliberate will. The elements of change are therefore about us in every direction, from the fundamental articles of our constitutions of government down to the by-laws of the humblest municipality.

Changes, then, may be wrought by public opinion wherever it shall lead us. They may be sudden, or they may be slow; they may be for the worse as well as for the better; they may be the solid growth of a sober review of public principles, and a more enlightened philosophy; or they may be the spurious product of a hasty and ill-advised excitement, flying from evils which it knows and feels, to those far greater, which it sees not, and may never be able to redress. They may be the artful delusions of selfish men, taking advantage of a momentary popularity, or the deep-laid plan of designing men to overthrow the foundations of all free institutions. This very facility of introducing changes should make us

[1] Cicero, Oratio pro Sextio, ch. 47.

more scrupulous in adopting innovations; since they often bring permanent evils in their train, and compensate us only by accidental and temporary good. What is safe is not always expedient; what is theoretically true is often practically false or doubtful; what at the first glance seems beneficial and plausible is, upon more mature examination, often found to be mischievous or inefficient; what constitutes the true policy and security of free governments lies not unfrequently so distant from immediate observation and experience, that it is rashly rejected or coldly received. Hence, it has been remarked, that a free people rarely bestow on good rulers the powers necessary for their own permanent protection, and as rarely withhold from bad ones those which may be used for their own destruction.

Again, independently of the common causes which are constantly at work in all governments founded upon the common passions and infirmities of human nature, there are in republics some peculiar causes to stimulate political discontents, to awaken corrupt ambition, and to generate violent parties. Factions are the natural, nay, perhaps the necessary growth of all free governments; and they must prevail with more activity and influence, just in proportion as they enlist in their ranks the interest and power of numbers. Where all the citizens are, practically speaking, voters, it is obvious that the destiny of public men and public measures must essentially depend on the contest at the polls, and the wisdom of the choice which is there made. We need not be told that many other influences are present on such occasions besides those which arise from talents, merit, and public services. We need not be told how many secret springs are at work to obstruct that perfect freedom and independence of choice which are so essential to make the ballot-box the just index of public opinion. We need not be told how often the popular delusions of the day are seized upon to deprive the best patriots of their just reward, and to secure the triumph of the selfish, the cunning, and the timeserving. And yet, unless the people do at all times possess virtue, and firmness, and intelligence enough to reject such mischievous influences; unless they are well instructed in public affairs and resolutely maintain the principles of the constitution, it is obvious, that the government itself must soon degenerate into an oligarchy; and the dominant faction will rule with an unbounded and desolating energy. The external forms of machinery of the republic may continue to exist, like the solemn pageantry of the Roman Senate in the times of the emperors; but the informing spirit will have departed, and leave behind it only the faded and melancholy memorials of irretrievable decay.

I have but glanced at these considerations, each of which might well furnish a topic for a full discourse. If the remarks already suggested are in any measure well founded, they establish the great truth, that, as in the American republic, the people themselves are not only the source of all power, but the immediate organs and instruments of its due exercise at all times, it is of everlasting importance to them to study the principles of government; and thoroughly to comprehend men as well as measures, tendencies, as well as acts, and corrupting influences, as well as open usurpations. To whom can we justly look for the preservation of our public liberties and social rights; for the encouragement of piety, religion, and learning; for the impartial administration of justice and equity; for wise and wholesome laws, and a scrupulous public faith; but to a people who shall lay a solid foundation for all these things in their early education; who shall strengthen them by an habitual reverence and approbation; and who shall jealously watch every encroachment which may weaken the guards or sap the supports on which they rest?

And this leads me to the next topic upon which I propose to address you; and that is, the practicability of teaching the science of government as a branch of popular education. If it be not capable of being so taught, then indeed well may patriots and philanthropists, as well as philosophers, sink into profound despair in regard to the duration of our republic. But it appears to me that we are by no means justified in arriving at such a desponding conclusion. On the contrary, we may well indulge a firm and lively hope, that, by making the science of government an indispensable branch of popular education, we may gradually prepare the way for such a mastery of its principles by the people at large as shall confound the sophist, repress the corrupt, disarm the cunning, animate the patriotic, and sustain the moral and religious.

It is true, that a thorough mastery of the science of government, in all its various operations, requires a whole life of laborious diligence. But it is equally true that many of its general principles admit of a simple enunciation, and may be brought within the comprehension of the most common minds. In this respect it does not materially differ from any of the abstract physical sciences. Few of the latter are, in their full extent, within the reach of any but the highest class of minds; but many of the elements are nevertheless, within the scope of common education, and are attainable by ordinary diligence. It is not necessary that every citizen should be a profound statesman. But it may nevertheless be of vast consequence that he should be an enlightened as well as an honest voter, and a disciplined thinker, if not an eloquent speaker. He may learn enough to guard himself against the insidious wiles of the demagogue, and the artful appeals of the courtier, and the visionary speculations of the enthusiast; although he may not be able to solve many of the transcendental problems in political philosophy.

In the first place, as to the constitution of the United States; (and similar considerations will apply, with at least equal force, to all the state constitutions,) the text is contained in a few pages, and speaks a language which is generally clear and intelligible to any youth of the higher classes at our common schools, before the close of the usual academical studies. Nay, it may be stated with confidence, that any boy of ordinary capacity may be made fully to understand it, between his fourteenth and sixteenth year, if he has an instructor of reasonable ability and qualifications. He may become possessed of the actual organization and powers of the government, under which he lives, to which he is responsible, and which he is enjoined, by every duty of patriotism and interest, to transmit unimpaired to future generations. He may practically learn the leading divisions of the great powers of all governments, into legislative, executive, and judicial. He may ascertain, in some general way, the definite boundaries and appropriate functions of each. He may understand yet more; that there are checks and balances everywhere interposed to limit power, and prevent oppression, and ensure deliberation, and moderate action. He may perceive that the House of Representatives cannot make laws without the coöperation of the Senate; that the President cannot make appointments without the consent of the Senate; and yet, that the President can, by his qualified veto, arrest the legislative action of both houses. He may perceive that the judiciary, in many parts of its organization, acts through, and by, and under the will of the legislature and executive; and yet, that it stands in many respects independent of each; nay, that it has power to resist the combined operations of both; and to protect the citizens from their unconstitutional proceedings, whether accidental or meditated. He may perceive that the state governments are indispensable portions of the machinery of national government; that they in some cases control it; and in others, again, are controlled by it; that the same supreme law which promulgates prohibitions upon certain acts to be done by the states, at the same time promulgates like prohibitions upon the acts of the United States. He may perceive that there are certain leading principles laid down as the fundamental rules of government; and that they constitute a solemn bill of rights, which must be obeyed and cannot be gainsaid. He may perceive that the trial by jury is preserved, as a matter of right, in all cases of crimes, and generally, also, in civil cases; that the liberty of speech and of the press are constitutionally vindicated; that no national religion can be imposed upon the community; that private property cannot be taken away without adequate compensation; and that the inviolability of public and private contracts is strenuously enforced.

Having arrived at this clear and definite view of the distribution of the powers of government, with the appropriate restrictions belonging to them, he can scarcely fail to ask, What are the reasons which induced the framers of the constitution to adopt them? It is scarcely possible that he should be so dull as not to have some desire to gratify, or so indifferent as not to have some curiosity to indulge such inquiries. When he is told, on every side, that this is the form of government best calculated to secure his personal happiness, and animate his love of liberty, it would be incredible that he should feel no interest in ascertaining why and wherefore it is so. Why, for instance, legislation may not as well be confided to one body, as to two distinct bodies? Why unity in the executive is preferable to plurality of numbers? Why the judiciary should be separated from the other branches? Why, in short, simplicity in government is destructive of public liberty; and a complex machinery of checks and balances is indispensable to preserve it? Inquiries of this sort, if they do not spontaneously rise up in his own mind, cannot be presented to it by his instructor without opening new and various sources of reflection. He will thus be conducted to the threshold of that profound science which begins and ends with the proper study of man in all his social relations.

And here, again, it may be confidently affirmed that there is not the slightest difficulty in unfolding to our youth the true nature and bearing of all these arrangements, and the reasons on which they are founded. Although they are the result of human wisdom, acting upon the most comprehensive human experience, and have tasked the greatest minds to discover and apply them, they are, nevertheless, capable of as exact a demonstration as any other problems of moral philosophy applied to the business of human life. It required the genius of Newton to discover the profound mystery of the universal law of gravitation; but every schoolboy can now reason upon it, when he bathes in the refreshing coolness of the summer stream, or gazes with unmixed delight on the beautiful starlight of the wintry heavens. So it is with political philosophy. Its great truths can be clearly taught and made familiar to the juvenile mind at the same time that they may well employ the most exalted powers of the human understanding. What more difficulty, for instance, is there in a scholar's comprehending the value of checks and balances, and divisions of power in a government, than in comprehending the value of good order and discipline in a school, or the propriety of trustees laying down rules to regulate and control the head master, and he other rules to guide and direct his ushers? The principles may not, indeed, always be obvious to the narrow circle of his thoughts; but they can be pointed out. They may lie too remote for his immediate observation; but he may learn the paths by which they may be explored. They may not, as yet, be within his grasp; but he can be taught how they may be reached by skill and diligence. He may not, as yet, see their full extent and operation; but his vision will gradually expand, until he can seize on the most distant objects, and bring them, as it were, under the eye of his mind with a close and cloudless certainty. Every element of knowledge which he thus gradually acquires will soon become incorporated into his former stock, until at last he has accumulated a capital upon which he may safely set up for himself; and, by widening, and deepening, and strengthening the foundations, he may, at length, acquire a character for political wisdom and ability which shall make him at once an ornament and a blessing to his country, even though he may never pass beyond the precincts of his native village. He may there be able to quiet the discontented murmurs of a misguided populace. He may there repress the inordinate love of innovation of the young, the ignorant, and the restless. He may there stand the unconquerable friend of liberty; recommending it by his virtues, and sustaining it by his councils. He may there withstand the village tyrant, too often disguised under the specious character of the village demagogue. And he may there close his life with the conscious satisfaction that, as a village patriot, he has thus filled up the measure of his duties; and has earned a far more enviable title to true glory than the conqueror, who has left the dark impressions of his desolations in the ruined hopes and fortunes of millions.

If, on the other hand, a higher destiny awaits him; if he is called to take a part in the public councils of the state or nation, what immense advantages must such preparatory studies and principles give him over those who rise into public life by the accidents of the day, and rush into the halls of legislation with a blind and daring confidence, equalled only by their gross ignorance, and their rash ardor for reform! For weal or for woe, our destiny must be committed to the one or the other of these classes of rulers, as public opinion shall decide. Who would willingly commit himself to the skill of a pilot who had never sounded the depths, or marked the quicksands of the coast? Who would venture to embark his all on board a ship on a short voyage, (far less on the voyage of life,) when the crew have not learned how to trim the sails, and there is neither chart nor compass on board to guide the navigation?

I am not aware that there are any solid objections, which can be urged against introducing the science of government into our common schools as a branch of popular education. If it should be said that it is too deep and difficult for the studies of youth, that objection assumes the very matter in controversy; and if the observations already made are well founded, it is wholly indefensible. If it should be said that it will have a tendency to introduce party creeds and party dogmas into our schools, the true answer is, that the principles of government should be there taught, and not the creeds or dogmas of any party. The principles of the constitution under which we live; the principles upon which republics generally are founded, by which they are sustained, and through which they must be saved; the principles of public policy by which national prosperity is secured, and national ruin averted; these, certainly, are not party creeds, or party dogmas; but are fit to be taught at all times and on all occasions, if any thing which belongs to human life and our own condition is fit to be taught. If we wait until we can guard ourselves against every possible chance of abuse before we introduce any system of instruction, we shall wait until the current of time has flowed into the ocean of eternity. There is nothing which ever has been, or ever can be taught, without some chance of abuse, nay, without some absolute abuse. Even religion itself, our truest and our only lasting hope and consolation, has not escaped the common infirmity of our nature. If it never had been taught until it could be taught with the purity, simplicity, and energy of the apostolic age, we ourselves, instead of being blest with the bright and balmy influences of Christianity, should now have been groping our way in the darkness of heathenism, or left to perish in the cold and cheerless labyrinths of skepticism.

If it be said, that there is not time, or means, suitable to learn these principles in our common schools, the true answer is, that, if the fact be so, (which is not admitted,) more time should be given, and more ample means be supplied, for the purpose. What is the business of education, but to fit men to accomplish their duties and their destiny? And who is there among Americans, that is not called to the constant performance of political duties, and the exercise of political privileges? He may perform, or use them, well or ill. But the results of the use and abuse are, and ever will be, mixed up with his own intimate interests. The perils, he may choose that others shall encounter, he must share in common with them. He is embarked in the same ship of state, and the shipwreck, which shall bury the hopes of others, will not spare his own. What blessings in human life can fairly be put in competition with those derived from good government and free institutions? What condition can be more deplorable than that, where labor has no reward, property no security, and domestic life no tranquillity? where the slave is compelled to kiss the chain which binds him to wretchedness, and smile upon his oppressor, while his heart is writhing in agony? Let not Americans forget, that Greece, immortal Greece, has been free; and yet, that thousands of years have already rolled over her servitude; that Italy, beautiful Italy, has been free; but where is now her republican grandeur? The Apennines still lift up their bold and rugged peaks; the sun still looks down upon her plains with a warm and cloudless splendor; — but the spirit of liberty is not there; and Rome has become, as it were, the vast sepulchre of her own perished glory.

But, independent of the grave considerations already urged, in favor of the introduction of political studies into our system of popular education, there are other collateral advantages, which should not be wholly passed by.

In the first place, there are no studies better fitted to discipline the mind, or to accustom it to severe and close investigation. They combine, in a very high degree, the speculations of philosophy with the varied events of history, and increase the separate interest of each. They have a tendency to enlarge and liberalize the mind, by familiarizing it with comprehensive views of men and things. They are capable of an indefinite expansion and variety; such as may employ the whole leisure of the most retired scholar, or suit the short and hasty intervals of the man of business. They gather up new materials in the daily intercourse of society;

and, at the same time, they enable us to expound its apparent anomalies, and classify its varied results.

In the next place, they have a powerful tendency to counteract the rash and hasty judgments, which youth and inexperience naturally produce in ardent and inquisitive minds. Nothing is so fascinating and so delusive, as the simplicity of theory, in the earlier stages of life. It not only flatters that pride of opinion, which results from a supposed mastery of important truths; but it gratifies that fresh and vigorous confidence, which hopeth all things, and believeth all things. The severe lessons of experience do, indeed, generally, correct, or demolish these visionary notions. But they often come so slow, that irreparable mistakes have been already committed; and the party is left to mourn over the blight of his own prospects, or the impending dangers to his country. Nothing can have a more salutary effect in repressing this undue pride and confidence, than the study of the science of government. The youth is there taught, how little reliance can be placed upon mere abstract speculations; how often that, which is theoretically true, becomes practically mischievous; how complicated is the machinery, necessary to carry on the operations of a good government; how many nice adjustments are required, to give full play and activity to the system; how slow every change must be, to be safe, as well as improving; and, above all, how often the wisest statesmen, the truest patriots, and the most profound reasoners, find defects, where they had least suspected them; and their labors, begun with energy and confidence, end in disappointment and mortification. Nay, systems of government, which have been apparently reared with consummate skill and solidity, have often been found buried in ruins, before the capstone has been placed upon them; and, while the architect has been still gazing on his own work, he has become the first victim of its ponderous magnificence.

Considerations of this sort cannot wholly escape an ingenuous youth, upon the most cursory examination of government, as it is read by the lights of history. They will naturally inspire caution, if they do not awaken distrust; and when, at every step of his advancement in political studies, he finds himself compelled to surrender some imagined truth, to discredit some popular dogma, and to doubt some plausible theory, he cannot but profit by the instructions which they hold out, and the admonitions which they silently inculcate. A nation, whose citizens are habitually attentive to the principles and workings of government, may sometimes be betrayed; but it can scarcely be ruined. At least, it cannot be enslaved, until it has sunk so low in corruption, that it will hail the presence of any tyrant, to escape from the terrible scourges of anarchy.

But it may be asked, and this is the last topic on which I propose to address you, In what mode is the science of government to be taught in our common schools? The answer may be given in a few words. It is by the introduction and constant use of suitable elementary works, which unfold the principles of government, and illustrate their application, and in an especial manner, with reference to the forms of the American constitutions. Such works should not only be read, but be studied as class-books. The instructor, if he possesses common skill and ingenuity, may easily make them, not a dry task, but an interesting exercise. By bringing constantly before the school, in the course of reading, and recitation, and occasional explanations, the leading principles of government, he will gradually make the pupils familiar with their bearing and value. They may not at once arrive at the various truths which are designed to be taught; but they will silently master them. And by the time they have passed through the usual preparatory studies of the school, they will have acquired a stock of materials for future use, of inestimable value — a stock, which will furnish perpetual sources for meditation, and enable them to lay a broad foundation for the due discharge of the duties of private citizens, and the more arduous employments of public life.

Lord Brougham, one of the most powerful advocates of popular education in our day, has made the following remarks, which cannot be more fitly addressed to the consideration of any other body than that, which I have now the honor to address. "A sound system of government," says he, "requires the people to read, and inform themselves upon political subjects; else they are the prey of every quack, every impostor, and every agitator, who may practise his trade in the country. If they do not read; if they do not learn; if they do not digest, by discussion and reflection, what they have read and learned; if they do not qualify themselves to form opinions for themselves, other men will form opinions for them; not according to the truth and the interests of the people, but according to their own individual and selfish interest, which may, and most probably will, be contrary to that of the people at large. The best security for a government, like ours, (a free government) and generally, for the public peace and public morals, is, that the whole community should be well informed upon its political, as well as its other interests. And it can be well informed only by having access to wholesome, sound, and impartial publications."

I shall conclude this discourse with a single sentence, borrowed from the great work of Cicero on the Republic, the most mature, and not least important, of his splendid labors — a sentence, which should always be present to the mind of every American citizen, as a guide and incentive to duty. "Our country," said that great man, "has not given us birth, or educated us under her law, as if she expected no succor from us; or, that, seeking to administer to our convenience only, she might afford a safe retreat for the indulgence of our ease, or a peaceful asylum for our indolence; but that she might hold in pledge the various and most exalted powers of our mind, our genius, and our judgment, for her own benefit; and that she might leave for our private use such portions only, as might be spared for that purpose."[1]

[1] Cicero, de Republicâ, lib. i. cap. 4.

LIFE, CHARACTER, AND SERVICES OF CHIEF JUSTICE MARSHALL.

A DISCOURSE PRONOUNCED ON THE 15TH OF OCTOBER, 1835, AT THE REQUEST OF THE SUFFOLK BAR.

THE funeral obsequies have been performed; the long procession has passed by, and the earth has closed over the mortal remains of Chief Justice Marshall. Time has assuaged the first agonies of grief of the immediate relatives who were called to mourn over so afflictive a loss; and others, who, looking to the claims of private friendship or to the public interests, were astounded at a blow, which, though not unexpected, came at last with a startling force, have had leisure to recover from their perturbation, and may now contemplate the event with a calm though profound melancholy.

It is under these circumstances that we are now assembled together to devote a brief space of time to the consideration of his life, character, and services; and then to return again to the affairs of the world, edified, as I may hope, by what he was, and warmed and elevated by a nearer approach to excellences, which, if we may not reach, we may yet gaze on with devout respect and reverence. I am not insensible of the difficulties of the task of worthily discharging the duties of the present occasion. I am but too conscious how much more successfully it would have been accomplished in other hands; and how little is my own ability to do justice even to my own feelings in attempting a sketch of such a man. I have not, however, felt at liberty to decline the part which has been assigned to me in the commemorations of this day, lest I should be thought wanting in readiness to do homage to one who was the highest boast and ornament of the profession. There is this consolation, nevertheless, in undertaking the task, that it requires no labored vindication of motives or actions. His life speaks its own best eulogy. It had such a simplicity, purity, consistency, and harmony, that the narrative of the events in their natural order invests it with an attraction which art need not seek to heighten, and friendship may well be content to leave with its original coloring.

Of the great men who have appeared in the world, many have been distinguished by the splendor of their birth or station; many by the boldness or variety of their achievements; and many by peculiarities of genius or conduct, which, from the extraordinary contrasts presented by them, have awakened the curiosity, or gratified the love of novelty of the giddy multitude. I know not, how it has happend, but so, I fear, the fact will be found to be, that high moral qualities are rarely the passport to extensive popular favor or renown. Nay; a calm and steady virtue, which acts temperately and wisely, and never plunges into indiscretion or extravagance, is but too often confounded with dulness or frigidity of temperament. It seems as if it were deemed the prerogative, if not the attribute, of genius, to indulge itself in eccentricities, and to pass from one extreme to another, leaving behind it the dark impressions of its vices or its follies. The deeper movements of the soul in the inmost workings of its thoughts are supposed to display themselves like volcanoes in the natural world, by occasional explosions which awe, but at the same time excite the crowd of eager spectators. They are struck with admiration of what they do not comprehend; and mistake their own emotions for the presence of superior power. They are bewildered by the shifting exhibition, alternately of brilliant deeds and debasing passions, of intellectual efforts of transcendent energy, and paradoxes of overwrought ingenuity; and being unable to fathom the motives or sources of anomalies, they confound extravagance with enterprise and the dreams of wild ambition with lofty and well-considered designs.

And yet if there is any thing taught us, either by the precepts of Christianity, or the history of our race, it is, that true greatness is inseparable from sound morals; that the highest wisdom is but another name for the highest talents; that the genius which burns with a pure and regulated flame throws far and wide its beneficent light to guide and cheer us; while occasional corruscations serve only to perplex and betray us, or (to borrow the language of poetry) serve but to make the surrounding darkness more visible. The calm and patient researches of Newton and Locke have conferred far more lasting benefits on mankind, than all the achievements of all the mere heroes and conquerors of ancient or modern times. One patriot like Epaminondas, Scipio, or Washington, outweighs a host of Alexanders, Cæsars, and Napoleons. The fame of Justinian as a fortunate possessor of the imperial purple, would have long since faded into an almost evanescent point in history, if his memorable Codes of Jurisprudence had not secured him an enviable immortality by the instruction which they have imparted to the legislation of all succeeding times. He who has been enabled, by the force of his talents and the example of his virtues, to identify his own character with the solid interests and happiness of his country; he who has lived long enough to stamp the impressions of his own mind upon the age, and has left on record lessons of wisdom for the study and improvement of all posterity; he, I say, has attained all that a truly good man aims at, and all that a truly great man should aspire to. He has erected a monument to his memory in the hearts of men. Their gratitude will perpetually, though it may be silently, breathe forth his praises; and the voluntary homage paid to his name will speak a language more intelligible and more universal than any epitaph inscribed on Parian marble, or any image wrought out by the cunning hands of sculpture.

Reflections like these naturally crowd upon the mind upon

the death of every great man; but especially of every one who may be justly deemed a benefactor and ornament of his race. In the present case, there is little occasion to point out the manner or the measure of their application.

JOHN MARSHALL was born on the 24th day of September, 1775, (a little more than eighty years ago,) in the county of Fauquier, in the State of Virginia. His father was Thomas Marshall, a native of the same State, and at the time of his birth, a planter of narrow fortune and retired habits. Of this gentleman, who afterwards served with great distinction during the revolutionary war, having been appointed to the command of one of the Continental Regiments of Infantry, it is proper to say a few words in this place. He was a man of uncommon capacity and vigor of intellect; and though his original education was very imperfect, he overcame this disadvantage by the diligence and perseverance, with which he cultivated his natural endowments; so that he soon acquired, and maintained throughout the course of his life, among associates of no mean character, the reputation of masculine sense, and extraordinary judgment and ability. No better proof, indeed, need be adduced to justify this opinion than the fact, that he possessed the unbounded confidence, respect, and admiration of all his children at that mature period of their lives, when they were fully able to appreciate his worth, and to compare and measure him with other men of known eminence. I have myself often heard the Chief Justice speak of him in terms of the deepest affection and reverence. I do not here refer to his public remarks; but to his private and familiar conversations with me, when there was no other listener. Indeed, he never named his father on these occasions without dwelling on his character with a fond and winning enthusiasm. It was a theme, on which he broke out with a spontaneous eloquence; and, in the spirit of the most persuasive confidence, he would delight to expatiate upon his virtues and talents. "My father," would he say with kindled feelings and emphasis, "my father was a far abler man than any of his sons. To him I owe the solid foundation of all my own success in life." Such praise from such lips is inexpressibly precious. I know not, whether it be most honorable to the parent, or to the child. It warms, while it elevates our admiration of both. What, indeed, can be more affecting than such a tribute of filial gratitude to the memory of a parent, long after death has set its seal upon his character, and at such a distance of time, as leaves no temptation to pious sorrow to exaggerate what he was, or to excite the imagination to paint what he might have been.

Colonel Marshall had fifteen children, several of whom are still living. Some of them, besides the one of whom I am mainly to speak, have attained high distinction as scholars and statesmen; and one, whom I do not feel privileged to name, enjoys the reputation of a thorough acquaintance with that most difficult of all studies, the Philosophy of History.

John was the eldest son, and of course was the earliest to engage the solicitude of his father. The means of obtaining any suitable education at the family residence were at that period scanty and inadequate. Fauquier was then a frontier county in the State; and whoever will carry back his thoughts to the dangers and difficulties of such a local position, far in advance of the ordinary reach of compact population, will readily comprehend the embarrassments and sacrifices, with which it was attended. Colonel Marshall was thus compelled exclusively to superintend the education of all his children; and perceiving the rapid development of the talents of his eldest son, he gave him a decided taste for the study of English literature, and especially for poetry and history. At the age of twelve, the latter had transcribed the whole of Pope's Essay on Man, and some of his moral essays; and had committed to memory many of the most interesting passages of that distinguished poet.

The love of poetry, thus awakened in his warm and vigorous mind, soon exerted a commanding influence over it. He became enamored of the classical writers of the old English school, of Milton, and Shakspeare, and Dryden, and Pope; and was instructed by their solid sense and beautiful imagery. In the enthusiasm of youth, he often indulged himself in poetical compositions, and freely gave up his leisure hours to those delicious dreamings with the muses, which, say what we may, constitute with many the purest source of pleasure in the gayer scenes of life, and the sweetest consolation in the hours of adversity. It has, indeed, been said by Sir James Mackintosh, that all men of genius delight to take refuge in poetry from the vulgarity and irritation of business. Without yielding to so general and sweeping a conclusion, it may be truly said, that it is not uncongenial with the highest attributes of genius, and is often found an accompaniment of its nicer sympathies.

One of the best recommendations, indeed, of the early cultivation of a taste for poetry, and the kindred branches of literature, is, that it does not expire with youth. It affords to maturer years a refreshing relaxation from the severe cares of business, and to old age a quiet and welcome employment, always within reach, and always bringing with it, if not the charm of novelty, at least the soothing reminiscences of other days. The votary of the muses may not always tread upon enchanted ground; but the gentle influences of fiction and song will steal over his thoughts, and breathe, as it were, into his soul the fragrance of a second spring of life.

Throughout the whole of his life, and down to its very close, Mr. Marshall continued to cultivate a taste for general literature, and especially for those departments of it, which had been the favorite studies of his youth. He was familiar with all its light, as well as its more recondite, productions. He read with intense interest, as his leisure would allow, all the higher literature of modern times; and, especially, the works of the great masters of the art were his constant delight. While the common publications of the day fell from his hands with a cold indifference, he kindled with enthusiasm at the names of the great novelists and poets of the age, and discussed their relative powers and merits with a nice and discriminating skill, as if he were but yesterday fresh from the perusal of them.

To many persons it may seem strange, that such a love of letters, and especially of works of imagination, should ever be found combined with the severe logic and closeness of thought, which belonged to his character, and gave such a grave cast to all his juridical labors. But the truth is, that the union is far less uncommon in the highest class of minds, than slight observers are apt to suppose. There is not only no incompatibility in pursuits of such opposite tendencies; but men of genius, more than any other persons, from their lively sensibility to excellence, are prone to have their curiosity awakened by any exhibition of it, in whatever department of knowledge or art it may be displayed. They feel the presence of superior power; they are touched by the sublime reaches of kindred spirits; they gaze on the wonders of that workmanship, whose exquisite proportions they understand, and whose difficulties of execution they appreciate. They see the glory of that eminence, which is so proudly won, and so bravely maintained. But they can also measure what few other persons can, what vast resources and uncounted labors have been exhausted in the attainment. Thus, their sympathies are excited by every triumph of the human intellect; and the very contrast of their own favorite studies and pursuits with those of others opens upon them new sources of pleasure, in surveying the variety, as well as the magnificence, of human genius. But to return to my narrative.

There being no grammar school in the neighborhood, young Marshall, at the age of fourteen, was sent for his education about a hundred miles from his home, and was placed under the tuition of Mr. Campbell, a clergyman of great respectability. He remained with him a year, and then returned home, and was placed under the care of a Scotch gentleman, who was just then inducted as pastor of the parish, and resided in his father's family. He pursued his classical studies under the care of this reverend pastor, as long as he resided in the family, which was about a year; and he had at that time commenced the reading of Livy and Horace. After this period, he was left to his own unassisted diligence; and his subsequent mastery of the Classics was accomplished without any other aids than his Grammar and Dictionary. He never had the benefit of any instruction in any college, or other public institution; and his attainments in learning, such as they were, were nourished by the solitary vigils of his own genius. In English literature, he continued to receive the fostering care and assistance of his father, who directed his studies, and contributed, in an eminent degree, to cherish his love of knowledge; to give a solid cast to his acquirements; and to store his mind with the most valuable materials. It is to this circumstance, that we are mainly to attribute that decided attachment to the writers of the golden age of English literature, which at all times he avowed, and vindicated with a glowing confidence in its importance, and its superior excellence. His father, too, at this period, was not only a watchful parent, but a most useful and affectionate friend; and he became the constant, as he was also almost the only intelligent, companion of his son. The time which was not thus passed in the society of his father, he employed in hardy, athletic exercises in the open air. He engaged in field sports; he wandered in the deep woods; he indulged his solitary meditations amidst the wilder scenery of nature; he delighted to brush away the earliest dews of the morning, and to watch the varied magnificence of sunset, until its last beams ceased to play on the dark tops of the noiseless forest. It was to these early habits in a mountainous region, that he probably owed that robust and vigorous constitution, which carried him almost to the close of his life with the freshness and firmness of manhood.

It was about the time, when young Marshall entered on the eighteenth year of his age, that the controversy between Great Britian and her American Colonies, which ended in the establishment of the independence of the latter, began to assume a portentous aspect. It could not fail to engage the attention of all the Colonists, whether they were young, or old, in the retirement of private life, or in the exercise of public political functions. It was a stirring theme of conversation, involving interests of such vast magnitude, and consequences of such enduring influence, that every patriot felt himself called upon by a sense of duty to arouse himself for the approaching exigency. Young Marshall could not be indifferent to it. He entered into the controversy with all the zeal and enthusiasm of a youth, full of the love of his country, and deeply sensible of its rights and its wrongs. Partaking of the spirit and energy of his father, he immediately devoted his time, with a prophetic foresight, to the acquisition of the rudiments of military manœuvres in an independent company of volunteers, composed of gentlemen of the same county, to the training of a company of the militia of the neighborhood, and to the diligent reading of the political essays of the day. For these animating pursuits he was quite content to relinquish all his literary studies; and the pages of Blackstone's Commentaries, to which he had already begun to direct his ambition, were forgotten amidst the din of arms, and the preparations for open hostilities.

In the summer of 1775, he was appointed the first lieutenant of a company of minute men, who were enrolled for active service, and assembled in battalion at the beginning of the ensuing September. In a few days they were ordered to march into the lower country, for the purpose of defending it against a small predatory force of regulars commanded by Lord Dunmore, and also of assisting in the relief of Norfolk, with some other provincial troops. Hearing of their approach, Lord Dunmore took an advantageous position on the north side of Elizabeth, near the great bridge, and at a small distance from Norfolk. A battle soon afterwards took place between the opposing bodies, in which the British were repulsed with great gallantry. On this occasion Lieutenant Marshall took an active part, and had a full share of the honors of the day. The provincials, immediately after the retreat of the British, made their way to Norfolk; and Lieutenant Marshall was present, when that city was set on fire by a detachment from the British ships, then lying in the river.

In July, 1776, he received the appointment of first lieutenant in the eleventh regiment on the Continental establishment; and in the succeeding winter he marched with his regiment to the Middle States, then the scene of an harassing warfare; and in May, 1777, he was promoted to the rank of captain. From this period he remained constantly in service until the close of the year 1779. He was present at the skirmish with the British light infantry at Iron Hill; and he fought in the memorable battles of Brandywine, Germantown, and Monmouth. During this period of his military life, he was often employed to act as Deputy Judge Advocate, a situation, which brought him to a large acquaintance with the officers of the army, by whom he was greatly beloved, and among whom he deservedly acquired an extensive influence. I myself have often heard him spoken of by some of these veterans in terms of the warmest praise. In an especial manner the Revolutionary officers of the Virginia Line (now "few and faint, but fearless still,") appeared almost to idolize him, as an old friend and companion in arms, enjoying their unqualified confidence.

It was during his performance of the duties of Judge Advocate, that he for the first time (I believe) became personally acquainted with General Washington, and (I am sure) with Colonel (afterwards General) Hamilton; for both of whom, it needs scarcely to be said, he always entertained the deepest respect, and whose unreserved friendship, at a subsequent period of his life, he familiarly enjoyed. His opinion of Washington is sufficiently manifested in his biography of that great man. Of Hamilton he always spoke in the most unreserved manner, as a soldier and statesman of consummate ability; and in a point of comprehensiveness of mind, purity of patriotism, and soundness of principles, as among the first, that had ever graced the councils of any nation. His services to the American Republic he deemed to have been of inestimable value, and such as had eminently conduced to its stability, its prosperity, and its true glory.

There being, in the winter of 1779, a great surplus of officers belonging to the Virginia line, beyond the immediate exigencies of the service, the supernumeraries, among whom was Captain Marshall, were directed to return home, in order to take charge of such men, as the state legislature might raise for their command. It was in this interval of military inactivity, that he availed himself of the opportunity of attending at William and Mary's College the course of law lectures of Mr. (afterwards Chancellor) Wythe, and the lectures upon natural philosophy of the then president of the college, Mr. (afterwards Bishop) Madison. He left that institution in the summer vacation of 1780; and soon afterwards received the usual license to practise law. In October of the same year he returned to the army, and continued in active service until after the termination of Arnold's invasion of Virginia. Finding, that the same redundancy of officers in the Virginia line still continued, he then resigned his commission, and addicted himself to the study of his future profession. The courts of law were suspended in Virginia until after the capture of Lord Cornwallis and his army at the memorable siege at Yorktown. As soon as they were reopened, Mr. Marshall commenced the practice of the law, and soon rose into high distinction at the bar.

In the spring of 1782, he was elected a member of the state legislature; and, in the autumn of the same year, a member of the state executive council. In January, 1783, he married Miss Ambler, the daughter of the then Treasurer of the state, to whom he had become attached, before he quitted the army. With this lady he lived in a state of the most devoted conjugal affection for nearly fifty years; and her death, not quite three years ago, cast a gloom over his thoughts, from which I do not think he ever fully recovered. About the time of his marriage, he took up his permanent residence in the city of Richmond. In the spring of 1784, he resigned his seat at the council board, in order to devote himself more exclusively to the duties of the bar. He was immediately afterwards elected a member of the legislature by the county of Fauquier, a tribute of respect from the spot of his nativity the more marked, because he had already ceased to have any thing but a nominal residence there. In 1787, he was elected a member of the legislature by the county of Henrico; and he soon embarked in all the perplexing political questions which then agitated the State.

It is to this period, — between the close of the war of the Revolution, and the adoption of the present constitution of the United States, — that we are to refer the gradual development and final establishment of those political opinions and principles, which constituted the basis of all the public actions of his subsequent life. He had entered the army with all the enthusiasm of a young man, ardent in the cause of liberty, devoted to his country, glowing with confidence in the wisdom and virtue of the people, and unsuspicious, that they could ever be seduced or betrayed into any conduct, not warranted by the purest public principles. He knew the disinterestedness of his own heart; and he could not believe, nay, he could not even imagine, that it was possible, that a republic, founded for the common good, should not, at all times and under all circumstances, be exclusively administered for this single purpose. The very suggestion of any doubt upon the subject led him to distrust, not his own judgment, but the intelligence or integrity of those, who ventured to breathe that doubt, even in the softest whispers. He had never heard of the profound remark of a great statesman, that a young man, who was not an enthusiast in matters of government, must possess low and grovelling principles of action; but that an old man, who was an enthusiast, must have lived to little purpose. He could have learned nothing worth remembering; or remembered only what was fit to be forgotten. Like the shepherd in Virgil, in the simplicity of his heart he thought, that all things were at Rome, as they were at Mantua; — *Sic parvis componere magna solebat.* Amidst the din of arms, he found no leisure to study the science of government. He deemed it useless to consider, how liberty was to be enjoyed and protected, until it was won. The contest for national existence was then instant and pressing. The only lights which were on the paths of the patriot, to guide or instruct him, were those which glanced from the point of his sword. The midnight hours were to be passed, not in the soft serenities of meditation, but in mounting guard on the outposts; in stealthy patrols along the lines of the enemy; or in repelling the deadly attack in the midst of the flashes and the roar of well-directed musketry and cannon.

"When I recollect," (said he, in a letter written long afterwards to a friend,) "the wild and enthusiastic notions, with which my political opinions of that day were tinctured, I am disposed to ascribe my devotion to the Union, and to a government competent to its preservation, at least as much to casual circumstances, as to judgment. I had grown up at a time, when the love of the Union, and the resistance to the claims of Great Britain, were the inseparable inmates of the same bosom; when patriotism and a strong fellow feeling with our suffering fellow-citizens of Boston were identical; when the maxim, 'United we stand, divided we fall,' was the maxim of every orthodox American. And I had imbibed these sentiments so thoroughly, that they constituted a part of my being. I carried them with me into the army, where I found myself associated with brave men from different States, who were risking life and every thing valuable, in a common cause, believed by all to be most precious; and where I was confirmed in the habit of considering America as my country, and congress as my government."

But the times were now arrived, in which the dreams of

his early manhood were to be rigidly compared with the sober realities about him. The Revolution, with its strong excitements, and its agitations of alternate hopes and fears, had passed away. The national independence had been achieved; and the feverish and restless activity of the past had given place to a state of languor and exhaustion, which made the advent of peace itself a period of renewed anxieties, and heavier cares. What had been gained by the sword was now to be secured by civil wisdom; by the establishment of wholesome laws, sound institutions, and well-regulated government. And deeply and painfully did every lover of his country then feel the truth of the remark of Milton,—"Peace hath her victories, no less renowned than War."

Whoever is well read in our domestic history, cannot have forgotten the dangers and difficulties of those days. The close of the war of the Revolution found the whole country impoverished and exhausted by the necessary expenditures of the contest. Some of the States had made enormous sacrifices to provide their own just contributions for the public service; and most of them had been compelled to resort to the ruinous expedient of a paper currency, to supply their own immediate wants. The national finances were at the lowest ebb of depression. The continental congress had issued more than three hundred millions of paper money, purporting on its face to contain a solemn pledge of the faith of the Union for its due redemption, which pledge had been as notoriously violated. And, indeed, this paper money had sunk to the value of one dollar only for one hundred; and at last had ceased in fact to circulate at all as currency. The national debt was not only not discharged; but was without any means of being discharged, even as to the interest due upon it. The army had been disbanded with long arrearages of pay outstanding; and the discontents of those noble bands, which had saved the country, were listened to, only to be disregarded. The very magnitude of the public evils almost discouraged every effort to redress them. The usual consesequences of such a state of things had been fully realized. Private, as well as public, credit was destroyed. Agriculture and commerce were crippled; manufactures could not, in any strict sense, be said to have an existence. They were in a state of profound lethargy. The little money, which yet remained in specie in the country, was subject to a perpetual drain, to purchase the ordinary supplies from foreign countries. The whole industry of the country was at a stand. Our artisans were starving in the streets, without the means, or the habits of regular employment; and the disbanded officers of the army found themselves, not only without resources, but without occupation. Under such circumstances, the popular murmurs were not only loud, but deep; and the general distress became so appalling, that it threatened a shipwreck of all our free institutions. In short, we seemed to have escaped from the dominion of the parent country, only to sink into a more galling domestic bondage. Our very safety was felt to be mainly dependent upon the jealousy, or forbearance of foreign governments.

What aggravated all these evils was the utter hopelessness of any effectual remedy under the existing form of the national government; if, indeed, that might be said to deserve the name, which was but the shadow of a government. The union of the States at the commencement of the revolutionary contest was forced upon us by circumstances; and from its nature and objects seemed limited to that precise exigency. The Confederation, which was subsequently framed, was conceived in a spirit of extreme jealousy of national sovereignty, and withal was so feeble and loose in its texture, that reflecting minds foresaw, that it could scarcely survive the revolutionary contest. Yet feeble and loose as was its texture, it encountered the most obstinate opposition at every step of its progress; and it was not finally adopted, until the war was about to close, in 1781. The powers of congress, under the Confederation, were, for the most part, merely recommendatory, and to be carried into effect only through the instrumentality of the States. It conferred no power to raise revenue, or levy taxes, or enforce obedience to laws, or regulate commerce, or even to command means to pay our public ministers at foreign courts. Congress could make contracts; but could not provide means to discharge them. They could pledge the public faith; but they could not redeem it. They could make public treaties; but every state in the Union might disregard them with impunity. They could enter into alliances; but they could not command men or money to give them vigor. They could declare war; but they could not raise troops; and their only resort was to requisitions on the States. In short, all the powers given by the Confederation, which did not execute themselves without any external aid, were at the mere mercy of the States, and might be trampled upon at pleasure. Even that miserable fragment of sovereignty, the power to levy a tax of five per cent. on imports, in order to pay the public debt, and until it was paid, was solemnly rejected by the States, though asked by congress in terms of humble entreaty, and the most affecting appeals to public justice.

The result was obvious. Without the power to lay taxes, Congress was palsied in all their operations. Without the power to regulate commerce, we were left to the capricious legislation of every state. Nay, more; our trade was regulated, taxed, monopolized, and crippled at the pleasure of the maritime powers of Europe. Every state managed its own concerns in its own way; the systems of retaliation for real or imaginary grievances were perpetually devised and enforced against neighboring States. So that, instead of being a band of brothers, united in common cause, and guided by a common interest, the States were everywhere secret or open enemies to each other; and we were on the verge of a border warfare of interminable irritation, and of as interminable mischiefs.

Such was the state of things in the times of which I have been speaking; and strong as the coloring may seem to those whose birth is of a later date, it falls far short of a full picture of the actual extent of the evils which the details of the facts would justify.

It was under these circumstances that the state legislatures were constantly called upon by public clamor and private sufferings, to interpose summary remedies to ward off the hardships of the times. The people, loaded with debts, and goarded on almost to madness by the thickening calamities, demanded measures of relief of the most extravagant nature. The relations of debtor and creditor, always delicate, became every day more embarrassed and more embarrassing. Laws suspending the collection of debts; insolvent laws; instalment laws; tender laws; and other expedients of a like nature, which every reflecting man knew would only aggravate the evils, were familiarly adopted, or openly and boldly vindicated. Popular leaders, as well as men of desperate fortunes, availed themselves (as is usual on such occasions) of this agitating state of things to inflame the public mind, and to bring into public odium those wiser statesmen who labored to support the public faith, and to preserve the inviolability of private contracts.

The whole country soon became divided into two great parties, one of which endeavored to put an end to the public evils by the establishment of an efficient national government; the other adhered to the state sovereignties, and was determined at all hazards to resist the increase of the national power. Virginia bore her full share in these political controversies. They were constantly debated in the halls of her legislature; and whatever might be the fate of any particular debate, the contest was perpetually renewed; for every victory was but a temporary and questionable triumph, and every defeat left still enough of hope to excite the vanquished to new exertions. At this distance of time it is scarcely possible to conceive the zeal, and even the animosity, with which the opposing opinions were maintained. The question, whether the Union ought to be continued, or dissolved by a total separation of the States, was freely discussed; and either side of it was maintained, not only without reproach, but with an uncompromising fearlessness of consequences. Those who clung to the supremacy of the States, looked without dismay upon a dissolution of the Union; and felt no compunctions in surrendering it. Those, on the other hand, who deemed the Union the ark of our political safety, without which independence was but a name, shrunk with horror from the thought of its dissolution; and maintained the struggle with a desperate valor, as the death-grapple for constitutional liberty.

It was in such times and under such circumstances that Mr. Marshall, while yet under thirty years of age, was called upon to take an active part in the legislative deliberations, as well as in the popular meetings in his native state. "My immediate entrance," said he, in the letter already alluded to, "into the state legislature opened to my view the causes which had been chiefly instrumental in augmenting those sufferings, [meaning of the army]; and the general tendency of state politics convinced me that no safe and permanent remedy could be found, but in a more efficient and better organized general government." Mr. Madison was at that time, and had for some years before been, a member of the state legislature; and stood forth on all occasions an inflexible and enlightened advocate for the Union; and General Washington was the acknowledged head and supporter of the same principles. Mr. Marshall at once arrayed himself on the side of these great leaders; and while Mr. Madison remained in the legislature he gave him a bold and steady support in all the prominent debates. The friendship which was thus formed between them was never extinguished. The recollection of their coöperation at that period served, when other measures had widely separated them from each other, still to keep up a lively sense of each other's merits. Nothing, indeed, could be more touching to an ingenuous mind than to hear from their lips, in their latter years, expressions of mutual respect and confidence; or to witness their earnest testimony to the talents, the virtues, and the services of each other.

It was by this course of action in state legislation at this appalling period, that Mr. Marshall was disciplined to the thorough mastery of the true principles of free government. It was here that he learned and practised those profound doctrines of rational, limited, constitutional liberty, from which he never shrunk, and to which he resolutely adhered to the end of his life. It was here that he became enamored, not of a wild and visionary republic, found only in the imaginations of mere enthusiasts as to human perfection, or tricked out in false colors by the selfish, to flatter the prejudices, or cheat the vanity of the people; but of that well-balanced republic, adapted to human wants and human infirmities, in which power is to be held in check by countervailing power; and life, liberty, and property are to be secured by a real and substantial independence, as well as division of the legislative, executive, and judicial departments. It was here that he learned to love the Union with a supreme, unconquerable love; a love which was never cooled by neglect, or alienated by disappointment; a love which survived the trials of adversity, and the still more dangerous trials of prosperity; a love which clung more closely to its object, as it seemed less dear or less valuable in the eyes of others; a love which faltered not, fainted not, wearied not, on this side the grave. Yes; his thoughts ever dwelt on the Union, as the first and best of all our earthly hopes. The last expressions which lingered on his dying lips breathed forth a prayer for his country.

> " Such in that moment, as in all the past,
> ' O, save my country, Heaven,' was then his last."

While these exciting discussions were absorbing the whole attention of the state legislatures, the Confederation was obviously approaching its final dissolution. It had passed the crisis of its fate; and its doom was fixed. As a scheme of government it had utterly failed; and the moment was now anxiously expected, when, from mere debility, it would cease to have even a nominal existence, as it had long ceased to have any substantial authority. The friends of the Union determined to make one more and final effort. A convention was called, which framed the constitution of the United States; and it was presented to the people for their ratification or rejection. This measure at once gave rise to new and more violent political controversies; and the whole current of popular opinion was impetuously hurried into new channels. Parties, for and against the adoption of the constitution, were immediately organized in every state; and the lines of political division were for the most part the same, which marked the former parties. Virginia, as a leading state, became the scene of the most active exertions; and, as many of her gifted and eloquent men were arrayed against the constitution, so its friends rallied for the approaching struggle with a proportionate zeal and ability.

Mr. Marshall was chosen a member of the convention of Virginia, which was called to deliberate upon the ratification of the constitution, under circumstances peculiarly gratifying. A majority of the voters of the county in which he resided, were opposed to the adoption of it; and he was assured, that, if he would pledge himself to vote against it, all opposition to his election should be withdrawn; otherwise he would be strenuously resisted. He did not hesitate for a moment to avow his determination to vote for the constitution. To use his own language — "The questions, which were perpetually recurring in the state legislatures; and which brought annually into doubt principles, which I thought most sacred; which proved, that every thing was afloat, and that we had no safe anchorage ground; gave a high value in my estimation to that article in the constitution, which imposes restrictions on the States. I was consequently a determined advocate for its adoption; and became a candidate for the convention." The opposition to him rallied with great force; but such was his personal popularity, and the sense of his integrity, or (as in his modesty he chose to express it) "parties had not yet become so bitter, as to extinguish the private affections, that he was chosen by a triumphant majority.

Few assemblies have ever been convened under circumstances of a more solemn and imposing responsibility. It was understood, that the vote of Virginia would have a principal and perhaps decisive influence upon several other States; and for some weeks the question of the adoption of the constitution hung suspended upon the deliberations of that body. On one side were enlisted the powerful influence of Grayson, the strong and searching sense of George Mason, and the passionate and captivating eloquence of Patrick Henry. On the other side were the persuasive talents of George Nicholas, the animated flow of Governor Randolph, the grave and sententious sagacity of Pendleton, the masculine logic of Marshall, and the consummate skill and various knowledge of Madison. Day after day, during the period of twenty-five days, the debate was continued with unabated ardor and obstinate perseverance. And it was not until it was known that the constitution had already been adopted by nine States, (which settled its fate) that Virginia, by the small majority of *ten* votes, reluctantly gave her own voice in its favor.

During the whole of this most arduous and interesting contest the leading debates were principally conducted on opposite sides by Henry and Madison. Mr. Marshall contented himself with a constant support of his leader. But on three great occasions, the debate on the power of taxation, that on the power over the militia, and that on the powers of the judiciary, he gave free scope to his genius, and argued in their favor with commanding ability. The printed sketches of all these debates are confessedly loose and imperfect, and do little justice to the eloquence or ability of the respective speakers. Yet with all their imperfections the most careless observer cannot fail to perceive, in what is attributed to Mr.

Marshall on these occasions, the closeness of logic, the clearness of statement, and the comprehensiveness of principles, which characterized his labors in the maturer periods of his life. I regret, that the brief space of time, allowed for the present notices, does not justify me in the citation of some passages to illustrate these remarks.

It is difficult, perhaps it is impossible, for us of the present generation, to conceive the magnitude of the dangers which then gathered over our country. Notwithstanding all the sufferings of the people, the acknowledged imbecility, nay the absolute nothingness of the Confederation, and the desperate state of our public affairs, there were men of high character, and patriots, too, who clung to the Confederation with an almost insane attachment. They had been so long accustomed to have all their affections concentrated upon the state government, as their protection against foreign oppression, that a national government seemed to them but another name for an overwhelming despotism. We have lived to see all their fears and prophecies of evil scattered to the winds. We have witnessed the solid growth and prosperity of the whole country, under the auspices of the national government, to an extent never even imagined by its warmest friends. We have seen our agriculture pour forth its various products, created by a generous, I had almost said a profuse industry. The miserable exports, scarcely amounting, in the times of which I have been speaking, in the aggregate, to the sum of one or two hundred thousand dollars, now almost reach to forty millions a year in a single staple. We have seen our commerce, which scarcely crept along our noiseless docks, and stood motionless and withering, while the breezes of the ocean moaned through the crevices of our ruined wharves and deserted warehouses, spread its white canvas in every clime; and, laden with its rich returns, spring buoyant on the waves of the home ports; and cloud the very shores with forests of masts, over which the stars and the stripes are gallantly streaming. We have seen our manufactures, awakkening from a deathlike lethargy, crowd every street of our towns and cities with their busy workmen, and their busier machinery; and startling the silence of our wide streams, and deep dells, and sequestered valleys. We have seen our wild waterfalls subdued by the power of man, become the mere instruments of his will, and under the guidance of mechanical genius, now driving with unerring certainty the flying shuttle, now weaving the mysterious threads of the most delicate fabrics, and now pressing the reluctant metals into form, as if they were but playthings in the hands of giants. We have seen our rivers bear upon their bright waters the swelling sails of our coasters, and the sleepless wheels of our steamboats in endless progress. Nay, the very tides of the ocean, in their regular ebb and flow in our ports, seem now but heralds to announce the arrival and departure of our uncounted navigation. We have seen all these things; and we can scarcely believe, that there were days and nights, nay, months and years, in which our wisest patriots and statesmen sat down in anxious meditations to devise the measures, which should save the country from impending ruin. The task was, indeed, most arduous; in which success was far more desired than expected. Obstinate prejudices were to be overcome; and popular influences were to be resisted. They could scarcely hope for their just rewards, except from a distant posterity. But they were governed by a supreme love of their country, and the consciousness of the inestimable value of the objects, if achieved. Events, indeed, have far outstripped their most sanguine imaginings. By the blessing of Providence we have risen, under the auspices of the Federal Constitution, from a feeble republic to a wide-spreading empire. Many of these patriots and statesmen went down to their graves without the consolation of having witnessed the glorious results of their labors. We owe them a debt of gratitude, which can never be repaid. They laid the broad foundations of our government upon public justice, public virtue, and public liberty. They reared the superstructure with consummate skill, and of the most solid materials. It is for us to say, whether it shall remain through all ages an enduring monument of political wisdom; or, toppling from its height, shall bury under its ruins the glory of the past and the hopes of the future. It can be preserved only by untiring watchfulness. It may be destroyed by popular violence, or the madness of party, or the deeper sappings of corruption. It may, like the fragments of other great empires, (may Heaven avert the evil!) it may

> "Leave a name, at which the world grew pale,
> To point a moral, or adorn a tale."

But these are topics, which, though not inappropriate upon the present occasion, are of themselves of too absorbing an interest to be discussed, as mere incidents in the life of any individual. They may be glanced at in order to do justice to eminent patriotism; but they essentially belong to that philosophy, which reads in the history of the past lessons of admonition and instruction for the ascertainment of the future. Tacitus in other days arrived at the melancholy conclusion, Reipublicæ Forma laudari facilius, quam evenire; vel si evenit, haud diuturna esse potest.[1]

As soon as the adoption of the Constitution had been secured, Mr. Marshall immediately determined to relinquish public life, and to confine his labors to his profession. To this resolution, which was urged upon him by the claims of a growing family and a narrow fortune, he was not enabled to adhere with the steadfastness which he wished. The hostility already evinced against the establishment of the national government, was soon transferred in Virginia to an opposition to all its leading measures. Under such circumstances, it was natural for the friends of the Constitution to seek to give it a strong support in the state legislature. Mr. Marshall was according compelled to yield to their wishes, and served as a member from 1788 to 1792. From the time of

[1] Tacitus, Annal. B. 4, n. 15.

the organization of the government under President Washington, almost every important measure of his administration was discussed in the Virginia legislature with great freedom, and no small degree of warmth and acrimony. On these occasions, it fell to the lot of Mr. Marshall to defend these measures, and to maintain the rights, duties, and powers of the national government against every attack; and he performed the service with great zeal, independence, and ability. In 1792, he again retired from the state legislature, and returned to his professional labors with increased activity; and soon found himself engaged in all the leading causes in the state and national tribunals. The excellent Reports of this period by my lamented friend, Mr. Justice Washington, exhibit ample proofs of his success in argument.[1]

But, although Mr. Marshall was for some years withdrawn from public life, yet he was still compelled to take an active part in political discussions. The French Revolution, which at its early dawn had been hailed with universal enthusiasm throughout America, had now burst out into extravagancies and butcheries, which disgraced the cause of liberty, and gave an unbounded license to ferocious mobs and demagogues. The monarchs of Europe, alarmed for their own safety, were soon leagued in a mighty confederacy to crush a revolution, dangerous to the claims of legitimacy, and the stability of thrones. It was easy to foresee, that if their enterprises against France were successful, we, ourselves, should soon have but a questionable security for our own independence. It would be natural, after their European triumphs were complete, that they should cast their eyes across the Atlantic, and trace back the origin of the evil to the living example of constitutional liberty in this Western hemisphere. Under such circumstances, notwithstanding all the excesses of the French Revolution, the mass of the American people continued to take the liveliest interest in it, and to cherish the warmest

[1] See also Mr. Call's Reports.

wishes for its success. These feelings were heightened by the grateful recollection of the services rendered to us by France in our own Revolution; and the consideration, that she was struggling to relieve herself from oppressions, under which she had been groaning for centuries. In this posture of affairs, there was infinite danger, that we should be driven from the moorings of our neutrality, and should embark in the contest, not only as an ally, but as a party, foremost in the fight, and in the responsibility. We were just recovering from the exhaustion, and poverty, and suffering, consequent upon our own struggle; and the renewal of war would be fraught with immeasurable injuries, not only to our present interests, but to our future national advancement. France saw and felt the nature of our position; and partly by blandishments, and partly by threats, endeavored to enlist our fortunes, as she had already succeeded in enlisting our feelings, in her favor. The other powers of Europe were not less eager in their gaze, or less determined in their future course. England, herself, had already adopted precautionary measures to compel us to support our neutrality in an open and uncompromising manner, or to assume the state of positive hostilities.

It was under these circumstances that President Washington, having determined to preserve our own peace, and to vindicate our rights against all the belligerents with an even-handed justice, issued his celebrated Proclamation of Neutrality. The whole country was immediately thrown into a flame; and the two great parties, into which we were then divided, engaged, the one in denouncing it, and the other in supporting it, with intense zeal. On this occasion Mr. Marshall found himself, much to his regret, arranged on a different side from Mr. Madison. He resolutely maintained the constitutionality, the policy, nay, the duty of issuing the Proclamation, by oral harangues, and by elaborate writings. For these opinions he was attacked with great asperity in the newspapers and pamphlets of the day, and designated by way of significant reproach, as the friend and coadjutor of Hamilton, a reproach, which at all times he would have counted an honor; but, when coupled (as it was) with the name of Washington, he deemed the highest praise. He defended himself against these attacks with an invincible firmness and ability proportioned to the occasion. He drew up a series of resolutions approving the conduct of the Executive, and carried them by a decided majority at a public meeting of the citizens of Richmond.

The result of this controversy is well known. The administration was sustained in its course by the sober sense of the majority of the nation; and the doctrine, then so strenuously contested and boldly denounced, has ever since that time been laid up as among the most undisputable of executive rights and duties. Probably, at the present day, not a single statesman can be found, of any influence in any party, who does not deem the measure to have been as well founded in constitutional law as it was in sound policy.

In the spring of 1795, Mr. Marshall was again returned as a member of the state legislature, not only without his approbation, but against his known wishes. It was truly an honorable tribute to his merits; but it was demanded by the critical posture of our public affairs. The treaty with Great Britain, negotiated by that eminent patriot, Mr. Jay, was then the subject of universal discussion. As soon as the ratification of it was known to have been advised by the Senate, the opposition to it broke out with almost unexampled violence. Public meetings were called in all our principal cities for the purpose of inducing the President to withhold his ratification; and if this step should fail, then to induce congress to withhold the appropriations necessary to carry the treaty into effect. Such a course, if successful, (it was obvious) would at once involve us in a war with England, and an alliance with France. The denunciations of the treaty were everywhere loud and vehement. The topics of animadversion were not confined to the policy, or expediency of the principal articles of the treaty. They took a broader range; and the extraordinary doctrine was advanced and vigorously maintained, that the negotiation of a commercial treaty by the Executive was an infringement of the Constitution, and a violation of the power given to congress to regulate commerce.

Mr. Marshall took an active part in all the discussions upon this subject. Believing the treaty indispensable to the preservation of peace, and its main provisions beneficial to the United States, and consistent with its true dignity, he addressed himself with the most diligent attention to an examination of all the articles, and of the objections urged against them. It was truly a critical period, not merely for the country, but also in an especial manner for the administration. Many of its sincere friends, from the boldness and suddenness of the attacks upon it, from the inflamed state of the public mind, and from a natural distrust of their own judgment upon topics full of embarrassment and novelty, remained in a state of suspense, or timidly yielded themselves to the prejudices of the times. It has been well observed in the biography of Washington, that it is difficult now to review the various resolutions and addresses to which this occasion gave birth without feeling some degree of astonishment, mingled with humiliation, on perceiving such proofs of the deplorable fallibility of human reason.

In no state in the Union was a more intense hostility exhibited against the treaty than in Virginia; and in none were the objections against it urged with more unsparing or impassioned earnestness. The task, therefore, of meeting and overturning them was of no ordinary magnitude, and required the resources of a well-instructed mind. In some resolutions, passed at a meeting of the citizens of Richmond, at which Mr. Chancellor Wythe presided, the treaty was denounced "as insulting to the dignity, injurious to the interest, dangerous to the security, and repugnant to the Constitution of the United States." At a meeting of the same citizens, subsequently held, Mr. Marshall introduced certain resolutions in favor of the conduct of the Executive, and supported them in a masterly speech; the best comment upon which is, that the resolutions were approved by a flattering majority.

But a more difficult and important duty remained to be performed. It was easily foreseen, that the controversy would soon find its way into the state legislature, and would there be renewed with all the bitter animosity of party spirit. So odious was the treaty in Virginia, that Mr. Marshall's friends were exceedingly solicitous, that he should not engage in any legislative debates on the subject, as it would certainly impair his well-earned popularity, and might even subject him to some rude personal attacks. His answer to all such suggestions uniformly was, that he would not bring forward any measure to excite a debate on the subject; but if it were brought forward by others, he would at all hazards vindicate the administration, and assert his own opinions. The subject was soon introduced by the opposition; and, among other things, the constitutional objections were urged with triumphant confidence. Especially was that objection pressed, which denied the constitutional right of the Executive to conclude a commercial treaty, as a favorite and unanswerable position. The speech of Mr. Marshall on this occasion has always been represented as one of the noblest efforts of his genius. His vast powers of reasoning were displayed with the most gratifying success. He demonstrated, not only from the words of the Constitution and the universal practice of nations, that a commercial treaty was within the scope of the constitutional powers of the Executive; but that this opinion had been maintained and sanctioned by Mr. Jefferson, by the Virginia delegation in congress, and by the leading members of the Convention on both sides. The argument was decisive. The constitutional ground was abandoned; and the resolutions of the assembly were confined to a simple disapprobation of the treaty in point of expediency.

The constitutional objections were again urged in congress, in the celebrated debate on the Treaty, in the spring of 1796; and there finally assumed the mitigated shape of a right claimed by congress to grant or withhold appropriations to carry treaties into effect. The higher ground, that commercial treaties were not, when ratified by the Senate, the supreme law of the land, was abandoned; and the subsequent practice of the government has, without serious question, been under every administration, in conformity to the construction vindicated by Mr. Marshall. The fame of this admirable argument spread through the Union. Even with his political enemies, it enhanced the estimate of his character; and it brought him at once to the notice of some of the most eminent statesmen, who then graced the councils of the nation.

In the winter of 1796, Mr. Marshall visited Philadelphia, to argue before the Supreme Court the great case of Ware *v.* Hylton, which involved the question of the right of recovery of British debts which had been confiscated during the revolutionary war. It is well known that the question was decided against the side on which Mr. Marshall was employed. On this occasion he was opposed by three of the ablest lawyers then belonging to the Pennsylvania bar. This was, of itself, under such circumstances, no small distinction. But the sketch of the argument delivered by him, as we find it in the printed Reports, affords conclusive evidence of his juridical learning. and the great skill with which he arranged his materials and sustained the interests of his client.

It was during this visit that he became personally acquainted with the distinguished men who were then in congress, as representatives from the Northern States. "I then became acquainted," says he, in a letter to a friend, "with Mr. Cabot, Mr. Ames, Mr. Dexter, and Mr. Sedgwick of Massachusetts, Mr. Wadsworth of Connecticut, and Mr. King of

New York. I was delighted with these gentlemen. The particular subject (the British Treaty) which introduced me to their notice, was at that time so interesting, and a Virginian, who supported, with any sort of reputation, the measures of the government, was such a *rara avis*, that I was received by them all with a degree of kindness which I had not anticipated. I was particularly intimate with Mr. Ames, and could scarcely gain credit with him, when I assured him, that the appropriations would be seriously opposed in congress." The event proved, that he was right. The high opinion which he then formed of these gentlemen, continued to be cherished by him through all his future life.

About this period President Washington offered him the office of Attorney-General of the United States; but he declined it on the ground of its interference with his far more lucrative practice in Virginia. He continued, however, in the state legislature; but he rarely engaged in the debates, except when the measures of the national government were discussed, and required vindication. Nor were the occasions few, in which this task was required to be performed with a steady confidence. One of them shall be mentioned in his own words. "It was, I think," said he, "in the session of 1796, that I was engaged in a debate, which called forth all the strength and violence of party. Some federalist moved a resolution, expressing the high confidence of the House in the virtue, patriotism, and wisdom of the President of the United States. A motion was made to strike out the word *wisdom*. In the debate the whole course of the Administration was reviewed, and the whole talent of each party was brought into action. Will it be believed, that the word was retained by a very small majority? A very small majority in the legislature of Virginia acknowledged the wisdom of General Washington!"

Upon the recall of Mr. Monroe as Minister to France, President Washington solicited Mr. Marshall to accept the appointment, as his successor; but he respectfully declined it for the same reasons as he had the office of Attorney General; and General Pinckney, of South Carolina, was appointed in his stead. "I then thought," said he, "my determination to remain at the bar unalterable. My situation at the bar appeared to me to be more independent, and not less honorable, than any other; and my preference for it was decided."

But he was not long permitted to act upon his own judgment and choice. The French government refused to receive General Pinckney; and Mr. Adams, (who had then succeeded to the presidency,) from an anxious desire to exhaust every measure of conciliation, not incompatible with the national dignity, in June, 1797, appointed Mr. Marshall, General Pinckney, and Mr. (afterwards Vice-President) Gerry, Envoys Extraordinary to the court of France. After no inconsiderable struggles in his own mind, (which are fully developed in a paper now in my possession,) Mr. Marshall accepted the appointment; and proceeded to Paris, and there, with his colleagues, entered upon the duties of the mission. It is well known, that the mission was unsuccessful; the French government having refused to enter into any negotiations. The preparation of the official despatches addressed to that government upon this occasion was confided to Mr. Marshall; and these despatches have been universally admired. They are models of skilful reasoning, clear illustration, accurate detail, and urbane and dignified moderation. They contain a most elaborate review of all the principles of national law, applicable to the points in controversy between the two nations. As state papers, there are not in the annals of our diplomacy any, upon which an American can look back with more pride, or from which he can draw more various instruction.

On his return home Mr. Marshall resumed his professional business, and had the best reasons to believe that it would be increased rather than diminished by his temporary absence. He was determined to pursue it with renewed ardor. But from this determination he was again diverted by a personal appeal made to him by General Washington, who earnestly insisted, that he should become a candidate for congress. After a conversation between them of the deepest interest and animation, and breathing on each side a spirit of the purest patriotism, Mr. Marshall reluctantly yielded to the wishes of General Washington, and became a candidate, and was elected after a most ardent political contest; and took his seat in congress in December, 1799. While he was yet a candidate, President Adams offered him the seat on the bench of the Supreme Court, then vacant by the death of Mr. Justice Iredell. He immediately declined it; and it was conferred on that excellent magistrate, Mr. Justice Washington.

The session of congress in the winter of 1799 and 1800 will be forever memorable in our political annals. It was the moment of the final struggle for power between the two great political parties which then divided the country, and ended, as is well known, in the overthrow of the federal administration. Men of the highest talents and influence were there assembled, and arrayed in hostility to each other; and were excited by all the strongest motives which can rouse the human mind, the pride of power, the hope of victory, the sense of responsibility, the devotion to principles deemed vital, and the bonds of long political attachment and action. Under such circumstances, (as might naturally be expected,) every important measure of the administration was assailed with a bold and vehement criticism; and was defended with untiring zeal and firmness. Mr. Marshall took his full share of the debates; and was received with a distinction proportioned to his merits. Such a distinction, in such a body, is a rare occurrence; for years of public service and experience are usually found indispensable to acquire and justify the confidence of the House of Representatives.

It is not my intention to enter into a minute detail of the debates, in which Mr. Marshall took a part, or to vindicate his votes or opinions. The duty is more appropriate for a different labor. On one occasion, however, he took a leading part in a most important debate, which acquired for him a wide public fame, and therefore requires notice in this place. I allude to the debate on the case of Thomas Nash, otherwise called Jonathan Robbins, who had been surrendered to the British government for trial for a supposed murder, committed by him on board of a British ship of war. Certain resolutions were brought forward, censuring the conduct of the Executive for this act, in terms of decided disapprobation, as unconstitutional and improper. Mr. Marshall, in the course of the debate, delivered a speech in vindication of the right and duty of the Executive to make the surrender, which placed him at once in the first rank of constitutional statesmen. The substance of it is now in print. It is one of the most consummate juridical arguments which was ever pronounced in the halls of legislation; and equally remarkable for the lucid order of its topics, the profoundness of its logic, the extent of its research, and the force of its illustrations. It may be said of that speech, as was said of Lord Mansfield's celebrated Answer to the Prussian Memorial, it was *Réponse sans replique*, an answer so irresistible, that it admitted of no reply. It silenced opposition, and settled then and for ever, the points of national law upon which the controversy hinged. The resolutions did not, indeed, fall lifeless from the Speaker's table, though they were negatived by a large majority. But a more unequivocal demonstration of public opinion followed. The denunciations of the Executive, which had hitherto been harsh and clamorous everywhere throughout the land, sunk away at once into cold and cautious whispers only of disapprobation. Whoever reads that speech even at this distance of time, when the topics have lost much of their interest, will be struck with the prodigious powers of analysis and reasoning which it displays; and which are enhanced by the consideration, that the whole subject was then confessedly new in many of its aspects.

In May, 1800, President Adams, without any personal communication with Mr. Marshall, appointed him Secretary of War. Before, however, he was called to enter upon the duties of that office, the known rupture took place between the President and Colonel Pickering; and Mr. Marshall was appointed Secretary of State in the stead of the latter. The appointment was every way honorable to his merits; and no one doubted, that he was eminently qualified for the discharge cf its arduous and important duties.

And, here, I cannot but take great pleasure in recording a circumstance equally honorable to all the parties concerned. Without intending in the slightest degree to enter upon the discussion of the controversy between the President and Colonel Pickering, I may be permitted to say, that the circumstances, necessarily attending the dismissal of the latter from office, were calculated to awaken a strong sense of injustice in the mind of an officer of unquestionable integrity and patriotism. The rupture grew out of a very serious difference of opinion upon very grave political measures; and Mr. Marshall entertained a decided attachment to the views of the President. Under such circumstances, it would have been not unnatural, that the late Secretary should have felt some prejudices against his successor; and that there should have been some withdrawal of mutual confidence and perhaps respect between them. No such event occurred. On the contrary, each, to the day of his death, spoke of the other in terms of enviable commendation; and their mutual frank and familiar friendship was never in the slightest manner interrupted. I have often listened to the spontaneous praise bestowed on Mr. Marshall by Colonel Pickering, (a man to whom might justly be applied the character, — *Incorrupta fides nudaque veritas, et mens conscia recti,*) in his own peculiar circle of friends with unmixed delight. It was full, glowing, and affecting. It was a tribute from one of such sincerity of thought and purpose, that praise, even when best deserved, came from his lips with a studied caution of language. His conversation, always instructive, on these occasions rose into eloquence, beautiful, nay, touched with a moral sublimity. When all the circumstances are considered, I think, that I do not overestimate the value of this example of mutual confidence and friendship, when I pronounce it as gratifying as it is rare. It prostrates in the dust all petty rivalry for public distinction. It shows, that great minds (and perhaps great minds only) fully understand that exquisite moral truth, that no man stands in another man's way in the road to honor; and that the world is wide enough for the fullest display of the virtues and talents of all, without intercepting a single ray of light reflected by any.

On the thirty-first of January, 1801, Mr. Marshall received the appointment of Chief Justice of the United States. It is due to his memory to state, that it was conferred on him, not only without his own solicitation, (for he had in fact recommended another person for the office) but by the prompt and spontaneous choice of President Adams upon his own unassisted judgment. The nomination was unanimously confirmed by the Senate; and the Chief Justice accordingly took his seat on the bench at the ensuing term of the Supreme Court. I trust, that I am not violating any private confidence, when I quote, from a letter of the distinguished son of this distinguished patriot, a passage on this subject, to which the whole country will respond without hesitation. It inclosed a judicial commission to a gentleman, now justly enjoying the highest professional reputation; and says with equal felicity and truth — "One of the last acts of my father's administration was the transmission of a commission to John Marshall, as Chief Justice of the United States. One of the last acts of my administration is the transmission of the inclosed commission to you. If neither of us had ever done any thing else to deserve the approbation of our country, and of posterity, I would proudly claim it of both for these acts, as due to my father and myself." The claim is, indeed, a proud claim to distinction. It has received, as it deserved, the approbation of the whole country. The gratitude of posterity will also do just homage to the sagacity, foresight, disinterestedness, and public spirit of the choice. It was in moral dignity the fit close of a political life of extraordinary brilliancy. In public importance it scarcely yielded to any act of that life, except the motion for the Declaration of Independence. Such honor from such hands was felt to be doubly dear. It was the highest praise from one, whose title to confer it had been earned by long services in the cause of liberty. The names of Adams and Marshall became thus indissolubly connected in the juridical and constitutional history of the country.

From this time until his death the Chief Justice continued in the discharge of the duties of his exalted office with unsullied dignity, and constantly increasing reputation. Notwithstanding his advancing years, no sensible inroad had been made upon his general health, until the last term of the Court, when it was obvious, that his physical strength had passed the utmost stretch of its vigor, and was in a state of rapid decline. His intellectual powers still, however, retained their wonted energy; and, though he was suffering under great bodily pain, he not only bore it with an uncomplaining spirit, but continued to take his full share of the business of the Court. No better proof need be required of his intellectual ability than his opinions, which stand recorded in the last volume of Reports.

At the close of the term he returned to his residence in Virginia; and he was afterwards induced, by the solicitations of his friends, to visit Philadelphia, in the expectation of receiving some aid from the distinguished medical skill of that city. His constitution, however, had become so shattered, that little more remained to be done, during the last weeks of his life, than to smoothe the downward path towards the grave. He died on the sixth day of July last past, about six o'clock in the evening, in the arms of his children, without a struggle; and, to use the expressive language of one who was present, his last breath was the softest whisper of a zephyr. Fortunately, by the considerate kindness of his friends, he was spared the knowledge of the death of his eldest son, who lost his life a few days before by a most calamitous accident; an event, which, from the high character of the son, and his strong affection for him, would have filled his last hours with inexpressible anguish.

He was fully aware of his approaching end, and prepared to meet it with a calmness built upon the fixed principles, by which he had regulated his life. Two days only before his death he wrote an inscription to be placed on his tomb, in the following simple and modest terms: "John Marshall, son of Thomas and Mary Marshall, was born on the 24th of September, 1755, intermarried with Mary Willis Ambler the 3d of January, 1783, departed this life the —— of ——, 18—."

What can be more affecting than these few facts, the only ones, which he deemed in his last moments worth recording! His birth; his parentage; his marriage; his death. His parents, to whose memory he was attached with a filial piety, full of reverence; — his marriage to the being, whom he had loved with a singleness and devotedness of affection never surpassed; — his own birth, which seemed principally memorable to him, as it connected him with beings like these; — his own death, which was but an event to re-unite him with those, who had gone before, in a world, where there should be no more suffering or sorrow; but kindred souls should dwell together, even as the angels in heaven.

I have now finished the narrative of the life of Chief Justice Marshall, a life which, though unadorned by brilliant passages of individual adventure, or striking events, carries with it (unless I am greatly mistaken) that, which is the truest title to renown, a fame founded on public and private virtue. It has happened to him, as to many other distinguished men, that his life had few incidents; and those which belonged to it were not far removed from the ordinary course of human events. That life was filled up in the conscientious discharge of duty. It was throughout marked by a wise and considerate propriety. His virtues expanded with the gradual development of his character. They were the natural growth of deep-rooted principles, working their way through the gentlest affections, and the purest ambition. No man ever had a loftier desire of excellence; but it was tempered by a kindness, which subdued envy, and a diffidence, which extinguished jealousy. Search his whole life, and you cannot lay your finger on a single extravagance of design or act. There were no infirmities, leaving a permanent stain behind them. There were no eccentricities to be concealed; no follies to be apologized for; no vices to be blushed at; no rash outbreakings of passionate resentment to be regretted; no dark deeds, disturbing the peace of families, or leaving them wretched by its desolations. If here and there the severest scrutiny might be thought capable of detecting any slight admixture of human frailty, it was so shaded off in its coloring, that it melted into some kindred virtue. It might with truth be said, that the very failing leaned to the side of the charities of life; and carried with it the soothing reflection — *Non multum abludit imago.* It might excite a smile; it could never awaken a sigh.

Indeed, there was in him a rare combination of virtues, such only as belongs to a character of consummate wisdom; a wisdom which looks through this world, but which also looks far beyond it for motives and objects. I know not, whether such wisdom ought to be considered as the cause, or the accompaniment, of such virtues; or whether they do not in truth alternately act upon, and perfect each other.

I have said, that there was in him a rare combination of virtues. If I might venture, upon so solemn an occasion, to express my own deliberate judgment, in the very terms most significant to express it, I should say, that the combination was so rare, that I have never known any man, whom I should pronounce more perfect. He had a deep sense of moral and religious obligation, and a love of truth, constant,

57 *

enduring, unflinching. It naturally gave rise to a sincerity of thought, purpose, expression, and conduct, which, though never severe, was always open, manly and straightforward. Yet it was combined with such a gentle and bland demeanor, that it never gave offence; but it was, on the contrary, most persuasive in its appeals to the understanding.

Among Christian sects, he personally attached himself to the Episcopal Church. It was the religion of his early education; and became afterwards that of his choice. But he was without the slightest touch of bigotry or intolerance. His benevolence was as wide as Christianity itself. It embraced the human race. He was not only liberal in his feelings, and principles, but in his charities. His hands were open upon all occasions to succor distress, to encourage enterprise, and to support good institutions.

He was a man of the most unaffected modesty. Although I am persuaded, that no one ever possessed a more entire sense of his own extraordinary talents and acquirements, than he; yet it was a quiet, secret sense, without pride and without ostentation. May I be permitted to say, that, during a most intimate friendship of many, many years, I never upon any occasion was able to detect the slightest tincture of personal vanity. He had no desire for display; and no ambition for admiration. He made no effort to win attention in conversation or argument, beyond what the occasion absolutely required. He sought no fine turns of expression, no vividness of diction, no ornate elegancies of thought, no pointed sentences, to attract observation. What he said was always well said, because it came from a full mind, accustomed to deep reflection; and he was rarely languid, or indifferent to topics which interested others. He dismissed them without regret; though he discussed them with spirit. He never obtruded his own opinions upon others; but brought them out only, as they were sought, and then with clearness and calmness. Upon a first introduction, he would be thought to be somewhat cold and reserved; but he was neither the one nor the other. It was simply a habit of easy taciturnity, waiting, as it were, his own turn to follow the line of conversation, and not to presume to lead it. Even this habit melted away in the presence of the young; for he always looked upon them with a sort of parental fondness, and enjoyed their playful wit, and fresh and confident enthusiasm. Meet him in a stage-coach, as a stranger, and travel with him a whole day, and you would only be struck with his readiness to administer to the accommodations of others, and his anxiety to appropriate the least to himself. Be with him, the unknown guest at an inn, and he seemed adjusted to the very scene, partaking of the warm welcome of its comforts, whenever found; and if not found, resigning himself without complaint to its meanest arrangements. You would never suspect, in either case, that he was a great man; far less that he was the Chief Justice of the United States. But, if perchance invited by the occasion, you drew him into familiar conversation, you would never forget that you had seen and heard that "old man eloquent."

He had great simplicity of character, manners, dress, and deportment; and yet with a natural dignity, that suppressed impertinence, and silenced rudeness. His simplicity was never accompanied with that want of perception of what is right, and fit for the occasion; of that grace, which wins respect; or that propriety, which constitutes the essence of refined courtesy. And yet it had an exquisite *näiveté*, which charmed every one, and gave a sweetness to his familiar conversations, approaching to fascination. The first impression of a stranger, upon his introduction to him, was generally that of disappointment. It seemed hardly credible, that such simplicity should be the accompaniment of such acknowledged greatness. The consciousness of power was not there; the air of office was not there; there was no play of the lights or shades of rank; no study of effect in tone or bearing. You saw at once, that he never thought of himself; and that he was far more anxious to know others, than to be known by them. You quitted him with increased reverence for human greatness; for in him it seemed inseparable from goodness. If vanity stood abashed in his presence, it was not, that he rebuked it; but that his example showed its utter nothingness.

He was a man of deep sensibility and tenderness; nay, he was an enthusiast in regard to the domestic virtues. He was endowed by nature with a temper of great susceptibility, easily excited, and warm, when roused. But it had been so schooled by discipline, or rather so moulded and chastened by his affections, that it seemed in gentleness, like the distilling dews of evening. It had been so long accustomed to flow in channels, where its sole delight was to give or secure happiness to others, that no one would have believed, that it ever could have been precipitate or sudden in its movements. In truth, there was, to the very close of his life, a romantic chivalry in his feelings, which, though rarely displayed, except in the circle of his most intimate friends, would there pour out itself with the most touching tenderness. In this confidential intercourse, when his soul sought solace from the sympathy of other minds, he would dissolve in tears at the recollection of some buried hope, or lost happiness. He would break out into strains of almost divine eloquence, while he pointed out the scenes of former joys, or recalled the memory of other days, as he brought up their images from the dimness and distance of forgotten years, and showed you at once the depth, with which he could feel, and the lower depths, in which he could bury his own closest, dearest, noblest emotions. After all, whatever may be his fame in the eyes of the world, that which, in a just sense, was his highest glory, was the purity, affectionateness, liberality, and devotedness of his domestic life. Home, home, was the scene of his real triumphs. There, he indulged himself in what he most loved, the duties and blessings of the family circle. There, his heart had its full play; and his social qualities, warmed, and elevated, and refined by the habitual elegancies of taste, shed around their beautiful and blended lights. There, the sunshine of his soul diffused its soft radiance, and cheered, and soothed, and tranquillized the passing hours.

May I be permitted also in this presence to allude to another trait in his character, which lets us at once into the inmost recesses of his feelings with an unerring certainty. I allude to the high value in which he held the female sex, as the friends, the companions, and the equals of man. I do not here mean to refer to the courtesy and delicate kindness with which he was accustomed to treat the sex; but rather to the unaffected respect with which he spoke of their accomplishments, their talents, their virtues, and their excellencies. The scoffs and jeers of the morose, the bitter taunts of the satirist, and the lighter ridicule of the witty, so profusely, and often so ungenerously, poured out upon transient follies or fashions, found no sympathy in his bosom. He was still farther above the commonplace flatteries, by which frivolity seeks to administer aliment to personal vanity, or vice to make its approaches for baser purposes. He spoke to the sex, when present, as he spoke of them, when absent, in language of just appeal to their understandings, their tastes, and their duties. He paid a voluntary homage to their genius, and to the beautiful productions of it, which now adorn almost every branch of literature and learning. He read those productions with a glowing gratitude. He proudly proclaimed their merits, and vindicated on all occasions their claims to the highest distinction. And he did not hesitate to assign to the great female authors of our day a rank, not inferior to that of the most gifted and polished of the other sex. But, above all, he delighted to dwell on the admirable adaptation of their minds, and sensibilities, and affections to the exalted duties assigned to them by Providence. Their superior purity, their singleness of heart, their exquisite perception of moral and religious sentiment, their maternal devotedness, their uncomplaining sacrifices, their fearlessness in duty, their buoyancy in hope, their courage in despair, their love, which triumphs most, when most pressed by dangers and difficulties; which watches the couch of sickness, and smooths the bed of death, and smiles even in the agonies of its own sufferings; — These, these were the favorite topics of his confidential conversation; and on these he expatiated with an enthusiasm which showed them to be present in his daily meditations.

I have hitherto spoken of traits of character, belonging in a great measure to his private life. Upon his public life we may look with equal satisfaction. It was without stain or blemish. It requires no concealment or apology, and may defy the most critical and searching scrutiny. He was never seduced by the allurements of office to a desertion of his principles. He was never deterred from an open vindication of them by popular clamor, or party cabal; by the frowns of power, or the fury of mobs. His ambition took a loftier range. He aspired to that fame which is enduring, and may justly be conferred by future ages; not to that fame which swells with the triumphs of the day, and dies away, long before it can reach the rising generation. To him might be applied the language of another great magistrate[1] — He wished for popularity; that popularity which follows, not that which is run after; that popularity which, sooner or later, never fails to do justice to the pursuit of noble ends by noble means. He would not do what his conscience told him was wrong to gain the huzzas of thousands, or the daily praise of all the papers which came from the press. He would not avoid to do what he thought was right, though it should draw on him the whole artillery of libels; all that falsehood or malice could invent, or the credulity of a deluded populace could swallow.

There was throughout his political life a steadfastness and consistency of principle as striking as they were elevating. During more than half a century of public service, he maintained with inflexible integrity the same political principles

[1] Lord Mansfield, 4 Burr. R. 2562.

with which he begun. He was content to live *by*, *with*, and *for* his principles. Amidst the extravagancies of parties at different times, he kept on the even tenor of his way with a calm and undeviating firmness, never bending under the pressure of adversity, or bounding with the elasticity of success. His counsels were always the counsels of moderation, fortified and tried by the results of an enlightened experience. They never betrayed either timidity or rashness. He was, in the original, genuine sense of the word, a federalist — a federalist of the good old school, of which Washington was the acknowledged head, and in which he lived and died. In the maintenance of the principles of that school he was ready at all times to stand forth a determined advocate and supporter. On this subject he scorned all disguise; he affected no change of opinion; he sought no shelter from reproach. He boldly, frankly, and honestly avowed himself, through evil report and good report, the disciple, the friend, and the admirer of Washington and his political principles. He had lived in times when these principles seemed destined to secure to the party to which he belonged an enduring triumph. He had lived to see all these prospects blasted; and other statesmen succeed with a power and influence of such vast extent, that it extinguished all hopes of any future return to office. Yet he remained unshaken, unseduced, unterrified. He had lived to see many of his old friends pass on the other side; and the gallant band, with which he had borne the strife, drop away by death, one after another, until it seemed reduced to a handful. Yet he uttered neither a sigh, nor a complaint. When, under extraordinary excitements in critical times, others with whom he had acted, despaired of the republic, and were willing to yield it up to a stern necessity, he resisted the impulse and clung to the Union, and nailed its colors to the mast of the Constitution.

It is no part of my duty or design upon the present occasion to expound or vindicate his political opinions. That would of itself furnish ample materials for a discourse of a different character. But it is due to truth to declare, that no man was ever more sincerely attached to the principles of free government; no man ever cherished republican institutions with more singleness of heart and purpose; no man ever adhered to his country with a stronger filial affection; no man in his habits, manners, feelings, pursuits, and actions, ever exemplified more perfectly that idol of chivalry, a patriot without fear and without reproach. But, on the other hand, no man was ever more sensible of the dangers incident to free institutions, and especially of those which threaten our national existence. He saw and felt where the weaknesses of the republic lay. He wished, earnestly wished, perpetuity to the Constitution, as the only solid foundation of our national glory and independence. But he foresaw what our course would be; and he never hesitated to express what his fears were, and whence the ruin of the Constitution must come, if it shall come at all. In his view, the republic is not destined to perish, if it shall perish, by the overwhelming power of the national government; but by the resisting and counteracting power of the state sovereignties. He thought with another kindred mind, whose vivid language still rings in my ears after many years, as a voice from the dead, that in our government the centrifugal force is far greater than the centripetal; that the danger is not, that we shall fall into the sun; but that we may fly off in eccentric orbits, and never return to our perihelion. Whether his prophetic fears were ill or well founded time alone can decide;—time, which sweeps away the schemes of man's invention; but leaves immovable on their foundations the eternal truths of nature.

Hitherto, I have spoken of the attributes belonging to his moral character, and the principles, which governed his life and conduct. On these, I confess, that I dwell with a fond and reverential enthusiasm. There was a daily beauty in these, which captivated the more, the nearer they were approached, and the more they were gazed on. Like the softened plays of moonlight, they served to illuminate all objects, at the same time that they mellowed and harmonized them. But, I am admonished, that the duties of the present occasion require me to dwell rather on his intellectual, than his moral qualities. He stands before us rather as the head of a learned profession, than as a private citizen, or as a statesman.

He was a great man. I do not mean by this, that among his contemporaries he was justly entitled to a high rank for his intellectual endowments, an equal among the master-spirits of the day, if not *facile princeps.* I go farther; and insist, that he would have been deemed a great man in any age, and of all ages. He was one of those, to whom centuries alone give birth; standing out, like beacon lights on the loftiest eminences, to guide, admonish, and instruct future generations, as well as the present. It did not happen to him, as it has happened to many men of celebrity, that he appeared greatest at a distance; that his superiority vanished on a close survey; and that familiarity brought it down to the standard of common minds. On the contrary, it required some degree of intimacy fully to appreciate his powers; and those who knew him best, and saw him most, had daily reason to wonder at the vast extent and variety of his intellectual resources.

His genius was rather contemplative, than imaginative. It seemed not so much to give direction to his other intellectual powers, as to receive its lead from them. He devoted himself principally to serious and profound studies; and employed his invention rather to assist philosophical analysis, than to gather materials for ornament, for persuasion, or for picturesque effect. In strength, and depth, and comprehensiveness of mind, it would be difficult to name his superior. He sought for truths far beyond the boundaries, to which inquisitive and even ambitious minds are accustomed to push their inquiries. He traced them out from their first dim lights and paly glimmers, until they stood embodied before him with a clear and steady brightness. His sagacity was as untiring, as it was acute; and he saw the conclusion of his premises at such vast distances, and through such vast reaches of intermediate results, that it burst upon other minds as a sort of instant, and miraculous induction. It was said, by a distinguished political opponent, who had often felt the power of his reasoning, that he made it a rule in argument, never to admit any proposition asserted by the Chief Justice, however plain and unquestionable it might seem to be; for, if the premises were once admitted, the conclusion, however apparently remote, flowed on with an irresistible certainty. His powers of analysis were, indeed, marvellous. He separated the accidental from the essential circumstances with a subtilty and exactness, which surprised those most, who were accustomed to its exercise. No error in reasoning escaped his detection. He followed it through all its doublings, until it became palpable, and stripped of all its disguises. But, what seemed peculiarly his own, was the power, with which he seized upon a principle or argument, apparently presented in the most elementary form, and showed it to be a mere corollary of some more general truth, which lay at immeasurable distances beyond it. If his mind had been less practical, he would have been the most consummate of metaphysicians, and the most skilful of sophists. But his love of dialectics was constantly controlled by his superior love of truth. He had no vain ambition to darken counsel, or encourage doubt. His aim was conscientiously to unfold truth, as it was, in its simple majesty; to strengthen the foundation of moral, religious, social, political, and legal obligations; and to employ the gifts, with which Providence had intrusted him, to augment human happiness, support human justice, and bind together in an indissoluble union the great interests of human society. In short, if I were called upon to say, in what he intellectually excelled most men, I should say it was in wisdom, in the sense already alluded to; — a wisdom drawn from large, extensive, sound principles and various researches; — a wisdom, which constantly accumulated new materials for thought and action, and as constantly sifted and refined the old. He was not ambitious of literary distinction. But his great work on the life of Washington shows his capacity for historical composition in the most favorable light. It will forever remain a monument of his skill, sound judgment, and strict impartiality; and must in the future, as in the past, be a standard authority for all other historians.

In contemplating his professional career it cannot for a moment be doubted, that he must have occupied the foremost rank among advocates. Such accordingly has been his reputation transmitted to us by his contemporaries at the bar. From what has been already said, his powers of argument must have ensured him entire success. In his manner he was earnest, impressive, deliberative; but at the same time far more intent on his matter than his manner. Never having known him, while he was at the bar, I should have silently drawn the conclusion, that his forensic arguments were more distinguished for masculine sense, solid reasoning, and forcible illustration, than for impassioned appeals, or touching pathos, even when the latter might fairly enlist the judgment of an advocate. But there have been times in private conversations and conferences, in which he has been roused by the interest of the subject to such a glowing strain of animated reasoning, that I am convinced that he was no stranger to appeals to the heart; and that when he chose, he could call up from the very depths of the soul its most powerful feelings.

In regard to eloquence, if by that be merely meant an ornamented diction, splendor of style, impassioned delivery, and fine flourishes of rhetoric, it could scarcely be said to belong to his forensic addresses. In the view of such a mind as his, there were graver duties to be performed, and more important interests to be secured. He loved the law as a science, and not as a trade; and felt the full dignity of being a minister at its altars. He deemed himself under deep responsibility, not to his client alone, but to the court, and to the cause of public justice. He studied to know what the precepts of the law were, that he might apply them to his cause, and not to pervert them to aid the triumph of injustice, or to swell the trophies of cunning, or avarice, or profligacy. His notions of professional morals and obligations were far different from such mean and debasing palterings with conscience. He argued *for* the law, and *with* the law, and *from* the law. He disdained to mislead the court or jury, if he could; and he gave to both on all occasions the support and the instruction of his ample studies.

But if by eloquence be meant the power to address other men's minds in language expressive and luminous; to present the proper topics of argument in their just order and fulness; to convince the understanding by earnest and sententious appeals; and, by the force of reasoning, to disarm prejudices, to subdue passions, and to dissipate popular delusions; if these be the attributes of eloquence, then, indeed, few men might more justly aspire to such a distinction. I would not claim for him, that he possessed the power to seduce men's understandings by persuasive insinuations or honeyed accents; but I affirm, that he withdrew their understandings from the potency of such artifices, so that they fell lifeless at his feet; —*telumque imbelle sine ictu.* To him may unhesitatingly be applied the language of Cicero, pronounced upon one of the greatest lawyers of Rome, that he possessed a mastery of the highest art of oratory; the art of analyzing, defining, and illustrating a subject; separating the true from the false; and deducing from each the appropriate consequences;—artem, quæ doceret rem universam tribuere in partes, latentem explicare definiendo, obscuram explanare interpretando; ambigua primum videre, deinde distinguere; postremo, habere regulam, quâ vera et falsa judicarentur; et quæ, quibus positis, essent, quæque non essent, consequentia. Hic enim attulit hanc artem, omnium artium maximam, quasi lucem, ad ea, quæ confuse ab aliis aut respondebantur, aut agebantur.[1]

But it is principally upon his character as a Magistrate,

[1] Cicero De Clar. Orator. Cap. 14.

presiding over the highest tribunal of the nation, that the solid fabric of his fame must rest. And there let it rest; for the foundations are deep, and the superstructure fitted for immortality. Time, which is perpetually hurrying into a common oblivion the flatterers of kings, and the flatterers of the people, the selfish demagogues, and the wary courtiers, serves but to make true greatness better known, by dissolving the mists of prejudice and passion, which for a while conceal its true glory. The life of the Chief Justice extended over a space rare in the annals of jurisprudence; and still more rare is such a life, with the accompaniment of increasing reputation. There was nothing accidental or adventitious in his judicial character. It grew by its own native strength, unaided by the sunshine of power, and unchecked by cold neglect, or unsparing indifference. The life of Lord Mansfield was one of the longest and most splendid in the juridical history of England. That of the Chief Justice was longer, and may fairly rival it in the variety of its labors, in the glory of its achievements, and in its rapid advancement of the science of jurisprudence.

The Chief Justiceship of the United States is a station full of perplexing duties, and delicate responsibilities, and requiring qualities so various, as well as so high, that no man, conscious of human infirmity, can fail to approach it with extreme diffidence and distrust of his own competency. It is the very post, where weakness, and ignorance, and timidity must instantly betray themselves, and sink to their natural level. It is difficult even for the profession at large fully to appreciate the extent of the labors, the various attainments, the consummate learning, and the exquisite combination of moral qualities, which are demanded to fill it worthily. It has hitherto been occupied only by the highest class of minds, which had been trained and disciplined by a long course of public and professional service for its functions. Jay, Ellsworth, and Marshall, have been the incumbents for the whole period since the adoption of the constitution; and their extraordinary endowments have in a great measure concealed from the public gaze the dangers and the difficulties of this dazzling vocation.

There is nothing in the jurisprudence of the States, which affords any parallel or measure of the labors of the national courts. The jurisprudence of each state is homogeneous in its materials. It deals with institutions of a uniform character. It discusses questions of a nature familiar to the thoughts and employments of the whole profession. The learned advocate, who finds himself transferred, by public favor or superior ability, from the state bar to the state bench, finds the duties neither new nor embarrassing in their elements or details. He passes over ground, where the pathways are known and measured; and he finds pleasure in retracing their windings and their passages. He may exclaim with the poet, *Juvat iterare labores;* and he indulges a safe and generous confidence in his own juridical attainments.

How different is the case in the national courts! With whatever affluence of learning a judge may come there, he finds himself at once in a scene full of distressing novelties and varieties of thought. Instead of the jurisprudence of a single state, in which he has been educated and trained, he is at once plunged into the jurisprudence of twenty-four States, essentially differing in habits, laws, institutions, and principles of decision. He is compelled to become a student of doctrines, to which he has hitherto been an entire stranger; and the very language, in which those doctrines are sometimes expressed, is in the truest sense to him an unknown tongue. The words seem to belong to the dialect of his native language; but other meanings are attached to them, either so new, or so qualified, that he is embarrassed at every step of his progress. Nay; he is required in some measure to forget in one cause, what he has learned in another, from its inapplicability or local impropriety; and new statutes, perpetually accumulating on every side, seem to snatch from his grasp the principles of local law, at the moment when he is beginning to congratulate himself upon the possession of them. Independent of this complicated intermixture of state jurisprudence, he is compelled to master the whole extent of Admiralty and Prize Law; the public and private law of nations; and the varieties of English and American Equity jurisprudence. To these confessedly herculean labors he must now add some reasonable knowledge of the Civil Law, and of the jurisprudence of France and Spain, as they break upon him from the sunny regions of the farthest South. Nor is this all; (though much of what has been already stated must be new to his thoughts,) he must gather up the positive regulations of the statutes and treaties of the national government, and the silent and implied results of its sovereignty and action. He must finally expand his studies to that most important branch of national jurisprudence, the exposition of constitutional law, demanding, as it does, a comprehensiveness of thought, a calmness of judgment, and a diligence of research, (not to speak of other qualities,) which cannot be contemplated without the most anxious apprehensions of failure. When these various duties are considered, it is scarcely too much to say, that they present the same discouraging aspect of the national jurisprudence, which Sir Henry Spelman has so feelingly proclaimed of the municipal jurisprudence of England, in his day; — *Molem, non ingentem solum, sed perpetuis humeris sustinendam.*

These, however, are but a part of the qualifications required of the man, who holds the office of Chief Justice. He must also possess other rare accomplishments, which are required of one who, as the head of the Court, is to preside over its public deliberations, and its private confidential conferences. Patience, moderation, candor, urbanity, quickness of perception, dignity of deportment, gentleness of manners, genius, which commands respect, and learning which justifies confidence; — These seem indispensable qualifications to fill up the outlines of the character. While I was yet shadowing them out in my own mind, my eyes insensibly turned (as it were) to the Judicial Hall at Washington, and to the very Chair appropriated to the office. The venerable form of Marshall seemed still seated there! It was but a momentary dream; I awoke; and found that I had but sketched the first lines of his portrait.

Yes, this great and good man was all, that we could ask, or even desire for the station. He seemed the very personation of Justice itself, as he ministered at its altars—in the presence of the nation—within the very walls, which had often echoed back the unsurpassed eloquence of the dead, of Dexter, and Pinkney, and Emmett, and Wirt, and of the living also, nameless here, but whose names will swell on the voices of a thousand generations. Enter but that hall, and you saw him listening with a quiet, easy dignity to the discussions at the bar; silent, serious, searching; with a keenness of thought, which sophistry could not mislead, or error confuse, or ingenuity delude; with a benignity of aspect, which invited the modest to move on with confidence; with a conscious firmness of purpose, which repressed arrogance, and overawed declamation. You heard him pronounce the opinion of the Court in a low but modulated voice, unfolding in luminous order every topic of argument, trying its strength, and measuring its value, until you felt yourself in the presence of the very oracle of the law. You heard, (if I may adopt the language applied to another great magistrate on a like occasion) you "heard principles stated, reasoned upon, enlarged, and explained, until you were lost in admiration at the strength and stretch of the human understanding."[1] Follow him into the conference room, a scene of not less difficult or delicate duties, and you would observe the same presiding genius, the same kindness, attentiveness, and deference; and yet, when the occasion required, the same power of illustration, the same minuteness of research, the same severity of logic, and the same untiring accuracy in facts and principles.

[1] Mr. Justice Buller, speaking of Lord Mansfield, in Lickbarrow *v.* Mason, 2 Term Rep. 73.

It may be truly said of him, as it was of Lord Mansfield, that he excelled in the statement of a case; so much so, that it was almost of itself an argument. If it did not at once lead the hearer to the proper conclusion, it prepared him to assent to it, as soon as it was announced. Nay, more; it persuaded him, that it must be right, however repugnant it might be to his preconceived notions. Perhaps no Judge ever excelled him in the capacity to hold a legal proposition before the eyes of others in such various forms and colors. It seemed a pleasure to him to cast the darkest shades of objection over it, that he might show how they could be dissipated by a single glance of light. He would by the most subtile analysis resolve every argument into its ultimate principles, and then with a marvellous facility apply them to the decision of the cause.

That he possessed an uncommon share of juridical learning, would naturally be presumed, from his large experience and inexhaustible diligence. Yet it is due to truth, as well as to his memory to declare, that his juridical learning was not equal to that of many of the great masters in the profession, living or dead, at home or abroad. He yielded at once to their superiority of knowledge, as well in the modern as in the ancient law. He adopted the notion of Lord Bacon, that "studies serve for delight, for ornament, and for ability," — "in the judgment and disposition of business." The latter was his favorite object. Hence he "read not to contradict and confute; nor to believe and take for granted; nor to find talk and discourse; but to weigh and consider." And he followed another suggestion of that great man, that "Judges ought to be more learned than witty; more reverend than plausible; and more advised than confident." The original bias, as well as the choice, of his mind was to general principles, and comprehensive views, rather than to technical, or recondite learning. He loved to expatiate upon the theory of equity; to gather up the expansive doctrines of commercial jurisprudence; and to give a rational cast even to the most subtile dogmas of the common law. He was solicitous to hear arguments; and not to decide causes without them. And no judge ever profited more by them. No matter, whether the subject was new or old; familiar to his thoughts, or remote from them; buried under a mass of obsolete learning, or developed for the first time yesterday; whatever was its nature, he courted argument, nay, he demanded it. It was matter of surprise to see how easily he grasped the leading principles of a case, and cleared it of all its accidental incumbrances; how readily he evolved the true points of the controversy, even when it was manifest that he never before had caught even a glimpse of the learning upon which it depended. He seized, as it were by intuition, the very spirit of juridical doctrines, though cased up in the armor of centuries; and he discussed authorities, as if the very minds of the Judges themselves stood disembodied before him.

But his peculiar triumph was in the exposition of constitutional law. It was here, that he stood confessedly without a rival, whether we regard his thorough knowledge of our civil and political history, his admirable powers of illustration and generalization, his scrupulous integrity and exactness in interpretation, or his consummate skill in moulding his own genius into its elements, as if they had constituted the exclusive study of his life. His proudest epitaph may be written in a single line — Here lies the Expounder of the Constitution of the United States.

I am aware of the force of this language; and have no desire to qualify it. The task which he had to perform, was far different from that which belongs to the debates in other places, where topics may be chosen, and pressed, or avoided, as the occasion may require. In the forum there is no choice of topics to be urged; there are no passions to be addressed; there are no interests to be courted. Critical inquiries, nice discriminations, severe inductions, and progressive demonstrations are demanded upon the very points on which the controversy hinges. Every objection must be met, and sifted, and answered, not by single flashes of thought, but by the closest logic, reasoning out every successive position with a copious and convincing accuracy.

Let it be remembered, that, when Chief Justice Marshall first took his seat on the bench, scarcely more than two or three questions of constitutional law had ever engaged the attention of the Supreme Court. As a science, constitutional law was then confessedly new; and that portion of it, in an especial manner, which may be subjected to judicial scrutiny, had been explored by few minds, even in the most general forms of inquiry. Let it be remembered, that in the course of his judicial life, numerous questions of a practical nature, and involving interests of vast magnitude, have been constantly before the court, where there was neither guide, nor authority; but all was to be wrought out by general principles. Let it be remembered, that texts, which scarcely cover the breadth of a finger, have been since interpreted, explained, limited, and adjusted by judicial commentaries, which are now expanded into volumes. Let it be remembered, that the highest learning, genius, and eloquence of the bar, have been employed to raise doubts, and fortify objections; that state sovereignties have stood impeached in their legislation; and rights of the most momentous nature have been suspended upon the issue; that under such circumstances, the infirmities of false reasoning, the glosses of popular appeal, the scattered fire of irregular and inconclusive assertion, and the want of comprehensive powers of analysis, had no chance to escape the instant detection of the profession. Let these things (I say) be remembered; and who does not at once perceive, that the task of expounding the constitution, under such circumstances, required almost superhuman abilities? It demanded a mind, in which vast reaches of thought should be combined with patience of investigation, sobriety of judgment, fearlessness of consequences, and mastery of the principles of interpretation, to an extent rarely belonging to the most gifted of our race.

How this gigantic task of expounding the Constitution was met and executed by Chief Justice Marshall, let the profession, let the public, decide. Situated as I am, I may not speak for others upon such an occasion. But having sat by his side during twenty-four years; having witnessed his various constitutional labors; having heard many of those exquisite judgments, the fruits of his own unassisted meditations, from which the court has derived so much honor; — *et nos aliquod nomenque decusque gessimus;* — I confess myself unable to find language sufficiently expressive of my admiration and reverence of his transcendent genius. While I have followed his footsteps, not as I could have wished, but as I have been able, at humble distances, in his splendid judicial career, I have constantly felt the liveliest gratitude to that beneficent Providence, which created him for the age, that his talents might illustrate the law, his virtues adorn the bench, and his judgments establish the perpetuity of the Constitution of the country. Such is my humble tribute to his memory. *His saltem accumulem donis, et fungar inani munere.* The praise is sincere, though it may be perishable. Not so his fame. It will flow on to the most distant ages. Even if the Constitution of his country should perish, his glorious judgments will still remain to instruct mankind, until liberty shall cease to be a blessing, and the science of jurisprudence shall vanish from the catalogue of human pursuits.

And this great magistrate is now gone — gone, as we trust, to the high rewards of such eminent services. It is impossible to reflect, that the places which once knew him, shall know him no more, without a sense of inexpressible melancholy. When shall we look upon his like again? When may we again hope to see so much moderation with so much firmness; so much sagacity with so much modesty; so much learning with so much purity; so much wisdom with so much gentleness; so much splendor of talent with so much benevolence; so much of every thing to love and admire, with nothing, absolutely nothing to regret?

And yet there are some consolations even in so great a loss. Cicero, in mourning over the death of his friend, the great Roman lawyer, Hortensius, did not hesitate to pronounce his death fortunate; for he died at a moment happy for himself, though most unfortunate for his country. Quoniam perpetuâ quâdam felicitate usus ille, cessit e vitâ, suo, magis quam suorum civium, tempore. Vixit tam diu quam licuit in civitate bene beateque vivere.[1] We may well apply the like remark to Chief Justice Marshall. He was not cut off in middle life, in the early maturity of his faculties, while he was yet meditating new plans of usefulness or glory. He lived to the very verge of that green old age, after which the physical strength sensibly declines, and the intellectual powers no longer reach their accustomed limits. He retained, to the very last hour of his life, the possession of all these powers in full perfection, without change — nay, without the shadow of change. Such had been his hope, earnestly and frequently expressed to his confidential friends, with deep solicitude; for no man more than he dreaded to add another to the melancholy lessons:

> "In life's last scenes, what prodigies surprise,
> Tears of the brave, and follies of the wise."

We may well rejoice, therefore, that a life, so long and so useful, should have come to its close without any exhibition of human infirmity. The past is now secure. It is beyond the reach of accident. The future cannot be disturbed by error, or darkened by imbecility. His setting sun loomed out in cloudless splendor, as it sunk below the horizon. The last lights shot up with a soft and balmy transparency, as if the beams, while yet reflected back on this world, were but ushering in the morn of his own immortality.

[1] Cicero De Clar. Orator. Cap. 1.

CODIFICATION OF THE COMMON LAW.

A REPORT OF THE COMMISSIONERS APPOINTED TO CONSIDER AND REPORT UPON THE PRACTICABILITY AND EXPEDIENCY OF REDUCING TO A WRITTEN AND SYSTEMATIC CODE THE COMMON LAW OF MASSACHUSETTS, OR ANY PART THEREOF; MADE TO HIS EXCELLENCY THE GOVERNOR, JANUARY, 1837.

THE three leading questions presented for the consideration of the Commissioners are:

1. The practicability of reducing to a written and systematic Code the Common Law of Massachusetts, or any part thereof.
2. The expediency of such a reduction, if practicable.
3. The plan or plans, by which the same can be best accomplished, if expedient.

Before proceeding to a direct examination of these questions, it seems proper to make some preliminary remarks, which may serve to explain the exact state of these questions, and to guard against any erroneous inferences, as to the nature and limits of the inquiries which they involve.

When our ancestors first emigrated to this country, then a wilderness, inhabited only by the Indians, who possessed no regular government or administration of laws, they brought with them the common law of the mother country, (England,) so far, as from its nature and objects, it then was or might be applicable to their situation, as colonists, distant from and possessing institutions and political arrangements varying from those of the parent country. It is obvious, that they could not bring with them the whole body of the English law then in force; for much of it must have been wholly inapplicable to their situation, and some of it was inconsistent with their policy and prosperity as colonies. Thus, for example, many of the feudal tenures, then in force in England, were never known here, all tenures of land here being from the beginning in free and common socage. So, the whole common law, applicable to the ecclesiastical establishment of England, never had an existence here, for a similar reason.

Nor was this an artificial principle assumed for the occasion to govern the colonies. It was a part of the general law of the land, at the time of the emigration of our ancestors, that all new settlements made by Englishmen, in desert and uncultivated regions, were to be governed by the law of England, subject to the qualifications already stated. It was also a principle, fully recognized in the charters granted to the colonies, either in direct terms, or by necessary implication. In most, if not in all of them, there will be found an express declaration, that no laws shall be made repugnant to those of England, (or some equivalent phrase,) but as near as may conveniently be, their laws shall be consonant with and conformable to those of England. There is also to be found in all the charters, except that of Pennsylvania, (where it was probably omitted by mistake or accident,) an express clause, declaring, that all English subjects and their children, inhabiting in the colonies, shall be deemed natural born subjects, and shall enjoy all the privileges and immunities thereof. This was specially true in relation to the colony of Massachusetts, whose successive charters expressly recognize these privileges and immunities as the right of all subjects and their children inhabiting therein, and authorize the enactment of laws not repugnant or contrary to the laws of England.

The common law, thus introduced into the colonies, was not, in a strict sense, the common law in its original form, but, as it was then existing in England, modified, amended and ameliorated by statutes; and it was claimed as the birthright and inheritance of all the colonists. The revolutionary Congress of 1774, accordingly, unanimously resolved, "that the respective colonies are entitled to the common law of England, and more especially to the great and inestimable privilege of being tried by their peers, in the vicinage, according to the course of that law;" and "that they were entitled to the benefit of such of the English statutes as existed at the time of their colonization, and which they have by experience respectively found to be applicable to their several local circumstances."

But notwithstanding this general adoption of the common law of England, it is obvious, that the qualifications annexed to it must have given rise to many very perplexing doubts and difficulties. What portions of the common law were applicable to the situation of the colonies, was an inquiry perpetually presented in the course of forensic discussions in former times. And though by the gradual operation of judicial decisions, and the positive enactments of the colonial, provincial, and state legislatures, the field of controversy has been greatly narrowed; yet there still remain some topics of debate upon which it would not be easy to affirm, whether the common law of England had been adopted here or not. Nor has the provision of the Constitution of this Commonwealth of 1780, that "the laws, which have heretofore been adopted, used, and approved in the province, colony, or state of Massachusetts Bay, and usually practised on in the courts of law, shall still remain and be in full force until altered or repealed by the legislature; such parts only excepted as are repugnant to the rights and liberties contained in this constitution," materially changed the grounds of difficulty and controversy; for the inquiry must still be made, what are the laws which have been so adopted, used, and approved, and usually practised on in our courts of law?

Besides the common law of England, there are to be found in Massachusetts some few local usages and principles, which properly constitute a part of our common law, though unknown to that of England. One of the most striking instances of this sort is the capacity of a married woman to dispose of her real property by a deed with the consent of her husband; whereas, by the common law of England, it can be done only by a peculiar process called a fine or a common recovery.

The common law of Massachusetts, then, properly embraces, in the first place, that portion of the common law of England, (as modified and ameliorated by English statutes,) which was in force at the time of the emigration of our ancestors, and was applicable to the situation of the colony, and has since been recognized and acted upon, during the successive progresses of our Colonial, Provincial, and State Governments, with this additional qualification, that it has not been altered, repealed or modified by any of our own subsequent legislation now in force. In the next place, it embraces those local usages and principles, which have the authority of law, but which are not founded upon any local statutes. The latter, indeed, are so few, and comparatively, in a general sense, so unimportant, that they may, for all our present purposes, be passed over without farther observation or notice.

The next inquiry is, what is the true nature or character of the common law, so recognized and established, and where are its doctrines and principles to be found. In relation to the former part of the inquiry, it may be generally stated, that the common law consists of positive rules and remedies, of general usages and customs, and of elementary principles, and the developments or applications of them, which cannot now be distinctly traced back to any statutory enactments, but which rest for their authority upon the common recognition, consent and use of the State itself. Some of these rules, usages and principles are of such high antiquity, that the time cannot be assigned, when they had not an existence and use. Others of them are of a comparatively modern growth, having been developed with the gradual progress of society; and others, again, can hardly be said to have had a visible and known existence until our own day. Thus, for example, many of the rights and remedies, which ascertain and govern the titles to real estate, are of immemorial antiquity. On the other hand, the law of commercial contracts, and especially the law of insurance, of shipping, of bills of exchange, and of promissory notes, has almost entirely grown up since the time (1756) when Lord Mansfield was elevated to the bench. And again, the law of aquatic rights and water courses, and the law of corporations can scarcely be said to have assumed a scientific form until our day.

In truth, the common law is not in its nature and character an absolutely fixed, inflexible system, like the statute law, providing only for cases of a determinate form, which fall within the letter of the language, in which a particular doctrine or legal proposition is expressed. It is rather a system of elementary principles and of general juridical truths, which are continually expanding with the progress of society, and adapting themselves to the gradual changes of trade, and commerce, and the mechanic arts, and the exigencies and usages of the country. There are certain fundamental maxims in it, which are never departed from; there are others again, which, though true in a general sense, are at the same time susceptible of modifications and exceptions, to prevent them from doing manifest wrong and injury.

When a case, not affected by any statute, arises in any of our courts of justice, and the facts are established, the first question is, whether there is any clear and unequivocal principle of the common law, which directly and immediately governs it, and fixes the rights of the parties. If there be no such principle, the next question is, whether there is any principle of the common law, which, by analogy, or parity of reasoning, ought to govern it. If neither of these sources furnishes a positive solution of the controversy, resort is next had (as in a case confessedly new) to the principles of natural justice which constitute the basis of much of the common law; and if these principles can be ascertained to apply in a full and determinate manner to all the circumstances, they are adopted, and decide the rights of the parties. If all these sources fail, the case is treated as remediless at the common law, and the only relief, which remains, is by some new legislation, by statute, to operate upon future cases of the like nature.

These remarks may be illustrated, by referring to some of the most familiar cases which occur in the every day business of life. In the common case of work and labor, done for any person, or goods sold and delivered to him, the common law implies an obligation or duty in the person, for whose benefit, and at whose request it is done, to pay the amount of the price of the goods, or the value of the work and labor. Now there is no statute from which this obligation or duty is derived. It is simply a dictate of natural justice, and from that source was adopted into the common law. The mode, by which this obligation or duty was enforced in the ancient common law, was by the remedy called an action of *debt*. But this remedy was in some respects, and under some circumstances, liable to embarrassments and technical objections. About three hundred years ago, it occurred to some acute lawyers, that another remedy, which would avoid these embarrassments and objections, might be applied. Accordingly, an action of trespass on the case, now well known by the name of an action of indebitatus assumpsit, was brought in the courts of Westminster Hall, to recover the amount of the debt. It was then very gravely debated, whether such an action would lie, and finally (after great diversity of opinion) it was settled in favor of the action. The principal ground of the decision was from the analogy to other well known forms of actions on the case, and the undertaking or promise of the debtor, implied by law, to pay the debt, the breach of which undertaking or promise was a wrong to the other party, for which he was entitled to recover, not technically the debt, but damages to the full amount of the debt. And this is now the common mode, by which debts of this sort are usually sued for and recovered.

Again: When a man borrows money of another to be repaid to the lender, the common law, upon principles of natural justice, holds him liable to repay it, upon his express or implied agreement to that effect. But cases occurred, in which money in the hands of one person, in justice and equity, belonged to another; but it had not been borrowed, nor had the possessor promised to pay it over. On the contrary, he resisted the claim. The question then arose, whether in such a case the money was recoverable. And the courts of law, at a comparatively recent period, held, that an action would lie for the recovery of it, and that the proper action was indebitatus assumpsit, for money had and received to the use of the party entitled. Here, again, the courts acted upon principles of natural justice, and founded themselves, both as to the right and the remedy to recover, upon the analogies of the law. They first inferred, from the principles of natural justice and the analogies of the law, an implied undertaking or promise to pay over the money, because in conscience and duty the holder was bound so to do; and next they applied the remedy by analogy to other cases where there was an express promise of a similar nature.

Again: Until the reign of Queen Anne, promissory notes, although payable to bearer or order, were held not to be negotiable; so that no person but the payee could maintain an action for the money due on the same. The ground of this decision was, that debts, technically called choses in action, are not assignable at the common law, a doctrine which can be traced back to its early rudiments. This, therefore, was a case, where, though the principles of natural justice might apply to create an obligation, the positive rules of the common law forbade it. Hence the interposition of the legislature became indispensable. Nay, even the payee himself could not, according to the rules of the common law, maintain an action directly on the instrument; but he could only use it as evidence of a debt in an action properly framed upon the consideration, for which it was given. When the Statute of 3d and 4th Anne, chapter 9, made such promissory notes negotiable, it was found to be so convenient, that it was generally, though not universally, nor without some exceptions and modifications, introduced either by statute or usage into the Colonies. In Massachusetts it was adopted by usage, and acted upon down to our day, without any other sanction than judicial recognition.

As soon as the negotiability of promissory notes was thus established, it gave rise to innumerable questions, as to the rights and responsibilities of the parties, which was either confessedly new, or but faintly indicated by antecedent principles. What were the nature and extent of the obligation of an indorser; what were the duties of the indorsee; when demand was to be made of payment of the maker; what notice was to be given, and how notice was to be given, by the holder to the indorser; these and very many questions of a like nature, were necessarily to be resolved. And so complicated and so various are the circumstances, which may attend cases of this nature, that notwithstanding the long course of decisions, which have in a great measure ascertained and qualified the rights and responsibilities of the parties, there yet remains a wide field for future discussions, growing out of the new and ever-varying courses of business. The principles of natural justice have furnished many rules for the exposition of the contract and obligations of the parties; the analogies of the common law have furnished others; the usages of the mercantile world have furnished others; and then again there have been anomalies, which could not be brought within the range of any well-defined principles, and therefore have been left to be regulated by legislative enactments. In this branch of the law, in an especial manner, will be found a striking illustration of the remark of an eminent judge, that the common law is a system of principles, which expands with the exigencies of society.

With these few preliminary observations, which seemed necessary to a just understanding of the subject, the Commissioners will now proceed to the direct consideration of the inquiries presented by their commission.

I. The first is, as has been already stated, the practicability of reducing to a written and systematic Code the Common Law of Massachusetts, or of any part thereof.

This inquiry involves, or at least may involve, two very distinct and widely different propositions, according to the sense in which we interpret the terms, "the Common Law of Massachusetts." If by those terms is to be intended not only all the general principles of that law, but all the diversities, ramifications, expansions, exceptions and qualifications of those principles, as they ought to be applied, not only to the past and present, but, to all future combinations of circumstances in the business of human life, it may require one answer. If, on the other hand, those terms are to be understood in a more restricted sense, as importing only the reduction to a positive code of those general principles, and of the expansions, exceptions, qualifications and minor deductions, which have already, by judicial decisions or otherwise, been engrafted on them, and are now capable of a distinct enunciation, then a very different answer might be given. In the former sense, the Commissioners have no doubt, that it is not practicable to reduce the common law of Massachusetts to a written code; in the latter sense, they have no doubt, that it is so practicable; and the expediency of doing it will come under review in a subsequent part of this Report.

As there appear to the Commissioners to be abroad in the community some erroneous notions on this subject, under both of the preceding aspects, they beg leave respectfully to suggest the reasoning, by which they have arrived at the conclusions above stated. It is not an uncommon opinion, that all law is capable of being reduced to a specific form, which shall apply with equal clearness and certainty to the solution of all cases, past, present and future. In short, it is frequently supposed and frequently asserted, that a code may be compiled of all the law, which is to regulate the rights and titles, the property, the business and the contracts of a nation, so definite, full and exact, that it shall furnish a complete guide, not only for the decisions of courts of justice, but for intelligent citizens throughout the country, in all cases, and shall supersede, if not the necessity of new legislation, at least the necessity of new rules, and the modification of old rules by courts of justice, to reach the exigencies of every variety of controversy. Why, it is often asked, cannot the law of a country be reduced to a positive form? If it is law, it must be known, or it ought to be known, so that every citizen may govern his conduct accordingly. If it is known to a few, why may it not be made known in a positive form to all persons? If not fully known to any persons, ought a free nation to remain subject to rules, of the nature and extent of which they are ignorant, and to allow their rights to be decided by doctrines now promulgated for the first time? Questions of this sort are often put, and suggestions of this character are often made. They wear an air of plausibility, and therefore should be deliberately examined, and the errors, to which they may lead, should be corrected by expounding the sources of them. It is very certain, that no nation, whose legal institutions are known to us, ever had a code of the nature above supposed, namely, one, which was comprehensive enough to embrace all the doctrines and details required for the private concerns and business of its whole population. That it never has been done, however, furnishes no absolute proof, that it cannot be done. But at the same time, since it is well known, that many partial codes or collections of laws have been made, the fair presumption is, that it has been deemed impracticable or unwise to attempt more.

In proportion as nations advance in civilization and commerce, the business of the people and the rights and modifications of property, become necessarily more complicated and difficult, and various in their relations and circumstances.

The principles of law, which might suffice for the ordinary transactions of one age, would be wholly insufficient to answer the exigencies of the next age. Of the innumerable questions which arise in any one age, and admit of forensic controversy and doubt, probably not one in a hundred, perhaps it would be more correct to say, not one in a thousand, ever comes before a court of justice to be there finally settled by adjudication. Many are settled by compromise; many by arbitration, or the intervention of friends; many are neglected or abandoned, from their comparatively slight importance, or the poverty of the claimants, or their ignorance of, or indifference to, their rights, or from other causes tending to suppress litigation. Hence it is, that the basis of the actual administration of justice in every country must comprehend principles of far more extensive reach than those which become the subjects of direct adjudication in courts of justice, and be capable of a progressive adaptation to new cases as they arise, or the most manifold public and private mischiefs must pervade the whole community.

It may be asked, why may not a nation require all the laws, which are to govern it, to be clearly made known and promulgated before they are acted upon? Certainly it is competent for a nation so to act. It may declare, that the administration of justice shall be applied only to rights and titles and claims which have been previously ascertained by the terms of express laws, leaving nothing to the judgment of courts of justice, beyond the direct application of the text to the very cases thus ascertained. But what would be the consequence of such a course of legislation? It would be, that every case of wrong and injustice and oppression, not thus foreseen and provided for, would be wholly remediless. And the mass of such cases would be perpetually accumulating, since positive legislation, however rapid and constant, can never keep up in any just proportion with the actual permutations and combinations of the business of an active, enterprising, and industrious people. Suppose, for example, the Legislature of

Massachusetts should declare, that there should be no other laws in force except what are contained in the Revised Statutes; it is obvious that the whole business of life must stop in this State; for that code does not provide for one case in a thousand, perhaps not for one in a hundred thousand, which is of daily occurrence and activity.

It is obviously impossible to make a positive code, which shall be adequate to the business and rights and modifications of property in any one single age, unless the Legislature can foresee every possible as well as every probable combination of circumstances applicable to every subject-matter in that age. Such a degree of wisdom and foresight belongs not to any human beings. If it were possible to foresee and provide for all such exigencies of a single age, having a determinate course of business, and institutions, no one would be rash enough to assert, that it was possible to foresee and provide for the exigencies, rights, duties, and business of the same nation throughout all time. A code, therefore, however full, would be perpetually growing more and more defective, unless resort was had to new legislation; and such legislation, to be either wise or effective, must allow a great number of cases of the same sort to arise under various aspects, before the proper remedy or principle, which ought to be generally applied, could be clearly perceived, or safely adopted. In short, unless it were possible to compel all men to act at all times in one way, and to prevent the occurrence of any new combinations of circumstances, (a condition morally and physically impossible,) and unless it were also possible for a legislature to foresee and provide for all the cases that had arisen, or could arise, (a condition equally impossible,) there is no pretence to say, that any written code could embrace all the provisions fitted for an active, commercial, and free people, advancing in civilization, wealth, and industry. And if any code could be framed, which should aspire to provide in detail for the common run of circumstances, it would be found in practice to be not only materially defective, but so voluminous in its precepts, that a whole life would be required to master all its provisions, and more than a whole life to accumulate the materials fit for its composition.

It has been already stated, that perhaps not one case in a hundred, which admits of doubt or controversy, ever comes before a court of justice for decision. Of the reported cases, which were decided in England before the middle of the last century, consisting principally of cases at the common law, an abridgment has been published in twenty-four folio volumes; and, after all, it is a very unsatisfactory and incomplete abridgment of those cases, probably not covering one half of the minute doctrines asserted and acted on in them. An abridgment of the reported cases at the common law, from that time down to the present, has also been published in fifteen volumes (royal octavo) which is equally imperfect and unsatisfactory. These voluminous works are but specimens of what a code must be, which should attempt to enumerate in detail the doctrines of the common law, which have been in dispute in courts of justice, and have been established by decisions. If the enumeration of these is so voluminous, we may readily see, what space would be required for those which are known and not disputed, and for those which are unknown, or uncertain in their application, and whose circumstances have never been discussed in tribunals of justice. A code, which should embrace the doctrines of all the reported cases of the common law, from the most important to the most minute, with accuracy and clearness, would of itself be exceedingly voluminous, and require many years, if not an age, for its preparation, and then would be mastered only by those, who could afford to devote a large portion of their lives to the study and exposition of it. For the purposes of common life, it would be like a sealed book, which would neither enlighten nor aid practical inquirers, and perhaps by a partial examination might mislead them. But if a code should attempt more, and be framed so as to comprehend, in all their details, all the known and undisputed doctrines of the common law, which on that account are only incidentally touched or alluded to in reported cases, it would probably be doubled in its bulk and extent. If it should attempt to go farther, and provide for the application of those doctrines to all other cases, which had arisen and were known, or which could be foreseen by the exercise of the most profound and varied wisdom and experience of the Commonwealth, it would not only be found upon its first promulgation exceedingly defective, but it would be of such vast size and accumulated materials, that it would serve to perplex rather than to clear away difficulties, and would import into the administration of justice more mischiefs and doubts, and stimulants to litigation, than it could hope to remedy. There would be this additional evil, that as the rules established for future cases would necessarily be founded upon general theories, and would not, as now, be adopted upon full argument, and modified from time to time, to meet the circumstances of each particular case, there would be infinite danger, that they would in practice be found to work ill, or to defeat the main objects, which the legislation was intended to accomplish.

The civil code and the commercial code of France are probably as perfect specimens of legislation as ever have been, or ever can be produced, having been prepared with great care and diligence, by the most learned jurists of France, after repeated revisions, and with the assistance of the ablest and the most experienced judges of the tribunals of all the departments of that extensive kingdom. Yet it is well known, that a great variety of questions, as to the true construction of the text, and a still greater variety of questions, arising from new and unforeseen cases, have been discussed in their judicial tribunals, which already occupy many volumes of reports, and must constitute a continually augmenting mass of materials, alternately for litigation and for legislation. This consideration furnishes no just objection, when properly viewed, to the establishment of codes; but it serves to show the utter impracticability of making any adequate provisions for all future cases; or of devising any forms of expression, which shall not be susceptible of some diversities of interpretation. Such is the unavoidable imperfection of all human language, and such the short-sightedness of the most deliberate efforts of human wisdom!

Considerations of this sort, which cannot fail to force themselves upon the mind upon a close survey of the subject, have led the Commissioners to the conclusion, that it is not possible to establish in any written code all the positive laws, and applications of laws, which are necessary and proper to regulate the concerns and business of any civilized nation, much less of a free nation, possessing an extensive commerce, and a great variety of manufacturing and agricultural interests, which are constantly undergoing new modifications, and are susceptible of being the subjects of infinitely diversified contracts, and rights of property and enjoyment. If it were possible to provide such a written code, the Commissioners are of opinion, that the present state of the common law does not furnish sufficient materials for the purpose. An infinite number of new rules and doctrines, and modifications, limitations and enlargements of old rules and doctrines, would be required even for an approximation to such a code. And after all, from what has been already suggested, it would be found full of defects, inconveniences and embarrassments, from the impossibility of foreseeing many new combinations of circumstances, or of providing in the most suitable manner for them, if foreseen, without the aid of long experience and thorough argument, and a nice discrimination and balancing of opposing reasons. It is upon these grounds, that the Commissioners have ventured to express their opinion, that, in the broad sense of the terms already indicated, the common law of Massachusetts is not capable of being reduced to a written and systematic code; and that any attempt at so comprehensive an enterprise would be either positively mischievous, or inefficacious, or futile. It seems to them, that private convenience as well as public policy requires, that the common law should be left in its prospective operations in future (as it has been in the past) to be improved, and expanded, and modified to meet the exigencies of society, by the gradual application of its principles in courts of justice to new cases, assisted from time to time, as the occasion may demand, by the enactments of the legislature.

But although in the broad sense of the terms, the common law of Massachusetts is not susceptible of being reduced to a written and systematic code, the inquiry is, in the opinion of the Commissioners, a very different one, whether the whole or parts thereof, in the narrower sense above stated, may not be beneficially reduced to such a code. In this last sense, the common law may be said to embrace two distinct branches, to wit: first, the well known and ascertained general principles of that law; and secondly, the well known and ascertained applications of those general principles to the circumstances of particular cases. The former are often denominated, in the juridical language of Continental Europe, emphatically as law; the latter as jurisprudence. The former are rather recognized than promulgated in our courts of justice. The latter constitute the mass of our judicial decisions, and can rarely be ascertained with perfect exactness from any other sources; though they necessarily compose a part of every elementary treatise upon any branch of the common law.

In respect to the general principles of the common law of Massachusetts, it may be affirmed, that they are not positively incapable of being generally collected into a code. We say generally, because there may still be some question, whether particular principles of the common law of England constitute a part of the common law of Massachusetts. But in relation to a very large mass, there is no difficulty whatsoever of this nature. These general principles are to be found, for the most part, collected in elementary treatises now extant, upon the whole or particular branches of the common law.

They are capable of being stated in the very form and language, in which they are there enunciated, as they have, from long examinations and critical trials, acquired a precision and exactness, which approach very near to scientific accuracy; and for all the ordinary uses of life, they are sufficiently clear in their interpretations and qualifications. To this extent, at least as far as these general principles have assumed such a precision and exactness, they may be embodied in a written code, with such a systematic arrangement, as the nature of the different subject-matters, to which they apply, may require.

In respect to the details of these general principles in their actual application to particular cases, where they have necessarily undergone modifications, exceptions and qualifications, as they are chiefly, if not exclusively, to be gathered from actual adjudications in courts of justice, it may also be affirmed, that they are not positively incapable, so far at least as reported cases go, of being generally reduced to a written code. We say generally, because here also there are, or may be great doubts, whether particular doctrines constitute a part of our common law; and because there are to be found conflicting decisions upon some points, so that it may not be easy to affirm, upon the weight of authority, what the true doctrine is; and because some branches of the common law of England have become so nearly obsolete, and so obscure from lapse of time and disuse, that, if they constitute a part of our common law, it would be very difficult to collect all the true doctrines, and to express them in an unexceptionable form. Time here, as everywhere else, has wrought such great changes in rights, remedies, institutions, and usages, that it would be almost a hopeless task to suit the ancient forms and the ancient language of particular doctrines to the present state of things. It is quite a different question, which will be presently considered, whether it would be useful or expedient, to attempt any codification of all the details of these general principles, as they are embodied in the decisions, which have been made by courts of justice in different ages.

These considerations naturally conduct us to the second and very important inquiry, as to the expediency of reducing the common law of Massachusetts, or any part thereof, (in the narrower sense already stated) to a written and systematic code, so far as the same is practicable. Upon this subject, the commissioners have employed a good deal of deliberation; and they now propose to state the results, to which they have arrived; to state the objections, which have been or may be urged against any system of codification, with the answers thereto; and lastly to state the reasons, on which their own results are founded.

I. The Commissioners are, in the first place, of opinion, that it is not expedient to attempt the reduction to a code of the entire body of the common law of Massachusetts, either in its general principles or in the deduction from, or the applications, of those principles, so far as they have been ascertained by judicial decisions, or are incontrovertibly established.

II. The Commissioners, are, in the next place, of opinion, that it is expedient to reduce to a code those principles, and details of the common law of Massachusetts in civil cases, which are of daily use and familiar application to the common business of life, and the present state of property and personal rights and contracts, and which are now so far ascertained and established, as to admit of a scientific form and arrangement, and are capable of being announced in distinct and determinate propositions. What portions of the common law properly fall under this predicament will be in some measure considered hereafter.

III. The Commissioners are, in the next place, of opinion, that it is expedient to reduce to a code the common law, as to the definition, trial and punishment of crimes, and the incidents thereto.

IV. The Commissioners are, in the next place, of opinion,

that the law of evidence, as applicable both to civil and criminal proceedings, should be reduced to a code.

And, in order to guard against any objections founded upon a misconception of the nature, objects, and effects of such a codification, the Commissioners propose to insert in such a code the following fundamental rules for its interpretation and application.

I. The code is to be interpreted and applied to future cases, as a code of the common law of Massachusetts, and not as a code of mere positive or statute law. It is to be deemed an affirmance of what the common law now is, and not as containing provisions in derogation of that law, and therefore subject to a strict construction.

II. Consequently, it is to furnish the rules for decisions in courts of justice, not only in cases directly (*ex directo*) within its terms, but indirectly, and by analogy in cases, where, as a part of the common law, it would and ought to be applied by courts of justice, in like manner.

III. In all cases not provided for by the code, or governed by the analogies therein contained, the common law of Massachusetts, as now existing, is to furnish the rules for decision, unless so far as it is repugnant to the common law affirmed in the code, or to the statute law of the state.

Such is the basis of the code proposed by the Commissioners, and such the principles, by which they propose, that those who shall be called upon to perform the duty of codification, should be guided.

The Commissioners are aware, that there are many objections, which have been and may be urged, not only against any codification of the common law, in the broadest sense of the terms, but also against any codification whatever, even of the limited nature and extent, which they have ventured to recommend. These objections have been urged not only at home but abroad; not only in countries governed by the common law, but in countries governed by the civil law, and by their own customary law; not only in public debates, but in elaborate treatises by jurists of distinguished reputation and ability. A proper respect, therefore, for the opinions thus promulgated, requires them to take notice of some of the most prominent objections, and to submit such answers as have occurred to them touching the subject.

One of the most general objections urged against the establishment of a code is, the utter impossibility of making it perfect, or applicable to all future changes in the condition, rights and property of a nation. It has been said, that no system of laws can remain for a great length of time unchanged; for the progress, or even the regress of civil society, must constantly call for new modifications of the existing laws; and that one of the peculiar excellences of the common law consists in its adaptation to all circumstances, and, in a general sense, to all the exigencies which civil society may present. It is not necessary to controvert the general truth of this remark. On the contrary, it may be fully admitted, and yet in no degree impair the reasoning in favor of a code. The fact, that no system of human laws can be made so perfect as not to require future revisions, modifications, amendments, and even partial repeals, in the new changes of society, furnishes no just objection to the adoption of some positive laws, providing for the ordinary concerns of a nation. It would be deemed little short of an absurdity to declare, that, because no perfect laws can be made, therefore no laws should be made. Even the common law does not pretend, in the slightest degree, to be a perfect system. On the contrary, it has undergone, and is constantly undergoing changes, to meet the new exigencies of society; and the aid of the legislature is constantly invoked to cure its defects, and improve its remedial justice. If the common law had the theoretical perfection and excellence attributed to it in the objection, (which can be admitted only with many qualifications and exceptions,) still, it is not perceived how this perfection and excellence are impaired by putting into a positive text, what is supposed, by the objection itself, to be clear and determinate, and to make it rest, not upon disputable deductions, but upon the positive sanctions of the legislature, declaring it to be the common law. In truth, the objection, though in its form general, seems principally addressed to a case, where a nation should establish a particular code of laws, and abolish all other laws not provided for in that code. In such a case, it may be admitted, that the unavoidable imperfections of the code would often produce very great mischief and injustice, and require incessant enactments by the legislature to overcome them. In this view the objection has no application to codification, as proposed by the Commissioners; for every thing not governed by the code is to be left precisely as it now is. Courts of justice are to be at full liberty to apply the existing common law to non-enumerated cases, exactly as they now do. And from the materials thus furnished by judicial decisions, improvements and additions may, from time to time, be engrafted by the legislature on the code itself. It will thus become, what it ought to be, a perpetual index to the known law, gradually refining, enlarging and qualifying its doctrines, and at the same time, bringing them together in a concise and positive form for public use.

Another objection, which has been urged by distinguished jurists of continental Europe, is, that the jurisprudence of a country (in their sense of the phrase) is perpetually changing its form and character with every succeeding age; and any attempt to give it permanency in its principles or its applications must make it inflexible, and unfit for the purposes of social justice. Thus, for example, it is asserted, that the customary law of some of the continental nations is in a perpetual though gradual state of change; and that this is a state most useful and salutary to be preserved; for otherwise the jurisprudence of one age would become obligatory upon another, and prevent the improvements in it, which might be best adapted to its prosperity and social advancement. This objection, whatever may be its force or value, when applied to the state of the customary law, in some of the countries of continental Europe, vanishes, when it is attempted to be applied to our common law. In America and in England, the common law is not, in the sense of the objection, of such a changeable nature. When once a doctrine is fully recognized as a part of the common law, it forever remains a part of the system, until it is altered by the legislature. A doctrine of the common law settled three hundred years ago is just as conclusive now in a case, which falls within it, as it was then. No court of justice can disregard it, or dispense with it; and nothing short of legislative power can abrogate it. With us the notion that courts of justice ought to be at liberty from time to time to change established doctrines, to suit their own views of convenience or policy, would be treated as a most alarming dogma, subversive of some of the best rights of a free people, and especially of the right to have justice administered upon certain fixed and known principles. Our ancestors adopted in its fullest meaning the maxim, that it is a wretched servitude, where the law is vague and uncertain. Hence it is, that precedents in our courts of justice are of very high authority, and, with rare exceptions, conclusive as to the principles, which they decide and establish; and subsequent judges are not at liberty to depart from them, when they have once become a rule of rights or of property. The whole of the judicial institutions in England and America rest upon this doctrine as their only solid foundation. But upon the continent of Europe, or at least in some parts of it, the case is very different. The decisions of courts of justice, (technically called jurisprudence) go no farther than to decide the merits of the particular case. They furnish no determinate rule for other cases of a like nature. Precedents are not of absolute authority, or, in a general sense, of any cogent obligation. The doctrines of the judges of one age may be, and are disregarded by those of another. And it is quite competent for an advocate to insist upon principles and reasonings which are adverse to a long train of decisions, and entirely subversive of their authority. The objection, therefore, so far as it can apply to America and England, is an objection, not to a code, but to the common law itself; for the common law has this very inflexibility of character, and permanence of doctrine, of which the objection complains. With us in Massachusetts, the common law is now just as much of general obligation, and of general fixedness in its doctrines, and as binding upon courts of justice, as it would be if reduced to a code, and no more. When new cases arise, they are governed (as we have seen) by such analogies to those which have already been decided, or by such principles of natural justice, as are properly applicable to them. When old cases arise, the established doctrines furnish the sole rule, by which they are decided.

But though this last objection is principally, if not exclusively, confined to the jurists of continental Europe, there is one of a kindred nature, which is sometimes pressed by the opponents of codification on both sides of the Atlantic. It is, that the moment, that the common law shall become the text of a positive code, it will cease to be common law; it will be inflexible in its applications, and subject to none of those implied and reasonable exceptions and modifications, which now constitute its peculiar character. This objection would certainly have much weight, if it were a necessary result, that the codification of the common law would thus destroy its flexibility, and reduce it to a hard and unyielding positive text. But the Commissioners are of opinion, that no such result would or ought to follow. On the contrary, they propose (as has been already suggested) that the reduction of the common law to a text should not be held to change the nature or character of the interpretation or application of its doctrines.

An objection of a different character, and which, indeed, is that, which in one shape or another is found afloat through the community, is, that every code of the common law must necessarily be imperfect, and leave much still to be explained by very imperfect lights; that so far as the principles and details of the common law are capable of codification, they are, or are supposed to be, now well known, and a code is not necessary to ascertain or promulgate them; that the benefits of a code must, therefore, be slight and unimportant, since it can provide for comparatively few cases of real doubt, and may even lead to mischievous errors in reasoning or application of the text.

This objection may perhaps be best answered by a consideration of the benefits which may be derived from a codification of the common law. It has been already admitted, that every such codification must, from the nature of things, be imperfect; for it never can embrace all the past, present, and future changes in society, which may require new rules to govern them. But this is an objection, in its general form, founded upon the absolute infirmity of human nature, for every purpose of perfect action, and is not limited to codification. It by no means follows, that, because legislation cannot do every thing, or foresee every thing, therefore no legislation should exist, either to remedy evils, to ascertain rights, or to secure property. The benefits proposed by a code may be summed up in the following propositions.

I. In the first place, certainty, clearness and facility of reference are of great importance in all matters of law, which concern the public generally. It is desirable, in every community, that the laws which govern the rights, duties, relations, and business of the people, should, as far as practicable, be accessible to them for daily use or consultation. No one, indeed, is so rash as to suppose, that, with the very different occupations, means of education, and opportunities of leisure, of the mass of the people, it is possible for them fully or accurately to understand all the laws in their full force and extent. This must, under all circumstances, require thorough study, laborious diligence, and a great variety of accessary knowledge. But it does not follow, that, because all cannot be attained, therefore the more general and useful rules may not be brought under the notice of the people, and, according to their attainments and leisure, be made the means of guarding them from gross mistakes in business, or gross violations of the rights of others. Now, certainly, if a rule or doctrine of the common law exists in a determinate form or with a determinate certainty, it is capable of being so expressed in the text of a code. If so capable, then it is not easy to perceive why it should not be so expressed, that it may furnish a guide for inquirers, to clear away a private doubt, or to satisfy a hesitating judgment.

But this is not all. At present, the known rules and doctrines of the common law are spread over many ponderous volumes. They are nowhere collected together in a concise and systematic form, having a positive legislative sanction. They are to be gathered from treatises upon distinct and independent subjects of very different merit and accuracy; from digests and abridgments; from books of practice and from professional practice; and above all, from books of reports of adjudged cases, many hundreds of which now exist, and which require to be painfully and laboriously consulted in order to ascertain them. These rules and doctrines may be well known and well understood by eminent lawyers and judges, by profound students, who possess an ample library of law books, and by others, who devote their whole leisure to the purpose. And yet men less eminent, less studious, or with less means to provide a library, or to consult it, may be unable to arrive at the same certainty, and may even be misled by their partial examinations into serious errors and mistakes. A leading rule may have some exceptions, which have escaped the researches of the party, and yet be as well established as the rule itself. Many law suits are now founded upon errors and mistakes of this sort, which the mere imperfection of the means within the reach of the interested party, or of his counsel, has unavoidably produced. A single line of a code, properly and accurately prepared upon such a subject, might at once have dissipated every doubt and uncertainty, as to the nature, extent, and operation of the existing rule.

II. And this leads the Commissioners to remark, in the next place, that one great use of a code of the common law, in its principal branches, will be the abridgment of professional as well as of private labor, in ascertaining and advising upon a rule or doctrine of that law. A vast deal of time is now necessarily consumed, if not wasted, in ascertaining the precise bearing and result of various cases, which have been decided touching a particular topic. If the result is at all contested by the adverse party, no counsellor would feel safe without a thorough examination of all the leading cases, (even though they should spread over centuries,) lest he should be surprised at the argument by a loose dictum, a questionable authority, or an ambiguous statement, either distinguishing or controlling the case before him. Hence it is, that lawyers in the fullest practice are compelled to the most severe studies, upon points upon which they do not entertain much if any doubt, lest, in the long array of cases which may be cited upon any disputed or undisputed point, there should be some intimation which might injuriously affect their client's rights or remedy. And yet, it is not too much to say, that often a single page of a code would contain, in a clear and explicit statement, all that the researches of a week, or even of a month, would scarcely justify them in affirming with an unfaltering confidence.

One great advantage, therefore, of a code, an advantage which in a practical view can scarcely be over-estimated, is, that it supersedes the necessity, in ordinary cases at least, of very elaborate researches into other books; and, indeed, it often supersedes in all cases, but those of rare and extraordinary occurrence, the necessity of consulting an immense mass of learned collections and digests of antecedent decisions.

This has accordingly been found to be one of the ordinary

results of codification, whenever it has been successfully accomplished. Thus, we are informed, that the codes of Justinian superseded for ordinary use some camels' loads of written Commentaries on the law. And it is notorious that the civil code of France, (commonly called the Napoleon code,) has, in like manner, thrown out of the daily consultation of jurists a voluminous bulk of treatises upon the customary and provincial law of that country. There are cases, indeed, in which now those voluminous collections must still be consulted. But the occasions are, probably, not one in a hundred of what they were before that code was promulgated. In like manner, it may be unhesitatingly affirmed, that the maritime and commercial ordinances of Louis XIV, of 1673, and 1681, not only put an end to a vast extent of litigation, in the different maritime provinces of that kingdom, but also furnished rules so clear and so equitable as to have been adopted as the basis of much of the maritime law of other countries, and especially of that of England.

III. In the next place, it may be stated, in connection with the preceding head, and as illustrative of it, that there are in the common law many points, which, though on the whole now established by a considerable weight of judicial authority, are not absolutely beyond the reach of forensic controversy, if learned counsel should choose to stir them. There are, for example, many questions which have given rise to litigation in different ages, and upon which there may be found in the reports, not only occasional diversities of judicial opinion, but many nice distinctions and differences, and many incidental dicta which serve greatly to perplex the inquiries of the ablest lawyers. Where authorities are to be found on each side of a point; where the circumstances of cases, very nearly resembling each other in most respects, are yet distinguishable from each other by nice shades of difference, or have been so distinguished, thus furnishing grounds for reasoning and controversy, as to the precise extent of a principle; no judges would feel at liberty to stop the argument, although, in their judgment, the weight of authority should be clearly against the suggested distinction or difference. Much of the time of courts of justice is consumed in arguments of this sort, where there are numerous cases, with some slight differences of circumstances, bearing on the same general rule, all of which may be required to be examined and distinguished. It was said by an eminent judge (Lord Eldon) upon one occasion, where some question of artificial or technical law was under discussion before him, that there were upwards of three hundred cases bearing on that question, which had already been decided. To master them, with all their minute distinctions of circumstances, would of itself be a vast labor. And yet it is not perhaps too much to say, that four or five lines of text in a code, stating the true general rule, deducible from the best of them, would at once have put aside the necessity of any further consideration of most of these cases.

There are, besides, numerous points, upon which there are now to be found conflicting decisions, or dicta of courts of justice, which shake the authority of certain doctrines. In cases of this sort, it seems desirable to establish, which of these decisions constitutes the true rule, or at least to give a positive affirmance of the true rule, when it can be fairly ascertained what that is. And perhaps also, in some instances of daily practical importance, where there is a real doubt what the true rule of the common law is, it may not be without use to fix it in a like positive form.

The Commissioners do not indulge the rash expectation, that any code of the known existing common law will dry up all the common sources of litigation. New cases must arise, which no code can provide for, or even ascertain. These must necessarily be left to be disposed of by courts of justice, as they shall occur in future. But the Commissioners are of opinion, that a code, which shall contain the clearly established principles of the common law, will be attended with great benefits to the public, for the reasons already stated.

It will show, what the existing law is, as far as it goes, in a clear and intelligible manner. It will have a tendency to suppress useless and expensive litigation. It will greatly abridge the labors of judges, as well as of the profession, by furnishing a starting point for future discussions, instead of imposing the necessity of constant researches through all the past annals of the law.

Having stated these general reasons in favor of the reduction to a code of the common law of Massachusetts, to a limited extent, we are next naturally led to the inquiry, what portions of the common law should or may be reduced to such a code?

For the purpose of a more exact consideration of this subject, the common law of Massachusetts may be distinguished into four classes.

I. That, which is potentially in existence, but, in a great measure, obsolete; and that, which is of rare occurrence in practice, or doubtful and obscure in regard to its nature, extent, and operation in the Commonwealth.

II. That, which, though positively in existence and known as a part of the common law, and admitting of general application, has yet been so modified or altered by the legislature, as to be of but limited use in practice.

III. That, which is of daily occurrence in the common business of life, and furnishes the rules for the rights of persons and the rights of property of the community at large — in civil cases.

IV. That, which defines and punishes crimes, and ascertains the rules of proceeding in criminal cases.

In regard to the first class, it seems to the Commissioners wholly unnecessary to attempt any codification of so much of our common law as falls within its reach. It would be extremely difficult to draw up any exact text of this portion of our common law, from the obscurity of the proper materials, and from the difficulty in many cases of ascertaining the exact boundaries between what is merely obsolete, and what is now a component part of that law. And, after all, if any codification thereof was made, it would rather be an incumbrance upon the general text, than any real aid to subsequent inquiries. Thus, for example, it may be a matter of some uncertainty, whether certain common law remedies, respecting real estate, are, or were a part of the common law in force here: — such as writs of assize, of common, of pasture, of admeasurement, of pasture, of partition, of admeasurement of dower, of cosinage, certain kinds of writs of entry, writs of ejectione firmæ, writs of warrantia chartæ, and others of a similar nature. Of others, again, there is no doubt of their actual legal existence; such as, for example, fines and common recoveries; and yet they are now scarcely known in practice, having been superseded by other more convenient modes of transferring real estate. And yet the learning of the common law upon the subject of fines and recoveries is full of intrinsic difficulties and niceties, and technical principles, which it would require many pages to state, and many more to make intelligible to the common reader. The same remarks are applicable to the common law respecting markets, outlawry, prerogative, voucher, waife, and other heads of a like nature, remote from our ordinary inquiries.

In regard to the second class, there seems to be equal doubt of the solid utility of any attempt at codification. The great extent, to which legislative enactments have gone in the modification, alteration and superseding of large portions of this class, directly or indirectly, would make the task of selecting that, which is in force, exceedingly embarrassing, and perhaps perilous. Thus, for example, the common law respecting amendments of process and proceedings, bail, distress, feoffments, and other common law modes of conveyancing, forfeitures, mesne and final process, sheriffs and trials, have undergone so many modifications, and alterations, and partial abrogations, that it is not easy to say, how much of the very complicated doctrines of the common law on most of these topics is now actually in force; for in practice they are of rare occurrence and application. But a still more striking illustration may be found in the subject of special pleading. It is well known, that this constitutes one of the most purely technical, acute and intricate subdivisions of the common law; and even the doctrines relative to a small branch only of it, that of abatement, though rare in practice, is full of nice and over curious learning. The legislature, by an act passed at its last session, have provided, that all matters of law or of fact in defence, in any civil action, may be given in evidence under the general issue, and no other plea in bar of such action shall be pleaded. The effect of this enactment is, to abolish so much of this branch of the law as relates to special pleas, technically so called. But it leaves in full force all the doctrines of pleading in regard to declarations, in regard to pleadings in abatement, in regard to the general issue, and in regard to general demurrers to the declaration. It would seem, under these circumstances, wholly unnecessary to reduce to a code the principles of pleading applicable to special pleas, technically so called. The reduction to a code of the doctrines relative to pleadings in abatement, which is full of intricacy, and to a considerable degree, obsolete in practice, would seem equally unnecessary. The doctrines of pleading still applicable to declarations, to general demurrers, and to the general issue, are of a very comprehensive nature, and abound with artificial and technical principles, and it would be a task of no small difficulty to say, in many cases, to what extent many of these principles reach, and how far they are governed by rules ordinarily applied to special pleas, technically so called. For these reasons, the Commissioners are of opinion, that it is not advisable, at present, to codify this branch of our jurisprudence. It would rather seem desirable, if any thing is to be done, to reduce it to a more simple form, and disembarrass it of some of its cumbrous and inconvenient appendages.

The third class is that, to which the Commissioners are of opinion, that the labors of codification should be strenuously and sedulously directed. This class comprehends three great branches of the law. I. That, which respects the civil rights, capacities and duties of persons, considered by themselves, or in their social and other relations to other persons; and the remedies resulting from those rights, capacities and duties. II. That, which respects the rights and titles to real and personal property, and the incidents thereto, and the remedies, by which they are protected and vindicated. III. The rights, duties and claims arising from contracts, in the largest sense of that term, comprehending express contracts, such as bonds and obligations, conditions, conveyances, covenants, and other positive stipulations between parties competent to contract; and implied contracts, which result by operation of law, either from the implied consent and intentions of the parties, or from the dictates of natural justice in furtherance of right, or in suppression of wrong. Connected with this branch necessarily is the consideration of the remedies applicable to the various kinds of contracts; some of which stand upon principles purely technical, and others again upon principles of a more general nature.

Many of the most important portions of our common law applicable to the first and second heads, are now so well ascertained and well defined, as to be capable of being reduced to a positive text. Some of them are indeed of great intricacy; but still capable of being in a great measure reduced to such a text. Perhaps the most complicated of these will be found to be, the rights, and capacities, and duties of guardians and wards, of infants generally, of husband and wife, of executors and administrators and administrations, of corporations, and the rights and titles growing out of last wills and testaments. The latter are of singular intricacy and nicety of detail, arising from the almost infinite variety of language and provisions to be found in last wills and testaments, from the ignorance, or peculiar views, or imperfect expressions of intention by different testators. And yet, it may with truth be said, that even the reduction to a code of the rules and principles, which have been deduced by a great writer (Mr. Fearne) from a most acute and close survey of a single head of this subject, that of contingent remainders and executory devises, in the very language, in which he has expressed them, would of itself be no inconsiderable advantage to the profession, as well as to the public. It would almost supersede, in cases constantly arising, the necessity of a daily consultation of authorities, spreading over centuries, and so numerous and various in their application, as to task the time and diligence of the ablest lawyers to a most exhausting extent. They would, at least, have a point of rest, at which they might repose, secure as to the past.

But it is principally in the third and last class, that the Commissioners are of opinion, that the benefits of a code will be most extensively felt, and in which the task may be performed with the greatest certainty of success. It is true, that some branches of the law of contracts contain rules and principles of a technical and artificial nature, not well adapted to the modern exigencies of society. Examples of this sort may be found in the law applicable to obligations, conditions, covenants, and certain classes of conveyances. But, in general, the law of contracts may be affirmed to be founded in sound sense, and adapted to the ends of social justice. Especially may this be affirmed of the law of contracts, which has been developed and established within the last century. Even the law of contracts, applicable to the old forms of obligations and covenants and conveyances, has been, by the cautious expositions of great judges in different ages, reduced to a high degree of certainty. But commercial contracts are eminently entitled to be deemed in this predicament; and under the forming hands of a succession of learned judges and jurists for the last century, they have attained a scientific precision, and accuracy, and clearness, which give them an indisputable title to be treated as a fixed system of national jurisprudence. In regard to commercial contracts, it may be affirmed without hesitation, that the general principles which define and regulate them, and even the subordinate details of those principles, to a very great extent, are now capable of being put in a regular order, and announced in determinate propositions in the text of a code. Among these contracts, the Commissioners would especially recommend as the subjects of a code the following titles, viz.: the law of agency, of bailments, of guaranty, of suretyship, of bills of exchange, of promissory notes, of insurance, and of partnership. They would also recommend, in like manner, the law of navigation and shipping and maritime contracts, including therein the law respecting the rights, duties and authorities of owners and part-owners, and masters, and seamen, and shippers, and passengers; the law of bottomry, of charter-parties, bills of lading, and other contracts of affreightment, including therein the law of freight; and the law of general average, of salvage, and of seamen's wages. These branches of commercial and maritime law are not only capable of being put into the form of a positive text, but of being condensed into a text of a comparatively small extent. It is not too much to affirm, that the whole law of insurance, as far as it has been ascertained and established by judicial decisions and otherwise, may now be stated in a text not exceeding thirty pages of the ordinary size of octavos. In point of fact, it is embraced in the commercial code of France in less than half that space, and most of the principles of that part of the code are the same as those of our law.

In the next place, the Commissioners are of opinion, as indeed they have already intimated, that the common law, as to crimes and punishments, and the incidents thereto, admits of being generally reduced to a code with accuracy and precision. If it can be done, it seems to the Commissioners, that the public at large have a right to claim from the legislature, that it shall be done. One of the most obvious dictates of reason is, that public crimes, which are to affect every citizen, should, as far as practicable, be made known to all. It is wholly unnecessary for the Commissioners to expound the importance of this truth, as it cannot well escape the notice of every intelligent legislator. It is fortunate, that in the present state of the criminal law, there is so much certainty as to the nature and punishment of crimes, at the common law, and the incidents and modes of proceeding therein, that it will not be found a very difficult task, to reduce most of the important doctrines and rules to a positive text.

Connected with these extensive branches of the common law, both civil and criminal, there remains the grave subject of the law of evidence, involving not merely questions respecting the competency and credibility of testimony, but the general rules for the admissibility of written and parol evidence on particular issues. Owing to the invaluable labors of the eminent judges of the last half century, this subject is now, with a few unimportant anomalies, capable of a scientific arrangement and determinate exposition in its general principles, and in many of its most useful details. The rules of evidence have been truly said to constitute the best, if not the only real security for the lives, the personal rights, and the property of all our citizens; and, therefore, the knowledge of them is of infinite moment to the public, as well as to the profession. Any code, which does not embrace them, must be pronounced to be in its very constitution radically defective. The Commissioners, therefore, earnestly recommend the codification of the law of evidence, as among the first objects for the deliberation of the Legislature.

The Commissioners have thus given a very summary view of their opinions respecting the codification of our common law. Every topic, which they have ventured to suggest, might easily have been expanded into a great variety of auxiliary considerations. But it has seemed to them sufficient to point out the general grounds of their opinions, and to leave to the wisdom of the legislature a full review of them.

In concluding this part of the subject, it seems proper for the Commissioners to suggest, though it does not exactly fall within the strict terms of their commission, that if a code should be framed upon any or all of the topics which they have ventured to recommend, it will afford a fit opportunity for the legislature to supply some of the acknowledged defects, to cure some of the admitted anomalies, and to correct some of the erroneous doctrines, which, in a long succession of ages, have gradually been ingrafted upon our common law. This, to be sure, ought to be done with a cautious and skilful hand, and with a deep sense of the delicacy of intermeddling with established principles. If, however, no changes are attempted except such as have the sanction of experience, and the support and approbation of enlightened judges and jurists, much may be done to introduce harmony, and consistency, and simplicity into the general system.

It now only remains for the Commissioners to express their opinion, as to the plan or plans, by which such codification, if undertaken, can be best accomplished. Looking to the extent and variety of the labor, as well as to the learning and ability required for the task, the Commissioners think, that it will be indispensable to employ at least five commissioners, of high standing in the profession, and otherwise suitably qualified, to reduce those portions of our common law to a code or codes, which the Commissioners have proposed. Much time must necessarily be devoted exclusively to the subject; and, with all the aids which can be obtained, several years will be required for the completion of the entire enterprise. During the progress of it, the Commissioners must have frequent meetings for discussion, as well as for a careful examination and scrupulous review of the labors of each other. Perhaps it may be found advisable to authorize the Commissioners occasionally to employ some assistants, having extraordinary qualifications, to bring together the materials of a particular head for the more deliberate consideration of the Commissioners. In this way the progress of the work might be greatly accelerated, at a comparatively small expense. And it may be properly left to the Commissioners to decide, whether it will be best to lay before the legislature the result of their labors, from time to time, as particular topics shall be reduced to a text; or to await the accomplishment of the entire scheme, and then to submit it as a whole to the legislature.

As the Commissioners may find it necessary to open a wide correspondence with members of the profession, in various parts of the United States, as well as to perform many incidental duties, requiring the aid of a secretary, it is respectfully submitted, that they should be authorized to appoint one, with a suitable compensation.

The Commissioners do not understand that they are required, by their commission, to lay before the legislature the details of the plan or plans, by which the system of codification should be carried into effect, or the particular branches of the common law, which it should embrace, or any analytical exhibition of the mode or arrangement, or contents of the code. They presume, that these matters will properly appertain, and indeed ought to appertain, to the duties of the Commissioners, who shall be appointed to prepare such a code, if the legislature should choose to sanction the project. It is obvious, that, in the progress of the investigations, necessary to complete so extensive a labor, many new views must continually arise, and many amendments and improvements of the first plan may be suggested by the experience of the Commissioners, and a more thorough and close examination of particular topics.

Such are the expositions, which the Commissioners have thought it their duty to present to the consideration of the legislature, upon the interesting and important subject of their commission.

All which is most respectfully submitted.

JOSEPH STORY,
THERON METCALF,
SIMON GREENLEAF,
CHARLES E. FORBES,
LUTHER S. CUSHING,
Commissioners.

SPEECH AT THE CENTENNIAL CELEBRATION OF HARVARD UNIVERSITY.

Mr. President, I rise with unaffected diffidence to address you on the present occasion, and to return thanks for the toast just announced from the Chair. The novelty of the circumstances under which we are assembled, as well as my own unexpected position at this moment, place me in a state of great embarrassment. In the first place, if invited here as a member of the Corporation of Harvard College, I had consoled myself with the reflection, that a matter of law would be my especial protection for an unbroken silence. I think that my Lord Coke has somewhere told us, and at all events the doctrine is assuredly as old as his day, that a corporation has no soul; nor has it any natural body; but only an artificial existence, or legal entity; so that it cannot manifest its intentions by any personal acts or oral discourse, and therefore it can act and speak only under its common seal, or at all events through its acknowledged living head; and through that head our Corporation has already powerfully and eloquently spoken this day. But although I have hitherto had great confidence in the law, as on my side, it seems that it has failed to be my security in the present emergency.

In the next place, I had placed equal reliance upon a matter of fact. I came here with a distinct understanding, that on this most interesting anniversary, all of us should move in procession, and take our places at the tables, in the order of our respective college classes; and well I knew, that, as a member of the class of 1798, in the midst of that phalanx, I should be secure from all intrusion from without, so that I might comfortably say, with honest John Falstaff, "Shall I not take mine ease in mine own inn?" But here, again, I have been mistaken in the matter of fact; for the place from which I now address you, abundantly proves, that the move and the remove have been greatly to my disquiet. In short, sir, I am in the same unhappy predicament here, in which many poor gentlemen find themselves in some other places, with a total failure of matter of law and matter of fact for my justification or defence, touching the demand for a speech.

But, not to trouble you with any further apologies, allow me in a graver tone to say, that few occasions could be of more deep and permanent interest than the present. When I look around me, and see the numerous assemblage of students and alumni who grace this celebration, I cannot but feel a lively sensibility and unaffected gratitude, in being permitted to witness such a scene, under such auspices. I cannot turn my eyes towards the neighboring collegiate halls and academical shades, without the most touching reminiscences of former days passed there, in the season of gay and unsuspicious youth. I realize in its full force the beautiful language of the poet: —

> "I feel the gales, that from ye blow,
> A momentary bliss bestow,
> As, waving fresh their gladsome wing,
> My weary soul they seem to soothe,
> And, redolent of joy and youth,
> To breathe a second spring."

Many of the topics, which naturally crowd upon the mind under such circumstances, have already been in a great measure exhausted in the excellent address to which we have just listened from the Chair, and in the elaborate and powerful discourse, which occupied our attention in the morning. At this late hour, I have little to add to what has been so well discussed in them. My worthy friend who last spoke (the learned Dean of the Faculty of Divinity) has placed before us the labors and the services of the Puritan clergy in establishing and protecting and aiding this University, in their true light. He has but done them the justice of bestowing warm praise upon their prompt zeal, their untiring fidelity, and their constant devotion to its interests. It was founded by them for the cause of religion and truth; and I trust it will forever remain steadfast and immovable in that cause.

In regard to the complimentary notice of the Law School of the University, in the toast from the Chair, I cannot but receive it with a deep consciousness of the kindness which dictated it, and of the small claim that I have to appropriate to myself personally the commendation which it implies. No one appreciates more fully than myself the general importance of the study of the law. No one places a higher value upon that science, as the great instrument by which society is held together, and the cause of public justice is maintained and vindicated. Without it, neither liberty, nor property, nor life, nor that which is even dearer than life, a good reputation, is for a moment secure. It is, in short, the great elastic power which pervades and embraces every human relation. It links man to man by so many mutual ties, and duties, and dependencies, that, though often silent and unseen in its operations, it becomes at once the minister to his social necessities, and the guardian of his social virtues. No one, therefore, can hold in more reverence than myself, the memory of that excellent man, the founder of the Professorship which I have now the honor to hold, whose bounty is worthy of all praise; for its noble object is to inculcate, through all generations, the doctrine of the supremacy of the constitution and laws. But although I am conscious of my own inability to carry into full effect his admirable design, I trust that it will not be thought presumptuous in me to indulge the hope, that there may hereafter be found, among the pupils of this school of jurisprudence, some master spirit, who will task himself to its accomplishment, and thereby secure to himself and the school an enviable immortality. To such a one I would say,

> "Bate not a jot
> Of heart or hope; but still bear up and steer
> Right onward."

But I confess that my thoughts have been led in a somewhat different direction from that of the law by the festivities of this day. The very spot where we are assembled is consecrated by a thousand endearing associations of the past. The very name of Cambridge compels us to cast our eyes across the Atlantic, and brings up a glowing gratitude for our unspeakable obligations to the parent University, whose name we proudly bear, and have borne for two centuries. To her we owe many of our earliest scholars and best benefactors, many of our civil rulers and our ecclesiastical leaders. They nursed our infant institution in their bosoms. They cherished the cause of letters and learning with a holy ardor and unconquered diligence, in this then scarcely reclaimed wilderness. They stamped the image of their own exalted piety and patient virtues upon their own age. They refined, while they animated, the strong lineaments of the Puritan character. They planted the precious seed, whose mature fruits we are now enjoying in a rich and luxuriant harvest. I do not say too much then, when I proclaim, that we owe unspeakable obligations to the ancient and venerable University of Cambridge in old England. Let it be recollected, that there our pious founder, John Harvard, of glorious memory, received his education. There, also, our second President, Charles Chauncy, gathered the solid learning, which he so liberally bestowed upon his pupils here. There, also, the first three ministers of the first parish of our own Cambridge, the Rev. Mr. Hooker, the Rev. Mr. Stone, and the Rev. Mr. Shepard, were matriculated, and in Emanuel College laid the foundations of that ample knowledge of things human and divine, which made them the ornaments of their own age, and the pride of succeeding generations. So numerous, indeed, was the class of educated men from this stock among our civil and clerical fathers, that it has been stated by one of our own historians, of almost unexampled minuteness and accuracy of research, that there were, as early as 1638, forty or fifty sons of that University dwelling in the sparse villages of New England, being one for every two hundred or two hundred and fifty inhabitants.

We may, therefore, indulge a just pride in claiming our kindred with and lineage from that University. Nor ought we to desire to trace back to any higher origin our instruction in literature and religion, or our love of science and liberty. That ancient University numbers among her sons some of the brightest names in the annals of British renown. Bacon, Milton, Newton, were her own. And where in the history, I do not say of England, but of the world, can we point to men of more extraordinary genius, more profound attainments, more comprehensive researches, or more enduring fame? It seems scarcely the coloring of poetry to declare, that

> "They passed the flaming bounds of place and time,"

and saw

> "The living throne, the sapphire blaze,
> Where angels tremble while they gaze."

Mr. President, I will not detain you or the company any longer. I beg leave to offer as a toast, —

"Our Ancient Mother, the University of Cambridge in old England. "*Salve, magna Parens, — magna Virûm.*"

LITERARY TENDENCIES OF THE TIMES.

A DISCOURSE PRONOUNCED BEFORE THE SOCIETY OF THE ALUMNI OF HARVARD UNIVERSITY, AT THEIR FIRST ANNIVERSARY, AUGUST 23, 1842.

There are few occasions, on which we could have been assembled, which would awaken more varied feelings, or possess a more profound interest, than that, which now brings us together. We stand here, at the distance of two hundred years, upon the very spot where stood the first class, having completed their academical course, ready to receive the earliest honors of this our parent University. From the pious lips of the first President, whose remains lie in the neighboring churchyard, they received their farewell benediction, — in the presence of the venerable founders of the colony, — amidst the deep shades of the surrounding forests, and under the roof of the simple edifice, first reared to God and the Church in this stranger land. Few, indeed, were they in number, but not faint or faltering in the support of religion and learning. The little Band of Nine may well be presumed upon that occasion to have sought utterance of their own thoughts in the very language of the Governor of the Colony (a short time afterwards) in his appeal to the General Court for aid to the College. "If this work of the College be thought fit to be upheld and continued, as we hope that considerations of the glory of God, the honorable interest of the country, the good of all posterity, and the experience of the benefits and blessings thereof, will constrain all men to say it is, then something must effectually be done for help in the premises."

And that something (said these youths) must be done by us, that we may establish the foundations, and perpetuate the fame, of this Institution. We are the first-born, and will not dishonor our parentage. Wherever our lots in life may be cast, to this blessed spot will we turn with a holy reverence. For the prosperity of this college shall our daily prayers ascend. Here shall our last thoughts repose. And whatever of earthly honors shall belong to us, to this altar shall they be brought, as the first-fruits of grateful children to the best of mothers. Worthily, indeed, were those vows performed. They went forth into the world with undaunted zeal to the great work, and became eminent in the church and the state. Their mouldering relics have, indeed, long since shared the common fate, and returned to the dust. But their good deeds still survive in the memories of good men, and shed a mild and balmy light over the annals of the past, as well as over the honors of the present days.

And we too, are assembled here, — for the first time, — on an occasion equally worthy of commemoration, and full of responsible duties. We meet to celebrate the first anniversary of the society of all the Alumni of Harvard. We meet without any distinction of sect or party, or of rank or profession, in church or in state, in literature or in science. We meet, as a band of brothers, educated in the bosom of the same indulgent parent, and drinking from the same fountain, which has from the beginning poured forth its pure and sparkling streams of knowledge to give life and glory to our land. Our fellowship is designed to be, — as it should be, — of the most liberal and comprehensive character, conceived in the spirit of catholic benevolence, asking no creed but the love of letters, seeking no end, but the encouragement of learning, and imposing no conditions, which may lead to jealousy or ambitious strife. In short, we meet for peace and for union; to devote one day in the year to academical intercourse and the amenities of scholars. We would shake off from our feet the dust, gathered, not only in the by-ways and highways of life, but in the fervid race for public distinction. We would lay aside for the hour, the garlands and the palms, and the emblems of victory. *Viridesque coronæ, et palmæ pretium victoribus.*

We would enter this temple with hearts overflowing with grateful recollections of the past, and earnest hopes of the future. We would lay upon this family altar our tribute of affection, and celebrate with our whole hearts the birthday of our matriculation. *Salve, — magna Parens, — magna Virûm.*

Under such circumstances I am but too conscious of my own inability to perform the duties assigned to me in a manner suited to the dignity of the occasion. It would have been far more grateful to me, that the task should, according to your first choice, have been executed by your venerable President, whose ripe scholarship, and rare endowments, and intellectual energy, have so long attracted the public admiration. He seems, indeed, to form the connecting link between the present and the past, standing, as it were, upon the verge of that dim twilight of life, where the twinkling stars, in our catalogue, alternately appear, and vanish, as the shades of the evening shut down upon the passing generations. *Sic itur ad astra.*

I am conscious, also, in whose presence I stand, and whose instructed judgments I am called upon to address. I see before me the veterans, who, having won the laurels of their day, seek now in retirement to enjoy the dignity and repose of learned leisure. I see before me those, who occupy the high ranks of professional life. The venerable ministers of the Gospel, whose critical spirit has illumined the dark passages of Scripture, and given new vigor to the sublime truths of religion. I see the professors of the medical art, whose genius has curiously studied the maladies of our race, and whose skill has administered succor to thousands, who were ready to perish. I see the jurists, who, in the judgment-seat, or at the bar, have applied their profound knowledge to the support of the civil institutions of society, to the protection of innocence, to the fearless vindication of right, and to the triumph of justice over popular clamor and political cabal. I see the statesmen, whose enlarged and comprehensive minds have maintained the glorious struggle for the support of the principles of the Constitution, which may, if any thing human can, perpetuate the blessings of liberty, and save us from becoming a byword and reproach among the nations of the earth. I see the elegant and quiet scholars, who have given their days and nights to illustrate the annals of the past, or imparted a warm and sunny glow to the literature of the present. I see the ambitious youth, who, having completed their preparatory studies, stand at the starting-post of the course, impatient of delays, and panting for the toils and the rewards of the victories of life. The Olympic dust has not as yet even soiled their sandals. Nor can they as yet feel the force of that solemn admonition: "Let not him, that girdeth on his harness, boast himself, as he that putteth it off."

It is, I repeat it, under such circumstances, that I feel with unaffected sensibility the difficulties of the task, which I have assumed. Amidst a crowd of topics, which rush upon the mind, I would fain select some one, not unworthy the interests and associations of the occasion. After some hesitation nothing has occurred to me more appropriate, than some suggestions on the dangers and difficulties and duties of scholars in our own age, and especially in our own country.

If I were called upon to say, in one word, what constitutes the predominant danger of our day, I should say, that it is the tendency to ultraism of all sorts, and in all directions. In all ages there have probably been found among men of letters three distinct classes in opposition to each other. But never until our day have the lines of separation between them been so broad, and so sharply defined. These classes are, — The lovers of the past, — the devoted admirers of the present, — the enthusiastic prophets of the future. It is of course, that the world of letters, like the natural world, should appear under very different aspects and relations to each of these classes. The antiquarian dwells with intense pleasure upon the olden times, as at once their historian and eulogist. He lives, as it were, among the dead, and esteems it his highest privilege to remember the forgotten, and to chisel deeper the inscriptions upon the tombs of the renowned. He gathers up the dilapidated fragments with a holy reverence, and finds in each of them the ruins of a lofty mind, more precious, because it is rescued from the remorseless hand of modern improvement, and speaks, in its broken language, the voice of departed ages. On the other hand, the fond admirer of the passing literature of the day deems little else worthy of his notice, and contemplates former works but as faded pictures, left to moulder on the walls, or at best, as serving to show the prejudices, or follies, or defects of taste of bygone times. And, again, the man of ardent temperament, regardless of the known and the tangible, casts his keen glances through the obscurities of the future, and prophesies the surpassing grandeur of the days to come, when new revelations of the human soul shall be unfolded, and new truths be proclaimed, which philosophy itself, in its boldest flights, has never yet dreamed of. He sees, that, after the lapse of nearly six thousand years, man is but in the infancy of his being; that he has learned little, which might not as well be forgotten; that the lights, which have hitherto guided him, are not from heaven, but false and delusive phantoms, which have led him astray; that he has yet to learn how to live, as well as how to die; and that this instruction is to be sought, not in the meditations and writings of the great minds of other ages, but in the depths and communings of his own spirit.

Now, I say, that these three classes of opinions, which, to some extent, have probably prevailed in all the epochs of literature, have acquired an unnatural impulse and acceleration in our day, from the vast powers of a free press, and the concentrated influences of a wide-spread education. If this state of things is to continue; if these three classes of opinions are to flow on in separate, yet neighboring channels; if they are to divide and distract the public mind and conduct; it is plain, that there is no small danger to the cause of solid learning, sound religion, and social institutions. Divide and conquer, is the cunning maxim of tyrants, in order to accomplish their nefarious purposes. But in the republic of letters the same rule must nourish factions at war with its safety and its advancement. If, for example, the human mind, (as we are sometimes proudly informed,) has never yet grappled with the great truths belonging to its character and destiny; if neither history, nor experience, nor philosophy, have hitherto even reached the vestibule of those inquiries, which are to guide us in the business of life, in the affairs of government, in the principles of public policy, in the development of national interests and resources, in the foundations of morals and religion, or (passing from these to less grave topics) if genius has never yet affixed the true value or importance to any of its own achievements in art, or science, or learning; and the mastery of its powers, as well as its means of excellence, are yet to be searched out, as unknown quantities; then, indeed, as it seems to me, man has lived in vain, and disquieted himself in vain. We can give no pledges of success in our present efforts, which former ages have not given. We can offer no securities, which may not hereafter crumble away, like the fabrics, which they reared only to perish, or left, as monumental ruins, to instruct us in the meanness of the end, compared with the magnitude of the labor.

Considerations not less discouraging must arise, if either of the other two extremes of opinion are to possess an enduring influence. The truth is, that the past is not every thing; nor the future every thing; nor the present every thing. The intellect of man is now neither in its infancy, nor in its decrepitude. Human knowledge, whether it be for ornament or use, for pleasure or instruction, is the accumulation of the wisdom and genius of all ages, and is, like the ocean, composed of contributions from infinitely various sources, whose currents have mingled together from the beginning, and must continue so to do to the end of time. Sound the depths as you may, they will be found not entirely the same, nor entirely different. The shoals and the quicksands may be removed from one side; but they have often only shifted to the other. The waters may have become more clear and transparent in some parts; but at the same time more turbid, and shallow in others. The general level has not materially changed in height or the current in its breadth, although occasional tides may have ebbed and flowed with irregular and sometimes desolating power. In some places the alluvial deposits have buried the ancient landmarks; while in others they have been worn away, or submerged. So, in some measure, has it been with the history of the human mind. What has been gained in one direction, has been almost simultaneously lost in another. The known of one age has become the obscure of the next, and the lost of the succeeding. The favorite pursuits and studies of one age have sunk into insignificance or neglect in another. The value, as well as the interest, of particular researches has fluctuated with the passions, and the theories and the fashions of the day. And while each successive generation has imagined itself to stand upon the shoulders of all that preceded them, and flattered itself with the belief, that it surveyed all things with a more comprehensive power, and a less obstructed vision, it has forgotten that on every side there is a natural boundary to the intellectual horizon, at which every object becomes obscure, or evanescent; and that, just in proportion as we advance in one direction, we may be receding from well-defined and fixed lines of light in the other.

I have said, that the tendency in our day is to ultraism of all sorts. I am aware, that this suggestion may appear to some minds of an easy good-nature, or indolent confidence, to be overwrought, or too highly colored. But unless we choose voluntarily to blind ourselves to what is passing before our eyes in the daily intercourse of life, it seems to me impossible not to feel, that there is much which demands severe scrutiny, if not serious alarm. I meddle not here with the bold, and yet familiar speculations upon government, and polity, upon the fundamental changes and even abolition of constitutions, or upon the fluctuating innovations of ordinary legislation. These might, of themselves, furnish out exciting themes for public discussion, if this were a fit occasion to introduce them. I speak rather of the interests of letters — of the common cause of learning — of the deep and abiding principles of philosophy. Is it not painfully true, that the spirit of the age has broken loose from the strong ties, which have hitherto bound society together by the mutual cohesions and attractions of habits, manners, institutions, morals, and literature? It seems to me, that what is old is no longer a matter of reverence or affection. What is established, is not on that account esteemed positively correct, or even salutary or useful. What have hitherto been deemed fundamental truths in the wide range of human experience and moral reasoning, are no longer admitted as axioms, or even as starting points, but at most are propounded only as problems, worthy of solution. They are questioned and scrutinized, and required to be submitted to jealous proofs. They have not even conceded to them the ordinary prerogative of being presumed to be true, until the contrary is clearly shown. In short, there seems to me, at least, to be abroad a general skepticism — a restless spirit of innovation and change — a fretful desire to provoke discussions of all sorts, under the pretext of free inquiry, or of comprehensive liberalism. And this movement is to be found not merely among illiterate and vain pretenders, but among minds of the highest order, which are capable of giving fearful impulses to public opinion. We seem to be borne on the tide of experiment with a rash and impetuous speed, confident that there is no risk in our course, and heedless, that it may make shipwreck of our best hopes, and spread desolation and ruin on every side, as well on its ebb, as its flow. The main ground, therefore, for apprehension is not from undue reverence for antiquity, so much as it is from dreamy expectations of unbounded future intellectual progress; and, above all, from our gross over-valuation and inordinate exaggeration of the peculiar advantages and excellences of our own age over all others. This last is, so to say, our besetting sin; and we worship the idol, carved by the cunning of our own hands, with a fond and parental devotion. To this cause, I think, may be chiefly attributed that bold, not to say reckless spirit of speculation, which has of late years spread itself with such an uncompromising zeal over our whole country. It is not indigenous to our soil; nor does it belong to the sober sagacity and patient judgment of the Anglo-Saxon race. There are many, even among the educated classes, and far more among the uneducated, who imagine that we see now, as men never saw before, in extent, as well as in clearness of vision; that we reason, as men never reasoned before; that we have reached depths and made discoveries, not merely in abstract and physical science, but in the ascertainment of the moral and intellectual powers of man, and the true structure and interests of government and society, which throw into comparative insignificance the attainments of past ages. We seem to ourselves to be emerging (as it were) from the darkness of bygone centuries, whose glow-worm lights "show the matin to be near, and 'gin to pale their ineffectual fires," before our advancing radiance. We are almost ready to persuade ourselves, that their experience is of little value to us; that the change of circumstances is so great, that what was wisdom once, is no longer such; that it served well enough for the day; but that it ought not now to be an object of desire, or even of commendation.

Nay, the comparison is sometimes eagerly pressed of our achievements in literature with those of former ages. Our histories are said to be more philosophical, more searching, more exact, more elaborate than theirs. Our poetry is said to surpass theirs in brilliancy, imaginativeness, tenderness, elegance, and variety, and not to be behind theirs even in sublimity, or terrific grandeur. It is more thoughtful, more natural, more suggestive, more concentrated, and more thrilling than theirs. Our philosophy is not, like theirs, harsh, or crabbed, or irregular; but wrought out in harmonious and well-defined proportions. Our metaphysical systems and mental speculations are (as we flatter ourselves) to endure forever, not merely as monuments of our faith, but of truth, while the old systems must fall into ruins, or merely furnish materials to reconstruct the new, — as the temples of the gods of ancient Rome serve but to trick out or ornament the modern churches of the Eternal City. Ay, — and it may be so. But, who will pause, and gaze on the latter, when his eyes can fasten on the gigantic forms of the Colosseum, or the Pantheon, or the Column of Trajan, or the Arch of Constantine? "It was among the ruins of the Capitol," (said the historian of the Decline and Fall of the Roman Empire,) "that I first conceived the idea of a work, which has amused and exercised near twenty years of my life, and which, however inadequate to my own wishes, I finally deliver to the curiosity and candor of the public." Among the ruins of the Capitol! He felt, indeed, that history was philosophy, teaching by example. He was willing to devote a whole life to the study of the dead, that he might learn how to instruct posterity in their dangers and their duties.

May I not stop for a moment, and ask if there is not much delusion and error in this notion of our superiority over former ages; and if there be, whether it may not be fatal to our just progress in literature, as well as to the permanent interests of society? I would not ask those who entertain such opinions, to accompany me back to the days of Aristotle and Cicero, whose works on the subject of government and politics alone have scarcely received any essential addition in principles or practical wisdom down to this very hour. Who, of all the great names of the past, have possessed so profound an influence and so wide an authority for so long a period? If time be the arbiter of poetical excellence, whose fame is so secure as that of Homer and Virgil? Whose histories may hope to outlive those of Thucydides and Tacitus? But I would limit myself to a far narrower space, to the period of the two centuries which have elapsed since our ancestors emigrated to America. Survey the generations which have since passed away, and let us ask ourselves, what have been their literary labors and scientific attainments? What the productions of their genius and learning? What the amount which they have contributed to ameliorate the condition of mankind, — to lay deep and broad the foundations of theology and jurisprudence and medicine, — to establish and illustrate the principles of free governments and international law, — and to instruct, as well as amuse, the leisure, and to refine the taste of social life? Unless I greatly mistake, a calm survey of this whole matter would convince every well-balanced mind, that, if we may claim something for ourselves, we must yield much to the scholars of those days. We shall find that much of our own fruits have been grafted on the ancient stocks. That much of what we now admire is not destined for immortality. That much which we deem new is but an ill-disguised plunder from the old repositories. And that much which we vaunt to be true, consists of old fallacies, often refuted and forgotten, or of unripe theories, which must perish by the wayside, or be choked by other weeds of a kindred growth.

The truth is, that no single generation of men can accomplish much of itself or for itself, which does not essentially rest upon what has been done before. Whatever may be the extent or variety of his labors, and attainments, much of them will fail to reach posterity, and much which reaches them will be felt, not as a distinct formation, but only as component ingredients of the general mass of knowledge. Many of the immortals of one age cease to be such in the next which succeeds it; and, at best, after a fitful season of renown, they quietly pass away, and sleep well in the common cemetery of the departed. What is present is apt to be dazzling and imposing, and to assume a vast importance over the distant and the obscure. The mind in its perspective becomes affected by the like laws as those of the natural vision. The shrub in the foreground overtops the oak that has numbered its centuries. The hill under our eye looms higher than the the snowy Alps which skirt the edge of the horizon.

But let us subject this matter to a little closer scrutiny, and see if the annals of the two last centuries alone do not sufficiently admonish us of the mutability of human fame as well as of that of human pursuits. What a vast amount of intellectual power has been expended during that period, which is now dimly seen, or entirely forgotten. The very names of many authors have perished, and the titles of their works are to be gathered only from the dusty pages of some obscure catalogue. What reason can we have to suppose, that much of our own labors will not share a kindred fate? But, turning to another and brighter part of the picture, where the mellowing hand of time has touched with its finest tints the varying figures. Who are there to be seen, but Shakspeare, and Milton, and Bacon, and Locke, and Newton, and Cudworth, and Taylor, and Barrow, not to speak of a host of others, whose works ought to be profoundly studied, and should illustrate every library. I put it to ourselves to say, who are the men of this generation to be brought into comparison with these, in the extent and variety of their labors, the powers of their genius, or the depth of their researches? Who of ourselves can hope to exercise an influence over the human mind as wide-spread as theirs? Who can hope to do more for science, for philosophy, for literature, for theology, than they? I put the argument to our modesty, whether we can dispense with the products of their genius, and wisdom and learning; or may cast aside their works as mere playthings for idlers, or curiosities for collectors of the antique?

I have but glanced at this subject. It would occupy a large discourse to unfold it in its various bearings and consequences. But the strong tendency of our times to disregard the lessons and the authority of the past must have any thing but a salutary effect upon all the complicated interests of literary as well as social life. It not only loosens and disjoints those institutions, which seem indispensable to our common happiness and security; but it puts afloat all those principles which constitute, as it were, the very axioms of all sound philosophy and literature. In no country on earth is the danger of such a tendency so pregnant with fearful results as in our own; for it nurses a spirit of innovation and experiment and oscillation, which leaves no resting-place for sober meditation or permanent progress. It was the striking remark of an acute observer of the human mind, that "He who sets out with doubting, will find life finish, before he becomes master of the rudiments;" and that, "He, who begins by presuming on his own sense, has ended his studies as soon as he has commenced them."[1]

But another danger in our age, and especially in our country, of no small extent, although certainly of a subordinate character, is the vast predominance of the taste for light reading and amusing compositions over that for solid learning and severe and suggestive studies. This has been gradually upon the increase ever since the commencement of the present century, and has become not only the fashion, but I may say, the passion of the day. It has been fostered by, and in its turn it has administered to, our periodical literature, which, from small beginnings, has at length accumulated to such a mass, as threatens to overwhelm all the other departments of literature and bury them under its avalanches. Novels and romances, and other exciting fictions, increase upon us with a fearful rapidity, and, in conjunction with periodicals, constitute the staple of nearly all the reading of the reading public. They are circulated in prodigious numbers through the cheap weekly and penny press. They are found with all the studied attractions and ornaments of

[1] Sir Joshua Reynolds, Discourses, p. 15.

letter-press and engraving upon the centre-tables of the refined and wealthy, piled up with a gay and varied profusion. They line the saloons of our hotels and boarding-houses. They fly on our railroads, and swim in our steamboats, with a dazzling and almost dizzy activity. Not a passenger-ship crosses the Atlantic, which is not freighted with the wet sheets of the last weekly or monthly, or quarterly, or the last story of the Jameses and Blessingtons and Bulwers. And, thanks to our good stars, sometimes they bring also, for our refreshment and delight, the thrilling pathos, and touching humor, of that marvellous genius of all work, the author of the " Old Curiosity Shop."

The consequence is, what might naturally be expected, that many of our best minds, and especially those, who pant for early distinction, devote all their thoughts and all their time to labors of this sort. They are seduced by the eager appetite of the public for novelty, and the ready returns both of money and reputation, to abandon more serious and less attractive studies. They turn with indifference or disgust from topics, which require profound investigation or severe criticism. They become impatient of the slow progress towards excellence, and of the long and cold researches, which satisfied the desires of the men of other days, who were content to bide their time, and await the award of posterity. They seek not to build the lofty poetry, which shall speak to the hearts of a thousand generations. They meditate not those high enterprises in philosophy, in history, in theology, or in jurisprudence, which, when once accomplished, will live on and instruct mankind, when the spot, which covers the ashes of their authors, shall be forgotten or obliterated from the records of time. They seek the ribands and the wreaths, and the shouts of applause of the passing crowd, and forget that they are not fame, — but, at best, mere glitter and show and sound. They come as shadows, and as such they will assuredly depart. The white foam of the combing billow dies away at the moment, when it breaks upon the shore. But the depths of the ocean remain undisturbed and noiseless; for they belong to the things of eternity.

Who, that looks around him does not perceive, what a vast amount of the intellectual power and energy of our own country is expended, not to say exhausted, upon temporary and fugitive topics, — upon occasional addresses, — upon light and fantastic compositions,— upon manuals of education, and hand-books of instruction,— upon annotations and excerpts, and upon the busy and evanescent discussions of politics, which fret their hour upon the stage, or infest the halls of legislation. Need we be told, that honors thus acquired, melt away at the very moment, when we grasp them; that some new wonder will soon usurp their place; and, in its turn, will be chased away or dissolved by the next bubble or flying meteor. I know, that it has sometimes been said, that "nothing popular can be frivolous; and that what influences multitudes must be of proportionate importance."[1] A more dangerous fallacy, lurking under the garb of philosophy, could scarcely be stated. There would be far more general truth in the statement of the very reverse proposition. We construct all sorts of machinery for the ready diffusion of science, and the circulation of philosophy. Our lecture-rooms and lyceums are crowded, day after day, and night after night, with those, who seek instruction without labor, and demand improvement without effort. We have abundance of zeal and abundance of curiosity enlisted in the cause, with little aim at solid results or practical ends. It seems no longer necessary, in the view of many persons, for students to consume their midnight lamps in pale and patient researches, — or in communing with the master spirits of other days, — or in interrogating the history of the past, — or in working out, with a hesitating progress, the great problems of human life. An attendance upon a few courses of lectures upon science, or art, or literature, amidst brilliant gas lights, or brilliant ex-

[1] See Sir J. Mackintosh's Life, vol. i. p. 131.

periments, or brilliant discourses of accomplished rhetoricians, are deemed satisfactory substitutes for hard personal study, in all the general pursuits of life. Nay, the capital stock thus acquired may be again retailed out to less refined audiences, and give ready fame and profit to the second-hand adventurer.

It is an old saying, that there is no royal road to learning; and it is just as true now, as it was two thousand years ago. Knowledge, deep, thorough, accurate, must be sought, and can be found, only by strenuous labor, not for months, but for years; not for years, but for a whole life. What lies on the surface is easily seen, and easily measured. What lies below is slowly reached, and must be cautiously examined. The best ore may often be required to be sifted and purified. The diamond slowly receives its polish under the hands of the workman, and then only gives out its sparkling lights. The very marble, whose massy block is destined to immortalize some great name, reluctantly yields to the chisel; and years must elapse before it becomes (as it were) instinct with life, and stands forth the breathing image of the original. To sketch the outlines of Hallam's noble Introduction to the History of Modern Literature, required studies so vast and various, that the libraries of all America would not at this very moment furnish the means of consulting, far less of mastering, the original authors. And yet we are apt to imagine, that few books need now be read in order to reach the depths of any art or science.

The consciousness of this very state of public opinion cannot but operate as a discouragement upon sensitive minds, and weaken their ambition for the attainment of high excellence. But, above all, that which, as I think, hangs with the deadliest weight upon the literary enterprise of American authors, is (what has been already alluded to) the perpetual necessity of catering to the false taste and morbid appetite of the mass of readers for temporary excitement, or for indolent amusement. How few, comparatively speaking, are found among our scholars, who devote their lives to the study of some great subject, with a view to embody their thoughts and acquirements, so that they may belong to the literature of future ages. How few are there, who can see, without dismay, the accumulation of materials around them, upon the mastery of which they are to found their own fame. How few can, with a calm and quiet consciousness of their own merit, see volume after volume fall from the press almost without notice or patronage, and yet be content to wait, until the voice of praise reaches them from a distance, — from the closets of the learned, and the schools of the philosophers. Speaking of the first volume of his great History of England, Mr. Hume, with quiet modesty, remarked: "My bookseller told me, that in a twelvemonth he sold only forty-five copies. I scarcely heard of one man in the three kingdoms, considerable for rank or letters, that could endure the book." But with the pride of a great mind, some years afterwards, he added: "I see many symptoms of my literary reputation's breaking out at last with additional lustre." What a cheering, what an impressive example!

I rejoice to say, that there are scholars in our country, who have avoided the beaten and dusty paths of every-day reputation, and have been willing to labor, — unseen and unheeded, — for a more enduring distinction. And they have gloriously won the prize. There are historians, and biographers, and mathematicians, and painters, and sculptors, and poets, and divines, who have been content for years to live on hopes, nourished in their own bosoms, or whispered only by the gentle spirit of private friendship, while they have been toiling for immortality. Meanwhile the press has rung its merry peals throughout the continent, for the favorites of the day. And where are these favorites now? They have perished, and their very names have died away, like the memory of an echo. There is a fine remark of Lord Bacon,[1] that "He that seeketh to be eminent among able men, hath a great task;

[1] 2 Bacon's Works, p. 345.

but that is ever good for the public. But he, that plots to be only the figure among ciphers, is the decay of a whole age."

And then again another danger, following close in the train of that, which I have been considering, is the feverish ambition for an artificial structure of style in all classes of composition. We no longer relish the quiet, easy, and idiomatic tones of the olden literature. The flowing grace and simplicity of Addison — the terse yet transparent style of Swift, — the natural yet elegant diction of Goldsmith, — the playful humor, and colloquial familiarity of Lamb, mixed up with deep reflections, and occasionally sprinkled with quaint phraseology, — these are no longer in the possession of the public favor. If they are not deemed dull, they are passed by with indifference. They are more often praised, than they are read. They hold, indeed, a certain conventional rank; but it is more as a matter of courtesy to escape debate, than of sincere love of what is true or beautiful. We require a more intense and exciting style, — strong and animated language — sudden and vivid contrasts, — abrupt changes, and unexpected turns of thought, — high coloring, and wild, and (it may be) startling figure of speech. And so that the story tells, and the narrative flies on, or the satire scorches, or the humor is broadcast in its lights, we are quite content, that the composition should be any sort of mosaic work, — interlaid with scraps of poetry or prose, — the classical or the new, — the quaint or the legendary, — the cant phrases of France or the mystical combinations of Germany. Everywhere we miss the raciness and richness of the Anglo-Saxon idiom, and even the ponderous vigor of the Roman roots forced into the native soil. To borrow the language of an eminent critic; "The grand defect is the want of repose, — too much and too ingenious reflection, — too uniform an ardor of feeling. The understanding is fatigued; the heart ceases to feel."[1]

And this again nourishes that dangerous facility of writing,

[1] Mackintosh's Life, vol. i. p. 407.

which is one of the most alluring temptations, and at the same time the most insidious foe of genius. He, who can throw off in a few hours the brilliant passages of his own mind upon transitory or local topics, and become the artificer of the leading article of a review, or miscellany, or annual, that flowers, and flourishes, and fades within the year; — he who puts forth his hasty pamphlet, upon the engrossing interest or stirring politics of the day; — he earns his passing fame with an easy promptitude, and may circulate freely among the wits of the club, and the coteries of the drawing-room. He, who writes well enough to please and pleases well enough to be paid, as well as to be read, is but too apt to forget, that nothing valuable is suddenly acquired; that what is enduring must be costly, in time, in labor, in design, in intellectual effort. The veriest tyro in colors can paint a picture with lights and shades and false brilliancies, which may attract and deceive the vulgar eye. The common sculptor may mould the human features with a light and facile hand, or carve them into the cold rigidity of stone. But the great artists of ancient and modern times wrought not out so their mighty labors. The Apollo, the Venus, the Gladiator, the Guliano, and Lorenzo de Medicis, grew not thus under the chisel of the artists. The Madonna, the Last Supper, the Day of Judgment, sprung not from the dashing touches of the moment. Time may truly be said, with these great minds, to have been the parent of immortality.

In close alliance with the foregoing will be found another and kindred danger to scholarship. If the public taste thus acts upon the studies and products of authors, and fashions their works for the market of the day,

"If those, who live to please, must please to live,"

it is not less true, that it reacts upon readers with a reciprocal malign influence. Their time is equally wasted in the indulgence of a varied and sometimes superficial round of reading, which vitiates, while it pampers the appetite. All is desultory and miscellaneous; crowded, and yet fleeting. The viands are dressed up in new form and fantasies; but still they are neither wholesome, nor satisfying. They cloy the taste without nourishing the soul. According to the temperament of the reader, his love of letters melts away under the soft sentimentalism of fiction, or wearies itself in drowsy indolence, or exhausts itself in private meditations, or rises into mystical reveries, very unintelligible, but not on that account less inviting.

It cannot admit of the slightest doubt, (at least in my judgment,) that the habit of desultory and miscellaneous reading, thus created, has a necessary tendency to enervate the mind, and to destroy all masculine thinking. Works of a solid cast, which require close attention and exact knowledge to grapple with them, are thrown aside, as dull and monotonous. We apologize to ourselves for our neglect of them, that they are to be taken up at a more convenient season; or we flatter ourselves, that we have sufficiently mastered their contents and merits from the last review, although in many cases it may admit of some doubt, whether the critic himself has ever read the work. Without stopping to inquire, how many of the whole class of literary readers now study with thoughtful diligence, the standard writers in our own language, and are not content with abridgments, or manuals, or extracts; I would put it to those, who are engaged in the learned professions, and have the most stringent motives for deep, thorough, and exact knowledge, I would put it to them to say, how many of their whole number devote themselves to the study of the great masters of their own profession. How many of them can, in the sober language of truth, say, We are at home in the pages of our profoundest authors, — We not only possess them to enrich our libraries, but we devote ourselves to the daily consultation of them. They are beside us at our firesides, and they cheer our evening studies. We live and breathe in the midst of their laborious researches and systematical learning.

If the seductive influences of this habit of desultory and miscellaneous reading and indulgence in general literature, were confined to persons of unbroken leisure, or indolent temperament, or moderate ambition, the evil would be far less felt, and the example far less mischievous. But it is apt to draw within its grasp the proudest spirits of the age. Many of the latter have the same insatiable appetite, if I may so say, for universal reading, — the same love of change, — the same eager search after novelty, which belong to the gay and the frivolous in their light pursuits. They amass vast treasures of knowledge, but use them, far less for composition, than for conversation; far less as materials, out of which they are to create works, destined for future ages, than as means for brilliant sallies in colloquial discourse, or for sunny disquisitions upon moral philosophy, or for picturesque sketches, or for off-hand contributions to the forthcoming periodical. They have learned well the lesson of Lord Bacon, that "Studies serve for delight, for ornament, and for ability. Their chief use for delight is in privateness and retiring; for ornament is in discourse; and for ability is in the judgment and disposition of business."[1] But they have forgotten the noble admonition of the same great mind, that "Wise men use their studies; and that there is a wisdom without them, and above them, won by observation. That they read, not to contradict or confute, nor to find talk and discourse; but to weigh and consider."[2]

There is, indeed, and for a considerable length of time, has been, a strong temptation to scholars to establish reputation by bringing their resources into full play in conversation among the higher circles of social life; and in our own times it has acquired a powerful impulse and acceleration among the affluent in learning and the elevated in genius. Dr. Johnson seems almost for the first time to have given it an attractive character by his own example and gigantic powers, both in

[1] Bacon's Essays. Essay 50, vol. ii. of his Works, p. 373. [2] Ibid.

reading and thinking. The glorious circle of great minds, who clustered around him, Reynolds and Burke and Goldsmith and Jones and Scott, and the gay wits of London, who listened with a just homage to his controversial dogmas, and untiring flow of thought, made it a fashionable object of ambition to become great in conversation. It may well be doubted, whether even Dr. Johnson, owing to this seductive influence, ever accomplished any thing commensurate with the powers of his understanding, or the variety of his knowledge. With the exception of his Dictionary, (a work of vast labor, if not of critical skill,) his best writings belong almost to the very close of his life; and if Boswell had not recorded his conversations with a graphical fidelity and fulness, which makes them the very familiars of our household, the fame of that great man, after a life of seventy-five years, would mainly rest upon two poems, in imitation of Juvenal, and upon his Lives of the Poets, which, with the exception of some half dozen Lives, wrought out with marvellous felicity and vigor, were but common task-work for the booksellers. I might mention Doctor Parr as another singular example of vast erudition, superior in this respect even to Johnson, and in general acquirements quite his equal, who has rendered himself famous for having exhausted his long life mainly upon a Spital sermon, and an edition of Bellendenus, neither of which is now read; and yet if he had loved reading and conversation less, and composition more, he might have stood in classical and other literature among the foremost of his age. He lives now, rather by the bright sayings, preserved by his biographers, and by his private letters, than by any literary achievement, worthy of remembrance.

But, for an example still more instructive, and far more interesting and affecting, let us turn to one of the most philosophical and polished scholars of our own day, I mean Sir James Mackintosh, whose genius has illuminated whatever it has touched, and touched almost every department of literature. Whoever has read the memoirs of that excellent man,

64*

written with an unassuming elegance, and a just filial reverence, by an accomplished scholar, must have risen from the perusal with mixed emotions of profound respect and profound melancholy. What do we here see, but a mind of the brightest order and most varied attainments, perpetually struggling with its own infirmity of purpose,—amassing, nay, devouring, all sorts of learning, with an eager and discriminating attention, sketching the outlines of the plan of some great work, and resolving at some future time to execute it,—rebuking its own delays, and yet persisting in the same course,—and at last, departing from the world, in a good old age, without having achieved any one of the loftier purposes, at which it aimed. Everywhere about us are the mighty fragments of his genius, like the mutilated Torso, exhibiting, in its broken proportions, the exquisite skill of the artist. His Introductory Lecture on the Law of Nations, the most magnificent discourse in our own, or perhaps, in any other language, is but a finished portico for the vestibule of a temple, destined never to be erected. And, again, his Historical Dissertation upon the Progress of Ethical Science, which it is impossible to read without kindling into enthusiasm, leaves us, with its bright but rapid lights, just on the threshold of the very inquiries, to which it points its way. And then, again, his contributions to the History of England seem but interludes between the acts and epochs of that great drama, where the curtain dops, just when the principal actors are about to play their parts on that grand theatre of human life. What can be more melancholy, or more full of regrets, than the contemplation of such a mind, so comprehensive in learning, so elevated in virtues, which has thus passed away, leaving so many admirable enterprises unaccomplished, and so many plans for immortality unfulfilled.

It may be said, that all this is the result of peculiar temperament. I think far otherwise; it is the natural result of the seductive influences, of which I have spoken, and of the profuse expenditure of intellectual power upon ends and aims, incompatible with enduring excellence, which is so much fostered by the spirit of our age. How difficult must it be to resist the temptations to universal reading, and the fascinations of colloquial discourse, when they win instant praise, and circulate freely to the very boundaries of the literary world. For one, who, with a stout heart and determined perseverance, could resist them, and die, like Sir Walter Scott, with his pen in his hand, there are hundreds who would surrender themselves the willing, or the reluctant, victims to their influence, and resolve and re-resolve, and yet close their lives in the midst of hopes deferred, and expectations blasted, and projects abandoned.

I have thus far spoken of some of the existing dangers to the permanent interests of learning and literature; and in so doing I have anticipated much which belongs to the consideration of the discouragements and difficulties of scholars in our day. Many other admonitory and interesting reflections might, however, be added upon the latter topic; but I shall content myself with a few suggestions only, addressed partly to our own peculiar national position, and partly to general causes at work throughout the world. One, indeed, which must strike even the most careless observer is the vast accumulation, in every department of knowledge, of new materials, which are to be mastered, in comparison with the old stock. The brief but pungent apothegm, that life is short, and art is long, could never come home to the bosoms and business of scholars with more significance than in the present age. Hitherto, the task of completing the round of studies for a well-disciplined mind in any one department, seemed to lie within a comparatively moderate compass. But the mass has now increased to an almost overwhelming size, (to use the language of Sir Henry Spelman,) *Molem non ingentem solum, sed perpetuis humeris sustinendam.* In some sciences whole branches have sprung into being within the last fifty years, while others have received such vast additions, that the old foundations have been buried under the substructions of the new. The learned professions have received a like augmentation of principles and materials. Five hundred volumes would, a half century ago, have been deemed sufficient for all the ordinary exigencies of study, where five thousand volumes would now scarcely meet the daily demands, for consultation or instruction. Medicine has changed, not merely its systems and theories, and its formularies, but, through the instrumentality of chemistry, it has created a new *materia medica*, and a new nomenclature. Anatomy and surgery, and physiological research, have elevated into science what seemed before but a humbler department of art. Theology, in its dogmatical, exegetical, and critical inquiries, has made our libraries groan under the weight and variety of its contributions. In former times the ablest divines might content themselves with a few solid bodies of divinity, the best sermons of the old school, and some helps to criticism and exposition, in the shape of common-place books or concordances, illustrated by the standard guides in Ecclesiastical History. How changed is all this now! Jurisprudence has unfolded its stores with an equal profusion; and it is scarcely too much to say, that it is now practically impossible to read all that is published; and the task of selection alone has become at once perilous and indispensable. In the mean time, the inquisitive and skeptical spirit of the age makes the duty of instruction, as well as that of the exposition and vindication of doctrines, full of labor and difficulty. Especially is this true in theology and the higher branches of philosophy. Here the scholar must give a life of patient diligence to the task; and will find, that if he is read by many, he will be praised by few. His very learning may make his labors repulsive; and the very depth of his researches may discourage his faltering followers. His deficiencies will be studiously proclaimed, while the profounder results of his analysis are unheeded. Here, he will offend the prejudices of the day by a bold and fearless criticism, and there, he will encounter a dogma, which staggers his faith, or brings into question his prudence or his judgment. If he appeals to posterity, he may, indeed, reap a just though distant reward, when the passions and parties of the day shall have passed away. But then it may happen, that the appeal may never reach that tribunal; or, if it should, the changes of fashions and feelings and opinions may make his claim a slender inheritance, even if it should be recognized and confirmed. Under such circumstances, well may he be inclined to shun the toil of the enterprise, and exclaim: *Ostendunt hæc tantùm fata, — neque ultra.*

Look for a moment upon the exhausting demands of the pulpit. Instead of listening to plain, calm, and practical expository discourses, as in former times, we have now become fastidious and exacting critics. We require, every Sunday, the exhibitions of varied talents, dressed up with all the polished elegance and refinement of an exquisite taste. We seek, I had almost said, we demand, one or more sermons to be produced every week, which would require the meditations of the most gifted mind for a whole month; and of such a quality of excellence, that probably no single mind, in the history of the profession, ever produced twelve of them in any one year. This is not all. The discourses must be wrought out with somewhat of dramatic power and effect. They must be eloquent, as well as instructive; pointed, as well as true; vivid, as well as thoughtful. They must win by their persuasive approaches, even more than they strike by their masculine reasoning. They may, indeed, reprove vice with a bold and fearless confidence, if it shocks by its grossness or revolting character. They may unmask hypocrisy, and denounce error, in good round terms. But they must deal gently with frailties, which are broadcast, and "just hint a fault or hesitate dislike," if it be a favorite folly of the day, which fashion has consecrated, and public opinion tolerates. Now, I think, that I do not exaggerate the difficulties and discouragements of the profession in our day, when I say, that the demands upon the preacher for ready compositions, and parochial duties, make it almost impracticable for him to attain eminence in biblical criticism, and disable him from writing works, which will be enduring monuments of his learning and ability, when he shall be gathered to his fathers.

Look again upon the scholar, who seeks eminence in classical studies. What a vast apparatus is now required to enable him to grapple with the intricacies of Grecian and Roman literature, its criticism, and its historical illustrations, or even the niceties of the grammatical structure of the language. It is a startling fact, that many a ripe scholar, even in patient and inquisitive and laborious Germany, will tell you, that there is not time, in any one life, to learn well more than a single language; that if one devotes himself to Greek, Latin is out of the question; and, that the study of a whole life may well be dedicated to the mastery of a single classical author, and even then, that much will be left untouched, or unexplained. Nay, Roman jurisprudence, which, after the criticisms of three centuries, seemed to have arrived at a fixed point in its expositions and principles, has now become suddenly changed in its aspects, and some of its elements have been displaced by the learned labors of living jurists, aided by the discovery of the Institutes of Gaius. And, as if ancient history itself were not secure against the inroads of modern speculation and industry, we are now told, that the historians of Rome totally mistook many of the facts, which they undertook to narrate from earlier traditions; and that we, in the nineteenth century, can by more profound researches, correct errors and explain transactions, which, for eighteen hundred years, were unquestioned, or were deemed irretrievably lost. It was not many years ago, that some of us were almost startled out of our proprieties by the doubt, whether any such person as Homer ever existed; and Niebuhr has so shaken the public confidence in the ancient historians, that a widespread alarm has infected our belief in the credibility of their chronicles.

Nor is the task of the instructor, or of the disciple, in intellectual or moral philosophy less formidable. If he could unfold the various systems of metaphysics, or of ethics, where is he to begin, or rather, where is he to end, his researches? His descent into the depths, and his ascent from them, are not among the facile operations of the human mind in our day.

> "In the lowest deep a lower deep,
> Still threatening to devour him, opens wide."[1]

If he has read half of what has been already written on these subjects, he has achieved a most gigantic enterprise. But if he would subdue the whole to his own purposes, and take but a moderate survey of the stores of scholastic logic and philosophy, deposited on the slumbering shelves of the public libraries of both continents, human life would not be long enough to complete his task. Here, at least, we must be content, not only, as Lord Bacon says, to read by deputy, but to think by deputy.

These are difficulties, which beset all scholars in our times from the profusion, and, as it were, from the very inundations, of learning. There are others, again, which press upon American scholars with peculiar force. Two opposite bands of disciplined troops break in upon our academical pursuits, as well as our literary repose, and threaten a protracted, if not a successful, warfare. They are embodied on one side under the leaders of what is called the Utilitarian System of knowledge, and on the other, under the clamorous advocates for an American literature, indigenous, exclusive, and national. Upon the former topic I do not purpose to touch. Upon the latter I would say a few words, as it constitutes the staple of so many of our public addresses, and ambitious essays. What do we mean by a National Literature? Do we mean by it a literature fostered and cultivated by American authors, addressing themselves to themes common to the world of letters? Or, do we mean by it a literature, which deals

[1] See Milton's Paradise Lost, B. 4, l. 76.

altogether in local topics, and busies itself only with institutions, and manners, and feelings, and discussions, peculiar to ourselves? If the former, it would be an idle waste of time to discuss the subject. The cultivation of literature in any country must essentially depend upon general causes, which rarely admit of much acceleration or retardation in their progress. An enduring literature must almost necessarily be of slow growth. It cannot be raised in the hot-beds of patronage or of power alone. It must spring up spontaneously, and be congenial to the soil. It can acquire excellence only, when the process of ripening is in a healthy air and a robust climate. It presupposes the existence of a large class of educated men, beyond what the steady demands of civil, political, and professional life require, for the advancement of the general interests of the society. It presupposes, that the rewards of other employments are not more certain and more tempting; more inviting from their relative facility of being reached; or more sure of conducting the aspirants to the repose and dignity of independence. It presupposes general wealth enough in the community to afford leisure to a large class of scholars to devote themselves to the highest pursuits of ambition, and the attainment of an imperishable fame; so that they may be content to wait for distant results. It presupposes, that it will afford a competent livelihood, to repay the exhausting labors of authorship,—for painful days, and wakeful nights, which move heavily on in the midst of secret and solitary studies, and indifference, and ill-health, and poverty. Until these things exist,—nay, until they in a great measure coexist, and act and react simultaneously upon each other, it is in vain to call for national literature and national authors. There must be patronage, liberal, constant, and comprehensive, as well as genius and talent, in the land. The public must be ready to reward authors as well as to praise them; to protect as well as to read their works; to encourage the domestic manufacture by giving it a reciprocal market abroad. Until this period shall arrive, it will be in vain to ask, or even to hope for a solid advancement in national literature. There may be, and there will be, occasional bursts of literary talent; but they will be irregular and transitory. There may be, and there will be, here and there, an author of exquisite elegance, or profound research; but for the most part, the lights will be flickering and faint, and do little more than skirt our horizon.

But if we mean by a national literature the other alternative before alluded to, a literature devoted to local thoughts, objects, interests, habits, and feelings, which shall stand out, like our lakes and rivers and waterfalls, with a sort of territorial magnificence or sovereignty (as is but too often the suggestion of national pride); then it might be worth while to consider, whether it were desirable, if attainable; or if attained, whether it would not sink us down to the level of a provincial dependency rather than elevate us to the rank of equals in the republic of letters. It is true, that the vanity of possessing the home market might lead us to address nothing to foreign minds, or to foreign sympathies; that we might clothe ourselves with the common fabrics and costumes, manufactured to the order and fashion of the day, without dreaming that they might possess neither grace nor dignity, and would be rejected by the taste, as well as be unsuited to the good sense of other ages. To the great author, seeking for permanent fame, may be addressed the same language which has been addressed to the great painter. "He must divest himself of all prejudices in favor of his age or country; he must disregard all local and temporary ornaments; and look only to those general habits which are everywhere, and always the same. He addresses his works to the people of every country and every age; he calls upon posterity to be his spectators; and says, with Zeuxis, '*In æternitatem pingo.*'"[1]

Nay, I will go farther, and venture to affirm, that no author

[1] Sir Joshua Reynolds's Discourses, p. 59.

of any nation has ever attained permanent celebrity, whose works have not in fact been addressed to sentiments, feelings, sympathies, and experiences, common to the human soul in all countries, and all ages. There may be found a few persons whose works paint transactions, which are purely local, or transient, and who may thus enlist the curiosity of the diligent antiquarian; but it is rather as specimens than as models. The mass of authors in ancient as well as in modern times, who are familiarly read, or extensively known,— are read and known, because their thoughts belong to all generations, and have inflamed the genius and warmed the hearts of the instructed as well as of the rude. The orators, the poets, the philosophers, and the historians of Greece and Rome are admired, not merely for the exquisite language in which their works are clothed, but for the lessons of wisdom which they teach; for the truths which they expound; for the beautiful and sublime imagery which they exhibit; and for the large results of human passions and human actions which they narrate or suggest. These are just as striking, and just as important and useful now as they were thousands of years ago. The works of Aristotle and Cicero have probably furnished more materials for instruction upon all the topics, of which they treat, than those of any other authors who have flourished before or since their times. There is not a single page of Sallust or Tacitus, even when professedly discussing motives, or recording events which now seem almost evanescent points of history, which are not replete with sound philosophy, with profound reflection, with acute analysis, of character, manners, and government, and with principles of universal application, which deserve to be treasured up as among the most valuable benefactions to the human race. To no nation on earth are the truths there unfolded, and the commentaries there condensed, of more importance than to ourselves. We may there see, how factions are engendered and how republics are ruined. How men in free governments become base, and servile, and corrupt, as well as, how they must act, in order to maintain the strength, the glory, and the well-balanced liberty of the State. Who does not read the common fate of republics, when Sallust, with searching severity, says; "Ubi labore atque justitia Respublica crevit, — sævire Fortuna, ac miscere omnia cœpit. Qui labores, pericula, dubias atque asperas res facilè toleraverunt, iis otium, divitiæ, optandæ aliis, oneri miseræque fuere. Igitur primo pecuniæ, deinde Imperii Cupido, crevit; ea quasi materies omnium malorum fuere."[1] Who does not see in his brief, but startling sketch of Catiline, the profligate demagogue of every age and country, at once crafty, selfish, variable, bold, and ambitious. "Animus audax, subdolus, varius, cujuslibet rei simulator ac dissimulator, alieni appetens, sui profusus, ardens in cupiditatibus, satis eloquentiæ, sapientiæ parum."[2] Who does not see the fawning sycophants and base retainers, waiting upon power and patronage, who pursue its triumph and partake its gale, in a single passage of Tacitus, of terrific grandeur, alluding to a period, when even fallen Rome yet affected liberty. "At Romæ ruere in servitium, Consules, Patres, Eques. Quanto quis illustrior, tanto magis falsi ac festinantes, vultuque composito, ne læti excessu Principis, neu tristiores primordio, lacrimas, gaudium, questus, adulatione miscebant."[3]

These great men wrote not to foster the pride, or the tastes, or the prejudices of their own country. They wrote not for Rome, but for the world; not for their own age, but for all posterity. Sallust avows this to be his own motive; conscious (as he says) that virtuous fame alone is immortal. "Mihi rectius esse videtur, ingenii, quam virium opibus, gloriam quærere, et quoniam vita ipsa, quâ fruimur, brevis est, memoriam nostri, quam maxume longam efficere. Nam divitiarum et formæ gloria fluxa atque fragilis; virtus clara æternaque habetur."[4] I have reserved (said Tacitus) a more

1 Sallust. Bell. Catil. § 10.

2 Ibid. § 6.

3 Tacit. Annal. Lib. 1, cap. 7.

4 Sallust, Bell. Catil. § 1.

fertile and secure subject for my old age, when, owing to the rare felicity of the times, you are at liberty to think what you please, and to speak what you think. "Uberiorem securioremque materiam senectuti seposui, rara temporum felicitate, ubi sentire quæ velis, et quæ sentias dicere licet."[1] A fit lesson to be learned even in this favored land; for, here, no mean courage is sometimes required, to speak what we think, when it strikes at some prevalent delusion; or to abstain from flattering the prejudices of the people, when the truth might offend them.

But I need not refer to the ancients. All countries and all ages furnish the same illustrations. There is not (I repeat it) a great author, who has come down to us with literary celebrity, whose pages are not addressed to interests, affections, and principles, common to all mankind. Tell me the author, who, since the revival of letters, has attained and still holds a settled eminence, in Italy, or Germany, or France, or England, whose writings are not felt to be the inheritance of the world? His works may have a strong flavor of the soil where they were produced; they may be tinctured with the colors of the age, in which they lived; they may even be soiled and stained by its vices, or its follies, or its affectations. But these blemishes and peculiarities are accidental and unfelt, and serve but to present in a broader light their intrinsic excellences,—as the blur in the diamond reveals its imperfections, without diminishing the vivid sparkles from its transparent surface. Who, for a moment, could imagine, that Dante, or Tasso, or Shakspeare, or Milton, or Locke, or Klopstock, or Goethe, or Schiller, or Racine, wrote solely for their own times and their own country; and did not possess the proud consciousness, that they would be read by future generations in every nation, where letters should be cherished, however refined and however remote. "My name and memory," (was the affecting and melancholy language of Lord

[1] Tacit. Hist. lib. 1, cap. 1.

Bacon, in his last will,) "My name and memory I leave to foreign nations, and to mine own countrymen, after some time be passed over."

There could not, indeed, be a more dangerous delusion, than the attempt on the part of American authors to build up an exclusive national literature in the sense, to which I have last alluded. Our just ambition should be to make our literature a component part of the literature of the world, for the use of all nations and all ages. Let it have the bold impress of American genius, and the masculine vigor, and the brave spirit of inquiry and expression, which fitly belong to a free government, and an unshackled press. But let it rise to the dignity and elevation of an appeal to the highest minds in their highest studies, wherever their nativity may be cast. Let it speak a universal language, and address passions, feelings, sympathies, and principles, which glow with equal fervor at the poles and at the equator. Let the thoughts be such, as may save the language itself from perishing. Let them live on, and bless, and improve mankind, and unfold to them their duty and their destiny, until the period shall arrive, when tyrants and barbarians shall consign all books to a common destruction, as an incumbrance upon anarchy or despotism.

And this leads me to say a few words, and but a few words, for

> "On our quickest decrees
> The inaudible and noiseless foot of time
> Steals, ere we can effect them,"

upon the duties of scholars in our day, and especially of American scholars. Much of what has been already said points its moral to this end and object. We have seen some of our dangers and difficulties. They may not be disguised, or concealed; but they must be met and confronted with a firm confidence and steady perseverance. The time has come, when the study of the ancient classics, of the great writers of Greece and Rome, is required to be reasoned out and vindicated anew. While it is advancing with a steady pace among a select class of minds, we cannot fail to see, that it is in a proportionate degree holding a less comprehensive influence with the community at large. The sympathies, as well as the attractions, of other pursuits, and the brilliant achievements of physical science, have cast it with the multitude into comparative obscurity. But a more sweeping and impetuous cause is the strong tendency of the day to popular education and popular schemes of instruction. Knowledge, it is now thought, may be acquired with far less labor and in a more brief space. Compendious systems have succeeded the tardy progress and rough discipline of former times. The youthful mind is now required to be crammed with all sorts of learning and science, at a period of life when it can scarcely digest any. We hurry on the work of education with an eager and crowded impatience, and seek to condense the labor of years into that of months. All things are to be taught at the same moment; *Dum fervet opus.* And the appointed course once run over, the preparations of active life are deemed complete; the prizes of life are already within reach; and superfluous study is dismissed, as equally without pleasure and without profit.

It is for American scholars to rouse themselves for the coming events, which cast their shadows before. They must press upon the public attention, with a fearless spirit of expostulation, the utter folly of all such expectations; they must proclaim the solemn fact, that facile methods of education are mere delusions, which cheat us out of our time, as well as impair the vigor of our understandings; that they will make us at once superficial and conceited, and enervate without filling the mind. It has been eloquently said, that "These noble studies preserve, and they alone can preserve, the unbroken chain of learning, which unites the most remote generations; the grand catholic communion of wisdom and wise men, throughout all ages and nations of the world."[1]

[1] Life of Mackintosh, vol. i. p. 119.

But a duty still higher, and more imperative, and urgent, is to stand forth as champions of truth, of sound morals, sound principles, and sound learning. It has been often suggested, as a matter of reproach, by foreigners, that our scholars and statesmen do not speak out to the public their real opinions. That they do not say, what they think, nor think, what they say. That our public harangues, and set pamphlets, and newspaper essays, are abundantly overlaid with flattery of vulgar errors, or popular delusions. That the people have perpetually trumpeted in their ears the praise of their wisdom and virtue and intelligence, when it is apparent, that there is the most sincere distrust of them all, and often the belief, that we are on the downward path of ruin. In short, that the whole body of our passing literature, and the spirit of our public discussions, are moulded and fashioned to suit the ever-varying forms of the popular will, and thus bring discredit upon our judgments, as well as upon our sincerity.

Admitting, that there is much of false and exaggerated statement in these suggestions, still there is truth enough at the bottom to challenge inquiry and demand reform. Has our literature in general a bold, healthy, solid, reflective, masculine character? Does it possess a fearless spirit of expostulation, or reproof, and a lofty avowal of principles, suited to the exigencies of our times? Does it tell the truth, the whole truth, and nothing but the truth, without fear, favor, affection, or hope of reward? Does it combat error, and expose folly, and resist visionary but captivating theories, by stirring appeals to the sober sense of the community, and the enlightened judgments of the wise? When the fundamental principles of republics, nay, of all governments, are assailed with presumptuous rashness, and the rights of property, and the securities of constitutions are assailed and questioned, does our literature come out, and unmask the deceit, and vindicate the truth, or does it lie by, and with indolent ease sleep over the evils, or silently evade its duty by hoping for the best, or softly whisper regrets, lest it should rouse opposition, or encounter obloquy? To these interrogatories let every scholar answer for himself. But let him remember, that these are not times to blink at questions, or to push aside inquiries. Not only is the schoolmaster abroad, but the skeptic is by his side, and the importunate reformer with his nostrums, and the enthusiast with his idealities and abstractions. Christianity itself is called upon, on one side, to buckle on its armor, not to maintain the mere creeds and dogmas of a peculiar church or sect, but to establish its facts and its miracles, nay, the reality of the character, if not the personal existence, of the Founder of its hopes and its consolations. On another side, Protestantism is again required, at the distance of three centuries after its noble triumphs, to show its title-deeds and its rights. It is put upon its defence, and asked for reasons and authority,—for its faith and its observances,—for its priesthood and its ordinances. The assaults come not from Rome alone. The battlements of Oxford frown upon its heresies, and forbid the banns of its alliance with the church. The warders upon her towers rebuke its backslidings, and demand a surrender of its banners and a renunciation of its errors. The blood of the martyrs has been spilled in vain. The warnings of the prophets have been proclaimed in vain. The Taylors, the Cudworths, the Chillingworths, the Barrows, and the Clarkes, have been but blind leaders of the blind. The Puritans and the Covenanters, the Presbyterians and the Congregationalists, the Calvinists and the Lutherans, are to lay down their spiritual arms, and submit to the sentence of the Vatican, pronounced on the banks of the Isis. These, then, are not the days for scholars, and least of all, for American scholars, to relapse into indolent indifference, or to send forth doubtful responses from their oracles, inviting double interpretations. The contest is no longer one with ignorance, or folly, or illiterate skepticism. The voices come from the seats of learning, from the deep studies of the closet, and from the bold speculations of gifted minds, capable of dealing with human rights and human belief. Learning must now be met by learning, talent by talent, genius by genius. The demand is for logic and reasoning, and historical truth, and not for mere dogmas or authority. Vague declamation will not suffice. There must be close, forcible, clear, convincing argumentation.

I might add, if time would allow me, that there are other duties, devolving upon our scholars and statesmen, which come home, at this very moment, to our business and bosoms. To master the great questions, which now agitate, not merely our public councils, but the minds of the whole nation, upon topics of political economy,—of national rights and duties,—of constitutional obligations,—and of social interests, there are required all the resources of our knowledge and experience, the powers of eloquence, the lights of history, the most thorough investigations of the principles of international law. Have there been, and are there now brought to the task, free from the admixture of all extraneous and impure ingredients, the profound and honest judgments of our best scholars and statesmen? Or have the passions and prejudices and interests of the day mingled in the strife, and disturbed all the just influences, which ought to govern the discussions? Has it been left to the great minds, and the enlarged experience, and the learned studies of our best men, to expound subjects, so full of delicate and difficult relations? Have not rash men leaped into the arena, where angels might almost fear to tread, and eagerly sought to forestall the public judgment, by appeals to popular or local interests, or by lofty denunciations of all, who dared to promote calm inquiry, or the severe analysis of principles? One should have thought, that the very gravity of such topics would have suppressed all arrogant assertion, and put to flight all dogmatism and theories; that we should have consulted the oracles of other times, and sought instruction from their wisdom; that we should have invoked the aid of Grotius, and Puffendorf, and Vattel, and Burke, and Adam Smith, and the authors of the Federalist, to enlighten our judgments, and purify our souls from debasing generalities.

And, again, it is the duty of our scholars to elevate the standard of our national literature; to engage it in themes more worthy of our destiny and rank in the republic of letters; to lift it above the petty strifes, the wild fantasies, and the vague novelties of the day. If we may not aspire to the highest efforts of human genius, to the sublimer walks of poetry and philosophy, which dazzle by excess of light, we may yet seek a more elevated region, and breathe a purer air, than broods over the barren plains and misty valleys of common life.

> "Largior hic campos Æther, et lumine vestit
> Purpureo, — Solemque suam, sua sidera nôrant."

Gentlemen, — I have done. As I close this discourse I cannot but turn my eyes to our venerable University, and ask, what she demands of us, her children, for the cause of religion, of letters, and of learning. She has stood forth for centuries, the glorious defender of truth, — unshaken, — unseduced, — unterrified. She has nourished in her bosom the wise, the eloquent, the renowned, the holy. In the days of her adversity, she has borne the brunt and burden without fear or faltering. In the days of her prosperity, she has been content to cultivate learning, and promote the arts of peace. Shall not her children rise up, and call her blessed! At this very moment I seem to see the shades of her departed sons pass slowly before me, — the long procession of two hundred years. They point with deep thoughtfulness to the past, and with earnest solicitude to the future. Their silence, more expressive than any human speech, addresses to us, at once, the language of admonition, — of exhortation, — of encouragement, — of entreaty. Methinks, as their shadowy forms glide away, the silence is for a moment broken, and I hear their united voices, in unearthly tones, utter, from beyond the grave,

> "O! Socii, — Antiquam exquirite Matrem."

SKETCHES OF JUDGES AND LAWYERS.

SKETCH

OF THE LIFE AND CHARACTER OF SAMUEL DEXTER.

[This sketch formed the concluding part of a Charge, delivered to the Grand Jury, at the Circuit Court holden at Boston, in the District of Massachusetts, in May, 1816; and was then published, at the joint request of the Grand Jury and the members of the Bar of the Circuit Court.]

I HAVE now finished the brief review of those offences which are most important in the criminal code of the United States. And happy should I be, if I could congratulate you on the peace and general prosperity of our country, without mingling emotions of a painful nature. But how is it possible to enter this hall of justice, and cast my eyes among my brethren at the bar, without missing one, who, for many years, has been its distinguished ornament?

On ordinary occasions of the loss of private or professional friends, we may properly bury our sorrows in our own bosoms. In such cases the public do not feel that deep sympathy which authorizes us to speak aloud our anguish and disquietude. But when such men as Mr. Dexter die, the loss is emphatically a public loss, and the mourners are the whole nation. To give utterance to our feelings is, therefore, a solemn duty. It is fit, that the example of the great and good should be brought forward, for the imitation of the young and ambitious; that gratitude for eminent services should find a voice as public as the deeds; and that exalted genius, when it has ceased to attract admiration by its living splendor, should be consecrated in the memories of those whom it has instructed or preserved.

I feel assured, therefore, that I am not stepping aside from the path of duty, or pressing unduly upon your attention, by devoting a few minutes of your time to a sketch of the history and character of this illustrious lawyer and statesman.

Mr. Dexter was descended from a highly respectable parentage. His grandfather was a clergyman. His father, the Hon. Samuel Dexter, was a merchant, and resided many years at Boston, where his son Samuel was born in the year 1761. The father early distinguished himself in the struggles between the Crown and the people of Massachusetts, previous to the Revolution; and, for his public services, was several times elected to the Council by the House of Representatives, and as often rejected by the royal governor of the province. He was at length admitted to a seat in the Council by the prudence or the fears of the executive; but in 1774 was again negatived "by the express command of his majesty." Towards the close of his life he retired altogether from public affairs, and engaged in a profound investigation of the great doctrines of theology. At his death he bequeathed a handsome legacy to Harvard University, for the encouragement of biblical criticism; and upon this honorable foundation, the Dexter lectureship has since been established.

Mr. Dexter, the son, after the usual preparatory studies, was matriculated at Harvard University in 1777, and received the usual degree of bachelor of arts in 1781. During his residence at the University, he gave ample promise of those talents, which shed so much lustre on his riper years. At a public exhibition he delivered a poem, which was at that time received with great applause, and is still considered as highly creditable to his taste and judgment. On receiving his degree, he was selected for the first literary honors in his class, which he sustained with increasing reputation.

He now determined to engage in the profession of the law, a science, whose acute distinctions and logical structure were wonderfully adapted to invigorate and develop the powers of his understanding. He passed the usual preparatory term at Worcester, under the tuition of the Hon. Levi Lincoln, then an eminent counsellor at the bar, and since Lieutenant Governor of the Commonwealth. During this period, and for several years after his admission to the bar, Mr. Dexter devoted himself with unceasing assiduity to acquire the elements of law; and, as may be easily supposed from his great abilities, he was completely successful in his purposes. Notwithstanding many discouragements of a public nature, which, at that time pressed heavily on young lawyers, Mr. Dexter rose rapidly into professional notice, and soon found himself surrounded with clients and business. In a short time he was chosen to the State Legislature; and his sound judgment and comprehensive policy gave him great weight and influence in all the deliberations of that body. From the State Legislature he was transferred to the Congress of the United States, being first elected to the House of Representatives, and afterwards to the Senate, by the suffrages of his native State. Perhaps there has been no period since the establishment of the government, which more imperiously demanded all the foresight virtue, and discretion of the ablest statesmen, than that in which Mr. Dexter was called to assist in the national councils. The first talents in the respective parties, which then divided the country, were drawn into Congress. The floors of the two houses became a vast amphitheatre, on which the struggles for political power and principle were maintained, with all the eloquence of rhetoric and strength of reasoning, which the zeal of party could enkindle in noble minds. The most deep and impassioned feelings took possession of the nation itself; and the same thrilling sensations which agitated Congress, electrified the whole continent. It seemed as if every power of the human mind was summoned to its proper business, and stretched to the most intense exertion. Many of you can recall the emotions of those days; and to those of us who were then reposing in academic shades, the light that burst from the walls of Congress, seemed reflected back from every cottage in the country. At no period of his life did Mr. Dexter more completely sustain his reputation for extraordinary talents. His clear and forcible argumentation, his earnest and affecting admonitions, and his intrepid and original development of principles and measures, gave him a weight of authority, which it was difficult to resist. Perhaps no man was ever heard by his political opponents with more profound and unaffected respect.

Mr. Dexter resigned his seat in the Senate, on his appointment as Secretary of War, under the administration of President Adams. He next received the office of Secretary of the Treasury; and, during a short period of vacancy, discharged also the functions of the Department of State. These were to Mr. Dexter new and untrodden paths. The habits of his life, and the pursuits of his mind, were ill suited to that minute diligence, and those intricate details, which the business of war and finance unavoidably impose upon the incumbents of office. He felt a great reluctance to engage in such employments, for which he professed no peculiar relish, and in which his forensic discipline and senatorial experience might not always guide him to correct results. His acceptance of these high stations was not, therefore, without much hesitation; but having accepted, he immediately employed the whole vigor of his mind to attain the mastery of all their multifarious duties. That he fully accomplished his purpose can be no surprise to those who knew him. Such was his intellectual capacity and discrimination, that what he had the wish to acquire cost him far less than any other man. The readiness, with which he received knowledge, seemed, at times, almost like instantaneous inspiration. He did not often choose to engage in laborious inquiries; but he had the necessary firmness and perseverance to attain whatever was essential to his ambition or public duties.

Towards the close of Mr. Adams's administration, he was offered a foreign embassy, which he declined; and upon the accession of Mr. Jefferson to the presidency, he resigned his public employments, and returned to the practice of the law with unabated zeal. From this period he engaged less in political controversies; and reserved himself principally for professional or theological researches. He had always accustomed himself to an independence of thinking upon all subjects, legal, political, and religious. He subscribed to no man's creed, and dealt in the dogmas of the school of no master; but he examined, and weighed, and decided every thing for himself. He observed, or thought he observed, that parties were gradually changing their policy and principles; and, on this account, he seems to have felt less desire to engage in controversies, where his judgment and political friendship might not always be reconcilable. On two memorable occasions, which are yet fresh in our recollections, he took an active political part. I refer to his opposition to the embargo and non-intercourse system, and his support of the late war. But, except in these instances, he rarely, if ever, appeared, after his return to the bar, as the strenuous advocate or opposer of any of the great political measures, which agitated the nation. It was not that he looked on with indifference, or sought to evade responsibility by equivocation or reserve. On the contrary, he was always frank, communicative, and decided. But his judgment was so little in unison with the wishes of any party, that he expressed his opinions, rather as guides of his own conduct, than from a hope to influence others. He was as incapable of deceiving others, as he was of deceiving himself; and would rather surrender the popularity of a whole life, than submit his own judgment to any sect in church or state.

It is not unusual, in men of eminence, after having withdrawn a few years from the bar, to find it difficult, if not impracticable, to resume their former rank in business. Nothing of this sort occurred to check the progress of Mr. Dexter. He was immediately engaged in almost all the important causes in our highest courts; and popular favor seemed to have increased, rather than diminished, during his temporary retirement. From the triumphs and victories of the State bar, his reputation soon carried him to the Supreme Court of the United States, where it has been my pride and pleasure, for many years, to see him holding his career in the foremost rank of advocates. This would entitle him to no ordinary praise; for that bar has been long distinguished by the presence of many of the most illustrious lawyers in the Union.

In no situation have the admirable talents of Mr. Dexter appeared with more unclouded lustre, than in his attendance on the Supreme Court at Washington. For several years he passed the winters there, under engagements in many of the most important causes. Rarely did he speak without attracting an audience composed of the taste, the beauty, the wit, and the learning, that adorned the city; and never was he heard without instruction and delight. On some occasions, involuntary tears from the whole audience have testified the touching power of his eloquence and pathos. On others, a profound and breathless silence expressed, more forcibly than any human language, the riveted attention of an hundred minds. I well remember with what appropriate felicity he undertook, in one cause, to analyze the sources of patriotism. I wish it were possible to preserve the whole in the language in which it was delivered. No one, who heard him describe the influence of local scenery upon the human heart, but felt his soul dissolve within him. I can recall but imperfectly a single passage; and stript of its natural connection, it affords but a glimmering of its original brightness. "We love not our country," said the orator, "from a blind and unmeaning attachment, simply because it is the place of our birth. It is the scene of our earliest joys and sorrows. Every spot has become consecrated by some youthful sport, some tender friendship, some endearing affection, some reverential feeling. It is associated with all our moral habits, our principles, and our virtues. The very sod seems almost a part of ourselves, for there are entombed the bones of our ancestors. Even the dark valley of the shadow of death is not without its consolations, for we pass it in company with our friends." In a still more recent instance, and, indeed, in one of the last causes he ever argued, he took the occasion of an appropriate discussion, to expound his own views of the constitution, and, dropping the character of an advocate, to perform the paramount duty of a citizen. He seemed, as if giving his parting advice and benediction to his country, and as if he had worked up his mind to a mighty effort to vindicate those solid maxims of government and policy, by which alone the union of the States can be upheld and perpetuated. It is deeply to be regretted, that his just and elevated views are now confined to the frail memories of those who heard him.

In the spring of 1815, Mr. Dexter was requested by President Madison to accept an extraordinary mission to the Court of Spain; but, from a reluctance to go abroad, he declined the appointment.

During the last winter, Mr. Dexter was, for a few days, afflicted with the epidemic prevailing at Washington; and was once compelled, from indisposition, to stop in the argument of a cause. He had, however, entirely recovered, and never seemed in better health. On his return from Washington, he went, with his family, to Athens, in the state of New York, to assist in the celebration of the nuptials of his son. He arrived there on Tuesday, the thirteenth of April, somewhat unwell; but no serious alarm for his safety existed until the day previous to his death. Finding his dissolution approaching, he gave the proper directions respecting his affairs, and prepared to meet his fate with the calmness of a Christian philosopher. He could look back on a life devoted to virtuous pursuits without reproach, and his regrets could only be for his family and his country. About midnight, on Friday, the third of May, he lost his senses; and, in three hours afterwards, he expired in the arms of his family, without a struggle or a groan.

Such was the life and such the death of Mr. Dexter. I forbear to give a minute account of the literary honors, which he received, and of the public institutions of which he was a member. I am aware, how little I am qualified for the office of his biographer; but I have this consolation, that he needs no other panegyric but truth. I will close these hasty sketches with a few remarks on his person, character, manners, and acquirements.

In his person, Mr. Dexter was tall, and well formed; of strong, well defined features, and bold, muscular proportions. His manners were, at a first interview, reserved and retiring; and this was sometimes mistaken by a careless observer for austerity or pride. But this impression vanished on a farther acquaintance; and it was soon perceived, that, though he made no effort to court popularity, he was frank, manly, and accessible; and at the bar conciliatory and respectful. His countenance was uncommonly striking; and yet, perhaps, scarcely gave at once the character of his mind. Unless awakened by strong interests, his features relaxed into a repose, which betrayed little of his intellectual grandeur. In such situations his eyes had a tranquil mildness, which seemed better suited to an habitual indolence of temperament, than to fervid thoughts. Yet a curious observer might read in his face the traces of a contemplative mind, sometimes lost in reveries, and sometimes devoted to the most intense abstractions of metaphysics. When roused into action, his features assumed a new aspect. A steady stream of light emanated from his eyes, the muscles of his face swelled with emotion, and a slight flush chafed his pallid cheeks. His enunciation was remarkably slow, distinct, and musical; though the intonations of his voice were sometimes too monotonous. His language was plain, but pure and well selected; and, though his mind was stored with poetic images, he rarely indulged himself in ornaments of any kind. If a rhetorical illustration, or striking metaphor sometimes adorned his speeches, they seemed the spontaneous burst of his genius, produced without effort, and dismissed without regret. They might, indeed, be compared to those spots of beautiful verdure, which are scattered here and there in Alpine regions, amidst the dazzling whiteness of surrounding snows. In the exordiums of his speeches he was rarely happy. It seemed the first exercise of a mind struggling to break its slumbers, or to control the torrent of its thoughts. As he advanced, he became collected, forcible, and argumentative; and his perorations were uniformly grand and impressive. They were often felt, when they could not be followed.

Such was the general character of his delivery. But it would be a great mistake to suppose, because his principal favorite was ratiocination, that his delivery was cold, tame, or uninteresting. I am persuaded, that nature had given him uncommon strength of passions. The natural characteristics of his mind were fervor and force; and, left to the mere workings of his own genius, he would have been impetuous and vehement. But he seemed early to have assumed the mastery of his mind; to have checked its vivid movements by habitual discipline; and bound his passions in the adamantine chains of logic and reasoning. The dismissal of the graces of fancy and of picturesque description were with him a matter of choice and not of necessity. He resigned them, as Hercules resigned pleasure, not because he was insensible of its charms, but because he was more enamored of wisdom. Yet, as if to show his native powers, he has sometimes let loose the enthusiasm of his genius, and touched with a master's hand every chord of the passions, and alternately astonished, delighted, and melted his hearers. Something of the same effect has been produced by what may be fitly termed, the moral sublimity of his reasoning. He opened his arguments in a progressive order, erecting each successive position upon some other, whose solid mass he had already established on an immovable foundation, till at last the superstructure seemed, by its height and ponderous proportions, to bid defiance to the assaults of human ingenuity. I am aware that these expressions may be deemed the exaggerations of fancy; but I only describe what I have felt on my own mind; and I gather from others, that I have not been singular in my feelings.

It would be invidious to compare Mr. Dexter with other illustrious men of our country, either living or dead. In general acquirements he was unquestionably inferior to many; and even in professional science he could scarcely be considered as very profound, or very learned. He had a disinclination to the pages of black-lettered law, which he sometimes censured as the scholastic refinements of monkish ages; and even for the common branches of technical science, the doctrines of special pleading, and the niceties of feudal tenures, he professed to feel little of love or reverence. His delight was to expatiate in the elements of jurisprudence, and to analyze and combine the great principles of equity and reason which distinguish the branches of maritime law. In commercial causes, therefore, he shone with peculiar advantage. His comprehensive mind was familiar with all the leading distinctions of this portion of law; and he marked out, with wonderful sagacity and promptitude, the almost evanescent boundaries which sometimes separate its principles. Indeed, it may be truly said of him, that he could walk a narrow isthmus between opposing doctrines, where no man dared to follow him. The law of prize and of nations were also adapted to his faculties; and no one who heard him upon these topics, but was compelled to confess, that, if he was not always convincing, he was always ingenious; and that, when he attempted to shake a settled rule, though he might be wrong upon authority and practice, he was rarely wrong upon the principles of international justice.

In short, there have been men more thoroughly imbued with all the fine tinctures of classic taste; men of more playful and cultivated imaginations; of more deep and accurate research; and of more various and finished learning. But if the capacity to examine a question by the most comprehensive analysis; to subject all its relations to the test of the most subtle logic; and to exhibit them in perfect transparency to the minds of others;—if the capacity to detect, with unerring judgment, the weak points of an argument, and to strip off every veil from sophistry or error;—if the capacity to seize, as it were by intuition, the learning and arguments of others, and instantaneously to fashion them to his own purposes;—if, I say, these constitute some of the highest prerogatives of genius, it will be difficult to find many rivals, or superiors to Mr. Dexter. In the sifting and comparison of evidence, and in moulding its heterogeneous materials into one consistent mass, the bar and the bench have pronounced him almost inimitable.

His eloquence was altogether of an original cast. It had not the magnificent coloring of Burke, nor the impetuous flow of Chatham. In moved along in majestic simplicity, like a mighty stream, quickening and fertilizing every thing in its course. He persuaded without seeming to use the arts of persuasion; and convinced without condescending to solicit conviction. No man was ever more exempt from finesse or cunning in addressing a jury. He disdained the little arts of sophistry or popular appeal. It was, in his judgment, something more degrading than the sight of Achilles playing with a lady's distaff. It was surrendering the integrity as well as honor of the bar. His conduct afforded, in these particulars, an excellent example for young counsellors, which it would be well for them to imitate, even though they should follow in his path with unequal footsteps.

His studies were not altogether of a professional nature. He devoted much time to the evidences and doctrines of Christianity; and his faith in its truths was fixed after the most elaborate inquiries. That he was most catholic and liberal in his views is known to us all; but, except to his intimate friends, it is little known how solicitous he was to sustain the credibility of the Christian system; and how ingenuous and able were his expositions of its doctrines.

As a statesman, it is impossible to regard his enlightened policy and principles without reverence. He had no foreign partialities or prejudices to indulge or gratify. All his affections centred in his country; all his wishes were for its glory, independence, and prosperity. The steady friend of the Constitution of the United States, he was, in the purest and most appropriate sense of the terms, a patriot and a republican. He considered the union of the States as the polestar of our liberties; and, whatever might be his opinion of any measures, he never breathed a doubt to shake public or private confidence in the excellence of the Constitution itself. When others sank into a despondency at the gloomy aspect of public affairs, and seemed almost ready to resign their belief in republican institutions, he remained their inflexible advocate. He was neither dismayed by the intemperance of parties, nor by the indiscretion of rulers. He believed in the redeeming power of a free constitution; and that, though the people might sometimes be deceived, to their intelligence and virtue we might safely trust to equalize all the eccentricities and perturbations of the political system. He had the singular fortune, at different times, to be the favorite of different parties, occupying in each the same elevation. It is not my purpose to examine, or vindicate his conduct in either of these situations. I feel, indeed, that I am already treading upon ashes thinly strewed over living embers. The present is not the time for an impartial estimate of his political conduct. That duty belongs, and may be safely left, to posterity. Without pretending to anticipate their award, we may with some confidence affirm, that the fame of Mr. Dexter has little to fear from the most rigid scrutiny. While he lived, he might be claimed with pride by any party; but now that he is dead, he belongs to his country.

To conclude;— Mr. Dexter was a man of such rare endowments, that, in whatever age or nation he had lived, he would have been in the first rank of professional eminence. It is unfortunate that he has left no written record of himself. The only monument of his fame rests in the frail recollections of memory, and can reach future ages only through the indistinctness of tradition or history. His glowing thoughts, his brilliant periods, and his profound reasonings have perished for ever. They have passed away like a dream or a shadow. He is gathered to his fathers; and his lips are closed in the silence of death.

I rejoice to have lived in the same age with him; and to have been permitted to hear his eloquence, and to be instructed by his wisdom. I mourn, that my country has lost a patriot without fear or reproach. The glory that has settled on his tomb will not be easily obscured; and if it shall grow dim in the lapse of time, I trust, that some faithful historian will preserve the character of his mind in pages that can perish only with the language in which they are written.

SKETCH

OF THE CHARACTER OF WILLIAM PINKNEY, OF MARYLAND.[1]

William Pinkney died at Washington on the twenty-fifth of February, of the present year, (1822,) in the fifty-eighth year of his age. He had been long distinguished among the statesmen of this country, and had enjoyed many public honors. He had been a Commissioner, under the British treaty of 1794; Minister Plenipotentiary, successively, at the Courts of Great Britain and Russia; and Attorney-General of the United States. At the time of his death, he was a Senator in Congress, from the State of his birth, (Maryland,) a situation, which he filled with the most distinguished ability.

Of his character, as a statesman, or a scholar, it is not the design of this sketch to present any outline. It is, as an advocate and lawyer, that he has a claim to receive a faint, but reverential memorial in these pages. For many years he stood at the head of the bar of Maryland; and, for the last ten years of his life, (the period during which he principally devoted himself to the business of the Supreme Court of the United States,) he was universally admitted to be in the first rank of the profession of the law, never supposed, by any one,

[1] This Sketch was originally written at the request of a friend, and sent to him. It is now printed from a rough copy, made at the time, with some few alterations.

to be excelled by any other advocate, and rarely deemed to be equalled. His person was strong, compact, and muscular, exhibiting great vigor of action, with no small grace and ease of movement. His countenance, without being strikingly interesting for its intelligence, or suavity, was manly and open; and, when excited by any discussion, was capable of the most powerful and varied expression, suited at once for the playfulness of wit, the indignation of resentment, or the solemn dignity of argumentation. His mind was singularly subtile and penetrating, equally rapid in its conceptions, and felicitous in the exposition of the truths, which it was employed to develop or analyze. In native genius, or, in other words, in the power to invent, select, illustrate, and combine topics for the purposes of argument, few men have been his superiors. But he did not rely exclusively on the resources of his genius. He chastened, improved, and invigorated it by constant study, and laborious discipline. He was from early life a diligent student, not only of the law but of general literature, and especially of classical literature. He was ambitious to be not only a good, but an exact scholar; not only a persuasive, but an elegant writer; not only a splendid, but a solid speaker; full of matter, as well as of metaphor; able to convince, as well as to instruct and please. His professional learning was very extensive, deep, and accurate. It was the gradual accumulation of nearly forty years' steady devotion to the science, as well as practice, of jurisprudence. He possessed a minute acquaintance with the ancient common law. Its technical principles, and feudal peculiarities, its quaint illustrations, its subtile distinctions, and its artificial, but nice, logic, were all familiar to his early thoughts, and enabled him, in the later periods of his life, to expound the abstruse doctrines of modern tenures and titles, with great facility and perspicuity. But his studies were not confined to mere researches into the doctrines of the old law. His reading was very extensive in all the departments of modern jurisprudence; and his practice, which was, perhaps, more various than that of any other American lawyer, led him to a daily application of all his learning in the actual business of the forum. Few men, in our country, had attained so exact, thorough, and methodized a knowledge, as he, of the general principles of the law of nations; of the doctrines of the prize and admiralty courts; of the broad and various foundations of equity jurisprudence; and of the admirable theories, as well as practical developments, of all the branches of maritime and commercial law.

In another department of professional learning, peculiar to these United States, he had attained a proud eminence. It was in the thorough mastery of the principles of constitutional law. His public life commenced about the period, when the Constitution of the United States was formed and adopted by the people. He was familiar with all the early controversies, to which it gave rise, and with the commentaries and glosses, as well of its enemies as of its friends. And his large experience as a statesman and advocate, gradually fixed in his mind all the rules for the true interpretation of its powers, its spirit, and its language. No one, perhaps, had weighed with more exactness or deliberation the bearing and tendency of its various complicated provisions. No one felt more deeply its absolute and indispensable importance to the existence of the nation. No one more sincerely and uniformly contended for a liberal exposition of its granted powers and privileges. Hence his arguments upon all constitutional questions in courts of justice, as well as in the halls of legislation, were characterized by an earnestness, a gravity, an eloquence, and force of reasoning, which convinced every man who heard him, that he spoke his own opinions, under the deepest sense of responsibility to his country, and that he sunk the advocate in the higher duties of the statesman. His last thoughts rested with an anxious solicitude upon the future destinies of his country. His last moments were employed in profound investigations, to sustain the constitution against the attacks, made upon it, in the then pending struggles for state sovereignty. And the writer of this sketch heard the declaration from his own lips, a short period before the illness, which terminated his life, that he was then preparing the materials, for a last and great effort on this subject, which, as a commentary upon the principles and powers of the constitution, he intended to bequeath to his country, as the closing labor of his political life.

The celebrity of Mr Pinkney, as a public speaker, requires some notice, in this place, of the nature and character of his oratory. It was, in manner, original, impressive, and vehement. He had some natural, and some acquired defects, which made him, in some degree, fall short of that exquisite conception of the imagination, a perfect orator. His voice was thick and guttural. It rose and fell with little melody and softening of tones, and was, occasionally, abrupt and harsh in its intonations, and wanting in liquidness and modulation. At times, his utterance was hurried on to an excess of vehemence; and then, as it were, *per saltum*, he would suffer it to fall, at the close of the sentence, to a low and indistinct whisper, which confused, at once, the sense and the sound. This inequality of elocution did not seem so much a natural defect, as a matter of choice, or artificial cultivation. But the effect, from whatever cause it arose, was unpleasing; and sometimes gave to his speeches the air of too much study, measured dignity, or dramatic energy. These, however, were venial faults, open to observation, indeed, but soon forgotten by those who listened to his instructive and persuasive reasoning; for no man could hear him, for any length of time, without being led captive by his eloquence. His imagination was rich and inventive; his taste, in general, pure and critical; and his memory uncommonly exact, full and retentive. He attained to a complete mastery of the whole compass of the English language; and, in the variety of use, as well as the choice of diction, for all the purposes of his public labors, he possessed a marvellous felicity. It gave to his style an air of originality, force, copiousness, and expressiveness, which struck the most careless observer. His style was not, indeed, like that of Junius; but it stood out, among all others, with that distinct and striking peculiarity, which has given such fame to that truly great unknown author. His powers of amplification and illustration, whenever these were appropriate to his purpose, seemed almost inexhaustible; though he possessed, at the same time, the power of condensation, both of thought and language, to a most uncommon degree. He never used his powers of amplification and illustration for mere ornament; but as auxiliaries to the main purposes of his argument, artfully interweaving them with the solid materials of the fabric. Occasionally, indeed, he would indulge himself in digressions, of such singular beauty and brilliancy, such a magnificence of phrase, and an appropriateness of allusion, that they won applause, even from those whose functions demand a severe and scrutinizing indifference to every thing but argument. In general, his speeches did not abound with rhetorical flourishes, or sparkle with wit, or scorch with sarcasm; though he possessed the faculty of using each of them with great skill and promptitude. But when the occasion seemed to him, from its extraordinary interest, or the state of public excitement, to require it, his speeches abounded with poetical imagery and ambitious ornaments, and were elaborated with all the studied amplitude of phrase of Burke and Bolingbroke.

But the principal and distinguishing faculty of Mr. Pinkney's mind, (in which few, if any, have ever excelled him,) and which gave such solid weight to his arguments, and carried home conviction to the doubting and the reluctant, was the closeness, acuteness, clearness, and vigor of his power of ratiocination. His luminous analysis of the merits of his case, his severe and searching logic, his progressive expansion of the line of argument, sustaining itself at every step, by a series of almost impregnable positions, and his instantaneous perception of the slightest infirmity in the arguments or concessions f his adversary, gave him, in most debates, a captivating, if not a dangerous superiority, and made him, at the bar, a formidable antagonist, always to be watched with jealousy, and always to be approached with caution.

Mr. Pinkney entertained the loftiest notions of the dignity and utility of the profession; and he endeavored, on all occasions, to diffuse among the members of the bar the deepest sense of its importance, and responsibility to the public. He was desirous of fame, of that fame which alone is enduring, the fame which reposes on sound learning, exalted genius, and diligent, nay, incessant study. Whatever might be the success of his oratory in the estimate of other persons, it never seemed to reach his own standard of excellence. He was, therefore engaged in a constant struggle, not merely to excel others, but to excel himself; and thus his orations (for such many of his speeches were) and his juridical arguments were perpetually enriched by the last accumulations of a mind, whose ambition never tired, and whose industry never slackened in its professional meditations and readings. In these respects, his example may fitly be propounded to all who seek solid reputation at the bar. He knew well that genius without labor could accomplish little; and that he who would enlighten others, or be foremost in the race of life, must quicken his own thoughts, by giving his days and nights, not to the indulgences of pleasure, or the soft solicitudes of literary ease, but to severe discipline, and the study of the great instructors of mankind in learning and science. His loss, in this edifying and cheering career, will long be felt. It has cast a gloom over the profession, which can be dissipated only by the rise of some other master spirit, to guide, to cheer, and to instruct us.

But it is time to close these hasty sketches. Peace to the memory of so great a man. Whoever recollects him, will, almost involuntarily, recur to a passage of Cicero, in his work on the famous orators of antiquity, descriptive of the character of L. Crassus: "Crasso nihil statuo fieri potuisse perfectius. Erat summa gravitas; erat cum gravitate junctus facetiarum et urbanitatis oratorius, non scurrilis, lepos; loquendi accurata, et sine molestia diligens, elegantia; in disserendo, mira explicatio; cum de jure civili, cum de æquo et bono disputaretur, argumentorum et similitudinum copia.[1]

[1] Cicero, De Claris Orat. cap. 38.

SKETCH

OF THE CHARACTER OF ROBERT TRIMBLE, ASSOCIATE JUSTICE OF THE SUPREME COURT OF THE UNITED STATES.

THE melancholy rumor of the death of Mr. Justice Trimble, of the Supreme Court of the United States, has at length been confirmed. That excellent man is no more. The nation has sustained a loss of no ordinary magnitude; and Kentucky may now mourn over the departure of another of her brightest ornaments, in the vigor of life and usefulness. It is but a few years since, that Hardin, who deservedly held the foremost rank at her bar, fell an early victim to disease. The death of that worthy and discriminating judge, Mr. Justice Todd, soon followed; and now Trimble is added, to complete the sad triumvirate. It is but two years since the latter took his seat on the bench of the Supreme Court, having been elevated to that station, from the District Court, solely by his uncommon merits. It is not saying too much to assert, that he brought with him to his new office the reputation of being at the head of the profession in his native state. Men might differ with respect to the rank of other lawyers; but all admitted, that no one was superior to Trimble, in talents, in learning, in acuteness, in sagacity. All admired him for his integrity, firmness, public spirit, and unconquerable industry. All saw in him a patience of investigation which never failed, a loftiness of principle which knew no compromise, a glorious love of justice and the law, which overcame all obstacles. His judgments were remarkable for clearness, strength, vigor of reasoning, and exactness of conclusion.

Without being eloquent in manner, they had the full effect of the best eloquence. They were persuasive, and often overwhelming, in their influence.

Such was the reputation, which accompanied him to the Supreme Court. Before such a bar, as adorns that court, where some of the ablest men in the Union are constantly found engaged in arguments, it is difficult for any man long to sustain a professional character of distinction, unless he has solid acquirements and talents to sustain it. There is little chance there for superficial learning, or false pretensions, to escape undetected. Neither office, nor influence, nor manners, can there sustain the judicial functions, unless there is a real power to comprehend and illustrate juridical arguments, a deep sense of the value of authority, an untiring zeal, and an ability to expound, with living reasons, the judgments, which the court is called upon to express. A new judge, coming there for the first time, may, under such circumstances, well feel some painful anxiety, and some distrustful doubts, lest the bar should search out and weigh his attainments, with too nice an inquisition. Mr. Justice Trimble not only sustained his former reputation, but rose rapidly in public favor. Perhaps no man ever on the bench gained so much, in so short a period of his judicial career. He was already looked up to, as among the first judges in the nation, in all the qualifications of office. Unless we are greatly misinformed, he possessed, in an eminent degree, the confidence of his brethren, and was listened to with a constantly increasing respect. And well did he deserve it; for no man could bestow more thought, more caution, more candor, or more research upon any legal investigations, than he did. The judgments, pronounced by him in the Supreme Court, cannot be read without impressing every professional reader with the strength of his mind, and his various resources to illustrate and unravel intricate subjects. Yet we are persuaded, that, if he had lived ten years longer, in the discharge of the same high duties, from the expansibility of his talents, and his steady devotion to jurisprudence, he would have gained a still higher rank; perhaps as high, as any of his most ardent friends could have desired. One might say of him, as Cicero said of Lysias, — "Nihil acute inveniri potuit in eis causis, quas scripsit, nihil (ut ita dicam) subdole, nihil versute, quod ille non viderit; nihil subtiliter dici, nihil presse, nihil enucleate, quo fieri possit aliquid limatius."

In private life he was amiable, courteous, frank, and hospitable; warm in his friendships, and a model in his domestic relations.

In politics, he was a firm and undeviating republican; but respectful and conciliatory to those, who differed from him. In constitutional law he belonged to that school, of which Mr. Chief Justice Marshall (himself a host) is the acknowledged head and expositor. He loved the Union with an unfaltering love, and was ready to make any sacrifice to insure its perpetuity. He was a patriot in the purest sense. He was; — but how vain is it to say what he was! — He has gone from us forever. We have nothing left, but to lament his loss, and to cherish his fame.

"Salve æternum mihi, maxime Palla,
Æternumque vale."

SKETCH

OF THE CHARACTER OF THOMAS A. EMMET.

(Copy of a Letter addressed to William Sampson, Esq.)

Washington, February 27, 1829.

DEAR SIR,

I had the pleasure of receiving your letter yesterday. I should long since have complied with your request in regard to Mr. Emmet if I could have found suitable leisure to sit down and make even a sketch of him, such as I thought him to be in character and attainments. Hitherto I have sought such leisure in vain.

It was in the winter of 1815 that I first became acquainted with Mr. Emmet. He was then, for the first time, in attendance upon the Supreme Court at Washington, being engaged in some important prize causes then pending in the court. Although, at that period, he could have been but little, if any, turned of fifty years of age, the deep lines of care were marked upon his face; the sad remembrances, as I should conjecture, of past sufferings, and of those anxieties which wear themselves into the heart and corrode the very elements of life. There was an air of subdued thoughtfulness about him that read to me the lessons of other interests than those which belonged to mere professional life. He was cheerful, but rarely, if ever, gay; frank and courteous, but he soon relapsed into gravity, when not excited by the conversation of others.

Such, I remember, were my early impressions; and his high professional character, as well as some passages in his life, gave me a strong interest in all that concerned him at that time. There were, too, some accidental circumstances which were connected with his arguments on that occasion, which left a vivid impression upon all who had the pleasure of hearing him. It was at this time that Mr. Pinkney, of Baltimore, one of the proudest names in the annals of the American bar, was in the meridian of his glory. He had been often tried in the combats of the forum of the nation; and, if he did not stand quite alone, the undisputed victor of the field, (and it might be deemed invidious for me to point out any one, as *primus inter pares*,) he was, nevertheless, admitted by the general voice not to be surpassed by any of the noble minds with whom he was accustomed to wrestle in forensic contests. Mr. Emmet was a new and untried opponent, and brought with him the ample honors gained at one of the most distinguished bars in the Union. In the only causes in which Mr. Emmet was engaged, Mr. Pinkney was retained on the other side; and each of these causes was full of important matter, bearing upon the public policy and prize law of the country. Curiosity was awakened; their mutual friends waited for the struggle with impatient eagerness; and a generous rivalry, roused by the public expectations, imparted itself to their own bosoms. A large and truly intelligent audience was present at the argument of the first cause. It was not one which gave much scope to Mr. Emmet's peculiar powers. The topic was one with which he was not very familiar. He was new to the scene, and somewhat embarrassed by its novelty. His argument was clear and forcible; but he was conscious that it was not one of his happiest efforts. On the other hand, his rival was perfectly familiar with the whole range of prize law; he was at home both in the topic and the scene. He won an easy victory, and pressed his advantages with vast dexterity, and, as Mr. Emmet thought, with somewhat of the display of triumph. The case of the Nereide, so well known in our prize history, was soon afterwards called on for trial. In this second effort, Mr. Emmet was far more successful. His speech was greatly admired for its force and fervor, its variety of research, and its touching eloquence. It placed him at once, by universal consent, in the first rank of American advocates. I do not mean to intimate that it placed him before Mr. Pinkney, who was again his noble rival for victory. But it settled, henceforth and forever, his claims to very high distinction in the profession. In the course of the exordium of this speech, he took occasion to mention the embarrassment of his own situation, the novelty of the forum, and the public expectations, which accompanied the cause. He spoke with generous praise of the talents and acquirements of his opponent, whom fame and fortune had followed both in Europe and America. And then, in the most delicate and affecting manner, he alluded to the events of his own life, in which misfortune and sorrow had left many deep traces of their ravages. "My ambition," said he, "was extinguished in my youth; and I am admonished by the premature advances of age, not now to attempt the dangerous paths of fame." At the moment when he spoke, the recollections of his sufferings melted the hearts of the audience, and many of them were dissolved in tears. Let me add, that the argument of Mr. Pinkney, also, was a most splendid effort, and fully sustained his reputation.

From that period I was accustomed to hear Mr. Emmet at the bar of the Supreme Court in almost every variety of causes; and my respect for his talents constantly increased until the close of his life. I take pleasure in adding, that his affability, his modest and unassuming manner, his warm feelings, and his private virtues, gave a charm to his character, which made it at once my study and delight.

It would ill become me to attempt a sketch of the character of Mr. Emmet. That is the privilege, and will be (as it ought) the melancholy pleasure, of those who were familiar with him in every walk of life, to whom he unbosomed himself in the freedom of intimacy, and who have caught the light plays of his fancy, as well as the more profound workings of his soul.

That he had great qualities as an orator cannot be doubted by any one who has heard him. His mind possessed a good deal of the fervor which characterizes his countrymen. It was quick, vigorous, searching, and buoyant. He kindled as he spoke. There was a spontaneous combustion, as it were, not sparkling, but clear and glowing. His rhetoric was never florid; and his diction, though select and pure, seemed the common dress of his thoughts, as they arose, rather than any studied effort at ornament. Without being deficient in imagination, he seldom drew upon it for resources to aid the effect of his arguments, or to illustrate his thoughts. His object seemed to be, not to excite wonder or surprise, to captivate by bright pictures, and varied images, and graceful groups, and startling apparitions; but by earnest and close reasoning to convince the judgment, or to overwhelm the heart by awakening its most profound emotions. His own feelings were warm and easily touched. His sensibility was keen, and refined itself almost into a melting tenderness. His knowledge of the human heart was various and exact. He was easily captivated by the belief, that his own cause was just. Hence, his eloquence was most striking for its persuasiveness. He said what he felt; and he felt what he said. His command over the passions of others was an instantaneous and sympathetic action. The tones of his voice, when he touched on topics calling for deep feeling, were themselves instinct with meaning. They were utterances of the soul as well as of the lips.

SKETCH

OF THE CHARACTER OF BUSHROD WASHINGTON, ASSOCIATE JUSTICE OF THE SUPREME COURT OF THE UNITED STATES.

THE death of Mr. Justice Washington is an event, which cannot but cast a gloom upon all the real friends of our country. He was born on the 5th of June, 1762, and was, of course, now in the sixty-eighth year of his age. It is well known, that he was the nephew, and, we have a right to say, the favorite nephew of President Washington. The latter bequeathed to him, by his will, his celebrated estate on the Potomac, Mount Vernon, which was the residence of this great patriot during the most brilliant periods of his life, the delightful retreat of his old age, the scene of his dying hours, and the spot, where, by his own order, his ashes now repose in the same tomb with his ancestors. To him also, President Washington gave all his valuable public and private papers, as a proof of his entire confidence and attachment, and made him the active executor of his will. Such marks of respect from such a man, — the wonder of his own age, and the model for all future ages, — would alone stamp a character of high merit, and solid distinction, upon any person. They would constitute a passport to public favor, and confer an enviable rank, far beyond the records of the herald's office, or the fugitive honors of a title.

It is high praise to say, that Mr. Justice Washington well deserved such confidence and distinction. Nay, more. His merits went far beyond them. He was as worthy an heir, as ever claimed kindred with a worthy ancestor. He was bred to the law in his native state of Virginia, and arrived at such early eminence in his profession, that as long ago as 1798, he was selected by President Adams, as a Justice of the Supreme Court, upon the decease of the late Judge Wilson, of Pennsylvania. For thirty-one years he held that important station, with a constantly increasing reputation and usefulness. Few men, indeed, have possessed higher qualifications for the office, either natural or acquired. Few men have left deeper traces, in their judicial career, of every thing, which a conscientious judge ought to propose for his ambition, or his virtue, or his glory. His mind was solid, rather than brilliant; sagacious and searching, rather than quick or eager; slow, but not torpid; steady, but not unyielding; comprehensive, and at the same time cautious; patient in inquiry, forcible in conception, clear in reasoning. He was, by original temperament, mild, conciliating, and candid; and yet he was remarkable for an uncompromising firmness. Of him it may be truly said, that the fear of man never fell upon him; it never entered into his thoughts, much less was it seen in his actions. In him the love of justice was the ruling passion; it was the master-spring of all his conduct. He made it a matter of conscience to discharge every duty with scrupulous fidelity and scrupulous zeal. It mattered not, whether the duty were small or great, witnessed by the world, or performed in private, everywhere the same diligence, watchfulness, and pervading sense of justice were seen. There was about him a tenderness of giving offence, and yet a fearlessness of consequences, in his official character, which I scarcely know how to portray. It was a rare combination, which added much to the dignity of the bench, and made justice itself, even when most severe, soften into the moderation of mercy. It gained confidence, when it seemed least to seek it. It repressed arrogance, by overawing or confounding it.

To say, that, as a judge, he was wise, impartial, and honest, is but to attribute to him those qualifications, without which the honors of the bench are but the means of public disgrace, or contempt. His honesty was a deep, vital principle, not measured out by worldly rules. His impartiality was a virtue of his nature, disciplined and instructed by constant reflection upon the infirmity and accountability of man. His wisdom was the wisdom of the law, chastened, and refined, and invigorated by study, guided by experience, dwelling little on theory, but constantly enlarging itself by a close survey of principles.

He was a learned judge. I do not mean by this that everyday learning, which may be gathered up by a hasty reading of books and cases; but that, which is the result of long-continued, laborious services, and comprehensive studies. He read to learn, and not to quote; to digest and master, and not merely to display. He was not easily satisfied. If he was not as profound as some, he was more exact than most men. But the value of his learning was, that it was the keystone of all his judgments. He indulged not the rash desire to fashion the law to his own views; but to follow out its precepts with a sincere good faith and a simplicity. Hence he possessed the happy faculty of yielding just the proper weight to authority; neither, on the one hand, surrendered himself blindfold to the dictates of other judges, nor, on the other hand, overruling settled doctrines upon his own private notion of policy or justice.

In short, as a magistrate, he was exemplary and able, one whom all may reverence, and but few may hope to equal.

But, after all, it is as a man, that those who knew him best will most love to contemplate him. There was a daily beauty in his life, which won every heart. He was benevolent, charitable, affectionate, and liberal, in the best sense of the terms. He was a Christian, full of religious sensibility, and religious humility. Attached to the Episcopal church by education and choice, he was one of its most sincere, but unostentatious friends. He was as free from bigotry, as any man; and at the same time that he claimed the right to think for himself, he admitted, without reserve, the same right in others. He was, therefore, indulgent even to what he deemed errors in doctrine, and abhorred all persecution for conscience' sake. But what made religion most attractive in him, and gave it occasionally even a sublime expression, was its tranquil, cheerful, unobstructive, meek, and gentle character. There was a mingling of Christian graces in him, which showed, that the habit of his thoughts was fashioned for another and a better world. Of his particular opinions on doctrinal points, it is not my intention to speak. Such as they were, though good men may differ as to their correctness, all must agree that they breathed the spirit of an inquisitive Christian.

He was a real lover of the Constitution of the United States; one of those who assisted in its adoption, and steadily and uniformly supported it through every change in its fortunes. He was a good old-fashioned federalist, of the school of the days of Washington. He never lost his confidence in the political principles which he first embraced. He was always distinguished for moderation, in the days of their prosperity, and for fidelity to them in the days of their adversity.

I have not said too much, then, in saying, that such a man is a public loss. We are not, indeed, called to mourn over him, as one who is cut off prematurely in the vigor of manhood. He was ripe in honors and in virtues. But the departure of such a man severs so many ties, interrupts so many delights, withdraws so many confidences, and leaves such an aching void in the hearts of friends, and such a sense of desolation among associates, that, while we bow to the decree of Providence, our griefs cannot but pour themselves out in sincere lamentations.

SKETCH

OF THE CHARACTER OF ISAAC PARKER, CHIEF JUSTICE OF THE SUPREME COURT OF MASSACHUSETTS.

Mr. Chief Justice Parker brought with him to the bench the reputation of an able, active, and learned advocate. He had well earned that reputation, by a course of long and honorable practice in the then District, now State of Maine. His talents, high as they were, were not his only recommendation. He possessed, what talents may adorn, but what talents, however shining they may be, never can supply, the *Mens conscia recti*, an inflexible integrity, a deep-rooted and enlightened virtue. His private life was without reproach, his honor without stain, his political and civil career straightforward and steady. His manners were frank, modest, and winning, without ostentation, and without affectation. Nature had given him a mild temperament, a quiet and moderated cheerfulness, an ingenuous countenance, and social kindness, which pleased without effort, and was itself easily pleased. But his most striking characteristic was sound sense, which, though no science, is, in the affairs of human life, fairly worth all others, and which had in him its usual accompaniments, discretion, patience, and judgment. In his professional harangues he was persuasive and interesting; he had the earnestness of one, who felt the importance of fidelity to his client, and, at the same time, the sincerity of one, who felt the dignity of truth, and of that jurisprudence, whose servant he was, and whose precepts he was not at liberty to disown, and was incapable of betraying. In the sense sometimes affixed to the term, he did not possess eloquence; that is, he did not possess that vivid imagination, which delights in poetical imagery, or in rhetorical flourishes, in painting the passions, or in exciting them into action. He was not addicted to a rich and gorgeous diction, or to coloring his thoughts with the lights and shades, or the brilliant contrasts, of a variegated style. But in a just sense, if we look to the means or the end, to his power of commanding attention, or his power of persuading and convincing the understanding, he might be deemed truly eloquent. His reasonings were clear, forcible, and exact; his language chaste, pointed, and select; his fluency of speech, uncommon; his action, animated; so that in their actual union they gave a charm to his arguments, which won upon the ears and captivated the judgment of his audience.

Such was the reputation and character, which he brought to the bench. He took his seat among distinguished men; and he sustained himself as a worthy and equal associate. He did more, and accomplished what few men do accomplish; he moved on with a continual increase of reputation, even to the very hour of his death. He lived through times, happily now past, of peculiar delicacy and difficulty; in the midst of great political changes and excitements, when the tribunals of justice were scarcely free from the approaches of the spirit of discord, and the appeals of party were almost ready to silence the precepts of the law. During this period, his firmness, moderation, patience, and candor secured to him the public confidence. When the office of Chief Justice became vacant by the lamented death of Mr. Chief Justice Sewall, all eyes were turned towards him as the successor. His appointment gave universal satisfaction. And yet, if he had died at that period, half of his real merits would have remained unknown. His ambition was now roused to new exertions by the responsibility of the station; his mind assumed a new vigor; his industry quickened into superior watchfulness; and he expanded, so to say, to the full reach of his official duties. It was a critical moment in the progress of our jurisprudence. We wanted a cautious, but liberal mind, to aid the new growth of principles, to enlarge the old rules, to infuse a vital equity into the system, as it was expanding before us. We wanted a mind to do, in some good degree, what Lord Mansfield had done in England, to breathe into our common law an energy suited to the wants, the commercial interests, and the enterprise of the age. We wanted a mind, which, with sufficient knowledge of the old law, was yet not a slave to its forms; which was bold enough to invigorate it with new principles, not from the desire of innovation, but the love of improvement. We wanted sobriety of judgment; but, at the same time, a free spirit, which should move over the still depths of our law, and animate the whole mass. Such a man was Mr. Chief Justice Parker. And whoever, in this age, or in any future age, shall critically examine the decisions of the Supreme Court, during the sixteen years in which he presided over it, will readily acknowledge the truth of these remarks.

There was in his mind an original, intrinsic equity, a clear perception of abstract right and justice, and of the best mode of adapting it to the exigencies of the case. He felt, as Lord Ellenborough before him had felt, that the rules, not of evidence merely, but of all substantial law, must widen with the wants of society; that they must have flexibility, as well as strength; that they must accomplish the ends of justice, and not bury it beneath the pressure of their own weight. There is in this respect much, very much, to admire, and, (if it were possible, in our reverence for the dead,) to envy, in his judicial career. Few men have ever excelled him in the readiness of grasping a cause, of developing its merits, or of searching out its defects. He may have had less juridical learning than some men; but no man more thoroughly mastered all that was before him, or expounded with more felicity the reasons even of technical doctrines. He had an almost intuitive perception of the real principle, pervading a whole class of cases, and would thread it through all their mazes with marvellous ability. His written opinions are full of sagacity, and juridical acuteness, at the same time that they possess a singular simplicity and ease. He rarely fails to convince, even when he questions what seems justified by authority. His judicial style is a fine model. It is equally remarkable for propriety of language, order of arrangement, neat and striking turns of expression, and a lucid current of reasoning, which flows on to the conclusion with a silent but almost irresistible force. In his more studied efforts, in some of those great causes, in which the whole powers of the human intellect are tasked and measured, he was always found equal to the occasion. There are not a few of his opinions, on some of these intricate subjects, which would bear a close rivalry with the best in Westminster Hall in our own times. There are some, which any judge might be proud to number among those, destined to secure his own immortality.

But we must stop; the time for mourning over such a loss cannot soon pass away. We have lost a great magistrate, and an excellent citizen. Vain is the voice of sorrow, and vainer still the voice of eulogy. They cannot recall the past. His place cannot be easily supplied; for it is difficult to combine so many valuable qualities in a single character. To sum up his in one sentence, we may say, that, as a judge, he was eminent for sagacity, acuteness, wisdom, impartiality, and dignity; as a citizen, for public spirit and elevated consistency of conduct; as a man, for generosity, gentleness, and moral purity. His fame must rest, where it is fit it should, upon the printed reports of his own decisions. These will go down to future ages; and though, perhaps, beyond the circle of the profession, they may not attract much general observation, (for the misfortune of the profession is, that great judges and great lawyers cannot enjoy a wide-spread popular favor,) they will yet be read and honored by the jurists of succeeding times with undiminished reverence, when those of us, who have known and loved him, shall be mingled with the dust, that now gathers round his remains. They will often recall to the classical reader the beautiful eulogy of Cicero, upon a great character of antiquity, so applicable to his: "Erat in verborum splendore elegans, compositione aptus, facultate copiosus; eaque erat cum summo ingenio, tum exercitationibus maximis consecutus; rem complectebatur memoriter, dividebat acute, nec prætermittebat fere quidquam, quod esset in causâ, aut ad confirmandum aut ad refellendum."

SKETCH

OF THE CHARACTER OF JOHN TODD, ASSOCIATE JUSTICE OF THE SUPREME COURT OF THE UNITED STATES.

MR. JUSTICE TODD possessed many qualities admirably fitted for the proper discharge of judicial functions. He had uncommon patience and candor in investigation; great clearness and sagacity of judgment; a cautious but steady energy; a well-balanced independence; a just respect for authority, and at the same time an unflinching adherence to his own deliberate opinions of the law. His modesty imparted a grace to an integrity and singleness of heart which won for him the general confidence of all who knew him. He was not ambitious of innovations upon the settled principles of the law; but was content with the more unostentatious character of walking in the trodden paths of jurisprudence; *super antiquas vias legis.* From his diffident and retiring habits, it required a long acquaintance with him justly to appreciate his juridical as well as his personal merits. His learning was of a useful and solid cast; not perhaps as various or as comprehensive as that of some men; but accurate, and transparent, and applicable to the daily purposes of the business of human life. In his knowledge of the local law of Kentucky, he was excelled by few; and his brethren drew largely upon his resources to administer that law, in the numerous cases which then crowded the docket of the Supreme Court from that judicial circuit. What he did not know, he never affected to possess; but sedulously sought to acquire. He was content to learn, without assuming to dogmatize. Hence he listened to arguments for the purpose of instruction, and securing examination; and not merely for that of confutation or debate. Among his associates he enjoyed an enviable respect, which was constantly increasing as he became more familiarly known to them. His death was deemed by them a great public calamity; and in the memory of those who survived him, his name has ever been cherished with a warm and affectionate remembrance.

No man ever clung to the Constitution of the United States with a more strong and resolute attachment. And in the grave cases which were agitated in the Supreme Court of the United States during his judicial life, he steadfastly supported the constitutional doctrines which Mr. Chief Justice Marshall promulgated, in the name of the Court. It is to his honor, and it should be spoken, that, though bred in a different political school from that of the Chief Justice, he never failed to sustain those great principles of constitutional law on which the security of the Union depends. He never gave up to party, what he thought belonged to the country.

For some years before his death, he was sensible that his health was declining, and that he might soon leave the Bench, to whose true honor and support he had been so long and so zealously devoted. To one of his brethren who had the satisfaction of possessing his unreserved confidence, he often communicated his earnest hope that Mr. Justice Trimble might be his successor; and he bore a willing testimony to the extraordinary ability of that eminent Judge. It affords a striking proof of his sagacity and foresight; and the event fully justified the wisdom of his choice. Although Mr. Justice Trimble occupied his station on the bench of the Supreme Court, for a brief period only, yet he has left on the records of the court enduring monuments of talents and learning fully adequate to all the exigencies of the judicial office. To both these distinguished men, under such circumstances, we may well apply the touching panegyric of the poet:

> Fortunati Ambo!——
> Nulla Dies unquam memori vos eximet Ævo."

SKETCH

OF THE CHARACTER OF HUGH S. LEGARÉ.

[The following remarks were made before the members of the Law School, at the lecture on the Constitution, June 22, which were taken down by a gentleman present, and afterwards published in the Law Reporter for August, 1843.]

When I last met you, I little anticipated the calamitous event, which has since occurred, in the death of a distinguished man, who expired in the city of Boston on Tuesday morning last. Whoever considers the principles of the Constitution can never forget him; for he was firm and true to its doctrines, and exhibited that elevated and comprehensive statesmanship, which the Constitution demands of its real friends. I refer, of course, to Mr. Legaré, the late Attorney-General, with whom I had the happiness to be intimately acquainted; whom I knew not only as an accomplished gentleman, but also as a great lawyer. I speak of him to you here, not merely to pay a deserved tribute to his worth, but because I know of no man whom I would sooner propound as an example to young men entering the profession, which he has so much adorned. I had indeed looked to him with great fondness of expectation. I had looked to see him accomplish what he was so well fitted to do, — what, I know, was the darling object of his pure ambition — to engraft the Civil Law upon the jurisprudence of this country, and thereby to expand the Common Law to greater usefulness and a wider adaptation to the progress of society.

Mr. Legaré was a native of South Carolina, and was graduated, I understand, at an early age, at Columbia College. He proceeded, soon after he left that institution, to

Edinburgh, where he devoted himself, with great diligence and intensity of study, to general and classic literature. He then went to the Continent and pursued the study of the Civil Law with great assiduity and success, and afterwards returned to South Carolina to practise, and became soon eminent at the Bar of that State.

It is a most singular circumstance, that eminence in general literature should, in the public mind, detract from a man's reputation as a lawyer. It is an unworthy prejudice, for certainly the science of jurisprudence may borrow aid as well as receive ornament from the cultivation of all the other branches of human knowledge. But the prejudice exists; — and yet one would think that the public had witnessed so many examples of men who were great scholars and great lawyers likewise, that the prejudice might be at this day disarmed of so much of its quality, as is apt to do injustice to the reputation of living men. Lord Mansfield was a most eminent scholar in general letters; but he was also unsurpassed in jurisprudence. Sir William Blackstone was so elegant a scholar, that his Commentaries are models of pure English prose; but they are none the less the invaluable mine of the Laws of England. Lord Stowell, the friend and executor of Dr. Johnson, was in various attainments exceeded by few; but his knowledge of general jurisprudence was greater than that of any man of his day. Some of the proudest names now on the English benches are some of England's best scholars. But there as well as here — though certainly it is far greater here — the public prejudice almost denies to a great scholar the right to be eminent as a jurist. Dr. Johnson has said, —

> "And mark what ills the scholar's life assail,
> Toil, envy, want, the patron and the gaol."

None of these were the evils of our friend. His only evil was, that his reputation as a lawyer was sometimes underrated, because of his great general attainments. But nothing could be more unfounded than this idea. He considered the law as his pursuit; as his object; as the field of his ambition. Fifteen years ago I knew him as an eminent lawyer. He afterwards went abroad in a diplomatic capacity; and, at Brussels, where he resided, devoted himself anew to the study of the Civil Law, with a view to make it subservient to the great object of his life, the expansion of the Common Law, and the forcing into it the enlarged and liberal principles and just morality of the Roman jurisprudence. This object he seemed about to accomplish; for his arguments before the Supreme Court were crowded with the principles of the Roman Law wrought into the texture of the Common Law with great success. In every sentence that I heard, I was struck with this union of the two systems. At the same time, the whole was wrought in a style, beautiful and chaste, but never passing from the line of the argument, nor losing sight of the cause. His argumentation was marked by the closest logic; at the same time he had a *presence* in speaking, which I have never seen excelled. He had a warm, rich style, but no declamation; for he knew that declamation belongs neither to the jurist nor to the scholar.

It was only during the last summer, that he wrote to me that he intended to translate Heineccius's Elements; for he wished, he said, to entice the American lawyer to the study of the civil law. He added, that he had nothing to gain by undertaking such a work, but that he would undergo the labor as a homage to his country. Knowing his eminent qualifications for the task, I advised him to make the translation, and to add to it notes of his own, so as to adapt the principles to the existing state of the common law; telling him that he would thereby confer a benefit on his country which no man of the age would be likely to exceed.

A few years since, he published a paper in the New York Review, on the origin, history, and influence of Roman legislation, and afterwards printed it separately from the Review itself. Whoever reads that essay — and I hope you will read it — will perceive his attainments in the civil law. You, who have not heard him, cannot judge of his attainments in the common law; but I, who heard his arguments, know that he devoted himself to the common law with a wise perception of its defects, and a purpose to ameliorate them with the riches of the civil law; and I may say of him, having seen his mastery of both systems of jurisprudence — that he walked with them triumphantly, the one in one hand, and the other in the other hand, in the path of a great jurist.

Although he might have had other places in the gift of the government — as I have been told — yet he desired only the office of Attorney-General, and he desired that for the sake of the law. When, therefore, the question is asked, was he eminent as a lawyer? I answer, no man more so. Do you ask, what was the secret of his eminence? I answer, it was diligence, profound study, and withholding his mind from the political excitements of the day.

To me, his loss is irreparable. How few do I see around me, severe in their studies in jurisprudence; willing to devote their days and nights to the mastery and improvement of it as a great science; and looking for the fame that comes from devotion like his. Such study is not fanned by the breath of popular applause, and so it is rare. But in him it shone most brilliantly. I pronounce him a great loss, as one of the most valuable lights of jurisprudence that it has been my happiness to know — my misfortune to lose.

It was but the day before yesterday — and before I had heard of his death, the news of which met me as I was going from my own house — that I had taken down *Cicero de Claris Oratoribus*, and had turned to the passage where he begins —

"As I was leaving Cilicia to go to Rhodes, I heard of the death of Hortensius." Hortensius, the great Roman lawyer, so much and so justly praised by Cicero, died as we are told, when his usefulness had been completed. How different from him, who has been taken from us when we had just learned to appreciate his inestimable value to the jurisprudence of the country. To Cethegus, another orator, Cicero applies the remark of Ennius —

> "Is dictus ollis popularibus olim,
> Qui tum vivebant homines, atque ævum agitabant,
> Flos delibatus populi."

I say of the Attorney-General, not Flos *delibatus populi;* I say of him, *Flos delibatus juris.*

As I looked a little farther, I came upon the passage, which, by a striking coincidence, expressed what has since been realized to my own feelings, as the full influence of such a life; a life, the only deep lamentation for which is, that it gave him so little time to make himself fully appreciated by the whole republic. I give you the English first, that I may afterwards give you the more beautiful Latin: "They therefore seem to me to have lived both fortunately and happy, not only in other States, but especially in ours, who have been permitted not merely to enjoy authority and the renown of action, but also to attain the praise of wisdom, whose memory and reputation, in our gravest and severest cares, have been truly grateful, whenever in history we have fallen upon them."[1]

I dismiss the subject, with the remark, that the Constitution has lost one of its best friends; the Supreme Court one of its brightest ornaments; the country an inestimable man, whose independence, whose public virtue, whose rare endowments, and whose freedom from all the arts of popularity gave full assurance of a life of the highest value to the State. To me, had my own career closed before his, a single word of praise from his lips, could I have looked back to know it, would have been as valuable a tribute as from any other human being.

[1] Itaque ii mihi videntur fortunate beateque vixisse, cum in cæteris civitatibus, tum maxime in nostra, quibus cum auctoritate, rerumque gestarum gloria, tum etiam sapientiæ laude perfrui licuit. Quorum memoria et recordatio in maximis nostris gravissimisque curis jucunda sane fuit, cum in eam nuper ex sermone quodam incidissemus.— Cic. *De Clar. Orat.* 2.

SKETCH

OF THE CHARACTER OF PHILIP P. BARBOUR, ASSOCIATE JUSTICE OF THE SUPREME COURT OF THE UNITED STATES.

THE family from which Judge Barbour was descended, was one of the oldest and most respectable in Virginia. His great-grandfather was a merchant of Scotland, who immigrated to this country. His grandfather was the pioneer and first settler of the country lying between the eastern base of the Blue Ridge and the Southwest mountains. His father, Thomas Barbour, inherited considerable wealth, and was a member of the old House of Burgesses, from the then very large county of Orange. He was one of those who, in 1769, signed the "Non-Importation Act" between this country and Great Britain. After the formation of the Union, he was elected to the legislature. Richard Henry Lee, in a letter to his brother, Arthur Lee, bore testimony to his worth, to the effect, "that he was glad that Thomas Barbour was in our state councils, for he was a truly intelligent and patriotic man."

On the maternal side, as his name indicates, Judge Barbour was related to the Pendleton family, his grandmother having been the aunt of the distinguished Judge Pendleton. Philip Pendleton Barbour was born on the 25th of May, 1783. Owing to his great hospitality, and a long series of disasters, his father was unable to afford him that liberal education which his talents and early promise would have justified. He was, however, sent early to school, where he soon developed many of those qualities for which he was afterwards so justly distinguished. He exhibited great aptitude for the acquisition of languages; and, with a correct taste and strong memory, sought out and retained through life the beauties of the Greek and Roman classics. Even in the performance of the tasks of a country school, he manifested that precision of information and depth of research, which, on a broader theatre, and carried to higher subjects, won for him a wide-spread and enduring reputation. He remained at school until the end of 1799. During the early part of 1800, he studied law at home; but in October, he determined to visit Kentucky, where, under great difficulty and embarrassment he commenced the practice of law. In the summer of 1801, he yielded to the persuasions of his friends to return to Virginia; and, having borrowed the necessary funds, spent one session at William and Mary College. In 1802, he resumed the practice of law in Virginia. In October, 1804, he was united to Frances T. Johnson, daughter of Colonel Benjamin Johnson, of Orange county, Virginia. During the next eight years he applied himself unceasingly to his profession. In 1812, he was elected to the Assembly, where he continued two sessions. In 1814, he was elected to Congress, where he continued until 1825. While there, he was chairman of the Naval and Judiciary Committees; and in 1821, was chosen speaker of the House of Representatives. About the year 1825, the University of Virginia went into operation. He was offered the professorship of law in that institution, and was pressed by Mr. Jefferson to accept it. He refused this station, however, and was appointed a Judge of the General Court of Virginia. In 1827, at the written request of a majority of his old constituents, he resigned his seat on the Bench, and was reëlected, without opposition, to Congress. In 1829, together with the illustrious Madison, he was chosen to represent the county of Orange, in the convention called to amend the constitution of Virginia. He presided over the deliberations of this body in a manner which elicited the approbation of its members. He was also president of the Anti-Tariff Convention which met in Philadelphia. In 1830, he retired from the practice of a profession which had yielded him considerable wealth, and of which he had been one of the brightest ornaments, and accepted the station of Federal Judge for the eastern district of Virginia. The chancellorship was offered to him and declined; as was also the post of Attorney-General. He refused the nominations for a seat in the Court of Appeals, the gubernatorial Chair, and the Senate of the United States. As Federal Judge, he won new honors, and showed himself worthy of the high and enviable station to which in 1836 he was called, that of Associate Judge of the Supreme Court of the United States. Having thus reached the height of the profession which he had chosen, he was unweariedly striving, with a virtuous ambition, to win that fame which great ability can only give when joined with pure principles, when death cut him off in his useful career, and robbed our country of one of its most distinguished sons.

It remains for us to take a brief notice of the professional attainments and judicial character of Mr. Justice Barbour. It has been already seen that no inconsiderable portion of his life was employed in active political duties and pursuits, which if not incompatible with, are (to say the least) by no means favorable to the cultivation of juridical knowledge, or to found a solid reputation in the law. He did not, however, at any time relax his vigilance in his professional studies, or become indifferent to professional success. On the contrary, he had the ambition to acquire all the knowledge which might be useful in his practice at the bar, and the persevering firmness to surmount every intervening obstacle. His mind was in a remarkable degree acute, sound, and discriminating, inclining to subtilty in disquisition, but not misled by it. He was earnest, candid, patient, and laborious in all his investigations; quick to discern the real points and merits of a case; but slow in arriving at his own conclusions. His talents were of a high order; but he was distinguished less for brilliancy of effort, than for perspicacious, close, and vigorous reasoning. He sought less to be eloquent than to be accurate; less to persuade by declamatory fervor, than to convince by clear and logical deduction. The learning, therefore, that he brought to the discussion of every cause, was pertinent, exact, and illustrative. It had point and force, and not merely remote or loose analogies to give it effect. When he was elevated to the Bench, he felt a deep and conscientious sense of his new duties; and was solicitous to master all the learning appropriate to discharge them in the best manner; and especially, after his appointment to the Bench of the Supreme Court, he devoted his leisure, with strenuous diligence, to attain all the various knowledge demanded for eminence in that station. Few men ever labored with more entire success in such a noble pursuit. During his brief career in that Court, he widened and deepened the foundations of his judicial learning to an extraordinary extent; his reputation constantly advanced, and his judgments were listened to with increased respect and profound confidence. If he had lived many years with good health, he could not have failed to have won the highest distinction for all those qualities which give dignity and authority to the Bench. It might be truly said of him, that he was not only equal to all the functions of his high station, but above them,—*par negotiis, et supra* ——. His country has lost by his death a bright ornament, and a pure and spotless patriot.

THE END.

www.ingramcontent.com/pod-product-compliance
Lightning Source LLC
LaVergne TN
LVHW102012210926
848483LV00011B/265
* 9 7 8 1 5 8 4 7 7 0 7 2 5 *